Missouri State Parks and Historic Sites

— Exploring Our Legacy —

The overlook at Trail of Tears State Park commands a sweeping view of the Mississippi River where the Cherokee crossed in 1838. *Denise Dowling*

Missouri State Parks and Historic Sites

— *Exploring Our Legacy* —

Editor
Susan Flader

Essays
John A. Karel, B.H. Rucker, Susan Flader,
R. Roger Pryor, and Charles Callison

Photographs
Oliver Schuchard and Others

Missouri Life Inc, Boonville, Missouri
and Missouri Parks Association, Columbia, Missouri

Missouri Life, Inc. and Missouri Parks Association
501 High St., Ste. A, Boonville MO 65233

 First edition 1992.

Library of Congress Control Number: 2015951674

ISBN 978-0-9968058-0-3
Printed in China

Book and Cover Design: *Missouri Life* Art Director Sarah Herrera
Editing: *Missouri Life* Project Editor Evan Wood
Missouri Life Editor-in-Chief Danita Allen Wood
Typefaces: Eames Century Modern and Scout

This paper meets the requirements of
ANSI/NISO Z39.48-1992 (Permanence of Paper).

MISSOURI PARKS ASSOCIATION

Missouri Life MEDIA

for Missourians who care

The sun's rays light Dillard Mill on a misty October morning. The mill was saved by Leo A. Drey for the people of Missouri. *Phil Kamp*

Missouri State Parks

Natural Divisions and Regions

This volume organizes the state parks and historic sites according to their location within six natural divisions and their regions, based largely on Thom and Wilson (1980), a widely recognized regionalization of the state used by state park officials for park planning beginning in the 1980s. The system aims to provide high quality representation of major characteristics, both natural and cultural, of each of the state's natural divisions and regions.

○ **State Parks**
□ **Historic Sites**

OZARKS
OZARK BORDER
MISSISSIPPI LOWLANDS
BIG RIVERS
OSAGE PLAINS
GLACIATED PLAINS

Regions

OZARKS
1. St. Francois Mountains
2. Upper Ozarks
3. Lower Ozarks
4. White River
5. Elk River
6. Springfield Plateau

OZARK BORDER
7. Mississippi River
8. Missouri River

MISSISSIPPI LOWLANDS
9. Lowlands
10. Crowley's Ridge

BIG RIVERS
11. Lower Mississippi
12. Upper Mississippi
13. Lower Missouri
14. Upper Missouri

OSAGE PLAINS
15. Osage Plains

GLACIATED PLAINS
16. Lincoln Hills
17. Eastern
18. Grand River
19. Western

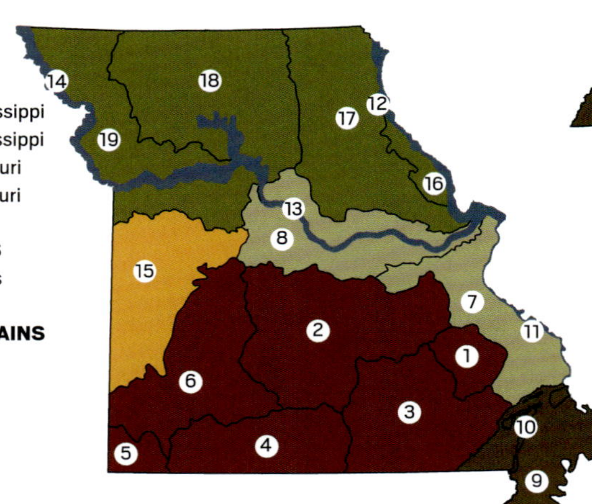

Contents

With more than 7,000 known caves, Missouri is called the cave state. State parks have at least 236 caves, including the premier show cave, Onondaga, a National Natural Landmark. *Ron Colatskie*

Parks Alphabetically

Compass plant, or *Silphium laciniatum*, punctuates the savanna-like border of Sherwood Prairie at Cuivre River State Park, the first place in the park system where controlled burning was practiced beginning in 1977. ***Bruce Schuette***

Preface

MISSOURI HAS ONE OF THE FINEST, most comprehensive systems of state parks and historic sites in the nation. Established in 1917 with the creation of a state park fund and starting in 1924 with the acquisition of the first park units, the system has grown to eighty-eight parks and historic sites totaling over 150,000 acres. The system annually records some eighteen million visits in a state with a population of six million.

The Missouri system of parks and historic sites is a reflection of the remarkable diversity of the state, both natural and cultural, and of its rich historical tradition. Missouri boasts some of the oldest rocks on the continent—the Precambrian igneous knobs of the St. Francois Mountains at the heart of the Ozarks—and some of the geologically youngest landforms—the big rivers and southeastern lowlands shaped by meltwaters of the great continental glaciers that covered the northern third of the state. In between are more caves and springs and clear natural streams than in probably any other state in the nation. The state is located on the border between the tallgrass prairies of the Great Plains and the extensive woodlands to the east, but it is also at the southern limit of some northern boreal plant species and the northern limit of some southern coastal plain species. All this makes for diversity.

Its commanding position at the junction of the two greatest rivers of the nation, the Mississippi and the Missouri, has given the state a vital role in nearly all of the currents of the country's human history. The first archaeologically undisputed contact of man and mastodon in the new world was found in a Missouri state park. Missouri was home to native peoples of both the woodlands and the prairies for more than ten thousand years; elements of the most sophisticated manifestation of native culture north of Mexico, the Mississippian, are found within its borders, as are key sites of the Osage, Missouria, Iliniwek, and other historic tribes.

Missouri was a key outpost and vital junction for French fur traders, miners, and farmers in the 1700s, a colony of Spain later that same century, and a magnet for Anglo-American settlers before and especially after the Louisiana Purchase of 1803. The Missouri River was the principal artery to the West for explorers and traders, and towns along its banks served as provisioning points for the great overland trails. With easy access by river, the state attracted a massive immigration from the upper South, complete with slaves. It also attracted large-scale migrations from Germany and the British Isles beginning around 1830, and then, with the advent of railroads, increasing numbers of settlers from non-slave areas of the United States—setting the stage for excruciating conflict during the Civil War. A rich agricultural state, Missouri also developed important mining and industrial activity, especially after the Civil War, but its small towns remained peculiarly vibrant and produced some of the nation's key leaders in war and politics and in literature and the arts. And in the twentieth century, the state became recognized for its outstanding recreational resources, attractive not only to its own citizens but also to visitors from afar.

One of the great strengths of the Missouri park system, like the national park system, has been the synergy of its combination of historic sites with natural parks. Although many states include some historic sites in their park systems, Missouri is one of relatively few states that have assigned all their state historic sites and parks, as well as outdoor recreation planning and historic preservation, to a single administrative agency, today the Division of State Parks—also known as Missouri State Parks—in the Department of Natural Resources. The system has functioned within the context of its multiple mission from the beginning, when it was a component of the state's Fish and Game Department, through the period 1937 to 1974, when it was an independent agency under a Missouri State Park Board, to the present arrangement. That mission, as currently stated, is "to preserve and interpret the finest examples of Missouri's natural landscapes; to preserve and interpret the finest examples of Missouri's cultural landmarks; and to provide healthy and enjoyable outdoor recreation opportunities for all Missourians and visitors to the state."

But the Missouri system of parks and historic sites is a product of more than happy conjunction of diverse natural and cultural resources with good administrative structure and management. Even more important, it is a legacy of people who have cared—cared enough to preserve for their own and future generations the best and most representative examples of their natural and cultural heritage. Behind each of Missouri's parks and historic sites—and behind many other areas that for one reason or another are not part of the system—lies a story of love and dedication and often remarkably effective action or splendid generosity by people who cared enough about their favorite place to secure its preservation. Every state, and the nation as well, has stories like this; but in Missouri, with its strong tradition of skepticism and its determination to hold the reins on government, the role of citizens who care has perforce been exceptionally strong.

Our purpose in this book is to explore each of Missouri's parks and historic sites and to capture its essence in words and in photographic images. We try to suggest not only what people saw in each park at the time of its establishment, but how the park or site itself and our thinking about it or uses of it may have changed over time. While the essays often describe the types of facilities available at the parks, our focus is primarily on natural and cultural resources and related recreational values, for it is these that have given the units statewide or even national significance and led to their inclusion in the system. State parks and historic sites would hardly be attracting eighteen million visits a year if they were not providing abundant recreation, but we hope through the stories in this book to expand people's awareness of the full range of recreational opportunities available at these parks, which includes understanding and enjoyment of natural and cultural features as well as sheer outdoor physical activity.

Beyond our focus on individual units, we seek to convey how the system as a whole reflects the natural and cultural heritage of the state. There are gaps, of course, some of which will surely be filled in the future. But we believe that Missouri comes closer to having a comprehensive system of state parks and historic sites than do most other states. Indeed, it is our hope that at least some readers will read this volume from beginning to end, rather than just dipping in here and there for particular parks or sites, and that they may gain thereby a fuller understanding of the natural and cultural history of the state and an appreciation for the vision and dedication of its citizens. We hope also that they will be inspired to visit places they have not yet seen, revisit others with new insights, ponder the particular nature of that which Missourians in the past have elected to preserve, and consider what they and others in the future might seek to add. Above all, we hope they will find reason to take pride in Missouri's state parks and historic sites and to protect and support them and the system of which they are a part.

Our intention, it should be stated, has not been to produce a guidebook, with detailed maps and locational information, lists of facilities, and addresses, telephone numbers, days and hours, and fees. Much of this information changes from time to time, and it is readily available in any case on the Missouri State Parks website and in brochures and other more timely and portable publications from the state or other sources. For the same reasons, we have not ordinarily provided exact figures for park acreages, but rather have rounded them.

This project had its inception several decades ago at a time of crisis for state parks in Missouri, when federal funds that supported many capital improvements during the 1960s and 1970s were suddenly withdrawn and state funds were constrained because of economic recession. The system was falling into decay and was in danger of dismemberment, with parks being proposed for transfer to another agency and historic sites presumably left hanging out to dry. The authors and editor believed that part of the problem was lack of widespread public understanding of the values at stake in the system as a whole, despite abundant evidence of Missourians' love for their favorite parks and a large reservoir of public goodwill. That love and goodwill have been amply demonstrated when Missourians voted in 1984 and again in 1988, 1996, and 2006 for a one-tenth-cent sales tax for state parks and soil conservation—a consistent source of funding that has led in recent decades to a genuine renaissance of state parks and historic sites in Missouri. But there is still limited public understanding of the system as a whole and of the part that each unit contributes to a much larger and more interesting picture, and it is that need that this book seeks to address.

The project began as a cooperative endeavor of the Missouri Parks Association, the Cultural Heritage Center at the University of Missouri-Columbia, and the Division of State Parks in the Missouri Department of Natural Resources (DNR). The Missouri Parks Association, a statewide citizens organization formed in 1982 in response to the crisis of the park system, initiated the project and has supported it financially and encouraged it throughout. The Cultural Heritage Center, which functioned from 1981 to 1995 to promote and facilitate multidisciplinary research on the heritage of the state and region, secured several grants to support research and to defray expenses. The park division has encouraged and facilitated the project throughout, its staff in both field and central office freely providing information and photographs and contributing to review of the manuscript.

The first edition of this volume was published by the University of Missouri Press in 1992, and over the ensuing decades it achieved many of the goals we set for it. But there are now eleven new parks in the system, and virtually every park has seen significant changes. Because reprinting the volume was no longer an option, Missouri Parks Association formed a new partnership with Missouri State Parks and Missouri Life Inc. in an effort to reach a new audience with a new book for a new generation. With two of the original authors deceased, B.H. Rucker joined the team of authors. In addition to the eleven essays for new parks, every essay has been revised, many of them substantially. While we have used some images from the original book, the vast majority—nearly 90 percent—are new.

Needless to say, the views expressed in this volume, as well as any errors that remain, are the responsibility of the authors and editor. While we have sought to be sensitive to the particular objectives and interpretive themes of individual units of the system and of the system as a whole, we have not hesitated to discuss problems and to offer critiques or judgments where they seemed warranted, sometimes going beyond particular sites to consider issues of regional or statewide interest. We agreed early on not to identify authorship of individual essays, in order to be free to critique, redraft, and expand on the work of our colleagues and thus to speak, insofar as possible, with a common voice.

We begin with a historical account of the evolution of the system to provide a context for the essays on the individual parks, many of which reflect the times in which they were established or developed. Missourians' image of their park system and its purposes matured with the years, and the philosophies that guided park development and management matured also. But despite changes in organizational structure and attitudes, there has also been a remarkable degree of continuity that has lent strength and resilience to the system.

The essays on individual units are arranged regionally and chronologically, following a generally accepted classification of the state into natural divisions and their regions, reflecting a largely watershed-based organization of the landscape. While state park naturalists now use a more sophisticated ecological classification system of national scope, it correlates well with the system of natural divisions used for the first edi-

tion and retained here. The natural divisions—Ozarks, Ozark Border, Mississippi Lowlands, Big Rivers, Osage Plains, and Glaciated Plains—are arranged roughly in order of their geologic and historical development, and parks within the divisions are also arranged roughly chronologically—or, in the case of the big rivers with their thousand miles in the state, by geographic progression up the Mississippi and then the Missouri. An essay at the beginning of each natural division discusses the characteristics of the division and briefly indicates the principal themes and the logic of the arrangement of individual parks and historic sites.

The scheme is far from perfect, and we have made some compromises. But we believe it is the most sensible one available to us in view of our stated objective to portray Missouri's state parks and historic sites as an integrated system. We rejected out-of-hand an alphabetical arrangement of units as being meaningless to the concept of a system. We also rejected an organization by type of unit—for example, with parks subdivided into natural parks, cave parks, and reservoir parks, and historic sites into Native American, ethnic, Civil War, mills, and the like. We especially resisted any effort to separate the historic sites from the parks because the sites are, in fact, legally parks and—far more important—there are cultural or historical resources in all of the parks and natural resources in virtually all of the historic sites. It would have been equally valid to convey the concept of a system through a wholly chronological arrangement—from the 1.5-billion-year-old Elephant Rocks to the studio where Thomas Hart Benton died at his easel in 1975. But it would not have been as practical because most of the parks exhibit significant features from many different time periods. In addition to the insights afforded by association of parks and historic sites within a meaningful framework, the regional arrangement has the added advantage of grouping essays on parks that readers may wish to visit on trips to particular parts of the state.

Missouri is unparalleled in the miles of high quality streams within its state park system, as here where the Meramec River curves along the base of Vilander Bluff, the river's highest bluff. ***Ron Colatskie***

We hope this book will stimulate some creative thinking about the interrelationships among parks and historic sites and among natural, cultural, and recreational resources and values. We also hope it will renew and inspire in its readers a greater appreciation of the state and its citizens, even as it deepens their understanding of this remarkable Missouri legacy. *

These extremely rare textile machines—two ring-frame ply twisters and a plain loom of 1860 vintage—demonstrate Watkins Woolen Mill's fame as America's finest preserved nineteenth-century textile factory. The mill has been designated a National Historic Landmark. *Ron Ginther*

Acknowledgments

THIS BOOK IN BOTH ITS EDITIONS has been a team effort with an ever growing and dedicated group of players. We should like to thank especially the Missouri Parks Association, the staff of Missouri State Parks, and the more than two hundred individuals and organizations who have encouraged and financially supported the publication.

Our greatest debt is to staff of Missouri State Parks, both current and retired, who viewed this book as another way of expressing their love for the state's parks and historic sites, to which many of them have devoted their entire careers. State Park Director Bill Bryan and former directors Wayne Gross and Doug Eiken steadfastly supported the project. Likewise, former Department of Natural Resources (DNR) Director Tracy Mehan encouraged publication of the first edition, as has Director Sara Parker Pauley the second.

This book began as the inspiration of then State Park Director John Karel, who guided its inception with insight and passion and later joined the team of authors. Paul Nelson, then chief of natural history, and B.H. Rucker, chief of historic sites, served as the principal coordinators of park staff contributions to the first edition and devoted untold hours to reviewing the manuscript, providing information, suggesting wording, and helping to secure photographs. David Kelly helped to coordinate park staff input to the current edition, Ken McCarty coordinated review of photos and captions, and B.H. Rucker, now retired, became an author. Two authors of the first edition, R. Roger Pryor and Charles Callison, are deceased, but their work lives on. Oliver Schuchard, whose large-format photographs made the first edition so stunning, is once again well represented in the second.

Among those who have provided photographs, Missouri State Parks graphics supervisor Stacy Bandelier and natural resource steward Allison Vaughn deserve special thanks for their help in securing photographs from various park and DNR sources. Former park naturalist Tom Nagel traveled the state for photos for the first edition, while natural resource steward Ron Colatskie and successive DNR staff photographers Nick Decker, Scott Myers, and Ben Nickelson also provided many images. Countless other staff members and former staff provided photographs and information and assisted in the review process. Among those who made special contributions are Bill Arnold, Jim Baker, Michael Beckett, Randy Becknell, Yvonne Bobbitt, Bill Bonnell, Carl Bonnell, Steve Bost, Annette Bridges, Cynthia Browne, Mary Bryan, Russell Burge, Walter Busch, Roxie Campbell, Matt Carletti, Michael Comer, Chris Crabtree, Chris Crocker, John Cunning, Ellen Davenport, Jim Denny, Mike Dickey, Steph Deidrick, Kim Dillon, Mary Donze, Wanda Doolen, Denise Dowling, Dan Drees, Meagan Duffee-Yates, Linda Endersby, Stan Fast, Chris Ferree, Don Fink, Tara Flynn, Richard Forry, Dawn Fredrickson, Janae Fuller, Jim Gast, Larry Grantham, Cindy Hall, Melissa Hall, Kerry Hays, Denzil Heaney, Art Hebrank, Orval Henderson, Blane Heumann, Dana Hoisington, Katy Holmer, Jamie Hubert, Sharon Hultberg, Almeta Jordan, Mathew Kantola, Quinn Kellner, Arne Larsen, Richard Love, Vicky Love, Nancy Masterson, Lesley McDaniel, Brian Miller, Ron Mullikin, Jim Newberry, Debbie Newby, Erik Otto, Anna Persell, Maria Potter, Janet Price, Donna Rausch, Debra Ray, Jim Rehard, Erin Renn, David Roggensees, Dakota Russell, Ed Schott, Bruce Schuette, Connie Schmidt, Don Schultehenrich, Michelle Soenksen, Bonnie Stepenoff, Don Stier, Brian Stith, Jerry Toops, Diane Tucker, Tom Uhlenbrock, Eugene Vale, Matt Vandevoort, Gary Walrath, Jennifer Weaver, Dustin Webb, Brian Wilcox, Lana Woody, and Tom Woodward. Former state park directors who offered insights and responded to queries for the first edition include Abner Gwinn, Joseph Jaeger, James Wilson, Fred Lafser, and Bill Palmer.

At the University of Missouri at Columbia, Diane Everman and Dennis Graham assisted with research for the first edition. Staff of the Western Historical Manuscript Collection, the State Historical Society of Missouri, the Missouri State Archives, the Missouri State Library, and Missouri State Parks facilitated research on documentary materials. Among others who supplied information or reviewed essays are Thomas Alexander, Jeffrey Ball, Robert Bray, Michael Cassity, Ben Duffield, Cam Fine, Townsend Godsey, Jean Hamilton, Harold Jordahl, James Keefe, David Leuthold, Bruce McMillan, Lynn Morrow, Osmund Overby, Gerald Rowan, Richard Sellars, William Wallace, and Ray Wood. Walter Schroeder of the University of Missouri at Columbia, Robert Mohlenbrock of Southern Illinois University at Carbondale, Ney Landrum of the National Association of State Park Directors, and Robin Winks of Yale University offered helpful comments on the first edition. For the current edition, Dru Buntin and Jennifer Johnson helped with essays for several parks, Denise Henderson Vaughn volunteered to make several special forays across the state for photographs, while Randal Clark, Greg Iffrig, Paul Jackson, Mike Leahy, Bill Naeger, Martin Turner, Cliff White, Eugene Vale, and Tom Vought also helped with photographs. At *Missouri Life*, Danita, Evan, and Greg Wood and Sarah Herrera shepherded the current edition to publication.

Financial support during various phases in the preparation of the first edition was provided by the sponsoring institutions, together with research grants from the Weldon Spring Research Fund of the University of Missouri and the University Research Council. The Watkins Mill Association, a friends group, pledged the first major support in aid of publication, and the Monsanto Fund followed with a generous challenge grant that in turn helped to stimulate other donations from more than one hundred individuals and organizations.

We are deeply grateful to Leo and Kay Drey, Pat Jones, and the Missouri Parks Association for major contributions toward publication of the current edition, as also for the first. The Conservation Federation of Missouri, the L-A-D Foundation, the Missouri Parks Association, and the Missouri State Park Foundation provided grants to support distribution of books to school libraries. More than two hundred individuals responded to a Kickstarter campaign to help with printing costs, with larger contributions from David and Nancy Bedan, Friends of Arrow Rock, Janice Gaston, Wayne and Jane Goode, James and Barbara Goodknight, Dr. Thomas B. and Margaret Hall III, Warren and Susan Lammert, Magnificent Missouri, Missouri Life, Inc., Beverly Miles, and Mary Still.

To all of these individuals and organizations we express our deepest gratitude. The manifold contributions to this project are yet another expression of Missourians who care. *

Above: From simple structures such as this gazebo overlooking Big River at Washington State Park to elaborate dining lodges, Missouri state parks are a treasure trove of Civilian Conservation Corps rustic architecture, a legacy from the first great era of park development during the Great Depression of the 1930s. ***Wikipedian Kbh3rd*** **• Right: When Henry Shaw donated Tower Grove Park to the city of St. Louis in 1868, a tradition of park philanthropy and planning was begun that in the next century would benefit the state park system. The park's fountains, artistic replicas of ruins, pergolas, and other Victorian design elements earned the park a designation as a National Historic Landmark.** ***Tower Grove Park Archives***

Evolution of the Park System

THE CONCEPT OF PUBLIC PARKS in Missouri gestated for half a century before Gov. Frederick Gardner signed an act of the Missouri General Assembly creating a state park fund on April 9, 1917, and our parks have continued to evolve for a century since. Yet despite the long and somewhat tortuous history of parks in the state and Missourian's attitudes about them, there are remarkable threads of continuity. The result is a system that reflects not only the natural diversity and rich historical currents of the state but, to a rather remarkable extent, the values and dedication of its citizenry and something of its political culture as well.

ORIGINS OF PUBLIC PARKS: MISSOURI AND THE NATION

For the origins of the movement for public parks in this country, we must look not to the national government or even to the states but to the great cities. New York established Central Park in the 1850s, and after the Civil War, a host of other cities joined in, not least among them St. Louis with Henry Shaw's Tower Grove Park in 1868 and Forest, O'Fallon, and Carondelet Parks in 1874. Kansas City, just beginning to grow in the 1860s, did not join the movement for public parks until the end of the century, but then it shot to the front ranks nationally with a visionary yet practical design for parks, boulevards, and residential and commercial districts conceived by landscape architect George Kessler and realized through a formidable array of civic, political, and entrepreneurial talents. The movement for urban parks was significant in that it drew on and nurtured notions of civic responsibility, planning, and design that would later pay dividends for state parks. George Kessler's successors in park, parkway, and urban planning—S.J. and S. Herbert Hare in Kansas City and Harland Bartholomew in St. Louis and their associates—would make crucial contributions to Missouri's state park system during the 1930s.

The movements for state and, later, national parks had an early tie to

the urban movement through the work of Frederick Law Olmsted, principal designer of New York's Central Park, who served as first head of the Yosemite Park Commission after Congress transferred Yosemite Valley to the state of California for protection and management in 1864. Olmsted realized that the prime value of Yosemite was its natural scenery, which the state therefore had an obligation to preserve "as exactly as is possible" and to guard from any constructions that would detract from it. Congress established the world's first national park in the Yellowstone country of Wyoming in 1872, again to protect the fabulous scenery and curiosities of nature from incompatible private exploitation.

At the urging of Olmsted and others, New York in 1885 voted to acquire a state reservation at Niagara Falls and to establish a state forest preserve in the Adirondacks. Michigan acquired its first state park, Mackinac Island, in 1885 by transfer from the federal government. Minnesota began acquiring state parks in 1889 with Birch Coulee, a battleground of the Sioux War, and then Itasca at the headwaters of the Mississippi in 1891, and Massachusetts established its Trustees of Public Reservations the same year to begin developing a system of public open spaces.

By the last decade of the nineteenth century and the first decade of the twentieth, the movement for public parks and forests gained momentum as part of a progressive era redefinition of the responsibilities of government. Virtually the entire system of western national forests dates from these decades; national parks were established at Yosemite, Mount Rainier, Crater Lake, Mesa Verde, and Glacier. Progressive states such as Wisconsin, Minnesota, California, New York, New Jersey, Maryland, Massachusetts, Pennsylvania, Ohio, and Illinois began or added to their systems of state parks and historic sites.

Missouri also experienced an upwelling of progressive sentiment among its citizenry, characterized especially by an emphasis on restraint of special interests and respect for law, but with the state's strong southern tradition of fiscal conservatism and distrust of government, its legislators continued to resist major new governmental programs. Herbert Hadley, a progressive elected in1908 as the state's first Republican governor since Reconstruction, led well-publicized annual outings on the Current and White Rivers in an effort to encourage Missourians' pride in their state and foster their commitment to protecting their resources. But he was thwarted in his efforts to establish state park and forestry programs by the parsimony of the old-line Democratic-controlled legislature, on one occasion failing by only one vote to gain a $160,000 appropriation from the game protection fund to purchase a 5,000-acre park at the fabled Ha Ha Tonka in Camden County.

Before leaving office in 1913, Hadley recommended a legislative commission to select "some of the natural wonders and beauties" of the state for purchase as parks, and a powerful Ozark Democrat, Sen. Carter Buford, won legislative approval for such a commission with himself as chair. The Buford committee visited and recommended acquisition of big parks of 5,000 acres or more at four sites: Ha Ha Tonka again, the Shut-Ins Club near Arcadia in Iron County, the Black River near Lesterville in Reynolds County (probably in the vicinity of Johnson's Shut-Ins), and Onondaga Cave in Crawford County. But the assembly was still unwilling to appropriate funds, and it would be a half-century or more before these prime areas would be secured for state parks.

The movement for state parks in Missouri may have gained impetus from the establishment in 1916 of the National Park Service in the Department of the Interior, which brought coherence and a sense of mission to the management of the national parks. The Missouri General Assembly in 1917 passed a bill providing that 5 percent of all fish and game license fees be transferred to a special state park fund, and this act is taken as the official establishment of the state park system. But seven more years would pass before the state would acquire its first parks. This delay was in part because the money accumulated slowly; after four years, there was still less than $40,000 in the fund. But it may also have been because too many people were mesmerized by the lure of Ha Ha Tonka, with its grandiose castle and thirty outbuildings, which was being heavily promoted by real estate interests but was out of reach at an asking price of $300,000. Not until Gov. Arthur Hyde

exerted his personal leadership and determination in the early 1920s did a park system begin to materialize.

In his efforts to acquire state parks for Missouri, Governor Hyde must surely have been encouraged by the calling of the first National Conference on State Parks in January 1921 at the invitation of the governor of Iowa. Twenty-eight states were represented, including Missouri, and the enthusiasm generated at this and subsequent conferences spurred the establishment of parks in at least twenty-five states during the 1920s. The movement for state parks was tied closely to that for national parks, in part to relieve the pressure on the national park system for new parks in every state, and also to the movement for better highways, which would connect the parks and open them for tourist development. Formerly an automobile dealer, Governor Hyde enjoyed his greatest successes in molding a modern highway system and a state park system for Missouri.

Realizing that the park fund was growing too slowly to acquire the

Gov. Herbert Hadley (seated, back) floats the Current River in a johnboat in 1909. He led well-publicized trips on Ozark rivers in an attempt to encourage Missourians' pride in their state and to foster their commitment to protecting their resources. He promoted establishing state parks and other conservation measures. *Herbert Hadley Papers, Western Historical Manuscript Collection*

"chain of parks" he now envisioned, Hyde succeeded in getting the state assembly in 1923 to increase the annual transfer of only 5 percent of fish and game license fees to 25 percent. During his last year in office, 1924, he appointed a new game and fish commissioner, Frank Wielandy, an Izaak Walton League leader from St. Louis who had been a park enthusiast for decades, and the two began canvassing the state—or at least the Ozarks—looking for the best lands to acquire with the $165,000 now in the park fund. Since they wanted five or six parks of 3,000 acres or more, including several of the largest springs, they certainly would not be

Ha Ha Tonka was still a majestic castle rather than ruins in the 1920s. With its superb concentration of caves, springs, sinkholes, and other karst topographic features and its grandiose castle, Ha Ha Tonka mesmerized Missourians with its potential as a park, perhaps thereby delaying the process of selecting other sites for the state's first parks. Decades later, the castle in ruins, Ha Ha Tonka finally joined the state park system in 1978. *State Historical Society of Missouri*

able to look at highly developed properties like Ha Ha Tonka.

As it happened, the first properties to move toward resolution were small historic sites in which local citizens had long been interested: the old tavern in Arrow Rock and the Mark Twain birthplace cabin in Florida. Like many historic sites that would come into state ownership over the years, each had a citizen support group—the Daughters of the American Revolution and the Mark Twain Memorial Park Association—that had secured the site and was willing to make a substantial contribution in the public interest. The 1917 act establishing the park fund had no language defining a park or clarifying its purposes; there would be no such language until 1953, although the fact that the fund originated from game and fish license receipts and was administered by the game and fish commissioner naturally led officials to think in terms of lands that also could be used to propagate game and fish. The eagerness of citizen groups to promote and support historic sites at the onset of the park program was thus critical to the development of a park system in Missouri that would eventually treat cultural resources on a par with natural resources.

Other than Arrow Rock and Mark Twain, which Governor Hyde happily accepted, he and his game and fish commissioner looked solely in the Ozarks for parks, because that is where land was cheap and where recreational and tourist potential seemed greatest. After looking at dozens of properties and turning down many more, Hyde and Wielandy by the end of 1924 had purchased or begun acquisition of six substantial parks in the Ozarks: Big Spring and Round Spring on the Current River, Alley Spring on the Jacks Fork, Bennett Spring on the Niangua, Deer Run near Ellington, and Indian Trail near Salem. Most of these areas had long been identified by their use as recreational sites and by public awe of them as natural wonders, the same kind of awe that led to public pressures for creation of the Adirondack Park in New York or the first national park in the Yellowstone country. Together they totaled nearly 24,000 acres and cost about $175,000.

During the next few years, a new game and fish commissioner, Keith McCanse, acquired five more parks: Montauk, Sam A. Baker, Meramec, Chesapeake, and Roaring River, the latter a magnificent 2,550-acre gift from Dr. T. M. Sayman of St. Louis, the first major donation to the system from a private individual. Thus by 1928, the state had fourteen state parks (including Sequiota, a fish hatchery reclassified as a park) totaling nearly 40,000 acres, acquired at a cost of about $335,000. Of twenty-six states that had created state parks by 1928, only four showed more acreage than Missouri—New York, South Dakota, Minnesota, and Wisconsin—and if state or federal lands reclassified as parks are omitted, Missouri was second only to New York. It was a stunning achievement, especially for a state as conservative as Missouri, an achievement that can only be explained by strong citizen support for saving park areas, unusual gubernatorial leadership, and the availability of splendid park resources at a remarkably low price. Another likely factor was the absence of competition from foresters, since Missouri, unlike most progressive states, had no state forest program whatever as of 1928.

Despite the state's initial success in acquiring a collection of superb parks, park leaders were under no illusion that the state was developing a comprehensive system. Except for Arrow Rock and Mark Twain, all the parks were in the Ozarks, and game officials, cognizant of the source of their funds, were at pains to point out that more than 95 percent of parkland was being used "strictly for game refuge purposes" and some 60 percent of park expenses were "chargeable directly to game propagation." Public and legislative pressures intensified during the late 1920s and early 1930s to acquire more historical properties and more lands north of the Missouri River, but game and fish officials found themselves

unable to justify using sportsmen's money for such purchases.

In 1932, following years of legislative efforts to force the purchase of parks north of the river, the Game and Fish Department acquired two small areas at Big Lake and Wallace, both of which were developed as fishing sites. The same year, two premier archaeological sites entered the system as gifts—Van Meter, a village site of the Missouria Indians, and Washington, known for its petroglyphs carved by Indians of the Mississippian tradition—but there was no mention whatever of the cultural significance of these sites in news accounts and reports from the Game and Fish Department. Meanwhile, the department felt constrained to demur on an appropriation for a historic site at Fort Osage, dating from the territorial period, on the grounds that it was "not a wise investment" when considered as a property for the Game and Fish Department.

As fish and game populations in Missouri continued to decline due to inadequate management and law enforcement and as departmental revenues fell off during the worst depression in the nation's history, Missouri sportsmen stepped up their efforts, dating back at least to the early 1920s, to take fish and game administration out of politics. By 1932, they were arguing as well against the diversion of license money to parks, as if that were a cause of the decline in harvestable fish and

The big Ozark springs were envisioned as jewels on a "chain of parks" connected by modern highways by Gov. Arthur Hyde and other park advocates of the 1920s. This is the spring branch and mill at Alley Spring. *Rex Gary, State Park Archives*

The state regent of the Daughters of the American Revolution, Ethel Massie Withers, showed this glass-lantern slide of the Federal-style Huston Tavern, built in 1834 at Arrow Rock, as she traveled the state around 1915 lecturing on Missouri's historic places. The DAR operated a tearoom here and encouraged the state to purchase the building, which it did in 1923, making it Missouri's first state historic site. *State Historical Society of Missouri*

game. What they wanted was more money for artificial propagation, a technique that leading professionals in the field already knew would not solve the problem. But once again, legislators failed to take action.

A NEW DEAL FOR STATE PARKS

Hunters and fishermen would have even more cause for concern after the inauguration of Franklin Roosevelt's New Deal in March 1933. Missouri, with its large acreage of parks ripe for development, was fortuitously poised to take maximum advantage of the Emergency Conservation Work (ECW) programs of the New Deal that in turn would mean even more expenditure of time, effort, and money on parks by the Game and Fish Department. Over the next few years, thousands of young men in work crews of the Civilian Conservation Corps (CCC), the Works Progress Administration (WPA), and other New Deal programs would literally give shape and definition to the parks, laying out and constructing roads and bridges, entrance gates, hiking and bridle trails, lakes with dams and spillways, swimming beaches, pools and bathhouses, campgrounds, picnic shelters, group camps, tourist cabins, dining lodges, water and sewage systems, comfort stations, and service centers. By the end of 1936, Game and Fish Commissioner Wilbur Buford, who served as state coordinator for the ECW, reported that more than $25 million in federal funds had been expended in Missouri, a considerable portion of it in state parks.

Virtually every park in the system benefited from the federal programs, and several new parks were added to take advantage of the open moneybags. The most grandiose plans centered on the huge new Lake of the Ozarks, formed after the completion of the Union Electric Power Company's Bagnell Dam on the Osage River in 1931. Foreseeing federal dollars, the company had hired the two leading architectural and planning firms in the state, Harland Bartholomew and Associates of St. Louis and Hare and Hare of Kansas City, known for their urban parks and parkways, to present recommendations for its property around the lake. The consultants recommended three separate state parks totaling 18,000 acres, preservation of large stretches of shoreline, and seventy miles of parkways. When the Missouri State Planning Board was established in late 1933 in response to federal mandates for state-level planning, Bartholomew and Hare were ready to serve as consultants and further their plans for Lake of the Ozarks as a focal point for tourism in the state. By 1934, when the New Deal began a program for federal purchase of submarginal agricultural lands for conservation purposes, including a system of Recreational Demonstration Areas conceived by the National Park Service, Lake of the Ozarks quickly emerged as a likely site. Missouri was second only to Pennsylvania in the number and extent of its demonstration areas, all of which would be developed by the National Park Service but were slated eventually to become state parks, which they did in 1946: Lake of the Ozarks, at 16,000 acres far and away the largest park in the system; Cuivre River, about 6,000 acres; and Montserrat (later called Knob Noster), 4,000 acres.

Other parks added during the early years of the New Deal included Sugar Lake (later renamed Lewis and Clark), donated by a group of Buchanan County sportsmen, and the Dr. Edmund A. Babler Memorial State Park in St. Louis County. Jacob Babler, who donated the park with his brother Henry, was well connected in St. Louis civic, planning, and political circles, and he clearly intended the park as a unit of the "outer park and parkway system" envisioned by civic leaders since the dawn of the century. He commissioned Harland Bartholomew to design the park

The tent camp at Sam A. Baker in the 1930s was temporary home to the young men of the Civilian Conservation Corps. The CCC built more than five hundred structures in Missouri Parks, such as the stable in the background. *State Park Archives* • A CCC crew works on a stone cabin at Big Spring. *National Archives*

and used his political influence to secure not one but two CCC camps and a WPA crew to develop it. Another park heavily promoted at the time by local park and civic groups in northern Missouri, as well as by the Missouri Chamber of Commerce, was intended as a memorial to a native son, Gen. John J. Pershing, but it had to await resolution of the tension between the state parks and game and fish interests before it, too, could take advantage of the federal development programs.

More significant even than the sheer quantity of development by the CCC and the WPA was the quality. All work was carefully planned in advance and supervised by professional architects, landscape architects, foresters, and civil engineers, most of them in the employ of the National Park Service. With NPS standards and criteria governing the work, the New Deal left a legacy of superb design and expert craftsmanship in rustic wood and stone. This fine CCC and WPA craftsmanship still enhances the parks and sets a standard for contemporary development.

NPS involvement during the New Deal era also influenced some of the management philosophy and policies of the parks, which now began to move—slowly at first—toward emphasis on biotic values and cultural heritage on the model of national parks, in contrast to some of the more manipulative forestry and game propagation practices favored by the Game and Fish Department. As it happened, quite unexpectedly, differences in management philosophies would have an opportunity to incubate over the years in two separate state agencies, one for game, fish, and forestry, the other for parks.

An effort for more than a decade to establish a citizen commission that would insulate the Missouri Game and Fish Department from politics and provide for more professional administration and policy continuity finally bore fruit in 1936, when a coalition of civic leaders and sportsmen secured passage by statewide initiative petition of a constitutional amendment establishing a four-member bipartisan Conservation Commission. The amendment took effect July 1, 1937, and gave the new commission authority to manage the bird, fish, game, forestry, and wildlife resources of the state, but it was totally silent about state parks.

Whatever the intentions of the promoters of the amendment, its effect was to force an alternative arrangement for the parks. The General Assembly in 1937 passed an emergency act to establish a State Park Board consisting of the governor, the attorney general, and the director of conservation, with the director of conservation to serve also as director of state parks. And for the first time, the assembly appropriated funds from general revenue for operation and development of the parks. Almost as if to proclaim the removal of the strictures that had guided the use of park funds derived from sportsmen's licenses, the assembly also made specific appropriations for acquisition of the long-sought Pershing Memorial Park, of a park to commemorate Gen. Enoch Crowder, of a new historic site at Fort Zumwalt, and of additions to Mark Twain and Van Meter. Thus the year 1937, which saw the sundering of the bonds between the Conservation Department and the state parks and the beginning of the long process of extrication, also witnessed one of the most successful legislative sessions in the history of the park system. Another park, Big Oak Tree, entered the system on an emergency basis later that year when citizens responded to a lumber company's plans to level the virgin forest surrounding the biggest oak in the state.

It was not clear how the new relationship between the State Park Board and the Conservation Commission would work out or even who would manage the parks. The attorney general advised that parks used exclusively for fish and game should be under the Conservation Commission and those used for recreation under the Park Board, while for those containing both wildlife and recreational resources—virtually all of the parks—the wildlife areas would be controlled by the Conservation Commission and the recreational areas by the Park Board. Obviously, there would be problems to sort out.

In retrospect, it appears that the newly elected governor of the state, Lloyd Stark, was supportive of parks and intent on placing them on a firm management footing. His four appointees to the new Conservation Commission included two who clearly were park-minded: A. P. Greensfelder,

A lumber company was about to cut down the biggest oak tree in Missouri when it and the eighty-acre remnant of Mississippi swamp forest on which it stood were rescued in 1937 by concerted citizen action. *State Park Archives* • Stonemasons in African American Civilian Conservation Corps Company 1743 built a gazebo and most of the park facilities at Washington State Park. *National Archives*

donor of Washington State Park and a member of the State Planning Board, and former Game and Fish Commissioner Wilbur Buford, who had won the respect of federal officials for his management of the ECW program in the parks. The governor, above all, did not want to do anything to jeopardize continued federal funding of park development. He let it be known that he favored the appointment of a professional with federal experience as conservation and park director, and the Conservation Commission eventually selected I. T. Bode of Iowa, a forester who had served with the US Biological Survey.

To develop in-house planning capability for parks, as was expected by the National Park Service, Bode and Stark selected an assistant director for parks, E. A. Mayes, who had experience with both the state and national planning boards, and hired several other professionals as well. The State Planning Board prepared a comprehensive plan for Missouri in 1938 and 1939, and Harland Bartholomew and S. Herbert Hare continued to consult on master plans for individual parks. Thus, park planning and administration advanced to a new level of professionalism in Missouri, one it would not see again until the 1970s, and federal dollars continued to flow, especially to develop the new parks in northern Missouri.

A review of the 1938 park plan suggests that despite the newfound professional basis of the state park system, modeled on that of the national park system, conceptions of the values of parks were still constrained by present realities. On a map of "lands suitable for recreation," for example, the parks are limited primarily to the scenic, "submarginal" Ozarks, while proposed units termed "recreational areas" (presumably not scenic enough to merit full park status) are scattered elsewhere in the state. The plan briefly mentions the desirability of including in the system distinctive natural features, such as native Missouri prairie, and important historic sites, but no such sites are identified among the proposed expansions. There is little sense of state parks as a system representing the full spectrum of the state's natural and cultural heritage. Full consciousness of the value of such resources had yet to evolve.

The plan also offers insights on the financing of the system. Nearly $20 million had been invested in the system through 1938, according to the plan: less than $1.5 million by the state ($550,000 in land acquisition and $915,000 in development and operation) and the remainder by the federal government. Of fourteen upper Midwest states selected for comparison, Missouri ranked second only to Illinois in the number of park service CCC camps it had been allocated, while it had spent only a third to a fifth as much per capita on parks from state revenues during the two-year period from 1937 to 1938. Missouri, with its superlative scenic resources, its strong tradition of urban parks and park planning, and its unabashed willingness to mine sportsmen's license fees to purchase parklands during a formative period, had managed to build a remarkable state park system with fortuitous federal assistance and incredibly little in the way of general state funds. The challenge now would be to come up with sufficient funds to maintain and develop that system.

RETRENCHMENT AND REDEFINITION

Although the 1938 park plan optimistically recommended enhanced state funding, an aggressive program of land acquisition, and stronger and clearer statutory authority for the Park Board (in a "confidential supplement," it suggested that the current board composed of major state executives was inadvisable and proposed a citizen board), in fact the park system would enter a period of severe constraints, retrenchment, and even crisis in the 1940s. It began with the election of 1940, in which a Republican, Forrest Donnell, won the governorship by a hair's breadth against the odds. With a new administration from a different political party, old arrangements were open to question, especially, as it turned out, the relationship between the Park Board and the Conservation Commission.

Since 1937, all major policy decisions, acquisitions, and appointments involving state parks had essentially been made out of the governor's office, with some patronage positions given to the attorney general. But day-to-day management during Stark's term was largely by administrators, including E. A. Mayes, whose appointments were split between conservation and parks and who reported to I. T. Bode in his dual capacities as director of conservation and of parks. The two agencies shared the same offices. There was talk of dividing the lands, but it was not done. For the most part, technicians in each agency plied their craft on the same lands. Without the management expectations of the National Park Service that came along with the federal funds it supervised, the management of parks and conservation would likely have been even more intermingled and confused than it was.

Under the new Republican administration beginning in 1941, the central offices, key staff positions, and land-management units of Conservation and Parks were formally and physically separated. The Conservation Commission took over the full salaries of all employees who had been on split appointments, and the Park Board hired a new chief, Fred W. Pape, former director of Forest Park in St. Louis. I. T. Bode retained his statutory authority as director of parks until a further reorganization in 1953, but he had little role in running the agency. The Park Board voted to surrender to the Conservation Commission its jurisdiction over Sequiota and Chesapeake state parks, which had been used primarily as fish hatcheries, and over 22,000 acres of forests at Deer Run and Indian Trail, which had never been developed for general recreation and had only a few thousand visitors each year.

There was discussion about other areas, including Big Lake, Lewis and Clark, Meramec, and Sam Baker, in which the Park Board authorized the Conservation Commission to continue certain management activities, but no other parks were transferred. After years of simmering controversy, an agreement in 1980 would give the Conservation Department the portion of Meramec east of the river for a state forest while Baker was retained exclusively under park management. The Conservation Department still retains jurisdiction and management of the trout hatcheries in Bennett, Montauk, and Roaring River State Parks and has regulatory jurisdiction over the fish and wildlife in other parks, subject to the land management authority of the state park system.

As the nation became preoccupied with World War II, the parks entered a holding pattern, or worse. Federal work relief programs came to an end, and labor costs suddenly more than doubled, if park workers could be found at any price. The entire professional staff left for the war effort. Personnel funds were nearly exhausted by March 1943, and the Park Board discussed closing up shop. In the end, the parks continued to operate, but just barely.

The pressing financial crisis of the parks was addressed in part by a

A park naturalist identifies special features within the landscape. The highly popular naturalist program began in 1937 and continued on a reduced basis even during the war years. ***Hadley K. Irwin, State Park Archives***

provision slipped into the state's proposed new constitution in 1944 by park benefactor Jacob Babler, a Republican delegate to the constitutional convention. It mandated an appropriation from general revenue each year for the next fifteen years of not less than one cent on each $100 of assessed valuation. This would provide about $400,000 a year, not a princely sum but several times more than parks had received during the war years. Babler also had a legislative bill introduced to create stronger, clearer statutory authority for the parks, along the lines recommended in the 1938 state park plan, and to establish a new bipartisan citizen park board. Missourians adopted the new constitution with its funding mechanism for parks in February 1945, and in May, the General Assembly passed Babler's park bill. Babler died on June 1, and on June 4, a new Democratic governor, Phil Donnelly, vetoed the park bill for technical and, so Republicans charged, political reasons.

The old Park Board headed by the governor thus continued at the helm. The board hired a new park director, Abner Gwinn, a highway department engineer selected for his ability to deal with the backlog of deferred maintenance. Gwinn would also have to set up state administration for the three former Recreation Demonstration Areas: Lake of the Ozarks, Cuivre River, and Knob Noster. The state was finally able to accept the latter in 1946 after funds from the new constitutional appropriation began to flow.

Once people began to sense that there was money, various groups appeared before the Park Board to promote new parks: Fort Osage, Wilson's Creek, Battle of Lexington, Sappington Cemetery, Confederate Memorial, Battle of Athens, and Fort Davidson. Historic sites such as these seemed over the years to attract more citizen initiative than other kinds of parks, but the board did not view itself as having the authority or the funds to acquire such sites. Nor was the legislature responsive, so there were no new parks until 1952. In that year, four new parks entered the system, mostly by donation: Thousand Hills, from the city of Kirksville; Confederate Memorial, transferred by the legislature; the Pershing boyhood home, purchased through the good offices of the Pershing Memorial Park Association; and Hawn, a surprise bequest from a country schoolteacher, Helen Coffer Hawn.

Throughout the postwar years, political charges continued to swirl around the Park Board, particularly regarding the patronage system and exorbitant profits made by park concessionaires, and numerous attempts were made to reform the system. Then in 1953, a bill similar to the Babler bill of 1945 passed the assembly and was signed by the same governor who had vetoed the earlier measure, Phil Donnelly, who had recently been reelected. In addition to setting up a bipartisan citizen commission of six members with staggered four-year terms, the new act provided a definition of a park that still forms the basic statutory expression of the mission of the park system: a park is "any land, site, or object primarily of recreational value or of cultural value because of its scenic, historic, prehistoric, archaeologic, scientific, or other distinctive characteristics or natural features."

Not only was it now clear that historic sites were included in the definition of a park, but it was also clear that the legislators intended the system to be broadly representative of the distinctive natural and cultural resources of the state, much as the national park system is representative of the nation. And it was clear that the criteria of significance for selecting new state parks related to their distinctive historic or natural features and the recreational or cultural values derived from them. This was nothing new; it was an expression in law of the park philosophy that had been evolving in the nation and the state to that time. But just as the 1916 act establishing the national park system mandated conserving "natural and historic objects" years before the National Park Service began acquiring deserts, grasslands, wetlands, and other non-forested, non-mountainous terrain and historic sites, so too Missouri still had a long way to go to realize the comprehensive array of natural and cultural resources implied by its mission statement in the 1953 act.

Under the new citizen commission, an array of new parks entered the system, beginning with the magnificent Johnson's Shut-Ins in 1955 from the Desloge Foundation. Later in 1955, Joseph Jaeger Jr., a Conservation Department forester, began a tenure as park director that would intersect the administrations of five governors, extending until 1973, except for a two-year hiatus in the mid-1960s. A dynamic and politically astute administrator, Jaeger sought, within the limits of available funds, to shape a more comprehensive system and to professionalize its administration.

During the next fifteen years, twenty-six new parks would enter the system, many of them historic or archaeological sites and nearly all of them donations, as the Park Board adopted a policy of accepting only donated units and, later, only donations for which the legislature would provide specific appropriations for initial development, in order to conserve its meager funds for operations and maintenance. Missouri voters in 1960 overwhelmingly approved a twelve-year extension of the constitutional one-mill appropriation for state parks instituted in 1945, but the funds were decidedly inadequate to support a rapidly growing system.

Citizens of Cape Girardeau County, undoubtedly encouraged by a local member of the Park Board, voted a $150,000 bond issue in 1956 to purchase a park on the bluffs of the Mississippi to commemorate the Cherokee Trail of Tears. Two reservoir parks were developed on leaseholds donated in 1957 by the Army Corps of Engineers: Lake Wappapello and Table Rock. The United Automobile Workers union donated Harry Truman's birthplace in Lamar in 1957, and the Anderson House and Lexington Battlefield Foundation gave the Battle of Lexington site in 1958. Three more parks were added in 1960: Pomme de Terre, another corps reservoir park; Wakonda, donated by the State Highway Commission; and Boone's Lick, a gift from Russell Clinkscales and Horace Munday. That same year, the governor also provided money from a special fund left over from the Spanish-American War to purchase the buildings that had housed the first state capitol in St. Charles.

In 1964 two parks that are now National Historic Landmarks entered the system: Watkins Mill, donated by the Watkins Mill Association and the citizens of Clay County, and Graham Cave, donated by Frances Graham Darnell. That year, county taxpayers and the St. Joseph Lead Company also donated the large St. Francois State Park.

After the Jefferson County court transferred the grave site of Gov. Daniel Dunklin to the state in 1965, the legislature in 1967 authorized the Park Board to maintain any grave of a former governor that was not within a perpetual care cemetery, as well as any covered wooden bridges donated to the state. These provisions resulted in the addition of the Burfordville, Union, Sandy Creek, and Locust Creek bridges to the system in 1967 or 1968.

Five other parks entered the system in 1967: Elephant Rocks through a gift by John Stafford Brown; Bollinger Mill from the Cape Girardeau County Historical Society; the Hunter-Dawson home from the city of

State park director Joe Jaeger, left, and University of Missouri archaeologist Carl Chapman examine a newly constructed shelter over the petroglyphs at Washington State Park in 1963. By this time, park officials were making concerted efforts to expand the system's representation, preservation, and interpretation of cultural resources. *Hadley K. Irwin, State Park Archives*

New Madrid; Rock Bridge from the Rock Bridge Memorial Park Association and with federal funds; and the Towosahgy archaeological site, also with newly available federal funds. In 1969, Fort Davidson was leased to the state by the US Forest Service, and Stockton became another corps reservoir park. In 1970 descendants of the Vallé and Rozier families donated the Felix Vallé home in Ste. Genevieve, and two more cemeteries with governors' graves, Sappington and Jewell, became historic sites.

THE RECREATION BOOM

The rapid expansion of the Missouri state park system during this period was not unusual compared with other states. In fact, the Missouri system expanded less than those of many other states that passed major bond issues or other special funding mechanisms for parks in the early 1960s. Even without any major funding for parks in Missouri, the expansion seemed fully warranted by the surge in attendance, which stood at only about half a million in 1945, down from a million before the war. But after the war, attendance exploded to a reported six million visitors by 1960 and over fourteen million in 1970, when a computer projection predicted future visitation at more than twenty-three million by 1980. Attendance figures can be notoriously unreliable, particularly in a state like Missouri that does not collect an entrance fee, and the figures from the 1960s, when officials were trying to win greater appropriations for their burgeoning system, are probably especially so. Yet anyone who visited the parks knew that they were popular and could see that they were being overwhelmed.

The dramatic increase in attendance at state parks in Missouri during the postwar years was part of a national surge toward outdoor recreation, spurred no doubt by the ready availability of automobiles and better highways, more leisure time, and other manifestations of what has come to be known as the "consumption society." In response to this phenomenon, the US Congress in 1958 created an Outdoor Recreation Resources Review Commission, which issued a battery of reports and recommendations including a proposal for a federal grants-in-aid program to assist state and local governments in the purchase and development of recreational lands. Congress followed through in 1964 by establishing the Land and Water Conservation Fund, which mandated state-level planning, as in the 1930s, but also insisted on one-to-one matching contributions.

The first $700,000 for state parks from the LWCF began flowing in 1966. Included in the first batch of projects, in addition to numerous small items for water, sewer, campground, and picnic area development at existing parks, were acquisition funds for Rock Bridge and Towosahgy. From then through 1981, Missouri would receive more than $68 million through the federal fund, nearly $18 million of which would be allocated to projects in the state parks, with most of the remainder going to local park systems. Annual apportionments to Missouri started modestly in the 1960s, increased to a high of nearly $7.5 million by the late 1970s (about a third of which went to state parks), dropped to nothing in 1982 during the administration of President Ronald Reagan, and then resumed at about $500,000 annually beginning in the mid-1980s, with all funds allocated to local parks. The total of about $18 million allocated to state parks from 1966 to 1981 helped the state to purchase ten new parks and to accept donations of several others that it might not have been able to develop without federal aid. In all, LWCF matching funds helped with acquisition or development projects involving fifty different state parks in Missouri.

The new era of federal aid also had another type of impact. Because it originated from a concern for outdoor recreation and provided so much funding for municipal and other local park systems, where the emphasis was heavily on intensive, facility-based recreation—playing fields, swimming pools, tennis courts, golf courses, fitness programs, and the like—the federal program shifted public attention and professional involvement toward the recreation aspect of the tripartite natural-cultural-recreational mission of the state park system. Acquisition

By the late 1960s, the explosion of recreational use in the parks put them in danger of becoming outdoor slums. Campgrounds like this one at Bennett Spring had no designated individual spots and were greatly overcrowded. *Hadley K. Irwin, State Park Archives* • Right: The pressures of recreational use, severe as they were by the 1960s and 1970s, were more widespread but probably no more intense than they had been at some popular getaways like Lincoln Beach on the lower Meramec River, where this photograph was taken around 1930. Thousands of St. Louisans flocked to the resorts near Castlewood Depot from 1915 to 1940. Castlewood joined the state park system in 1974 when the federal Land and Water Conservation Fund helped states acquire additional lands for recreation. *St. Louis Post-Dispatch, State Park Archives*

and development funded through LWCF had to be justified in terms of a contribution to public recreation, rather than to resource preservation or cultural interpretation. And most of the newly trained recreation professionals available for state park positions were products of programs that emphasized facility-based rather than resource-based recreation.

Fortunately for the state's rather vulnerable new ventures into preservation and restoration of historic sites, the federal government during the late 1960s also gave impetus to cultural concerns through the Historic Preservation Act of 1966, which established a National Register of Historic Places and a modest program of matching grants to help states prepare preservation plans, conduct surveys, and assist in preservation of sites. This program, like the outdoor recreation grant program, was administered in Missouri by the state park director, thus offering potential for coordination with park programs. Missouri was one of the first states to establish a state office of historic preservation under the new act and to inventory sites statewide that might qualify for the register. The National Park Service sent preservation staff from other states to learn Missouri methods, and the state became a leader nationally in restoration efforts.

The late 1960s and early 1970s were years of heightened interest nationwide in preservation of natural as well as cultural and recreational areas—indeed, ecology became a household word by 1970—but there seems to have been relatively little focus on ecological matters at the time with respect to Missouri's state parks, among either the park staff or the citizenry. Citizen attention regarding natural resources and environmental matters was focused more on federal agencies and, within the state, on the Conservation Department, which was engaged in a concerted effort in the early 1970s to broaden its mission and public appeal through what would become known as the "Design for Conservation." Conservation and environmental organizations in Missouri paid little attention to state parks.

Thus, there was scant public objection when as of January 1, 1970, the Park Board conveyed three of the original big-spring parks—Alley

Spring, Big Spring, and Round Spring—to the National Park Service for management as focal points of the Ozark National Scenic Riverways. Congress had passed the bill protecting the Current and Jacks Fork Rivers in 1964, making them the first federally protected, naturally free-flowing streams in the nation and a model for the National Wild and Scenic Rivers Act of 1968. Some park officials viewed the transfer as a way to get additional federal dollars for recreation development in Missouri, thus freeing state funds for other state parks. That three state parks were deemed worthy of inclusion in a unit of the national park system was a point of pride, but for some, this loss of three of Missouri's "crown jewels" would be a source of considerable angst.

The pressure of recreational use on the parks seemed almost overwhelming by the early 1970s. Whether or not there were fourteen million visitors annually as attendance figures indicated, it seemed as if there were and as if the number could only grow. In fact, the figure dipped to nine million by the mid-1970s, though there didn't seem to be fewer people in the parks. Whatever the numbers, picnic areas, swimming beaches, and campgrounds were bursting at the seams, with campers pitching their tents or parking their vehicles wherever they could find a spot of ground. To reverse this destructive trend, the Park Board decided to establish strict carrying capacities for campgrounds, with clearly marked, designated spaces, and to turn latecomers away if necessary. Then they announced the system's first general user fee, $10 a year per vehicle or $1 per day effective January 1, 1973, in order to fund a program of park development.

A new governor was inaugurated in January 1973: Christopher Bond, the first Republican since 1940. During his campaign, Bond had let it be known that there would be a new park director if he was elected, and he also challenged the legality of the user fee, which was subsequently rescinded. When Jaeger tendered his resignation as park director, the Park Board hired James Wilson, a personable young administrator with a degree in marketing, who had considerable experience with urban parks in St. Louis and also strong Republican credentials.

Wilson was decidedly recreation-minded. He was intent on developing park facilities to make them attractive to people from the cities, and at the same time, he wanted to teach people from the cities how to enjoy the parks. He also liked to acquire land, and during his four years at the helm, he secured several popular recreational parks: Finger Lakes and St. Joe, former mine lands especially attractive to dirt bikers; Castlewood and Bothwell, long famed as recreational retreats for urban visitors; Battle of Athens, acquired initially for its recreation potential; and Harry S Truman, on a corps reservoir. He also added four fine cultural properties to the system: Mastodon through the efforts of the Mastodon Park Committee; Jefferson Landing through the efforts of historic preservationists; Dillard Mill, by donated lease from the L-A-D Foundation of Leo A. Drey; and the Thomas Hart Benton home and studio, by purchase after the artist's death.

But Wilson had little opportunity to manage the parks, for he was caught up almost immediately in struggles over the reorganization of state government. After the legislature decided to transfer parks to a new super agency, the Department of Natural Resources (DNR), he became the first director of the department effective July 1, 1974. Like Wilson, his assistant William Wight was also interested in recreation and marketing. Wight took over as state park director and began new special events, learn-to-camp programs, and other efforts to attract more urban residents to the parks.

The 1974 reorganization had little to do with parks per se, having been dictated primarily by the need to consolidate agencies for more efficient government, but it had a significant impact on the parks nevertheless. The Park Board became an adjunct and eventually ceased to exist; later, a new advisory board appointed by the governor functioned from 1987 to 2008. Park personnel fared much better, being grandfathered into the state's merit system, where they received substantially higher salaries, salary levels that for the first time made possible the recruitment of professional career employees for virtually all supervisory positions.

As one of five divisions—the Division of Parks and Recreation—of a department concerned largely with regulatory functions involving air and water quality, solid waste, toxic substances, land reclamation, and the like, the parks would on occasion become the unintended victims of controversies not of their making. But the new department also provided opportunities for mutual cooperation and synergism. It was an innovative and exciting place to work in the mid-1970s, and it attracted more than its share of bright young professionals. Among them were three new employees in the planning division—Fred Lafser, John Karel, and Wayne Gross—who would serve as successive directors of the park system, beginning a period of appointment from within the agency.

STEWARDSHIP OF PARK RESOURCES

The mission of the Department of Natural Resources, wise stewardship of Missouri's resources, became the touchstone also of the park program under Fred Lafser, an environmental engineer who took over as park director in 1977 during the administration of Gov. Joe Teasdale, a Democrat. Without retreating from the commitment to make the parks accessible for recreational enjoyment, Lafser intended to place new emphasis on planning, management, and interpretation of natural and cultural resources, "with the protection of the integrity of the resource a paramount consideration."

Though preservation of distinctive scenic, historic, archaeological, or scientific features was enshrined in state park statute and the system from the beginning had protected such features, in fact, most park staff thought of themselves as managing recreational facilities and people rather than land and resources. The prevailing notion was that land would automatically be preserved if it were protected from destruction by people. To the extent that fish, wildlife, or forest management was required, the experts in the Missouri Department of Conservation (MDC) stood ready. Over the years, they did a fair amount of fish stocking, planting of wildlife food plots, and thinning of forests, and they conducted deer and turkey hunts in some of the parks as well. In this respect, Missouri park administration was no different from the early National Park Service, which also had not thought it necessary to have scientific expertise on staff but instead relied on professionals in the Forest Service and other agencies for advice and for resource management. The National Park Service was criticized by scientific groups as early as the 1920s for commodity-oriented management practices inappropriate to national parks, and in the 1930s, it began some modest park-oriented scientific research. As late as the 1960s, it was taken severely to task in several prestigious reports for failing to restore and maintain ecological integrity in the parks.

It was general awareness of new policies and perspectives nationwide on ecological land management that informed Lafser's efforts to focus more attention on stewardship in Missouri's parks. Following the lead of John Karel, whom he asked to head a new natural history program in the park division and subsequently appointed division director, he initiated an inventory of natural areas in the parks. This led in turn to designation of numerous natural areas in the parks by the Missouri Natural Areas Committee, established in 1977 by MDC and DNR along with the US Forest Service and National Park Service to administer the new interagency Missouri Natural Areas Program. Lafser and Karel also initiated a State Wild Area System in 1978, modeled on the federal wilderness system, which would grow in the next two decades to some 23,000 acres in eleven areas, all in state parks. Numerous rivers and streams in state parks won designation as Outstanding State Resource Waters under a program of the Missouri Clean Water Commission beginning in the late 1970s.

To administer these and other new stewardship efforts, Lafser and Karel developed new management policies geared toward preserving and restoring natural biological communities, including old-growth forests and natural grasslands and wetlands. They hired substantial numbers of naturalists, historians, and other resource-minded professionals who could develop management and interpretation appropriate to the mission of the park system. In 1980 park officials decisively assumed full management responsibility for all lands and waters in the parks, except for the hatcheries in the trout parks, though they continued to cooperate with the Conservation Department on many matters of mutual concern.

The resource consciousness of this period was reflected in park acquisitions, which included the superb karst features of Ha Ha Tonka, added to the system in 1978 after literally seven decades of effort, even though its castle was now in ruins; the stunning tallgrass landscape of

By the late 1970s, a heightened consciousness of the need to maintain the ecological integrity of the parks led to a pioneering program of experimentation in techniques of ecological stewardship that included the use of prescribed fire or controlled burning under the direction of park scientists. Fire restored long dormant native grasslands and woodlands, as here at Prairie State Park. This scruffy, brushy area is now magnificent tallgrass prairie. *Paul W. Nelson*

Prairie State Park, negotiated in 1978 and purchased in 1980 with the help of the Nature Conservancy; Robertsville with more than two miles of frontage on the Meramec River, purchased in 1979; Weston Bend along the Missouri River, acquired in 1980; and two parks in 1982, Long Branch, on a corps reservoir in north Missouri, and Onondaga, the fabulous show cave identified for its park potential along with Ha Ha Tonka by the Buford commission of 1915.

Acquisition of all of these parks benefited from the Land and Water Conservation Fund, like many other parks during this era. Two fine German buildings donated to the state in 1978 by the Brush and Palette Club of Hermann became the core of Deutschheim State Historic Site, though another state historic site, Fort Zumwalt, was transferred to the city of O'Fallon. Three other important properties came into the system in the early 1980s after many years of negotiations: the Scott Joplin house, donated in 1983 by Jeff-Vander-Lou, Inc., a neighborhood development corporation; Grand Gulf, donated in 1984 by Leo Drey's L-A-D Foundation; and Osage Village, purchased in 1984 from the Archaeological Conservancy, which had acquired it for the state.

By the time most of these negotiations took place, Lafser, who was a master at arranging funding from a variety of sources, had become director of the Department of Natural Resources in 1978, and he continued to arrange deals for new parks. In his stead as park director, he appointed Arlin Epperson, associate professor of recreation and park administration at the University of Missouri at Columbia, who served for a year, after which natural history coordinator John Karel took over as park director in 1979.

Karel, who would serve for six eventful years under both Democratic and Republican administrations, was committed to continuing the stewardship emphasis. With degrees in history as well as wildlife ecology, he was determined to bring cultural resources to equal billing with natural and recreational resources and to develop a fully integrated system. As the sixth park director in a little over six years during a period of major change, he was especially conscious of the need to forge a sense of unity, professionalism, and pride in the parks among the division's staff by heightening their consciousness of the special mission of the system. Thus early in his tenure, he worked with the staff to study the history and statutory basis of the system to develop the simple statement of the threefold mission of state parks that would guide policy and development from then on: "To preserve and interpret the finest examples of Missouri's natural landscapes; to preserve and interpret Missouri's cultural landmarks; and to provide healthy and enjoyable outdoor recreation opportunities for all Missourians and visitors to the state."

Among other efforts to integrate the elements of the mission and forge a sense of unity, Karel and the staff engaged in a conceptual planning process that entailed regular discussions of the character and direction of each of the parks and established priorities for development; this process still continues—now as part of a general management planning process—and among other advantages, provides guidelines and goals for each of the units of the system. The division also completed an ambitious natural heritage inventory of the system and launched an equally ambitious survey of CCC and WPA architecture in the parks. The natural heritage inventory led not only to greater staff consciousness of the value of the natural resources in the parks but also to a ground-breaking program of ecological restoration. Following experimental prescribed burning at Cuivre River beginning in 1977, nine remnant prairies totaling more than 2,200 acres in five parks were burned in 1980 under the direction of park naturalists to remove woody growth and encourage regeneration of native grasses and wildflowers, and the program grew with the years, extending to woodlands, glades, and marshes.

The survey of New Deal architecture resulted in the 1984 nomination of 11 historic districts and nearly 350 separate structures to the Na-

Gov. Christopher Bond discusses the issue of the day with a young activist for the parks and soils sales tax in 1984. ***L. T. Spence, St. Louis Post Dispatch***

tional Register of Historic Places—the most extensive multiple resource nomination in the nation up to that time. It was especially effective in heightening the staff's awareness of and pride in cultural resources throughout the system. Prior to the survey, most staff in the natural parks probably had never even thought of their parks as having cultural resources; after it, these fine New Deal structures and historic buildings from other eras took their place in park plans as priority candidates for restoration, most of which has since been undertaken one or more times. Staff throughout the system began to appreciate that all units, whether predominantly natural or historic, contained both natural and cultural resources that deserved careful stewardship.

For all the creative leadership and substantial federal funding of the late 1970s, the park system continued to struggle financially. Federal funds went toward acquisition and development, not operation and maintenance. Despite the creative use of donations, the fifty-fifty matching requirement for federal funds meant that at least some state funds had to be used as well. Meanwhile, state funds from general revenue, which provided the main day-to-day support of the system, rarely increased and, at a time of heavy inflation, actually decreased in real terms. The result was a slowly growing system with a declining base of support. And the situation would get worse before it would get better, reaching a nadir in 1982 when federal funds dried up and recession forced a series of cuts in state support. The $7.7 million park budget for fiscal 1982 was little more than half what it had been in the late 1970s.

In every legislative session during the early 1980s, numerous proposals were introduced to deal with the crisis of the parks. To some legislators and others, an obvious solution was to transfer the parks to the Conservation Department, where they could be funded out of the one-eighth-cent sales tax the citizens of Missouri had voted in 1976 to fund that department's "Design for Conservation," which included an ambitious program of land acquisition. To some conservative Missourians who disliked extensive acquisition of land by government, support of the park system seemed a preferable use for the money, while to some conservation officials, who had long thought they could do a better job of managing the parks, taking on this obligation seemed also to be a way to forestall perennial attempts to repeal the tax, though no one even broached the matter of historic sites, which conservation officials would be unlikely to accept. To DNR and park officials, who were just as concerned to preserve the distinctive mission and management philosophy of the parks as they were to solve the fiscal crisis, the apparent willingness of some conservation officials to provide for the parks suggested a preferable strategy: transfer a portion of the conservation tax to parks for their continued management within the Department of Natural Resources. To many citizen groups, including the powerful Conservation Federation of Missouri, which had led the effort to create the Conservation Commission in 1936 and then to pass the tax in 1976, any proposal to use the conservation tax seemed an intolerable raid on funds the citizens had voted for the Conservation Department, but there were differences between and even within groups as to whether the parks would be better off under DNR or under MDC.

Most citizen groups, including the Conservation Federation, which typically supported the Conservation Department, and the Sierra Club, which was more environmentally inclined, had simply not focused their attention on state park issues up to that time. Although awareness was beginning to spread, many members had little understanding of park resources or the new stewardship programs and thus did not think of parks as particularly relevant to their concerns. Park officials had traditionally looked to recreational user groups and to local historical and civic associations as their constituencies, most of which related to individual parks more than to the needs of the system as a whole and hence were not much engaged in the funding and organizational issues of the early 1980s.

In the heat of the legislative crisis of 1982, some Missourians began to appreciate the extent to which the park system had been neglected by the existing citizen organizations, and at the urging of State Park Director Karel, they determined to rectify the problem by organizing a Missouri Parks Association in October 1982. The first citizen group devoted solely to the state park system, MPA would seek to foster public understanding of the values embodied in the parks and historic sites and to serve as a watchdog and support group for the park division and for the integrity of the system. Swept immediately into the fray, the organization has generally been credited with making a significant difference for the parks.

Over a period of years of high tension in the conservation fraternity and through an extraordinary sequence of legislative maneuvers that no one could have predicted, several seemingly unrelated solutions to the funding crisis were developed that left parks by the mid-1980s poised for a remarkable renaissance. In fact, Karel and other park officials had laid the groundwork for the various solutions in their conceptual planning for the system early in the decade, but even they would not have dared predict the outcome.

The first measure to navigate the shoals was a $600 million bond issue for capital improvements known as the Third State Building Fund, which passed the assembly in 1981, was refined in the 1982 session, and then was approved by voters at a special election in June 1982, followed by three years of controversy and uncertainty over specific appropriations from the fund. DNR director Fred Lafser had played a crucial role early on in helping to shape the measure, and the park division would eventually gain nearly $60 million from this source for the largest rehabilitation and building program in the parks since the CCC and WPA of the 1930s.

The second measure was a joint resolution for a constitutional amendment to establish a parks and soils sales tax similar to the MDC tax. It passed in 1983 and was narrowly approved by voters in August 1984 after a long campaign led by the Missouri Parks Association and other groups cooperating under the banner of the Citizens Committee for Soil, Water, and State Parks. It provided for a one-tenth-cent sales tax to be split evenly between state parks and soil and water conservation efforts, both administered by the DNR. These funds, which began flowing in July 1985, were expected to provide about $13.5 million per year initially, to relieve the hard-pressed operations of the parks as well as to help with capital improvements.

The third measure, necessitated when a new governor, John Ashcroft, recommended eliminating funding for park personnel from the state's general revenue, involved the successful restoration of more than $6 million in general revenue support by the 1985 assembly.

As a result of the combination of these three measures, the fiscal 1986 appropriation for parks was far and away the largest in the history of the state park system, a stunning $64 million, much of which, however, was intended for multiyear construction projects.

RENAISSANCE OF THE PARKS

The challenge of building upon his predecessor's remarkable success in putting these funding systems into place and charting a course for the future fell to a new park director, Wayne Gross, who was promoted from deputy director after Karel was released in July 1985 by Governor Ashcroft, immediately following Karel's extraordinary legislative accomplishment. With degrees both in recreation and park administration and in public administration, Gross was an excellent manager of people and programs. He was a firm believer in the tripartite mission of the park system, and by all accounts, he was evenhanded in advancing it.

The planning, design, and construction of all the new facilities funded by the bond issue and the sales tax, especially coming all at once as they did in the extraordinary fiscal 1986 appropriation, presented a formidable task. Gross's challenge was to build with a sustained excellence that would carry the Missouri system of parks and historic sites to national prominence. In developing their plans for the use of these funds, which would not have been appropriated if legislators had doubted the need for them, park officials years earlier had made several strategic choices. Most critical was a decision, inspired perhaps in part by the firestorm of legislative opposition to the Conservation Department's ambitious program of land acquisition but also by compelling need, to emphasize development of parks currently in the system rather than acquisition of new parks. Although much of the development would be for improvement of basic infrastructure like roads, campgrounds, and water and sewer systems, there was also a conscious decision to emphasize visitor services that would put out the welcome mat for visitors from afar as well as for old friends. This would be accomplished through attractive, graciously staffed visitor centers with state-of-the-art exhibits and special programming to draw visitors into contact with the distinctive natural and cultural resources of each park. There was also a strong commitment to restore basic resources, especially the CCC structures, other historic buildings, and the ecological integrity of park landscapes.

The challenge for the division's small staff was complicated by the pressing need to show satisfactory results on the ground within a year or two in order to make a case for renewal of the sales tax, which due to a last-minute amendment in the assembly, was set to expire in only four years. But even as that gargantuan task was undertaken by both office and field staff, park officials and citizen groups repeatedly had to enter the halls of the capitol to defend the hard-won park funds against attempted assaults on what became known as the "park barrel," the trough of riches at which it was supposed anyone with any sort of park-related need could feed.

Local groups and legislators attempted to gain appropriations from park funds for local parks, museums, golf courses, zoos, community centers, swimming pools, and other projects that could not possibly meet the park mission's test of statewide significance; most but not all were vetoed by the governor if they survived the legislature. There were also efforts by legislators to use park funds for a veterans memorial (successful) and for tuck-pointing the stonework on the state capitol (successfully resisted). And there were determined efforts in the legislature to tap into the proposed renewal of the sales tax for funds for local parks and cultural institutions, storm sewers, and other endeavors that might well have doomed the measure to defeat at the ballot box. Finally, it became necessary for citizen supporters of state parks and soil conservation to undertake the arduous task of circulating an initiative petition in order to place a simple renewal of the parks and soils tax before the voters. That effort resulted in November 1988 in an overwhelming two-to-one mandate for a ten-year renewal of the tax. Clearly, Missourians loved their parks and approved of the way they were being developed.

After renewal of the sales tax and completion of most of the development funded by the bond issue, it was time for public officials and citizen supporters to examine the system and focus anew on the future. Fortunately, they had for guidance a major study of state parks nationwide published in 1989 by the Conservation Foundation, *State Parks in a New Era*. The report offered a comparative analysis of the growth and development of state park systems, especially in the period from 1955 to 1985, and examined three major areas of concern common to all of the states: stewardship of natural and cultural resources, innovations in funding, and strategies for tourism and economic development. Missouri had a special place in this study, as its parks and soils tax was featured

in the discussion of funding. No other state had a dedicated sales tax at the time, though park officials in several states expressed interest in trying to emulate Missouri.

The Conservation Foundation report revealed that the total acreage in state park systems nationwide had quadrupled between 1955 and 1985, or tripled, if the huge Alaska system is excluded from the calculation. Missouri's park system, by contrast, grew by little more than half in the same period, from about 66,000 acres to 103,000. While only nine states had surpassed Missouri in acreage in 1955 (up from four in 1928), by 1985, twenty-five states had larger state park systems. Missouri had grown more slowly because it had not initiated any major bond issues or other special funding mechanisms when many other states were doing so during the 1960s and 1970s, and when it finally did gain special funding in the 1980s, it used the money for rehabilitation and facility development rather than expansion. The story on comparative attendance was quite the reverse. In the nation as a whole, state park attendance in 1985 was three-and-a-half times as great as it had been in 1955, while in Missouri it was nearly five times as great, and by 1990, it would be seven times as great. Visitors were attracted to Missouri's state parks out of all proportion to acreage, a source of pride to be sure, but also a cause for concern if the resources that attracted visitors were to be protected for future generations.

The identification, monitoring, restoration, protection, and interpretation of park resources, collectively termed stewardship, came to be recognized by the 1980s as an urgent need of park systems nationwide. The President's Commission on Americans Outdoors, a successor to the Outdoor Recreation Resources Review Commission a quarter-century earlier, warned in its 1987 report that the condition of the nation's outdoor estate was precarious, owing in part to "too much use with too little

Funding made available by late 1985 through the parks and soils sales tax and a bond issue supported major refurbishment and development of the parks, like this handsome new visitor center under construction at Watkins Mill. ***Cindy Browne***

attention" and in part to pervasive long-term threats from outside the systems: toxic chemicals, air and water pollution, erosion and sedimentation, unsightly or intrusive development on inholdings or along the boundaries of parks, and the like. The Conservation Foundation report focused on California as a state that had begun to address the problem of stewardship in the early1980s, but it could as well have selected Missouri, which by 1990 had progressed perhaps even further than California in its stewardship results.

Despite concerted stewardship efforts throughout the decade, however, a study begun in 1988 identified more than fifteen hundred threats to Missouri's state parks and historic sites, such as soil erosion, sedimentation of streams and marshes from flooding, water and noise pollution, scenic degradation, commercial encroachments, invasions by exotic plants and animals, and in places, overuse by visitors. When DNR and the park division released the threats study in 1991, they boldly recommended that 90,000 acres be added to existing parks to help protect the integrity of their resources. The 1980s had witnessed a substantial effort to rehabilitate and develop the human-built infrastructure of the parks; the 1990s would require a major shift in emphasis to add more acreage and protect the natural and cultural resources of the parks from threats emanating from both within and beyond their borders.

The burgeoning attendance and other threats to the parks suggested a need to determine not only which parks could be expanded but also what new parks should be added to fill gaps in the system's representation of the natural and cultural heritage of the state and to

Among the more than fifteen hundred threats to the parks enumerated in a comprehensive study issued in 1991 is this horror story at Pershing State Park, where heavy sedimentation caused by land clearing, poor agricultural practices, and channelization in the Locust Creek watershed smothers the floodplain forest and other wetland ecosystems. *Tom Nagel*

relieve some of the pressures on other areas. With one exception, the period from August 1984, when Missourians first approved the parks and soils tax, until halfway through 1990 was the longest time span since the war years of the 1940s without the addition of new parks to the system. The war period had ended with the transfer to the state of 25,000 acres of Recreation Demonstration Areas at the same time, something unlikely ever to be repeated. The park division had kept its word, given during the sales-tax campaign of 1984, and spent its money taking care of what it had. The one exception was the small-in-acreage but extensive-in-reach, 200-mile-long Katy Trail, acquired in 1987 and developed with a $2.2 million donation from Edward D. Jones. It was time now to revisit the long-range plan for expansion of the system.

Among the criteria for selection of new parks, the most important were statewide significance and integrity of the proposed park's resources, but factors such as its contribution to the geographic and thematic balance of the system and its suitability for public interpretation and recreation were also vital. Obvious needs that emerged during the expansion study were parks to represent northern Missouri prairie, northern Missouri forest, Crowley's Ridge in the Mississippi Lowlands, the Elk River Hills in the southwestern Ozarks, the White River glades, and bottomland forests and sloughs along the big rivers. Chronologically and thematically, the most obvious cultural gap in the system was the lack of any site reflecting the French colonial period of the eighteenth century. Better representation was needed for the Woodland archaeological period and the era of early white contact with Native Americans. The system was also deficient in sites relating to early white settlement in the interior, many types of economic activity (notably the fur trade, forestry, and various types of manufacturing), and the experiences of women and ethnic groups. Among the areas of greatest recreation need, the plan identified the upper Mississippi and lower Missouri Rivers, the Taum Sauk Mountain region, and various rivers not yet represented in the system, such as the Gasconade and the North Fork.

Ste. Genevieve was the national poster child for the traumatic flood of 1993, which swamped most Missouri parks and communities along the big rivers from June through September. The historic town survived behind a levee that was hastily thrown up that spring, but French vertical log buildings such as the Bauvais-Amoureux and the Green Tree Tavern, which were outside the levee, stood in floodwaters for months. When the waters receded, preservation experts discovered the old French buildings were in much better shape than many newer frame structures, and the Amoureux was donated to the state. *Bill Naeger*

As the park division prepared to celebrate the seventy-fifth anniversary of its founding in 1992, it was fortunate to have an able and enthusiastic new DNR director, G. Tracy Mehan, who understood the need to acquire additional acreage and enjoyed access to Governor Ashcroft. Still, when the DNR requested legislative appropriations for new parks and expansion of existing parks in 1989 and subsequent years, it was greeted with strong support from some legislators, equally strong resistance from others, and alternative pet projects from yet others. Money was available from the sales tax for modest expansions, but legislators were willing to approve only a fraction of those requested: Taum Sauk Mountain and the Nathan Boone homestead in 1990 and additions to Taum Sauk and Crowder in 1991. Legislators also mandated a new Civil War park at Carthage that had not been a high priority for acquisition because the most important battlefield acreage was not available. In 1992 the state was finally able to fill important gaps in far southwest and far northeast Missouri with the acquisition of Big Sugar Creek State Park in the Elk River Hills and the Iliniwek Village site along the Des Moines River, which had been visited by Father Jacques Marquette and Louis Jolliet in 1673.

BELT-TIGHTENING AND CONSOLIDATION

The promise of consistent funding for park operations and maintenance from the combination of general revenue and the park sales tax, with modest funds remaining to address threats to the parks and even acquire some additional acreage, began to fade in 1990 when Governor Ashcroft, during a budget crisis, again proposed eliminating all funding for parks from the state's general revenue on the grounds that parks were now relatively well-off, as they were at the time. The senate at first restored the general revenue, from which the salaries of most park staff were paid, but the statewide budget crisis deepened. In the end, that time-honored source of funding was lost. With the loss, the park sales tax had to absorb not only the salaries of nearly the entire staff but also staff benefits, which had previously been paid from general revenue allocated to the state Office of Administration (OA), not from the park budget. And there were more blows. Other state agencies, including OA and even the park division's parent DNR, began charging the costs of their oversight of various functions to the park tax. To make matters worse, tax revenues failed to grow at the rate expected because of continual sales tax exemptions for special interests through legislative or court action, a problem that would grow with the years.

At the federal level, the new Americans with Disabilities Act (ADA) of 1990 required new physical accommodations at public facilities nationwide. Though the Missouri legislature created a special fund from which other state agencies could draw for ADA compliance, the park division was deemed ineligible owing to its dedicated tax. So the sales tax had to fund more than a thousand special ADA projects in the state park system, which had so many facilities and visitors. Also, shortly after the bond issue and the park sales tax were approved in the mid-1980s, the state made a policy decision to allocate all money from the federal Land and Water Conservation Fund to local units of government, keeping none at the state level, a decision that would not be revisited for decades despite the exhaustion of bond funds and the loss of general revenue for state parks.

Park supporters in 1993 toted up the unanticipated losses at nearly $15 million annually, including some $7 million in general revenue, $5 million in diversions or transfers to other agencies, and nearly $7 million in ADA compliance, the latter over two years. For fifteen years, funds allocated to capital improvements had approximately equaled operating funds, but the prospect now was for less than one-fourth of the total for capital improvement costs. That ratio would shrink further over the years. It was obvious that state parks were in for a period of belt-tightening, with little money for adding staff or land or for addressing threats.

Then came the massive and prolonged flood of 1993, which damaged twenty-one parks and historic sites, including nearly every park along the big rivers, the new Katy Trail most of all. The bill was estimated at more than $4 million, only a portion of which was covered by federal disaster-aid programs. That fall, heavy rains in the eastern Ozarks damaged ten more parks, including Washington and Sam A. Baker. So it would go over the years, with the increased frequency of extreme weather events.

The challenge of dealing with the necessary period of consolidation ahead fell to a new park director, Douglas Eiken, who took over in March 1994 from acting director Bill Palmer. Eiken was the first director appointed to the post without prior Missouri ties, and by the time he retired fifteen years later in June 2009, he would be the longest-serving park director in state history, having edged out Joe Jaeger, the previous longest-tenured director, by several months. Eiken had been state park director in North Dakota and president of the National Association of State Park Directors, reflecting the esteem in which he was held by his professional colleagues. With his perspective on park systems nationwide, the new park director identified the strength of the mission of the Missouri system and its vibrant citizen support network as its greatest assets, but he pointed to serious shortfalls not only in funds but also in staff salaries as compared with other state park systems. He intended to work on restructuring park administration for greater efficiency and on salaries, but first there was the pressing need to secure renewal of the parks and soils sales tax, on which state parks were now utterly dependent.

With state finances even more constrained by the Hancock Amendment, which limited total state revenues, legislators again, as back in the 1980s, considered combining parks, soils, and conservation in a single department with a combined tax, with funds from the tax also allocated to local parks and urban storm-water control. It was a period of high tension in the conservation fraternity, with organizations jockeying for part of the conservation and parks and soils taxes—a struggle that seriously jeopardized the renewal. The pressure was somewhat relieved when the legislature in 1995 authorized cities and counties to pass their own sales taxes of up to one-half cent for local parks or storm-water purposes. In the ensuing decades, more than 150 Missouri communities would pass local park taxes, inspired in large part by the success of the state park tax, and like the state tax, with strong citizen engagement and support. With the turmoil in the capitol ended, hundreds of park lovers from the Missouri Parks Association, the Conservation Federation, and other organizations came together to gather more than 270,000 signatures on an initiative petition for simple renewal of the state parks and soils tax. The renewal came to a statewide vote in November 1996 and again passed by an overwhelming two-to-one margin.

Once the petition drive was underway, Eiken began restructuring park administration: streamlining regions, reducing middle management, and raising park operations to a direct line of supervision by the division director. The aim was to reduce the distance between park field staff and the central office, the time required for decisions, and the costs of administration. Other changes would take longer to implement: reducing the number of job classifications—for example, combining naturalists and historians into a category of interpretive specialist, to create more opportunities for staff advancement that in turn would help to increase staff salaries—and combining nearby parks into clusters that could be managed by fewer staff. The changes generally improved park operations and staff morale, though over the years, some staff thought they

led to reduced attention to preservation and restoration of cultural and natural resources. Eiken also established the Joseph Jaeger Academy, named in honor of the longest-serving park director up to that time, to provide training programs for park staff; developed a more structured role for the State Park Advisory Board; and encouraged the establishment of a Missouri State Park Foundation to raise funds for special projects in the parks.

Another new initiative was establishment of urban outreach offices in St. Louis and Kansas City to develop new partnerships and programs for previously underserved segments of the urban population. It was an effort to inform new demographics about the resources of the state park system and encourage and facilitate their engagement with parks in the area. The effort began in Kansas City with a proposal to establish a civil rights museum at the Bruce Watkins Center, an African American cultural center that had been built with state park funds but was operated by the city. A dynamic new urban affairs coordinator, Cheryl Simmons, quickly demonstrated the potential for the museum by engaging a wide range of partners and community leaders in mounting a major exhibit that first year, 2001. Then, only days after the opening, she suddenly collapsed and died. Unable for a time to sustain the coalition, park officials turned to St. Louis, where they mounted a new outreach effort headquartered at the Scott Joplin site. Several years later, they resumed Kansas City programming from the Discovery Center, a Conservation Department facility in which DNR had office space. Both

To make state parks more welcoming to underserved demographics, staff established new urban affairs offices in Kansas City and St. Louis in the 1990s and cooperated with the Urban Populations Outreach Program of the Missouri Parks Association. Here, St. Louis youth learn about aquatic life. *St. Louis UPOP*

offices cooperated over the years with the Missouri Parks Association's Urban Populations Outreach Program, designed to introduce inner-city children to the wonders of state parks and the natural world, as well as developing numerous other partnership efforts.

Meanwhile, threats to the system continued apace. The problems of loss of prairie, savanna, glade, and woodland character and diversity in the absence of fire and the encroachment of invasive species in a landscape increasingly fragmented by urbanization and rural development were admirably addressed by park naturalists and managers, under the leadership of central office natural history staff at the forefront of the new practice of conservation biology and land restoration. By the late 1990s, more than 67,000 acres in twenty-six state parks—half the acreage in the entire system—were benefiting from regular ecological stewardship practices, including continual planning, research, and monitoring; removal of invasive cedars from glades and of exotics such as honeysuckle and garlic mustard from urbanizing boundaries, utility corridors, and roadsides, often by armies of volunteers; restoration of more natural hydrology in marshes and other wetlands and streams; reintroduction of native herbivores such as elk and bison; and especially the use of prescribed fire to mimic wildfires formerly characteristic of the system. Within years, the parks responded with greatly increased diversity of native grasses, wildflowers, birds, and other species, not to mention sheer beauty. By the time Missouri hosted the National Association of State Park Directors in 2004, it was indisputably a leader among the states in landscape-scale restoration. This stewardship required staff with knowledge and dedication and an administration supportive of their efforts, but fortunately it did not require much money beyond regular staff time.

Other threats placed greater financial stress on the system. Extreme weather events such as devastating floods, ice storms, tornadoes, and drought came with increasing frequency and severity in an era of global climate change. They required expensive cleanup and repair of facilities in addition to taking a major toll on vegetation. After the record flood of 1993 put 117 miles of the Katy Trail under water—washing out the trail, bridges, and trailhead facilities—massive floods struck again in 1995, fortunately with a bit less damage because some facilities had not yet been repaired from two years previous, and then again in 2011 and 2012. Windstorms hit with ferocity in 2004, 2008, and especially 2009, when the most massive windstorm on record swept across the Ozarks, causing major devastation at Stockton, Johnson's Shut-ins, Taum Sauk, and Babler. An ice storm in 2009 brought down much of the tree canopy at parks in the Bootheel, and droughts throughout the first decade of the twenty-first century took a major toll.

The park system was clearly in consolidation mode. During Eiken's first seven years, there were only two relatively small new parks added to the system, both of them gifts. In 1997, the Missouri DNR transferred to parks the former dioxin-laced Superfund site of Times Beach on the Meramec River, after it was cleaned up; it is now Route 66 State Park. And in 1999, Springfield businessman Jim D. Morris gave a park to the system to represent Crowley's Ridge in the Bootheel. Neither park required much development beyond modest parking areas, restrooms, and a few trails, as they were intended for day-use only.

Then in 2001, in anticipation of the bicentennial of the Lewis and Clark expedition, a long-sought, highly significant park at the point of the confluence of the Mississippi and Missouri Rivers came into the system, again largely through donations. A combination of gifts and grants from the Danforth Foundation, the Department of Interior, Great Rivers Greenway, the Army Corps of Engineers, and Pat Jones provided for acquisition and development, and much restoration planting was done with the help of volunteers. Reenactors of the historic voyage of discovery participated in the 2004 dedication of the Edward "Ted" and Pat Jones—Confluence Point State Park (now more than 1,000 acres) and continued upriver past other state parks, including another 13-acre tract

Prescribed fire has been used every two or three years for decades at Hawn State Park, and it has restored this stand of shortleaf pine, once one of the most common and sought-after trees in the Ozarks but now reduced to a fraction of its former extent. Stewardship crews have applied fire to nearly a quarter of the acreage of the state park system since the 1980s. ***Ken McCarty*** **• The Missouri (right) and Mississippi Rivers join at the new Edward "Ted" and Pat Jones—Confluence Point State Park, dedicated during the bicentennial of the Lewis and Clark expedition in May 2004. State Park Director Doug Eiken and his staff coordinated several events at Missouri state parks and nationwide as part of the bicentennial commemoration.** ***Missouri State Parks***

The failure of AmerenUE's upper Taum Sauk Reservoir in December 2005 caused the greatest devastation ever to occur in any Missouri state park, when 1.3 billion gallons of water roared down the mountainside, scouring the forested slopes clear to bedrock and depositing the trees, rock, and other debris in the beloved Johnson's Shut-Ins State Park. *Scott Myers*

donated to the system in anticipation of the bicentennial, the Clark's Hill/Norton State Historic Site. Doug Eiken and other state park staff played a major role in coordinating national Lewis and Clark commemorations all the way upstream, largely because of Eiken's prior work and connections in states along the route.

YEARS OF TRAUMA

In the wintry predawn blackness of December 14, 2005, one of the most popular parks in the system, Johnson's Shut-Ins, was utterly devastated when AmerenUE's mountaintop Taum Sauk Reservoir on nearby Proffit Mountain suddenly collapsed and sent 1.3 billion gallons of water roaring down the mountain and through the park. The icy torrent scoured the forested mountainside clear to bedrock, smashed the home of the superintendent to smithereens, and swept the parents and three young children hundreds of yards into a field where, miraculously, they were all found and rushed to a hospital in St. Louis. It created a dammed-up lake where there had been a river, obliterated the campground and other facilities, and deposited thousands of tons of boulders, trees, and debris in the beloved shut-ins. It was the worst disaster ever to strike a Missouri state park.

For more than four years, park staff from the central office and elsewhere in the system were diverted from their other responsibilities to help in the cleanup, planning, and reconstruction of Johnson's Shut-Ins. After protracted settlement negotiations, Ameren insurers picked up the $130 million tab for the cleanup and reconstruction of the park, but the trauma of the event and the ecological damage to the park would require far longer to heal. The 2007 settlement also included partial funding for the development of two new parks: a Rock Island Trail connector from the Katy Trail to Pleasant Hill in the Kansas City suburbs on right-of-way owned by Ameren; and Current River State Park, 780 acres with a mile of river frontage upstream from Round Spring transferred to DNR by

Supporters of the effort to secure another ten-year renewal of the Parks, Soils, and Water Sales Tax in 2006 gather at a rally in St. Louis. Of the Missouri citizens who voted on the measure, 71 percent approved the renewal, which will come to the ballot automatically every ten years. ***Missouri State Parks***

the Missouri Conservation Department. But a number of complex issues prevented development of either new park for years.

Another new park bought in 2008 with state funds, the 40-acre site of the African American encampment at the Civil War Battle of Island Mound, was delayed in its development too, for lack of funds. Then in May 2009, as construction of new facilities was underway at Johnson's Shut-Ins, more than 1,000 acres of wild and natural areas in the park that had been high and dry during the Taum Sauk deluge were devastated by the most severe windstorm to strike the Ozarks in recorded history; several other parks, including Taum Sauk, were severely damaged by the storm as well. With as much as 90 percent of the tree canopy toppled in some areas, it required years just to reopen the trails.

As if these man-made and natural disasters were not enough, the worst economic crisis since the Great Depression began in 2008 and by fall 2009 necessitated the elimination of 20 percent of park division staff positions (121 full-time-equivalent positions from a workforce of 600), resulting in major trauma not only to those who lost their jobs but to those who had to relocate and assume the responsibilities of colleagues who left. Fortunately, the parks and soils sales tax had been resoundingly renewed in 2006 by 71 percent of Missouri voters, so there was a base of dedicated support. Even so, it was clear that the tax could no longer support the full operating costs of the system. Sales tax revenues, which fund more than 75 percent of the system's budget, had plummeted more than 10 percent, and park earnings from campsites, lodging, and other services, which fund much of the remainder of the budget, were also down as visitors and visitor expenditures declined during the financial crisis.

But the decline in revenue, which was expected to continue for several years, was not the worst of the problems. There was also a massive backlog of needed infrastructure rehabilitation that had been mounting ever since the loss of state general revenue funds for parks in 1990, coupled with escalating diversions and exemptions from the park sales tax. The needs included water, wastewater, and electrical systems; dams, roads, and trails; buildings and recreation facilities; and especially the bed, bridges and culverts of the Katy Trail. Park officials initially estimated the backlog at about $200 million, counting only the top priority project from each unit of the system. Several years later in 2012, they calculated the backlog more accurately at $400 million.

Citizen supporters in the Missouri Parks Association and allied organizations began to advocate in the General Assembly for inclusion of state parks in a bill that would establish a new State Building Bond Fund to replace the Third State Building Fund, which had contributed so much to the renaissance of the park system in the 1980s and was now nearly paid off. State parks had been allocated about 10 percent of the earlier bond fund, so "Ten Percent for State Parks" became the rallying cry. After all, more than half of the buildings and two-thirds of the drinking water and wastewater systems under the jurisdiction of the State Office of Administration were in state parks, they argued. And with interest rates at record lows during the recession and the economy in desperate need of the jobs that would be created statewide by expenditure of the bond funds, what better time was there than now? The bond bill passed the house and came to the floor of the senate in the last week of the 2009 session, where it died under threat of filibuster. Each year after that, a similar bill was introduced, but it failed to get even that far at a time of growing political resistance to any form of debt.

BUILDING FOR THE FUTURE

With little prospect for a major infusion of new money into the system, state parks would have to search for more efficiencies and innovative partnerships. As it happened, a new state park director with close ties to Gov. Jay Nixon took over from interim director Dan Paige in the fall of 2009—just in time to oversee the termination of 20 percent of the system's staff positions, which had been previously selected but not yet announced. The terminations were a devastating blow to staff morale but also a move that could increase the new director's flexibility in budgeting available funds, if revenues improved. Bill Bryan, who had been deputy chief counsel for environmental protection under Attorney General Nixon, was appointed to the dual role of director of state parks and deputy director of the Department of Natural Resources. It was a combination that would give him an opportunity to forge partnerships with other agencies and DNR divisions at a time when federal "pass-through" funds for work relief and economic stimulus were available.

That first year, $2.5 million in federal funds for water system infrastructure came to parks, plus $1.4 million in transportation funds for Katy Trail bridges and culverts. The governor announced establishment of a State Park Youth Corps (SPYC) that would employ a thousand young people in the parks, using $3.3 million in federal stimulus funds in a partnership with the Department of Economic Development (DED), a program reminiscent of the Civilian Conservation Corps during the Great Depression. SPYC workers roofed and painted buildings, repaired trails, removed invasive species, mowed lawns, led tours, assisted in offices and visitor centers, and won for Missouri the 2010 President's Award of the National Association of State Park Directors. That was also the year that the economic crisis led the National Trust for Historic Preservation to declare state parks nationwide among America's most endangered historic places, with Missouri's infrastructure crisis as one of three prime examples, but by the end of the year, Missouri was

showing other states innovative ways to deal with the crisis.

Each year after that, Bryan, DNR, and the governor managed to cobble together funds from various sources—federal, state and private—to continue the SPYC program in order to provide their stressed, multitasking staff with much needed support on the ground as well as healthy summer jobs in the out-of-doors for youths who would otherwise have gone unemployed. Each year they managed to find modest funds for special projects in the parks from new sources beyond the park sales tax and park earnings. When the beloved CCC-era Camp Pin Oak Lodge at Lake of the Ozarks burned to the ground after a lightning strike in 2010, for example, it was rebuilt as close as possible to the original design and craftsmanship through a creative partnership with the DED, which provided a $1.5 million federal block grant, and State Fair Community College, whose construction technology students received valuable training, experience, and college credit in exchange for their labor. And when Pershing State Park's Locust Creek began to suffer from sedimentation as a result of erosion from agricultural lands and massive logjams in drainage ditches upstream, the park and other lands benefited from cooperative watershed projects involving the Natural Resources Conservation Service, the Environmental Protection Agency, MDC, DNR's Our Missouri Waters program, and AmeriCorps. These programs together added 1,700 additional acres to the park and helped restore them to more natural hydrologic function and ecological diversity. Then in early 2012, a beautiful, rugged tract in the LaBarque Creek watershed southwest of St. Louis came to the system as a bequest of St. Louis entrepreneur Don Robinson; valued at more than $5 million, it was among the largest gifts in the history of the park system.

As of 2012, the National Association of State Park Directors' annual statistical survey of the nation's state park systems revealed that the Missouri system, in terms of operating funds and acreage, ranked where it was back in 1985, before revenues from the parks and soils tax or the bond issue had begun to flow. In annual operating expenditures, Missouri ranked twenty-fifth among the fifty states, compared with twenty-fourth in 1985, and in acreage it ranked twenty-third, the same as in 1985, while the state ranked eighteenth in population. This means the Missouri state park system was considerably behind where it should have been in per capita revenues or acreage. Yet Missouri in 2012, as in 1985, ranked tenth highest among state park systems in attendance, a tribute to the quality and diversity of its resources and the excellence of its management, which put its best, most welcoming face forward and hid the festering infrastructure problems. Park staff were adept at keeping crumbling infrastructure functioning at least minimally "with duct tape and baling wire," as they liked to say.

The quality of resources and excellence in planning and management of Missouri's state park system have been recognized nationally by its selection six times as a finalist in the National Gold Medal Award competition for state park systems, more times than any other state. But Missouri has yet to win the Gold Medal, which has been awarded every other year since 1997 by the American Academy for Park and Recreation Administration and the National Recreation and Park Association. Of the seven state systems that have won the medal, all are considerably larger than Missouri in both annual operating budget and acreage, except Virginia, which in 2012 had half the acreage and one-third the attendance as Missouri but a 22 percent greater operating budget. Florida, which has won the award three times, had nearly three times the operating and capital budgets and five times the acreage of Missouri parks in 2012 but only 30 percent higher attendance. Missouri was also selected in 2012 for a Readers' Choice Award for Favorite State for Camping by the New York Times Company and in 2013 as Best Trails State by American Trails. The Missouri Parks Association in 2011 received the President's Award of the National Association of State Park Directors for its efforts on behalf of the state's parks. Clearly, Missouri State Parks were doing a lot that was right while struggling with inadequate funding. An economic impact study in 2012 showed that spending by state park visitors had an overall annual impact of more than $1 billion in sales, $307 million in payroll-related income, and $123 million in local, state, and federal taxes. For every dollar spent to operate the system, $26 was returned to the state's economy, a stunning return on investment.

In 2013, with the proposed bond issue for state buildings again stymied in the General Assembly, parks were allocated $20 million from an unexpected year-end windfall of state revenue. This was the first significant general revenue for parks since 1990, and it was slated to help with infrastructure rehabilitation in facilities across the state. In 2014, the legislature finally authorized a state bond issue but left specific allocation to the next session, when leaders decided on $50 million for parks. Then at the very end of the session, in a display of pique toward Governor Nixon, the house zeroed out not only the long-sought park funding through the bond issue but also the reappropriation of funds needed to complete projects already begun, a stunning $65 million blow to the system. Cooler heads were able to restore only $10 million in the time remaining. It was a sobering reminder that parks are subject to political whims, and that despite the relative stability provided over the years by the park sales tax for general operations, funding for infrastructure and other capital needs will remain a problem requiring solution.

As Missourians prepared to celebrate the centennial of the 1917 founding of the state park system, they could look back on a record of exceptional accomplishment built through struggle and dedication, and they could look forward to more of the same. To a remarkable degree, the Missouri system of state parks and historic sites achieves its goal of representing Missouri—both its natural and cultural heritage and the values and dedication of its citizenry. Missourians have built over the years a system of parks and historic sites that reflects the diversity of a remarkably diverse state. While there are still notable landscape features that are not well represented, the system offers its visitors a lifelong laboratory of carefully restored historic landscapes for study and appreciation of the state's natural heritage. It is perhaps inherently more difficult to reflect the cultural heritage of a state in all its richness because history keeps happening and not all aspects of culture may be embodied in particular sites, but the Missouri system, with its long tradition and its growing commitment to preservation and interpretation of cultural resources in the parks as well as in the historic sites, offers a fine starting point for those who would take the measure of the Show-Me State.

Parks are powerful symbols of a society, a measure of those aspects of their heritage in which people, individually and collectively, have taken pride. Fully two-thirds of the acreage and more than two-thirds of the units in the Missouri system came as gifts. The parks are a legacy of families like the Van Meters and the Grahams, who had long owned land that they and others knew was special; of wealthy individuals like Jacob Babler or Leo and Kay Drey or Ted and Pat Jones, who realized there were certain resources that ought to be the property of all the people; of individuals of modest means like Helen Hawn or Don Robinson or the women of the Mastodon Park Committee, who cared enough to buy or to mount a fundraising campaign for places they loved; of private industries and other units of government, which transferred some of their lands to the state for management as parks; of organizations like the Daughters of the Confederacy, the Pershing Memorial Park Association, or Jeff-Vander-Lou, which wished to honor people they admired; of local citizens who voted bond issues or donated funds to make Trail of Tears or Watkins Mill or Big Oak Tree available to all; and of members of numerous friends associations like Friends of Arrow Rock or of Rock Bridge, whose volunteer efforts help to sustain the parks each year into the future.

Left: With unemployment rampant and park staff and budgets stressed by the worst economic crisis since the Great Depression, Missouri in 2010 began a State Park Youth Corps reminiscent of the Civilian Conservation Corps of the 1930s to engage young people in healthy outdoor work in the parks. Here, SPYC workers scrape and paint at Felix Vallé State Historic Site. ***Susan Flader***
Above: Volunteers plant trees along Kiefer Creek in Castlewood State Park to restore bottomland forest to protect water quality in the creek. ***Lorin Crandall***

But a park system is more than a collection of individual sites. It involves an image of the system itself and of institutions for perpetuating it, including processes for selecting some sites and not including others, for funding and developing and maintaining the parks, and for interpreting them and making them accessible to the public. If the history of the Missouri system of state parks and historic sites seems to have been a continuing series of crises and struggles and political gamesmanship, perhaps it is because of the state's political culture—its fundamental conservatism and individualism and distrust of bureaucracy and, above all, its love of a fight. Yet the history of the state park system is also a record of remarkable continuity, sense of mission, and strength of tradition, despite frequent reorganizations and battles over ways and means. For that mission and tradition, one must look to the very idea of public parks and of a park system as worked out in the great urban parks and the national parks, as developed and perpetuated in the state's own system by a succession of talented park leaders and hundreds of dedicated career employees, and as strengthened by the pride that Missourians feel but rarely voice in their state and its heritage.

It is the state's citizens who are ultimately responsible for the park system that represents them and their heritage, citizens acting as individuals, organized in groups, functioning through their elected representatives, and when necessary, asserting their collective will directly through the initiative or referendum processes. It is worth recalling that when their own political culture of conservatism and individualism and skepticism has threatened on occasion to strangle their parks, Missourians have found a way to act directly to preserve what they value. The Missouri system of state parks and historic sites is thus above all a legacy of Missourians who care. *

OZARKS

THE OZARK HIGHLAND IS THE OLDEST REGION of Missouri geologically and, in some ways, the least altered. It is also the largest of the natural regions, embracing 40 percent of the state, and it is the most ecologically diverse. Henry Rowe Schoolcraft, who explored the area in the early nineteenth century, exulted in the beauty of the landscape: "The traveller in the interior is often surprised to behold at one view cliffs and prairies, bottoms and barrens, naked hills, heavy forests, rocks, streams, and plains all succeeding each other with rapidity, and mingled with the most pleasing harmony."

At the geologic core of the Ozarks stand the St. Francois Mountains, high rounded knobs of granite and rhyolitic rock formed by volcanic activity some 1.5 billion years ago. In comparison, the Appalachian Mountains began forming less than 500 million years ago, and the Rockies about 140 million years ago. The ancient peaks of the St. Francois Mountains, once as high as ten thousand feet, stood as an island archipelago during repeated incursions of the Paleozoic seas, in which the sediments that formed the limestones, dolomites, and sandstones of the Ozarks were deposited during hundreds of millions of years. During much of that time and for more than 200 million years since the last sea drained from the land, the Ozarks have both slowly warped upward into a vast low dome and just as persistently eroded away, the rivers cutting down through the varied sedimentary and igneous layers. The result is a highland of deceptively flat horizons but rugged, sometimes dramatic drainages, with successively younger rocks at the surface radiating concentrically outward from the ancient core.

Because of the varied rock types, drainage patterns, and topographic features of the Ozarks and also because the land has been above sea level and unglaciated for more than 200 million years—and thus available for occupation by plants—the region boasts the greatest diversity of flora and fauna of any region of the state. Indeed, many scientists regard it as one of the most significant centers of biodiversity on the North American continent. Forest, glade, and woodland dominate a landscape rich in endemic species, plants and animals found nowhere else on earth. Caves, springs, sinkholes, sinkhole ponds, and fens provide smaller, more specialized habitats for yet other species, while ancient streams in varied rock types also harbor distinctive life forms.

But millennia of ceaseless erosion, especially in the water-soluble rock that covers most of the area, have also left the Ozarks with thin, often stony, soils. The rugged topography has been relatively inhospitable to manipulation for human ends—save for mining the mineral wealth and lumbering the forests. Although many parts of the Ozarks have been settled nearly as long as other regions of the state, the way of life there has tended to be at once more attuned to natural rhythms and more precarious. And the Ozarks, though by no means escaping the onslaught of modern civilization, still retain in places a measure of what attracted people there in the first place.

Our exploration of Missouri parks and historic sites in this region begins in the St. Francois Mountains at the geologic core of the Ozarks, with the weathered pink boulders of Precambrian granite at Elephant Rocks. From there, we move to the broad wooded heights of Taum Sauk Mountain State Park and the river-scoured gorges of Johnson's Shut-Ins.

From a lichen-covered glade on Wildcat Mountain in Taum Sauk Mountain State Park, a hiker views the wildest vista in the Ozarks. ***Ron Colatskie***

> *"It is not important if our Ozarks are the most, or merely the next-most ancient of American hills. It matters only that they are here in the mellow beauty of great age; that they burn slowly and give off great heat like a log in deep ash; that they are the red reminiscent coal which is the best part of fire."*
> —Ward Allison Dorrance, *Three Ozark Streams*, 1938

The iron-rich igneous knobs in the fertile Arcadia Valley, characteristic features of the St. Francois knob-and-basin region, were strategic factors in both the location and the conduct of the crucial Civil War Battle of Pilot Knob, now a state historic site. Sam A. Baker State Park, an outlier at the southern boundary of the St. Francois Mountains, combines the elements typical of the region with its own unique flora and classic rustic-style architecture.

From the St. Francois Mountains, we move outward to the younger dolomites and limestones with caves, springs, sinkholes, underground streams, natural bridges, and other features characteristic of the karst topography of most of the remainder of the Ozarks as well as the Ozark Border. Karst topography is named for the Karst district of the Adriatic coast in Europe where the characteristic features produced in water-soluble rocks like limestone and dolomite were first described.

In this large extent of karst topography, we turn first to streams of the upper Ozarks that flow north and east, beginning in the Meramec River Hills. Meramec State Park, named for the scenic and aquatically diverse river that courses several miles along its borders, has more than fifty known caverns and many other karst features. Onondaga, a short distance upstream, displays Missouri's preeminent individual cave. In the cleft of a dolomitic ledge along Huzzah Creek, a tributary of the Meramec, lies one of the most picturesque gristmills in the Ozarks, Dillard Mill State Historic Site.

Farther to the west, near the north-flowing Niangua River in the Osage River Hills, is Bennett Spring, the fourth largest spring in the Ozarks, once the site of a thriving mill community and now a major trout-fishing mecca. Downstream on the Niangua is Ha Ha Tonka State Park, which has the greatest concentration of karst features in the state as well as beautiful orchard-like woodlands and glades with prairie grasses and wildflowers. Farther north, the Osage River's rugged, dissected hills frame the state's largest park on the Grand Glaize arm of Missouri's most famous impoundment, the Lake of the Ozarks.

The streams of the lower Ozarks, like those of the upper Ozarks, drain the Salem Plateau. Here are high-gradient, south-flowing streams that have carved deeply into otherwise broad, gentle uplands. Montauk State Park, centered on a cluster of springs at the headwaters of the Current River, is the only one of the four original big-spring parks in the Current River watershed remaining in the system, the other three having been transferred to the federally managed Ozark National Scenic Riverways. But the new Current River State Park with its historic complex of Alton Box Club buildings, just upstream from Round Spring, marks a welcome return of Missouri State Parks to the Current River Hills. Also in the Current River Hills, an innovative and unique arrangement allows Missouri State Parks to access more than fifty miles of trails for primitive recreation in the 62,000-acre Roger Pryor Pioneer Backcountry, a working forest owned by the L-A-D Foundation.

Lake Wappapello State Park, downstream from Sam A. Baker on the St. Francis River, just before it flows into the Mississippi Lowlands, offers an intriguing mix of typical Ozark vegetation with some bottomland species characteristic of the lowlands. To the west and just a few miles from the Arkansas line is Missouri's dramatic Little Grand Canyon, now Grand Gulf State Park, formed when a cave system collapsed and pirated a former surface stream, a spectacular instance of the interchange of surface water and groundwater typical of a karst landscape.

If the St. Francois Mountains are the geologic core of the Ozarks, many would say the cultural heart of the region is the White River Hills of southwestern Missouri, where the White River and its western tributaries have carved one of the most rugged, sharply dissected landscapes in the state. Among the most distinctive natural features of this region are its dolomite glades and cedar breaks, an area of concentrated natural diversity, with a mixture of southwestern plants and animals among the more typical Ozark species. These Missouri balds, as famed in legend as in the annals of science, form the scenic backdrop for one of the state's most popular tourist regions. Table Rock State Park, on the beautiful White River reservoir of that name, provides a base for exploring cultural facets of the region, while Roaring River State Park, at the abrupt juncture of the relatively level Springfield Plateau to the north and a sudden descent off an escarpment into the White River Hills, offers a primer in geology and ecology.

In the far southwestern corner of the state are the Elk River Hills—represented by a park named for Big Sugar Creek, which drains to the southwest-flowing Elk River and then to the Arkansas River—with distinctive topography and southwestern affinities.

North and west of the White River Hills is the Springfield Plateau, its younger Mississippian-age bedrock less dissected than that in other parts of the Ozarks and its flora exhibiting influence from the neighboring prairies of the Osage Plains. While nearly 30 percent of this area was presettlement prairie, much of the remainder was covered in post-oak flats and natural tree-dotted savannas. The oak groves, containing their own biotic flavors, slowly succumbed to brush, pasture, and impoverished woods resulting from long-term overgrazing and fire suppression. Nathan Boone, son of the famous pioneer, was attracted to the rolling Springfield Plateau when natural savanna still mantled the land, and now that his homestead is a state historic site, that older landscape is being restored. Battle of Carthage, a small historic site at a spring in the city of Carthage, highlights the strategic importance of the southwestern Ozarks in the Civil War era when it was a contested battleground between contending forces.

Stockton, Pomme de Terre, and Harry S Truman state parks are located on reservoirs constructed in the postwar era by the Army Corps of Engineers on the Springfield Plateau. Stockton, with its steady breezes from the southwest, offers some of the best sailing in the region while Pomme de Terre and Truman, in addition to the boating and fishing typical of reservoir parks, are models of success in the restoration of oak woodland with the help of prescribed burning. At the northwestern edge of the plateau, Truman offers an especially diverse representation of prairie-forest border landscape.

Covering such a large swath of the state and harboring so many charming cultural and natural landscapes and attractions, the Ozarks have for many visitors conjured the image of Missouri as a whole. The state parks have long conserved much of the best of this wonderful region, and they continue to welcome and inspire those who explore them. *

The collared lizard, an emblematic species of open, rocky glades on Taum Sauk Mountain and elsewhere in the Ozarks, has benefited from stewardship efforts of state park staff. ***Chad Doolen***

Elephant Rocks State Park

ELEPHANT ROCKS STATE PARK PROVIDES a veritable geological classroom. Here the visitor can see and touch some of the oldest rocks on the earth's surface. Here one can learn how even the hardest rocks remain at the mercy of the elements. And here one can contemplate the origin of the "elephants," the Ozarks, and the earth itself.

Geologists tell us that Missouri's red granite is about 1.5 billion years old. The granite was formed by the slow cooling of molten rock, called magma, as it intruded into the earth's crust. During this slow cooling, vertical and horizontal cracks, called joints, developed in the rock. The vertical joints developed in two different directional sets: one set trends toward the northeast, the other toward the northwest. Where the joints crossed each other, the granite separated into a huge stack of oblong blocks—all while still buried beneath the surface and further covered through the eons by layers of rock formed from sediments in ancient seas.

The Ozarks—and the elephants we know today—are the product of uplift and erosion. As the Ozarks warped upward into a gigantic dome and eroded over hundreds of millions of years, the granite blocks were brought closer to the surface. A combination of groundwater and chemical weathering began to decay the rock near the joints and fractures. Corners began to round, like the edges of a melting ice cube, and the spaces between filled with sand and grit, called grus. Once the fractured granite was exposed at the surface by further erosion, natural weathering by rainwater, freezing, thawing, sunlight, and wind continued rounding the blocks and removing the grus, some of which may still be seen between exposed joints. Even trees and shrubs, growing in the cracks, contribute to the slow disintegration of the ancient granite, one of the hardest rocks in the known universe. As weathering and erosion continue relentlessly over the eons, more of the herd yet buried beneath the surface may be freed.

These pachyderms remain fascinating despite the fact that the geologic explanation puts to rest more fanciful theories of their origin. The elephants were not moved here, either by giants or by glaciers. Glaciers can carry boulders and leave them behind as the glaciers retreat—such boulders are called erratics—but the glaciers never reached as far south as the St. Francois Mountains. No, the elephants were formed right where they stand—residual boulders resisting the elements. At Elephant Rocks State Park in Iron County, one can see all the various stages in the formation and weathering of boulders. The largest, which some know as Dumbo, leader of the herd, stands some twenty-seven feet tall and weighs an estimated 680 tons.

The state park contains several old granite quarries and is surrounded by even more; the town adjacent to the park is named Graniteville. Local homes and walls and gravestones are often made

* A HUNDRED YEARS TO GROW AN INCH

A measure of the slowness of the process of weathering these giants may be seen in the lichens that cover some of the boulders. Some lichens require as much as a hundred years to grow an inch, but they can be crushed by human hands and then washed away by the next rain. The elephants no longer sport as many of these elegant timepieces as they once did.

Right: Ancient pink granite boulders dominate the park. ***Oliver Schuchard*** **• Left: Dark green mosses and pale green lichens form intricate quilts over the granite. Each species is attuned to micro-differences in light and water.** ***Blane Heumann*** **Above: You can see how Elephant Rocks State Park got its name.** ***Paul Nelson***

Children love playing on the elephants. *Scott Myers* • Above: A short trail leads to the ruins of a granite-block engine house. *Missouri State Parks* • From the high rocks, you can view the characteristic flat horizon of the Ozarks. The scene is a reminder that these ancient mountains were leveled over eons to a plain, then gradually warped upward into a gigantic dome that was persistently eroded, leaving this deceptively flat horizon in a land of rugged hollows. *David Stoner*

of the pink Missouri stone. The largest granite quarry, just outside the park, was opened in 1869. It has furnished paving stones for some of St. Louis's streets, and they are still visible in the Laclede's Landing area. It also provided massive blocks for the piers of the Eads Bridge across the Mississippi at St. Louis and for the state capitols of Iowa and Illinois. B. Gratz Brown, who owned one of the quarries and was governor in 1871 when the state's impressive Second Empire–style governor's mansion was built in Jefferson City, donated four turned pink granite columns for the portico. Other quarries have furnished stone for major buildings in St. Louis and many other cities.

Missourians have been clambering around on the elephant rocks since long before the area became a state park, stretching back to the earliest white settlers, and probably Native Americans before them. By the 1870s, St. Louis artists were producing "views of the elephants," and the beloved old weathered boulders were the inspiration for the lifelike settings developed to house and display the hoofed animals at the St. Louis Zoo, built as a part of the 1904 World's Fair.

The area was suggested for a state park in 1924, but fourteen years later when Secretary of the Interior Harold Ickes came to Missouri to dedicate Babler Memorial State Park near St. Louis, he lamented, "Years ago this state should have set aside the Elephant Rocks, which have now been hammered to pieces." Fortunately, he was not entirely correct, and in 1967 a remnant of the site came into the state park system, fittingly enough through the generosity of a geologist who loved the rocks and appreciated their significance. John Stafford Brown, retired chief geologist for St. Joseph Lead Company, purchased 120 acres and presented it to the state. The small park of only 134 acres officially opened three years later in 1970 and now welcomes some 400,000 visitors a year.

State park planners have done an excellent job of designing the trails and other necessary improvements so that they have minimal effect on the natural resource. Elephant Rocks State Park was also the first park in Missouri to feature a Braille trail. Opened in 1973, the trail was specially designed to provide access for people with visual and physical disabilities. It features a paved surface with gentle grades and guide ropes or railings where necessary. Astroturf patches in the path alert users to Braille signs and tactile opportunities nearby, including a blindman's bluff play area. Also noteworthy are the picnic tables scattered among the rocks instead of massed in the open; they nearly disappear in the landscape while providing privacy for those using them.

At the center of the park, encircled by the Braille trail, is the seven-acre Elephant Rocks Natural Area. It is geologically an isolated hill—or tor—and is by far the most significant granite tor in Missouri. A spur off the trail leads to an overlook of an area where granite was quarried until the early 1900s. Another half-mile loop trail leads to the ruins of an old granite-block engine house where railroad cars, engines, and the steam engine used in quarry operations were serviced.

But it is the rocks that beckon, urging you to experience the joy of exploring or to ponder their origins. Here, among the ancient boulders of Elephant Rocks State Park, you can lose yourself in the weathered maze and ponder that you're standing in the very core of the Ozarks. *

ELEPHANT ROCKS STATE PARK • 7406 HIGHWAY 21, BELLEVIEW

Taum Sauk State Park

THE GEOLOGIC PHOENIX OF THE OZARKS, Taum Sauk Mountain was born of volcanic fire 1.5 billion years ago, then rose eons later at the very center of the Ozark dome. If Elephant Rocks is where one goes into the core of the Ozarks amid the pink granite boulders, Taum Sauk is where one ascends to the apex of the Ozark dome and surveys the world around. Located at the center of the 5,000-square-mile St. Francois Mountains with thirty nearby summits, Taum Sauk—likely a reference to the Sauk tribe, possibly meaning Big Sauk—is the state's highest point at 1,772 feet above sea level. Nowhere else in Missouri does such a panorama of nature's wild treasures and earthly forces combine.

Some forty local landowners willingly agreed to part with their properties spanning Iron and Reynolds Counties for the 8,730-acre Taum Sauk Mountain State Park beginning in 1990. The area had been recommended for acquisition as a national forest or state park as early as 1914. Then in the 1940s, Missouri writer and conservationist Leonard Hall proposed a 60,000-acre roadless wilderness preserve in the St. Francois Mountains, in a grand arc from Bell and Lindsay Mountains in the north through Goggins on the west to Taum Sauk and on, but the plan faltered owing to multiple ownerships. Interest in the area became even more widespread after 1958, when the twenty-eight-mile Taum Sauk Boy Scout Trail was dedicated; it stretches from Elephant Rocks in the north to Taum Sauk Mountain, and on west to Johnson's Shut-Ins State Park, which was new at the time. Since 1958, tens of thousands of Scouts and numerous other hikers have taken the trail. For the hardy, hiking the fourteen miles from Taum Sauk Mountain to Johnson's Shut-Ins is the best way to take the measure of the park and of yourself.

The 7,028-acre St. Francois Mountains Natural Area is exceptionally important for songbirds that depend on large blocks of undisturbed forest, woodland, and glades.

The drive to the mountain is not direct, no matter from which quarter of the state you begin, and therein lies a geography lesson. You will negotiate frequent hills and curves as the highway threads through the forest, with only the rare elevated ridge cleared of trees providing an overlook of the river valleys. When you can see out, you note a distant horizon made uniformly flat by the succession of deeply dissected ridges and valleys mingled into one. This is the great geologic dome of the Ozark interior, its ancient ocean-deposited limestones, shales, and sandstones lifted upward only to be deeply incised by spring-fed rivers and streams. If you can imagine the valleys and hollows filled with rock and grit until they were level with each successive ridge, a tabletop landscape would result—the Ozark plateau. But the fill has long since been removed by hundreds of millions of years of ceaseless erosion, creating today's rugged landscape.

As you approach closer to Taum Sauk Mountain from any direction, you begin to see distinctly elevated knobs in the distance: these are the St. Francois Mountains, the time-gentled igneous remains of ancient volcanoes here at the geologic core of the Ozarks. As your car ascends the mountain flank, every break in the trees reveals the massiveness of the broad, rounded summits. Just before the road curves into the parking area in Taum Sauk Mountain State Park, there is an overlook above

Arcadia Valley to the north with numerous St. Francois knobs in view and an exhibit identifying them. At the parking area at the trailhead, you jump out, eager to stretch your legs and explore this vastness afoot.

A short spur off the popular Mina Sauk Falls Trail takes you up to Missouri's highest point. At the summit, the mountain is flat. While its height is not sufficient to demonstrate life zones at different elevations, its height above the surrounding Ozark plateau teases the atmosphere enough to show subtle climatic differences. While the summer temperature on top of the mountain often reaches ninety degrees Fahrenheit, winter's weather is like that of Kirksville in northeastern Missouri, and local residents may witness the mountaintops capped in snow. All around, tree limbs lie scattered about the mountain crest, having shattered under the weight of frequent ice storms. Nearly every tree shows

the influence of wind and ice breakage and the scars of lightning strikes.

Then, take the three-mile-loop trail to the falls, which gradually descends the mountain's west flank onto successive glades of exposed igneous rock, here and there dotted by dwarfed trees and grasses resulting from the shallow, droughty soils. Smoke and Church mountains loom through the veil of a low cloud cap south of the Taum Sauk Creek valley. To the north are Wildcat Mountain and Weimer Hill, and in the distance, the northeast-trending arc of Proffit Mountain, their level summits falling just a little short of the highest point on Taum Sauk. This is one of relatively few vantage points from which one can see a portion of the unnatural high white wall of Ameren's Taum Sauk hydroelectric storage reservoir—located not on its namesake mountain but at the southern end of Proffit Mountain. Your attention may be pleasantly diverted by a pair of turkey vultures riding fixed on an invisible wave of mountain air.

Autumn glory spreads in a panorama from atop Taum Sauk Mountain, looking west toward Smoke Mountain (left) and Church Mountain. ***Ken McCarty***

After about four hundred feet of progressively steeper descent from the top of Taum Sauk, a timeless roar signals that Mina Sauk Falls is near. At the crest of the falls, rainwater collects in a small stream before plunging down a series of volcanic rock ledges positioned at right angles across ancient faults and rock fractures. The total drop of the falls is 132 feet, making this Missouri's tallest waterfall. This wind-swept, pine-crowned cascade stands sentinel above the Taum Sauk valley. Here, you can gaze with wonder at the massive knobs on each side of the deep

Above: Taum Sauk Creek, an Outstanding State Resource Water, reveals ancient layers of sedimentary rock as well as volcanic outcrops. ***Mick Sutton*** **Left: Taum Sauk Mountain is a paradise for Boy Scouts and other groups. Since 1958, more than 25,000 youths have hiked Missouri's wildest walk, fourteen miles from the mountain to Johnson's Shut-Ins.** ***Paul Nelson*** **• Right: A lichen-covered igneous glade on the west flank of Taum Sauk Mountain overlooks Taum Sauk valley with Church Mountain in the distance.** ***Pat Whalen***

valley below. The pink-layered rock underlying the falls is ash that spewed forth from some ancient volcano more than a billion years ago.

At the top of the falls, the Taum Sauk section of the Ozark Trail, following parts of the old Boy Scout Trail, comes down the southwest slope of the mountain into Taum Sauk Creek valley. You have a choice—best made before you start—whether to continue looping back up the mountain to your car on the Mina Sauk Trail or to follow the Ozark Trail down to the valley below and across Proffit Mountain to Johnson's Shut-ins. Only the hardy and well prepared should go all the way to the shut-ins, but if you do, you will be richly rewarded with indelibly imprinted memories of vistas and natural features.

Taum Sauk Creek valley is Missouri's deepest valley, measuring one thousand feet from the mountain summit to the mouth of the creek on the East Fork Black River some seven miles southwest. The upper five-and-a-half miles of the creek within the mountain fastness—so remote and unsuited to agriculture that the area was never settled—has been designated an Outstanding State Resource Water. Its waters are crystal clear, and it retains nearly all of its biotic integrity. Ozark witch hazel, a shrub that brings forth its sweet-scented red and yellow blossoms as early as January, lines its banks. Shortly after reaching the creek at the base of the falls, the trail passes through Devil's Tollgate, an eight-foot-

wide gap in a mass of pink igneous rhyolite some thirty feet high and fifty feet long. Not surprisingly, this is a popular lunch spot.

An off-trail climb from Devil's Tollgate to open barrens on Smoke Mountain south of the creek provides a spectacular view of Wildcat Mountain with its jagged mile-long rampart around its crest. This is Devil's Wall, thought to be evidence of a great collapsed volcanic caldera. From this vantage point, you can see why this place became a state park. In one view, you see Taum Sauk Mountain, the highest point in Missouri; Mina Sauk Falls, the tallest waterfall; Devil's Wall high on Wildcat; and the state's most extensive igneous barrens on Weimer Hill to the northwest. The barrens span a half-mile swatch on the southwest face of Weimer and rise nearly five hundred feet above the stream below. A thick mantle of prairie grasses and wildflowers covers the slope, here and there dotted with oaks, pines, and cedars. One of the rarest plants in the country, Mead's milkweed, flowers in late May on this glade. Despite their small stature, many of the twisted, gnarly post oaks and eastern red cedars exceed three hundred years in age.

Virtually the entire area seen from here and more was designated by the interagency Missouri Natural Areas Committee in 1996 as the St. Francois Mountains Natural Area, at that time by far the largest such area in the state. At 7,028 acres, it includes most of Taum Sauk Mountain State Park, Conservation Department land on Proffit Mountain, and the northeastern-most 80 acres of Johnson's Shut-Ins, plus more than four miles of the headwaters of Taum Sauk Creek. Its unusually large size was testament to its remarkable geologic and natural integrity. It also reflected a new scientific understanding of the importance of preserving a landscape-scale mosaic of the natural communities that make this part of the Ozarks one of the greatest centers of biodiversity on the continent. State park naturalists conduct prescribed burns annually in portions of the area to mimic the natural wildfires that maintained the open woodlands and glades, which once again have ground cover rich in native legumes, grasses, sedges, and wildflowers.

Back on the trail about a mile west of Devil's Tollgate, hikers have another choice: to continue on the Boy Scout Trail that crosses and recrosses the tree-shaded creek before going up and over Proffit Mountain to Johnson's Shut-Ins, or to follow the Ozark Trail as it skirts the

A naturalist engages children within a glade on Taum Sauk Mountain. *Ron Colatskie* • The rare Mead's milkweed flourishes on glades in the St. Francois Mountains Natural Area. *Mike Currier* • Water cascades down ledges of ancient volcanic rock at Mina Sauk Falls, Missouri's tallest waterfall. A three-mile loop trail gradually descends from the trailhead to the falls, where you can enjoy a view of the valley before climbing back out. Marbled veins of pink and dark purple atop the falls bear witness to ancient lava flows. *Glenn Curcio*

lower slopes of Weimer Hill and then ascends and traverses the long arc of Proffit Mountain through state forest and back again into Taum Sauk Park before dropping into the East Fork Black River valley and the shut-ins.

The view to the south for much of this distance along the Ozark Trail is Church Mountain, 1,300 acres of it owned by Ameren Missouri (formerly Union Electric) but leased since 1990 to the state as part of Taum Sauk Mountain State Park. In 2001 Ameren applied for federal and state permits to build a second hydroelectric storage plant with reservoirs atop Church Mountain and in Taum Sauk Creek valley, where they would be visible from nearly every vantage point and would obliterate the Boy Scout Trail along the creek. Aghast at this impending intrusion of industrial civilization into the oldest, wildest, and most ecologically diverse landscape in the state, conservationists mounted a multifaceted campaign, including preparation for legal action, intended to persuade Ameren and federal and state decision-makers that a second power plant with mountaintop and valley reservoirs in this area was simply unthinkable in the wake of the major public investment in the wild lands of this region and the heightened understanding of their extraordinary natural and cultural heritage. Much as they hoped and fought for a favorable outcome, citizen groups were astonished when Ameren within a month withdrew its permit applications, saying they had listened to the voices of the people.

Taum Sauk Mountain State Park offers unsurpassed scenery, genuine backcountry, delicate igneous barrens, an unspoiled headwaters creek, and diverse woodlands. Additional loop and connector trails are being built across Church Mountain to provide another route of access to the interior. Well-known to Scouts for more than half a century, this extraordinary mountain landscape at the geologic heart of the Ozarks continues to beckon all, whether for a hike along trails deep into the wilds or to admire and enjoy the views from roadside overlooks. *

TAUM SAUK STATE PARK • 148 TAUM SAUK TRAIL, MIDDLE BROOK

Johnson's Shut-Ins State Park

THIS PARK IS A PHOENIX, REBORN OF FLOOD and wind rather than fire. Since its inception in the 1950s, Johnson's Shut-Ins in Reynolds County has been among the best-known state parks in Missouri, but the chutes and potholes of its photogenic shut-ins were ravaged by one of the more cataclysmic dam failures in American history. In the frigid predawn blackness of December 14, 2005, the Taum Sauk Reservoir atop nearby Proffit Mountain suddenly collapsed and in only twelve minutes sent 1.3 billion gallons of water roaring seven thousand feet down the mountainside and into the heart of the park. The rocks, trees, and other debris carried by the water created an immense scour channel and were deposited in the famous shut-ins. Then, just as the cleanup of the park and reconstruction of facilities neared completion, the park's mountainous wild areas took a direct hit on May 8, 2009, from an extraordinarily powerful windstorm that toppled as much as 90 percent of the oak and pine canopy in some areas. In spite of all this, Johnson's Shut-Ins is being reborn.

Located in the St. Francois Mountains at the geologic core of the Ozarks, the park is justly famed for its rocks. Pink granites, porphyries, and blue-gray rhyolites offer testimony to an era of primordial volcanism more than a billion years ago. Upstream of the park, the East Fork of the Black River flows through a relatively broad valley, the same valley followed by Route N leading to the park. But as the stream leaves the more easily eroded dolomitic bedrock and meets the resistant igneous rocks of the ancient ash and lava flows, the valley becomes narrow and canyon-like. The water has had to fight ceaselessly, laboriously, for every fracture, every weak joint, straining to find the least resistant course to follow. Sometimes, it has made right-angle changes in direction, creating eddies and crosscurrents. The resulting gorges and rock gardens have come to be called shut-ins. There are other shut-ins in the St. Francois Mountains region, but Johnson's, named for nineteenth-century homesteaders who actually were the Johnstons, are the most famous.

This rugged, nearly impenetrable area was once part of the largest Spanish land grant in Missouri. Sixteen square leagues (nearly 100,000 acres) on the forks of Black River were awarded in 1799 to Father James Maxwell, the Irish Catholic priest of French Ste. Genevieve, who intended to rescue indigent Irish Catholics from British tyranny and establish them here under a benign Spanish monarchy. But Spain transferred the land to France, who sold it to the United States, and the Irish settlement never materialized. There is scant evidence of Euro-American activity in this hardscrabble region until a few homesteaders trickled in decades later. The land was still relatively wild, uncut, and inaccessible when it was first proposed as a state park in 1915.

Much of the original park, including the shut-ins and two miles of river frontage, was assembled over the course of seventeen years and donated to the state in 1955 by Joseph Desloge, a St. Louis civic leader and conservationist from a prominent lead-mining family. The family subsequently donated funds for needed improvements.

Most visitors to Johnson's Shut-Ins see only a small part of the park—the visitor center, the picnic grounds, the campground, and the shut-ins overlook. The more adventurous wade, swim, and play in the creek, climbing and sliding on the smooth and slippery volcanic rocks, sitting in the swirling waters of the gravel-scoured potholes—a poor man's Jacuzzi, especially appealing on a hot summer day.

But the vast majority of the park's 8,780 acres is a near-wilderness paradise welcoming those hardy enough for vigorous hiking. Nearly three-quarters of this acreage is included in the East Fork and Goggins Mountain Wild Areas. The East Fork Wild Area is generally that part of

Right: Gravel, sand, and rocks swirling in the river's currents have sculpted and smoothed chutes and potholes into the igneous rocks left by ancient volcanic activity. *Oliver Schuchard* • Above: In the heat of the summer, the dancing waters of the shut-ins beckon park visitors for a cool splash. *Susan Flader*

Hikers admire the vista from the Ozark Trail, which crosses the 5,000-acre Goggins Mountain Wild Area. *Paul Barbercheck* • The December 2005 collapse of the Taum Sauk Reservoir sent 1.3 billion gallons of water and debris roaring down Proffit Mountain into Johnson's Shut-Ins State Park, scouring a path down the forested mountainside to bedrock and obliterating the park superintendent's home and the campground in the valley. *Scott Myers*

These are two species unique to the Ozark Plateau. Above: This spiderwort species, or wild crocus, is common on the wooded slopes at Johnson's Shut-Ins. *Allison Vaughn* • Right: Striking Ozark witch hazel, which is adapted to frequently flooded gravel washes, blooms as early as January. *Jim Rathert*

the park, excluding developments, between Route N and the river. The Goggins Wild Area of nearly 5,000 acres includes the sprawling, four-domed Goggins Mountain northwest of Route N, which was acquired in 1993 through a $1 million gift from the Richard King Mellon Foundation's American Land Conservation Program. It also includes the southern dome of Bell Mountain and adjoins the 9,000-acre Bell Mountain Wilderness Area of the Mark Twain National Forest.

The thirty-three mile Taum Sauk section of the Ozark Trail traverses these wilderness and wild areas and continues east through the huge St. Francois Mountains Natural Area to Taum Sauk and Ketcherside Mountains, making this one of the most significant blocks of wild land east of the Rocky Mountains. Here in these rugged, wooded hills, you can find solitude and wildness—endangered resources in today's hectic world.

Johnson's Shut-Ins is a rich botanical reserve with over nine hundred recorded species of trees, shrubs, vines, grasses, wildflowers, and ferns, more species than any other Missouri state park. Why this diversity? This question is best answered by exploring several of the park's seven trails, which cross a variety of rock types, topographic features, aquatic areas, and elevations. Just below the shut-ins, for example, one can find Ozark witch hazel blossoming in January. One of several different shrubs growing on the gravel washes, Ozark witch hazel has adapted to the frequent rampaging floods by simply yielding its buoyant, rubbery stems to the forceful torrents. This gravel-wash natural community is part of Johnson's Shut-Ins Natural Area.

A hike into the East Fork Wild Area on the Horseshoe Glade loop trail will take you to igneous rock barrens. On a sunny winter's day, you'll pause a moment here to bask in the warmth. On a sunny summer day you'll hasten through the barrens back to the shade. Herein lies another key to the park's botanical diversity. Arid land plants adapted to conserving precious water make their home here. In contrast to these rhyolite rock barrens, the Dolomite Glade Natural Area just off the Ozark Trail is in the southwest corner of the wild area. This is also a hot and open spot, but the soils overlying the sedimentary dolomite rock support several plant species different from those on the igneous rhyolite barrens, including the haunting Missouri evening primrose, which blooms at night.

In late winter or early spring, a hike to the East Fork Wild Area may reveal blackened hills, scorched by fire. Park staff perform prescribed burns to mimic the natural fires that once shaped the extensive pine and oak woodlands of this region. Without fire, woody thickets and dense leaf litter would inhibit germination of shortleaf pine and shade out and choke the prairie and woodland wildflowers that grow here.

Upstream in the day-use area is yet another unusual community, an eighteen-acre boggy forest designated as the Johnson's Shut-Ins Fen Natural Area. Permanently wet soil fed by cool calcareous groundwater is the key to the fen. Here, the coolness simulates the boreal

ONE-THIRD OF OUR NATIVE FLORA

Johnson's Shut-Ins is home to more than nine hundred plant species, almost one-third of Missouri's entire native flora. Twenty terrestrial natural communities occur here, which is nearly a quarter of those that have been identified anywhere in the state. Here are the twenty terrestrial communities:

1. Dry-mesic Chert Forest
2. Dry-mesic Igneous Forest
3. Riverfront Forest
4. Dry Limestone-Dolomite Woodland
5. Dry Chert Woodland
6. Dry-mesic Chert Woodland
7. Dry Igneous Woodland
8. Dry-mesic Igneous Woodland
9. Dry-mesic Bottomland Woodland
10. Dolomite Glade
11. Igneous Glade
12. Dry Limestone-Dolomite Cliff
13. Moist Limestone-Dolomite Cliff
14. Dry Igneous Cliff
15. Moist Igneous Cliff
16. Igneous Talus
17. Gravel Wash
18. Stream Bank
19. Ozark Fen
20. Forested Fen

List by Paul W. Nelson, based on *The Terrestrial Natural Communities of Missouri* (2010 edition), by Paul W. Nelson

conditions of southern Canada, which were more common in Missouri during glacial times and which nurture plants such as swamp wood betony, bottle gentian, tall sweet William, and blue smooth violet.

This fen, the campground located nearby, and the entire East Fork Black River through the park, including the shut-ins, were obliterated by the debris-filled torrent that roared down the mountain that wintry morning in 2005. It was one of those rare nights when there were no campground occupants, or there would surely have been many lives lost in the raging torrent.

As it was, the orchid-filled forest in Buzzard Rock Hollow on the west face of Proffit Mountain, down which the deluge roared, was scoured clean to bedrock, and a debris dam some twenty feet high blocked the park entrance road and the river nearby. Downstream, more debris and sediment clogged the river, forcing it out of its channel, but it reclaimed an older channel, as rivers will sometimes do. The entire campground was obliterated and strewn with mud and debris, as was the fen nearby. The resistant rhyolite of the shut-ins was still there beneath the murky water, but the shut-ins were now filled with concrete, rubble, plastic, and rebar from the reservoir wall and trees and boulders from the scour channel. The boardwalk along the shut-ins was destroyed, as was virtually all the riparian vegetation. Media coverage was national in scope, and the entire park was closed until further notice.

AmerenUE (now Ameren Missouri), the owner of the reservoir, accepted responsibility for the cleanup and redevelopment of the park, but park staff engaged for years in a protracted tug of war with the engineers hired by the power company to do the job. When sediments kept washing down from the edges of the scour channel, the engineers wanted to stabilize them with fabric and special plantings, but park naturalists insisted on a slower, more natural course. When the river changed channels after the deluge, the engineers wanted to put it back and harden it in place with concrete, but park managers argued instead for gently encouraging it to seek its own meandering course through its new floodplain. When test excavations of the deeply buried Johnson's Shut-Ins Fen Natural Area suggested that the original plants were still in place under many feet of sediment, park naturalists guided crews with excavation equipment and dump trucks and then with shovels and hand trowels in the painstaking removal of the debris and sediment to uncover the fen plants and give them another chance at life. Some of the fen's characteristic plants survived, but it remains to be seen whether the fen will resume its natural hydrologic functioning. On downstream in the shut-ins themselves, an extraordinary amount of debris was removed, some of it with helicopters, to avoid further disturbing the area and to make it safe once again for swimmers.

Meanwhile, park facilities were completely redesigned and rebuilt. The old campground along East Fork Black River was abandoned, and a new one was installed a mile north on the Goggins tract well out of the floodplain, complete with new camper cabins, an equestrian area, and links to a ten-mile equestrian and hiking loop trail on the east slope of Goggins Mountain. The day-use area along the creek was enlarged, though it will take decades for the shade trees to grow, and the boardwalk along the shut-ins was rebuilt. There is a new Black River Center with exhibits about the park, the St. Francois Mountains, and the reservoir collapse. A new trail with an interpretive pavilion and overlook provide access to the scour channel, and there are exhibits along Black River and elsewhere in the park as well. All of this new development inevitably has a raw and unshaded aspect, but nature will gradually soften and beautify the park.

Ameren has rebuilt its Taum Sauk Reservoir, and the plant is once again producing electricity. Its high white walls and lights are much more intrusive on the natural scene than the old reservoir, but Ameren insurance picked up the astounding $130 million tab for the cleanup and the reconstruction of park facilities. A complete natural recovery, though underway, will require generations or possibly centuries.

Above: Wild hyacinth blooms in spring and brightens Horseshoe Glade. ***Allison Vaughn*** **• Right: Winter brings a hush to Johnson's Shut-Ins, and you'll likely have the pleasure of the park entirely to yourself.** ***Oliver Schuchard***

A year before the 2010 dedication of the new park facilities, the park was struck again, but this time with the massive storm of May 8, 2009, which included gale-force, straight-line winds with some forty companion tornadoes extending more than a thousand miles from Kansas across the Ozark Highland to eastern Kentucky and Tennessee. It was of a magnitude so far beyond that of any similar event ever before recorded by the National Weather Service that experts called it a super derecho. Well over 100,000 acres were severely impacted in the southeastern Ozarks, including more than a thousand acres in the East Fork Wild Area, on Goggins, and in neighboring Taum Sauk State Park. Elsewhere in the Ozarks, logging crews scrambled for years to salvage downed timber. In the state park, it took park crews and volunteers years to reopen the more remote trails. The oak and pine canopy was damaged over a broad acreage, but prairie forbs and grasses not documented in the original floral survey in 1977 flourished under the newly opened canopy. Within two years, breeding birds showed greater abundance and diversity than in nearby areas not impacted by the wind. There was also new reproduction of shortleaf pine that historically characterized this area. The extraordinary response of vegetation after the great windstorm has encouraged staff to extend prescribed burns to additional areas to facilitate natural recovery of the native oak and shortleaf pine woodlands.

Johnson's Shut-Ins had been loved nearly to death by the 1970s. It was closed for a time in the 1980s and redesigned as a controlled-access park limited to one hundred cars at a time to ensure a better experience and reduce impact. When the park was again closed for several years after the deluge, the traffic pattern was redesigned to accommodate more vehicles for camping and day-use in other areas, but the parking lot for the shut-ins is still limited to just one hundred cars.

If you should find a line for the shut-Ins when you arrive, especially in summer, there are other places to park to walk the trails and also other beautiful parks in the vicinity. Johnson's Shut-Ins is being reborn in the wake of disaster, and the process is as fascinating as it is complex. Come and experience the healing and the joys of this fabulous park. *

JOHNSON SHUT-INS STATE PARK • 148 TAUM SAUK TRAIL, MIDDLE BROOK

Battle of Pilot Knob State Historic Site

THE TIME-GENTLED REMAINS of Fort Davidson lie in the shadows of the granite knobs of the St. Francois Mountains, near Pilot Knob in the Arcadia Valley. Standing on the grass-covered slope of what was once a wall with a moat, you try to comprehend the carnage that took place here and down along Knob Creek on the afternoon of September 27, 1864, when Maj. Gen. Sterling Price stormed the fort.

Lack of discipline and lack of arms, horses, and perhaps even shoes conspired with geography against Price and his army. The one-time Missouri governor had entered Missouri from Arkansas on September 19 with a force of more than twelve thousand men, including some three thousand Arkansas conscripts and deserters pressed into service. Thousands of his troops were said to have been without adequate footwear, and fully one-quarter of the complement was without arms. Price planned to march his three divisions north to take the federal arsenal at St. Louis, a much-needed prize for the failing Southern cause, and then install the Confederate governor-in-exile in Jefferson City, rallying Missourians to his side as he progressed through the state. From a broader Confederate perspective, the intent of the campaign was to tie up federal troops in the West in order to relieve the desperate situation in the East, and Price succeeded in this, though at a terrible cost.

The Battle of Pilot Knob was one of the bloodiest in the Civil War in Missouri, and it marked the beginning of the end for the Confederate forces under Maj. Gen. Sterling Price.

After reaching Fredericktown, having encountered little resistance, Price and his staff debated whether to move directly to St. Louis or to turn west to seize the Union fortification at Pilot Knob. Afraid to leave this enemy fort on his flank, Price made the fateful decision to assault the stronghold twenty-two miles to the west. On September 26, he sent one division northwest to cut the railroad to Pilot Knob, but Union Brig. Gen. Thomas Ewing Jr., a brother-in-law of renowned Union Gen. William Tecumseh Sherman, and a small detachment of infantry reinforcements had reached Fort Davidson by train before noon that very day. This was the same Thomas Ewing who had provoked the passionate hatred of Missouri Southerners by his issuance of the infamous Order No. 11, which forced the depopulation and destruction of four heavily pro-South counties along the Kansas border in western Missouri.

Fort Davidson with its hexagonal nine-foot earthen walls and dry moat had been built the previous year by federal forces. It guarded the Ironton gap between Shepherd Mountain on the west and Pilot Knob on the east and marked the terminus of the Iron Mountain Railroad, which hauled the abundant minerals of the St. Francois Mountains region north to St. Louis. An approaching army would have to pass through hundreds of yards of open ground to reach the walls of the fort. Still, the fort was vulnerable to artillery attack from either of the flanking knobs, which had no forts because the ones that had been planned were never built.

Ewing had about 1,400 men to hold his position. He also possessed formidable artillery and plenty of ammunition. Shortly after his arrival at the fort, he sent two companies through the gap to patrol the road to Fredericktown. They quickly engaged the rebels' advance troops along the Stouts Creek Shut-Ins just east of Ironton. Skirmishes continued around the Iron County courthouse and back up the gap toward the fort. Price gave Ewing an opportunity to surrender early on September 27, but Ewing refused. Price launched a frontal assault on the Union forces. The bloody assault was short—some say only twenty minutes—but the casualties quickly mounted, numbering from five hundred to a thousand, mainly among Confederates storming the fort.

Having learned a bitter, costly lesson in this ill-advised frontal attack, Price decided to bombard the fort with cannons from Shepherd Mountain the next day. But at two o'clock on the morning of September 28, a loud explosion roused his forces. At daybreak, they found the fort empty with a giant smoldering hole in the center—all that was left of the Union powder magazine.

During a drizzly, dark night, with the wheels of their cannons and wagons muffled, the federal troops sneaked right through the disorganized rebel lines. When the squad left behind blew the powder magazine, General Ewing was already miles away. Outraged, General Price sent a division after the fleeing forces, but Ewing managed to fight his way safely to Leasburg after several days.

With many of his troops lost and the rest in disarray after this disaster, Price abandoned his plans to take St. Louis. He turned instead to a secondary prize, Jefferson City, only to be turned away by a newly reinforced Union garrison. From there, Price continued westward, pursued by Union forces. He suffered major defeats on October 23 at Westport, the biggest battle west of the Mississippi, and two days later at Mine Creek, Kansas, before retreating into Arkansas, all hope for reclaiming Missouri now shattered.

In 1905 the Pilot Knob Memorial Association, an organization of Civil War veterans who hoped to encourage federal preservation of the battlefield, purchased the site. Even though Ewing's son was a principal player in this endeavor, broad support for creating a national battlefield was apparently not forthcoming. In 1938 and 1939, Ewing's son and his wife, still hoping the site would someday become a national park, donated it to the US Forrest Service, which was acquiring land in the vicinity. State

Pilot Knob loomed above one of the bloodiest Civil War battles in Missouri. In the foreground during a reenactment, Confederate troops advance toward Fort Davidson, located at the terminus of the Iron Mountain Railroad. *Nick Decker*
Left: Confederate reenactors replicate the doomed assault, stalling out in the dry moat surrounding the fort, just as soldiers did in 1864. *Ben Nickelson*

park planners apparently prepared a master plan for the site as a cooperative endeavor, but the State Park Board was not interested in taking it over at the time. There was little development except for a small pull-off with a historical marker.

The modern reawakening of the site began with cannon fire and rousing speeches before a large crowd at a gathering to mark the centennial of the battle in 1964, and in 1969, the State Park Board agreed to take responsibility for managing and interpreting the two-acre site of the fort. Renewal of the ten-year permit from the Forest Service in 1980 led to increasing interest in making this fascinating site a more meaningful experience for visitors. In 1987 the state obtained title to the entire fifteen acres originally purchased by veterans in 1905 for the memorial, and in 1990, an adjacent nineteen-acre city park was added as well, providing a site for a new visitor center. In 1997 national Civil War organizations donated forty acres to the east, formerly owned by Hanna Mining Company. The site now covers eighty acres.

The state also has an agreement with the US Fish and Wildlife Service, which owns substantial acreage on Pilot Knob, that allows for guided hikes up the mountain to see remnants of iron mining and Civil War activity and to gain a panoramic overview of the St. Francois Mountains and of the Fort Davidson earthworks. The city of Pilot Knob now owns Shepherd Mountain, from which Price's troops intended to bombard the

fort. In 2013 the city opened a two-mile loop hiking trail on the northeast face overlooking the battlefield. The state has also acquired two acres at Stout's Creek Shut-Ins where forces from the two sides skirmished before the fateful battle, though public access awaits road changes in the area.

The site of Fort Davidson was renamed Battle of Pilot Knob State Historic Site in 2014 on the occasion of the sesquicentennial of the battle. Your tour there should begin in the visitor center, equipped with an audiovisual program and a fiber-optic battle map as well as other exhibits and artifacts. Included is a Confederate six-pounder cannon that had been dragged to the top of Shepherd Mountain only to be hit by uncannily accurate Union cannon fire from the fort before it could be brought into action. The building, of subtle classical design, is located some distance from the fort to minimize its impact while still providing a formal and dignified entry to the battlefield.

The approach to the fort itself is over a pleasant walking path across the ground that was once contested so fiercely. From the path toward the fort, the strategic nature of the narrow notch in the mountains becomes apparent. The mass of Shepherd Mountain looms ahead, blocking the horizon, while the jagged-toothed, mined-out summit of Pilot Knob rears up behind. When Cyrus Peterson in his book about the battle referred to it as the "Thermopylae of the West," he spoke not only in

Fort Davidson was originally equipped with siege guns similar to this pair now displayed near the fort. Pilot Knob and the visitor center emerge from a morning fog. Above: Nearly fifty thousand people—perhaps the largest crowd ever to attend a state park event—gathered for the sesquicentennial reenactment in 2014. Right: During that event, a Union color guard marches across the battlefield, as color guards often did during Civil War battles. *All Ben Nickelson*

classical allusion but also with considerable topographical accuracy.

The sharp-edged reality of armed conflict to the contrary, the fort today evidences a curious softness, the result of years of weathering and the healing miracle of grass covering the entire earthwork. Early morning and late afternoon visits are most rewarding, when the low angle of the sun's rays heightens the relief of the remaining features. Then, the moat lies in shadow while the tops of the walls where the parapets once stood are still bathed in sunlight, bringing forth the clear outline of the once embattled hexagon.

Even the earthen platforms for the thirty-two-pounder siege guns at the corners become visible in the slanting rays. The deep shadow marking the crater in the center of the fort serves as compelling evidence of the magnitude of the blast that startled the resting Confederates during that rainy night following the afternoon's carnage.

Extending from the fort's south wall was a rifle pit, really a trench some two hundred yards long and deep enough for men to walk in and fire from. Now it is visible only from the air as a faint shadow in the green grass, reaching out from the fort and stretching south toward Shepherd Mountain in the distance. Several hundred Confederate soldiers still repose within it, resting forever on the battlefield where they made the ultimate sacrifice for their principles on that warm fall afternoon in Missouri, September 27, 1864. *

BATTLE OF PILOT KNOB STATE HISTORIC SITE • 118 EAST MAPLE, PILOT KNOB

Sam A. Baker State Park

ON THE SOUTHERN FLANK OF THE ST. FRANCOIS Mountains, Sam A. Baker offers visitors the freedom to wander at will in spacious, wild lands, savor old-time park hospitality in rustic comfort, enjoy the refreshing tingle of a clear Ozark mountain stream, and ascend the blue granitic hulk of Mudlick Mountain. Because Mudlick stands alone, separated from the concentration of domes surrounding Taum Sauk to the north, you can survey virtually the entire panorama of the St. Francois Mountains, while to the south and east you scan the deeply dissected hills of the Ozark border to the abrupt escarpment that drops off into the Mississippi Lowlands beyond.

This classic Missouri state park stands out in bold relief, encompassing all of Mudlick Mountain and the adjacent streams. On the east side, the park fronts on the St. Francis River and for about five miles on its tributary, Big Creek, which is an Outstanding State Resource Water. Huge boulders of Precambrian Mudlick dellenite, locally called blue granite, litter the hillsides and tumble into the canyons. The waters of the creeks rush and swirl around them, polishing them to a beautiful sheen.

Because the park was established under the old Missouri Game and Fish Commission, a large portion of the mountainous area was initially set aside as a big-game refuge. Here, in scattered small plots, standing grain enhanced efforts to increase the state's decimated deer herd, and a state turkey farm was established to help restore what was once an almost extinct species. In talking about the park and the wildlife when he was a boy, Gov. Sam A. Baker made it clear that he wished "to make available for this and future generations something that was commonplace to the youth of forty years ago." Today, deer and wild turkey have returned to their former abundance, both inside the park and in the surrounding area, and no longer require artificial measures for their propagation. Jointly managed for decades by the Conservation Department and the old Park Board, Baker since 1981 has been entirely in state park hands.

Cultural as well as natural resources make this park a Missouri classic. The first major construction came during Franklin Roosevelt's New Deal when the park became the site of Civilian Conservation Corps (CCC) Camp 5, set up in June 1933 in the valley near the present-day visitor center. By 1935, CCC enrollees had built barracks, installed telephone and water lines, laid out trails, planted trees, fought fires, and built a number of well-crafted rustic structures, including bridges, cabins, barbecue pits, restrooms, trail shelters, a gatekeeper's stand, a stable, and the beginnings of a timber and blue granite dining lodge. After the CCC company pulled out in October 1935, Works Progress Administration (WPA) workers completed many projects, including the lodge.

Most of these handsome, sturdy, Depression-era structures continue to function in the park today. Indeed, they set the tone for the whole place. Many have been restored, and others will be. The dining lodge, formerly known as the Black Lodge because of the dark blue dellenite stone, is an evocative structure, as is the old stable with its three-story octagonal tower and two projecting wings, now converted to a visitors center. Mudlick fire tower, a distinctive CCC-era landmark, is still used to spot smoke in the region's heavily timbered hills. Owing to the integrity of the preserved CCC and WPA workmanship, the entire 4,860 acres of the 1930s park has been designated the Sam A. Baker State Park Historic District on the National Register of Historic Places.

This view looks south from Big Creek Glade across the creek toward the 4,420-acre Mudlick Mountain Wild Area, one of the largest wild areas in the state park system. The twelve-mile Mudlick Trail winds around the mountain. ***Ron Colatskie***

One of the best ways to enjoy Sam Baker is to hike the trail that begins across from the dining lodge. The trail descends first to the floodplain of Big Creek, hugging the base of Mudlick Mountain. To the right are the majestic sweetgums, sycamores, Shumard oaks, and cottonwoods of a southeast Ozark terrace forest; on the left is the rich vegetation of the

shaded mountain base. The trail passes several steep rocky draws where huge purple and bluish boulders of the Mudlick dellenite are jumbled like a giant's toy blocks.

In the spring, these draws are alive with the rush of clear waters cascading over glistening rocks, moistening scattered patches of moss into puffy emerald cushions. These cool patches provide the rare and colorful four-toed salamander—a glacial relict species more common in Missouri during the colder climate of the Ice Age—with ideal shelter beneath which to breed and deposit its eggs. Later in the spring, the lower slopes of Mudlick display the lovely yellowwood tree, its luxuriant yellow-green compound leaves contrasting with fragrant pea-like white blossoms. Baker is one of the few places in Missouri to find this Appalachian species in its natural habitat.

Soon the trail turns left up a slope and begins a series of switchbacks across a bulging shoulder of the mountain. As the trail climbs, the forest soil gradually becomes thinner, rockier, drier. It then traverses several small glade openings filled with sun-loving grasses and flowers. From the openings, you may look back and see the valleys of

Above: The striking Civilian Conservation Corps-era stable with its three-story octagonal tower serves now as a visitors center with exhibits about the human and natural history of the park. The CCC also built well-crafted bridges, cabins, barbecue pits, trail shelters, a gatekeeper's stand, and restrooms. *Scott Myers* Left: The Black Lodge, built of local blue Mudlick dellenite, was the focal point of the 4,860-acre 1930s park, which has been enrolled on the National Register of Historic Places because of the quality and integrity of its CCC-era structures. *Tom Nagel* • Right: Mudlick Creek, a beautiful Ozark stream, gurgles through a rocky hollow in the Mudlick Mountain Wild Area. *Michelle Soenksen*

WHO WAS SAM A. BAKER?

Life was hard in rural Wayne County where Sam A. Baker was born, grew up, and later taught school. The work of firing a furnace to pay for his board at the state teachers college in Cape Girardeau undoubtedly fired his determination to succeed. After working his way up from teacher to principal to superintendent, he became state superintendent of public schools and then in 1924 was elected governor of Missouri. During his term, many of the first-generation of state parks were acquired—not least of them the forested, mountainous tract of canyons, shut-ins, and rushing streams in Wayne County, close to the village of Patterson where the governor was born. Baker himself encouraged friends and relatives to sell or donate their land to the state beginning in 1926, and the first 4,000 acres cost the state only $23,000. The park later grew to more than 5,300 acres.

Big Creek and, farther off, the St. Francis River. Reentering the oaks and hickories, the trail emerges suddenly at the brow of a point, where a small stone cabin seems to have grown right out of the mountainside. Its dellenite walls and floor, wood-shingle roof, and sturdy rock fireplaces all welcome hikers after a steep climb up the trail. It is actually a three-sided shelter, and as you sit resting under the eave on the raised lip of the stone floor, you might notice that there is an open ledge not far in front of you. Step closer to the edge, and a spectacular panorama reveals the wild canyon of Big Creek, as you look upstream toward the cliff-lined narrows and across at the pine-strewn slopes on the opposite bank. This shelter is one in a series of three strung out along the trail in an arc across the flank of Mudlick. Each is a joy. For a really special experience, you can arrange to camp overnight in one of them during the winter backpacking season.

This area is all part of the 4,420-acre Mudlick Mountain Wild Area, one of the largest wilderness preserves in the state park system, and a third of it is also a state-designated natural area. The twelve-mile Mudlick Trail, now a national recreation trail, contours around the mountain, with a spur to the fire tower at the top. Near the top of the mountain on its westerly flank are gnarled, stunted, weather-sculpted white oaks, many exceeding two hundred years of age and showing signs of the violent winds, lightning strikes, and heavy ice storms that pummel the mountain crest. Amazingly, most of the trees survive, providing numerous hollow trunks that serve as nature's hotels for a variety of birds, mammals, reptiles, and invertebrate fauna.

On the south ridge of the mountain, the trail leads through an area ravaged by a tornado in 1984. Hundreds of centuries-old oaks and

Riders enjoy seventeen miles of equestrian trails. Three stone hiking shelters overlook the Mudlick Trail. The St. Francis River at Baker is so gentle that families and small children can swim or float on rafts or tubes. A park naturalist—or else the snake—entrances children. *All Scott Myers*

hickories were toppled, just part of a never-ending natural sequence. Within two years, a profusion of flowering dogwood burst into bloom, because of the great increase in sunlight. The fallen trees and newly sprouted thickets supplied habitat for dozens of species. Today, the path of that tornado is hardly discernible to most hikers, though like all such events, it is recorded in the structure of the forest.

Sam A. Baker State Park is a great place for a family vacation. Its cabins and campgrounds offer a wonderful base of operations, its dining lodge a tempting respite from camp cooking. Big Creek is gentle and shallow enough for kids to play in, and the St. Francis River beckons canoes, kayaks, or rafts, which can be rented at the park store. The park offers six trails, short and long with varied loops and connectors, for hiking, biking, or horse riding. The nature center has hands-on exhibits, and the park staff offers great programs and guided hikes. Sam Baker would be proud of his namesake park and the authentic Ozark experience it offers Missourians. *

SAM A. BAKER STATE PARK • ROUTE 143, PATTERSON

Meramec State Park

ONE OF FIVE STATE PARKS ALONG THE MERAMEC River, Meramec State Park is one of the oldest, best known, and most popular of Missouri's state parks. The other parks along the river are Onondaga Cave, Robertsville, Route 66, and Castlewood. At nearly 6,900 acres, this park is one of the largest in the state, lying across parts of Franklin, Crawford, and Washington Counties. The park is named for the river that flows eight miles through it and along its borders, which is fitting, as the Meramec River is the dominant natural influence over the park's varied features. The river was also the centerpiece of a bitter public controversy resolved in favor of the free-flowing stream, one of the most biologically diverse in the Midwest.

The museum in the visitor center, dedicated in 1989, provides an outstanding introduction to the park and the river. It has an educational and fun mix of exhibits and activities for people of all ages. Especially popular are the large aquariums that display the amazing variety of aquatic life in the river—from predatory bass to minnows of rainbow colors—with a clarity and closeness that you otherwise might not experience. Large murals and complex dioramas present the broad sweep of history, both human and natural, in the Meramec River valley.

A good way to enjoy the park is by river. The river has an undeserved reputation as being treacherous, probably because of accidental drownings on the lower, deeper sections near St. Louis. But the Meramec is as safe as any other Ozark stream. If you launch your boat at Sappington Bridge and take out down at Cane Bottom, you can see much of the park in a good day's float or a more leisurely two-day float trip.

As you drift downstream, you will see Hamilton Creek coming in from the right. A bit more than a mile up this creek are the ruins of the old Hamilton Iron Furnace, not far from Hamilton Spring. The ironworks, one of many in the Meramec basin, was built in 1873 and was soon followed by a town that grew in size to some 150 people in the late 1880s. Ironworks are dependent upon the economy, and this one died young. It remains an intriguing site to visit, with the brick crucible still visible in the stone furnace and with the sites of several auxiliary structures still visible as well. The walking trail has signs identifying the features.

Beyond the mouth of Hamilton Creek, a massive dolomite cliff rises on the right bank. In the cliff is one of Missouri's most impressive cave openings, Green's Cave, well worth a stop. Wild caves such as Green's are managed to protect the bats that hibernate in them. Some are closed and others are open, but always check with park staff before exploring.

At this point, the river makes a large bend to the left and then back to the right, which geologists call an entrenched meander. Such bends speak of the natural history of the area. Rivers on relatively flat terrain tend to meander, whereas rivers in rough terrain tend to follow a straighter course. Most of the Ozark rivers were formed when the area was a broad plateau, so they meandered back and forth. As the region slowly became elevated over millions of years, the rivers—meanders and all—cut their way into the dolomite bedrock, thus "entrenching" themselves.

This is a good place to see the hydrologic power of the Meramec. On the outside bend of the meander, the water relentlessly wears away soil and rock on the bank. Large sycamores that have been undercut wait to tumble into the stream with the next flood. On the inside bend, the opposite is occurring. Silt and chert gravel are being deposited, often forming large bars with willows and other plants anchoring the new alluvial land. You cannot see it, but the river actually flows in a corkscrew motion as it rounds the bend. The rugged landscape of this state park owes its character to the persistent force of the Meramec River over the eons.

Meramec State Park could well be called "the cave park" as it has some four dozen named caves within its boundaries—more than any other state park in Missouri and second in the nation.

Down a little farther, you float past what was to have been the site of the Meramec Park Dam. This controversial federal water project was effectively killed in 1978 when the public voted "no" by a margin of two to one in a regional, twelve-county referendum. Respecting the citizenry's desires, elected officials deauthorized the project several years later. In fact, all of the state park land along the stretch of river just described had been purchased by the Army Corps of Engineers for the proposed 12,600-acre lake. The corps transferred several thousand acres of the land to the state for the park, along with a scenic easement, referred to by Ozarkers as a setback, of six hundred feet on each side of the river. Other lands were returned to private ownership through public auction.

Many factors figured into the dam's demise, but one is worthy of mention here: caves. In addition to more than four dozen known caves in the park area, countless caves with no surface entry probably exist.

The Meramec River flows more than eight miles through the park and along its borders. *Ron Colatskie* • Bleeding shiners, characteristic of the cool, clear Meramec, display their breeding colors. *William Roston* • The silent Hamilton Iron Furnace hints at the once thriving industry. *Missouri State Parks*

A formation in Fisher Cave shows some broken speleothems. ***Scott Myers***
Volunteers have painstakingly pieced together and then reattached more than 175 broken speleothems, using special adhesives. ***Shelly Colatskie***

Critics of the dam pointed out the cavernous nature of the hills that the earthen dam would have abutted, but Army engineers insisted that with enough concrete grout any cavity could be sealed. Drilling for a dam abutment accidentally confirmed a major cavern in one hillside, a cavern with chambers fifty feet high in places. Today that pristine cave, Moore's Cave, is protected as part of the state park and is closed to the public. It can only be entered by rope through a hundred-foot shaft.

Meramec State Park traces its beginnings to 1927, when the State Game and Fish Commission started acquiring land along the river near the site of the old mining town, Reedsville. Indians and early French and American settlers had mined for lead, and later also for iron and copper. Some ten thousand people in two thousand cars reportedly attended the park dedication in 1928, and Meramec, with ready accessibility from St. Louis, quickly became one of the state's most popular parks.

The Civilian Conservation Corps (CCC) built many of the facilities in the 1930s. Most of these structures, including the dining lodge, cabins, and river shelter, have been restored and are still in service. The vintage lodge offers a fine view of the river. Newer facilities such as the park store, the Hickory Ridge Conference Center, and the visitor center were designed to carry on the CCC heritage of handsome craftsmanship.

Near the riverside campground is the entrance to Fisher Cave, one of Missouri's oldest show caves. The cave features many speleothems (rock forms) with troglobites and stygobites (cave creatures). Fisher Cave was key in the 1950s studies of prominent geologist J. Harlan Bretz when he was developing his theory of speleogenesis, or cave origin.

State park naturalists conduct guided tours of the cave's subterranean splendor in the summer. Fisher Cave was closed temporarily in an effort to slow the rapid spread of white-nose syndrome, a disease caused by a fungus that was unknown to science as recently as 2007 and that is highly lethal to certain species of bats that hibernate in caves. Rigorous screening measures are now in place in state park show caves to minimize the spread of the syndrome, and the caves are closed in other seasons when bats are present. Most wild caves that harbor bats have been closed year-round. Until the disease and its transmittal are better understood, scientists prefer to err on the side of caution.

Outside the caves, wildlife abounds in the park, and you will have a good chance of seeing ospreys, mink, or river otters. September is often the best month to be on the river. Typically, skies are sunny, both air and water temperatures are mild, and the river is clear and uncrowded. In mid-September, the peak of the hummingbird migration usually coincides with the peak blooming of the cardinal flower. This common riverside plant is so sought after by hummingbirds that you will rarely watch for five minutes before a hummer shows up.

Even at midday on a summer weekend, you can experience the rich diversity of the Meramec by putting on snorkeling goggles and submerging into the clear waters. With over one hundred species of fish and numerous species of turtles, salamanders, crawfish, and mussels, the Meramec is considered Missouri's Amazon of aquatic life.

Back from the river is an extensive mature forest. On slopes that face east or north, the forest often reaches an impressive size and density. Here in early May, a healthy population of the exquisite yellow lady's slipper orchid flourishes. On the south sides of several ridges are several thin-soiled rocky glade openings in the forest. In mid-April, red Indian paintbrush embellishes the glades. In early June, the long rays of purple coneflower blossoms unfold, providing a second peak of color.

Some of the best places to experience the harmonious blend of glades and majestic trees are the park's two natural areas, the 460-acre Meramec Upland Forest Natural Area and the 830-acre Meramec Mosaic Natural Area. They represent some of Missouri's finest examples of the forest and woodland communities that typically grow on well-drained cherty soil formed from dolomite rock. Meramec Mosaic contains diverse natural communities, including fens, cliffs, caves, springs, creeks, lush bottomland forests and, on the uplands, woodlands with native grasses and gnarled chinkapin oaks and glades with dazzling wildflowers, thanks to stewardship by park staff and volunteers. The Mosaic area may be entered on the mile-long Natural Wonders Trail near the visitor center while the ten-mile Wilderness Trail traverses the more remote Upland Forest area and adjacent backcountry in the northern part of the park.

Although the woods and the caves provide an extra measure of enjoyment for a Meramec State Park outing, it is ultimately the river that defines not only the experience but also the park itself. Like one of the river's meanders, the park has come nearly full circle, from its first modest attempt to preserve the riverine environs for the public, through the speculative fevers of dam construction, back to the real heart of the matter: the Meramec. The natural values of the river and its rugged watershed have prevailed. *

MERAMEC STATE PARK • 115 MERAMEC PARK DRIVE, SULLIVAN

A chinkapin oak woodland with an open prairie-like understory of grasses and forbs adorns the Meramec Mosaic Natural Area. *Paul Nelson*

Onondaga Cave State Park

THE CROWN JEWEL IN MISSOURI'S underground treasure chest is Onondaga Cave. Meramec State Park, just twenty miles downstream, has the greatest number of caves, but Onondaga Cave State Park has the preeminent cave. For more than seventy-five years before its 1982 acquisition as a park, Onondaga Cave was one of the major public attractions in the Midwest, and it still is.

More than a geologic curiosity is preserved at Onondaga Cave State Park. Here is a memorial to a disappearing style of roadside showmanship that is peculiarly American. It is impossible to separate Onondaga Cave, the natural phenomenon, from Onondaga Cave, the showplace of a vintage twentieth-century frontier-style capitalism. The colorful cave forms are the results of millions of years of geologic history, and the human story of the cave is every bit as colorful. Appreciation of this state park in Crawford County is greatly magnified by knowledge of both.

More than thirty known caves are in this 1,300-acre park, more than any other park except Meramec. Two are well-known, Onondaga and Cathedral, and both had long histories of commercial operation as show caves. They occur in separate forested ridges divided by two small but deep valleys and a third ridge with nearly three hundred feet of relief.

The geologic story of these caves is like that of many others in the state. In prehistoric times, much of what is now Missouri was inundated by a series of shallow, warm seas. Over millions of years, shells and exoskeletons from a whole host of aquatic plants and animals were deposited as layer upon layer of sediments. Ages passed, and these deposits became the limestones and dolomites of the Ozark Plateau. The Paleozoic seas receded, and the land rose upward. Groundwater, which had become mildly acidic from percolating through decayed organic material on the new dry land, found its way along cracks and within the horizontal seams separating the sedimentary rock layers. The water slowly dissolved away the calcareous material, forming larger cracks and, finally, tunnels and chambers.

While this subsurface rock was being dissolved by groundwater, surface runoff began to cut valleys forming the Ozarks we know today. As the valleys deepened, the water table dropped, and some of the water-filled tunnels drained. As air replaced water in the passages, they became what we know as caves—like Onondaga and Cathedral. The

Stone lily pads in the cave have formed drop by drop over eons. ***Scott Myers***

mouths of the caves are the points where valley streams have cut across the passages, opening them to daylight. But the work of water was not done. Streams within the caves continued to erode both stone and clay fill, enlarging the cave passages and finally emerging as springs at the cave mouths.

Water carrying dissolved minerals from the ground could also seep into the caves, frequently depositing carbonate rock forms known technically as speleothems, or more familiarly as stalactites (hanging from the ceiling) and stalagmites (rising from the floor, due to drips from above). The color and variety of these dripstones and flowstones lend a decorator's touch to the cave interiors. Cave formation is an almost magical process: water dissolves and erodes the rock, forming the caves, and water can eventually fill the cave back up with redeposited stone.

No one really knows when the first explorers entered Onondaga Cave where its spring exited, but this entrance area was host to several mills during the latter half of the nineteenth century. In 1886 Charles Christopher, John P. Eaton, and Miles Horine began exploring what was then called Davis Cave, after William Davis, who owned and operated a mill at the spring and had built a dam to create a millpond at the cave's entrance. Eaton and his friends used a johnboat to gain entrance. Later, Eaton and Christopher acquired several hundred acres north of the Davis property, land under which much of their beautiful discovery was located. Plans were made to mine the cave onyx (calcite flowstone) from the plentiful formations, but lack of mining expertise and funds forced them to sell their holdings after the turn of the century.

One of the buyers was a St. Louis man, George Bothe, who formed a mining company to remove and market cave onyx for use, among other places, at the 1904 Louisiana Purchase Exposition in St. Louis. But a number of factors, including the brittleness of the calcite when removed from the constant cool temperature and humidity of the cave, led Bothe to look for some other way to exploit his underground treasure. He advertised the cave as an attraction for fairgoers, and he arranged for them to ride there from St. Louis on the Frisco Railroad, in which he had also invested. Thousands of visitors rode the Frisco to the little town of Leasburg where they were met by surreys or wagons for the five-mile trip to the cave. The success of the cave as a fair attraction convinced Bothe to keep it open for public viewing. He acquired the mill property from William Davis's widow and promoted the cave in railroad literature.

An interesting aspect of the ownership of caves is that owning the entrance to a cave is not the same as owning the cave: the cave belongs to whoever owns the land it is under. The sprawling nature of the Onondaga Cave system and a lack of knowledge in the early days about its extent led to what would be a long and convoluted struggle over ownership. After the Bothe ownership there were no less than a half-dozen owners, even including a St. Louis hospital, often with rival and competing claims to the land above the cave. A separate entrance was used to develop what was called Missouri Caverns—in reality, just a different portion of the same cave. There were cave wars above ground in the courts and below ground in the cave. Rival owners' cave guides sometimes engaged in rock throwing across the barbed wire fences that divided some passages of the cave, while above ground, roadside hucksters attempted to lure unsuspecting tourists to competing attractions. Legal action proceeded all the way to the Missouri Supreme Court. The cave wars finally ended in the 1940s, when the Crawford County Caverns Company acquired ownership of all the competing claims.

In 1949, Onondaga Cave began its ascent to national notoriety when it was sold to Lyman Riley and Lester B. Dill. Under their leadership, Onondaga reached its commercial apogee in the 1950s and 1960s as a nationally known show cave. Dill became sole owner in the late 1960s, and his remarkable personality has left its indelible mark on Onondaga Cave and Missouri's tourism industry. Dill had an Ozark wit and a legendary gift for telling tall tales. He always told what he called the Ozark truth—something between the honest truth and a bald-faced lie—like the time he promoted a 102-year-old Oklahoman named J. Frank Dalton as the real, still-living Jesse James. His stubborn resistance to the Army Corps of Engineers helped save the cave and much of the surrounding Meramec River valley from permanent flooding by the proposed Meramec Dam.

Lester Dill became known as "America's Number One Caveman," but he always referred to himself as a "caveologist." He had started exploring caves as a young boy giving torch-lit tours of Fisher Cave in Meramec State Park, where his father, Thomas Benton Dill, was a former landowner and the first superintendent. In 1933 Dill bought the old saltpeter Cave near Stanton and turned it into Meramec Caverns, set in what he called La Jolla Natural Park. Dill took the idea of highway advertising and set a standard for cleverness and saturation rarely equaled on the nation's highways. Billboards and painted barns heralded "See Jesse James' Hideout—Meramec Caverns" and "Visit Onondaga Cave, Daniel Boone's Discovery." He was instrumental in founding the National 66 Association to promote tourist attractions along old Route 66, dubbed the Main Street of America.

A naming contest in conjunction with the World's Fair in 1904 settled the cave's name as Onondaga, which is the name of a tribe of the Iroquois and means "spirit of the hills."

Stairs allow visitors to get close to the Queen's Canopy, a massive 40-foot-tall flowstone, which formed as water flowed down the wall. *Eric Spradling*

In 1980, Onondaga Cave won designation by the National Park Service as a National Natural Landmark, a testament to its value to science and to Dill's respect for the natural integrity of the cave despite his marketing prowess. Even before his death that same year, Dill had already begun talks on turning Onondaga Cave into a state park. With the cooperation of the Dill estate, the Nature Conservancy, and the Missouri legislature, his desire to preserve Onondaga for future generations was at last realized with the dedication of Onondaga Cave State Park—and presentation of the national landmark plaque—in 1982.

Shortly after acquiring Onondaga, park system scientists began working closely with the concessionaire and park staff to develop a cave stewardship plan. The plan ensured that the public would continue to enjoy the cave while its delicate biota and fragile geologic treasures

Left: Volunteers help restore rimstone dams in Onondaga Cave. *Greg Hanson* Above: Cathedral Cave takes its name from this 25-foot-high, 15-foot-wide formation known as the cathedral. *Missouri State Parks* • Right: • Eastern red cedars, some five hundred years old, have survived the ages on the 250-foot-high cliff edge at Vilander Bluff Natural Area. *Paul Nelson*

RESTORATION SUCCESS

Recently, in the course of removing gravel from old walkways in the cave, park staff uncovered large rimstone dams. The day after cleaning out one such dam, it filled with water, and a grotto salamander had already moved in—instant restoration gratification! On another occasion, volunteers from speleological society grottoes statewide helped relocate and install new bat-friendly gates on Onondaga and Cathedral Caves, which resulted in considerably increased bat numbers within a few years.

were preserved. For decades, countless thousands of visitors had caused physical damage to natural features and cave organisms—not maliciously but through lack of knowledge. New corrosion-resistant metal railings were installed along walkways, and new lighting circuits with low-intensity lights reduced the unwelcome green algae that covered areas around the old lights. The Missouri Speleological Society and other groups of cavers volunteered to remove trash and debris brought into the cave through the decades, thus reducing chemical contamination to groundwater. The practice of tossing coins into the pools in the unique lily-pad room was prohibited; cave guides were trained to explain how this activity had disrupted the delicate chemical process that formed the stone lily pads. Smoking was prohibited to eliminate air pollutants harmful to cave life. Unneeded shafts once used for transporting gravel into the cave were sealed, and airtight entry doors were installed to restore natural air currents, humidity, and temperature and to prevent drying of the cave.

In 1983, after deauthorization of the Meramec Dam, the Army Corps of Engineers added to the park another 380 acres downstream, including a large dolomitic bluff, the tallest bluff on the Meramec River. Many a canoeist is awed by the hulking dark-stained cliff face of Vilander Bluff with its projecting overhangs looming above. Along its rocky, broken slopes and atop the 250-foot cliff, eastern red cedars grow in timeless fashion. Seventy of them exceed three hundred years in age, with some up to five hundred years old. Dislodged skeletons of these ancient trees lie scattered here and there at the base of the cliff, their extremely slow decay allowing dendrologists to study the effects of bluff weathering on the trees.

Beware. Below the cliff is no place to camp. Cross sections of the base of these deceased cedars reveal scar wounds interrupting the tree rings about every six years, on average. The cause? Falling rocks.

A 206-acre portion of this tract was designated in 1993 as the Vilander Bluff Natural Area; it includes a mile of bottomland forest along the Meramec River, the bluff, caves, and an upland chert woodland and savanna that are accessible by trail.

Missouri celebrated 1990 as the "Year of the Cave," when its five-thousandth cave was officially recorded. Gov. John Ashcroft proclaimed Missouri "The Cave State" and urged Missourians to become aware of the fascinating mysteries and wonders underground. This proclamation aptly coincided with the dedication of an attractive new visitor center at the entrance to Onondaga Cave, which contains elaborate exhibits explaining Missouri's underground wonderland. By 2015 Missouri had nearly seven thousand known caves, and Onondaga is still preeminent among them.

Park staff recently discovered yet another passage in Onondaga, which added 310 feet to the known cave. The new addition contains remains of several ice age animals, further contributions of the cave to scientific discovery. In the mid-1990s, the park took over the former concession operation, and its naturalists and interpreters now lead cave tours. And then in 2012, the park attracted thousands of people to a Missouri Bat Festival sponsored by the U-Haul Corporation, at which the firm unveiled what it calls its Missouri SuperGraphic, a gigantic red bat flying over a map of Missouri that would be featured on 1,900 new moving vans nationwide—mobile billboards, in effect—to celebrate Missouri and attract even more visitors to Onondaga Cave State Park.

This National Natural Landmark, saved from fate as a mine by becoming a major attraction at a world's fair and then surviving as a show cave with creative marketing, still continues to awe park visitors today. *

ONONDAGA STATE PARK • 7556 ROUTE H, LEASBURG

Dillard Mill sits on a dolomite outcrop that separates the upper and lower millponds, with its millrace cut through bedrock. *Oliver Schuchard* • Above right: It is the only mill in the Missouri Ozarks with original machinery intact and in operating condition. These functioning roller machines on the main floor ground the grain to the desired consistency. *Missouri State Parks*

Dillard Mill State Historic Site

NESTLED AMONG THE OZARK HILLS along a rocky stretch of Huzzah Creek is one of the state's most picturesque gristmills. Dillard Mill was added to the state park system through a donated lease from the L-A-D Foundation, a private land preservation organization, in 1975. State park officials undertook a massive overhaul of the mill's mechanical systems, and today the machinery—almost all of which is original to the mill—is in good working order. Visitors delight in the creaks and moans as the turbine begins to spin, belts move, and the mill inches its way slowly back to life.

Reflections of the mill's barn-red metal siding shimmer in the clear waters of the ponded Huzzah Creek and are a muse to photographers and artists alike. The setting of this Crawford County mill is extraordinary. There are two ponds, one upstream and one downstream of the mill, separated by a narrow outcrop of rugged dolomite that continues to the east and south as a pine-covered bluff. As the bluff peters out, the small tributary Crooked Creek enters Huzzah Creek. At one time, the Huzzah wound past the miller's house and formed a large gooseneck. Eventually, the erosive work of the water breached the rocky ledge, and the Huzzah took a shortcut down a beautiful waterfall, the same route it used during many flash floods. Some attribute the cleft in the dolomite to a lightning bolt, but it is a classic case of a cutoff of an entrenched meander, leaving an isolated "lost hill" where the mill now stands.

Regardless of the rock gap's origin, it presented an obvious site for a small dam and water-powered mill. The millrace, where the sluice gate is located, was cut into the bedrock. The present-day mill was preceded by another mill built just north and below today's location. The first mill is credited as having been built by Francis Wisdom, who owned the property from 1853 to 1869. Joseph Dillard Cottrell and James Cottrell purchased it in 1881. Joseph ran the mill, while James opened a store just to the north. The local economy took an upswing with the 1880 opening of the Sligo iron furnace ten miles west in Dent County. In 1887 the first post office was established near the mill, and the small town of Dillard was born, named for the mill's operator, Joseph Dillard Cottrell. In 1890 the Cottrells sold the mill to Andrew Jackson Mincher and his son Jesse, but in 1895, the old mill burned. Around this time, the Sligo Furnace Company built a spur line connecting Sligo and Dillard to the St. Louis, Salem, and Little Rock Railway, thereby providing access to more distant markets and increasing migration into the area—until the Sligo Furnace, the last surviving iron furnace in Missouri, closed in 1923. The railroad spur ceased operating around 1930.

In 1980, a millwright came to inspect and repair the machinery. He was amazed to find the mill exactly as the previous owners had left it, with all of the machinery still in place.

The present mill was completed in 1908 by Emil Mischke, a German-Polish immigrant. He took a job at Sligo in 1899, bought the mill property, moved there in 1901 to operate a sawmill, and then built the new gristmill.

Power from the turbine is transmitted to the mill machinery through a pair of main bevel gears made from circular iron frames. The horizontal gear has iron teeth, while the vertical gear has wooden ones, which allowed easy breakage to avoid greater damage to other machines and also easy repair. ***Susan Flader***

Mills were traditional community gathering places, and Dillard still serves that purpose. *Yvonne Bobbitt* • Right: Huzzah Creek flows from the southeast to Dillard along a dolomite bluff before spilling over a milldam or being channeled through the millrace. Left: Marie Mischke served as the miller for more than twenty years, negotiating deals and operating machinery. She is buried in Dillard Cemetery alongside many of her customers. *Both Susan Flader*

It was state-of-the-art, powered by a turbine instead of a waterwheel and crushing grain between a series of steel rollers instead of buhrstones. Mischke and his sister and partner Marie operated the mill together, though lore tells that Marie was the miller. She was a full partner in the enterprise from 1908 until its sale, weighing the customer's grain, collecting the miller's share of the final product, and operating the machinery. In 1927, Emil at age sixty-seven sent for a mail-order bride. Anna Pressler from Los Angeles never became accustomed to the rugged Ozarks, and in 1930, she persuaded Emil to sell the mill and move to California. Marie continued to live in Dillard until her death in 1944 and is buried in the old Dillard cemetery, which is surrounded by the historic site but privately maintained.

The new owners, Lester E. and Virginia Klemme of St. Louis, operated the mill off and on with hired millers, although by the mid-1930s it was producing more cattle feed than flour. Taking advantage of the scenic beauty, they began operation of Klemme's Old Mill Lodge for city folks who wanted an escape. Following an unsuccessful attempt to get in on the health-food fad in the 1950s, Klemme closed down the mill operation for good around 1956. Then in 1962 after his wife died, he closed the Old Mill Lodge.

Sometime later, the State Park Board became interested in acquiring the mill. The plan was for the US Forest Service to buy the entire Klemme tract for the surrounding national forest and lease the mill to the state to operate as a historic site, but the Forest Service was not authorized to acquire the historic property. In 1974, St. Louis forest owner and environmentalist Leo Drey and his L-A-D Foundation stepped in to purchase the Klemme tract and donate a lease to the state. Park officials secured the services of internationally known millwright Derek Ogden in 1980 to inspect and repair the machinery. Ogden was amazed to find the mill exactly as Mischke and Klemme had left it, with the underwater turbine, generator, and all machinery, elevators, and spouts still in place. As Ogden said, "I have never before seen such a complete mill and have not seen one to match Dillard Mill since."

Today, the 132-acre Dillard Mill State Historic Site offers a fully operational turbine-powered roller mill, which visitors can tour for a nominal fee, and a mill store built around 1899 by Jacob Adams. Klemme's Old Mill Lodge and several other historic buildings are used as staff residences and offices. The site also has a day-use picnic area with a shelter and a mile-and-a-half hiking trail through a glade and wooded uplands east of the mill. The trail affords a scenic overview of the mill and its ponds. The park is bordered on the east and north by Mark Twain National Forest, and there have been discussions about leasing or buying more land for hiking trails and special events. To a greater extent than perhaps any other mill in the state, Dillard Mill still functions as a community center.

Dillard Mill stands as a reminder of a not-so-long-ago era, when man and nature cooperated to produce one of society's needs. Of the more than 900 mills that dotted Missouri's landscape at the turn of the century, the sites of only about 150 are known today. Many of the mill buildings are but skeletal remains. Some are used as houses or other businesses, but all hark back to a simpler time. Along with the other mills preserved in the state park system, Dillard Mill is a treasure. *

DILLARD MILL STATE HISTORIC SITE • 142 DILLARD MILL ROAD, VIBURNUM

Bennett Spring State Park

APPROACHING FROM ROUTE 64 WEST OF LEBANON, you wind down an entrance road past several private cottages and a tackle shop, then emerge from the upland into the hill-cradled valley of Bennett Spring. Across the manicured valley floor, you see the racing, tree-lined stream, almost always host to attentive figures garbed in waders and other accouterments of the devout angler. They stroke the waters lovingly with their lines and, with rods extended, twitch the tips from time to time—homage to the sacred trout.

Wooded slopes rise steeply on either flank, home to a diverse array of songbirds and other wildlife. On your right, you pass a sandstone-buttressed nature center, and the road curves over the stream on a graceful bridge of concrete and native stone, a now historic structure built in 1934 by the Civilian Conservation Corps (CCC). Upstream to your left is a low dam, successor to earlier milldams, usually lined with

The largest spring in the state park system, Bennett gushes on average 100 million gallons of water daily, its temperature holding steady at about fifty-seven degrees Fahrenheit.

anglers—literally shoulder to shoulder at season's opening and on pleasant weekends. Nearby are the brown buildings of the fish hatchery where the rainbow trout are spawned and nurtured. The hatchlings are rotated by age groups in a network of artificially fed ponds, and some are grown to lunker size before being released into the stream for enticement by anglers' lures.

Over the bridge, you enter the village-like heart of the park. The lodge, containing a restaurant and meeting room, is another architectural gem from CCC days, its decorative chandeliers featuring a trout motif. In the park store, the concessionaire sells tackle and other supplies to visitors and rents cabins and canoes for use on the nearby Niangua River; there is also a classroom for fishing instruction. Past these buildings, one road winds around the hill to stone cabins of modern construction and a few renovated ones built in the CCC years. The main park road extends downstream along the riffles and pools of the spring branch, recrosses it via a low bridge near the point where it empties into the Niangua River, then goes back up the hill and rejoins the main highway. Along this route through the park, you will also pass a swimming pool, campsites with electric hookups, and a spur road that leads to more campgrounds, including sites for tent campers and less mechanized vacationers.

Without spending a thoughtful hour or two studying the old photographs, maps, and artifacts in the nature center, you could scarcely imagine how this inviting and popular park evolved from a little mill town. The town faded away when big companies in Minneapolis and Kansas City began cheaply producing and distributing flour and other cereal products and when the automobile and improved roads led residents of the area into Lebanon or Buffalo to do their shopping. But the great spring has been a constant in the history of the area, and the rainbow trout became a catalyst for change. The same roads that once led toward bigger towns with more goods and services now enable hundreds of thousands of visitors to come to this appealing valley for recreation.

This was once territory of the Osage Indians and earlier native peoples, whose legends suggest a special reverence for the spring. The Osage had already ceded their lands in Missouri when an early settler named James Brice arrived with his wife and their two young daughters around 1837. Originally from Virginia, Brice recognized an economic opportunity in the strong and steady flow from the spring. Even before obtaining his first land patent, Brice erected a small gristmill on the spring branch, likely near the spring, about one-and-a-half miles upstream from its confluence with the Niangua River. He secured his first deed for 121 acres in Dallas County—a parcel that included the spring and part of the spring branch—from the federal government on December 11, 1846. In later purchases from the government and from a neighbor, Brice increased his holdings to 427 acres straddling the Dallas-Laclede county line.

Peter Bennett and his son soon established another mill downstream on the Niangua from the confluence. Both mills were swept away by floods in 1852. Brice began a new mill about a half mile downstream from the spring but died a year later, bequeathing his land and mill to his daughter Anna, who later married Peter Bennett Jr., entwining the two families.

In those days, the spring was known as Brice Spring, and the town that grew by the mill was called Brice. During the Civil War, according to old newspaper files, Peter Bennett Jr. constructed a larger, three-story mill on the spring branch with a timber dam and millrace. This family operated the mill until it burned in 1895 in what was rumored to be arson. The local Atchley family leased the land from the Bennetts and built the last in the historic succession of mills at Brice in 1900.

It was during the period from about 1900 until the Great Depression, according to regional historians, that Brice enjoyed its greatest prosperity. The focus of the area began to shift toward recreation after trout were introduced in 1900. The town had not only the mill but also a hotel and a store—both owned and operated by the Bennetts—a blacksmith shop, a church, and perhaps a second general store. In addition to farmers who came to get their grain milled and to shop in the general store, tourists began to arrive in buggies and later in Model Ts and Model As to stay at the Brice Inn and enjoy fishing and relaxing in the scenic valley.

The popular name of the spring had long since changed from Brice to

Trout fishermen have been casting their lines beneath the triple-arched bridge since it was built by the Civilian Conservation Corps in 1937. *Nick Decker* • Left: The great spring at Bennett has always lured fishermen. *Missouri State Parks*

Bennett, but the settlement was called Brice until its demise after it was bought by the state for a park in 1925. The last mill ceased making flour and cornmeal sometime in the 1920s but continued to grind food for fish and to generate electricity until it, too, was destroyed by fire in 1944. The church still stands in the park on one acre donated by the Bennetts in 1917 and remains an active place of worship for the community. It was veneered with locally quarried orange-brown sandstone in 1940 to blend with the CCC-built structures.

The trout that brought prosperity to the town and later to the park apparently came initially from a federal fish hatchery at Neosho, Missouri. *The Laclede County Sentinel* reported in January 1900 that the state fish commissioner "stopped by" and released forty thousand mountain trout. Although unrecorded, there were probably other releases of trout before Charles Furrow, a dentist and fishing enthusiast from Tulsa, Oklahoma, leased a site along the spring branch from the Bennetts and built a fish hatchery in 1924.The hatchery at Neosho provided fifty thousand rainbow trout eggs for Furrow's new hatchery troughs and placed another fifty thousand brook trout eggs from Wisconsin into the stream.

Bennett Spring was one of the first state parks acquired by State Game and Fish Commissioner Frank H. Wielandy with funds set aside under a legislative act from hunting and fishing license revenues. The initial acquisitions included eight acres from Josephine Bennett Smith in 1924 and 565 acres in 1925 from William Sherman Bennett, who had added to the acres that his parents inherited from James Brice. The

Flowering dogwood flourishes under a white oak canopy in a cove at Bennett. ***Pat Whalen*** **• Ten miles of loop trails take hikers through Spring Hollow woodlands ablaze with fall colors to a natural tunnel.** ***Scott Myers***

state also acquired Dr. Furrow's hatchery, which was operated until 1937 by the Game and Fish Department and after that by its successor agency, the Missouri Department of Conservation.

Little improvement took place in the new state park after its purchase until a CCC company composed of nearly two hundred out-of-work veterans of World War I arrived on the scene in November 1933. During the next four years, according to a CCC yearbook, the vets built "an $8,000 dam, a $13,000 bridge, a $14,000 dining lodge, six beautiful cabins, a store and post office building, shelter houses, roads, and trails." They also renovated the Atchley mill, enlarged the fish hatchery, and built a custodian's residence, as well as a stonemasonry latrine and rustic trailside benches. In addition, they razed and carted away the now dilapidated and deserted buildings of the old town of Brice. Most of the CCC structures still grace the park, many of them on the National Register of Historic Places.

The State Park Board administered land, facilities, and operations in the park, except for the hatchery, until 1974 when its successor agency, the Park Division of the Missouri Department of Natural Resources, took over. The Department of Conservation still operates the hatchery, licenses anglers, sets limits, seasons, and fishing hours, and enforces regulations. The daily release of catchable trout is based on the number of trout tags sold, so anglers are always assured of a well-stocked stream.

After the initial acquisitions in 1924 and 1925, the state continued to pick up adjacent tracts as they became available, and by early 1988, the total stood at just over 1,400 acres. This included the 160-acre Bennett Spring Savanna, located several miles south of the park along Route OO, an outstanding natural feature leased to the state by the Nature Conservancy in 1984 as one of the best examples known of a historic native Ozark open oak woodland.

Then a breakthrough: in 1988, the park division bought 1,660 acres from three willing sellers, adding native woodlands and glades that include most of the watershed of Spring Hollow extending southeast

This 300-foot-long natural tunnel was created by the partial collapse of an ancient cave. ***Diane Tucker*** **• The rich ground flora on the Bennett Spring Savanna is similar to days of old and results from frequent ground fires going back more than fifty years. The savanna is one of the state's best examples of a native Ozark open oak woodland.** ***Paul Nelson***

from the spring. Dye-trace studies in the late 1980s delineated a nearly 300-square-mile area south and east of the spring, including the city of Lebanon, that provides recharge to the spring, making Spring Hollow important for watershed and water quality protection. The acquisition more than doubled the opportunities for hiking and added significant natural history features, including a natural tunnel one hundred yards long, several shallow caves used for shelter by Native Americans and more recent huntsmen, and a spring-fed pond. On the uplands are substantial remnants of high quality open oak woodlands similar to those on the Nature Conservancy land, which has also since been enlarged to 920 acres, now contiguous with the park. Both park and Nature Conservancy lands are being restored and maintained by their respective staffs with the use of prescribed fire.

The Natural Tunnel and Savanna Ridge Trails, totaling some ten miles with several loops, provide access to Spring Hollow and its associated woodlands seasonally abloom with wildflowers. Part of the trail goes through a twisting valley with steep cliffs, which are actually remainders of a collapsed cave system; the natural tunnel carved through the dolomite strata by the stream over geologic ages is in fact a cave, one that has been cut off by erosion of deeper valleys at each end. Inside, the tunnel is forty to fifty feet wide in places with a ceiling up to sixteen feet high. Even during the driest times of the year, spring-fed pools within the tunnel are populated by small fish and other aquatic organisms. These cave remnants are connected to a much more extensive underground labyrinth that feeds the great spring at Bennett.

At the spring, visitors are fascinated by the powerful surge of water that issues mysteriously from the earth. A wayside exhibit profiles the depths of the spring, explored by qualified scuba divers who have descended more than a hundred feet into its cave-like passage that often

The chandeliers feature a trout motif at the handsome dining lodge built by the Civilian Conservation Corps. The lodge still serves tasty meals. ***Scott Myers***

Mist rises from Bennett Spring on a wintry morning. ***Diane Tucker***

contains trout and native crayfish. At the bottom, a torrential spring flow erupts through a narrow cleft at the base of a dolomite wall, its passage largely unexplored because the current is too swift. Here, nature performs her own polishing of rock jewelry, tumbling small pieces of chert in the upward-rushing currents, resulting in smoothly rounded stones.

You can learn more about a natural Ozark cold-water spring at the nature center, where staff can answer most questions. An illuminated plastic bubble in the center simulates spring water with its microcosmic underwater universe, its algae and insects magnified two hundred times to enhance understanding of the beginnings of the food chains that feed the larger animals we can see. Invisible to the human eye but around the legs of every angler wading in the stream is a fascinating array of brilliantly colored water mites, daphnias, and other creatures that drift among colonies of algae.

Exhibits also explain how the fractured layers of soluble limestone and dolomite in the region's natural plumbing system capture surface water not only from natural rainfall but also from garden sprinklers and septic tanks. An understanding of this process helps citizens of nearby Lebanon to appreciate the importance of protecting the area's water quality to ensure the continued health of Bennett Spring.

The one-and-a-half-mile branch from the springhead to the Niangua River has been altered in places by damming for mill purposes, by dredging to create deep holes for trout, and by both natural and man-induced changes in stream-side and emergent vegetation, but certain stream segments are left as natural riffle zones to preserve the aquatic plants and animals native to the cold-water spring branch.

In 1982, the Missouri Natural Areas Committee designated a small area of five acres on a series of dolomite ledges on the steep hillside along the spring branch as the Bennett Spring Hanging Fen Natural Area, which is saturated by seeps of cool, calcareous ground water that allow unusual fen plants to thrive. It may be viewed from the Spring Trail on the west side of the branch, which takes you from the spring past a CCC-era stone gauge house to the hatchery area. The straight and geometric concrete races for trout are of course entirely human artifacts, but the swarms of rainbow trout, all swimming in place against the constant current, are fascinating to watch.

Anglers and their families predominate among the almost 800,000 visitors at Bennett annually, but many others come to relax in the dining lodge, cabins, and campgrounds, to float the Niangua River, or to hike the trails through the scenic woodlands, awash in dogwood blooms each April. Everyone who comes, though, senses that the park is here because of the spring. And so are the trout. ⁕

BENNETT SPRING STATE PARK • 26250 ROUTE 64A, LEBANON

Ha Ha Tonka State Park

NEARLY SEVENTY YEARS PASSED after Ha Ha Tonka was initially proposed as a park before it was finally acquired by the state. A Missouri representative had promoted the area in Camden County as a national forest in 1903, and Gov. Herbert S. Hadley recommended it to become Missouri's first state park in 1909. Then in 1915, a special committee of the state legislature, appointed to investigate sites for potential state parks, recommended Ha Ha Tonka as its first choice. Other attempts at state purchase were made during subsequent years, all to no avail. The property changed hands frequently, with many owners failing to realize their development dreams. As one St. Louis realtor and conservationist pointed out, the tract seemed cursed. But in 1978 the curse was broken, and Ha Ha Tonka became Missouri's sixty-first state park.

Ha Ha Tonka contains Missouri's most outstanding examples of karst topography, named for the Karst region in the Balkans but characteristic also of the limestone-laden Ozarks. Here is found a honeycomb of tunnels, caverns, springs, sinkholes, and other limestone features created by water dissolving the soluble rock. The park also contains the state's best examples of glades, open areas with exposed bedrock dominated by drought-adapted herbs and grasses. Ha Ha Tonka is mantled in grasslands, occasionally shaded by oaks; these oak orchards, as some call them, were once one of Missouri's most widespread natural communities but are now among the least common.

No other state park has a more fascinating, if convoluted, history. Native Americans, early explorers, frontiersmen, outlaws, turn-of-the-century capitalists, and twentieth-century real estate speculators are all part of the park's history and folklore. And for good measure, it offers the storybook ruins of a castle.

For vintage Missouri hyperbole, consider the praise lavished on Ha Ha Tonka by Dr. Walter Williams, founder of the journalism school at the University of Missouri, who would later undertake the naming of Missouri's seven scenic wonders—Ha Ha Tonka being number one. Having visited the area many times beginning in the 1870s, he wrote that it contained "more natural curiosities than in any other similar share of the earth's surface" and chastised Missourians for their obliviousness:

> *If Hahatonka were on a railroad it would have thousands of visitors where now it has one. Here is a cave more wonderful than Mammoth Cave, a spring surpassing in size any in the State, a natural bridge superior to the famous Virginia Natural Bridge.... Yet Missourians will wander off to the distant sections of the country to see caves, waterfalls, lakes, and mountains far inferior in beauty.*

It is little wonder that the Osage and other tribes frequented the area. It remained Osage territory until the early nineteenth century, when most of their lands were ceded to the federal government. Early white visitors likely included Daniel and Nathan Boone, who spent the winters of 1801 and 1802 trapping beaver along the Niangua River, and Lt. James B. Wilkinson of the Pike Expedition, who described it in his official report. Legend says a band of counterfeiters, the infamous "Bank of Niangua," used the area in the 1830s and that the gang's leader, a fellow named Garland, built a gristmill on the spring branch.

During a railroad survey around 1894, Col. R.G. Scott explored the area and, taken with its beauty, amassed a large tract in partnership with a Civil War comrade from the area. Local residents petitioned the postmaster general in 1895 to name the new post office at the settlement near the spring Ha Ha Tonka. The name was supposedly derived from Osage words meaning "smiling waters," though others say the words in Osage would be closer to "big laugh."

High on a bluff overlooking the spring and the Niangua River—now the Niangua arm of Lake of the Ozarks—are the ruins of a massive stone mansion and its companion structures. Giving the park the look and mood of a back lot for the filming of a Gothic romance, these ruins represent what is probably the most intriguing episode in Ha Ha Tonka's fascinating history. They also represent the origin of the supposed curse.

Robert M. Snyder, a wealthy businessman from Kansas City, first visited the area in 1903 on a hunting trip. He stayed at a hotel in nearby Lebanon, where he learned about the wonders of Ha Ha Tonka. Immediately captivated, Snyder set out to acquire some sixty different tracts of land, beginning with the tract that included the spring and eventually totaling more than 5,000 acres. He envisioned a private retreat with a huge, European-style castle, which was designed for him by Kansas City architect Adrian VanBrunt. With native stone quarried on the site and stonemasons from Scotland, the 85-by-115-foot structure began taking shape in 1905. In addition, an 80-foot-high stone water tower was constructed, and greenhouses and stables were designed and begun. Snyder apparently intended to spare no expense, as everything about the project was on a grand scale.

But in 1906, Snyder was killed in an automobile accident. All work at Ha Ha Tonka ceased, and the fate of the place was in doubt. A group of St. Louis investors came close but ultimately did not buy the unfinished

Far right: Ha Ha Tonka's castle ruins highlight the cliff above the spring branch, now the Niangua arm of Lake of the Ozarks. *Tom Nagel* • Right: The natural bridge is a cool delight on a hot summer day. Nowhere else in the state has such a variety of karst features—springs, sinkholes, chasms, caves, underground streams, and natural bridges—in such a concentrated area. *Nancy Masterson*

Yellow coneflowers grace Lodge Glade, a fire-restored landscape, part of the 3,000-acre Ha Ha Tonka Oak Woodland Natural Area. *Nancy Masterson*

EXPLORE THE PARK

Ha Ha Tonka is a park best explored on foot. There are fourteen different trails totaling nearly eighteen miles, four of which are wheelchair accessible. Short trails, most less than a mile and with overlooks and interpretive panels or brochures, take you to the castle, the water tower, and key geologic features such as the spring, the natural bridge, and the Colosseum, Whispering Dell, Devil's Kitchen, and River Cave sinkholes. You can reach the natural area on several longer loop trails, including the Quarry and Dolomite Rock Trails and the seven-mile Turkey Pen Hollow Trail. For those who come by boat, there are docks with trailheads on either side of the Niangua Arm of Lake of the Ozarks.

property for $156,000. Eventually, Snyder's sons finished the castle, though not to their father's sumptuous specifications. Still, it was a luxurious white elephant, and they tried repeatedly to unload it on the state—for $160,000, $200,000, $300,000—always more than the state could afford. Using the mansion as a summer home, the Snyder family sued Union Electric when Bagnell Dam, completed in 1931, backed the Lake of the Ozarks up the spring branch. The Snyders settled out of court for $200,000. As the years passed, they used the home less and less, finally leasing it as a summer hotel. Tragedy struck again in 1942 when the wooden shingles on the roof of this supposedly fireproof building caught fire and the entire interior was gutted. The crumbling stone walls have maintained a lonely vigil ever since.

After the fire, the property changed hands several times, with each new owner planning to cash in by commercializing its natural wonders. Various groups tried unsuccessfully to purchase the land as a park or refuge or Scout camp. Each succeeding owner did little with the property except cause the price to rise. Meanwhile, the area was prey to trespassers, and many of the structures were vandalized. Shortly before the state acquired the land, the water tower was burned. But in 1978, with a grant from the federal Land and Water Conservation Fund and a sizable donation that allowed a tax write-off for its owner, the James T. Barnes Investment Company of Detroit, the entire 2,500-acre tract (then valued at nearly $2 million) finally became a state park.

Governor Hadley's effort to secure a $160,000 appropriation for the park in 1911 had failed by one vote; having cleared the Missouri Senate, the measure died in the House. Other governors failed as well, including Frederick Gardner in 1921 and Phil M. Donnelly in 1947. So Gov. Joseph Teasdale had every right to be proud when he announced in December 1978 that the state had finally acquired the fabled Ha Ha Tonka—and for just about the same dollar amount of state funds as the failed appropriation of 1911.

Since the site's acquisition by the state, it has become apparent that its scenic grandeur and the saga of the castle, however appealing to the public, are not the park's only claims to significance. In a single square mile, the park contains more classic karst features—caves, springs, chasms, sinkholes, underground streams, and natural bridges—than any other place in the state. The park has several major caves and other smaller ones with numerous passages, underground streams, and exemplary formations, including River Cave with an underground natural bridge and an immense columnar stalagmite thirty feet high and twenty-four feet in circumference. There is also a natural bridge on the surface spanning sixty feet with a ceiling height of thirteen feet, and numerous water-carved cliffs, sinks, and springs exposed to the surface when the roofs of other parts of the cave system collapsed. By no means least of the park's geologic wonders is the Ha Ha Tonka Spring, counted among the state's dozen or so largest springs and discharging an average of some fifty million gallons of fresh, cold water every day. Mantling the rugged topography are the finest and largest natural oak woodlands and glades in the state—a wildflower-carpeted wonderland with over five hundred species of plants harkening back to presettlement times in the western Ozarks.

Repeated fires, naturally occurring and set by native tribes, gave this landscape its special character. For centuries, periodic fire shaped a mosaic of post, white, chinkapin, and blackjack oaks and other species into a harmonious intermingling of open rocky glades, grasslands with widely spaced individual trees, or open woodland on steep north-facing slopes where fire is somewhat less frequent. The post oaks and, to a lesser degree, other oaks have evolved bark thick enough to protect their trunks from fire, while their limbs sprawl just out of harm's way. Beneath the oaks flourish prairie plants—tall grasses such as big bluestem, Indian grass, and little bluestem and myriad prairie wildflowers, sometimes as many as two hundred species on a single acre.

Animal life in this fire-dependent landscape is equally diverse. Prior to white settlement, the once extensive woodland zone stretching along the eastern plains from Texas to Wisconsin was home to many species that are today associated with brushy thickets and the woodland edges of fields. The eastern bluebird (Missouri's state bird), cardinal, redheaded woodpecker, prairie warbler, screech owl, and many other species prefer open natural orchards to denser forests. Tree hollows, created by insects, bacteria, and fungi that enter trees scarred by fire, provide refuge for nearly a hundred species of cavity-nesting vertebrates. Flying, gray, and fox squirrels, raccoons, opossums, broad-headed skinks, chipmunks, and certain bats are plentiful here.

The oak woodland is in part a cultural landscape. For thousands of years, American Indians used fire presumably for practical reasons: to make hunting better, to promote berry and fruit production, and to prevent acorn weevils from destroying acorns—a precious food source for humans and animals alike. After white settlement, the open woodlands were converted to farmland, and fire prevention allowed various woody species to form thickets. But in this rough region of the Ozarks, a tradition of woods burning persisted despite the best efforts of conservation officials to stamp it out, thus unintentionally preserving vestiges of the woodland community. Indeed, coring samples from old trees in the park suggest that fires burned the area every five to twenty years for millennia. Since 1983, park staff have introduced a prescribed fire program and have worked closely with conservation officials to educate local citizens about the use of controlled burning to restore a biologically unique and valuable component of Missouri's presettlement heritage.

Shortly after the park was acquired by the state, three small natural areas were designated in 1981 by the Missouri Natural Areas Committee: Red Sink, an eight-acre sinkhole with a mature sinkhole-floor forest; Lodge Glade, a 20-acre dolomite glade with several calcareous sinks; and Ha Ha Tonka Karst, a 70-acre collapsed cave system with a natural bridge, caves, springs, and sinkholes. Then, after park naturalists introduced prescribed fire in portions of the glades and oak woodlands, the response of the natural ground flora was so remarkable that by 1990, a 953-acre area won designation as the Ha Ha Tonka Savanna Natural Area. In 2012 this area was expanded to nearly 3,000 acres as the Ha Ha Tonka Oak Woodland Natural Area, which incorporates each of

The storied ruins of Ha Ha Tonka would melt away to rubble within decades if not for stabilization using a sophisticated post-tensioning method being tested here on the stable. Note the steel plates at top and bottom, rods, and new mortar. ***Susan Flader*** **• The Ha Ha Tonka woodland evolved with natural and Native American fire and now is maintained with prescribed fire.** ***Allison Vaughn***

The castle seemed cursed. The wealthy businessman who started it in 1903 died before it was completed. His sons eventually finished it, but tragedy struck once again when it burned in 1942. *Gary Sumpter* • Left: Once common, these open oak orchard landscapes once covered about one-third of the state, but they are now rare. Botanists have recorded more than 250 species of native wildflowers in this "prairie in the shade," here with fire-tolerant 300-year-old post oaks. The woodland is now restored and maintained by prescribed burns. *Ken McCarty*

the previously designated natural areas in the park and encompasses each part of the park that is managed with prescribed fire. The park's geologic and natural history features are so significant that it has also been nominated as a National Natural Landmark, the highest level of national designation, which has been accorded to only three other state parks—Big Oak Tree, Onondaga Cave, and Grand Gulf. Ha Ha Tonka, if it wins designation in the exhaustive process, would be the largest landmark site in the park system and the only one interrelating geological, biological, and cultural significance.

In addition to its continuing landscape stewardship program, the park division has invested nearly a million dollars in the highly professional but virtually invisible stabilization of the castle ruins so beloved by visitors. Without the sophisticated post-tensioning technique using steel plates and reinforcing rods bonded several feet deep into the bedrock with epoxy cement as tension devices to stabilize the stone walls, it would only have been a matter of years before the castle was reduced to a pile of rubble. Considering the lengths to which park designers and estate planners in the nineteenth century went to deliberately create false ruins in the landscape, as at Tower Grove Park in St. Louis or Andalusia outside Philadelphia, it is perhaps not surprising that Missourians should want to preserve the real ones so spectacularly situated at Ha Ha Tonka.

The park's karst features have also been protected. Visitors used to cause damage by climbing the scarps to the springs, cliffs, and bluff-top castle. Today, a series of boardwalks and stairs give them better access. You can now descend into River Cave or climb from the spring to the castle on wooden steps. The boardwalk going up over the cliff at the spring is a truly amazing sight—316 steps to the top.

Even without campgrounds, cabins, or a restaurant, and with only a small open-air informative pavilion, the 3,752-acre Ha Ha Tonka is a remarkably popular park, with more than half a million visitors annually. Ha Ha Tonka is a wonderland that will not disappoint. *

Left above: Ha Ha Tonka Spring, the state's tenth largest, may be viewed from a boardwalk overlook. *Randal Clark* • Left: Mosses, ferns, and wildflowers flourish in a sinkhole under a canopy of ancient oaks. *Paul Nelson*

HA HA TONKA STATE PARK • 1491 STATE ROAD D, CAMDENTON

Lake of the Ozarks State Park

MISSOURI'S LARGEST AND MOST VARIED state park is an inheritance from the Great Depression. The farm economy was collapsing even before the historic stock market crash in 1929, the event often cited as triggering the economic decline that prostrated not only America but most of the industrialized world. Swept into the presidency by an unhappy electorate in 1932, the pragmatic and innovative Franklin D. Roosevelt quickly launched a series of programs aimed at relieving unemployment and widespread human distress.

Some of these New Deal programs were designed to relieve problems in rural America. Crop and livestock prices had collapsed, and small-town banks were going broke. Mortgage foreclosures had turned thousands of once landowning farmers, the descendants of proud homesteaders, into impoverished renters or unemployed wanderers. Roosevelt and his advisers were sensitive to problems of both farmers and land misuse. One of their programs was to buy tracts of land in areas where the terrain and the soil—steep, rocky, and thin—made them submarginal for agriculture. The farmers would move to better lands or into different occupations, and the acquired lands were turned into primitive parks or public recreation areas.

As part of the National Industrial Recovery Act of 1933, a system of Recreational Demonstration Areas (RDAs) was authorized to test the feasibility of converting submarginal farmlands near large population centers into outdoor recreation areas suitable for transfer later to the states or other units of government. By 1939 there were forty-six such areas in twenty-four states, including three in Missouri, all managed by the National Park Service. Beginning in 1942, they were conveyed to the states; the ones in Missouri were transferred in 1946.

In addition to this RDA, assembled in 1934 around the Grand Glaize Arm of the Lake of the Ozarks, the others were Cuivre River State Park in Lincoln County and Knob Noster in Johnson County. While this area wasn't as close to either St. Louis or Kansas City as the other two, one special feature surely attracted the New Deal planners to this region in hilly Miller and Camden counties as they were thinking about recreation: the lake itself. It was formed in 1931 as the Union Electric Company of St. Louis completed construction of Bagnell Dam on the Osage River, the largest hydroelectric impoundment in the Midwest.

The new dam backed water up the meandering main stem of the Osage and its many tributaries that descended through precipitous little valleys, creating a reservoir of 55,342 surface acres with some 1,150 miles of shoreline. Grand Glaize Creek was one of the more scenic tributaries, and it had already been identified as a potential park site by planners working for Union Electric. Fifteen linear miles of the creek and eighty-five miles of shoreline were to be encompassed within the federal recreation area. Thus it could have charming lake vistas,

Right: Public Beach Number 1 provides solitude for a couple of people on a quiet day. ***Oliver Schuchard*** **• Above: Fishermen cast lines into the morning mist. While some might associate the Lake of the Ozarks with speedboats, with 1,150 miles of shoreline, there are still plenty of quiet coves for fishing boats.** ***Nick Decker***

swimming beaches, facilities for boating and fishing as well as camping and picnicking, and miles of trails for nature lovers and seekers of solitude. Lake of the Ozarks State Park has all of these within its 17,600 acres—making it far and away the largest park in the system.

In the 1920s, Union Electric, empowered with a license from the Federal Power Commission, had gone about aggressively buying all the

Far left: Missouri's official state tree, the flowering dogwood, welcomes spring visitors. *Oliver Schuchard* • Rocky bluffs offer magnificent views to boaters. *Missouri State Parks* • Seventeen miles of trails please riders. *Scott Myers*

land needed for its new reservoir. It acquired most of it in fee, some by condemnation, but took only "flowage easements" in some cases where only a small part of a farm would be inundated at the lake's highest level. Thus, while the federal agencies were purchasing other lands in the planned recreation area, they also negotiated with Union Electric for its previously acquired lands in the Grand Glaize area. The company's land records show that the transfers to the federal government took place from 1935 to 1937, mostly at a nominal price since this was at the depth of the Depression and submarginal farmland wasn't worth much for any purpose. At any rate, Union Electric was required by federal regulations to divest itself of lands not actually needed for operation of its hydroelectric project. Future fortunes were to be made in resort, commercial, and residential development around the lakeshores, but not by Union Electric.

Although the utility company could condemn land, and did, the federal agencies chose not to exercise the power of eminent domain for RDAs. Despite the economic straits of the era, a few landowners chose to hang on to their property. There remain today a number of private parcels within the park boundaries.

Group camps constructed in the 1930s by the Civilian Conservation Corps (CCC) are a distinction and attraction shared with the other two former federal RDAs and several other parks. Perhaps because it is the largest, Lake of the Ozarks has the most: Camps Red Bud, Pin Oak, Clover Point, Rising Sun, and Hawthorne. Another, Pe-He-T'se, has now been dismantled, and Hawthorne has been closed. Hawthorne was used from 1982 to 2005 to house low-security prisoners employed for maintenance tasks in the park through an arrangement with the state Department of Corrections. The camps are frequently reserved in warm weather months by Girl Scouts, Boy Scouts, Future Farmers, and 4-H clubs but are available for rental by other youth and adult organizations. Red Bud, the smallest, can accommodate groups as small as twenty or as large as forty-four. Rising Sun can take as many as two hundred. Clover Point, often used by adult groups such as the Audubon Society of Missouri, was renovated in the early 1980s by the Young Adult

Above: A ten-mile aquatic trail runs the length of the Grand Glaize Arm and is marked with buoys keyed to a guide. ***Cindy Hall*** **• Right: Twelve land trails totaling more than forty miles attract bicyclists, mountain bikers, horseback riders, wheelchair users, or hikers. Here, the picturesque and short Bluestem Knoll Trail near the trail center crosses restored bluestem glades and post oak woodlands typical of this region in earlier times.** ***Susan Flader***

Conservation Corps, a federal program reminiscent of the CCC.

Pin Oak, long known as the Girl Scout Camp, features primitive cabins in the woods, tastefully spaced along the shoreline so the young campers could go to sleep listening to the night music—owls, whippoorwills, and the lapping lake waters—rather than voices in a neighboring cabin. It was restored to its original CCC integrity in 1989 but with modernized dining and bathing facilities. The State Park Youth Corps, another program reminiscent of the CCC, was working on cabins at Pin Oak and in other group camps in the park in 2010 when the Pin Oak dining lodge, considered one of the finest examples of CCC architecture in the park system, was struck by lightning and burned to the ground the night of September 3. Gov. Jay Nixon pledged to rebuild, despite the most severe financial trauma since the Great Depression. By 2013, the lodge was rebuilt on the original footprint, as close in style and materials to the original lodge as possible but with modern improvements. This was accomplished by a remarkable partnership—also reminiscent of the CCC—between Missouri State Parks, State Fair Community College, and the Missouri Department of Economic Development, which provided a $1.5 million federal block grant. The college's construction technology students traded their labor for college credit and construction experience.

The park is a treasure trove for social and architectural historians of the twentieth century; in fact, some old log buildings that were salvaged by the CCC date from the nineteenth century. Other new ones were carefully crafted to match closely the older structures. The park and its main road, Route 134, have been designated a historic district on the National Register of Historic Places in recognition of the prime examples of CCC-era, hewn-log construction, the beautiful rustic bridges, and the extensive network of CCC-built stone ditch-dams that provide erosion control and add to the charm of the beautifully designed road. All of Camp Pin Oak and the central area of Camp Hawthorne are separate historic districts on the National Register. Many other CCC-built structures in the park—such as the park office, the log trail center, and features associated with Public Beach No. 1—also appear on the register.

As a water-based park, Lake of the Ozarks offers excellent opportunities for swimming and boating. Grand Glaize Beach and Public Beach No. 1 are longtime favorites of park users. The park offers a popular full service, concession-operated marina at Grand Glaize Beach, which also includes one of the larger boat ramps on the lake and provides access to miles of undeveloped shoreline favored by fishermen. A smaller marina at Public Beach No. 1 and other boat launch areas are used by campers and

day users. Public access is an important factor, given that most of the lake's shoreline is privately owned.

Away from the waters of the reservoir, the landscape is largely the dry upland chert woodlands common in this part of the Missouri Ozarks. Oak species predominate, but in April when the oaks are just budding, an understory of flowering dogwood and serviceberry blossom into breathtaking beauty. A visitor who takes the trails finds fascinating natural diversity in numerous small glades (more than twenty have been counted in the park), sundry calcareous wet meadows and fens, dolomite bluffs reaching down to the lake, and marshes, spring-fed or in the shallow fringes of the impounded water. Historically, the park would have had open woodlands with widely spaced trees and an understory of prairie grasses, and a few such areas have been restored by park staff with prescribed fire. Each terrain supports its characteristic community of wildflowers, grasses, or sedges and other plant life. The fauna, naturally, is also diverse. Aside from offering glimpses of white-tailed deer or the stealthy wild turkey, this park is noteworthy among birders for migrating hawks in the fall. In winter, bald eagles are easily seen soaring over the secluded coves. And, standing three feet high, the great blue heron accents primordial misty lakeshores early in the morning.

Befitting the largest park in the system, there are twelve trails totaling more than forty miles, several providing access for bicyclists, equestrians, and wheelchairs, and for good measure in a water-based park, a ten-mile aquatic trail running the length of Grand Glaize Arm and marked with buoys keyed to a guide. The longest trails, about thirteen miles each, are the Trail of Four Winds in the northeast part of the park, open for biking and horse riding as well as hiking, and the Honey Run Trail in the southwest, suitable for mountain biking as well

OZARK CAVERNS & COAKLEY HOLLOW

The Lake of the Ozarks State Park was augmented in 1978 by the acquisition of Ozark Caverns, a major Missouri cave that had been commercially operated from 1951 until its transfer. With the cave came 350 acres on the southern edge of the park. It is one of three show caves in the state park system, in addition to Onondaga and Fisher Cave in Meramec State Park. All were once privately owned and operated commercially for the tourist trade.

Ozark Caverns was never as splashily illuminated or as much modified inside as some show caves, and park managers have removed the electrical wiring. Here, visitors carry lanterns and view the speleological wonders as the first explorers did, with candles or miner's lamps.

Seeps from the sides and ceiling dissolving and redepositing carbonate materials have created a typical cave wilderness of stalactites, stalagmites, "soda-straws," helectites, and cave corals. The most famous formation is Angel's Shower. In this speleothem complex, a massive group of stalactites "rains" a continuous shower that falls free for eight feet to be caught in a shining (when lighted) crystalline basin rising from the floor of the cavern. Built up over who knows how many thousands of years, Angel's Shower is highly unusual, a type of formation found in few other places in the cave world.

The guided tour traverses about a half-mile, round-trip. En route, you might see a sleeping bat, usually the tri-colored bat, a solitary species clinging to the ceiling, or perhaps a little brown bat or a big brown bat. Rare gray bats, mostly male, often inhabit an unvisited part of the cave. The visitor may also glimpse the blind grotto salamander in the cave stream. A few small invertebrates live in the darkness, and what appear to be claw marks in soft clay suggest that bears once visited.

Ozark Caverns was originally known as Coakley Cave, named for an Irishman who settled in the little valley, still called Coakley Hollow, shortly after the Civil War. The cave was known before that, as names inscribed on a "name wall" date back to the 1850s. Coakley installed and operated a gristmill until about 1890, when he moved the mill and machinery to a site near the thriving town of Linn Creek—now submerged beneath the Lake of the Ozarks. Remnants of a milldam can still be seen just downstream from the confluence of the cave stream with the larger spring-fed Coakley Hollow Creek, an Outstanding State Resource Water.

Boggy open meadows, or fens, dot the creek. Fed by cold, seepy groundwater, they resemble boggy wetlands found to the north in Minnesota or Canada. Rare plants like Riddell's goldenrod, swamp wood betony, and various sedges are relicts perhaps left behind thousands of years ago when glaciers retreated from northern Missouri. Where once an old house stood in front of the cave entrance, today there lies a lush fen restored by removing the fill gravel placed there decades ago. So unique is this spring-fed valley that the stream and its fens have been designated Coakley Hollow Fen Natural Area. A loop trail explores the hollow and the nearby uplands, home to an area of upland flatwoods that has also been a focus of restoration for more than a quarter century. An inviting visitor center with a museum, situated fifty yards from the cave entrance, orients visitors to the forces that created not only the cave but also the entire park.

Left: The Angel's Shower formation in Ozark Caverns entrances a tour group. *Scott Myers* • Above: Golden ragwort and Indian paintbrush bloom along spring-fed Coakley Hollow Creek in Coakley Hollow Fen Natural Area. *Cindy Hall*

as hiking. The latter traverses not only hilly post oak woodlands and bottomland communities along Honey Run Creek but also an unusual type of ridge-top wetland community called upland flatwoods, in which the frajipan soil structure causes water to pool on the surface during the rainy season but crack when it becomes dry, favoring plants adapted to both wet and dry conditions. The three-mile Woodland Trail loops through a portion of the 1,275-acre Patterson Hollow Wild Area, while across the road from the trail center the short Bluestem Knoll Trail meanders through woodlands and glades that have been carefully restored with prescribed fire. Other short trails follow the lakeshore and traverse uplands in the vicinity of campgrounds, cabins, beaches, and picnic areas.

In the eastern end of the park is an unusual, possibly inappropriate, feature for a state park, the Lee C. Fine Memorial Airport. The airport is operated in partnership with the city of Osage Beach and serves the resort area around the lake. Named in honor of a popular official who died suddenly in 1966 in his second year as director of state parks, it is a reminder of the days of grandiose planning in the 1960s when federal dollars flowed freely for regional economic development. Officials envisioned a $5 million convention center and luxury resort at which the governor could host his colleagues at the national governors' conference. The jetport that was to trigger an "economic explosion" in the lake region was built, but legislators turned thumbs down on the convention center. The state proved unable to attract private investors to build a resort on park land.

Even so, the lake area is one of the most intensively developed playgrounds in the United States, with many lake roads lined with lodges, restaurants, tackle and curio shops, and a variety of rides, water slides, and other places of entertainment. Indeed, what was once an area catering seasonally to the fishing, boating, swimming, and sunning crowd has now become urbanized with extensive shopping centers and a growing year-round residential population.

Thus, it is all the more remarkable that just a short turnoff from the Highway 54 Expressway, one finds the state park, a 17,600-acre oasis of natural beauty and tranquility where there are no corny signs, no garish neon or billboards, and no angry honking of horns. It is the public's great good fortune that the Grand Glaize shores and surrounding lands were kept in the public domain and in their natural state. *

LAKE OZARK STATE PARK • 403 MISSOURI 134, KAISER

Montauk State Park

ORIGINATING IN A SERIES OF SPRINGS adjacent to Pigeon Creek in Dent County, the Current River begins its journey south in Montauk State Park. More than forty million gallons of cool, clear water bubble up daily from the ancient dolomites lying under this park. Many more springs add their flows to this "running river" as it hurries toward Arkansas. French settlers knew it as *la rivière courante*. The river twists and turns, entrenched in the hilly landscapes of the Ozarks, and its rugged beauty has made it the most popular of Missouri's float streams. Leonard Hall, the dean of Missouri's conservation writers, put it best: "One thing which makes Current River unique is that it lives out its entire life within the heart of the Ozark highland and thus is always in character."

The name Montauk is an Algonquin word meaning "island country" or "fort country." Some of the early pioneers came from Montauk Point in Suffolk County on Long Island, and their new post office in Missouri was named after their old New York home.

The National Park Service manages much of the Current River as part of the Ozark National Scenic Riverways. Established in 1964, the Riverways, comprised of the Current River and its tributary, the Jacks Fork, marked the first attempt by the federal government to create a linear river park. Three of the oldest and most popular Missouri state parks—Big Spring, Alley Spring, and Round Spring—were ceded to the new federal Riverways. But Montauk, where the river is born, remains a state park.

One of the first-generation of parks, acquired by the state in 1926, Montauk is perhaps best known as one of Missouri's four trout parks. Two others, Bennett Spring and Roaring River, are also in the state park system, while Maramec Spring is managed by a charitable foundation. The secluded setting has over three miles of fishing stream and stunning woodlands that surround the spring branch, which give Montauk a more primitive feel than the state's other trout parks. The long, cold spring branches of Montauk provide an ideal habitat for hatchery-bred rainbow trout. The Civilian Conservation Corps (CCC) constructed the handmade stone dam and spillway that control the outflow of water from the rearing ponds in 1935. As at Bennett Spring, the CCC company at Montauk was composed of veterans of World War I, including several experienced stonemasons. The rustic character of the stonework, which gives the

Above left: Fishermen work the White Oak Pool at Montauk Spring. Rainbow trout are released from the hatchery in the park, keeping the pool supplied. *Oliver Schuchard* • Top: Current River, alluring in spring when the redbuds bloom, flows from Montauk State Park into the Ozark National Scenic Riverways. *Larry Sportsman* • Left: The Montauk Mill is the sole survivor of a thriving village that was once located here. *Dave Dawson* • Above: The mill store and machinery can be seen on free guided tours of the mill, mostly on weekends. *Steve Bost*

Top: The Pine Ridge Trail climbs through the Montauk Upland Forest Natural Area, a mature pine, oak, and hickory woodland, to a scenic summit. ***Susan Flader*** **Above: The harmless midland water snake is characteristic of Ozark streams.** ***Missouri State Parks*** **• Right: Montauk Spring was once one big spring outlet, but a torrential downpour in Crabtree Hollow in 1892 washed sand, gravel, and debris into the spring. The filled-up spring belched for days before the water bubbled back out in multiple springs. This is the largest, flowing to Current River.** ***Katy Holmer***

impression of a natural formation rather than a man-made feature, has merited its inclusion on the National Register of Historic Places.

Almost any weekend from early spring to late fall, anglers from Missouri and other states flock to the park and line up along the "runs," trying to catch one of the delectable beauties released to the wild every day by the Missouri Department of Conservation, which manages the fishery. The most extraordinary spectacle is the old-fashioned trout opening-day ritual on March 1 each year. Thousands of ardent anglers descend on the park the day before, and some stay up all night visiting with friends and readying equipment, the better to jockey for position in the cold dawn as they wait for the opening siren. It used to be mainly a male-bonding ritual, with young boys proudly accompanying their fathers to their first opening, but nowadays there are many mothers and grandmothers fishing alongside young boys and girls. Surely one of the most colorful events, opening day at the trout parks has come to signal the beginning of a new year for the entire park system.

Rising from the springs and hatchery area, steep wooded ridges hem in the fledgling Current River, forming a narrow valley of superb, scenic beauty. The slopes are covered with a mature woodland of white oak, shortleaf pine, black oak, northern red oak, and maple. In places, the river flows below tall pine-capped bluffs of stained dolomite. The park is well-known for its spring wildflower display—the fire pinks, blue phlox, white and yellow dogtooth violets, yellow bellwort, Solomon's seal, trillium, columbine—and, of course, flowering dogwood, wild plum, serviceberry, and redbud. Beginning in the late 1990s, park staff initiated ecosystem restoration efforts involving prescribed fire in the heart of the high quality woodlands at Montauk. Successive fires have opened the understory to reveal woodland wildflowers, such as the spectacular royal catchfly,

which regularly appeared throughout this part of the Current River Hills before European settlement and now flourishes again.

Montauk Spring today really consists of multiple springs, but back before the turn of the twentieth century, there was a single big spring outlet. Legend says someone made a sounding that proved that spring to be at least 250 feet deep. Then in 1892, a torrential local downpour in Crabtree Hollow washed sand, gravel, and debris into the spring. The filled spring reportedly belched for several days before the bubbling water formed the multiple springs we see now.

No doubt it was the presence of the spring that attracted the first white settlers to the valley, not far into the nineteenth century. Most of the settlers were from Kentucky or Tennessee, although settlers from New York named the village of Montauk, which was the second town established in Dent County.

The rushing waters from Montauk Spring were ideally suited to powering gristmills, and the little valley was home to four different mills. The first was built in 1835 and operated by A. W. Hollerman. Twenty-five years later, the Stephenson family built and operated both a gristmill and

A cold morning's mist surrounds an ardent fisherman. ***Scott Myers*** **• Kids of all ages love to fish for trout here, even during winter.** ***Steve Bost***

a turbine sawmill. Tim Hickman purchased the old Hollerman mill with its large wheel, but then in 1865 he built a third mill powered by turbines. The new mill was destroyed by fire in 1895. Undaunted, Hickman sent for a Missouri millwright, William J. Furry, who rebuilt the mill, and it is this one still standing. Completed in 1896, this mill was of the roller type and had fairly elaborate machinery.

The same CCC company that built the dam and spillway in 1935 restored the 1896 mill and set into the new stone foundation two old buhrstones filled with concrete. In the center of one is the inscription: "Veteran Co. 1770 Sec. 2 Feb. 10, 35." The company also built roads, cabins, foot trails, and shelter houses.

The mill, the last remnant of the once thriving village of Montauk, is now open to the public. Much of its machinery is still intact, although the steel rollers were removed in 1942 for the war effort. When the mill was operating, bucket elevators moved the grain to a bin at the top of the mill. Then the grain dropped through many pairs of horizontal steel rollers, which crushed it. As it passed between each pair of rollers, vibrating silken screens called bolts sieved the grain. So the wheat passed from roller to roller, becoming finer and finer, and the bolts sifted the wheat, separating it from the bran and removing impurities. On the main floor, workers sacked the flour, middlings, shorts, and bran. Over the years, the state has undertaken further restoration of the mill and the mill store.

The 2,100-acre Montauk State Park offers a variety of accommodations: campgrounds, housekeeping cabins, a motel, and the Dorman L. Steelman Lodge. The facilities are open year-round, and a meeting room is available for small conferences. During the winter months, catch-and-release angling is available. During the regular fishing season, there are trout derbies and mill tours, hikes, and amphitheater programs led by interpreters. Montauk is popular, having the highest occupancy rates for its campgrounds and lodgings of any state park.

That is no surprise, given the allure of the trout fishing, the mill, the headwaters of the Current River, and the well-developed trail system here. Opening day or any day, Montauk State Park is a treasure. Even the eagles like it here at the gateway to the Current River. *

MONTAUK STATE PARK • 345 COUNTY ROAD 6670, SALEM

Top: A pair of eagles built their nest on a ridge-top pine in 2000 and have been successfully raising young here ever since. *Larry Sportman* • Left: A trail from the lodge to the campground goes through a classic bottomland forest. *Scott Myers* • Above: Tiny Pigeon Creek combines with the springs in Montauk State Park to form the headwaters of the Current River. *Steve Bost*

Current River State Park

WHEN GOV. ARTHUR HYDE and his new game and fish commissioner Frank Wielandy began searching in 1924 for sites to purchase for Missouri's first state parks, they looked especially at the beautiful springs and riparian forests along the Current and other Ozark rivers. By the end of the year, they had acquired the crown jewels of Round Spring and Big Spring on the Current, Alley Spring on the Jacks Fork, and Bennett Spring on the Niangua. Forty-six years later, all but Bennett were transferred to the National Park Service as part of the deal that created the Ozark National Scenic Riverways. On the Current River, the state park system retained only Montauk at the headwaters—probably because it was a "trout park" with a trout hatchery and rearing facilities run by the Missouri Department of Conservation (MDC).

Since then many park lovers have yearned for state parks to return to the Current River. That happened in 2007 when Gov. Matt Blunt approved the transfer of the former Alton Club property on the Current River—just upstream from Round Spring—from the MDC to the Missouri Department of Natural Resources (DNR). The transfer included club buildings plus 780 wooded acres west of Route 19 for a new state park.

The property includes a lodge and about twenty other rustic wood structures built in the 1930s as a corporate retreat for the Alton Box

This richly diverse new state park has almost two miles of frontage on the Current River and encompasses more than a mile of Sinking Creek, a bluff-lined, meandering tributary.

Board Company, the largest producer of paper box board in the United States. MDC purchased it in 1996 from a successor firm and operated it as the Presley Education Center, beloved by the many teachers and others who attended workshops and meetings there. But when MDC sought to tear down the old Alton Club buildings and start over with new construction, historic preservationists and river lovers protested that the complex of buildings was a rare intact survival of a type of rustic private retreat once common along Ozark streams. And besides, the buildings were on property under scenic easement to the National Park Service and thus could not legally be replaced. To prove their point, they nominated the Alton Club to the National Register of Historic Places and won approval by the Missouri Advisory Council on Historic Preservation after several tense hearings. The complex of buildings on about thirty-five acres was listed on the register in 2005.

The historic complex in the rustic style common to the National Park Service and to Civilian Conservation Corps structures built in the 1930s includes a lodge with dining facilities, a living room with original finishes (wood paneling and floors and a massive fireplace with stalactites in the stonework), a sleeping wing, and a veranda facing the Current River. Perhaps the most architecturally significant building is a 40-by-90-foot gymnasium with oak tongue-and-groove floor, knotty pine-paneled walls, and a barrel-vault lamella roof designed by St. Louis architect Gustel Kiewitt, a design used also in the old St. Louis Arena, now demolished. Other buildings include a dormitory, a pool hall turned classroom, a screened barbecue house with built-in stone grill, and a lake house that appears to be suspended above the swimming and fishing lake. There was also a tennis court, a skeet-shooting range, and a barn for horses or boats. The thirty-five-acre developed area on the riverfront is landscaped with local limestone and fieldstone retaining walls and walkways.

Except for the developed area, the park preserves a remarkably intact and diverse wooded terrain steeply carved through four hundred feet of vertical relief from Route 19 to the river. There are three tributary streams through Broad Shoal, Jones, and Dugan hollows with terrestrial and aquatic communities deserving of natural area status. A fourth stream, through Slick Shoal Hollow on an MDC tract adjacent to the park on the west, is also managed by park staff; the hollow contains an important cave, Bat Cave, a major hibernaculum for gray and Indiana bats. The hillsides are heavily mantled in oak with numerous small dolomite glades, springs, seeps, fens, rock outcrops, bluffs, and bottomland forests, and the bluffs and outcrops expose a broad spectrum of Ozarks geologic history. In the broader sections of hollows are some old farm fields now regenerating, several of which have been planted with shortleaf pine. The spring-fed Current River and its tributaries are remarkably

clear with high gradients and abundant riffle and bluff pool habitats. The extreme aquatic diversity, physiographic complexity, large expanse of contiguous woodland, and high degree of endemism—species unique to this region—make the Current River Hills a globally significant center of biodiversity, and this park is an excellent place to see that.

Though the Current River in its deep valley tended to protect the parkland lying to its east from wildfire carried by west winds, there is evidence in the park of deep archaeological deposits suggesting as much as ten thousand years of human habitation, which would likely have provided a human source of ignition, accounting for the fire-adapted oak and pine woodlands in the area.

Early settlers raised livestock on the open range and also burned the woods to encourage forage. The greatest era of industrial logging in this area was from 1890 to 1920; the sawmill at West Eminence on the Jacks Fork some fifteen miles to the south, which began operations in 1909, attracted some twelve thousand people to the town. When the boom ended, settlers continued their tradition of burning woods to clear them for pastures until state and federal forestry officials made a concerted effort to end the burning, beginning in the 1930s.

The Current River Hills, viewed here from a fire tower on a ridge overlooking the park and the river, are rugged and remarkably intact. The Ozarks are a globally significant center of biodiversity with a large number of terrestrial and aquatic species found nowhere else in the world. ***Ken McCarty***

Alton Box had initially acquired its land as a source of pulpwood for its operations, but managers soon realized the recreational values of the property were more important. They began protecting the regrowing forest. As a result, trees and understory are today more dense than they probably ever were before, and the glades have partially filled in with red cedar and elm. Park naturalists have begun reintroducing fire and restoring the landscape to a more natural condition.

State park officials planned to restore the Alton Club to its heyday from about 1938 to 1955. They talked of using the new park as a hub for a network of trails in the area, especially along the Current River and

Top: Mixed shortleaf pine and oak was common on some high ridges with sandy soils until the logging era. You can still find scattered mature trees and a few seedlings and saplings here in a scarlet and black oak woodland. Clear-water streams, like this one flowing through a fen in Jones Hollow, grace three steep hollows as they dance along on their way to the Current River. *Both Ken McCarty*

in the Roger Pryor Pioneer Backcountry just east of Route 19. They recognized that camping or lodging facilities would have to be limited, though, because of the rugged topography of the area and Scenic Riverway easement restrictions on more level land near the river. Planners considered draining a man-made lake upslope of the easement zone to allow room for parking, an amphitheater and multipurpose building, campsites, cabins, and an innovative "reciprocating wetland wastewater facility," vegetated at the surface and with subsurface disposal. They envisioned a landing for canoes to pull in to visit the historic area.

Because the Alton Club property had been purchased with Conservation Department funds, the Missouri DNR agreed to allow hunting for a minimum of sixty days each year. Park officials had estimated the cost for initial restoration and infrastructure at some $7 million, money not available in the park division budget, so it would have to be raised privately or from special sources. One possibility was a monetary settlement then being negotiated by the state with AmerenUE in the wake of the 2005 breach of Ameren's Taum Sauk Reservoir that tore the heart out of Johnson's Shut-ins State Park.

Then in late 2007, in the interval between the announcement and the actual transfer—after MDC staff pulled out but before state park officials established a presence—a Shannon County road crew brazenly bulldozed a road from Route 19, beginning only a hundred yards south of the current entrance road, down a steep hill, and through the new park's Jones Hollow nearly to the Current River. The road went through an area where park planners had intended to locate a group camp, through a fen and potential natural area, and part of the way in the creek bed itself, causing major damage. Stunned, park officials tried to block access, but

Top: The intact Alton Club Lodge and about twenty buildings were listed on the National Register of Historic Places in 2005 as a rare example of private retreats once common along the Current River. ***Susan Flader*** **• Above: A lake house appears to be suspended above the man-made lake. Right: The gymnasium has an unusual barrel-vault lamella roof.** ***Both Missouri State Parks***

within hours, a county crew reopened it. The issue of whether the route was or was not a legitimate county road was then referred to the attorney general's office where it languished through an election, a change in administration, and the worst stock market crash since the Great Depression—the start of a devastating recession that would last years.

Thus the park remained gated and undeveloped, while the county continued blocking the road. The state had few funds and little interest in investing in the park without resolution of the road issue, and planners talked increasingly about the difficulty of developing facilities and the expense of wastewater treatment in such a sensitive area.

With the road issue still unresolved, park officials finally talked with Shannon County commissioners in 2012 to see if some accommodation could be worked out. The result was the state conceding on the road, but the county agreeing to reroute it to avoid the most sensitive areas and to keep it gated during the summer season and at certain other times. That June, the park finally opened on weekends for day use, still without new development.

Then in 2013, word came that the US Marshals Service would be conducting an online auction of property seized in a drug raid—the old Camp Zoe property just east of Route 19 less than a mile from Current River State Park. Here was a beautiful 330-acre tract with some relatively flat land that had already been disturbed, some infrastructure already in place, and much of Sinking Creek with its fine sand beaches. It seemed the perfect answer to the vexing problem of developing camping, lodging, and other visitor service facilities on the steep, sensitive terrain of the Alton Club tract, and the money saved in development costs could more than equal the price of the additional land. So the state, through an agent, entered the bidding process and ended with the winning bid—though the marshals insisted on more, a total of $640,000.

The purchase for state park use was generally greeted with favor, especially by former campers at Camp Zoe who had fond memories of their time there. Camp Zoe, named for the mother of one of the owners,

Left: The dramatic Echo Bluff along Sinking Creek, part of the former Camp Zoe, is a focal point of the new park. *Susan Flader* • Above: Current River State Park offers ridges with memorable views of the Current River, seen here through an ancient cedar. Right: As naturalists explored the ridges and hollows of the new park, a fritillary butterfly lit on a sprig of white crownbeard on their map, a nice omen. *Both Ken McCarty*

opened as a girls camp in 1929, run by three teachers in Webster Groves and Kirkwood schools, so it early attracted many St. Louis youngsters, some of whom attended year after year. They enjoyed horseback rides to a swimming hole, sitting around the campfire at night, bunking in the screened cabins, and participating in all the other activities of camp life. In 1967 the camp was sold to two couples from the Ozarks, who began to admit boys as well as girls and operated it until 1986. After a period of intermittent rentals, a frontman for a rock band bought it in 2004, and they organized five or more weekends of jam-band festivals there annually, each attended by upward of seven thousand people, many of them teenagers. Federal authorities closed the festivals in 2010 after the owner pled guilty to "maintaining drug-involved premises."

After the state's purchase, park officials wasted no time in cleaning up the place, dismantling decrepit facilities, and planning for new infrastructure and visitor service amenities, including campsites, cabins, and a lodge. Only two significant buildings from old Camp Zoe remained, the stone and timber lodge on the hill and the barn in the valley, along with a local cemetery from the pre-Zoe era. Construction of road and visitor facilities estimated at $52 million began in early 2015, attended by controversy concerning the scope, speed, and secrecy of the project, expected to be complete in 2016.

How the plans for the Zoe property will be meshed with those previously made for Current River State Park remains to be seen, but the vision is to create a center for Ozark cultural and natural interpretation and recreation, including a staging area for long distance trails through the park, the Roger Pryor Pioneer Backcountry, and the Ozark National Scenic Riverways. Bluff-lined Sinking Creek is a perfect place for family fun in the water and for short floats. The Current River is right there for longer floats and fishing, and the old Alton Club is a fascinating historic complex. Round Spring, Montauk, and other beloved sites are nearby. Current River State Park, featuring the Current River and the Current River Hills, will no doubt become an unparalleled treasure. *

CURRENT RIVER STATE PARK • SHANNON COUNTY ROAD 19-D AT HIGHWAY 19, SALEM

Trails of the Roger Pryor Pioneer Backcountry

DEEP IN THE MISSOURI OZARKS, the region surrounding the Current River includes the most extensive forests and some of the most rugged topography in the state. If Missouri can be said to have a "big woods," this is it. Parts of these woods are owned and managed by a variety of public agencies, including the US Forest Service, the National Park Service, and the Missouri Department of Conservation (MDC), but a large swath of this landscape is a private working forest known as Pioneer Forest. At more than 140,000 acres, it is the largest holding of private land in Missouri, and it is owned by the L-A-D Foundation. Of that forest, the most expansive and primitive block of 62,000 acres is designated as the Roger Pryor Pioneer Backcountry, comprised of mile upon mile of wooded, hilly country, all draining to the Current River by way of three unspoiled streams.

More than fifty miles of trails wind through this sprawling Shannon County landscape. The Missouri Department of Natural Resources (DNR) leases and Missouri State Parks administers the trails for public use. Though this trail system is not a state park in the usual sense, it is a significant recreational resource for Missouri, especially for those in search of an experience in a remote and undeveloped Ozark area.

The story of this resource is part of a saga of Missouri conservation history, one that centers upon the vision and tenacity of a mild-mannered and self-effacing but determined conservationist named Leo A. Drey. In the early 1950s, Drey began to acquire the Ozark lands that became Pioneer Forest. These lands, like much of the Ozarks, had been logged heavily and were in poor condition. Drey's resolve was to restore them to health and productivity, and he sought advice from various professionals, especially foresters and conservationists. His goal was to demonstrate that such Ozark land could be managed conservatively as a viable economic enterprise, using single-tree selection harvests, while at the same time restoring its natural integrity. After more than sixty years, the results are manifest for all to see: vigorous timber, clean water, abundant wildlife, and scenic beauty.

One of Leo Drey's trusted advisors regarding environmental issues was another St. Louisan named R. Roger Pryor. Pryor was a passionate and highly knowledgeable spokesman for the Missouri outdoors and a larger-than-life figure as not only an activist but also a folk musician, raconteur, and general outdoorsman. Shortly after his untimely death in 1999 at age fifty-four, Drey selected the largest contiguous block of Pioneer Forest and designated it as the Roger Pryor Pioneer Backcountry. His purpose was to provide an enduring reserve of wild Ozark land, a largely primitive setting available for visitors to explore and enjoy but that would remain a productive working forest.

In 2004 Drey donated Pioneer Forest, including the Backcountry, to the L-A-D Foundation, an institution he formed in 1962 to carry his conservation mission into the future. The foundation continues to manage this property faithful to Drey's vision and principles. L-A-D also owns nearly 4,000 acres of natural areas and other special designation lands, including nearly thirty-five miles of frontage on the Ozark National Scenic Riverways under scenic easement to the National Park Service, seven state-designated natural areas and related lands leased to MDC, and the core properties at Dillard Mill State Historic Site and Grand Gulf State Park, leased to the DNR's state park system.

Part of Drey's vision includes the lease of the extensive trail system in the Backcountry, which a DNR director expressed an interest in helping to administer for public use in 2001. These trails provide access to a remote and scenic setting about as far removed from modern surroundings as one can get in Missouri. Despite periodic selective timber harvesting, the Backcountry remains primitive and even isolated, a place where one must be observant and careful to avoid getting lost. But here is a landscape that is undeveloped, unconfined, and full of appeal and adventure for some.

Finding these trails is part of the fun. Heading south from Salem along Route 19, one of Missouri's original state highways and the first to be designated as an official Scenic Highway, you begin to leave the open rolling Salem plateau and enter a new type of country. This is a region of steeper hills and essentially unbroken forest and woodland, with only occasional openings and settlements. This landscape holds firm all the way through Shannon County and into central Oregon County, not

Forest researcher Richard Guyette at the University of Missouri has called this area of the Ozarks "the heart of roughness." This remote, rugged, and scenic setting offers remarkable hiking and backpacking on more than fifty miles of trails on 62,000 acres for fit and experienced adventurers.

Far left: You can hike to this view of Current River from Bee Bluff on a spur from the Brushy Creek Trail. ***Neal Humke*** **• At the Himont Trailhead in 2001, landowner Leo Drey (third from right) dedicated the Roger Pryor Pioneer Backcountry as a working forest with long-distance hiking trails available for public use, while the Department of Natural Resources director at the time, Steve Mahfood (right), announced an intent to develop a lease agreement for State Parks to administer the trail system for primitive backcountry recreation.** ***Susan Flader***

Sierra Club volunteers have built and maintained trails in the Backcountry each year for decades. ***Robert Gestel*** **• A volunteer from the Show-Me Missouri Back Country Horsemen marks the Blair Creek Equestrian Trail.** ***Jim Attebury***

breaking out again into more open uplands until south of the breaks of the Eleven Point River.

Along the way, you pass Current River State Park and enter the Ozark National Scenic Riverways. Just south of the bridge across Sinking Creek, the first public road heading east from Route 19 is known as the Camp Zoe Road. It leads across the Backcountry about twelve miles to the Himont Trailhead. This gravel road is among the prettiest of autumn drives when the colors of the changing oak leaves contrast with the dark green needles of Missouri's native shortleaf pine. The first major low-water crossing along Camp Zoe Road is Big Creek. From there the road climbs out of the valley, crosses broad Polk Ridge, winds around the uppermost reaches of the Brushy Creek drainage, and continues east. Himont was once the site of a fire tower, but all that is left are its concrete bases that now surround a fire pit used by hikers and hunters.

As the largest contiguous block of wild country in the state, the Backcountry spans thirteen miles east to west and eight miles north to south. It includes three sizable tributaries to the Current River and all of the associated hollows, ridges, bluffs, springs, and caves. The vegetation here reflects the Lower Ozarks with hickory, ash, black gum, shortleaf pine, and a broad array of oak species. A highlight of the native fauna amid these hollows is the American black bear, one of Missouri's last remaining populations and a real symbol of wildness.

Pioneer Forest and state park staff have assisted many volunteers in building and maintaining the trails you find here. The three streams that drain the area, spring houses, old homeplaces, cemeteries, traces followed by early travelers, and even an old logging tram route are all part of the trails that the public can now explore.

Motorized travel is allowed only on county gravel roads, but the hiking opportunities are abundant and colorful. Thirteen miles of the Blair Creek Section of the Ozark Trail traverse the eastern portion of the Backcountry. This section of the Ozark Trail was among the first to be constructed in Missouri during the late 1970s by volunteers from the Missouri Chapter of the Sierra Club. They return each year to help with signage and

Above: The Current River Natural Area with its 300-year-old white oaks was the first natural area designated in Missouri. The now enlarged 265-acre area is accessible from the Brushy Creek Loop Trail. *Greg Iffrig* • Right: Backpackers hike along the Blair Creek section of the Ozark Trail. *George Denniston*

maintenance. As this section of the trail enters Pioneer Forest from the Mark Twain National Forest it drops down into the valley of Blair Creek and passes several dolomite bluffs, wending its way south toward the Current River. McIntyre Spring, also known as Harper Spring, near the mouth of Jim's Creek, is one of the largest along the trail and emerges from within the remains of an old springhouse. Past the mouth of Holmes Hollow, the old Blair Creek Cemetery remains in use.

Sierra Club volunteers also helped with the Laxton Hollow Trail. This easy two-mile route leaves from Himont Trailhead and winds its way around a side hollow before heading into its namesake hollow, crossing the dry gravel-bottom stream, then out to its mouth where it merges with the larger Blair Creek. Here, across Blair Creek, the trail joins the Ozark Trail, but those interested in a shorter hike may return to Himont.

Volunteers of the Show-Me Missouri Back Country Horsemen have helped with the design, maintenance, and signage for the Blair Creek Equestrian Trail. There are two equestrian trailheads with parking for several horse trailers, one just north of the Backcountry on the Mark Twain National Forest and the other to the south on MDC land near Owls Bend. Riders may travel through the Backcountry for nearly twelve miles, in places generally paralleling the hikers-only section of the Ozark Trail. Although there is no overnight horse camping in the Backcountry itself, designated areas are nearby on the Mark Twain National Forest.

The nineteen-mile Brushy Creek Loop Trail begins at Himont and takes hikers down Brushy Creek Valley along an abandoned narrow-gauge tram bed to the long-deserted company town of Brushy, some remnants of which are still discernible. Logs were loaded on rail cars here during the first major timber harvest in this area in the early 1900s. The eastern Satterfield Hollow loop offers hikers an alternative return route and passes through part of the 265-acre Current River Natural Area, an area saved by Leo Drey from imminent harvest when he purchased a large tract that included what is now the Backcountry from National Distillers Products Corporation in 1954. A ten-acre tract here was initially recognized by the Society of American Foresters in 1955 as one of its first Research Natural Areas, and it was the very first such preserve in Missouri. This important area protects a rare remnant of old-growth forest, featuring some impressive white oaks up to four hundred years old. Hikers then cross into the bottom of the Middle Prong Brushy Creek near Hog Cave Hollow before heading back to Himont.

A new trail still under construction, the Current River Trail, uses part of the Brushy Creek Trail, then follows the Current River and, in places, Big Creek for twelve miles to Round Spring. It is a cooperative effort of the L-A-D Foundation, Missouri State Parks, and the Ozark National Scenic Riverways. There are splendid views of the Current River, and lucky hikers may see wild horses grazing in open areas along the river. Plans are to continue this route farther from Round Spring to the old Camp Zoe and then on to Current River State Park. Once completed, those seeking more adventure may be able to combine overland and river travel. Other trails are envisioned, for example, to Jerktail Mountain, affording striking views across the Current River watershed, and another trailhead is planned at Camp Zoe.

About fifty years ago, a newspaper writer from Kansas City hiked through the Brushy Creek area of the Backcountry and returned home to write that it was "the most remote place in all of Missouri." The trails of this Backcountry offer a unique experience, where you can explore for miles or for a short distance. Either way, a powerful sense of ancient wooded hills and lonely spaces will linger long and pleasantly in your memory. *

TRAILS OF THE ROGER PRYOR PIONEER BACKCOUNTRY • CAMP ZOE ROAD, SALEM

Lake Wappapello State Park

THE ST. FRANCIS RIVER once flowed freely through the piney ridges of the southeastern Ozarks below Sam A. Baker State Park before dropping into the lowlands of Missouri and Arkansas on its way to the Mississippi. Native Americans gave the river its name of Cholo-Holley or Smoky Waters.

Before 1936 and the building of a dam, there were a number of small communities in the Ozark portion of the St. Francis River, including one called Wappapello. In 1936 Congress passed the Overton Act, which authorized the Army Corps of Engineers to develop the St. Francis Basin Project to control flooding on the lower Mississippi River. Accordingly, the Memphis district began construction of a dam across the St. Francis River near Wappapello in 1938, the first of the large corps dams in Missouri. This was also the site of the first government-funded archaeological survey of a reservoir area in the state, conducted by an undergraduate student at the University of Missouri, Carl Chapman. Chapman would later become the dean of Missouri archaeology and would be credited with lobbying the Archaeological and Historic Preservation Act of 1974 through Congress. The act has provided millions of dollars for cultural resource surveys and mitigation at federally funded reservoirs and other construction projects throughout the nation. State parks at two more recent corps reservoirs in Missouri, Harry S Truman and Mark Twain, have benefited from studies funded with more than $1 million each under this program.

Lake Wappapello is named for a small Wayne County railroad town named Wappapello, reportedly after a friendly Shawnee chief who hunted the area during early pioneer times.

In addition to submerging archaeological remains, the Wappapello project displaced several towns, eight schools, and hundreds of farms and homes. As is the case with most reservoirs that flood river bottomland, many complained that the best farmland in Wayne County was being destroyed. Nevertheless, the 2,700-foot-long, 109-foot-high dam was completed in 1941, and it created an 8,400-acre lake at what engineers would call normal pool. The lake can reach more than twice that size at high water, backing up almost to Sam A. Baker State Park some twenty miles north.

Notwithstanding the loss of a free-flowing river and its rural communities, Lake Wappapello is one of the more beautiful corps reservoirs in Missouri. The water is all from the Ozarks, and clear. The hills surround-

The fishing is excellent, especially for largemouth bass, crappie, white bass, and bluegill. A beach offers swimming and water fun, and you can hike a trail to the Allison family cemetery on the ridge above the lake. *All Lauren Stroer*

ing the lake are steep and scenic. The forests that cover these slopes are rich and diverse. With the Mississippi Lowlands not far away, the addition of southern cherrybark oak, sweetgum, and devil's walking stick add an interesting bottom-country component to the typical Ozark flora of shortleaf pine, white oak, and sour gum. The fishing is excellent, especially for crappie, white bass, and bluegill, as well as largemouth bass and catfish.

Not far from the dam itself—though more than fifteen miles by road from the town of Wappapello near the former logging boomtown of Chaonia—is a ridge known as Allison's Peninsula, named for the family that once lived there, and their cemetery still remains on the ridge. In this area, the state of Missouri operates Lake Wappapello State Park on 1,854 acres provided by the corps as a donated lease in 1957. Along with Table Rock State Park, leased to the state on the same day, it is the oldest of the corps reservoir parks in the system.

This state park is well-known and popular among people in southeast Missouri, southern Illinois, and western Kentucky and Tennessee; but still, it is seldom crowded and offers a relaxing hideaway, especially if you enjoy lake fishing, boating, and hiking. The facilities include two campgrounds, one on the ridge and one nestled near the lake, picnic areas, a swimming beach, and tidy little kitchen-equipped cabins that are perfect for a family escape.

Several trails in the park lead along the lake and into the Ozark forest. One leads also to the old Allison family cemetery. The sunsets over the lake from this point are superb. Trails up Asher Creek valley and along an arm of the lake that is a designated waterfowl winter refuge offer sightings of eagles, ospreys, ducks, and other wildlife. Another longer trail, which heads north along the lake and loops back through adjacent public lands, connects with a spur of the Ozark Trail and beckons mountain bikers, equestrians, and backpackers.

In addition to the intrinsic attraction of a quiet, wooded, lakeside park, Wappapello also is a convenient point from which to explore nearby features. The lake is virtually surrounded by Army Corps of Engineers land, most of which is undeveloped. One such area, the Johnson tract, is a large expanse of little-disturbed forest that is being managed as a natural area. The Poplar Bluff unit of the Mark Twain National Forest is just to the west, and Sam A. Baker State Park is to the north. The fascinating bottomlands of Mingo National Wildlife Refuge are just across the dam to the east, and the former University Forest, now operated by the Missouri Department of Conservation, is to the south.

At the state park itself, there is a special quality of early morning light that will lift you from any doldrums. Arise early, walk to the water's edge, and enjoy the golden shafts of light piercing the cool morning mists, sparkling the dew on numberless leaves across the dark green or radiant autumnal hills and then steadily creeping across the still waters of the deep-shaded cove. Then you may agree that lovely Lake Wappapello State Park is still the Smoky Waters. *

LAKE WAPPAPELLO STATE PARK • ROUTE 172, WILLIAMSVILLE

Grand Gulf State Park

After a heavy rain, runoff pours into Grand Gulf, known as Missouri's Little Grand Canyon, sometimes nearly filling it to the top. *Matthew Kantola*

LOCAL OLD-TIMERS knew it all along. The stream of Grand Gulf canyon a few miles north of the Missouri-Arkansas line, which disappears into subterranean caverns, reemerges nine miles south as the famous Mammoth Spring that bursts from the earth in Arkansas. In 1941, folklorist Otto Rayburn reported a local experiment: people dumped sacks of oats into the stream in the canyon and then observed the oats emerge in the spring. Later investigators confirmed the experiment with fluorescein dye.

Although it had been considered as early as 1939, Missouri's "Little Grand Canyon" in Oregon County was added to the state park system in 1984. It has a long history as a public attraction and a source of pride and wonder to nearby Ozark residents. The area is steeped in folklore and is a popular picnic and sparking area. Unlike the Grand Canyon, which is wider than it is deep, Grand Gulf is truly a chasm, deeper than it is wide.

Comparisons to the Grand Canyon aside, Grand Gulf is a striking landscape. To understand its story, one must turn to geologists for an explanation. It began, like the rest of the Ozarks, with the deposit of sediments that eventually formed limestones and dolomites, the uplifting of those layers, and the dissolving action of mildly acidic groundwater, which carved fissures and channels in the bedrock. Here at Grand Gulf is a cave system whose roof collapsed thousands of years ago. The result is a vertical-walled canyon about three-quarters of a mile long. Bussell Branch, a surface stream draining some twenty-eight square miles that once flowed above the cave system, became diverted into the chasm in a process geologists call stream piracy. Over the years, the gulf was further altered by the pour-off from the Bussell Branch watershed.

"A lost river, born in Missouri, reborn in Arkansas," is how folklorist Otto Rayburn described it in Ozark Country, *1941.*

All of this water still today passes through a 250-foot natural tunnel—the part of the cave that remains intact—and emerges into a large circular chasm, another remnant of a collapsed cave chamber. Here the stream submerges back into the cave system and begins its Stygian journey toward rebirth in Mammoth Spring.

The walls of the canyon are festooned with herbaceous greenery and, in the lower sections, flood debris. These cliffs rise as much as 130 feet at the natural bridge.

The steep walls required explorers to make their way upstream for some distance to gain safe access. Then, walking downstream, they could enter the tunnel, which at ordinary water levels is some seventy-five feet high. If they happened to notice that the flood debris had reached this same height, they'd have known to scan the sky for possible thunderheads before proceeding. The ceiling height drops to only about ten feet on the downstream end of the tunnel. Entering into the chasm and coursing past large blocks of dolomite—part of the collapsed roof—the stream reaches the extant portion of the cave, which acts as a drain for all the water flowing into the gulf.

This passage from the chasm to the cave long fascinated scientists and spelunkers. How could so massive a cave system pinch out into such a small, unimpressive end? Fortunately and intriguingly, accounts by earlier explorers give us the answer. In her now classic *Cave Regions of the Ozarks and Black Hills* (1898), the young scientist Luella Agnes Owen recounted her exploration along with two companions. She described what they saw after entering the cave at the downstream end of the gulf and proceeding perhaps six hundred feet farther downstream:

Left: Seen from an overlook, the cave explored by geologist Luella Agnes Owen is no longer accessible. ***Denise Vaughn*** **• Greenery festoons the natural bridge, which links two parts of the collapsed cave system.** ***Lauren Stroer***

"The ceiling dipped so we were not able to stand straight, and the guide said he had never gone farther; but to his surprise here was a light boat, which I am ready to admit, he displayed no eagerness to appropriate to his own use, and swimming about it, close to shore, were numerous small eyeless fish, pure white and perfectly fearless; the first I had ever seen, and little beauties."

Bravely, Luella determined to use the boat to explore the underground stream even further, leaving her nephew and the guide behind holding an attached coil of slender twine that would be her only lifeline to return against the current. Luella continued in the boat along a narrow, rocky, twisty channel until she came to an even smaller passage where she could lodge the boat sideways against the rocks and enjoy "an astonishing multitude" of the fearless eyeless fish. Then, acceding to the shouts of her guide that he feared the twine could be severed by the rocks, she let him pull her back

The boat had apparently been left by an earlier exploration led by Maj. M. G. Norman, who owned the property surrounding the gulf. Access to the first part of the cave was available, according to local residents, until the early 1920s when a great storm filled the gulf with downed trees and other debris. Ever since, that stream and Luella Owen's "little beauties" have remained unviewed. In the 1990s, state park officials employed a robot that toted a camera and digging tool to try to find a way past the flood debris and into the cave. They eventually gave up, deciding that any effort to break up the plug could risk havoc at Mammoth Spring and the adjacent town during floods.

Heavy rains can fill the entire gulf to depths exceeding one hundred feet. Several times in recent years, even the 130-foot-high observation platform has been covered. As the gulf begins to drain after a storm, waterfalls of seventy to eighty feet may be observed.

In 1959, the Missouri General Assembly narrowly defeated a locally sponsored measure to allow the state to acquire Grand Gulf as a state park. But local interest in creating a park continued unabated. In 1970 St. Louis forest owner and conservationist Leo Drey purchased the land in order to assure its preservation. The following year, the US Department of the Interior designated the gulf as a National Natural Landmark, the first of Missouri's sixteen natural landmarks to win this coveted distinction. And finally, in 1984 the land came into the state park system through a lease agreement between Drey's L-A-D Foundation and the state, thus assuring its continued availability for public enjoyment and enlightenment.

Park managers have laid out trails and installed wheelchair-accessible boardwalks and overlooks at this 322-acre day-use park, so some sixty thousand visitors a year can get close to the edge of the gulf without endangering themselves or the environment.

A hike on the mile-long woodland trail surrounding the gulf reveals evidence of debris that has floated along the shorelines, indicating past high-water marks of this huge, temporary natural bathtub. The Spanish oak-dominated woodlands that surround the chasm are relatively dry, and park managers are treating them with prescribed fire to encourage the unusually interesting ground flora, providing visitors an opportunity to walk through a landscape rare in Missouri.

Outdoor exhibits at the trailhead provide artistic renderings of the geology, so visitors can visualize the processes that produced Missouri's "Little Grand Canyon." *

GRAND GULF STATE PARK • ROUTE W, THAYER

Table Rock State Park

THE GEOGRAPHIC REGION KNOWN AS THE OZARKS has various definitions, depending upon one's point of view. There is a generalized area that most people can agree is the Ozarks, but the geologist, botanist, and historian always seem to draw the outer boundaries differently, and they differ also about where the true heart of the area lies. From a cultural point of view, many would argue that the heart of the Ozarks, the cultural core if you will, would be in the upper White River valley, straddling the border between Missouri and Arkansas.

This valley is physically near the center of almost anyone's definition of the Ozarks—except the geologist, who would look to the oldest rocks in the St. Francois Mountains. The people who settled the White River country were relatively homogeneous, at least in comparison to Ozark border areas. The White River settlers were old-stock Americans primarily from the southern Appalachians. They were migrants from the same rugged country that Horace Kephart described in his classic study, *Our Southern Highlanders*. These folk dominated most of the Ozark region, and in the White River valley, the highland stock was nearly undiluted.

In addition to its ethnic character, the valley's geography has encouraged a sense of region. The White River blithely ignored state boundaries, and to some extent the settlers saw themselves as White River valley residents—not in place of but at least in addition to being Missourians or Arkansans. This is one Ozark area where people readily identify themselves as Ozarkians.

This sense of regional identity was further established by several literary works. One of the first of the literate explorers of the Ozarks was Henry Rowe Schoolcraft, who traversed the region on horseback in 1818 and 1819 and was enamored of the area. The writer Harold Bell Wright in 1907 produced a romantic and enormously popular novel, *Shepherd of the Hills*, set in the White River country, which for good or ill shaped the image of the people of the Ozarks for the national public and, eventually, the self-image of Ozarkians themselves, in part. It was seekers of

> *This small 350-acre park annually attracts more than a million visitors from all over Missouri and throughout the country, more than any other state park except the largest, 17,600-acre Lake of the Ozarks State Park, fifty times the size of Table Rock.*

Wright's Ozarkian fantasy who constituted the first wave of tourism into the White River country. In fact, the centerpiece of Wright's tale, Old Matt's Cabin, was located only a few miles from where Table Rock State Park would be established a half-century later. A more academic but often amusing look at Ozark culture was provided by Vance Randolph, who spent years collecting the music, stories, and traditions of the Ozarks, focusing a lion's share of his attention on the White River country.

The White River is long and sinuous, originating in northern Arkansas, flowing north into Missouri, then south back into Arkansas, with several loops back into Missouri, finally leaving Missouri for good, and then sliding out of the hills and through the lowlands of eastern Arkansas to join the Mississippi River. The upper valley is generally the region near the state line, embracing the whole length of the river in Missouri plus some of the major tributary valleys, including all or parts of Barry, Stone, Taney, Christian, Douglas, and Ozark counties.

The promise of power and the peril of flooding eventually drowned the White River. The first dam on the White was Powersite, constructed in 1912 and creating Lake Taneycomo. It was Missouri's first hydroelectric dam, and it is still owned by Empire District Electric Company. Later, the Army Corps of Engineers, under the authorization of the Flood Control Acts of 1938 and 1941, constructed four more major dams in the upper White River valley: Norfork, Bull Shoals, Table Rock, and Beaver. Because of these reservoirs, not a single mile of the original White River still flows free in Missouri. The headwaters of some of its tributaries are all that are left of this once great river system.

At 252 feet, Table Rock Dam in Taney County is by far the highest dam in the state, and it is the only one of these four corps dams constructed within the boundaries of Missouri. Opposition to the dam was fierce, but a powerful combination of utility and Chamber of Commerce interests prevailed, and the 43,000-acre hydroelectric and flood-control reservoir was completed in 1959. The dam and lake take their name from a high rock shelf along the White River just downstream from the dam.

The construction of Table Rock and other corps lakes in Missouri provided an opportunity for the Missouri State Park Board to acquire several state parks at little or no cost in the 1950s and 1960s when there were no funds available for acquisition of new state parks. These lake parks provided a different sort of recreation than most of the existing state parks from earlier eras, featuring large acreages of flat water perfect for every aspect of boating or water sport. At Table Rock State Park, the 1957 leasehold from the Corps of Engineers consists of about 350 acres along the northeast shore of the lake near the dam, about eight miles south of Branson. The park provides a full array of lake-oriented

Above: The upper mile of Lake Taneycomo below Table Rock Dam is as good a representation of the original upper White River valley as remains in Missouri. ***James Little*** **• Left: Table Rock Lake is famed for its clear water.** ***Tom Nagel*** **Right: Mountain bikers navigate the White River Trail.** ***Carl Bonnell***

facilities, including camping and picnic areas amid the oaks and hickories along the winding lakeshore, a boat launch, and the largest full-service marina in the state park system. Visitors can rent a kayak or a ski boat, try a para-sailing ride, take an excursion on a catamaran, get trained and outfitted for scuba diving, or even rent a bike.

For those who enjoy their recreation on solid ground, tiny Table Rock park offers access to more than fifteen miles of trails in addition to its lakeshore camping and picnicking facilities. The Chinquapin Trail provides a taste of Ozark woodlands and glades for people walking from one part of the developed area to the other, while the Lakeshore Trail is a paved hiking and biking trail that follows the shoreline from the park marina to the Corps of Engineers Visitor Center at the Table Rock Dam two miles to the north. Like the Lakeshore Trail, the twelve-mile White River Valley Trail uses corps as well as state land and offers a fair sampling of rugged White River woodlands and glades. This hiking and mountain-biking trail, which consists of four interconnected loops, was awarded national Coalition for Recreational Trails honors upon its completion in 2011. The park has some of the best glades in the Branson

area and is one of the few places in the park system where one can find the showy American smoke tree, a signature species of the White River Hills. It also has a small area of riverfront forest with the eye-catching yellowwood, another signature species, and a canebrake where the rare Swainson's warbler has been spotted.

You can rent a boat at the largest marina in the park system and then enjoy the crystal waters, rocky shores, and glade-dotted hills. Because the park is next to Branson, chances are you will hear some country music. *All Missouri State Parks*

Table Rock Lake, for all the controversy that attended its birth, is a beautiful body of water. It is known for the stunning clarity of its waters, a fact that scuba divers will attest. The fishing is excellent, especially for bass and, in nearby Lake Taneycomo, for trout stocked by the Department of Conservation's Shepherd of the Hills Hatchery close to the park. And of course, it is a favorite for swimming, boating, and water-skiing. The lake has suffered serious water quality problems at times, due to all the development in its watershed coupled with leakage from septic systems, agricultural runoff, and the city of Springfield twenty-five miles to the north. But to their credit, civic organizations and citizens of southwest Missouri recognized the threat this posed to their tourism-based economy and have become strong supporters of measures to greatly improve Springfield's sewage-treatment system and to reduce pollution and runoff.

Construction of these large lakes spurred the boom in tourism that had begun on a smaller scale with Lake Taneycomo in the 1920s. With

Table Rock Lake is a great lake for families and swimming and all sorts of activity in and on and beside the water. *Missouri State Parks*

new roads for access and the attraction of the lake, plus the allure of the scenic hills and the Ozark mystique, Forsyth, Branson, and other area communities underwent revolutionary change. The Herschend family leased Marvel Cave, a show cave in Branson, in 1950 and developed the Ozark-themed Silver Dollar City to complement it, beginning in 1960. Shortly thereafter, Presley's Country Jubilee became the first of what within forty years would be more than one hundred country music and other theaters in Branson, making it a national destination for live music and other entertainment.

No longer an isolated region, the White River country became instead a fringe of the Sun Belt and faced a new invasion from the North, this time of tourists, vacationers, and retirees. Harold Bell Wright came to the "Shepherd of the Hills Country" by taking the train to the end of the tracks and then proceeding on horseback. Modern pilgrims will find their way there on a new four-lane highway that would have made a highway engineer's jaw drop only a few years ago. Mountains have been cleft, valleys filled, and a concrete ribbon now leads like an arrow to the heart of this tourist mecca.

The intensity of the industrial-scale tourism around Branson must be seen to be believed. For miles along certain roadways, there are wall-to-wall attractions ranging from miniature golf emporiums and fast-food franchises to country music palaces. Needless to say, much of the original culture of the valley has been displaced. Ironically, a commercialized version of rustic Ozark culture serves as a chief theme of the local tourist industry. If real Ozarkians are now scarce, numerous imitations, some in fair earnest, are nevertheless offered in abundance. "Hillbillies," some in neon and some in genuine homespun, are all over the place in Ozark Mountain Country.

Nestled in the midst of all the bustle lies Table Rock State Park. Admittedly, many visitors to the park are attracted by abundant entertainment in the vicinity. But that they appreciate what the park itself has to offer may be indicated by ballots cast in 2010 by readers of the *AAA Midwest Traveler* magazine, who voted Table Rock the best park in the Midwest by a nearly two-to-one margin. (The second and third place winners were also Missouri state parks, Lake of the Ozarks and Ha Ha Tonka.)

Table Rock State Park is indeed worth a visit. It provides the perfect access to a storied region—and while you're there, be sure to take in a naturalist-led walk or evening program. You may enjoy the abundant tourist attractions of Branson, but when you need a break, you can hike the park trails or find along some backwoods byways much that is still unspoiled and inviting in the White River Hills. *

TABLE ROCK STATE PARK • 5272 ROUTE 165, BRANSON

Roaring River State Park

IT DOESN'T "ROAR"—BUT IT ONCE DID. Or so they say. The spring once gushed from a cleft in the dolomite bluff, twenty million gallons daily that tumbled and cascaded over, under, and around a rocky escarpment, down to the streambed below. But in the 1930s, the Civilian Conservation Corps (CCC) built a dam in front of the cleft in the bluff, and the cascade was submerged beneath the deep, blue pool we see today. A small trickling flow from the bluff high above falls into the pool, spraying and refreshing the clumps of ferns, columbines, and mosses that line the dolomite ledges that extend into the shallow, cave-like cleft in the rock. This grotto of blue and silver water, gray rock, and delicate green ferns in quiet indirect light is as lovely a scene as any in the park system.

Roaring River is one of the "grand old ladies" of the Missouri state park system, dating back to the 1920s. A classic in many ways, it has a breathtaking setting: a deep, narrow valley framed by high, forested slopes—the look of mountainous terrain. Because of its age and size, it was a logical choice for development by the CCC during the Great Depression. In addition to the dam at the spring, built in support of the trout-raising operation that stocks the spring branch running through the park, there are many rustic timber and stone structures built in the traditional CCC style. Coupled with a modern lodge of rustic appearance, the buildings stamp Roaring River as a park developed in the golden age of park design and construction.

It is a popular park, drawing visitors from Missouri and beyond to engage in many forms of traditional state park recreation. The adjacent Mark Twain National Forest provides a valuable buffer against commercial development. And the park, with its large, long-protected acreage, harbors a remarkable assortment of native southwest Ozark species and natural habitats, including a large complex of open dolomite glades.

Left: The spring emerges in a peaceful grotto. ***Oliver Schuchard*** **• Above: Secluded cabins on the hillside above the dam built by the Civilian Conservation Corps overlook the popular fishing pool below the dam.** ***Missouri State Parks***

The intensely rugged hills that embrace the valley of Roaring River are part of the White River Hills region of the Ozarks, distinguished by the large scale of its scenery, the dramatic depth of its valleys, the size and openness of its glades, and the unusual wealth of its native plant life, with both Appalachian and southwestern species.

> *At Roaring River, the insight of the old Ozark adage becomes clear: "Our mountains ain't that high, but our valleys sure are deep!"*

Driving south toward the park from Cassville on Highway 112, you pass through gently rolling uplands, and then, very near the park boundary, the mild upland abruptly falls off into steep, hilly terrain. You travel down into the mountains at Roaring River.

Since people first arrived in the southwestern Ozarks, the rushing cold purity of the river has been a magnet. American Indians camped there, and later, European settlers found utilitarian work for the waters of the spring branch, developing mills for grain, saw timber, wool, and locally grown cotton. But despite these developments, the river still attracted people to its beauty and restfulness.

Barry County itself has not always been a very restful place. The Butterfield Overland Express crossed it on the main street of Cassville in its brief but exciting life in the late 1850s. Early in the Civil War, the pro-Confederate majority of the Missouri General Assembly convened briefly in the county courthouse at Cassville after adjourning from

The park has twenty-six cabins available for overnight guests. ***Kyle Spradley***
Hoarfrost forms as mist rises from the spring and coats trees in the Roaring River valley, which winds through the beautiful, rugged hills. ***Merle Rogers***

Neosho, having earlier been driven out of Jefferson City by the Union army. Gov. Claiborne Jackson signed the Missouri Act of Secession at Neosho on October 31, 1861, paving the way for Missouri's acceptance by the Confederacy as its twelfth state. The hills around Roaring River served as hideouts for wartime guerrillas and outlaws, and large-scale troop movements traversed the countryside nearby, going north and south.

Sometime after the war, the spring branch was stocked with trout, and a small resort community grew up in the valley. Part of the valley floor was subdivided into hundreds of tiny lots for cottages and commercial development. By the turn of the twentieth century, wealthy businessmen from Kansas City and St. Louis used Roaring River as a sporting retreat. One of these St. Louis businessmen, Dr. Thomas M. Sayman, tried to interest Gov. Arthur Hyde and his game and fish commissioner, Frank Wielandy, in purchasing the area as one of the state's first parks in 1924, but the price was too steep. Sayman then appeared somewhat mysteriously at a courthouse sheriff's sale of much of the Roaring River property in 1928 and won the bid for $105,000. Rumors that the eccentric and spectacularly bald promoter planned to develop an elaborate tourist resort were laid to rest when he promptly donated more than 2,500 acres to the state of Missouri.

In the 1930s, the primary development of the park was undertaken by Company 1713 of the CCC and by crews of the Works Progress Administration. This work, under the supervision of the National Park Service, illustrates the rustic style of CCC park architecture. It included a fish hatchery and related structures, rental cabins, Deer Leap and other trails, picnic shelters, restrooms, and the original three-story park lodge of native stone and timber, now being renovated. The CCC camp enrolled hundreds of young men from 1933 until 1939, and for the most part, the facilities they built are still sound and in service. Even the officers' barracks area has survived as Camp Smokey, a group camp. Near a CCC shelter in a picnic area now stands a larger-than-life bronze statue of a CCC worker, dedicated in 2013 in tribute to the tens of thousands of workers who built facilities in most of the state parks in the Depression years of the 1930s.

One CCC effort, however, had a rather tortuous history. In 1936, the crew began construction of a thirty-acre artificial lake, contoured to the steep slopes of the narrow valley and with a beach and a large bathhouse. By early 1939, park officials realized that the lake was silting up too fast to be successfully maintained—a consequence of erosion from the unprotected, overgrazed land near the headwaters—and they pro-

posed construction of a swimming pool in order to make use of the impressive bathhouse. Later that year, a disastrous flood damaged much of the CCC work in the valley, and crews were diverted to cleanup and repair of higher priority facilities. The bathhouse became a clubhouse, and then was beautifully renovated as the Ozark Chinquapin Nature Center, where visitors can learn about the perils of land abuse and about the still abundant natural wonders of the White River Hills.

For most visitors, the central attraction at Roaring River is fishing for rainbow trout that are regularly stocked in the spring branch. Many of the more than half a million visitors each year from Arkansas, Oklahoma, Texas, and Missouri try their luck with the trout. Others enjoy hiking the trails, camping, and eating or relaxing in the handsome Emery Melton Lodge completed in 1998.

From its beginnings, Roaring River State Park harbored a treasure trove of natural features beyond the developed areas, in the wilder reaches of the hills. Besides the spring itself and the mountains, this 4,300-acre preserve shelters more than its fair share of interesting rocks, plants, and animals. The park has many small caves, several small springs, and rocks from at least six different formations. At about the 1,200-foot elevation, a contact zone between two of these layers has produced a "bench," or narrow level rim along the side slopes of the mountains. This bench is a good place for examining such outcroppings as Compton limestone and

Chattanooga shale, as well as shelter caves and small springs. Cloaking the hills are several distinct plant communities with a total of more than six hundred different species. Animal life in the park is generally characteristic of the Missouri Ozarks, with the addition of several southwestern species including painted buntings and greater roadrunners. Two uncommon species of salamander, the gray-bellied and the rare Oklahoma salamander, live in the park's clear, shallow streams. In the winter, bald eagles roost regularly in the valley.

Some 2,075 of the park's 4,300 acres are protected as the Roaring River Hills Wild Area, a designation that forever protects and preserves the wildness, naturalness, and rugged character of the hills by prohibiting roads and mechanical equipment that would disrupt the sanctity of solitude found within the area. This wild area, one of twelve in the state park system totaling almost 23,000 acres, became a kind of test case for wild area values and management in the early 2000s. The area harbors hundreds of acres of dolomite glades that had for many years been invaded by eastern red cedar, a native species that had formerly been kept at bay on the glades by frequent wildfires. In the 1990s park managers sought to restore the open character and biodiversity of the glades with prescribed fire, a practice that has generally been permitted in wilderness and wild areas. But when the more mature cedars proved able to resist the fires, managers sought a waiver of the wild area policy to allow the physical removal of the cedars with chainsaws and motor transport, possibly even by commercial logging operators.

This proposal predictably led to passionate discussion among park staff and representatives of several conservation organizations with varying views about the management of wildness and biodiversity, which are usually mutually reinforcing but occasionally diverging. Over a period

A lone fisherman enjoys solitude as the sun's early rays pierce the morning fog. ***Kyle Spradley*** **• A glade in the Roaring River Hills Wild Area offers an expansive view of the White River hills.** ***Allison Vaughn*** **• Former Civilian Conservation Corps workers and current State Park Youth Corps members join Gov. Jay Nixon in dedicating a statue honoring CCC workers.** ***Missouri State Parks***

of several years, a new wild area policy was developed for the system. To get to that point, several large meetings and an on-site retreat were held, and a work group including citizen members was appointed. Federal wilderness managers held training programs in wild area management for park staff. The process also resulted in a new management plan for Roaring River. Reached through compromise, the plan provided for minimal use of tools to remove cedars on up to 170 acres of glades within the wild area and restoration of more glades beyond. Most important was an acknowledgment that wildness itself is a value worthy of respect independent of biodiversity, especially in designated wild areas.

Today, glade restoration continues, and prime examples of this significant landscape feature can be found throughout the park. Uncommon plants such as poppy mallow and Trelease's larkspur grow in abundance on the restored glades.

As a grand and venerable place, Roaring River guards multiple treasures, stories, and impressions. Probably no other Missouri state park has as many legends associated with it as Roaring River—from old mountain hermits and outlaw hideouts to eccentric millionaires and adventurous CCC youths. Discover memories and reveries of your own here, too. Linger when you visit, and visit more than once and in different seasons. This is good advice for all the state parks, but especially so for one of the "grand old ladies." *

ROARING RIVER STATE PARK • 12716 FARM ROAD 2239, CASSVILLE

Big Sugar Creek State Park

ENTER INTO A BYGONE OZARK ERA. The uplands are sparsely populated with oaks and hickories. Sunlight trickles down the valleys to meet purple coneflowers amidst green and golden grasses. Dip your hands into a stream alive with spring water seeping from an underground passage, and feel the chill of time immemorial drip from your fingertips. Inhale the rich scent of fallen oak leaves, wildflowers, and mossy limestone. Watch the swooping flight pattern of a resident pileated woodpecker, its wild laugh welcoming you into Big Sugar Creek State Park.

Like the crystals of a geode within an ordinary rock, Big Sugar Creek is a treasure amid far southwest Missouri's remote hills. It boasts a diverse array of living communities, such as cherty woodlands and limestone glades that harbor rare, endangered, and regionally restricted plants and animals that flourish in this distinct Ozark landscape. The rugged hills of McDonald County have also given rise to legends, tall tales, and a fascinating history, with considerable uncertainty as to which is which.

There are stories of Pine Wars, with battles fought over rights to valuable pine timber, and a real war, when Northern and Southern armies marched through the county and no one could be safely neutral. The courthouse was burned by bushwhackers in 1863, and in 1939, many scenes in the famous movie *Jessie James* were filmed nearby because Hollywood executives thought Pineville and the Big Sugar country looked more like 1870s Clay County than Clay County did. There were disputes over land titles and rough justice meted out by "slickers" and vigilantes. A place on the river known as Penitentiary Bend is claimed by some as the site where a sheriff's posse rounded up a band of outlaws; others maintain as stoutly that miserable prisoners from a Civil War skirmish were once confined there. So this fascinating corner of southwest

Far left: In the southwest corner of Missouri, early spring reveals the rugged Elk River Breaks Woodland Natural Area with limestone outcrops, dry cherty slopes, and oaks with scattered shortleaf pine. *Allison Vaughn* • Above: Big Sugar Creek journeys southwest into the distinctive Arkansas River drainage area from the wild and rugged Elk River hills. *Susan Flader* • The roadrunner and other species found here are more commonly seen to the south and west. *El Brujo*

Missouri boasts a cultural history as intriguing as its natural history, but some local legends provoke as many questions as answers.

The idea for the park dates to the 1970s when naturalists and planners analyzed the park system to identify gaps in its representation of the natural and cultural heritage of the state. The Elk River Hills ecoregion in Missouri's far southwestern corner emerged as such a gap. Years later, in southern McDonald County five miles east of Pineville, some land became available along Big Sugar Creek that was the best remaining sizable example of the native landscape in the Elk River Hills. Park officials acquired 717 acres in 1991, and subsequent acquisitions brought the total to 2,047 acres by 1994. In 2000, the multiagency Missouri Natural Areas Committee recognized the significance of the park's remarkable biodiversity by designation of a 1,613-acre portion of the park as the Elk River Breaks Woodland Natural Area. The area includes 345 different species of plants and 134 confirmed species of birds, coupled with the distinctive aquatic fauna of Big Sugar Creek and its tributaries.

The park includes two-and-a-half miles of riverfront, a fine setting for river play and exploration, but unlike most rivers in the Missouri Ozarks that drain north, east, and south to the Missouri, Mississippi, and White Rivers, Big Sugar Creek drains southwest into the Elk River and then on to the great Arkansas River drainage, a distinct and powerful landscape. As a result, this beautiful, clear-water, bedrock stream harbors some aquatic species unique to this area of the state, including the redspot chub, bluntface shiner, cardinal shiner, Neosho midget crayfish, and mucket mussel. Big Sugar Creek itself is a compelling resource, but equally significant is the range of steep hills and rocky hollows that cradle the Big Sugar valley and provide habitat for a rich array of species and communities, including the rare Ozark Chinquapin. A variety of interesting and unusual animals also find refuge within the Big Sugar Hills, including the gray bat, Oklahoma salamander, and pine warbler.

In an effort to restore the integrity of dwindling glade and woodland habitats, park naturalists in the mid-1990s began a prescribed-burn program for the park. By reintroducing fire, which was part of the natural cycle in this area, they encouraged some of the original native vegetation.

Left: Children explore this lone surviving outbuilding of the Shady Grove School and limestone ledges dripping with moisture on a misty day. The building is one of the few remnants of Cyclone, a nineteenth-century hamlet near Big Sugar Creek. *Both Denise H. Vaughn* • Above: This rare Anisota moth, a southern species, is found only in burned landscapes. *Allison Vaughn* • Right: These leaves and burs are from the rare Ozark chinquapin, which still survives at Big Sugar. Naturalists are propagating the trees in the wild so they can reintroduce them to other areas within the tree's range. *Steve Bost*

Unfettered by competition for sunlight, the remaining trees flourished, and grasses and wildflowers appeared once again on the hillsides. The results of this burn program are evident along the Ozark Chinquapin Trail, which in part follows a ridge through native grasses under an open canopy of oaks and shortleaf pines.

The park has been only minimally developed over the last two decades. Future plans include a canoe launch and various facilities for visitors, but the bulk of the park, including the natural area, is proposed as the park system's twelfth wild area. A key feature of the park and wild area is the rugged three-mile Ozark Chinquapin Trail that winds through the Big Sugar hills. The trail gives you a chance to experience this rough terrain as Native Americans and early explorers may have, traversing ancient ridges and valleys through which spring water and rainwater flow in myriad deep hollows to Big Sugar Creek. You might chance upon a whitetail buck along the trail or see a flock of wild turkeys foraging in the woods. Chipmunks scamper through leaves and underbrush to their nests in dead oaks and limestone outcroppings, and armadillos shuffle along, searching for food under the leaves.

This beautiful rugged topography that makes McDonald County such a joy to visit today also somewhat slowed its settlement by pioneers. The uplands, known generally as barrens or flatwoods to the early settlers, were thought to be unfertile and not suited to agriculture, so it was the rich bottomlands along the creeks that attracted the first settlement. On Big Sugar Creek in the vicinity of what would later become the state park, the first land patents were taken out in the 1830s and 1840s. By 1860, there was a low dam across Big Sugar providing water power for a gristmill and later for a sawmill. A small commercial establishment provided store-bought goods for the neighborhood. This little hamlet seems not to have had a formal name until about 1883. In that year of winds and waters, a post office was begun, and even though the village has long since disappeared, this vicinity is still known by that acknowledgment of adverse weather: Cyclone.

Only a few remnants of these earlier times can still be found in the park. A rock outbuilding that served as a woodshed for Shady Grove School still stands at the Ozark Chinquapin trailhead. About a half-mile along the trail, hikers with a keen eye can discern vestiges of the rock foundation of a house. And across the trail from the house foundation is the concrete foundation of a granary. On the whole, though, nature has reclaimed the man-made structures, and the overall sense of this place is wild and natural.

Ancient Ozark chinquapins stand in winter like gaunt statues on spare bony ridges, their remnant twisted branches a testament to hardiness. In the draws, chickadees and nuthatches titter as the tinkling streams wind their way to the big creek, where colorful and unusual fish remind us of Missouri's position as a true crossroads, including links to the great Southwest. Big Sugar is a landscape of rugged beauty and much remaining mystery. It deserves a visit from Missourians curious about the fascinating nooks and crannies of their wonderful state. *

* THE RARE OZARK CHINQUAPIN SURVIVES HERE

In open, rocky terrain, vestiges of the rare Ozark chinquapin survive as scrubby stump sprouts, which may be viewed from the tree's namesake hiking trail. Once revered for its tasty nuts, the Ozark chinquapin succumbed to chestnut blight in the 1950s and 1960s, and it continues to be ravaged by this disease, which inhibits survivors from reaching their normal sixty-foot height. In fact, Big Sugar Creek State Park is one of the relatively few places in Missouri in which this species still survives, and it may provide a seed source for efforts underway to reestablish this charismatic plant throughout its former range. Other rare plants found in the park include Ozark corn salad and climbing milkweed.

BIG SUGAR CREEK STATE PARK • BIG SUGAR CREEK ROAD, PINEVILLE

Nathan Boone Homestead State Historic Site

HE CAME TO THE PRAIRIE not so much by design as by necessity, probably driven as much as drawn. Col. Nathan Boone, soldier, surveyor, explorer, and son of the famous pioneer, was starting over again at the age of fifty-seven. It was his second experience of this sort, having been uprooted from a Kentucky home as a young man when he and his sixteen-year-old bride followed his land-bereft father into Missouri at the turn of the nineteenth century, and now again when he had to sell his handsome stone house and land in St. Charles County and move his family to a hand-hewn log cabin northwest of Springfield. In fact, it is a historical irony that the Boones—several generations of them—probably blazed more new trails, discovered more new caves, springs, and mountains, and walked over more unclaimed land than any other single family in American history, and wound up with very little of it for their trouble.

Col. Daniel Boone—the storied frontiersman and hunter—and his enterprising sons left indelible marks on the history and geography of Missouri. Such places and names as Boonville, Boonesboro, Boone County, the Boone's Lick Trail, and the Boone's Lick Country mark their enterprises and explorations. Prominent among the family's cultural legacies is this frontier homestead near the town of Ash Grove, in Greene County northwest of Springfield, with the log house that was home to Nathan's family for the last nineteen years of his strenuous life. Although never the subject of tall tales and sometimes fanciful biographies like his illustrious father, this son of Daniel Boone rivaled his father in contributing to the development of the American frontier.

Daniel Morgan, the seventh child and third son, and Nathan, the tenth and youngest, helped their parents move to Missouri (then the Spanish colony of Louisiana) in 1799 after Daniel the elder had lost his holdings in Kentucky in a land-title dispute. The Boones had been drawn to Missouri by the promise of grants of land from the Spanish authorities. Daniel was given land in the beautiful Femme Osage valley, and his sons and other relations secured neighboring grants.

The elder Boone's land difficulties surfaced one last time late in his life when the land commission for the newly created Territory of Missouri refused to confirm his claim to the one thousand arpents of real estate given him by the Spanish authorities. It took an act of Congress in 1814 to give Daniel title to his land as an honorarium for the "arduous and useful services" he had rendered to his country. Unfortunately, the good news arrived almost simultaneously with his creditors from earlier land problems in Kentucky, and after the sale of his newly patented property, he was left virtually penniless at the age of eighty.

Thus it was that he lived with one or another of his children. As he felt his days numbered, he last moved in 1820 to Nathan's newly completed three-story stone house on a hill overlooking the Femme Osage and Nathan's Spanish grant lands. It was in this new house that Nathan's famous father died shortly thereafter, a circumstance that has led to it being called the Daniel Boone home. This imposing structure still stands and is now operated by Lindenwood University as a heritage center.

Long before building his new home on the prairie, Nathan had met success as a hunter and trapper—harvesting nine hundred beaver from Ozark streams in a single season in 1803—and then as a manufacturer of salt with his brother Daniel Morgan at the salt springs (now Boone's Lick State Historic Site) in the central Missouri region that bears their name. He was selected by William Clark in 1808 to guide a military expedition to establish Fort Osage on the Missouri River and to help persuade the Osage to come to the fort from their village on the Osage Plains to negotiate a treaty of cession for most of the land that would become Missouri and Arkansas.

When Native American attacks on white settlements were incited by British agents in the War of 1812, President James Madison appointed Nathan as a captain in the US Rangers for the new territory of Missouri. After Nathan's command, along with all mounted troops in the US Army, was disbanded at the end of the war in 1815, he prospered in civilian life as a surveyor and farmer in St. Charles County, built his big stone house, and served as a delegate to the convention in 1820 that drafted Missouri's first constitution.

Nathan and Daniel Morgan were contracted by William Clark to build the Kansas Indian Agency in 1828; then in 1832, Clark hired Nathan again to survey a neutral ground to keep the Sioux apart from the Sac and Fox tribes. But when the Sac and Fox under Chief Black Hawk took arms later that year against a federal order to leave their lands in northern Illinois and Wisconsin, Nathan reentered the US Army as captain of a company of dragoons. He was at this time in midlife, fifty-one years of age, and would remain in the military for the next twenty years, mostly in Indian Territory, helping to make treaties with the tribes of the Great Plains and carving out lands for the resettlement of tribes forced west as

Black-eyed Susan and wild bergamot brighten Nathan Boone's last homestead on the open, rolling Springfield Plain. The little house remains mostly unchanged since it was built in the 1830s on the prairie. ***Both Scott Myers***

THE DOGTROT HOUSE

The hewn log house here, likely built by Nathan Boone's sons and their slaves, was a far less grand accommodation than the one he'd left in St. Charles County. The house is comfortable, but not very large. Architectural historians call this a double-pen log cabin. That is, the rooms are two square log rooms separated by a center hallway, or "dogtrot," the whole covered by one roof. The center passageway originally had open ends like a breezeway when the house was constructed, but later was enclosed. A chimney and a fireplace at each end serve the two rooms. The facade of the house facing the hillside is plain, but the side facing to the southeast, toward the creek and down the valley, has a veranda. The house sits gently on the land, emphasizing the horizontal rather than the vertical as the landscape itself seems to do. The house is sited—as good pioneer houses tended to be—so that it is tucked under the brow of the low rise to the northwest, somewhat protected from the brunt of winter winds.

The house was originally sided with hand-riven walnut clapboards, and these survive intact on the protected wall under the veranda roof. The clapboards remind us once again of the care and importance that in past times were accorded small details, since each is beaded at its bottom edge. That is, a molding plane was applied by hand to every board individually in order to finish its edge with a rounded groove.

The interior of the house is simply two large rooms, each some seventeen feet square, with the hallway between. The degree of survival of the historic fabric on the interior is stunning as you realize the original fireplace mantels, doors, and woodwork trim are in place, and all demonstrate the care and precision of handmade work. The trim boards are beaded, and all of the doors are made of planks with Z-braces. In one corner of the hallway a winding stair leads to a large one-half-story loft above.

Several courses of logs on the walls extend above the loft floor, dividing it into three spaces—perhaps bedrooms—except for one small chamber at the head of the stairs. The purpose of this little eight-foot-square room is uncertain, but its construction is interesting. Its walls are covered with hand-cut walnut boards, and even in the gloomy light of this attic space, you need only run your fingers over the surface to feel rather than see the shallow hills and valleys that proclaim the entire wall has been painstakingly shaped by hand with a smoothing plane.

Olive Boone's loom would have been in the breezeway or the living room of the dogtrot, though it had its own room in the big stone house in St. Charles County. The loom here is from another Boone family line. An heirloom garden reminds visitors that settlers grew most of their own food. *Both Bonnie Roggensees*

Snow covers Olive's and Nathan's graves. The Boones and the people they kept as slaves are buried in separate cemeteries on the property. *Dakota Russell*

a result of President Jackson's removal policy. It was likely while en route to Fort Gibson in present-day Oklahoma that he noted the beautiful ash grove on the rolling prairie northwest of Springfield and encouraged several of his sons to check out the area.

During this time, he was facing what seemed to be a recurrent family nightmare. When a German traveler visited his wife Olive to inquire about buying her appealing limestone house, she told him that Nathan had signed a security for a friend who later absconded, leaving him with a debt of $5,000. Whether to retire the debt, to leave an area rapidly filling with German immigrant settlers, or to locate his family closer to the region of his military service, in 1837 Nathan sold his home and 700-acre farm in the Femme Osage Valley for $6,120 and headed to Ash Grove with his wife, teen-aged daughters, ninety-eight-year-old mother-in-law, and several slaves to start all over again.

The site of the new Boone farm was in a shallow swale formed by an ephemeral tributary of Clear Creek, which runs west to the Sac River a mile and a half away. The landscape, now partially restored to native prairie flora with small limestone glades that harbor thriving populations of the endangered Missouri bladderpod, probably looks today much as it did when Nathan first saw it. Patches of trees stand along the creek, and small woodlands mark the position of the family burial plot and several springs on the property. Prairies like this had remained largely unsettled by pioneers until a fairly late date owing to the common perception that a lack of trees indicated lesser fertility. The difficulty of turning heavy prairie sod also made these lands less attractive until the availability of the steel plow. At the site today, an heirloom garden and orchard demonstrate the transition to agriculture.

Nathan was able to enjoy his new home on the prairie only on sporadic furloughs between his army assignments. Soon he was headquartered for several years at Fort Leavenworth and then again at Fort Gibson, from which he led three companies of dragoons on a seventy-nine-day horseback reconnaissance over the western prairies and up the Arkansas River to provide protection for traders using the Santa Fe Trail. He then led his dragoons on a dangerous mission "to preserve the peace among the Cherokee," who were divided and bitter after suffering thousands of deaths during their forced removal from Georgia to Oklahoma on the Trail of Tears. Preventing outright civil war among the factions may have been the greatest accomplishment of this son of Daniel Boone.

Back at Ash Grove, Olive cared for her aged mother (who lived to 104), her younger daughters, and several orphaned grandchildren while managing the farm and the slaves during Nathan's long absences. Indeed, some state park staff argue that this place should be called the Olive Boone State Historic Site, since she was the one who looked after her extended family of fourteen children, numerous grandchildren, other relatives, and five to fifteen slaves, as well as numerous hogs, cows, sheep, horses, oxen, and several hundred acres of land producing corn, oats, potatoes, and wheat.

Finally in 1848, having recently been promoted to major, Nathan took sick leave and returned to his homestead at Ash Grove. After years of rugged army life on the frontier, the old soldier's health was failing. Still on leave, he was promoted in 1850 to lieutenant colonel but never again served on active duty, and in 1853 at age 72, he resigned his army commission. During his final years, he rode over his farm checking on crops, livestock, and slaves when he was able and enjoyed sitting on the veranda telling stories of his incredible life.

In late 1851, the roving frontier historian Lyman Copeland Draper journeyed to Ash Grove and spent three weeks with Nathan and Olive, interviewing them about the legendary Daniel Boone to get the real story. While recording some three hundred pages of notes, subsequently deposited at the Wisconsin Historical Society, Draper also captured some of Nathan's equally remarkable life and, perhaps even more important, something of the more elusive experience and voice of Olive Boone.

Though feeble with "dropsy"—probably heart failure—for years, Nathan lived to age seventy-five at his final homestead, and then after he died in October 1856, was buried a few hundred yards north of the house. Two years later, he was joined by Olive, once his sixteen-year-old bride. There they still lie, amid some of their children and grandchildren. Nearby is another cemetery with at least eleven graves for slaves or former slaves of the family, a number of whom took the name Boone after they were emancipated at the end of the Civil War and remained on or near the Boone farm.

The luck of Boones with land had never run smoothly, and even this last homestead was entangled in a court fight among Nathan and Olive's children and then left the Boone family entirely in 1897, when it was sold at auction at the courthouse door in Springfield to cover the indebtedness of one of their grandchildren. Perhaps fate finally smiled when on August 15, 1991, the Missouri Department of Natural Resources took title to 370 acres of original Boone land. Only 160 acres, including the house, had been part of Nathan's nearly 1,000 acres, while the remainder, including the cemeteries, were part of his son Howard's adjoining farm. One feels an inner satisfaction in knowing that there now will be a Boone homestead on the map in perpetuity, as if the grateful citizens of their adopted state are holding in trust for this illustrious pioneer family the land that eluded them in their own lifetimes. *

NATHAN BOONE STATE HISTORIC SITE • 7850 NORTH HIGHWAY V, ASH GROVE

Battle of Carthage State Historic Site

In a state with a fairly high percentage of families whose ancestors weathered the Civil War in Missouri and whose descendants still live here, the legacy of that conflict is an ever-present aspect of the family lineage. And for newcomers or even visitors, the lingering perception of those times may still fascinate today.

For thousands of Missourians, the most important Civil War site may be the one closest to where they live or where their own ancestors took a stand—and it is likely unmemorialized if it was not a major battlefield. These sites include skirmishes, guerrilla actions, politically significant places, key garrisons, and important buildings. Nearly twenty years ago, recognizing that it is infeasible and unnecessary for the state to own all these places, park officials embarked on a Civil War marking program, focusing their efforts on sites not already marked by other organizations. Dozens of markers have been erected, and others are planned.

The Battle of Carthage illustrates the problems of preserving and interpreting a site that isn't a concise, well-bounded battlefield. At Carthage on July 5, 1861, the action was fierce, but it lasted less than a day—never more than an hour or so at any one point—and it swept down nine miles of country road leaving no permanent marks. State park authorities felt it was an ideal candidate for a marker, but local interests wanted more. In 1990, legislation established an eight-acre historic site focused on Carter Spring in the city of Carthage in Jasper County where federal and pro-South state forces ended the day's hostilities and where both sides bivouacked on different nights.

But the battle was much bigger than the Battle of Carthage State Historic Site and amorphous as well, as is often the case in the chaos of combat. As a result, the presentation is multifaceted. Park officials have placed an interpretive display at the state-owned spring site, but visitors also will want to see a city-owned Civil War museum near the square and take a self-guided auto tour along Civil War Avenue, driving the nine miles north to other scenes of action at Spring River, Buck Branch, and Dry Fork. Dry Fork, in particular, survives almost unaltered, its farm fields and creek probably looking much as they did on the day of the battle.

What actually happened at Carthage on that long July day in 1861 and why was it important? The battle was one in a series of armed conflicts, beginning at Boonville in June and culminating in September at Lexington, where militia forces sympathetic to the South, organized for the most part as the Missouri State Guard, sought to wrest control of the state from federal forces that included among their number some of the hated Yankees from northern states and the "damned Dutch" (regiments made up of German immigrants) from St. Louis, but also a good many ordinary Missourians who remained loyal to the Union.

The battle at Carthage was hardly earth-shattering; it did not produce a clear victory, nor was it particularly well fought. The inexperience of both sides was revealed, and that is not surprising considering how early in the war the battle took place. Bull Run, often referred to as the first battle of the war, did not occur until two weeks after Carthage.

Before the encounter at Carthage, events were going strongly in favor of the Union. Federal troops had driven Gov. Claiborne Fox Jackson and his pro-Southern forces from the capital at Jefferson City, routed them at Boonville, and sent them fleeing toward the southwestern corner of the state. Now a Union detachment under Col. Franz Sigel, encamped on July 4 at Carter Spring in Carthage, was trying to prevent Jackson from linking up with other Missouri forces and with a Confederate army under Gen. Ben McCulloch in northwest Arkansas. At Dry Fork Creek about nine miles northwest of Carthage, at eight-thirty in the morning on July 5, Sigel's and Jackson's forces met and squared off.

Jackson had about six thousand men, mainly recruits, eager to fight but inexperienced and undisciplined, most armed only with their flintlocks and squirrel rifles and fully a third with no arms at all. Sigel's force

Left: Both federal and state troops, who were in conflict with each other, bivouacked in this meadow by Carter Spring on successive nights, July 4 and 5, 1861. *Bonnie Roggensees* • Nationally known for history paintings, Missouri artist Andy Thomas portrays the federal retreat through Carthage. • Visitors can walk on the bluff above Carter Spring from which Union artillery fired the final battle shots, covering their withdrawal. *Denise H. Vaughn*

was much smaller, numbering about eleven hundred, most of whom were St. Louis Germans, well armed and well drilled. As the firing began, Sigel, noting an attempt by Jackson's superior numbers to encircle him and cut off his supply train, commenced an orderly retreat. Thereupon the action shifted southward several miles to the next creek crossing, over Buck Branch, then another three miles to Spring River, and finally into Carthage, where Sigel's rearguard artillery positioned on the bluffs above Carter Spring continued to cover his withdrawal masterfully.

The battle went down in history as a victory for Governor Jackson's State Guard. Although his ragtag recruits could not defeat the smaller but better trained and equipped enemy, they had their way on the field and proceeded without further hindrance to their rendezvous with Gen. Sterling Price and the rest of the Southern forces. There they would train, organize, and regroup for the coming advance north.

The Battle of Carthage was an important turning point for the cause of the South in Missouri, even if only for a few months. It raised Southern hopes, and the Missouri State Guard gained a momentum that carried it to Lexington, the high water mark of the Confederacy in Missouri.

And only at Carthage did a sitting governor personally and successfully lead state troops against a US army. Carthage made it clear that Union occupation of Missouri would not be uncontested; resistance would be ferocious and unremitting throughout the long war.*

THE CIVIL WAR IN MISSOURI

More Missourians fought in the Civil War, in proportion to the state's population, than was the case in any other state. Some 60 percent of eligible men saw action—at least 50,000 served the Confederacy and 109,000 the Union. More than 8,000 black Missourians enlisted in Missouri regiments, and others enlisted in other states. About 14,000 Missourians gave their lives for the Union, and even more for the Confederacy.

Over 1,100 battles or skirmishes were fought here, a number exceeded only in Virginia and Tennessee. And the vengeful guerrilla warfare here—described by one historian as the "war of ten thousand nasty incidents"—drew virtually every man, woman, and child into the maelstrom.

Of the literally hundreds, perhaps thousands, of sites in Missouri associated with the Civil War, the state park system focuses on six:

- Battle of Carthage, July 1861
- Battle of Athens, August 1861, in far northeast Missouri, possibly the farthest north conflict in the war
- Battle of Lexington, September 1861, which marked the high tide of the Southern cause in the state
- Battle of Island Mound, October 1862, where African American troops for the first time anywhere in the nation experienced Civil War combat
- Battle of Pilot Knob, September 1864, the encounter that doomed Confederate dreams of reclaiming Missouri
- Confederate Memorial, to honor the dead.

Many other Missouri parks have Civil War history: Hunter-Dawson, Jefferson Landing, Bollinger Mill, Roaring River, St. Francois, Mark Twain, and Arrow Rock, to name a few. The National Park Service protects the battlefield at Wilson's Creek as well as Whitehaven, the home of General Ulysses Grant.

BATTLE OF CARTHAGE STATE HISTORIC SITE • CHESTNUT STREET, CARTHAGE

Stockton State Park

SAILING MAY NOT BE the most common water recreation in Missouri, but a sizable group of freshwater sailors pursue the sport here in southwest Missouri at Stockton Lake, an Army Corps of Engineers reservoir. The lake's ultra-clear waters and wooded shorelines lure sailors from Missouri and neighboring states.

Headquarters for most Stockton sailors is Stockton State Park, 2,175 acres of land leased from the corps and developed for recreation by the state of Missouri. The full-service marina welcomes visitors. In addition to the traditional campgrounds and picnic areas, the park also offers a camp store, a restaurant on the dock, and several lodging options ranging from duplexes with kitchens to rustic camper cabins.

Many claim Stockton Lake offers the best sailing in the lower Midwest. The key is the steady southwest breeze off the Springfield Plateau that sweeps over 25,000 acres of open water.

Beyond sailing, the park is popular with recreational boaters and lake fishermen, who enjoy the unspoiled shoreline and elbow-room of the uncrowded lake. Canoeists and kayakers can spend their time paddling the park's seven-mile water trail along the shore of a cliff-lined peninsula, with launch points on either side only a mile apart. The park also offers hiking trails with lake vistas and naturalist-led walks, evening programs, and junior-naturalist activities during summer months.

Stockton State Park is located on a long north-south peninsula that once was known as Umber Point, a prominent ridge dividing the valleys of the Sac and Little Sac Rivers in Cedar County. Sources vary about whether Umber derives from a settler's surname or from the Latin *umbra* or French *ombre*, meaning "shady place." We do know that Cedar County is named for a creek west of the Sac and, in turn, for the eastern red cedar that grows so abundantly all over southwest Missouri. Located in the western Springfield Plateau region of the Ozarks, Cedar County is, in fact, not as shady as some other places, being a transition zone for prairie, savanna, and open woodland.

Extensive archaeology performed in conjunction with the reservoir construction project in the 1960s revealed this area to have a complex prehistory, but one typical of the rest of the Osage River basin. There is evidence of human occupation for at least ten thousand years, with changing ways of life as climate and vegetation changed over time. This was Osage country when French explorers first learned of it in the seventeenth century, but the Cherokee, Chickasaw, and Choctaw from the Southeast moved into the region late in the next century. The area was part of the Osage Cession of 1808, but the first permanent Anglo-American settlements were not established until the 1830s.

The recorded history is meager, but we know that citizens changed the name of the county seat twice, first from Lancaster to Fremont in

Above: The state park marina rents boats of all types for sailing, fishing, cruising, or paddling. Left: Kayakers enjoy the water trail around Umber Point, with its many quiet coves and places for swimming and fishing. *Both Scott Myers* Right: Sailboats brighten the breezy waters at Stockton Lake. *George Denniston*

1847, shortly after the establishment of the county, and then in 1859 from Fremont to Stockton. Captain John C. Fremont and Commodore Robert F. Stockton were both associated with the conquest of California in 1846 and 1847 during the Mexican-American War. Fremont, the son-in-law of Missouri's powerful senator Thomas Hart Benton, was leader of the Bear Flag Revolt to establish a Republic of California, and Stockton was the naval officer who proclaimed California a US territory. The name change to Stockton might have been in protest over Fremont's leadership of anti-slavery forces as the first presidential candidate of the Republican party in 1856. The town was partly burned during the Civil War by Confederate Gen. J. O. Shelby and then later rebuilt.

Apparently, before the turn of the century, a small crossroads settlement named Umber gathered itself into temporary existence on the Umber ridge before fading away after World War II. A few old cemeteries remain on the ridge.

Since the Civil War, the biggest event by far in the county has been the construction of Stockton Lake by the Corps of Engineers. Authorized by the Flood Control Act of 1954 for that purpose and also to provide power, water supply, and recreation, the dam across Sac River was completed in 1972. Since then, the Sac and Little Sac Rivers have formed one of the clearest lakes in the state. Umber Point is now in the state park, and sailboats brighten the breezy waters on sunny summer days. *

STOCKTON STATE PARK • 19100 HIGHWAY 215, DADEVILLE

Pomme de Terre State Park

BEFORE THE FIRST WHITE SETTLERS came to southwest Missouri, wandering French trappers and traders had visited and explored the area's many beautiful rivers, including one they apparently named for a tuberous plant that grew in the vicinity and fed the local American Indians. The plant might have been the widespread groundnut or American potato bean (*Apios americana*) or the now rare prairie turnip (*Pediomelum esculentum*), also known as Indian breadroot or wild potato. Potato in French is *pomme de terre*, which means apple of the earth, and thus a fine western Ozark river was named.

For thousands of years, American Indians lived along the river. They left evidence of their passing not only in the usual middens (refuse from their campsites), but also in some intriguing burial cairns built of stone. The Indians have been gone a long time now, and the few wandering French were replaced in the 1820s and 1830s by aggressive settlers from the hills of Tennessee and Kentucky. An old history book describes them: "Democrats of the Andrew Jackson type—men who partook more of the stern nature of the old hero of New Orleans; resolute, fiery, and unconquerable by nature." Inspired by Jackson's nickname, Old Hickory, these folks named their county Hickory, and they called their county seat Hermitage, after Jackson's beloved Tennessee homestead.

What we find today at Pomme de Terre is not a river but a remarkably attractive, clear lake of some 7,800 acres dating from the 1960s, compliments of the Army Corps of Engineers. The state park at

Pomme de Terre offers a fishing opportunity unique in Missouri. Some time ago, northern muskies were stocked here; these fish, native to the northern Great Lakes region, survived and now provide exotic sport. Some real lunkers have been taken.

"Pommey"—as the locals know it—consists of 735 acres in two separate parcels, one on the Hermitage side, the other on a peninsula accessible from the south, or Pittsburg, side of the lake.

The emphasis at Pomme de Terre is on water recreation, and the park offers a setting of quiet, usually uncrowded, beauty. The two park units are separated by several miles of road and function almost independently. Each has a full set of facilities for visitors. The park has more campsites than any other Missouri state park, over 240. The Pittsburg area also offers an alternate camping experience with its fabric-covered yurts. Part of the reason that camping is popular at Pomme de Terre is the shoreline location that many of the sites enjoy—bacon seems to smell better frying here in the early morning when its aroma mixes with the fog off the lake. Both campgrounds offer nearby beaches and fine swimming.

Pomme de Terre also offers a fishing opportunity unique in Missouri. Some time ago, northern muskies or muskellunge were stocked in this Ozark lake; the species survived and now provides exotic sport for those who seek this large and unusual fish, which is native to the northern Great Lakes region. A number of real lunkers have been taken. A marina consisting of a camper store and grill offers boat, equipment, and slip rentals.

Located in the western Springfield Plateau section of the Ozarks, the land around the lake is rolling rather than mountainous, and the woodlands show the influence of the prairies of the nearby Osage Plains to the west. Today, park staff use prescribed burning to unveil a landscape once dominated by ancient 350-year-old post oaks. The trails and picnic area of the park's south side are an outstanding outdoor classroom where each spring visitors can witness a renewal of this once widespread oak parkland, now replete with wildflowers and rich prairie grasses. There is also a trail to the ridge-top earthen burial mounds and rock cairns of the Native Americans who occupied this area. Excavations of several of the mounds have revealed materials from the Late Woodland period (AD 500 to 1000), while materials in the rock cairns are from the later Mississippian cultural tradition.

All in all, Pomme de Terre, with its evocation of French traders and Native Americans who roamed the prairies and oak woodlands, is a pleasant park that offers an idyllic setting for a family camp-out. *

Water-skiing, fishing, and canoeing are all popular here. A naturalist teaches children about some of the critters they may encounter at a park swimming beach. ***Both George Denniston***

POMME DE TERRE STATE PARK • ROUTE 64B SPUR, PITTSBURG, MISSOURI

Top: Two-hundred-year-old post and chinkapin oaks are in their element with a rich ground cover of prairie grasses and wildflowers. During the 1900s, the ground flora had been smothered by dense vegetation, but prescribed fire has once again opened the landscape. *Allison Vaughn* • "Pommey," as the locals call it, is a favorite park for camping and picnicking near the water. The park has more campsites than any other state park, and most are next to the water. *Scott Myers* Adventurous swimmers jump off cliffs; anyone jumping into unknown waters should always check the depth before jumping in. Marinas and beaches allow visitors to enjoy other kinds of water recreation, too. *George Denniston.*

Harry S Truman State Park

THE VISITOR ARRIVING BY CAR at Harry S Truman State Park meanders for miles along the curvy spine of a narrow ridge. Close to the park, steep valleys alternating on either side of the road provide nickelodeon glimpses of Truman Lake in the distance. A great bend of the Osage River has created a long peninsula so pinched at one point that one can see the lake reaching close through valleys on both sides. Suddenly the park entrance appears, and the landscape opens into upland prairie. One now has a choice, as the road splits to follow two different prongs of the ridge. Along its outer margins, as seen either from a vehicle through winter's leafless woods or from a boat nosing into U-shaped coves, the undulating ridges of the peninsula end abruptly in steep bluffs or sheer cliffs.

The landscape and culture of the upper Osage basin is complex and diverse. The basin lies primarily on the Springfield Plateau of the Ozarks, with some headwaters in the tallgrass prairie country of eastern Kansas and western Missouri. In the vicinity of the dam site, the Osage valley is deeply cut and surrounded by rugged, mostly tree-clad terrain. Glade openings are frequent and help support abundant wildlife.

Early natives probably hunted Ice Age mastodons and ground sloths here. The famed Rodgers rock shelter south of Warsaw, which revealed some ten thousand years of nearly continuous occupation by Native Americans, has water lapping into it at full pool. Subsequent native people, the Osage, gave their name to the river. A powerful and far-ranging tribe, the Osage played a key role in the early fur trade and exploration conducted by Frenchmen such as Charles du Tisné who led an expedition through the area in 1719. American pioneers began permanent settlement in the 1830s.

In the 1840s, a protracted series of fights between outlaws and vigilantes came to be known as the Slicker Wars after the habit of one side to strip and whip, or slick, the bare backs of their captured foes with hickory switches. Although the area was overwhelmingly southern in background, the Civil War brought divisions of allegiance and murderous guerrilla warfare. The town of Osceola, seat of neighboring St. Clair County, was probably most notable in this regard. In 1861 the notorious Kansas jayhawker and later US senator from Kansas, James Lane, descended upon Osceola, plundered everything of value, and then burned the town to the ground. It was in retaliation for this Union atrocity that the far more widely known raid by Missourians on Lawrence, Kansas, took place in 1863. Much of this basin history and prehistory, plus a good deal of Army Corps of Engineers showmanship, is displayed at the corps visitor center perched atop Kaysinger Bluff.

The corps leased the parkland to the state, and the park, which opened in 1983, is well run and highly attractive. The 1,440-acre park consists of a two-lobed peninsula jutting into the central part of the lake close to Truman Dam in Benton County. Park planners took advantage of a superb location and easily controlled access to create one of Missouri's finest reservoir-based state parks. There are abundant, tidy campsites, clean sand beaches, shady picnic areas, convenient boat launches, and a

Left: A shady bluff provides a peaceful view. ***Nick Decker*** **• Above: A wind surfer catches a breeze.** ***Scott Myers*** **• Picnickers enjoy the view.** ***Missouri State Parks***

A lone fisherman enjoys a quiet sunset. Truman Lake offers peaceful solitude, in comparison to its bustling neighbor, the Lake of the Ozarks. *Nick Decker*

THE CONTROVERSIAL DAM AND RESERVOIR

This idyllic park is an outcome of a hotly contested dam and reservoir project in a region of the state no stranger to controversy. The Osage River was dammed for the first time in 1931 by a private utility corporation, Union Electric of St. Louis. The resulting reservoir, Lake of the Ozarks, backs up from Osage Beach more than fifty miles west nearly to Warsaw. Some years later, the Army Corps of Engineers proposed a second dam at Warsaw, and the Flood Control Act of 1954 authorized Kaysinger Bluff Dam and Reservoir as part of a larger scheme for flood control in the Missouri River basin. In 1962 the purposes of hydroelectric power and recreation were added to the project, and construction began in 1964. Along the way the name of the project was changed, perhaps as a public-relations gesture, from Kaysinger Bluff to Harry S Truman Dam and Reservoir.

The project was truly gargantuan. The new reservoir would permanently cover 55,600 acres in four counties, about the size of Lake of the Ozarks, but at full pool it could flood more than 200,000 acres, much of it farmland. The waters would consist of the backed-up flows of several major streams, including the South Grand, the Pomme de Terre, the Sac, and the Osage itself. More than four thousand archaeological sites along the rivers would be submerged, and several thousand families dislocated. The opposition was strong, but belated and ultimately unsuccessful, and in December 1979, Truman Dam generated its first kilowatts of hydroelectric power.

fully equipped marina. Fishing, sailing, and pleasure boating are all popular, and trails wind through the woods and out to rocky overlooks.

Perhaps because of the park's semi-isolated peninsular setting, wildlife is not threatened and allows close observation. It is not uncommon to see deer, wild turkeys, fox squirrels, and cottontail rabbits feeding along the grassy shoreline near the campground beach. In the winter, numerous bald eagles roost on the tall limestone bluffs bordering the lake.

Truman State Park captures the character of both the prairies to the west and the Ozark woodlands to the east. Fires once swept across the Osage Plains from the west, at times likely set deliberately by Native Americans to stimulate ground flora and direct wildlife movements for hunting, with the result that the fires' frequency and intensity inhibited the growth of trees on the plains. But in the deeply dissected hills along the entrenched Osage River and its tributaries where Truman State Park is located, the fires burned with less intensity. North-shaded slopes and steep valleys gentled the fires often enough to allow oaks to flourish in a relatively open setting. By 1980, however, after decades of effective fire suppression, portions of the park had become dominated by red cedar and oak thickets. Beneath these thickets under a blanket of leaf debris, diminutive prairie plants and small clumps of native grasses barely survived, kept alive by their well-developed root systems and just enough light. It was a perfect setting for prescribed fire, which park naturalists began in the early 1980s and still continue.

Today, widely spaced oaks once again shade a mantle of prairie grasses and wildflowers. The brilliant orange beauty known as western wallflower dots the limestone barrens here in May and June. This member of the mustard family and other species such as stickleaf, Missouri spurge, and plains muhly occur in no other state park. Thanks to the fossiliferous limestone and dolomite exposed throughout the area, a dense cover of the small, single-leaved adder's-tongue fern blankets the ground in spring. This tiny fern owes its name to a serpent-like fruiting stalk protruding from its single leaf. When you enter the park, you drive for several miles through a beautifully restored landscape.

It is somehow fitting that this superb park, which anchors the reservoir on the Osage River named for the only president from Missouri, should once again exhibit an oak woodland and prairie landscape like the one here when Osage Indians hunted the area or when Harry Truman was born not far from here. *

HARRY S TRUMAN STATE PARK • 28761 STATE PARK ROAD, WARSAW

Top left: Stickleaf mentzelia from the Great Plains is found here. Top right: Rough-seeded clammyweed is a signature plant of Truman's glades. Above: Prairie and savanna landscapes are being preserved. ***All Allison Vaughn***

OZARK BORDER

> *"Nature has undoubtedly intended this Country to be not onely the most agreeable and pleaseing in the World, but the Richest also.... She has the Richest Lead Mines in the World ... Salt Springs ... Iron Ore.... A Country thus Rich by Nature cannot be otherwise then Wealthey with a moderate shere of Industry."*
>
> —Moses Austin, "A Memorandum of M. Austin's Journey ... to the Lead Mines," (1796-1797)

COMPRISING ABOUT 13 PERCENT OF THE STATE, the Ozark Border natural division is a broad belt to the north and east of the Ozark region. Although geologically part of the Ozark Highland, the characteristic species of the Ozarks grade into those of adjacent natural regions here. This is owing to a complex arc of successively younger geologic formations marking the northeastern rim of the Ozark dome. Located along the lower Missouri and Mississippi Rivers, the region is characterized in part by highly dissected hills with narrow, loess-covered ridges and deep valleys, covered in presettlement times by a mosaic of denser forest areas in valleys, more open woodlands, and some notable prairies and glades. An aerial view of the river hills also reveals narrow, linear bands of sandstone glades that snake along mid-ridge contours, especially along the lower Missouri River. In an arc beginning in St. Louis County near the Meramec River and running southeast to Perryville are prominent dolomite glades, as well as some extensive exposures of Lamotte sandstone.

Culturally, this region experienced millennia of significant occupation by native peoples, who left evidence of their activities in many places. It was among the earliest regions settled—and in places, mined—by the French and old-stock Americans, though they avoided some of the roughest river hills and sought out the valleys and the broader plains more distant from the bigger rivers. After about 1830, significant numbers of Germans settled in the region. The region divides readily into areas drained by the Mississippi and the Missouri Rivers.

We start with the wilds of Hawn State Park, in the area bordering the Mississippi River in the rugged hills of western Ste. Genevieve County. Located east of the Precambrian core of the Ozark dome, Hawn is characterized by picturesque cliffs and ledges carved from the ancient Lamotte sandstone of the Cambrian period, its acidic soils clad in pines and draped with ferns, mosses, orchids, and other unusual plant and animal species. The Pike Run Hills of St. Francois State Park, a refuge for both plants and people, are characteristic of the Ozark Border landscape, with a rich assemblage of plant species on the steep slopes, across glades, and in significant fens along Coonville Creek.

Previous page: Ozark Border streams en route to the Missouri and Mississippi Rivers have carved deep hollows or valleys, as here in the Gans Creek Wild Area at Rock Bridge Memorial State Park. *Randal Clark*

Our next two parks are prominently associated with native peoples. At Mastodon in Jefferson County, human artifacts have been found in direct association with the bones of extinct Ice Age mammals dating from about twelve thousand years ago. At Washington, American Indians of the Mississippian tradition carved birds, animals, and other ceremonial symbols on the surfaces of exposed slabs of dolomite bedrock sometime between AD 1000 and 1600.

Bollinger Mill on the Whitewater River of western Cape Girardeau County, originally constructed by a Swiss-German settler from North Carolina in 1799 and twice rebuilt, illustrates the early and continuing importance of gristmills in rural areas, especially here in the Ozark Border where streams have steeper gradients as they flow off the Ozark Dome to the big rivers. The associated Burfordville Covered Bridge and the Sandy Creek bridge in Jefferson County reflect an important era of nineteenth-century transportation history.

Missouri Mines State Historic Site and St. Joe State Park in the old lead belt in St. Francois County offer opportunities to explore the fascinating mining history of Missouri, from the French enterprises of the eighteenth century to the industrial behemoths of the twentieth, and to ponder the impacts on the economy and the landscape. Missouri Mines, with its dozens of hulking structures, is one of the finest mining museums in the nation, while the 8,000-acre St. Joe, which has long attracted off-road-vehicle users to its mined-out lands, also offers several thousand acres of surprisingly high quality woodlands.

At the northern margin of the region, four state parks anchor the Meramec Greenway (formerly known as the Meramec River Recreation Area), a linear series of open spaces along the Meramec corridor that restores and protects resources and provides public recreation for the St. Louis metropolitan area. Castlewood, long a recreational magnet for St. Louisans in the days of travel by rail, was the initial centerpiece of this ambitious effort and the focus of significant restoration activity. It is still a recreational magnet. Route 66 State Park, located where the historic Mother Road crossed the Meramec River and headed west, came to the park system in 1997 as a remediated Superfund site. In a marked contrast of histories, Don Robinson at his passing in 2012 donated to Missouri State Parks his unspoiled scenic acreage in the LaBarque Creek watershed, which drains to the Meramec just a few miles upstream of Route 66. And some miles farther upstream is Robertsville State Park, purchased in 1979 as part of the state's commitment to the Meramec Recreation Area.

In the portion of the Ozark Border region draining to the Missouri River, we move generally upstream from east to west, beginning in western St. Louis County with Dr. Edmund A. Babler Memorial State Park, an exemplar of highly dissected river hills, luxuriantly forested due to rich loess soils that have developed from windblown deposits of silt. North of the river in Montgomery County is Graham Cave, a commodious rock shelter in a sandstone exposure in the Loutre River valley where ten thousand years of human habitation have been documented archaeologically.

And in Boone County in central Missouri are three quite disparate parks. Rock Bridge Memorial State Park well represents the broken wooded terrain and the sinkholes, caves, and other karst features of the northern Ozark Border. Jewell Cemetery, a peaceful place just off the main north–south road through Columbia, is the burial place of Gov. Charles Hardin and several other prominent leaders and their black servants, all of whom came up the Missouri River to settle in what would become Missouri's Little Dixie region. And Finger Lakes, an old mine just at the northern edge of the Ozark Dome where coal seams in younger Pennsylvanian rock were close enough to the surface to be strip-mined, has been repurposed for motorcycle and all-terrain vehicle recreation as well as for swimming, fishing, canoeing, and kayaking.

Rich in both natural and cultural history, the Ozark Border is near the larger population centers of the state. This ensures that the diverse state parks of this region have a grateful and appreciative constituency, as they well merit. *

Yellow lady's slipper orchids may be found in acid soils on wooded slopes of Hawn and other parks in this natural division. ***Randal Clark***

Hawn State Park

SOME STATE PARKS CAN BE EXPERIENCED by canoe, by motorboat, by car, or by trail bike, but there is only one way to really take in the pleasures of Hawn State Park, and that is by foot. True, the campgrounds and picnic areas, some of the most pleasant in the park system, are accessible by automobile. But to see the bulk of this park and to savor its riches, the visitor must leave the family sedan behind and strike out across the sandy forest floor, strewn with pine needles.

Arriving by car at the northern end of this foot-traveler's park in the rugged hills of western Ste. Genevieve County, you are treated to one of the loveliest vistas in the state. After passing the park office, the entrance road turns south and descends a steep slope to the campground and picnic area located in the valley of Pickle Creek. The rolling forested hills of the eastern Ozark Border provide a wide-angle, windshield-framed spectacle that immediately tells you that this place is something special.

Hawn State Park preserves Missouri's most exemplary concentration of distinctive Lamotte sandstone landscape features. Lamotte is the name of the very old, coarse-grained sandstone formation that overlies the ancient igneous rocks of the Precambrian era. The Lamotte is composed of sands weathered from the Precambrian granites, and its sculpted outcrops provide a contrast to the more usual dolomites and limestones that poke through most of Missouri's landscape. The park's principal streams, Pickle Creek and River aux Vases, have carved steep-sided ravines into the thick beds of the Lamotte, reaching the more erosion-resistant igneous rock in places to create shut-ins.

The unique ability of this sandstone to hold groundwater moisture and to produce acidic soils allows for distinctive flora. The park supports a mixed pine and hardwood forest and a whole assembly of unusual and rare plants. In some places the oak and pine forest gives way to pure stands of mature shortleaf pine—Missouri's only native pine. These stands are among the finest anywhere in the state. Parts of the park have a forest floor literally carpeted with needles over the whitish sands of the Lamotte.

Prior to settlement, the park was covered with enormous pines, some of their trunks measuring four feet thick. Much of the landscape was more open than it is today, mantled in a mosaic of wildflowers and shrubs amid the pines. Visitors can visualize what some of the landscape must have looked like at the open pineries near the picnic shelter, around the amphitheater, and in the extensive grove at Botkin's Pine Woods Natural Area.

The park is beautiful year-round, but especially in the spring. Both dogwood and redbud are plentiful, and they are joined by the fragrant blossoms of the rose azalea, one of Missouri's showiest flowering shrubs. Hawn is the only state park where you can find these azaleas. Along the sandstone bluffs, you may also find the rare eastern clubmoss called ground cedar *(Lycopodium tristachyum)*. In Missouri, it has been found only in Ste. Genevieve County at three sites in and near the park.

In a few remote corners of the park, the erosive action of water on sandstone has produced box canyons that are cooler, damper, and shadier than the surrounding hillsides. These microhabitats provide refuge for plants and animals usually found in more northern states, left behind when the Ice Age glaciers retreated. They have become living museums.

Among the rich plant life are many species of ferns: cinnamon, royal, sensitive, lady, broad beech, bracken, Christmas, common polypody,

Far left: Rose azaleas accent a fern-covered ledge. *Tom Nagle* • Hikers cross the Lamotte sandstone of Pickle Creek in its upper reaches. *Ron Colatskie*

The Lamotte Sandstone Barrens Natural Area features many sandstone glades. *Paul Nelson* • Pickle Creek cascades through shut-ins formed by erosion-resistant Precambrian granite in the Pickle Creek Natural Area. *Ron Colatskie*

bulblet, silvery, ebony, pinnatifid, marginal shield, and common woodfern, narrow-leaved and Scott's spleenwort, and two rare species, hay-scented fern and spinulose shield fern. The beautiful showy orchids and other orchids are abundant; two of them are quite rare—green adder's mouth and rattlesnake plantain. Other relicts include partridgeberry and Canadian white violet.

Even the creeks themselves are special. Pickle Creek provides a distinctive habitat with its clear water, sandy bottom, shaded surface, and lack of much aquatic vegetation. Fish biologists report that the creek supports at least twenty species of fish—various minnows, darters, and shiners—even an occasional smallmouth bass. It has been designated an Outstanding State Resource Water, and nearly sixty acres of its corridor comprise the Pickle Creek Natural Area.

The diversity of the flora and fauna is important, probably more so to the scientist or naturalist than to the average park visitor. But almost everyone will recognize Hawn State Park as a distinctive natural setting. Park visitors will find opportunity for solitude and for primitive recreation. Recognizing the importance of these values, park officials have designated more than half of the park as the Whispering Pines Wild Area.

Hawn State Park is named for Helen Coffer Hawn, a rural Ste. Genevieve County public school teacher who lived with her mother and brother in a rented cottage but dreamed of creating a "little park" for the people of Missouri. Through her will after her death in 1952, she gave nearly 1,500 acres of magnificent wild hills and streams to the state. She had acquired them tract after tract in at least twelve separate purchases between 1932 and 1941 and had hoped to acquire still more that landowners were unwilling to sell, including the impressive columnar Chimney Rocks.

Development at Hawn was held up for more than a decade by the state's inability to acquire the Chimney Rocks, which were thought at the time to be essential for "park appeal." When the area was finally opened to the public, it was called an outdoor recreation area rather than a park, and the Park Board shared its management with the Conservation Department for timber-stand improvement and hunting as well as other recreation. After four years and a number of citizen complaints, the Park Board took over sole management. Thirty additional purchases by the state in the years since Helen Hawn's extraordinary gift have brought the total holdings to almost 5,000 acres, still without the Chimney Rocks. But no one today would think of suggesting that Hawn lacks park appeal.

Motorists rarely discover the park accidentally; it is situated about halfway between Highway 67 and Interstate 55. For years, people learned of Hawn most often by word of mouth, and the visitors singing its praises were interested in less-developed recreational areas and appreciative of its natural amenities. Respecting that tradition and those values, park officials have ex-

ercised great care in developing the park. In addition to adding more acres to protect the watershed of Pickle Creek from encroaching development, they have kept the campground modest, avoided more elaborate accommodations, and limited trail use to pedestrians. Even so, the park attracts more than ninety thousand visitors a year and shows signs of wear, erosion, and loss of natural vegetation in places. You can help by staying on trails, resisting the temptation to climb on moss-and-lichen-covered slopes and ledges.

As park managers and visitors have come to appreciate the extraordinary natural qualities of the park, management goals have centered increasingly on landscape restoration and protection. There are four state-designated natural areas in the park, three of them within the wild area. With a beautiful trail along its length, Pickle Creek is the most readily accessible. Since the diverse flora and fauna of the pine and mixed woodlands on the Lamotte sandstone in this area developed and thrived by adapting to repeated wildfires, which were suppressed for many decades here and throughout the Ozarks, park managers began in 1988 to restore fire by prescribed burns, preceded in places by mechanical thinning of dense vegetation. Since then, they have conducted dozens of such burns in various areas of the park, both within the wild area and on lands more recently acquired, restoring a much more open, diverse understory. Scientists from nearby universities have conducted dozens of research and monitoring projects, many assessing diversity of species and responses to fire, making Hawn one of the most carefully studied of our state parks as well as one of the most beloved.

The 2,880-acre Whispering Pine Wild Area offers more than fifteen miles of interconnected loop trails. ***Ron Colatskie*** **• Prescribed fire has been used here to preserve pine woodlands and sandstone glades.** ***Kevin Sink***

If you hike about a mile south from the campground, the trail leads up a remnant erosional knob of sandstone called Evans Knob. You're only about three hundred feet above Pickle Creek and not that far from the park comfort station, but standing there in that old forest—mostly white oak, shortleaf pine, and scarlet oak with a sprinkling of flowering dogwood and wild blueberry—you feel transported back in time, back to the mid-nineteenth century before this remote, rugged terrain was settled and when the nearest hint of spreading civilization was the old plank road several miles to the north (now Route 32). You are too far away to have heard the wagons hauling pig iron from Iron Mountain to the river at Ste. Genevieve, just as now you cannot hear the automobile traffic speeding between Farmington and Weingarten. Or you may be transported back further, to the days of ox-drawn French *charettes* hauling lead from Mine La Motte—named for Antoine de la Motte Cadillac, the governor of Louisiana who discovered the mine that in turn gave its name to the sandstone so characteristic in the region—or back even further, when Native Americans roamed free and stalked game in the piney woods. That is the magic of Hawn State Park. *

HIKING AT HAWN

Hawn State Park features some of the finest hiking trails anywhere in the state. The Whispering Pines Trail, built and maintained with the cooperation of the Ozark Chapter of the Sierra Club, consists of two loops—one about six miles and the other less than four—and leads south toward the River aux Vases. A shorter trail leads up Pickle Creek from the picnic grounds to the scenic shut-ins. White Oaks Trail connects with both Pickle Creek and Whispering Pines Trails, leading hikers through a diverse mixed hardwood and shortleaf pine woodland. Hikers like the changing landscapes: terraced cliffs covered with ferns and moss, miniature terrarium-like gardens overhanging rock shelves along clear streams, shattered blocks of sandstone and volcanic talus, distant pine-clad hills, and uplands here and there broken by sandstone boulders and exposed slabs of bedrock.

HAWN STATE PARK • 12096 PARK DRIVE, STE. GENEVIEVE

St. Francois State Park

DESCRIBING HIS CIVIL WAR HIDE-OUT in the Pike Run Hills of St. Francois County, Sam Hildebrand in 1870 is reported to have said, "They look like the fragments of a broken up world piled together in dread confusion, and terminating finally in an abrupt bluff on the margin of Big River."

These hills have been a hideout and a refuge for a long time. Ten thousand years ago, as the last ice age ended and the climate moderated, the spring-fed seepages along the narrow, shaded valleys of Pike Run became isolated strongholds for delicate water-loving plants that had perished elsewhere in the warmer and drier Ozarks.

Much later, when Americans began to settle the eastern Ozark Border region, the rough and remote hills surrounding the Pike Run tended to attract people seeking refuge, permanent or temporary, from the outside world. And during the Civil War, these same hills were the favorite refuge for one of Missouri's most notorious Confederate guerrillas.

In 1964, the St. Francois County Court conveyed about 1,350 acres at the heart of this wild and rugged region to the people of Missouri for a state park, following a local drive for funds to purchase the land. This was matched by another 1,050 acres with three miles of frontage along the Big River donated by the St. Joseph Lead Company. In a sense, these valuable gifts ensure that the Pike Run Hills will continue to be a refuge—for the rare and beautiful plants along the streams, for the wild animals of the forests and hills, and for refuge-seeking people. Folks today don't visit here to escape the long arm of the law but rather to find refreshment and renewal amid the beauty of these ancient hills beside the waters of Pike Run, now known as Coonville Creek, and along the banks of the historic Big River.

St. Francois State Park is named for the county in which it is located, not for the ancient mountains just to the south. The park is a superlative example of the intricately dissected topography so characteristic of this part of Missouri, especially along the larger streams. The underlying bedrock has been carved over millennia by water draining to the Big River. The resulting hills and hollows are cloaked in forests and woodlands of oak, hickory, and red cedar, with several glade openings on south-facing slopes.

The soul of this landscape and the setting for its most exciting natural features is the valley of Coonville Creek; an inviting trail leads up the valley. One of the first things that will strike you about this small stream is the clarity of its waters. Another will be the beauty of its musical flow over bedrock ledges, not rushing and turbulent in normal seasons, but gentle and refreshing. Pausing at one of the many pools, you can lose yourself in the aquarium-like world of graceful native fish, aquatic insects, and delicately floating leaves. Over eighteen kinds of fish live here, including the colorful southern redbelly dace, the orangethroat darter, and the nocturnal slender madtom.

Locals knew a stream here as Pike Run, but government mapmakers called it Coonville Creek, probably after the nearby Coonville School. You won't find Pike Run on a map, but it lives on in the local name Pike Run Hills, used for the isolated, rugged, and wild region of which the stream is the heart.

Along the valley, the trail passes a number of small springs and seeps. These cool, dependable waters help account for the steady clear flow of the stream. Around some of the seeps, boggy soils support plant communities called fens. Growing in these fens are botanical rarities such as the grass pink orchid, swamp wood betony, and swamp thistle. The rarest jewel in this valley is the queen of the prairie, with its luxuriant deep green foliage and tall summer-flowering spikes bearing dense clusters of pink blossoms. All of these features render Coonville Creek one of the premier small streams in the Ozarks. It has been designated an Outstanding State Resource Water for its aesthetic and scientific value,

Left: The low rays of the winter sun cast long shadows along Coonville Creek in the rugged Pike Run Hills. ***Ron Colatskie*** **• Above: Flowering bluebells border the Swimming Deer Trail in St. Francois State Park.** ***Scott Myers***

This woodland in Coonville Creek Natural Area invites exploring, and you can hike along scenic Coonville Creek on the Mooner's Hollow Trail. *Jamie Hubert*

and its valley is the Coonville Creek Natural Area. But Coonville wears its titles lightly. It is a friendly stream that will call you again and again to wander in its valley and along its banks.

The same rugged isolation that helps to explain the unique natural character of Coonville Creek also made the Pike Run Hills a hideout for human refugees. The most famous of these by far was the notorious outlaw Sam Hildebrand. Hildebrand came from an established and respected family in the Big River valley—the imposing 1832 Hildebrand home of ashlar stone still stands today very near the park boundary—and as a child Sam roamed all over the Pike Run Hills. When the Civil War broke out, the terrible division of Missouri cleaved right through the Big River neighborhood.

Though sympathizing at first with the Union cause, Sam turned to the Confederacy when Union militia killed three of his noncombatant brothers in cold blood and drove his mother from their family home. He became a bitter rebel bushwhacker who killed for revenge, and he was so deadly that his small band tied down large numbers of Yankee troops all over southeast Missouri. When federal soldiers were hot on his trail, Sam often headed for the Pike Run Hills. The small cave where he reputedly hid is still concealed in the park, high on a bluff above the Big River.

In the early twentieth century, the narrow hollows and coves of these hills proved ideal for the time-honored Ozark custom of making moonshine whiskey. Up one of the side hollows off Coonville Creek, a lovely spring emerges from a shaded, mossy grotto. Moist ledges glisten with ferns and liverworts. Dogwood branches and wild hydrangeas nod overhead, and the gurgle of spring water over shiny pebbles soothes the ear. Perhaps old John Thomas Forshee enjoyed the peaceful quiet of this beautiful spot as much as he appreciated how perfect it was for the moonshine still that he set up there in the 1920s. The "revenuers" eventually caught John Thomas and sent him to prison. But Forshee Spring is still hidden in the hills, and it's as alluring as ever.

The 2,735-acre St. Francois State Park provides an immaculately kept campground and lovely picnic sites, and the Big River provides wading and swimming holes as well as easy canoeing. More than 80 percent of the park has been designated the Coonville Creek Wild Area, accessible via the ten-mile Pike Run Trail. Park visitors can enjoy an outstanding interpretive program and many activities.

Hikers explore the Pike Run Trail. *Scott Myers* • Top right: This fen in the natural area is one of the largest and richest in the park system. *Ken McCarty* • Bottom right: Blazing star graces a glade in the wild area. *Ron Colatskie*

Whether your interest is natural history and you enjoy the unusual local plants, animals, and geology, or your imagination is fired by the lonely vigils of Sam Hildebrand and John Thomas Forshee hiding in these ancient hills, St. Francois State Park is waiting to welcome you and your family to your own refuge, a place of exploration and refreshment. *

ST. FRANCOIS STATE PARK • 8920 US HIGHWAY 67 NORTH, BONNE TERRE

A full-size replica of a mastodon skeleton looms over smaller exhibits in the museum. Mastodon bones and spear points found at the site yielded the first undisputed evidence that humans were here in North America at the same time. Bones from other extinct species also have been found here. *B.H. Rucker*

Mastodon State Historic Site

"BESIDES THE MASTODON'S HEAD, I have found near the same place, several highly interesting remains of antediluvian animals, one of which especially merits attention. It is the head of a nondescript animal, which appears to have been superior in size to the largest elephant, and which resembles somewhat the Mastodon in the hind part of the head, but the front part is entirely different; and until it is recognized or proved to have been previously discovered, I shall name it Koch's Missourium, in honor of the state it is discovered in, and intend, in a very short time to give a minute description to it, as well as of a great many relics not herein mentioned."

This is how self-styled naturalist Albert C. Koch, writing in 1839, described the giant creature he found just south of St. Louis in Jefferson County. He eventually called it Leviathan Missouriensis. Koch was not hindered by a scholar's knowledge of anatomy (or any other science, for that matter). Thus, he was free to fill in gaps in his creature's reassembled skeleton with bones from other animals and other locations.

Koch eventually agreed to sell his collection to the British Museum for several thousand dollars along with an annual stipend. The true scholars at the British Museum were not impressed with Koch's fanciful creations, but they recognized what was clearly a significant collection of Pleistocene animal bones. Koch's Missourium, properly reassembled, turned out to be a mastodon (*Mammut americanum*) after all. It still resides in London, where it has often been on public display at the Natural History Museum.

Koch made his most famous discovery at the base of a limestone bluff near the junction of Rock and Black Creeks, close to the village of Kimmswick and not far from the Mississippi River. Many prehistoric animals traveled to this site, probably attracted by the sulphur springs and salt licks. And many died there, perhaps trapped in the marshy ground.

Over the years following Koch's initial diggings, many would-be paleontologists, and some fast-buck artists, were attracted to the ancient bones at the site. For nearly ten years beginning in 1897, Charles W. Beehler of St. Louis conducted extensive excavations and established a small museum there. During this period, it was not unusual for teams of visiting scientists to make the twenty-two-mile train trip down the Iron Mountain route to view the marvelous fossils. Perhaps to increase interest in this strictly commercial venture, the promoters claimed that human bones and some stone tools had been found in association with the bones of extinct species of animals, but professional scientists remained skeptical owing to inadequate controls and documentation—especially after later examination demonstrated that the purported human bones were not from humans.

From 1940 to 1942, Robert McCormick Adams, a St. Louis archaeologist, conducted scientifically oriented excavations at the Kimmswick site with Works Progress Administration funding. Though he discovered a projectile point from the Early Archaic period—circa 7,000 to 5,000 BC—in undisturbed loess above the bone bed, he did not find any direct evidence for the association of humans with mastodons or other species. Then the discussion rested for a time, though other scientists and untold amateurs continued to pick over the site.

The initial 418 acres of Mastodon State Park, including most of the old bone beds, were acquired in 1966 by the State Highway Department as part of the right-of-way for the new Interstate 55 heading south out of St. Louis. Four years later, after completing the new highway, the department declared the acreage surplus property and made plans to auction it off. Local residents, long proud of the historic significance and scenic beauty of the area, organized the Imperial Improvement Association to try to save the land as a park. The Highway Department was determined to realize a financial return on the tract and would not consider simply transferring the property to another state agency. But they agreed in the fall of 1970 to delay any sale to give county officials time to explore the park option.

A state archaeological survey presented to the State Park Board a month later dashed cold water on the dreams of the local residents. Despite the generous volume of bones retrieved from the site over the previous 140 years, the report expressed doubts concerning the extent of undisturbed Pleistocene deposits remaining. To try to put to rest the putative connection of mastodon bones with human artifacts, the survey report stated, "No cultural material has ever been found at the site to show man's involvement and contemporaneity with these mastodons."

> *Self-styled naturalist Albert C. Koch called his sensational find at what became known as the Kimmswick Bone Bed the Leviathan Missouriensis. He traveled the country displaying his beast and other fossil discoveries with a flair for showmanship that P. T. Barnum would have hailed.*

Local advocates were neither pleased nor deterred by the negative report. One bright spot was a tentative endorsement by Robert McCormick Adams. Although not sure what was left of the bone-bearing deposits, he thought the development of the bone beds as an interpretive area would "keep alive the vast importance of this site to American history."

Local enthusiasm for a park continued unabated, but action lagged. In spring 1974, the Highway Department finally went ahead with its auction, and some St. Louis developers delivered the winning bid of more than $568,000. An explosion of activity ensued, including a lively

A walk through the beautiful woods at Mastodon State Park offers respite from the rapid urbanization of Jefferson County. *Christina Pick*

protest before the highway commission. Four area women—Dorothy Heinze, Marilyn King, Hazel Lee, and Rita Naes—took it upon themselves to form the Mastodon Park Committee to shepherd the project. Within a few months, the women had secured a commitment from the highway commissioners to delay awarding the bid for eighteen months to see if the committee could equal the amount offered. In addition, they secured an agreement by state park officials not only to accept the property as a state park but to request half the purchase price in the form of a grant from the federal Land and Water Conservation Fund.

Holding dances and other events, often with fabulous home-cooked meals, and appealing to all sorts of individuals and organizations, the women of the Mastodon Park Committee started raising money. After three months, they had about $24,000. The 1970 archaeological report still haunted the project; was all this effort justified? One conservation organization solicited for help responded that it was a "quite ordinary and common site" not meriting state park status. And indeed, without continuing archaeological significance, the site was nothing special; it was cut by roads in several directions, had sewer easements on it, was crossed by a large power line, and had been dug over for lime. More recently, it has been surrounded by urban development.

Fortunately, in retrospect, the local park promoters did not listen to all the expert advice they were receiving but kept plugging away. Their ceaseless lobbying of local representatives and other efforts were acknowledged in 1975 when the legislature appropriated $200,000 in state funds toward the purchase. By the deadline, they had raised enough money on their own, including a $28,000 pledge from the McDonnell Douglas Personnel Charity Trust, to meet the bid with funds to spare. The committee presented a check to the state, and Mastodon State Park became a reality in July 1976. It was reclassified in the 1990s as a state historic site.

The successful effort led Gov. Christopher Bond to declare the "campaigning and fund raising for saving of the historical site ... one of the finest projects to celebrate the Bicentennial in the state." But the Mastodon Park Committee did not rest on its laurels; the four women continued to raise money to help in developing the recreational and interpretive resources of the new park, insisting on new archaeological excavations to search especially for evidence of possible human association with the mastodons.

Since leading Missouri archaeologists considered the site too compromised to be worth their time, state park officials contracted for initial reconnaissance with a research team headed by Russell Graham of the Illinois State Museum, much to the consternation of the Mastodon Park Committee. After a century of pilferage, they were reluctant to see any bones leave Missouri, even if only temporarily. But they soon became enamored of the scientists. Almost immediately after beginning work, in May 1979 the Illinois researchers discovered a Clovis spear point, a very

Left: The visitor center displays artifacts from the site, including a mastodon tooth that children may touch. *Christopher Ferree* • Above: Giant ground sloths once roamed the Midwest. *B. H. Rucker* • Top right: A 12,000-year-old Clovis spear point was found in direct association with a mastodon bone. *Missouri State Parks* • Center right: Department of Natural Resources Director Fred Lafser (left), Russell Graham (center), and R. Bruce McMillan examine the site where the point was found in 1979. *K.W. Cole* • Below: A volunteer helps visitors investigate rocks with fossils during a special event. *Missouri State Parks*

ancient and distinctively shaped projectile, in direct association with mastodon bones. Halting all excavation, they put out a call to the dean of Missouri archaeologists, Carl Chapman, and other specialists who raced to the scene along with a gaggle of TV, radio, and newspaper reporters to examine the stunning find.

The discovery at Mastodon State Historic Site is now considered the first undisputed evidence of the association of humans and mastodons in North America. The 1979 excavation and two subsequent ones have yielded two Clovis points, other tools, and waste flakes resulting from the manufacture of chipped stone tools, as well as bones from a species of sloth, a bison, a miniature horse, a wild pig, a stag moose, and a giant armadillo. While no datable organic materials have been recovered, it is believed that the site dates to about twelve thousand years ago, based on the similarity of the points to others recovered in the West. The finds were especially significant at a time when scientists from many disciplines were interested in the phenomenon of widespread extinction of large mammals at the end of the Ice Age and were considering the possibility that early humans may somehow have been involved.

Prodded and aided by the Mastodon Park Committee, park officials built a beautifully designed visitor center at the crest of the hill above the discovery site. Octagonal in shape, the structure leads the visitor back through the epochs of human and natural history in the area, past a life-size replica of a mastodon skeleton, through an exit to a self-guiding trail that wends past the Charles Callison Memorial Bird Sanctuary and down the hill to the excavation site at the base.

What remains of the archaeological deposit is being preserved, and at present, there are no plans for further excavation. Friends of the site would undoubtedly like to see excavations continue—we like to know and accomplish all we can in our own lifetimes—but preserving a portion of exceptionally significant sites such as Mastodon is necessary so that future generations of scientists, armed with technologies we can scarcely imagine, may make yet more stunning discoveries. *

MASTODON STATE HISTORIC SITE • 1050 CHARLES J. BECKER DRIVE, IMPERIAL

Washington State Park

AMERICAN INDIAN ROCK CARVINGS are found in a few other places in the state, including Thousand Hills State Park, but this one park along the Big River in northeastern Washington County contains almost two-thirds of all the petroglyphs discovered in Missouri so far.

The glyphs are carved in horizontal slabs of limestone bedrock ledges in the rocky, barren glades of this Ozark Border park. One large group of about two hundred glyphs is situated precariously close to Highway 21, which probably obliterated some others during its construction. Another group of about forty is east of the park's entrance road at the south end of the visitor center. The third and largest group, numbering some 238,

Washington is the petroglyph park, with three different groups containing almost five hundred carvings depicting animals, thunderbirds, humans, turkey tracks, snakes, arrows, and more.

occurs on ledges overlooking Maddin Creek. The glyphs depict animals, birds—including dozens of thunderbirds—turkey tracks, snakes, human figures, footprints, hands, phallic and vulvar motifs, arrows, maces, cups, houses, geometric shapes, and other abstract symbols.

The carvings have been known since the first lead miners and farmers arrived in the area. Two groupings have been protected in the park since the first tract was donated to the state in 1932 by A. P. Greensfelder, a civic-minded St. Louis engineer and planner, and the third grouping, known as the Creswell grouping, was added in a combination purchase and donation from John and Mildred Graff of Boulder, Colorado, in 1990.

The petroglyphs have been analyzed by numerous archaeologists over the years, yet they remain something of a mystery. Although there is abundant evidence of peoples from the Woodland and even earlier traditions in the area, archaeologists believe the thunderbirds and other ceremonial symbols are the work of people of the Middle Mississippian culture during the period between AD 1000 and 1600. They seem to have been related in some way to the great center of Mississippian culture at Cahokia, Illinois, across the river at St. Louis, and to many other Mississippian settlements, such as those at Towosahgy and Lilburn in the Mississippi Lowlands. The Big River is the only other river in Missouri with large Mississippian villages along its length.

Archaeologists speculate that these villages in the "old lead belt" along Big River may have been part of a trade network for galena crystals, which have been found in Mississippian sites throughout the central part of the country. But because of key differences between Big River and Mississippian sites, some scholars believe that what we see at Big River is evidence not of the migration of peoples but of the diffusion of Mississippian ideas into an indigenous Woodland culture.

Whatever the connections with more distant areas, the petroglyph complexes at Washington State Park were almost certainly major ceremonial sites. Young men may have been initiated into secret societies here, the glyphs serving as memory aids for the complex sequences of songs and rites that were part of the ceremonies and the directional arrows perhaps pointing the way through the maze. Ceremonies may

Above: Blue-eyed Mary and wild sweet William flourish on the rich soils of moist forests in the Washington Upland Hardwoods Natural Area. ***Ron Colatskie***

American Indians of the Mississippian cultural tradition carved hundreds of symbols, including thunderbirds, snakes, animal tracks, and more in the ancient limestone bedrock of Washington State Park. *Missouri State Parks, Glenn Curcio (top right), and Renee Bronaugh (left)*

Big River flows sometimes languidly but elsewhere speedily through riffles along Washington State Park's eastern and northern borders. *Missouri State Parks*

Glade coneflowers flourish on one of the park's many glades. *Ron Colatskie*

also have related to fertility of humans and harvests, such as the Green Corn ceremony with its rich oral tradition, carried into historic times by the Osage and eastern tribes related to Missouri. There is much we do not know about the petroglyphs here, but we can feel their power and sense that this place was sacred.

The petroglyphs are not the only examples of masterful craftsmanship in stone at Washington State Park. Not long after the land was donated to the state for a park, an all African American company of the Civilian Conservation Corps (CCC) set up camp and began to develop the rugged tract along Big River for recreational use. Inspired by the petroglyphs in the park, the members of the company named their barracks area Camp Thunderbird and titled their camp newspaper the *Thunderbird Rumblings*. Between 1934 and 1939, these young men, aged eighteen to twenty-five, built many rustic stone structures that blend well with both the rock carvings and the natural rock outcroppings in the park. Among the truly notable features in this park is a lodge, now a park store, constructed of rough random-cut ashlar stone, with a thunderbird symbol carved in the stone facing at the gable end and repeated in interior details such as the handmade iron door hinges. The park also boasts handsome rental cabins, an octagonal lookout shelter of random-cut native limestone, open on all sides to views of the campground, bluffs, and Big River, another shelter of native stone resembling a natural outcropping of rock, set into a hillside and offering a spectacular view of the river valley, and a 1,000-step trail winding up the hill behind the shelter. The highly ambitious, labor-intensive construction of these structures blends beautifully into the natural park environment.

The African Americans in Company 1743 of the CCC were known for their high morale and consistently hard work, and they won an outstanding reputation. All of their work within the original 1932 boundaries of the park, including fourteen buildings and extensive stone roadside work, is now recognized as the Washington State Park Historic District on the National Register of Historic Places. But racial prejudice was never far from the surface in the 1930s. When the company completed its work at Washington and was transferred to Mark Twain State Park in northeastern Missouri, citizens in some nearby communities protested the stationing of black Americans in the park. But other citizens, both near

Mark Twain and in lead belt towns such as DeSoto, Cadet, and Blackwell, countered with petitions of support for the black workers on the grounds that the company's work and conduct at Washington were exemplary.

The landscape now at Washington State Park is not entirely the same as that which greeted the American Indian rock carvers or perhaps even the black stonemasons. The bluffs and rocky outcrops are still there, of course, but the hills have become much more densely forested so that the vistas are not as open. Here is how the naturalist Henry Rowe Schoolcraft described the country when he traveled in the vicinity of Potosi in 1818 and 1819: "The growth of prairie grass in the open post-oak woods and prairies is of the most luxuriant kind.... The barrens are also covered with a profusion of wild fruits ... and wild flowers." He also noted that the "growth of grass in the woods affords ample range for cattle and horses, and they are kept constantly fat."

Place names like Old Mines, Cannon Mines, Baryties, and Mineral Fork remind us that this was mining country. The French mined lead seasonally in this area in the eighteenth century, their shallow "diggings" dotting the landscape. In the early nineteenth century, they were joined by Anglo-Americans following the lead of Moses Austin, who introduced more efficient smelting methods.

In 2001, the state acquired the ruins of a rare lead-smelting furnace located on a tract of land at the west end of the park. Built in 1838, the furnace is of the "Scotch hearth" variety, of which only a few have survived, and it represents an important improvement in smelting technology. In conjunction with the twentieth-century equipment and exhibits at Missouri Mines State Historic Site some twenty miles south, this furnace further illustrates the history of lead mining in Missouri.

With permanent settlement around the turn of the nineteenth century, the vegetation began to change. Miners greatly increased production, requiring ever more wood to fuel their furnaces, while farmers brought with them cattle, goats, horses, and hogs to feed on the lush grasses. More than a century of lead mining and open-range grazing wiped out most of the original woodlands, grasslands, and wildflowers. Subsequently, without thick ground cover and fire to suppress them, growths of eastern red cedar, sugar maple, and oaks formed dense thickets.

In some of the prominent rocky glades scattered along the park's hillsides, naturalists found remnants of the once dominant cover of prairie grasses and wildflowers. In the late 1980s they began preliminary clearing of invading cedars on the glade located near the petroglyph parking area. Although at first the glade appeared ragged, persistence in continued brush removal and several prescribed burns paid off. In the spring of 1991 the glade erupted in a grand floral display, as if the wildflowers were rejoicing in their release from woody bondage. Such restoration has continued on this and other glades in the park and also in the woodlands where deeper soils allow the stately post, chinkapin, and white oaks to thrive. One of the park's best and most accessible examples is the open woodland north of the park road between the visitor center and the road to the petroglyph shelter, where wild bergamot, goldenrod, and a variety of asters create a colorful mosaic beneath the oaks.

Among the many flowering species are some found in few other parks, including the thick-leaved Fremont's leather flower, the delicate blue-violet nemastylis or celestial lily, and a rare primrose, *Oenothera triloba*. The animal life of the glades is unusual, too, with the top of the food chain represented by the coachwhip snake and the swift eastern collared lizard. The collared lizard has long been a favorite of visitors; it folds its front legs up against its chest like a little tyrannosaurus and sails along on hind legs, jumping over rocks in its path. But by the early 2000s, it was nearly extirpated from the park, a victim of poachers collecting specimens illegally for the pet trade, though it does not survive well in artificial settings. Through public education, protection, and habitat restoration, park staff hope to create conditions that will allow its recovery.

Celandine poppies grace the 1000 Steps Trail, which was painstakingly laid by the Civilian Conservation Corps. ***Ron Mulliken***

Washington Upland Hardwoods Natural Area lies along the limestone bluffs and talus slopes that face the Big River and offers a strong contrast to the drier woodlands and glades typical of most of the park. This rich, north-facing slope has produced a mature stand of hardwoods with a luxuriant ground cover of ferns and wildflowers. Tall specimens—up to a hundred feet—of elm, bur oak, sugar maple, basswood, and Kentucky coffee tree are common. Mid-story trees include pawpaw, Ohio buckeye, and American bladdernut.

In spring, this area hosts the park system's showiest display of woodland wildflowers. Everywhere, just before the leaves unfold on the trees, is a carpet of green interspersed with blue-eyed Marys, purple trilliums, smooth yellow violets, candle anemones, wild ginger, and bright yellow celandine poppies, among dozens of other species. The best way to view this area is to walk the trail—part of the thousand steps so carefully laid by the CCC stonemasons—down from the picnic shelter to the Thunderbird Lodge. Part way down the hillside, you will encounter the old stone CCC shelter house, where a breathtaking view of the river valley below lies just beyond the parapet wall.

At 2,158-acre Washington State Park, the landscape that inspired Native American rock carvers, African American stonemasons, and the naturalist Henry Rowe Schoolcraft still works its magic. *

WASHINGTON STATE PARK • 13041 HIGHWAY 104, DE SOTO

Bollinger Mill State Historic Site

THERE IS SOMETHING CAPTIVATING about covered bridges and old gristmills; they hark back to what we think of as simpler times—before automobiles, before electricity, when roads and bridges were designed for slower, horse-powered vehicles and when running water was the usual power source for local commerce.

In western Cape Girardeau County, two of these historic features have survived side by side in a classic picturesque setting. The Burfordville Covered Bridge, completed around 1868 after nearly ten years of delays brought about by the Civil War, spans the Whitewater River just upstream from the four-story Bollinger Mill, built at the same time on the foundation of a much older structure.

Despite the name, there is no white water to be found on this river on its forty-mile run through Perry and Bollinger Counties to the mill in Cape Girardeau County. Sixteen miles farther downstream, a diversion channel intercepts the river and takes its water directly east to the Mississippi, part of the public works system designed to drain the Missouri Bootheel for agriculture. But the area was still wilderness in the 1790s when a twenty-five-year-old Americanized German named George Frederick Bollinger arrived.

German and Swiss families from North Carolina established here what may have been the first German Reformed Church in Missouri. They became the nucleus of a prosperous farming community known as the Whitewater Dutch.

Surviving nineteenth-century mills and covered bridges are rare, and even rarer side by side. *Jim Diaz* • The original buhrstones imported from France are still at the mill. The upper stone, shown here turned upside down for sharpening, would be flipped over onto the lower stone behind it for use. *Denise H. Vaughn*

Bollinger received a Spanish land grant from the commandant at Cape Girardeau on condition that the land be developed and settled. He built the first mill and dam of logs at the turn of the nineteenth century, and he also brought twenty German and Swiss families from his home state of North Carolina to the new settlement along with German-speaking slaves of their households. These settlers were known as the Whitewater Dutch, and they have descendants who remain in the area. Settlers living on the St. Francis and Black Rivers up to a hundred miles away are said to have brought their corn and wheat to Bollinger's mill, the largest in the area.

Bollinger went on to serve as both an officer in the War of 1812 and as a statesman. He was elected to all four territorial assemblies and, after statehood, served in the Missouri senate, rising to president pro tem.

By 1825 Bollinger had replaced the original mill and dam with a much more substantial timber-framed structure upon a limestone foundation. More locally quarried stone was used for the dam that impounded water for the wheel used to generate power. After Bollinger died in 1842, his family continued to operate the mill for two more decades. At the beginning of the Civil War, one of his Confederate grandsons was involved in an attack on a wagon traveling by the mill. The wagon was part of a column of federal troops headed toward the county seat at Jackson. Union forces retaliated and burned the mill in September 1861. Only the masonry foundation survived.

In 1865, Solomon R. Burford purchased the property from Sarah, the original Bollinger's daughter. Two years later, Burford rebuilt the mill with brick on the old limestone foundation, and this is the structure that visitors enjoy touring today. The adjacent settlement, which became known as Burfordville, had a post office, several stores, a blacksmith shop, a

Above: In the attic of the mill, the belt elevators, enclosed in wooden boxing, reach the top, dump their grain, and make a U-turn to start back down empty. Right: Visitors can inspect this Leffel turbine, which is like the one submerged in the river that ran the mill and still turns the stones today to grind cornmeal. *Both Denise H. Vaughn* • Far right: The Howe truss design seen clearly here is used by three of Missouri's four remaining covered bridges. Patented by William Howe in 1849, the truss derived its strength from massive diagonal wooden compression members, made mainly of yellow poplar, used with vertical iron rods in tension. *Martin Turner*

two-room school, several churches, and of course, the mill.

The 140-foot-long Burfordville Bridge was originally built by Joseph Lansmon, who was commissioned by the Cape Girardeau McAdamized Road Company to construct the private toll bridge for travelers on the road between Cape Girardeau and Greenville. He used the Howe truss design, in which diagonal wooden compression members (mainly yellow poplar) are used with vertical iron rods in tension to form trusses. Tolls were charged until 1906 when local farmers, tired of waiting for the court to abolish tolls, broke down the gates and used the road and bridge without paying. The state highway commission rehabilitated the bridge in 1950, adding a corrugated metal roof, later restored to wood shingles.

The adjacent mill continued in commercial use until about 1948, operated by the Cape County Milling Company. A descendant of Bollinger, Julia Vandivort, and her husband, Clyde, purchased the mill in 1953, and in 1961, their son Paul gave it to the Cape Girardeau County Historical Society, which in 1967 donated the twenty-one-acre historic site to the state. That was the same year the Missouri legislature authorized the state park agency to maintain Missouri's remaining wooden covered bridges as historic sites. With later additions, including the Bollinger family cemetery, the park is now about forty-four acres.

Bollinger Mill is an impressive structure rising four stories above the Whitewater River. Part of the river was diverted through the old lime-

stone-block catacombs beneath the mill where the turbines provided power for the mill. All grain entering the mill was moved to the top floor by elevators, which were moving belts with small metal cups attached. From the top of the mill, grain was gravity-fed downward through the milling processes—cleaning, grinding, sifting—on lower floors. Finally, after passing through the buhrstones on the second floor, the freshly ground grain dropped into wooden bins on the first floor.

Exhibits on the second floor interpret almost two centuries of milling on the banks of the Whitewater River—a history that parallels the industrialization of milling. The upper floors of the mill contain examples of machines, some salvaged from other mills in Missouri and the Midwest, that performed the various steps in the milling of grain. This collection of roller mills, sifters, separators, bran dusters, and other devices is representative of a major evolution in the milling process that contributed to the decline of thousands of small rural mills and the growth of large milling centers in Minneapolis, St. Louis, and Kansas City. The capacities of these large merchant mills provided enough surplus to export around the world.

The old buhrstones and one of the turbines found in the mill were expertly restored by English millwright Derek Ogden and are used today to demonstrate the nineteenth-century process of making stone-ground cornmeal. The "run" of stones, originally imported from France, consists of two stones, each forty-two inches in diameter, placed one over the other. Corn is fed into the center of the upper "runner" stone and is ground between it and the lower "bed" stone as the runner stone turns. A pattern of shallow grooves cut in the facing surface of each stone creates a shearing action as the grooves cross each other. These same grooves move the meal outward from the center, and it is collected around the outer edge of the stones as it exits from the slight gap between them.

There are other fascinating features too. Leaving the mill, you notice a different kind of signature. To the left of the main door, carved in the limestone, are the initials SRB—left by Solomon Richard Burford.

Bollinger Mill and Burfordville Covered Bridge provide the visitor with a step back in time to experience the sounds of grist milling, the smell of freshly ground cornmeal, a stroll through the oldest covered bridge in Missouri, and a peaceful rest along a tree-lined stream. *

BOLLINGER MILL STATE HISTORIC SITE • 113 BOLLINGER MILL ROAD, BURFORDVILLE

Sandy Creek Covered Bridge State Historic Site

MOTORISTS HEADING SOUTH FROM ST. LOUIS toward Hillsboro may not realize when they cross Sandy Creek on State Route 21 that located just a short distance downstream is one of Missouri's last remaining covered bridges. Once fairly numerous, the covered bridges still standing numbered only eleven by 1942. The decline continued until 1967, when the Missouri legislature authorized the state park system to preserve the four remaining structures. Sandy Creek Covered Bridge, originally built in 1872, still carried traffic until 1984.

The bridge was constructed of white pine by John Hathaway Morse for $2,000. The 76-foot-long structure followed the Howe truss design and reportedly could handle up to seventy tons. Fourteen years after it opened, it was destroyed during spring floods. But Henry Steffin was able to salvage about half the original timbers and rebuild the bridge for only $889.

After another flood in 1940, the wooden piers were replaced with concrete supports. And once again in 1952, the bridge was renovated, this time by the Jefferson County Chamber of Commerce, who protected it with a corrugated metal roof and placed a historical marker on it. Following restoration by the park division in 1984, the barn-red bridge now has a wood shingle roof as it did originally.

Sandy Creek takes its name from the St. Peter sandstone exposed along the south-facing slopes of a long ridge south of the creek, known locally as Sandy Ridge or Sand Ridge.

The bridge is located on the old Hillsboro-Lemay Ferry Road. Before bridges, ferries were often used in Missouri, especially on the larger streams, and some of the first bridges were often built by ferrymen as toll bridges. Although guidelines for bridge construction were included in many of the early road laws, bridge building didn't really catch on until the state's first public bridge code was established in 1825. The code required that any structure costing more than $25 be built by the county court. By the mid-1840s, most of the state had caught bridge-building fever. The first covered bridge was reportedly a span built by Travis Burroughs in 1851 across Perche Creek in Boone County on a road that followed the old Boone's Lick Trail.

Although several structural designs were popular, by far the most successful was the Howe truss, which is represented in three of the four covered bridges still standing in Missouri—Burfordville at Bollinger Mill in Cape Girardeau County, Locust Creek in Linn County, and Sandy Creek. The design was patented in 1840 by William Howe, whose nephew Elias made substantial advances to the sewing machine with his 1845 model.

The essential feature of the Howe truss was its use of metal verticals functioning as tension members and wooden diagonals functioning as compression members. With the iron truss rods, Howe

The covered bridge provides a bright focal point against the snow or, in the summer, the deeply shaded picnic area. *Ron Colatskie* • Glade coneflowers and coreopsis adorn a glade on nearby Fort Hill. *Missouri State Parks*

truss bridges are often considered to be transitional from wood to iron. But covered bridges were practical as well as quaint; the addition of roof and sides served to protect the structural timbers from the elements.

The Sandy Creek site includes about two hundred acres of undeveloped land adjoining the bridge. Sandstone outcroppings have formed glades and rocky barrens with characteristic dryland flora and fauna. Part of the site runs about a mile south of the creek to a local prominence called Fort Hill. The conical little hill crowned by an escarpment displays a small prairie glade typical of the kind found in this eastern Ozark Border region of Washington and Jefferson Counties. In early May, the glade on Fort Hill is given to displays of purple and gold: on close inspection, the purple really comes from the pale violet petals of the glade coneflower and from the lavender bells of Fremont's leather flower, while the gold turns out to be sand tickseed.

No formal trail system leads into the Fort Hill area of the site, but visitors are encouraged to explore it on short hikes of their own. With a lunch in the creek-side picnic area, a stroll through the old bridge, and a hike into the woods, this small historic site can provide all the requirements for whiling away a lazy afternoon. *

SANDY CREEK COVERED BRIDGE STATE HISTORIC SITE • OLD LEMAY FERRY ROAD, GOLDMAN

Missouri Mines State Historic Site

MISSOURI'S EARLIEST EXPLORATION and development were fueled by two commercial enterprises. The first of these, the fur trade, is widely known and acknowledged. Many Americans seem to be at least generally familiar with the romantic saga of the traders and their adventures in penetrating the region's rivers and hills, dealing with the natives, and competing for territory and trading grounds. Less familiar is the story of the other great thrust of European enterprise on the Missouri frontier: mining. The passion to find and retrieve Missouri's underground wealth, especially lead and iron ore, was every bit as responsible as the fur trade for the region's exploration, and it was a greater factor in its settlement, beginning with the French in the eighteenth century.

The story of mining in Missouri rings with courage, innovation, and achievement, as well as with a measure of greed, exploitation, and abuse. We have here an epic tale of a process that fundamentally shaped the state: Missouri was the world's largest lead producer for a time. This important story needs to be told, and Missouri Mines State Historic Site is dedicated to that mission.

Federal Mill No. 3 in Flat River (now Park Hills) was built by the Federal Lead Company in 1907, at a time when fifteen different mining companies operated in the so-called "old lead belt" of southeastern Missouri. Surrounded by communities with names like Leadwood, Rivermines, and Leadington, this large industrial complex in St. Francois County processed the rich ores mined in the region. In 1923 the facility was purchased by the St. Joseph Lead Company, which had been active in the area since 1864, and it grew to become a major lead-concentrating complex with more than thirty significant buildings and structures and large equipment spread over twenty-five acres. It was the largest plant of its type in the world, the hub of an enterprise with one thousand miles of multilevel mine tunnels and three hundred miles of underground mainline railroad track connecting the various shafts and mills. The company bought out all of its competition by 1933 and was the sole employer for thousands of mine workers in the region.

From 1907 when the Federal Mill opened to the present, Missouri has been the largest producer of lead in the United States, most of the time accounting for more than 80 percent of US production. At one time, Missouri was the largest lead producer in the world. China has surpassed all other countries in recent decades.

From its inception, St. Joseph Lead Company has been involved in many aspects of the communities in which it has operated, from water supply and fire control to education, public health, parks, and community celebrations. Its many workers in the lead belt and their families have generally appreciated this engagement—earning the firm a reputation as "the venerable St. Joe," or in local parlance, "Uncle Joe."

Around the middle of the twentieth century after more than two hundred years of productivity, the local veins began to play out, and St. Joe discovered and developed a "new lead belt" some thirty-five miles to the west and south around the tiny hamlet of Viburnum. The functions of the Federal Mill facility dwindled, and in 1972 operations ceased. However, just about the same time, St. Joe's Viburnum Trend made Missouri the largest lead producer in the world.

In 1975 the expanded St. Joe Minerals Corporation offered the entire Federal Mill complex, along with over eight thousand acres of land, to the state of Missouri for recreational purposes. For several years, the state wrestled with the problem of how to convert this huge acreage, part of which was covered with the unsightly remains of mining operations, into a public park. With proper facilities and management, much of the acreage offered a range of outdoor recreation possibilities. An obvious focus

was on an already established pattern of use by off-road recreational vehicles on the most altered lands, especially the broad expanses of sandy tailings, which are a by-product of ore processing. As plans proceeded to develop the park for these and other uses, the question still remained of what to do with the huge and now derelict industrial facility at the

The maze of buildings and other structures at Federal Mill No. 3 comprises one of the most extraordinary mining museums in the United States. It's located in the "old lead belt," a legendary mining region in the United States. ***Ron Colatskie***

Federal Mill complex on the north end of the property.

Some park professionals and many locals dreamed of a mining museum, and indeed, before St. Joe pulled out, it allowed park staff to select any items they wished to keep for a museum—locomotives and ore cars, diggers, mechanized shovels, and drills. But the mill complex was still a headache—an invitation to vandalism and injury. The many run-down buildings were ugly to some and incredibly expensive either to renovate or remove. Over time, park officials began to appreciate that this industrial complex, with its large number of mining-related buildings, its many gigantic implements of industrial technology, and its location in the heart of one of the most legendary mining regions in the United States, ought to be retained in its entirety and developed to tell the story of mining in Missouri. What had been perceived by some as an awkward liability began to be transformed into an exciting resource and an interpretive opportunity perhaps unrivaled anywhere in the country.

Once this fundamental direction was set, a long process of research and evaluation followed. Park staff discovered that the Federal Mill complex was even richer in potential than they had dreamed. At the same time, making these valuable resources meaningful and accessible to visitors would require a significant investment of funds. The very scale of the artifacts and historic structures rendered the resource extremely difficult to work with.

Fortunately, enthusiasm for the project swelled within the park system and also among many local community leaders and state legislators. St. Joe and the state mining industry council took an interest, donating funds to assist development. Now, Missouri Mines State Historic Site is on its way to becoming one of the most important interpretive centers for industrial mining technology and architecture in the United States. A tremendous amount of work remains to be done, but the potential has been revealed. And visitors are in for a real treat.

Driving down the entrance road from Route 32 in Park Hills, one is immediately struck by the immensity of the mill complex sprawling in the valley, with its powerhouse, headframe, crushers, foundry, machine shop, and all the other buildings used for crushing, grinding, and concentrating the ore and for maintaining the widespread operations. Entry for visitors today is through the gatehouse area, just as it was for thousands of mill workers for more than half a century. In the mill yard are the aging buildings and all the apparatus overhead, quiet now, but still showing the signs of former enterprise. In the powerhouse is an extensive museum of Missouri mining geology, history, and equipment. Site staff and, on some occasions, former miners explain things to visiting families, schools, churches, bus tours, and other groups. Plans exist to renovate some of the more significant structures to give a sense of the milling process, and other plans are in place for more historical exhibits.

The story at Missouri Mines focuses, of course, on the long-enduring boom of the old lead belt that the mill so dramatically portrays. As funds become available, the museum is intended to include the whole story of mineral wealth and its development in the state. It begins with basic geology, which the unparalleled rock and mineral collection in the powerhouse helps to illustrate. Missouri's underground resources include not only lead and iron, but also copper, silver, barite, zinc, granite, limestone, and coal. Clay, sand, and gravel are also highly important and valuable mineral resources. Human use of these resources began with American Indians, who quarried flint and mined richly hued ores to make paints.

The French developed the first lead mines in eastern Missouri in the early 1700s, and Anglo-Americans joined with enthusiasm by 1800, using Moses Austin's technological innovations. He first made his mark—

Top: Housings that once contained conveyor belts form geometric patterns. *Oliver Schuchard* • The Powerhouse Museum displays massive equipment such as this St. Joe shovel. The mechanical loader on tracks was designed for conditions here but has been used in mines worldwide. *Missouri State Parks* Right: Mill buildings and machinery that once processed most of the world's lead ore now stand silent. *Oliver Schuchard*

and then went bankrupt—in the Missouri lead region before securing a Spanish charter in 1821 for a colony in Texas. After the Civil War, the rowdy, western-style boomtowns of far-southwest Missouri exploited lead and zinc in the Tri-State District at the junction of Missouri, Oklahoma, and Kansas, but the old lead belt continued to produce as well.

The mining districts of the state influenced immigration patterns, encouraging people from the mining cultures of Wales and central Europe to settle in Missouri. Newly discovered resources of barite in southeastern Missouri and coal in the northern and western parts of the state began to be exploited. The importance of all this activity was reflected in the establishment of three institutions at Rolla: the Missouri Geological Survey in 1853; the School of Mines in 1870, now known as the Missouri University of Science and Technology; and the US Bureau of Geology and Mines in 1889. Successors of these institutions still remain in Rolla today.

Missouri Mines has the potential to be one of the best museums of mining and minerals in the country. With its extraordinary physical plant and mineral collections, it already is, in many respects. Mining has been from the beginning an integral part of the state's heritage, intimately related to its settlement, development, economy, and environment. Missouri Mines State Historic Site tells the exciting story of that epic saga, amid the hulking structures and machinery that were so much a part of it. *

MISSOURI MINES STATE HISTORIC SITE • 4000 STATE HIGHWAY 32, PARK HILLS

St. Joe State Park

IN 1972, WHEN THE ST. JOE MINERALS CORPORATION shut down its great lead-processing mill at Flat River, having largely exhausted nearby ore deposits, the future of the mined-out area had been forecast by popular usage. Aficionados of the new and versatile off-road vehicles (ORVs)—dune buggies, all-terrain vehicles (ATVs), and motorcycles—found a challenging playground in the abandoned piles of mine waste, or chat, and hundreds of acres of tailings that formed a desert-like surface when pumped in behind a dam. Why not, company officials asked themselves, donate the whole area to the state for a park?

Mining and the disposal of spoils had transformed about 1,200 acres lying south of the great mill in St. Francois County. But flanking the mined land on the east, west, and south, the company owned more than 7,000 additional acres, largely second-growth Ozark woodland but mostly natural, nevertheless. At its southern tip, the property even included a short reach of the St. Francis River in its scenic valley. Encouraged by the Missouri Department of Natural Resources, the company offered the whole tract to the state, including the deteriorating but still impressive Federal Mill, now Missouri Mines State Historic Site. Gov. Christopher Bond announced acceptance of the gift in December 1975; the deed of transfer was recorded in September 1976.

Thus, Missouri acquired a highly diverse recreational area accommodating many different uses. Shortly after the transfer, the Southeast Missouri Regional Planning and Economic Development Commission at Perryville secured funding to study the economic, social, and physical impact of the new park and to develop a master plan for it. In the commission's March 1979 report, the planners predicted the park could expect "nearly 500,000 visitors each year when fully developed." St. Joe reached a high of 855,362 visitors in 2006 and regularly welcomes more than 600,000 a year. A third of the visitors come from out of state.

ORV enthusiasts, well over half of them in family groups, make up most of the visitors and probably always will, as this is one of the few parks that allows them. Another state park also acquired in the mid-1970s welcomes them: Finger Lakes, in an old coal-mining area north of Columbia. Motorcycles and other ORVs had once ranged through many of the parks, causing numerous complaints, but the General Assembly effectively excluded them in 1971 when it passed a law restricting all motor vehicles to park roads and to a maximum speed of twenty miles per hour. The provision of two parks for ORVs helped win public acceptance of the new restrictions.

The 2,000-acre ORV riding area at St. Joe is made up of about 800 acres of tailings sand flats and 1,200 acres of wooded slopes. Trails in the area have been created by riders, although wider vehicles such as dune buggies and four-wheelers are instructed to stay out of the wooded areas. With the help of dedicated volunteers, the wooded trails and perimeter gates have been mapped and posted with signs. Grants for recreational trails have also been used by volunteer groups, including Friends of St. Joe State Park and Missouri Dirt Riders, and park staff to improve and maintain trails and develop other amenities, such as a children's riding area, an ORV education website, and a concession building. ORV users have a designated campground with direct access to the riding area.

Four small clear-water lakes—Jo Lee, Pim, Monsanto, and Apollo—were formed in the upper arms of Shaw Branch behind the tailings deposits pumped into the arms of the little valley. All are popular with anglers, yielding the typical pond species: black bass, crappie, bluegill, and channel catfish. Monsanto and Pim lakes have excellent swimming beaches, their sandy bottoms sloping gradually into deeper water. Monsanto, at twenty-five acres the largest lake, has an Americans with Disabilities Act-accessible fishing dock and trail for bank fishing. There are also several picnic areas with playgrounds for children.

Left: Off-road riders from across the Midwest come to enjoy many miles of hilly, wooded trails that encircle the tailings sand flats. *Missouri State Parks* • Above: Significant stands of shortleaf pine here are among the park system's best examples of botanically diverse native Missouri pine woodlands. *Allison Vaughn*

St. Joe has become one of the premier off-road vehicle areas in the Midwest and is Missouri's fourth largest state park, now 8,243 acres. The park also accommodates hiking, biking, horseback riding, camping, bird-watching, and nature study.

Eleven miles of paved bicycle and hiking trails encircle the ORV area, created on the abandoned beds of logging roads and a railroad used by the mining company to haul raw ore from the producing mines to the processing mill. Approximately six miles of spurs lead to Missouri Mines State Historic Site, the Pim day-use area, and to Farmington. Several other hiking, biking, and equestrian trails totaling more than seventeen miles traverse the rugged oak and hickory woods in the western and southern portions of the park. Mountain biking is growing in popularity, and cycling clubs in nearby lead-belt cities and from as far away as

Above: The ruggedness of St. Joe State Park's extensive acreage, with its mosaic of shortleaf pine and oak woodlands, is accentuated by a mantle of snow. ***Ron Colatskie*** **• Right: An eleven-mile paved bicycling and hiking trail, with nearly four miles accessible to wheelchairs, encircles the park. Four small lakes formed behind the tailings deposited in the upper arms of Shaw Branch are excellent for fishing, swimming, and wildlife viewing.** ***Both Scott Myers***

St. Louis schedule events here. Equestrians have a specially equipped campground and staging area at the southern end of the park. Also in the south end is a flying field for radio-controlled devices.

A number of special events, generally hosted by user groups, are held at St. Joe annually, including several national motorized competitions that draw ORV riders from across the nation. There are also various mountain biking and equestrian events, and of course, the usual hiking, birding, and wildflower group activities.

Scientific advancement in the twentieth century identified the dangers of exposure to lead; as a result, lead testing, including air monitoring, has been ongoing throughout the park's history. Between public health concerns and a tenuously constructed dam, St. Joe could have been the site of more than a few catastrophes. Fortunately, the problems have been remedied in time, and the park is now safer than ever and, perhaps, more beautiful too.

For more than a hundred years, this "old lead belt" area of Missouri provided the nation with the majority of its lead needs. Miners extracted the rocks in which galena was embedded and hauled them to the surface for processing. At the mill, the ore was crushed to a fine grit. It was then mixed with water and chemicals to separate the galena from the rest of the material. After the galena concentrate was dried, it was hauled to a smelting plant elsewhere and heated, burning off the sulfur and leaving pure lead. The waste material left behind at the mill, known to the miners as slime, was ready for disposal.

In those simpler times, it was just piped as a slurry into the four upstream arms of the nearby valley of Shaw Branch, which had been blocked with a rubble rock dam. The water from the slurry drained through the dam, leaving the tailings behind. In time, after about sixty years, the mining and milling activity completely filled the valley with 1,200 surface acres of tailings, 800 behind the dam, in some places a hundred feet deep, and another 400 acres downstream from the dam.

The dam had been cobbled together over the decades by adding material as needed at the top. A 1992 Army Corps of Engineers study of mine dams in the Big River basin found that only one of forty-five dams was safe and twenty-seven dams were high-hazard, of which the dam in St. Joe State Park posed perhaps the greatest danger of catastrophic failure and would be the most expensive to renovate, at an estimated $14 million. Fortunately, the study recommended federal help through Superfund, the federal program enacted in 1980 for cleaning up hazard-

At this family-friendly park, these tailings flats are a favorite place for kids to ride their motor bikes and all-terrain vehicles. *Martin Turner*

ous wastes, and in 1997 the dam was stabilized.

But the 1,200 acres of tailings still required remediation. The work began in the 1990s with removal of chat from campsite pads and playground areas and replacement with rock or mulch. In 2005 the beaches at Pim and Monsanto lakes were covered with clean sand, and grassy areas and concrete walkways were built, in each case with work done cooperatively by park crews and the Doe Run Company, successor to St. Joe as the result of a 1986 merger. Finally in 2011, the Environmental Protection Agency approved funding for a $7 million tailings cleanup plan submitted on behalf of Doe Run and the Missouri Department of Natural Resources. The plan provided for covering tailings with rock on certain slopes and in drainages, establishing vegetation on the flats, and surfacing the ORV trails with clean material.

During the same decades that the lead tailings remediation was occurring, the natural history values of this diverse park increasingly attracted the attention of park naturalists, who in 1992 began restoring several thousand acres of woodlands with many glades and occasional prairie openings on the broadest of the high flat ridges. Glades with their distinctive communities of grasses and wildflowers can be found on rocky sunny slopes, mostly on the west side of the park. Naturalists have learned that significant stands of native shortleaf pine and oak woodlands in the eastern and southern parts of the park are the most botanically diverse of any in the park system. A single one-fourth of a square meter plot in this area holds the park system record for the largest number of different plant species in a single monitoring plot: thirty-six.

On the western side, the Harris Branch watershed, which is almost completely contained within the park, is considered to be a significant potential natural area. It has a healthy colony of colorful dark-sided salamanders and glades with large populations of prairie iris. The park also harbors a breeding population of the eastern wood peewee, and its entire vicinity has been designated an Important Bird Area. The challenge for the future will be to prevent erosion, trampling, and encroachment by ORVs, horses, and invasive species, while park stewardship crews continue their efforts to reintroduce fire and restore the richness, diversity, and beauty of this large, contiguous expanse of surprisingly diverse Ozark woodland.

The remarkable range in outdoor recreation and natural and cultural resources makes St. Joe State Park a destination for people throughout the Midwest. From its not-so-propitious beginnings as a mined-out expanse, the park has developed into a safe, enjoyable haven for family recreation and an Ozark Border landscape of memorable beauty and interest. *

ST. JOE STATE PARK • 2800 PIMVILLE ROAD, PARK HILLS

Castlewood State Park

IMAGINE YOURSELF BACK ON THE FOURTH OF JULY, 1922. Your family has planned a weekend vacation to a river resort not far from St. Louis. Early on Saturday morning, you arrive at the Missouri-Pacific station in Webster Groves where you load your supplies onto one of the special resort trains. Another car will carry the family canoe. After a short ride, the train unloads its reveling vacationers—up to ten thousand a weekend—at the several small resort depots along the Meramec River in western St. Louis County.

Your family gets off at Castlewood Depot at the grand staircase that leads up to the big hotel and clubs; you are staying at the Castlewood. As soon as everyone is settled in, you all change into bathing suits and hurry back down the staircase to the bottom of the palisade bluffs, where you take a ferry across the river to the large sandbar downstream known as Lincoln Beach. The Meramec River is dotted with floating swimmers and canoes; the beach is covered with sunbathers and kids building sandcastles.

You have just imagined the reality from 1915 to about 1940, when St. Louisans by the thousands flocked to the Castlewood area for weekends of canoeing, swimming, dancing, partying, and some gambling.

Views are magnificent from the limestone glades and the bluffs known as the "castle fortress," which likely gave one resort and thus the park its name. The park anchored the recovery of the lower Meramec River. ***Both Scott Myers***

After World War II, many of the hotels and clubhouses declined, and the natural beauty and recreational value of the lower Meramec River went unappreciated as the area became a kind of industrial dumping ground.

Today, after decades of effort by citizens and government alike, much of the dormant potential of the river has been rediscovered. In 1975 Gov. Christopher Bond announced a plan to coordinate the recovery of more than a hundred miles of the lower Meramec River and formally designated it as the Meramec River Recreation Area (now known as the Meramec Greenway in its lower reaches). The centerpiece of this effort was and is Castlewood State Park. The park includes much of the old resort area, including Lincoln Beach and the site of the old Lincoln Lodge. The park also offers more than thirty miles of hiking and biking trails, eleven of which are open to horseback riders.

A hike along the River Scene Trail leads one atop the white cherty limestone bluffs—the "castle fortress," maybe the origin of the park's name—where a truly majestic view awaits. Look south across the river's floodplain into the wooded alcoves of Tyson Valley, upstream as the bluffs arc to the southwest or downstream as far as Fenton—a scenic panorama lies in every direction as the Meramec meanders in great loops, back and forth, across its valley.

Across the river some 250 feet below—now grown up in willows—is the old Lincoln Beach, a sandy byproduct of the Union Sand and Gravel Company's gravel-mining activity in the river upstream. Mounds of gravel and some remaining equipment, hidden by the bottomland forest, bear witness to the Meramec's contribution to Missouri's leading mineral industry—the Meramec alone has been the source of nearly a quarter of the gravel mined in the state.

Cottonwoods and also the uncommon green hawthorn grow along the river's bank. Unfortunately, so does the prolific bush honeysuckle, public enemy number one in many parks in the St. Louis region and across the state. An invasive exotic species from Asia once planted by suburbanites for its form and attractive bright red berries, it has spread rapidly and competes with our native flora, often leaving the forest floor barren of other plant life. At Castlewood, park staff and volunteers have begun to confront the invasion with brute force. Armed with brush saws, loppers, and herbicide, they have begun to chip away at the green invader. Where bush honeysuckle is removed, the native flora eagerly returns, reclaiming the natural character of these Ozark Border forests and woodlands.

On the south side of the river near the old community site of Morschels is a stand of native bottomland forest. Most such stands were long ago

Volunteers plant native bottomland trees in a bend of Kiefer Creek to help restore an eroding bank and to demonstrate conversion to native species. *Lorin Crandall*

cleared away for agriculture or industry, but here at Castlewood, the visitor can still experience the feel of a mature floodplain forest with its silver maple, box elder, black willow, white ash, sycamore, huge cottonwood, slippery elm, and hackberry. By contrast, as you enter the park via Ries Road from the north, a beautiful drive along Kiefer Creek's canyon-like descent, you pass through the more typical upland forest of the eastern Ozark Border, dominated by white oak, northern red oak, and shagbark hickory. If it is spring, the drive will be highlighted by the floral displays of the redbud and dogwood. The road descends these dissected hills and arrives in the park as the canyon widens into a relatively flat valley.

Castlewood State Park incorporates old resort areas and remnants of the grand staircase and is a vital park, being both alongside the Meramec River and near an expanding metropolitan area. It encompasses 1,800 acres in different sections on both sides of the river and stretches for nearly five miles.

But not all has been well with sparkling little Kiefer Creek, so inviting for play on a hot summer day. It is downstream from an area of rapid urbanization along and south of Manchester Road that causes intense storm-water runoff. That and leaks from antiquated septic systems of clubhouses, since converted to year-round homes, can result in bacteria levels in the creek during high flows that exceed safe levels for swimming. Missouri Coalition for the Environment staff discovered that data collected by the US Geological Survey showing extremely high bacteria concentrations in the creek had not been used to evaluate water quality in the park—because the data had been collected just upstream from the park on a stream segment that had never been classified by the state. This proved to be a particularly egregious instance of a larger problem of unclassified streams on which the coalition had been working for years. Thus was born the Kiefer Creek Watershed Restoration Project.

Funded by a series of grants from various sources beginning in 2010 and involving multiple public and private partners, an expanding group of coalition staff, interns, and stakeholders developed a watershed plan, which included land stewardship and riparian restoration projects. Volunteers from the coalition, St. Louis Audubon Society, Master Naturalist chapters, and corporate partners began to remove invasive species, restore riparian vegetation, and monitor bird and animal populations in the park, as well as work with upstream landowners.

In comparison with nearby watersheds where urbanization had occurred earlier and problems were far more advanced, there was hope for Kiefer Creek, which turned out to be one of the few remaining watersheds in the St. Louis region that was still functioning with a semblance of normality. If the group could reach local decision-makers and citizens with a case for smarter development policies and funds for watershed improvements, might they yet be able to arrest the degradation and improve the watershed and the park? It seemed worth a try, and the coalition and its partners began the task, committed to carrying on into the future.

It is the valley of Kiefer Creek within the park that was the section first opened to the public and is still today the heart of the park. It was once part of a large estate assembled by David Ranken from a sprawling collection of private parcels adjacent to the hotels, clubhouses, and boathouses of the Castlewood development. The Ranken holdings had more than once fueled state park speculations—beginning in the 1930s when the Lake Meramec Association proposed a dam near the river's mouth to create a twenty-mile-long lake for urban recreation. None of the proposals came to fruition, and the area continued to decline.

Finally in 1973, when parcels from the estate were offered for sale, a new citizen conservation group, the Open Space Council of St. Louis, recognized the possibility of creatively combining funding from various sources for a park. Through a large bequest to its foundation, the council

Top: Thirty miles of trails invite all kinds of recreation. *Both Missouri State Parks* Kiefer Creek is a magnet for children on a hot summer day. *Scott Myers* • You can still find remnants of the old staircases that connected resort lodging with the old Castlewood depot and Meramec beaches. *Missouri State Parks*

was able to help the state acquire two of the tracts—nearly 1,100 acres—for more than $1.3 million, half of which came from the federal Land and Water Conservation Fund. The land was transferred to the state in 1974, and during the next decade, ten additional tracts were added to the park through the continued efforts of the Open Space Council and the park division. The council also organized an annual Operation Clean Stream, continued now for more than four decades, to engage hundreds of volunteers each August in removing tires, refrigerators, industrial castoffs, and flood debris from the banks and bed of the river.

The success story at Castlewood and the vision of a Meramec Greenway prompted the addition to the Meramec corridor of other open-space lands acquired by the state and by counties, municipalities, and private institutions. More than 50,000 acres of such lands have been protected along the Meramec, including Robertsville, Route 66, and Don Robinson State Parks. Though progress slowed in the 1980s with the decrease in federal matching funds for recreation lands, a citizen initiative in 2000 for a one-tenth percent sales tax for the even larger vision of a Great Rivers Greenway, of which the Meramec is a part, breathed new life into the effort. Approval by voters in 2013 of another initiative to increase the tax an additional three-sixteenths percent gives hope of even more progress, especially when coupled with the remarkable volunteer efforts the river and its parks have inspired.

The dream of a greenbelt along more than a hundred miles of the lower Meramec with both public and private recreation facilities and interconnecting trail systems still lives and thrives. And Castlewood State Park is still the anchor of the effort. *

CASTLEWOOD STATE PARK • 1401 KIEFER CREEK ROAD, BALLWIN

Route 66 State Park

NO OTHER UNIT of the Missouri state park system has had so strange a genesis as Route 66 State Park. Once a natural and beautiful stretch of Meramec River frontage, curving in a gentle, mile-long arc with scenic bluffs lining the other side of the stream, it grew into a town, stimulated by a newspaper publicity stunt, and later was numbered among the nation's most seriously contaminated Superfund sites, requiring massive cleanup by the Environmental Protection Agency (EPA). Against all odds, it wound up reverting to nature once again as one of the most popular parks in St. Louis County.

Today, the ash mounds that resulted from the incineration of the dioxin-contaminated soil have settled and compacted to such an extent that they barely register as mounds, and the joggers, dog-walkers, and cyclists on the road passing by the big field scarcely give a thought as to how this corduroy landscape came into being.

So do the ruins of the town or the magnitude of the environmental disaster overwhelm the park visitor? Not at all. What meets the eye is a pleasant vista of mixed woods and open fields, with park-like amenities and pleasant walking paths along the river and amid the trees and fields. Only occasionally does something strike the eye, something not quite right about the woods. For example, a long, straight corridor leading to the river is filled with young trees or sometimes only tall grass, with larger trees all along the sides; one realizes this must have once been a street. The small trees are more recent, having grown since the town was abandoned, while the large ones were individual yard trees, much older and larger, that once shaded houses. Park planners have cleverly worked with the town grid, and the new park plan of trails and roads, parking areas, picnic shelters, and open clearings for special events has taken advantage of the landscape as it was already subdivided, with features in places that lent themselves to recreation. Eventually, this townscape will evolve into a natural landscape, just as old farm fields revert to nature at other state parks.

Alongside one straight run of park road is a peculiar earthen structure, twelve or fifteen feet high and thirty feet wide, grass covered, and stretching a quarter-mile along the road. It is an interesting landscape feature, mimicking an Etruscan tumulus or a Native American burial mound, since it contains all that remains of the city of Times Beach, mashed, compacted, and safely interred. It is ironically known as the town mound, a gift for future archaeologists. In the meantime, vent pipes at either end carry away any methane gas the debris might generate.

How did it happen that over 2,200 people once called this place home?

On the morning of July 25, 1925, the *St. Louis Times* hit the streets with a screamer topping the front page: "Greatest Subscription Offer Ever Made." With purchase of a six-month subscription to the paper, the buyer could also purchase a 20-by-100-foot building lot for only $67.50 ($10 down, $2.50 monthly) in the "new summer resort devel-

The Route 66 bridge over the Meramec River was an engineering marvel in its day, but today, park lovers fight for its survival. In the water beneath the bridge, pier supports from the 1900-era bridge are still visible. *Scott Myers* • Cattails line a former borrow pit, where topsoil was removed to cover the incinerated remains of Times Beach. *Lauren Stroer* • These bicyclists were photographed from the now grass-covered town mound. *Missouri State Parks*

oped by the *St. Louis Times* for its readers." The paper explained that all lots, wherever located, would be sold at the same price, and all would have equal rights to the beach, a riverfront park, and membership in a community lodge. The *Times* had platted the development so that there were some thirteen streets laid out in arcs paralleling the river. Across these arced streets at right angles ran a half-dozen principal streets that radiated out like spokes from a common area near Eureka. The result was a town shaped like a slice of pie but with a subdivided grid that looked on paper somewhat like one fourth of a spider web, containing nearly one hundred blocks and more than a thousand lots.

At first, the owners of the new lots built mainly fishing shacks and small cabins, often on stilts in case of floods. As time went by and major floods didn't come, more substantial dwellings began to appear, houses for year-round residents, not just summer places. In 1933 one of the principal radial streets became the corridor through town for the newly designated Highway 66, headed for Los Angeles. The town continued to grow, the landscape to harden, and by the 1970 census, there were several hundred houses, two trailer courts, and over two thousand residents—although no paved streets. In 1972 and 1973, the city arranged to have the streets sprayed with waste oil, so that dust from the gravel streets and dirt lanes would not annoy the residents.

Then calamity struck, or to borrow the phrase from "The Raven," by Edgar Allen Poe, "unmerciful disaster followed fast and followed faster." Ten inches of rain in four days created a massive flood in 1982, huge beyond any previous expectation, inundating the entire town from one end to the other. The December crest of twenty-four feet above flood stage on the Meramec has never been equaled, before or since. At nearly the same time, suspicions long held by the EPA were confirmed: the waste oil sprayed on the streets ten years earlier had been contaminated with potentially deadly amounts of dioxin. Residents received letters from the Centers for Disease Control: if they were still in town, leave; if they were out of town because of the flood, do not return. This was the deathblow to the little settlement begun in 1925. Eventually the town board voted for disincorporation, and the EPA announced a $33 million buyout of the entire town. Times Beach would be no more.

But then what?

Officials determined that the best method for disposal of dioxin and dioxin-contaminated soil and other material was high temperature incineration. At extreme temperatures, dioxin, an organic compound, simply decomposes into its constituent elements and a harmless residue of ash. Because of the huge volume of earth to be burned, the EPA contracted to have a high temperature incinerator constructed on-site. Fed into a rotating kiln, the contaminated earth slowly progressed from one end of the kiln to the other, enduring an hour at 1,250 degrees Fahrenheit. At the far end, it emerged into a secondary combustion chamber

A Route 66 special edition motorcycle and a Phillips 66 sign are displayed in the 1935 roadhouse that is now the park's visitor center. ***Don Fink*** **• Domestic daylilies abound in the woods and will last a century or two. Archaeologists use them as a marker to find old house sites. Top Right: A trail follows the straight line of a former road through a pleasant meadow.** ***Both Lauren Stroer***

where it received a final blast of 1,750 degree heat before any remaining gases and ash were finally quenched in a water bath. The resulting ash sludge was then entombed in three mounds covered with earth and grass, each nearly a quarter-mile long.

Other nearby farms and subdivisions had also pursued the same dust-settling waste oil treatment in the 1970s, but on a smaller scale than Times Beach. Rather than dismantling and re-erecting the kiln repeatedly, the EPA determined instead to haul the contaminated earth from these sites to the kiln at Times Beach for incineration. Altogether, dioxin-contaminated earth from twenty-seven different sites was incinerated at Times Beach, a total of 265,000 tons at a cost of $110 million, one of the most expensive Superfund projects in America at that time.

By 1997 testing showed that there was no longer any dioxin contamination, and the cleaned-up real estate was deeded to the state of Missouri for a state park that same year. Trying to turn a corner from less happy times, the park was named in homage to the era when "the Beach" was linked to a proud national phenomenon—Route 66, America's great Mother Road. Nearly a half-mile of the original highway remains in the park. There are also 418 acres of fields and woods, youngish woods to be sure, but attractive and pleasant for strolling the unnaturally straight byways that crisscross the park.

Some 200,000 visitors per year use the park, and they are a little different crowd than one finds in many more rural state parks. The park's status as a day-use area is obvious—people aren't as settled in or relaxed as they are when visiting a park for a few days or a week of camping. At Route 66, the visitors seem busy: walking, pushing strollers, walking the dog, jogging, running, or biking. These are mostly city people, here for an hour or two for exercise or some fresh air, for a quick stretch of the legs and a bit of blue sky. Then it's back into the car and off to town again. Nonetheless, the deer and turkeys that have taken up residence seem unconcerned with the intensity of the visitors, and the birds and other small wildlife seem to move at their usual pace. The river itself suggests more leisurely activity, with a walking trail along its gently curving bank and a ramp access for launching boats.

The town and the park have always been about the road and the river. First the town and then later the park were established where the road crossed the river on its way from St. Louis to Eureka. From the earliest days, there was always a route out of the city to the southwest, and a steel truss bridge with oak floor planks crossed the Meramec here in 1900. Today when the river is low, you can see the remains of several piers of that bridge, lying low in the water. But when this southwestern road out of the city was designated for the routing of Highway 66, a new bridge was needed, one capable of carrying the heavy traffic loads of the modern highway that was coming. In 1932 a new bridge was completed: a riveted, Warren deck truss bridge, a type wherein the truss structure of

the bridge was beneath the roadway, rather than above it.

Not long after the bridge had been completed in 1935, an establishment was built at the east end of the bridge that is still in use, now serving as the park's headquarters and visitor center. It was built as the Bridgehead Inn but probably achieved its most lasting fame as Steiny's, a classic roadhouse of the 1940s. During the dioxin crisis, it served as headquarters for the EPA and the contractor's staff. Long before it became part of the state park, the building already had been heavily remodeled, and today, its vinyl siding and pop-in windows are rather incongruous with the style of the architecture. Nonetheless, visitors enjoy the gallery inside, where many interesting exhibits and artifacts of Route 66's heyday, as well as materials explaining the dioxin problem and its remedy, are on display.

The new bridge carried the highway over the river for three decades or so, until the coming of Interstate 44, which bypassed the town one lane at a time and crossed the Meramec just downstream a few hundred yards. After that, the old bridge continued to serve the town, and then just the park until 2009 when it was entered into the National Register of Historic Places. Ironically, it was condemned that same year, because of advanced deterioration. Highway engineers had determined that the old truss system beneath the road deck was too weak to any longer support traffic. The bridge was still property of the Missouri Department of Transportation (MODOT) but was no longer part of the highway system, hence the determination that it be demolished. However, because the bridge played such a vital role in the park operation, connecting segments of the park on either side of the river, and is also an important link in the Meramec Greenway Trail, being the only place the trail can cross the river, MODOT offered a deal: the bridge and some of the $600,000 set aside for its demolition could be given to any entity capable of taking responsibility for it and raising the millions of dollars for repairs. In hopes that some group or agency would step forward, MODOT used some of the $600,000 to remove the heavy bridge deck, lightening the load on the truss structure to avoid possible collapse in the meantime.

Thus, we leave Route 66 State Park at a juncture, a crossroads so to speak. The old bridge looks forlorn, with no roadway over it, its rusty steel trusses open to the weather, an airy lacework hanging between the sky and the river. The park is split in half, with no direct connection between the visitor center headquarters on one side and the acreage of woods and fields on the other, and the park system has no money to repair the bridge. Visitors wanting to enjoy both halves of the park must venture out onto several miles of busy Interstate 44, using two different exits a couple of miles apart, one exit for the visitor center and a different one for the recreation area. It is inefficient and inconvenient for both park staff and visitors and an obstacle for the Meramec Greenway Trail. Yet, where can the millions of dollars be found that are needed to repair the bridge? Once again, "the Beach" finds itself at the center of a drama.

The state park staff has taken well-earned pride in meeting the challenge of turning this area once nearly universally considered a disaster into a pleasant, increasingly attractive recreational asset enjoyed by hundreds of thousands of visitors annually. It seems likely that this same can-do spirit, in cooperation with the Meramec Greenway organization and other urban partners, will likewise find a solution to the bridge problem. Stay tuned. *

ROUTE 66 STATE PARK • 97 NORTH OUTER ROAD E, EUREKA

Don Robinson State Park

IN THE RUGGED LABARQUE CREEK HILLS, tucked away in the upper watershed of northwest Jefferson County, is one of the newest jewels in the state park system. Don Robinson assembled the 843 acres as his personal retreat over the years since his initial purchase in 1964, and then he willed them to the people of Missouri as a state park upon his passing in March 2012. With an estimated value of more than $5 million, the land is among the largest gifts in the century-long history of the system. Don Robinson joins the pantheon of state park heroes, another of those civic-minded individuals who had acquired special places of beauty and interest in Missouri and then donated them to the park system.

Robinson was struck by the ruggedness of the surrounding landscape when he bought his first 320-acre parcel in 1964. Fondly recalling his first visit, he explained, "It was so cold out the beer was freezing on top of the cans. I thought, well, this is really prehistoric—I just gotta get it." As he continued to add adjacent parcels, he realized he was getting close to a tract the exact size of New York City's famed Central Park—843 acres—and at that he stopped, though he continued to buy, develop, and sell property in the vicinity of his own retreat.

Robinson was known for his utterly unique yet direct, humorous, and scrupulously honest personality. He made his money producing, marketing, and distributing a stain remover called Off, a concoction he made himself with simple equipment, first in rented space in Kirkwood with the assistance of local boys who kept their hours on the honor system, and later, in a room under the concrete deck of a raised swimming pool he built on his property. He was an early user of infomercials in the 1970s, producing and appearing in his own spots to demonstrate his product and paying television stations in Missouri and nearby states to run them. He thought nothing of loading up his station wagon with Off and driving to Iowa to stock the supermarket shelves himself. He also made an energy drink, Jyro Cola, which he distributed by truck with the help of local kids. Although he sometimes claimed he didn't want neighbors, he was actually quite hospitable to a variety of friends and neighbors, interested in getting to know people, very well-read, and generous with the use of his land. In return, when he lived alone in the woods in his senior years, local folks watched out for him.

His home, where he lived alone for nearly half a century, sits on one of the most striking vistas of the park. He described it as "just a cut above camping—but I like it that way." The lower stone portion of the house had been built in 1928, but he added a second floor and, later, a clerestory of his own design. The changes he made to the house and the surrounding landscape, including partial construction of a colonnade on the deck of the pool, demonstrated his interest in architecture and his frugal use of recycled materials and found objects; he even hired Kirkwood boys to chip terra cotta ornaments off an old hotel being taken down in St. Louis. One change he never made to the house was adding a finished ground floor—the floor was literally the bedrock knoll on which the house sat. In 1997 an elaborate treehouse in his woods graced the cover of *Smithsonian* magazine, and several years later, the dust jacket of a hardcover book about outstanding treehouses. Sadly, it no longer survives.

Several intermittent tributaries of LaBarque Creek—French for "the boat," a reminder of the French heritage of the St. Louis region—originate in the park. The creek flows six miles northeast to the Meramec River. With forty-four species of fish, it is considered one of the healthiest and highest quality streams in the St. Louis area, and its thirteen-square-mile, steep, wooded watershed has remained largely undeveloped. Although the watershed is less than forty miles from downtown St. Louis and lies in the path of rapid suburban growth, it has been the focus of concerted efforts in recent years by public agencies, conservation organizations, and private landowners to protect its outstanding qualities, and nearly half its acreage has come into public ownership. Don Robinson's land may have been the least disturbed, most beautiful of all, and he cared deeply about its future. As he put it, "I had to do something about it, or else my melon-headed cousins out of nowhere would come out of the woodwork and sell the place over a weekend or something."

The geology of the park and the LaBarque watershed includes outcroppings of limestone, dolomite, and sandstone that give rise to a rich mosaic of ecosystems. The St. Peter sandstone in particular, a formation that developed as part of the shoreline of a Paleozoic sea, has been sculpted by erosion over time into a variety of noteworthy features, including dry open glades and moist box canyons, cliffs, waterfalls, chutes, pools, and overhangs. The park has an impressive diversity of flowering plants, ferns, liverworts, and a fourth of all the moss species and nearly a third of the lichen species known in the state. There are also outstanding bird and other wildlife resources here, though more comprehensive surveys are needed. Indeed, much of the park is considered to have potential natural area quality. Given its complex geology and hilly topography, a visitor can hike through a range of ecological communities in an hour or two.

Several rare or unusual plants, including rock firmoss, Forbe's saxifrage, partridgeberry, sensitive fern, and sphagnum moss, appear in several sandstone box canyons. The cliff walls and the flora that have

Right above: An overhang sculpted in St. Peter sandstone harbors mosses, lichens, liverworts, and in winter, icicles. ***Ron Colatskie*** **• Left: Don Robinson's home showcases his architectural interests.** ***Susan Flader***

taken root here are highly sensitive to any disturbance. Rock climbing in particular is one of the biggest threats, as the lightest of tread can dislodge what little soil supports these delicate plants, leaving the walls devoid of plant life. Downstream from these canyons, rich moist forest unfolds, where thickets of spicebush, pawpaw, and other native flora offer a different atmosphere, and perhaps a glimpse of migrating warblers in spring and fall.

Signature features at Don Robinson State Park are the several sandstone box canyons carved into the landscape. Over the eons, water has sliced through the grainy sandstone beds to form steep canyons with some walls exceeding eighty feet in height.

Ascending from the shady environs of the box canyons, you will find a sharp contrast on the many dry glades. Sandstone glades are rare, and high quality examples such as those at Don Robinson State Park are even rarer, as the sensitive sandy soils are easily eroded. On these sites, gnarled blackjack and post oaks dot the dry sandy slopes, along with the occasional prickly pear cactus. In places, stunted and twisted eastern red cedars stand guard over the bare sandstone. These sandy, acidic sites harbor a suite of small plants adapted to these specific conditions, including rock spikemoss, fame flower, dwarf dandelion, and rough buttonweed. Glades perched on dolomite outcrops have a slightly different character. Here on the dry alkaline rocks and soils, wildflowers put on a colorful show throughout the summer months, with prairie dock, rosinweed, Missouri coneflower, glade coneflower, and the rare Fremont's leather flower as highlights. These small glades are modest relative to open glade landscapes elsewhere in the Ozarks, but they are a special part of this landscape.

The park's woodland communities occupy a continuum between the strongly contrasting forests and glades. While not as open as the glades or as thick and lush as the forests, the woodlands reflect a smooth transition between the two. Here you will find stately white oaks and northern red oaks, and on drier sites chinkapin and post oak, over a rich understory of shrubs, grasses, and wildflowers. Historically, fire moved through these woodlands, creating an open park-like look. Perhaps set by humans over the millennia or ignited by lightning, these fires would burn through the woodlands before expiring on the moist, deeply shaded canyon slopes.

Restoring the natural role of fire is a priority for park staff and an important part of restoring the diversity of the park's glades and woodlands. Over recent decades, fire had been suppressed as the countryside developed, and fire-intolerant species such as sugar maple began to creep upslope. Gradually, the park's glades and woodlands became crowded with rank growth of trees and shrubs, shading out the ground flora. Luckily, many of these plants still found a refuge on thin soils, roadsides, and in the occasional open field. As the park develops, ecologists will seek to restore these ecosystems to their original diversity of plant and animal life.

Don Robinson's unusually intact and scenic property has attracted naturalists for decades, some of whom became friends of his and

Left: Pawpaws and other native flora flourish in moist, forested bottomland downstream from the canyons. The prickly pear cactus may be found on more acidic sandstone glades, while the rare Fremont's leather flower may be found on alkaline dolomite glades. Several other rare or unusual plants can also be found in the park, which is known for its diverse environments. Above: A park planning team examines an intriguing sandstone feature. *All Ron Colatskie*
Right: This waterfall spills down into a sandstone box canyon. *Allison Vaughn*

returned repeatedly to survey its flora and fauna. The Webster Groves Nature Study Society has led botanical field trips here since the mid-1960s. The Missouri Native Plant Society, St. Louis Audubon Society, and Friends of LaBarque Creek Watershed have also highlighted the natural riches found here. Their attention helped to illuminate the potential of this property as a state park.

Development of this area will no doubt focus primarily on the stewardship and interpretation of its unusual natural history and scenery. Walking trails invite exploration of the rugged terrain and fascinating plant and animal habitats. Other public and protected lands in the vicinity, including several adjacent or nearby Conservation Department areas, offer much potential for cooperative effort in protecting the remarkable Missouri heritage of the LaBarque Hills region. The Friends of LaBarque took the lead in bringing various public and private entities and local landowners to the table to develop the 2009 LaBarque Creek Watershed Conservation Plan, which serves as a template for efforts in the area.

Don Robinson spent years considering what to do with his property and ultimately decided that Missouri State Parks would fulfill his vision of preserving this beautiful landscape for future generations to enjoy. On a peaceful knoll just a short walk from his former home, he rests for eternity, having become a part of the wild acres he so loved. Now his legacy is available for you and your family to enjoy as well. ✻

Robertsville State Park

SOUTH OF A GREAT BEND in the Meramec River and just a mile upstream from the Shaw Nature Reserve is a pleasant little park. The initial 1,100-acre tract of Robertsville State Park in east-central Franklin County was purchased by the Missouri Department of Natural Resources in 1979 as part of the state's commitment to the Meramec River Recreation Area, a string of parks, conservation areas, and other recreational facilities along the lower Meramec, anchored by Castlewood State Park. Robertsville is at the upstream end, a mile above the Missouri Botanical Garden's Shaw Nature Reserve.

This land was once part of a large plantation. For much of the nineteenth century, the River Hills Plantation was the home of Edward James Roberts, who came to Missouri from Virginia in 1830 at the age of fourteen. Seventeen years later, he married Ann M. Robertson of St. Louis County. On their sprawling farm of more than 3,000 acres on the rich bottomland along the Meramec, they raised horses, mules, cattle, swine, wheat, corn, Irish potatoes, sweet potatoes, oats, and hay. Agricultural records show that the plantation yielded 10,000 pounds of tobacco in 1850. The 1860 census indicates that Roberts held twenty-five slaves. The Roberts family cemetery remains within the park, and some descendants of the plantation workers still reside in the vicinity.

Naturally, such a substantial landowner was active in civic affairs; Roberts served as a local tax collector and as an election judge, and he was also a master Mason. When the Frisco Railroad extended west from St. Louis, it established a station on his property, giving Roberts the opportunity to develop an all-purpose business listed as "Mill-Store-Money Lending." The station survives today as Robertsville, an unincorporated town, but the trains no longer stop. Much of his land north of the railroad remained under single ownership for years. The state bought it with the help of the Land and Water Conservation Fund from a group of investors whose plans for a resort and golf courses failed to materialize.

Spicebush Trail, less than a mile long, passes beneath a tall canopy of white, pin, and bur oaks, with scattered large sycamore, hackberry, elm, and maple trees. The namesake spicebush, a Missouri native deciduous shrub, is prominent in the understory, and autumn brings its bright red berries.

The Meramec River borders the tract on the north and west, while Calvey Creek forms the eastern boundary. Much of the land is situated in the floodplains, where several sloughs provide fine wetland habitat attractive to a variety of waterfowl. In one isolated area, some cottonwoods and other trees host nests of great blue herons. Heronries are very sensitive, so no trails intrude into this area.

As a floodplain landscape, Robertsville does not include dramatic topography, but in the central area of the park, a small hill rises about 160 feet above the surrounding lowlands. This hill represents an erosional remnant—often called a lost hill—formed by the changing courses of the Meramec River and Calvey Creek. When one stream cuts off another or occupies the channel of another, the resulting stream piracy will often

The Roberts family cemetery is a reminder of the park's earlier days as a nineteenth-century plantation. *Oliver Schuchard* • The park provides more than two miles of Meramec River frontage. *Missouri State Parks* • The Spicebush Trail traverses one of the best bottomland forests in the park system. *Erik Otto*

leave a remnant of dissected ridge that then becomes an independent hill.

Part of the old agricultural character of Robertsville remains pleasantly reflected in the broad openings that greet the visitor at the park entrance. Vistas across gentle grassy meadows dotted with dark green cedars carry the eye to the low, wooded campground hill, and then farther to the tall hardwoods nearer the Meramec.

One way to really experience the Robertsville landscape is to explore the Spicebush Trail that traverses some of the park's rich, lower woods. Along with the spicebush, thick, dark hanging vines of wild grapes appear almost jungle-like in places—an atmosphere that certainly goes with the heat, humidity, and insects of midsummer. Spring is beautiful, with carpets of wildflowers and a host of forest-loving birds in full song. You'll almost surely hear the high-pitched call of the red-shouldered hawk. You'll also see native woodpeckers in the tall timber. There's even a good chance to see some wild turkeys slipping through the bottoms.

With more than two miles of frontage on the Meramec River, Robertsville has great access to the river for boating and fishing. It's also the perfect spot for a waterside picnic in the shade on a summer evening. But you'll have to experience that for yourself to know what it's really like. *

ROBERTSVILLE STATE PARK • 900 STATE PARK ROAD, ROBERTSVILLE

Dr. Edmund A. Babler Memorial State Park

MANY THINGS ABOUT BABLER STATE PARK are special—its origin, its funding, its facilities, its rich botanical diversity, and its location in St. Louis County on the fringe of Missouri's largest metropolitan area. Babler is one of the most heavily visited parks in the system. When it was dedicated in 1938, the park was a long drive into the country. Now, it is an open-space oasis amid a rapidly expanding suburban landscape.

The park was given to the state as a living memorial for St. Louis physician Edmund A. Babler by his two brothers, Jacob and Henry. Their father, Henry J. Babler Sr., was a Swiss émigré to Wisconsin who settled in Eldorado Springs, Missouri, in the 1870s. The family prospered in Missouri, the brothers establishing themselves as leaders in St. Louis by the early twentieth century.

Jacob went into law and urban planning and later became a prominent figure in the insurance business and in Republican politics, with oil and real estate interests on the side. Beyond his efforts at Babler Park, he made many other contributions to state parks, including a critical donation to the campaign for Big Oak Tree in 1938 and powerful support for both a constitutional provision in 1944 for state parks funding and for a bill in 1945 to create stronger statutory authority for state parks, which ultimately became law in 1953. Henry was also in insurance, while Edmund earned his medical degree from the Missouri Medical College—now Washington University School of Medicine—in 1902 and became a renowned and beloved surgeon, known for his service to the poor and his advocacy for more outdoor recreation for young and old.

The brothers started acquiring land in the drainage of Wild Horse Creek in 1926 with the idea of creating a park. After Edmund's sudden death from pneumonia at age fifty-four in 1930, Jacob and Henry were determined to complete an attractive park in his memory for the people of Missouri. They donated the first tract of 868 acres to the state in

In 1942, a military police battalion used one area of the park as a prisoner-of-war camp for German and Italian soldiers captured in Africa. More recently, the old Babler Lodge has served as a residence for juveniles on a work-release program. The youths receive counseling while working on park maintenance.

1934 and added nearly 800 acres more within two years. Since then, the state has acquired additional tracts, bringing the total to nearly 2,500 acres.

The mid-1930s were the years of New Deal-sponsored work relief in the parks, and Jacob Babler, through his friendship with Congressman John J. Cochran of St. Louis, arranged for a substantial allocation of labor from the Civilian Conservation Corps (CCC)—more than for any other park in Missouri—to develop Babler Memorial Park. To help ensure superb development of the park and provide for its operation into the future,

The Edmund Babler monument in its carefully manicured park setting also includes sculptures of people the doctor helped. ***Oliver Schuchard***

DOCTOR
EDMUND A. BABLER
1874 – 1930
DEDICATED TO THE MEM-
ORY OF A GREAT SURGEON
AND HUMANITARIAN
HE THAT CARETH FOR THE
SICK AND THE WOUNDED
WATCHETH NOT ALONE.
THERE ARE THREE IN THE
DARKNESS TOGETHER
AND THE THIRD IS THE LORD

he established the Jacob L. Babler Perpetual Endowment Trust Fund in 1937 with an initial contribution of $1.5 million. The trust agreement provided that the state would own the land but the park would be funded and supervised by the trustees, including Jacob and Henry Babler, with provision for eventual surrender of the park to the state. For decades to come, Babler was listed as a state park but funded and managed by the Babler Trust—an utterly unique arrangement in the park system. After Jacob's death, additional funds from his estate augmented the trust.

The evidence suggests that Jacob Babler took a decidedly proprietary interest in the park, visiting the CCC crews at work there almost daily, meeting with Harland Bartholomew, who designed the park for him, commissioning a noted New York sculptor to create a statue of his brother, and even traveling to Washington, DC, to discuss plans with Conrad Wirth, head of land planning and CCC activities for the National Park Service. Wirth was so taken with Babler's enterprise that he personally supervised "cutting the vistas" at Babler Park. At the dedication ceremony in 1938, the principal speaker was Secretary of the Interior Harold L. Ickes.

The park that Babler built is a fascinating mix of urban and rural. The massive stone gateway, the entry avenue wider than a city boulevard with stone gutters and curbing, the gravel pathways and manicured landscaping against a forest backdrop, the full-length bronze statue of Dr. Edmund Babler—all are evocative of great urban parks such as St. Louis's Tower Grove and Forest parks.

The rambling stone lodge and the stone and timber picnic shelters, stable, restrooms, bridges, and underpasses have the rustic mien and

Left: The rich Missouri River hills at Babler are known for their massive oaks, and more than a dozen miles of hiking trails entice visitors. ***Christina Pick*** **• Above: Babler hosts many school groups, who learn about natural communities.** ***Nick Decker*** **• Right: The pool at the Babler Outdoor Education Center is accessible for people with disabilities.** ***Rockwood Community Education Department***

unobtrusive siting of typical CCC construction. And while the CCC structures in this park are representative examples of their era, they are somewhat more elaborate and certainly more numerous here than in any other park, a credit to Jacob Babler's good connections.

Twenty-two structures from the CCC era are now part of the Babler historic district on the National Register of Historic Places, including the stone lodge, which now serves as a boys camp operated by the state Division of Youth Services.

Jacob Babler shared the vision of St. Louis planners and civic leaders of a great outer loop of parks interconnected by parkways. Accordingly, he continued to buy tracts and secure right-of-way donations for an extension of Clayton Road to the park and for a corridor from the park to the Missouri River, but he was unable to realize this larger vision before he died in 1945. Some two decades after his death, when full control of the park and remaining assets of the trust passed to the state, the State Park Board began to sell off the outlying tracts, much to the consternation of those who still shared the larger vision. Despite some opposition, the state preferred to consolidate its holdings and use the funds to undertake more extensive development at the park.

The trust fund established by Jacob Babler—administered until 1968 by a special board of trustees—provided for maintenance and development but with some special management provisions. The Bablers placed certain restrictions on use of the land: they wanted the park limited to day use with no camping. No hunting was to be allowed, and the park was intended "for the Caucasian race," though the trustees could at their discretion provide additional facilities for other races in segregated areas. Other state parks, like many public facilities, were also in effect segregated at the time, but the trust provisions created concern for a time after the Supreme Court anti-segregation decision in 1954. Today, people of all races and backgrounds enjoy the park, and overnight camping is permitted, though the campground was built on additional land purchased by the state.

One of the special distinctions of Babler Park is the Jacob L. Babler Outdoor Education Center for the Disabled, a barrier-free resident camp

The rugged loess hills of Babler, here with a vernal carpet of spring beauties, are characteristic of an Ozark Border landscape. *Matt Faupel* • Beautiful Civilian Conservation Corps stonework enhances the grounds. *Missouri State Parks*

The four-sided fireplace presides inside the new Alta picnic shelter, which was rebuilt with local materials to Civilian Conservation Corps specifications after lightning destroyed the original. *Both Missouri State Parks*

with special facilities constructed on state-purchased land in the early 1970s. The year-round center includes sleeping cabins, recreation and dining facilities, a mile-long nature trail, and an accessible swimming pool. Now operated by the Rockwood School District as the Babler Outdoor Education Center, it is available to any nonprofit organization and is used some ten thousand camper-days per year. The work they do there will warm your heart and at times make you cry.

The park also offers the usual picnic areas, more than a dozen miles of hiking trails—half of which are shared with equestrians—a two-mile paved bike path, and facilities more typical of a city park, such as ball fields. Park staff also run one-day summer camp experiences called Babler Outdoor Adventure for inner city children.

The CCC-era stable no longer houses an equestrian concession but instead is used by Rockwood School District as an outpost for Babler Wild, a series of week-long summer camps. An impressive visitor center completed in 1991 houses special exhibits about the natural history of the park. A walk-through diorama, for example, explores the intricate interrelationships among birds, mammals, reptiles, insects, microorganisms, and other creatures in an old-growth forest environment.

Babler State Park represents a classic Ozark Border landscape: rugged with rocky loess-mantled hills and highly dissected ridges. These river hills drain to the Missouri River, a short distance to the north. On southern and western slopes, the forest is typically Ozarkian in character with stunted oaks and hickories. Shadbush and lowbush blueberry signal that other plants of the rocky, cherty Ozarks can be found. Yet hidden on the north and east slopes and in deeper valleys is a taller, more luxuriant forest, essentially untouched for nearly a century. The massive trees in Babler's deep ravines exhibit a timeless character that complements the stately design of the park entrance and other public areas.

Natural area surveys in the 1970s identified eight different areas of the park as significant natural communities. One—Babler Southwoods Hollow—was officially designated a state natural area in 1978. It was described as an old-growth forest dominated by white oak and sugar maple with a sparse understory. At the time, it seemed the best approach to these areas was to protect them from development and let them be.

By the 1990s and increasingly in the present century, as Babler became ever more an island in a sea of suburban residential development, park naturalists became concerned about high deer densities (approaching eighty per square mile, when fifteen to twenty would be more sustainable), habitat degradation by horses and humans, and encroachment of exotic honeysuckles, garlic mustard, and other invasive species that inhibit native flora. They also began to notice that sugar maple, formerly present in deep coves, was now moving up the ravines and along the drier wooded ridges where the species was shading out native understory and inhibiting reproduction of the park's signature oaks.

After lightning struck the Alta shelter in 2008, about twenty acres of surrounding woods that had been burned in the fire subsequently exploded with a beautiful array of native grasses and wildflowers. Park officials knew it was time to rethink a decision three decades earlier not to use prescribed fire in the woods at Babler.

This island in a sea of suburbia is now undergoing rather intensive efforts to restore some of the rich diversity that attracted the Babler brothers in the 1920s and to maintain it for park visitors in generations to come. Regular monitoring of deer populations and browse damage has led to carefully managed culling by special deer hunts most years since 1997. Volunteers monitor water quality in the streams and help to remove invasive species, and park crews use prescribed fire to restore glades and woodland communities on rocky slopes facing west and south.

To experience Babler's continuum of ecosystems, hike the relatively steep two-mile Dogwood Trail or the shorter and gentler Hawthorn Trail, which starts from the parking lot near the rebuilt Alta Shelter. You begin in a dry cherty woodland where the acidic soils are rich with legumes such as tick trefoils and goats rue. Bearing left at the fork in the trail, you encounter a dry limestone woodland high above Wildhorse Creek, where you wind through one of the park's small glades carpeted in grasses and wildflowers and with chinkapin oaks, white oaks, and the occasional wooly buckthorn on drier sites. Then the trail takes a quick turn around the end of the narrow ridge to the north slope where tall white oaks, ashes, hickories, and colonies of pawpaws flourish in the richer loess soils characteristic of the Missouri River Hills.

These high quality natural features immediately adjacent to the St. Louis metropolitan area, coupled with classic park design and distinctive recreational opportunities, make this a true gem of the state park system, thanks to the splendid vision of the Babler brothers. *

DR. EDMUND A. BABLER MEMORIAL STATE PARK • 800 GUY PARK DRIVE, WILDWOOD

Graham Cave State Park

IN THE HILLS ABOVE THE LOUTRE RIVER in Montgomery County, a few miles north of the Loutre's confluence with the Missouri River, is an outcrop with a large cave created at the contact zone between St. Peter sandstone and Jefferson City dolomite. Caves in dolomite or limestone are common enough, but a sandstone cave is less common. What happened here is that the dolomite below was more soluble and slowly dissolved away, leaving a cavity under the sandstone. Some of the sandstone crumbled and collapsed into the cavity, enlarging it, and leaving an arch-like entrance 120-feet wide and 16-feet high. Originally the cave extended about a hundred feet into the hill. An accumulation of debris and dust over the years then filled the lower part of the cave with about seven feet of deposit.

What is noteworthy, though, is not so much the cave, rare as it is, as what has been found in the debris on its floor. This cave, like others so favorably situated, was an admirable shelter for animals and people through the years—just how many years would one day be discovered.

The cave was a mile north of the early nineteenth-century settlement of Loutre Lick, now known as Mineola, then noted for its mineral springs with reputed medicinal powers. This "lick" was owned by sons of Daniel Boone, whose claims dated from 1802 during the Spanish colonial era. The Boone's Lick Trail, the trail they took west from St. Charles, went right past the Loutre Lick and on to the more famous Boone's Lick salt works, which they also operated.

Dr. Robert Graham, a Scotsman who came to Missouri from Kentucky in the wave of migration that followed the War of 1812, settled in the area in 1816 and purchased from Daniel Morgan Boone a portion of his rich bottomland along the Loutre River. Loutre—French for otter—is the name by which the river was known as early as the French explorer Étienne de Veniard sieur de Bourgmond's 1723 trip up the Missouri River to the mouth of the Grand River, where he would found Fort Orleans.

THE CAVE ONCE SHELTERED PEOPLE AND LIVESTOCK

D. F. Graham, son of the cave's original owner, kept hogs in the cave during winter and early spring. Then his son Benjamin used the cave to shelter sheep and store machinery. Benjamin's son-in-law began bulldozing to enlarge the livestock area. Archaeologists got wind of this and persuaded him to stop until they could conduct excavations. They found well-stratified materials revealing almost continuous human occupation over the last ten thousand years. The lower levels contained a thick record of human presence from about ten thousand to nine thousand years ago. These discoveries were the oldest known in Missouri up to that time and led to the cave becoming the first archaeological site in the nation designated as a National Historic Landmark.

The land in this area declines rapidly in agricultural potential as it leaves the river, climbing to the rugged and rocky escarpment that rims the edges of the valley—so much so that Graham did not pursue ownership of the ridge-top quarter-section that contained the cave until 1847, when it was still available directly from the US government. Graham raised black Angus cattle brought from Kentucky and is said to have mined saltpeter from the cave to sell to St. Louis gunpowder factories.

Graham's son, D. F. Graham, became interested in archaeology, digging numerous Indian mounds in the vicinity and even making a test excavation in the cave. His collection of artifacts grew so large that his wife made him build another structure, the "relic house," to store them. After his death, his son Benjamin, who had studied at the University of Missouri, offered the artifact collection to the university. Professors Jesse E. Wrench and J. Brewton Berry, who were interested in archaeology, visited the cave in 1930 to assess its potential, but did little digging. This was before the formation of the Missouri Archaeological Society or

any formal archaeological study at the university. Benjamin's daughter Frances married Ward Darnell. After World War II, archaeologists were much better organized when they learned Darnell was bulldozing the debris in the cave. Fortunately, they persuaded him to hold off.

From 1949 through about 1955, archaeologists Wilfred Logan and Carl Chapman of the University of Missouri and the Missouri Archaeological Society conducted extensive excavations in the cave. The results were staggering. Within a deep portion of the deposits, they found evidence of the oldest known humans in Missouri up to that time. These discoveries were being made just as the new carbon-14 technology for dating organic material such as bone or wood was substantially revising archaeologists' notions of when early people had arrived on the continent. It had once been thought that they had arrived less than three thousand years ago, but discoveries in New Mexico were forcing scientists to push their estimates backward. The hard evidence came with radiocarbon dating at places like Graham Cave.

In the floor of Graham Cave, a sandstone rock shelter that is now a National Historic Landmark, archaeologists have uncovered a record of almost continuous human habitation over the last ten thousand years. ***Ben Nickelson***

The lowest deposits in the cave belonged to the Dalton Period—named for Missouri Supreme Court Judge S. P. Dalton, himself an amateur archaeologist who first studied the distinctive projectile point that characterized the period. During that time, native people were adjusting to the rapidly changing climate, vegetation, and animal life after the retreat of the glaciers. Another adjustment in thinking was involved here because before carbon-14 dating became available, scientists thought the last glaciers had retreated perhaps as much as twenty-five thousand years ago; now they were finding evidence of the last, or Wisconsin, glaciation still in Wisconsin as recently as ten thousand years ago, at the same time as the early occupation of Graham Cave.

The extremely significant discoveries at Graham Cave, including not

Glades and open oak woodlands, here with gray-headed coneflowers, are being preserved in the Graham Cave Glades Natural Area. *Bruce Schuette*

only the oldest materials but also the remarkable evidence of ways of life and adaptations to the environment over ten millennia, were recognized in November 1961 when Graham Cave became the first archaeological site in the nation to be designated a National Historic Landmark. Frances Graham Darnell, great-granddaughter of Dr. Robert Graham, took pride in the discoveries made on her land and donated 237 acres—land that had been in her family for nearly a century and a half—to the state in 1964. This was the core of what is today Graham Cave State Park.

From 1967 to 1968, further excavation was conducted by archaeologist Walter Klippel, in part to test whether changes in the environment during the Archaic period—ten thousand to three thousand years ago—were reflected in cultural material. Analysis of soil deposits in the cave indicated that this area underwent rapid warming from the cool glacial period after about eight thousand years ago, and that until about five thousand years ago, this area shared a warm dry period that allowed the eastward extension of prairie grasses across northern Missouri, Iowa, and Illinois in what has become known as the Prairie Peninsula. During this time, faunal remains in the cave showed a gradual but marked change from forest mammals to species that prefer an edge habitat, reflecting a change from forest to mixed prairie and woodland. Study of the types of stone tools, however, suggested that the cave was used for generally the same purposes through time. More than 99 percent of the stone used for the tools was locally available, though the manner of manufacture changed over time, suggesting that people may have adapted in place to their changing environment rather than dying or moving out and different cultural groups migrating in.

For interpretive purposes, the 1960s excavations were left open behind a protective barrier, instead of being backfilled. Because of this, they've been degraded by burrowing animals and erosion, so park managers have recently begun a stabilization program. These were probably the best-preserved deposits from this time in the state, and undisturbed portions of the site being banked for future excavation may still retain that distinction. We likely have more to learn from Graham Cave.

Today, the 386-acre park protects not only the cave that sheltered early inhabitants but also vestiges of the landscape that supported them. A rich bottomland forest along the Loutre River changes into oak woodlands upslope, and then into rocky, sun-drenched glades. Glades within the park are found on sandstone, several limestones, and dolomite bedrock that outcrop here at this northern edge of the Ozark Border. The glades on each type of rock produce their own characteristic plant and animal life. Unique to the park system are isolated carpets of a moss-like fern called spikemoss, which grows on dry, exposed sandstone glades.

A shelter explains cultural and natural features of the park, and visitors explore a sandstone bluff covered with mosses and lichens. *Both Missouri State Parks*

The importance of these remnant glades—among the best glades in Missouri—has led to the designation of an 80-acre tract as the Graham Cave Glades Natural Area. Park managers have restored not only the glades but also the open woodlands around them by removing the young thickets of eastern red cedar and using prescribed burns to keep them open for sun-loving plants that thrived here for millennia when wildfires were more prevalent.

A walk through the natural area passes by some of the park's glades. Another short trail leads from the popular campground to the Loutre River and a boat-launch area, and a trail from the lower picnic area to the cave passes a shelter with exhibits about the park's archaeology and natural history. The visitor center displays artifacts from the excavations, and a diorama of the cave area tells the story of both the natives and the landscape they inhabited for nearly ten thousand years. *

GRAHAM CAVE STATE PARK • 217 HIGHWAY TT, DANVILLE

Devil's Ice Box Spring Branch trickles under the natural bridge that gives the park its name in the stillness of a winter morning. ***Oliver Schuchard***

Rock Bridge Memorial State Park

BECAUSE OF ITS ODDITY, the area south of Columbia was probably destined to become a state park, if not preserved in some other way, although this is hindsight, of course. There are so many natural phenomena here to excite human curiosity. Flowing creeks disappear underground. Natural shallow ponds called sinkholes act like funnels, holding water for only a short time after heavy rains. Deep holes in the earth open into extensive caverns. Bats boil out of these caves at dusk. There's a spectacular chasm where a stream emerges from the foot of one cliff only to flow toward another one and beneath a massive arch of limestone topped by trees. This is the centerpiece, the rock bridge that gave the park its name. All are characteristics of a karst landscape underlain by porous and water-soluble limestone.

The first recorded owner of this curious landscape was Nathan Glasgow, who bought it from the federal government for $1.25 per acre before Missouri became a state in 1820. Stone quarried from a flanking bluff was used to build a low dam across the upstream end of the natural bridge, thus enhancing the power of the water to operate a gristmill. This was the first of a succession of mills at the site over the next century. A paper mill operated in the 1830s but didn't last long. It was followed by a whiskey distillery built by James McConathy, who marketed his product as McConathy's Rye, touting its quality derived from the pure water of Little Bonne Femme Creek (now Devil's Icebox Spring Branch).

The distillery was raided by Union soldiers in 1863 and destroyed by fire in 1889, but it was rebuilt two years later by a new owner and continued to prosper until the Missouri legislature passed a local-option liquor law. In 1908 Boone County declined to vote itself wet, and the distillery fell into ruin. In the late nineteenth century, there were at times both a general store and a post office at the little town of Rock Bridge Mills. It was an active community center, a place for political rallies, celebrations, and family picnics, and gatherings continued even after the old distillery shut down and the store closed. The geologic wonders were an enduring attraction.

Jess and Mary Calkins came from Nebraska in 1922 to buy the Rock Bridge and 860 adjoining acres. The Calkinses opened a "gay, modern amusement park," according to an announcement in the *Columbia Evening Missourian* of July 23, 1922. It offered "a merry-go-round, doll racks, popcorn, and fairy floss candy machines" and also "elaborate fireworks in the evening." They soon added a dance floor, built beneath the branches of an ancient oak, and it became a popular attraction.

When the Calkinses' daughter Naomi married Columbian Dennis Ingrum, the newlyweds received as a wedding gift a deed to the Rock Bridge and 320 acres. In all the years that Dennis Ingrum farmed the land, he always made visitors from town feel welcome, sometimes entertaining the "city girls" from Stephens College with a demonstration of making molasses from sorghum cane. A field trip to Rock Bridge and Devil's Icebox was standard for geology classes, and university students would return with their dates for a lark. "Dad always wanted to share the beauty of the place with others who loved it, too. He wasn't interested in getting rich," daughter Mary Toalson told a reporter, explaining why Dennis Ingrum rejected big offers from developers but agreed to sell his land at a modest price for a state park.

Although always privately owned, the actual rock bridge and its neighboring caves had been a semipublic area for more than a century when in 1961, sudden tragedy struck a Columbia family, starting a movement to preserve the area permanently for public use. That is why the word "memorial" appears in the official park name. Lewis Stoerker was a popular professor of speech and dramatic arts at the University of Missouri when his daughter Carol, age nine, was struck and killed by a car. Grief-stricken, Stoerker and his wife Dorothy conceived the idea of establishing a park to memorialize their beloved Carol, a place where children could run and play in safety. He knew about Rock Bridge and approached landowners in the area. Dennis Ingrum quickly said he would sell—for a park.

The Stoerkers and their daughter had many friends, young and old, who rallied to the cause. They held auctions, teenagers collected money, 4-H clubs and scout troops helped, and Columbia businesses made gifts. At one point, Dr. Frederick Middlebush, a former president of the University of Missouri, handed Professor Stoerker a check for $10,000. By 1966 the fund exceeded $85,000, and a committee went to see the State Park Board. The board agreed to accept the proposed park provided the citizens group could raise a total of $175,000 to match another $175,000 the board would seek from the recently enacted federal Land and Water Conservation Fund to acquire the needed land.

Stalactites and stalagmites meet to form curtains here in the deep haunts of Devil's Icebox Cave. *Scott Schulte*

A VITAL WILD CAVE

Devil's Icebox is the seventh longest cave in Missouri, nearly seven miles including side passages. In a state with nearly seven thousand known caves, Devil's Icebox ranks among the most diverse caves. It harbors three federally endangered species of bats and boasts a flatworm, the pink planarian, not known to be anywhere else in the world. The cave has been closed to visitors since 2010, because of the threat of white-nose syndrome to bats. Wild cave tours, formerly offered by trained park staff and volunteers on a limited basis, were suspended indefinitely until more is understood about the disease.

The Devil's Icebox boardwalk leads up and over the rock bridge and then down into the collapsed entrance to Devil's Icebox and Connor Caves. Displays along the way explain the geology. *Scott Myers* • Kids search for aquatic life in Devil's Icebox Spring Branch, which is popular with groups. *Susan Flader*

Although such arrangements rarely work out exactly as planned, the Rock Bridge Memorial Park Association donated more than 1,100 acres to the state during 1967 and 1968, and the state purchased several hundred acres more.

Public use of the area increased after the initial acquisitions were completed and the state park became official. On April 10, 1974, at a celebration of the fiftieth anniversary of the state park system, Gov. Christopher Bond dedicated a stone monument and plaque at the park in "appreciation to the Rock Bridge Memorial Park Association, Inc., and the Columbia community" and "in memory of Carol Stoerker." Piece by piece, the park was expanded until by 2000 it totaled more than 2,270 acres.

Next to the famous bridge itself and only a short distance from it, the outstanding geologic feature of the park is a precipitous entrance to a steep, rocky chasm known as the Devil's Icebox. A boardwalk now leads to the Icebox—a sinkhole that collapsed into a cave—and then descends into it by sturdy plank steps installed by the park division to prevent damage to the fragile plant life that clings to the rock walls. At the bottom is an entrance into the cave system, and in midsummer, one perceives at once how the Icebox got its name. The cave stream runs by, accompanied by a steady flow of chilling air. Explorers in 1926 and later determined that the cave extended three and a half miles along its main channel, and it has lengthy side passages for a total length of nearly seven miles, making it the seventh-longest cave in Missouri.

While protecting caves for bat habitat was probably not what motivated park founders, they nevertheless accomplished it. Devil's Icebox Cave is used by a maternity colony of endangered gray bats for raising their young each year from April through August. Other species that hibernate in the cave are the big and little brown bats, the tri-colored bat, and the endangered Indiana and northern long-eared bats. A small flatworm, the pink planarian, has been found only here in the entire world. The pink planarian and other troglobites of the cave—including a spider, a millipede, and a springtail—lack eyes and complete their life cycles living solely in caves. Along with surface species that accidentally find their

way into the cave, the animal life of the Icebox ranks among the most diverse of any Missouri cave.

The stream that issues from Devil's Icebox is visible for only a few feet before it again flows underground through Connor's Cave, only about 150 feet in length, then emerges as a spring that flows through a valley created by the collapse of a section of cave roof—the event that separated the Rock Bridge from the rest of the cave system. If these karst features seem complex, a visit to the boardwalk with its explanatory panels will make them more clear. While subject to change, Connor's Cave is open from April 13 through October 13, and is often used for school tours and bat programs.

The surface watershed that recharges the Devil's Icebox stream is dotted with hundreds of sinkholes, funnel-shaped depressions that drain water directly into the cave system. Through dye-tracing studies, park officials have learned that Bonne Femme Creek also loses water to the underground cave system, bringing the total acreage in the watershed to more than 8,500 acres. To protect the stream and its cave life from pollution by agricultural chemicals, lawn fertilizers, or human wastes draining into these sinkholes, the state was able to acquire nearby parcels of the watershed on several occasions since 1975. These tracts of "sinkhole plain" make up the areas where the Grassland, Karst, and other trails run. Native grassland, interesting in itself for its wildflowers and bird life, has been restored on parts of these tracts. Water quality in the cave, where the pink planarian lives, continues to be a concern as lands around the park are developed.

To help protect Gans Creek, a tributary of Little Bonne Femme Creek flowing through the park from the east, 750 acres of bottomland forest, limestone bluffs, and wooded hills have been designated the Gans Creek Wild Area. Gans Creek, along with Devil's Icebox Spring Branch and nearby Bonne Femme, Bass, and Turkey Creeks, is an Outstanding State Resource Water. The wild area is an excellent place for hiking, birding, botanizing, or even cross-country skiing during winter snows. When the City of Columbia acquired 320 acres along Gans Creek directly east of the wild area for its park system, conservation and civic groups participated enthusiastically in the planning process from 2007 to 2010 to ensure that the watershed in the hills along the creek would be preserved in a natural condition to protect the creek and the state park.

Rock Bridge State Park attracts more than 300,000 visitors a year, including many school groups who learn about caves, bats, karst systems, and water quality. It has day-use areas with two picnic shelters and other picnic sites, a playground, and a log cabin of uncertain origin—the Hickam Cabin—that was dismantled and rebuilt in 2014 by the park's support organization, Friends of Rock Bridge. Here and there in the park are sites of other cabins or barns. The park offers a special-use area for nonprofit youth groups interested in primitive camping. Eight hiking trails totaling some twenty-two miles provide access to all areas of the park, with some available also for mountain biking and horse riding when conditions permit.

The Friends of Rock Bridge was organized in 1991 to help protect the park from inappropriate or high-density development on its borders and to encourage the use of the park for recreation and education. The organization developed a vision early on for a nature discovery center, with classrooms and exhibits to serve as a base for groups visiting the park, but for various reasons was unable to realize it. Then in 2013, officials of Missouri State Parks and Columbia Public Schools jointly announced plans for an innovative partnership to build a new experimental elementary school in the park rooted in nature and science education. The school would house one hundred fifth graders selected by lottery, who would be immersed in nature-themed education, both indoors and outdoors, across the curriculum. The facility would be available for other groups or park events during nonschool hours.

To an extent that early visitors to the Icebox and even citizens who contributed their dollars for the park in the 1960s could scarcely have imagined, Columbia has sprawled southward in recent decades and now borders the park on parts of its north, east, and west boundaries. Developers in 2013 proposed a Parkside Estates subdivision adjacent to the northwest corner of the park that state park officials regarded as the

From top: Hundreds of sinkholes in the park and the surrounding plain funnel surface runoff directly into the Devils Icebox Cave system. ***Ben Nickelson*** **Children tour Connor Cave to learn about caves and the special creatures they harbor.** ***Missouri Parks Association*** **• The pink planarian flatworm found here but nowhere else worldwide is threatened by polluted surface water.** ***Tony Elliott***

most dense development directly adjacent to a state park anywhere in the state. Although that density would not have been permitted under either the tract's former county zoning or the provisions of the painstakingly crafted and approved plan for the Bonne Femme Watershed of which it is a part, the proposal was approved by the Columbia City Council subject to a limit of no more than 15 percent impervious surface and other provisions such as use of native vegetation, no chemical fertilizers, and measures to limit runoff. This is a chance—and a challenge—for city officials and Columbia citizens, who almost universally love Rock Bridge Park, to show that such a development can be successful over time without harming the park.

Despite the challenges of accommodating a growing regional population, Rock Bridge remains a delightful destination. Its landscape of entrenched creek valleys, massive limestone bluffs and caves, and rolling grassy uplands intrigues and charms, especially if you are on foot. Countless fond memories of this park derive from springtime visits by students from the nearby universities; something powerful draws young people when the air softens, wildflowers blossom, and birds call from greening woodlands. It could also be a good time for you and your family to make memories of your own. Try a picnic near the natural bridge followed by exploration of nearby trails. Listen for spring peepers, watch for Virginia bluebells, and catch the fragrance of wild plum. *

The Gans Creek Wild Area with its bottomland forest, wooded hills, and limestone bluffs offers serene vistas. Gans Creek has been designated an Outstanding State Resource Water. *Randal Clark* • Devil's Icebox Cave has been closed since 2010 because of white-nose syndrome to protect these Indiana bats and other bat species until more is known about the disease. *Roxie Campbell*

ROCK BRIDGE MEMORIAL STATE PARK • 5901 SOUTH HIGHWAY 163, COLUMBIA

IN MEMORY OF
CHARLES H. HARDIN.
CHRISTIAN-STATESMAN-
PHILANTHROPIST. AS LAWYER.
LEGISLATOR. STATE SENATOR.
AND GOVERNOR.
FAITHFULLY HE DISCHARGED HIS
DUTY. IN 1880. HE LAID DOWN AT
THE FEET OF JESUS. ALL HIS
EARTHLY HONORS.
AND ATTACHED HIMSELF TO THE
BAPTIST CHURCH.
WHEN THE SUMMONS CAME FOR HIM
TO ENTER THE CHURCH TRIUMPHANT.
GLADLY HE OBEYED AND NOW RESTS
ON THAT BRIGHT SHORE. WHERE
ALONE PEACE SHEDS HER LIGHT.
AND ONE LONG DAY UNDIMMED BY
NIGHT. FAREWELL FOR A LITTLE
WHILE. MARY.
JULY 15. 1820—JULY 29. 1892
HARDIN
WIFE OF
CHAS HARDIN
GEORGE WALTER
Son of

Jewell Cemetery State Historic Site

SOUTH OF DOWNTOWN COLUMBIA is a small cemetery where Missouri's twenty-second governor is buried, as is the founder of William Jewell College. The site is bordered by a low stone wall with an iron gate. The cemetery was once part of the estate of George Jewell, who founded one of Missouri's early dynasties. In 1841, he deeded the cemetery to his son William and grandson Thomas. More than forty descendants of George Jewell are buried there. A plaque on the gate reminds visitors that only Jewell kin are to be buried within. The most noteworthy are William Jewell and Charles Hardin.

William Jewell (1789 to 1852) was a man of many callings: physician, politician, reformer, architect, and ordained minister. As mayor of Columbia, Jewell pushed for surveying and paving the city's streets. As a minister, he helped establish the first church in Columbia. As a state legislator, he worked for prison reforms and more humane punishments. He served as an army surgeon in the Black Hawk War from 1831 to 1832. In 1833 he helped establish Columbia College, a precursor to the University of Missouri, which absorbed its land and buildings when it was established in Columbia in 1839. Indeed, Jewell chaired the Boone County committee to raise subscriptions for the state university and pledged $1,800 to the fund.

Deeply committed to education, Jewell also tendered $10,000 worth of land—provided that the Baptist Church would match his contribution—for the establishment of a Baptist college. By 1849 his offer was more than matched, including $7,000 by the citizens of Clay County, so the college was chartered in Liberty and named for Jewell, who as an architect supervised construction until his death. He was joined as a supporter and early trustee of the college by, among others, Waltus Watkins, who built Watkins Mill, now a state historic site, and the Reverend Robert James, Frank and Jesse's father.

Left: Charles Hardin, a Missouri governor and nephew of William Jewell, is buried in the nineteenth-century Jewell family cemetery. *Oliver Schuchard* • Above: William Jewell was a physician, politician, minister, architect, and patron of many colleges, including the one in Liberty named for him. *Missouri State Parks*

Another trustee of William Jewell College was William's nephew, Charles Henry Hardin (1820 to1892), who was practicing law in Fulton when he was elected to the Missouri legislature—first to the house of representatives and later to the senate. At the outbreak of the Civil War, Hardin, a Constitutional Unionist, introduced in the senate a successful amendment intended to prevent a precipitous decision in favor of secession. He was the only senator present at Neosho in October 1861 to vote against secession, but when he was considered a Southern sympathizer and disfranchised, he returned to his farm near Mexico in Audrain County. In 1872 he returned to the senate, part of the Democratic resurgence in postwar Missouri, and in the fall of 1874, he was elected governor, having previously defeated ex-Confederate Brig. Gen. Francis M. Cockrell for the Democratic nomination.

> *Gov. Charles Henry Hardin, interred here, is known for reducing a large state debt from the Civil War and for the sale of bonds for railroad construction. He also issued a "grasshopper proclamation," in which he encouraged citizens to pray for the end of a plague of Rocky Mountain locusts. People gathered in churches to pray on June 3, 1875, and within days, it began to rain and the grasshoppers left.*

An advocate of education like his uncle William Jewell, Charles Hardin founded the Hardin College for women in Mexico, Missouri, and contributed substantially to it. In 1889 he led the fundraising campaign for the establishment of the Missouri Military Academy, also in Mexico. He earned his right to burial in the cemetery through his mother, a daughter of George Jewell.

Jewell Cemetery came under state management in 1970 after the state legislature in 1967 mandated the State Park Board to "suitably mark and maintain every grave of a former governor of this state, which is not within a perpetual care cemetery." In addition to Dunklin's Grave and Sappington Cemetery, which like Jewell are state historic sites, the park division also has a program to mark with plaques all governors' graves in the state and even those out-of-state. There are two governors' graves in California.

Jewell Cemetery is a tiny, half-acre remnant of the nineteenth century amid the twenty-first-century sprawl of south Columbia. But within its stone walls, the site retains its integrity. The earliest grave dates from 1822, and the most recent from 1968. At the back of the cemetery are about twenty unlettered but neatly quarried blocks of native limestone, thought to be markers for the graves of slaves or former slaves of the Jewell family. Jewell freed some of his slaves in 1836 and the remainder upon his death in 1852. If these are slave graves, they represent an unusual exception to traditional nineteenth-century practices, as slaves were usually not buried inside walled-in family enclosures. Perhaps these stones bear mute testimony to the humanitarian ideals of William Jewell. *

JEWELL CEMETERY STATE HISTORIC SITE • SOUTH PROVIDENCE ROAD, COLUMBIA

Finger Lakes State Park

NO DOUBT THERE ARE VISITORS to Finger Lakes State Park who do not recognize this area, just north of Columbia, as a man-made landscape. A half-century has passed since the Peabody Coal Company shovels ripped up the northern Boone County soil and rock to reach the coal below. Since then, there has been some recovery, both from natural seeding and from human-assisted replanting. Still, the rugged terrain—steep ridges and deep ravines, many of which are water-filled—is the telltale aftermath of a resource-extraction process known simply as strip mining.

The park represents a creative and successful recycling of strip-mined land for recreational use, attracting off-roaders who coexist remarkably well with those who prefer fishing, swimming, kayaking, bicycling, and hiking.

Coal has always been one of Missouri's most abundant fuels, and coal mining has been an important industry here, even though it is also followed by controversy. The state ranks among the top ten in quantity of coal reserves. Coal deposits lie under most of northern and western Missouri, although these coal beds are not as massive or of as high quality as those found in some states to the east and west. The coal is found in seams interbedded with shales, sandstones, and limestones dating back in time to the Pennsylvanian period, when large, salamander-like amphibians and early reptiles were the dominant land creatures.

In just a little more than three years, beginning in 1964, the Peabody Company removed some 1.2 million tons of coal from its Mark Twain Mine. The mine tapped into one of Missouri's major coal fields—one that stretches from western Callaway County northwest across Boone, Howard, Randolph, and Macon counties. After ceasing mining, Peabody undertook some initial reclamation, planting the barren piles of waste and stocking some water-filled pits as fishing lakes.

In the early 1970s, the US Department of the Interior initiated a program to recycle strip-mine areas as "reclamation for recreation" demonstration projects. The State Park Board surveyed potential sites and identified the Mark Twain Mine as a good candidate. During the negotiation and planning period that ensued, the Peabody Company agreed in 1973 to donate about one thousand acres to the state of Missouri, a donation that was matched with funds for development provided by the federal Land and Water Conservation Fund. Plans for the new park sought to complement decisions that had already been made for Rock Bridge Memorial State Park south of Columbia, which emphasized types of recreation compatible with its outstanding natural and geologic features. At Finger Lakes, by contrast, the emphasis would be on reconfiguring the topography and reclaiming the mined lands for off-road motorcycling and water recreation.

Finger Lakes will never be a natural area like nearby Rock Bridge, but it is a real success as a recreation area. Peabody Lake, one of the larger lakes, was developed with a sand swimming beach and a changing

Dirt bikers race across the mine spoil at a motocross event. ***Oliver Schuchard***
Kayakers follow the water trail along one of the fingers. ***Tom Uhlenbrock***

A mountain biker enjoys the new Kelley Branch trail. *Ben Nickelson* • This bird's-eye view above the middle of the park shows the finger-shaped lakes to the south. *Paul Jackson* • Swimmers find the lake attractive, too. *Denise H. Vaughn*

house. For several decades, it was the most popular swimming hole in the Columbia area until the city developed its own swimming beaches on lakes in town. Several of the finger-shaped pits in the eastern half of the park were connected to form a canoe trail nearly five miles long where the fishing is good and visitors have a chance of spotting great blue herons, beavers, raccoons, or deer; there is a boat launch area and the park now rents canoes and kayaks. A pleasant tree-shaded campground has been developed at the north end of the park.

But the real measure of the park's popularity lies in its use for off-road vehicles (ORVs): four-wheel vehicles with handlebars also known as all-terrain-vehicles (ATVs) and motorcycles of the dirt-bike variety. There is a five-mile designated, marked, and maintained trail from the campground to the motocross track, the staging area, and south to the park office, but ORV users have pioneered some seventy miles of challenging routes across the steep hills and ravines of the strip-mined spoil area.

The motocross track, developed by professional riders and state park planners, is close to Highway 63 in the western part of the park. This area hosts special events each year, co-sponsored by the park and a volunteer motocross parents group. The event draws both professional and amateur riders from across the country. In many places and to many people, ORVs in parks are quite controversial. Perhaps it is fitting, then, that this lively sport has found a home in a park born of controversy over strip mining. Here, motorcycle and ATV enthusiasts can enjoy a challenging landscape without harming some fragile, natural setting, leaving other more natural parks like Rock Bridge less pressured as a result.

The trees at Finger Lakes have grown over the years, and some wildflowers have taken root. The park has come to look more natural—too natural to suit the avid dirt bikers and ATV riders, who worry that it will be taken over by nonmotorized recreationists. The Department of Natural Resources listed the Kelley Branch as an impaired stream in 1998 under terms of the Clean Water Act and Missouri water quality standards, due to excessive sedimentation. As a result, a ninety-acre area of wooded hills buffering the creek was encircled by guardrails and closed to ATVs and off-road motorcycles; the area had been a favorite for riders who loved to cross, recross, and ride in the creek. Over a period of years, the eroded areas and vegetative cover were restored, and a three-mile-loop hiking and mountain-biking trail with just a single crossing of Kelley Branch was built by park staff and State Park Youth Corps workers with help from a local mountain-biking club. Still, most of the 1,130-acre park remains open to ORV use.

Lying on the sandy beach after a swim, a visitor realizes, almost subconsciously, that the background music one hears is the whining drone of the small-engined dirt bikes, modulating in pitch as they alternately climb and descend the hilly motocross track a few ridges away. One can't help but compare them mentally with the giant shovels that roamed this landscape a half century ago, the roar of their great diesel engines reverberating as they lifted dirt and rock and scooped the rich black coal into waiting trucks. *

FINGER LAKES STATE PARK • 1505 PEABODY ROAD, COLUMBIA

MISSISSIPPI LOWLANDS

> *"One can drive a hundred miles from north to south through the middle of the Missouri Delta and see hardly more than a wood lot. It was all or nearly all heavily timbered swamp land only forty years ago."*
> —THAD SNOW, *FROM MISSOURI*, 1954

THE MISSISSIPPI LOWLANDS AREA in far southeastern Missouri is mostly a flat alluvial plain shaped by outwash from the great glaciers. About thirty to fifty million years ago, this region was part of the Mississippi Embayment, similar to today's delta, emptying to the Gulf of Mexico. The region is now the northernmost reach of the Gulf Coastal Plain and harbors many species characteristic of that region. Clearly set off from the Ozarks and the Ozark Border to the west and north by an escarpment 100 to 250 feet high, this is the most physiographically, biologically, and culturally distinctive region of Missouri.

The natural vegetation that occupied this low-lying region less than two centuries ago was unlike any found elsewhere in the state. Imagine a vast, deep forest of massive oaks, ancient bald cypress swamps, and impenetrable thickets of giant cane stretching five hundred miles southward to the Gulf Coast. The massive glacial outwash that shaped this landscape during more than a million years carried in its waters silts ground fine in thousands of miles of braided channels, then carried aloft by strong winds to create sand dunes and ridges. Even after the glaciers retreated, floodwaters from the Mississippi and from rivers draining the southeastern Ozarks continued to nourish the landscape. Though interrupted by north-south-trending sandy ridges, some elevated only a few feet above the surrounding terrain—except one, Crowley's Ridge, which stands some 100 to 150 feet high—most of the land was low, bathed annually in nutrient-rich floodwaters. The resulting bald cypress and tupelo gum swamps and tall bottomland forests dominated by elm, sweetgum, oak, and other hardwoods were lush and diverse, containing many species at the northern or western limits of their range. The wildlife was abundant and diverse.

The region is distinctive also in having been the most thoroughly altered by human beings through deforestation, ditching, and draining, with most of the alteration occurring in the twentieth century. Because it has undergone such rapid transformation so recently, the area has had a demographic and social history unlike that of any other region of the state. And because it is different and also remote from most of the state's population, the region is probably the least known and understood by most Missourians.

The Mississippi Lowlands have two distinct land types: the lowlands themselves, poorly drained and of slight relief, and Crowley's Ridge, an elongated line of steep uplands that arc across the region from the Mississippi south of Cape Girardeau southwest to the lower St. Francis River. Three units of the state park system are in the lowlands and one is on Crowley's Ridge.

The first is Big Oak Tree State Park in Mississippi County, one of the few spots anywhere in the lowlands where one can experience the magnificent bottomland forest and bald cypress swamp that covered virtually the entire area before the headlong deforestation that began in the late nineteenth century. Not far from Big Oak Tree is Towosahgy State Historic Site, located on a natural sand ridge along an oxbow of the Mississippi, where archaeological excavations have documented a fortified ceremonial center of the town-dwelling peoples of the Mississippian tradition, who occupied this area and much of the southeastern part of the country between about AD 1000 and 1400.

The Hunter-Dawson home in New Madrid, built in the late 1850s and occupied by the interrelated Hunter and Dawson families until the 1960s, evokes the character of the region in the antebellum period and reflects the lives and activities of entrepreneurial families that were deeply involved in virtually all aspects of the stunning transformation of the Mississippi Lowlands from "swampeast" Missouri to the richest agricultural region in the state.

For years, the state sought a park on Crowley's Ridge, a series of hills that once bordered an earlier channel of the Mississippi on its west side. Today, a small but fascinating tract near Malden, Morris State Park, provides some representation of this feature. The park and the much longer ridge of which it is a part are of great interest both geologically and biologically, and because the ridge stood above the swampy lowlands, it was one of the earliest corridors for human movement and agricultural settlement.

Missouri's Mississippi Lowlands make a compelling landscape, linking our upper South border state to the deeper delta South. Despite drastic alterations of the region's natural features, the state park system preserves superb highlights of original forest and ridge scenery, prehistory, and historic architecture worthy of every Missourian's time and exploration. *

The swamp forests that were formerly characteristic of the Mississippi Lowlands have been reduced to tiny remnants, like this one at Big Oak Tree State Park, where yellow butterweed still thrives in saturated soils. ***Ken McCarty***

Big Oak Tree State Park

PICKING OUT THE BOUNDARIES of Big Oak Tree State Park is easy as you drive south on Route 102 from East Prairie, across the billiard-table-flat farmlands of Mississippi County. The 1,000-acre preserve stands out as an oasis of tall trees surrounded by miles of cropland, a living time capsule for an environment that once stretched across the entire Bootheel of southeastern Missouri. Big Oak Tree is a monument both to the original forested wilderness of "swampeast" Missouri and to the dedication of citizens who wished to ensure that at least a small fragment of that vast wilderness would be forever protected from logging and agricultural development. The park also stands as testimony to the difficulty of trying to protect a dynamic ecosystem no longer connected to many of the processes that shaped it over time.

Your first impression is of the height of the forest and the size of the trees. The canopy rises to 120 feet, with some of the park's giants grabbing another twenty feet of sky. For a time in the 1960s, this small park in Missouri's Mississippi Lowlands was home to nine reigning national champions on the American Forestry Association's roster of big trees; that is, nine trees were the largest recorded representatives of their species anywhere in the nation. Little Big Oak Tree State Park outranked Olympic National Park, which had seven champions on nearly a million acres, and it was in turn outranked only by Great Smoky Mountains National Park, with fifteen. Today, sadly, Big Oak Tree is home to only one national champion, a pumpkin ash, and several state champion trees.

The park was named for a giant bur oak that survived until 1952. Another bur oak along the boardwalk rivaled that one with a circumference of more than twenty feet and a crown spreading nearly a hundred feet, but it toppled over on Christmas in 2009. Fortunately, it left behind a nearby twin almost as big.

The great bur oak that inspired the park lived there for 396 years. Once scheduled to be cut down as a curiosity for fair goers to the 1904 Louisiana Purchase Exposition in St. Louis, the stately tree survived another half-century before finally succumbing in 1952 to lightning strikes and tree rot. The big oak and the other incipient champions were found on an 80-acre tract of virgin hardwoods that in 1937 became the object of an urgent campaign by local residents to save some remnant of their natural heritage. Reaching the front page of the *St. Louis Post-Dispatch* and other newspapers, the effort to save the big oak became a statewide crusade, even enlisting Gov. Lloyd Stark, a prominent nurseryman in private life, who fired off a telegram to the Mississippi Valley Hardwood Company of Memphis asking it not to destroy the tree. Though some doubtless thought only in terms of that single tree, many people realized that what was at stake was a part of Missouri's legacy—the magnificent swamp forest of the Bootheel—that was in imminent danger of disappearing forever.

Logging had begun with a vengeance in the area as soon as railroads crisscrossed the lowlands in the 1880s. New legal mechanisms for drainage in the early twentieth century and an extraordinary cotton boom in the 1920s, when the boll weevil farther south pushed large-scale production upriver into Missouri, resulted in the nearly complete transformation of Bootheel lands from about 70 percent "unusable" in 1907 to only 3 percent by 1930. Logging continued on the last patches of forest, spurred no doubt by economic pressures of the Great Depression. The Mississippi Valley Hardwood Company and associated firms had already cut nearly three-quarters of a million acres in the area when they were asked to spare the 80-acre tract surrounding the big oak.

Missouri officials could not afford to pay $100 to $125 per acre for the key tract and sufficient land that had already been logged but would serve as a buffer or game refuge—especially at a time when parkland in the Ozarks cost only $2 to $5 per acre. The State Park Board and the Conservation Commission, with help from a private donor, Jacob Babler, agreed to split the cost of the original 80-acre tract provided local citizens could raise enough money for a 920-acre buffer. Thus began a campaign for donations to save the big trees. Area schoolchildren contributed their small change, and business leaders gave their big change. Everyone wanted to help, it seemed, despite the depression. In 1938, the 1,000-acre park was dedicated.

Virtually the entire undeveloped portion of the park totaling about 940 acres was officially recognized as a state natural area in 1977, one of the earliest and largest areas designated by the Missouri Natural Areas Committee. In 1986 the 80-acre tract of virgin forest won designation as a National Natural Landmark; it is the only bottomland hardwood forest to survive essentially uncut out of the 2.5 million acres in Missouri of the Mississippi embayment forest that once stretched from southeastern Missouri to the Gulf of Mexico.

The general characteristics of the park—the poorly drained clayey soil, the dense understory, and of course, the big trees—are so different from anything else in the park system that even casual observers find themselves wanting to explore this unique environment. An elevated boardwalk and a longer loop trail allow even the less adventurous to experience

Above: This majestic bur oak towers over younger maple and ash trees in the rich bottomland forest and is a worthy successor to the original big oak for which the park was named. Its limbs reach as high as 120 feet. *Ron Colatskie* • Left: Bald cypress dominated the swamps of what used to be called "swampeast" Missouri before they were drained for agriculture. Today, cypress swamp is still the most characteristic natural community in the park. *Ken McCarty*

these dense, damp woods and gaze, awestruck, at the towering canopy. Some find it almost spooky to be there; others find it more cathedral-like.

In the wetter areas, the forest is made up mostly of bald cypress trees with their odd-looking "knees," along with cottonwood and willow. But on the higher ground—six inches is enough to make a difference here—forest inundation is more seasonal. This periodic flooding with slow drying provides a richly diverse overstory of mixed hardwoods: shellbark hickory, pecan, slippery elm, sweetgum, hackberry, persimmon, pawpaw, possumhaw, blue beech, and pumpkin ash, as well as the great bur, cherry-bark, overcup, and swamp chestnut oaks. Various kinds of vines draped throughout the understory create a jungle-like setting, and colonies of resurrection fern cling to the giant trees up near the canopy. The fern is only one of the epiphytes—plants that grow on other plants without damaging their hosts—found in Big Oak Tree.

Bird-watchers from all over the country visit Big Oak Tree to record some of its more than 150 known species, including several rare in Missouri. The chirp of the hooded warbler is hard to describe but easy to remember, and the bird's bright yellow plumage makes it easier to spot than some other warblers, such as the rare and secretive Swainson's. The woods are sometimes pierced by a loud "cuh-cuh" from the fish crow. And high overhead, you might see the Mississippi kite gathering a meal of insects on the wing. More common species include the prothonotary warbler, pileated woodpecker, rose-breasted grosbeak, wintering bald eagle, and a host of other waterfowl, especially wood duck.

For all its marvels, Big Oak Tree State Park today remains an endangered landscape, just as it was in the 1930s. Many of the park's oaks have been growing older and dying, with virtually no young ones to replace them. Many of the massive bald cypress trees are not doing well and are likely to be replaced by a young growth of willow, sugarberry, and

Left: In 2011, the New Madrid Floodway was activated by controlled detonations that opened the levee, and floodwaters engulfed the park and the round man-made lake, as they would have frequently before levees walled the river off. *Missouri State Parks* • Above: A boardwalk leads visitors into the swamp. *Scott Myers* • Right: After the 2011 flood destroyed the lake berm, it began reverting to a more natural swamp pond, and cypresses began recovering. *Ron Colatskie*

red maple; numerous other swamp species show little regeneration. The problems began even before creation of the park. Flood-control levees and drainage ditches for large-scale agriculture on the rich bottomlands disrupt normal intermittent hydrologic cycling. Park officials contributed to the problems in the 1950s when they acquiesced to political pressures for a fishing lake in the heart of the swamp. The 22-acre lake, constructed in 1960 in a biologically rich natural bayou known as Grassy Pond, was surrounded by a perfectly circular levee with a pumping system to maintain water levels. Fishing for species stocked by the Missouri Department of Conservation was fine for the first few years, but the lake never functioned properly and required continual stocking, pumping, and until halted in 1987, herbicides. Ironically, the best fishing came to be not in the lake but in borrow pits all around it.

Compounding the problems, park officials further agreed to build a drainage ditch through the swamp because some adjacent farmland became flooded when water levels were high. Beavers dammed the ditch and burrowed into the lake berm, causing leaks, so park staff obligingly dynamited the dams and trapped the beavers. In the 1980s, however, park resource professionals observed that the swamp was dry for most of nearly every year, owing to the disruption of natural flood cycles by the drainage canals circling and bisecting the park. They stopped the dynamiting, offering instead to buy the affected farmland, though farmers were unwilling to sell. And they initiated studies to determine whether different water cycles might encourage regeneration of oaks, cypress, pumpkin ash, and other hardwoods.

In the early 1990s, park officials began to discuss with the Army Corps of Engineers a project to surround the park with a levee that, with pumps and culverts, would enable better control of water levels in the park to mimic more natural hydrologic cycles. They even secured a $1.5 million state appropriation for such a project, but the effort became entangled in the corps' plan to close a 1,500-foot gap in the New Madrid levee a few miles southwest of the park. This gap was the last remaining connection of any sizable part of the Mississippi River floodplain in the entire state that remained open to backwater flooding, a priceless lifeline for the natural biota of Big Oak Tree and tens of thousands of other wetland acres in the area. The project, stoutly supported by regional agricultural and political leaders, was strongly opposed by the US Fish and Wildlife Service and other agencies and organizations because of its destruction of wetland values. Despite opposition, the corps proceeded, dangling the prospect of acquisition of 1,800 acres surrounding the 1,030-acre Big Oak Tree State Park to enable construction of the ring levee, pumps, and culverts. But it became apparent that the park project would not go forward because farmers were still unwilling to sell the needed land, and then in 2007, a federal court ruled against the corps' entire project and ordered all work deconstructed. Meanwhile, the state appropriation had long since disappeared.

During the next few years, the park was buffeted by an unprecedented series of extreme events, both natural and man-made, especially problematic for a small island like Big Oak Tree, so vastly different from the agricultural monotypes surrounding it and harboring such iconic resources. Hurricane Ike toppled many trees in the park and damaged the boardwalk in 2008. Then a record-making ice storm in January 2009 knocked down so many trees and branches that the forest canopy was reduced from an estimated 90 to 98 percent closure to only about 45 to 60 percent. A major windstorm that July uprooted more trees, and then over Christmas during a relatively modest wind, with no witnesses, the champion bur oak came down.

The next year was mild, but in spring 2011, nearly constant rains raised floodwaters in the Mississippi so high that the Corps of Engineers was forced to breach the mainline levee at several points for the first time since 1938—the year the park was established—so the New Madrid Floodway could serve its intended purpose, to absorb some of the excess water in order to save cities and levees both upstream and

down. A breach close to the park allowed floodwaters to enter with such force that they destroyed all the park buildings and equipment, including the boardwalk, the lake berm, and pumps. The flood left deep sand amid the trees in the southern end of the park.

Park officials became more philosophical in the wake of the deluge of extreme events, chastened by the limits of their ability to protect the park's iconic resources but resolved to do whatever they could to encourage more natural resilience in the system. With the man-made lake nearly empty and its ring levee heavily damaged, they decided to allow it to naturally disintegrate, perhaps removing sections of the berm to allow more free flow of water to recreate something approximating the earlier Grassy Pond with its native fishes and amphibians. Intermittent flooding and drying might then promote the growth of native bald cypress. The oaks and rich assemblage of species in higher areas could be encouraged by prescribed fire of the sort that occurred naturally in centuries past.

With the ice storm having reduced the tree canopy by nearly half over much of the park, numerous sun-loving plants sprouted, including giant cane, which is forming thickets or canebrakes like the ones described by early explorers. The cane in turn is creating habitat for the rare Swainson's warbler, which was seen frequently at Big Oak as recently as the 1970s but rarely since then. The boardwalk has been rebuilt and visitors may once again walk deeply into the heart of the forested swamp. The struggle by the corps and political leaders to close the gap in the New Madrid levee continues, but park officials and their supporters remain determined to encourage more natural ecosystem processes in the park.

With support, Big Oak Tree State Park will endure and remain a remarkable and unique testament to the presettlement biological richness of "swampeast" Missouri. It will not be the same, but it will still hold amazing stories about how this extraordinary landscape has adapted to human and natural challenges. The grandchildren and great grandchildren of those who worked so hard to save the big oak trees from annihilation in the 1930s will still be able to read those stories in the park landscape and help protect this remnant of the swamp-forest ecosystem in which those oaks were born. *

BIG OAK TREE STATE PARK • 13640 SOUTH ROUTE 102, EAST PRAIRIE

Towosahgy State Historic Site

THE MOUND BUILDERS INSPIRED A LIFE-LONG curiosity in Thomas Beckwith, born in 1840 on a farm in the Missouri Bootheel. People of his day called the prehistoric people Mound Builders because their villages featured large earthen mounds. Their villages were found throughout the southeastern United States, and especially in the Mississippi River valley. He seemed to have come by this curiosity honestly; in 1823, his grandfather Newman Beckwith had sent to the American Antiquarian Society in New England a prehistoric pot he had found eroding out of a Mississippi riverbank.

The investigation of these mounds and the people who built them became the younger Beckwith's passion. He dug into scores of these mounds, mostly in Mississippi County, both on his own extensive landholdings and on neighboring places. One wonders how he found the time to farm, given the time he devoted to his avocation. Late in life, he even wrote a book outlining his ideas about the origin of these villages and mounds and depicting his huge artifact collection. Unlike many people in those days, Beckwith correctly understood that the mounds had been built by American Indians and not by some mysterious vanished race.

The Native American builders of these mounds were part of what is now known as the Mississippian cultural tradition that had spread up and down the river from its center, the great ceremonial city at Cahokia, in Illinois. These Indians were urban dwellers, and their towns were scattered as far north as Wisconsin and as far south as the mouth of the Arkansas River, also east as far as Georgia and west to Oklahoma. Their villages, frequently surrounded by log palisades, included mounds of various sizes, the largest apparently built as platforms for buildings of ritual significance and perhaps residences for persons of high status. Smaller mounds were built for other purposes, including burials. The economy of these villages was based upon crops of beans, maize (corn), squash, sunflowers, and native grasses with edible seeds grown in fields outside the village walls. To this diet, they added wild game, fish, river mussels, persimmons, wild plums, and a variety of nuts. A trade network gave access to salt, mineral paint, chert for tools, and ceremonial materials. Large dugout canoes provided most of the transportation.

The site of one of the largest of these Mississippian villages in the Bootheel was situated on one of Thomas Beckwith's farms. Located on a ridge of sand known as Pinhook Ridge, the ancient village was bordered on one side by an extinct channel of the Mississippi River, an oxbow slough at that time, and consisted of seven mounds surrounding a central plaza, all at one time having been enclosed within a palisade and moat wherever not protected by the slough. The large ceremonial mound on the north end of the plaza was over 250 feet long, and still stands to this day a full 16 feet high—built of many tons of soil moved by hand labor from a nearby borrow pit. Arranged around the plaza and among the mounds had once been the many homes of the ordinary people of the village. These small family houses were typically constructed of "wattle and daub"—a lattice of tree branches plastered with clay. Like the rest of the Mississippi Lowlands, the village was surrounded by a primeval swamp forest of sweetgum, cypress, and sycamore, with their crops being grown in the open sand prairies higher on the ridge.

Because of its size and large temple mound, this site attracted early attention from artifact hunters. Beckwith himself had dug extensively on the site, known as Beckwith's Fort, and in the 1880s, Cyrus Thomas and the Smithsonian Institution Bureau of Ethnology's Division of Mound Exploration excavated aggressively there. Ironically, despite these previous excavations and considerable illegal pot hunting over the years, by the mid-twentieth century, Beckwith's Fort had become the best preserved and last relatively intact Mississippian village left in the state of Missouri. Other sites, especially in the Bootheel, had been destroyed by intensive agricultural practices such as land-leveling and subsoiling, while the many mounds in St. Louis, once known as Mound City, had long since been flattened and paved over.

At the urging of Dr. Carl Chapman of the University of Missouri, the State Park Board purchased the site in 1967, with grant assistance from the Land and Water Conservation Fund (LWCF). The sixty acres acquired encompassed the central area of the village, including the mounds and the visually apparent peripheral stockade line. At Chapman's suggestion, the park was named Towosahgy, a word borrowed from the Osage language meaning "old village."

> *"A regular mining fever at once broke out and spread so rapidly that in some instances as many as twenty-five or thirty men, women, and children could be seen digging for pottery in one field at the same time."* —CYRUS THOMAS

A facility master plan was developed calling for a museum and visitor center with offices and a laboratory, a service area with garage and workshop, and residential quarters for a site administrator and archaeological staff. As required by LWCF funding, a recreational walking trail around the site would lead to the mounds and various features reconstructed through archaeological exploration. Park officials envisioned a major presentation of Missouri's prehistory and ongoing collaboration with the University of Missouri's Division of American Archaeology. They selected a PhD archaeologist as administrator and formulated a policy of basic preservation, permitting only limited excavation necessary to develop the site for public visitation. Despite the fact that people had been digging

Left: This humble hill is the largest of Towosahgy's mounds. The Mississippian Indians conducted ceremonies upon it until about AD 1420. ***Oliver Schuchard***
When the Army Corps of Engineers dynamited a levee to activate the New Madrid Floodway in May 2011, forty-three deer, four turkeys, and two coyotes shared the shrinking top of the tallest mound during the height of the flood. The ancient Mississippian people knew what they were doing when they built their mounds on this ridge, out of reach of most floods. ***Chris Crabtree***

TOWO-1989-UMC
23MI2
XU-4 AREA
7.875SD
EARTHQUAKE
CRACK

there for a century and a half, mostly pot hunting, there was minimal recorded data about any features that might have been discovered. So officials planned small excavations to verify and locate the construction of the log palisade around the village, to define one or more of the small houses, and to test the big ceremonial mound for evidence of structures on top. Excavations at the south end of the village revealed the palisade; in fact, they showed that the palisade had undergone several phases of expansion. Remains of the palisade and several small houses found near the log wall were then "ghosted" by placing modern poles in the imprints where ancient posts once stood. Small excavations were also made at the north end of the property and on the big mound. There were plans for future excavations at the north and south ends of the village to make sure the visitor center and support buildings would not impinge upon important archaeological features. Signs were erected near the ghosted palisade lines and houses, and a steady trickle of visitors began finding their way to this out-of-the-way spot.

Then in the late spring of 1973, the river began to rise. By June, only the tops of the largest mounds protruded above a seemingly endless expanse of water. It was one of the worst Mississippi River floods in history, covering a large expanse of the Bootheel, including nearby Big Oak Tree State Park, where most facilities were destroyed. After the flood, the master plan was reevaluted, and a decision was made not to erect the planned structures and to provide only a passive visitor experience.

The ruined signs were removed, and any open excavations were closed. Towosahgy was put totally into preservation mode, with no visitor access to the site. A new sign at the north end of the property provided information about the village site and its history, but visitors were limited to viewing the site over the fence from the county road running alongside, from which only the larger mounds were clearly visible. For more than a decade, the site was mowed and kept clear of brush, but no further developments were undertaken.

Eventually, in response to continuing interest in the site and in deference to the LWCF grant, a new round of excavations began in the late 1980s that would lead to reopening the site to visitors. Excavations at the north and south ends conclusively determined that there was a moat on the outside of the log palisade, while excavation in the large ceremonial mound showed that what was thought to have been a ramp on the plaza side was actually much more interesting: the remains of one or more buildings that once stood on top. These buildings had been demolished by the inhabitants and pushed over the front side of the mound, after which the debris pile and the entire mound had been sealed with a thick cap of clay in a ritualistic manner of unknown significance. The mound excavation also recovered many objects of ceremonial importance, including natural crystals of various types, ear plugs and spools, a tobacco pipe, and effigy pottery. A surprise finding was evidence of early earthquakes associated with the nearby New Madrid Fault—fissures filled with sand pushed up from below, from two different earthquake events between AD 300 and 900. Finally, new radiocarbon dates indicated that the village had been occupied much longer than previously thought, roughly a thousand years from AD 400 to 1400.

The site once again welcomed visitors with a new entry road, parking, and toilet facilities along with a redefined walking trail, renewed ghosted

Top left: This 1971 excavation at Towosahgy revealed the rectangular pattern of a small house near the stockade that enclosed the village. Two different periods of stockade construction located in earlier excavations are marked by colored posts. ***John Cottier*** **• Excavations at the front of the large mound in 1989 revealed dramatic evidence of prehistoric earthquakes along the New Madrid Fault more than a thousand years ago, leaving fissures like the one running diagonally across the upper right. White sand from farther below was blown upward into the darker deposits found at higher levels.** ***James E. Price***

Visitors climb the temple mound at Towosahgy. ***Missouri State Parks***

palisade lines, and a dozen new interpretive panels presenting the latest research. Because of the probability of flooding, the facilities were designed for submersion and subsequent return to use.

It was good that they were: in the flood of 2011, the Army Corps of Engineers determined it was necessary to activate the New Madrid Floodway by dynamiting the Bird's Point Levee along the Mississippi. Once again, both Towosahgy and Big Oak Tree went under water—and stayed that way for weeks. At Towosahgy, only the tops of the two largest mounds showed, the big temple mound harboring a collection of refugee deer, turkeys, and coyotes. This time, when the river receded, the waterproof facilities were hosed off. Duplicates of the explanatory panels were rehung, and the site was soon back in business.

In archaeology, there is always a tension between preservation and excavation. Excavation is destruction. This may be less evident in dealing with a Roman amphitheater or highway, made from massive stone blocks, than in a Native American site, where an archaeological resource may often be only marked by a subtle change in color or texture of the soil itself. Excavation means trading the physical survival of the site for the knowledge gained about it. Caution dictates to excavate only as much as is necessary and with care so that the knowledge gained will become preservation of a different sort.

Thomas Beckwith was a mixed blessing for Missouri archaeology. His diggings were not excavations in the sense of modern professional archaeology. Regrettably, much information was lost in his ambitiously random pursuit of relics. But Beckwith's somewhat naive approach to archaeology must be contrasted with his contemporaries. As Cyrus Thomas noted, people around Charleston, Missouri, discovered that collectors would pay top dollar for Mississippian pots. Many sites were virtually destroyed, and thousands of Mississippian pots were sold on the open market and dispersed across the country and the world, many forever lost to modern archaeology. In contrast, Beckwith dug carefully, kept good provenance records for the objects he found, and in the end, donated his thousands of artifacts to Southeast Missouri State University for scholarly study. In the context of his times, Thomas Beckwith left a valuable legacy. Given his passion for Missouri's mound builders, he, and Grandpa Newman too, would likely be pleased to know that his fort is now held in public trust, to be permanently preserved. *

TOWOSAHGY STATE HISTORIC SITE • COUNTY ROAD 502, EAST PRAIRIE

Hunter-Dawson State Historic Site

THE HUNTER-DAWSON HOME IN NEW MADRID reminds us that Missouri, a border state with many upper South affinities, also had ties with the deeper delta South. Featuring bald cypress lumber from nearby swamp forests, construction on this fifteen-room mansion was begun in 1859 by William Washington Hunter, a fifty-two-year-old successful Bootheel businessman. Although Hunter died before the house was completed, his widow, Amanda Watson Hunter, moved in with some of her seven children just before the outbreak of the Civil War. In 1876, the house passed to their daughter Ella Hunter and her husband of two years, William W. Dawson. It remained in the Dawson family until it passed to the city of New Madrid in 1966 and then to the state in 1967.

The frame house was built by the combined labor of Hunter's slaves and hired craftsmen. It displays traces of many architectural traditions—most notable are Georgian, Greek Revival, and Italianate influences. Hunter also built the grain house and privy that remain on the twenty-acre site. Mrs. Hunter selected most of the furnishings in the spring of 1860, according to records in the family papers. Much of this furniture, which came from the Cincinnati firm of Mitchell and Rammelsberg, is still in the home.

The house features nine fireplaces, family and formal dining rooms, a kitchen, seven bedrooms, a sunroom, a sitting room, and double formal parlors. Typical Bootheel trees grace the estate.

The grounds feature many large trees, such as oaks, gums, elms, and pecans, many of which were present long before Hunter began construction of the house, though some have been lost as a result of severe wind and ice storms in recent years.

Without knowing something about the people who lived there, historic houses seem little more than empty shells. The Hunter and Dawson family stories breathe life into the old mansion, for these were families intimately associated for more than a century and a half with virtually all aspects of the development of the southeastern lowlands of Missouri.

The iconic front hall features portraits of Amanda Hunter's parents, Robert Goah and Jane Watson, plus a hall tree and pocket chairs that were original to the house. The Hunter-Dawson families had a remarkable impact on the area. *Michael Comer*

William Washington Hunter came to New Madrid in 1830 from Washington County, where his parents had settled six years earlier after leaving their native Virginia. He went to work in a fur-trading post and mercantile store owned by Robert Goah Watson, and he rose quickly as a merchant. His success was no doubt aided when he married the boss's daughter, Amanda Jane, in 1836. Amanda's father was born in Scotland but came to America to work for his uncle, who in 1805 sent him to New Madrid to operate his Indian trading post. The New Madrid earthquakes of 1811 and 1812 devastated the area, and most of the residents fled, never to return, but Robert and his wife stayed to rebuild their business. After Watson's death in 1855, William Hunter and Amanda's brother continued the business in partnership.

With his own brother, A. S. Hunter, William established a general mercantile store, the Crystal Palace, where the latest products off of steamboats could be purchased. He also entered into partnership with R. B. Turner for the trade of dry goods, produce, and furs from their steamboat on the Mississippi River. And along St. John's Bayou, east of New Madrid, he operated Hunter Mill Farm, a steam-run sawmill and gristmill. This was where much of the cypress for his home was milled. William Hunter combined his business dealings with an interest in civic matters, and in 1855, he helped organize the Dunklin and Pemiscot Road Company, which constructed a plank road through the swamps to settlements farther south in the Bootheel. An acquaintance of the Austin family, probably from their Washington County years, Hunter had encouraged the early settlement of Texas, where he acquired land holdings. When he died in 1859, Hunter owned at least fifteen thousand acres in Missouri, Arkansas, and Texas. He also owned thirty-two slaves, who were inherited by his widow and seven children in the division of his estate.

After William died and Amanda and the children moved into the house, family tradition maintains that during the Civil War, Union forces under Maj. Gen. John Pope forced the Hunter family from its two-year-old home so that it might serve as a military headquarters, though there is no direct evidence. Control of the Mississippi River was key to both sides' strategies during the war, and New Madrid and nearby Island No. 10 were scenes of battle during the conflict. Amanda's son, William Colson Hunter, along with many other local men, including William Dawson's father, joined the Confederate forces.

Above: The families who lived in this antebellum home helped transform the Mississippi Lowlands from colonial times to the twentieth century. *Michael Comer* • Left: Many furnishings originally selected by Amanda Hunter in 1860 for her new home, like this full-canopy Mitchell and Rammelsberg bed, were still in the home when it became a state historic site. *Brian Sirimaturos* • Right: The table and much of the tableware are original to the house. *Missouri State Parks*

William Dawson married Amanda Hunter's daughter Ella in the house on Christmas Eve in 1874. When they moved into it in 1876 after Amanda's death, they brought another distinguished lineage into association with this storied mansion. Dawson's great-grandfather on his mother's side, Pierre Antoine Laforge, came to New Madrid in 1791 just after the community was founded in Spanish Louisiana; he served as an interpreter and, after the Louisiana Purchase, as civil commandant and judge of the court of common pleas. His grandfather on his father's side, Dr. Robert Doyne Dawson, was a physician and lawyer who came to New Madrid from Maryland in 1800 to represent a client who had several Spanish land grants. He served in both the territorial and state legislatures and represented New Madrid at Missouri's constitutional convention in 1820. With his wife's brother, John H. Walker, he helped to assure that the Bootheel, where Walker grazed thousands of cattle, was included as part of Missouri.

William Dawson, educated at Christian Brothers College in St. Louis, followed in his grandfather's footsteps by serving three terms in the Missouri General Assembly from 1878 to 1884, when he was elected to the US Congress for one term. Despite continuing agricultural interests, he served also in other civic capacities and, beginning in 1914, for three terms as circuit clerk of New Madrid County. He was succeeded in that office by his daughter, Lillian, whom he trained. His son, William Dawson Jr. was involved in agriculture all his life, but he also served for more than twenty years as cashier of Hunter's Bank and in 1933 became owner of the New Madrid Oil Company. A bachelor until late in life, he lived with his mother in the house after his father's death in 1929 and then was joined by his sister Lillian after their mother's death in 1933. William died in 1956 without children, and Lillian passed in 1975.

As early as 1960, efforts had begun to interest the State Park Board in acquiring the house as a state historic site. Then in 1966, the city of New Madrid bought the decaying old home for $15,000, with many of Amanda Watson Hunter's 1860 furnishings still intact, and donated it to the state a year later. City officials were undoubtedly encouraged by state park director Lee C. Fine, who had grown up just down the street from the stately old mansion and who was distantly related to the Hunter family.

A bare-bones summation can scarcely suggest the manifold connections these remarkable families—and their equally remarkable home—had with the settlement and development of the Mississippi Lowlands from Spanish times to our own. More remains to be discovered through additional historical research. The Hunter-Dawson home, beautifully restored to the period of 1860 to 1880, reflects the success of the earlier generations and carries their tradition proudly into the future. *

HUNTER-DAWSON STATE HISTORIC SITE • 312 DAWSON ROAD, NEW MADRID

American beech trees typical of the Appalachians grow in the woodlands here in Morris State Park as well as elsewhere on Crowley's Ridge, though many have been lost during recent extreme droughts and ice storms. ***Allison Vaughn***

Morris State Park

ABOUT FIFTEEN MILES SOUTH OF CAPE GIRARDEAU on Interstate 55, a remarkable sight appears. Drivers heading south through the rolling Benton Hills get a big visual jolt upon reaching the crest of a moderate rise, when suddenly the whole earth seems to spread out before them. It turns out this last hill was small only on its north side. Once over the crest, there is a long downgrade, until the land is nearly totally flat in every direction. A first thought is that this is a river bottom, but it's much too large. This is not just a river bottom; it's a remnant of prehistoric delta land. Something like what happened in modern times a hundred miles south of New Orleans once happened here, about 50 million years ago.

Here in the heart of the continent, Gulf of Mexico waters once formed a huge bay that geologists call the Mississippi Embayment. It reached Missouri at its northwest edge. How this bay formed, filled in, eroded out, and left behind a bedrock, gravel, and soil spine several hundred feet high and some 150 miles long down its middle is a geological story both amazing and complex. That spine, known as Crowley's Ridge, is a striking landscape feature of Missouri's Bootheel region. On that ridge, a few miles east of Malden, is Morris State Park, a small but important remnant of this landscape. Jim D. Morris, a Springfield businessman who grew up picking peaches and cotton near Campbell four miles to the south, donated the land in 1999.

Geologists ascribe the formation of the embayment to plate tectonics, the means by which large plates of the earth's crust, with continents riding on them, move slowly over the semi-liquid mantle far below. By this mechanism, continents are formed, split, reformed, and generally moved about. More than 700 million years ago, North America was nearly torn in half by tectonic forces. This "rift" did not succeed, but the attempt resulted in a sunken scar up the middle of the continent that

Here in southeastern Missouri, waters of the Gulf of Mexico once lapped at the base of Ozark hills. A huge bay in Cretaceous times covered major portions of Louisiana, Arkansas, Mississippi, and Texas, as well as parts of Missouri, Kentucky, and Tennessee.

was then filled with sediments that became rock. Reactivation of this rift, the Reelfoot Rift, during Cretaceous times around 100 million years ago, created a new lowland, which, combined with rising sea levels, allowed seawater from the Gulf of Mexico to pour into the depression and form the bay. This same rift failure, with its weakened rock structure or "fault" deep in the earth, was responsible for the notable New Madrid earthquakes of 1811 and 1812 and the ongoing seismic activity in this part of Missouri.

The bay was an ideal habitat for shallow, warm-water organisms, their exoskeletons gradually building up layers of calcareous clay, marl, and chalk on the bottom. At the same time, nearly two-thirds of what would become North America was draining into the embayment through precursors of great rivers yet to come. Delta formation by all these streams, large and small, gradually began to fill in the bay, building up layers of sand, gravel, and silt, mixed with the calcareous strata deposited by the marine organisms.

Then, about 34 million years ago, the seas retreated, draining the embayment, and the present coastline of the Gulf of Mexico began to

Above: An eroding cliff in the park tells part of the story of Crowley's Ridge, showing a sequence of deposits but no visible bedrock. You can see the deposits of sands and clays with a band of pebbles and a loess cap above. ***Chris Crabtree***
Right: Crowley's Ridge extends for about 150 miles through the Mississippi Lowlands of Missouri and Arkansas. It was carved by the ancestral Mississippi River flowing to its west and the Ohio River to its east. ***Wikipedian Kbh3rd***

materialize. During this time, sediments were eroded rather than deposited, until new deposits began forming less than five million years ago, before and during the last ice age. The river systems that had carried the sediments into the bottom of the bay continued processes we see today, alternately cutting away the materials they had earlier deposited and depositing new materials in turn. The great rivers of today began to form: the Mississippi, Missouri, Ohio, Arkansas, and many smaller ones meandered back and forth across the plain, cutting and depositing materials in the great central valley.

But one thing was very different in this last ice age period. The proto-Mississippi River stayed to the west side of the valley, while the Ohio kept to the east, not joining together until they finally met well within the boundary of present-day Louisiana. As the two rivers meandered back and forth, they often came within ten or twelve miles of meeting, but it just didn't happen. Instead of one alluvial valley, two were formed, divided by this thin strip of elevated land between them. As the valleys eroded lower, the strip of land separating them became relatively higher. During glacial winters, when drought prevailed and monstrous windstorms swept the land, silt from the alluvial plain was swept up and later dropped as loess on the high ground of the ridge and on the bluff lines along the rivers, making the high spots even higher.

But this elevated strip between the rivers—Crowley's Ridge—may not have been formed solely through erosion by the ancestral rivers. Geologists now think that earthquakes in the New Madrid Seismic Zone may have thrown up the ridge's steep hillsides, called scarps. Earthquakes along the faults may have helped raise these parts of Crowley's Ridge above the surrounding bedrock, now buried by sediments from the ancestral Mississippi and Ohio Rivers. Landslides along these steep hills, including one in Morris State Park, may be related to more recent earthquake activity.

The geologic story of Crowley's Ridge was nearly complete, but there was one last act in the drama. More than ten thousand years ago, the Mississippi River finally did break through the ridge, near Cairo, Illinois. Once through, it never returned to the west side. The Mississippi captured the Ohio River's valley—and kept it—from Cairo all the way to the Gulf. Crowley's Ridge was now an isolated cresting, some 150 miles long (partially in Missouri but mostly in Arkansas), a dozen miles wide, and rising several hundred feet above the alluvial plain, which bordered it on each side. Some miles to the east, the Mississippi-Missouri-Ohio combination flowed, and still flows, to the sea.

The bedrock, clays, and gravels that form Crowley's Ridge have a wide range of geologic ages, varying from 600-million-year-old bedrock to silt that's less than twenty thousand years old. The geologic sequence visible in Morris State Park begins with sandstones that formed in a delta environment, clays that were formed in a near-shore marine environment, and gravels left by the ancestral Mississippi and Ohio Rivers and their tributary streams. Some silt deposits are loess, wind-blown powdered rock left behind when the glaciers retreated.

The Beech Tree Trail loops through a woodland of southern red oak and other oaks, with Hercules club among other plants in the understory. The trail leads to a scenic overlook above the alluvial plain. ***Ken McCarty***

So Morris State Park, a small one at 161 acres, has a big geologic story to tell. Although the park is small, it provides a pleasant and interesting visit. It nestles on the east flank of Crowley's Ridge amongst surrounding peach orchards and is nearly all wooded. As a resource-preservation park, little development is planned; its main offering is a two-mile ramble on Beech Tree Trail.

The loop trail provides an accessible scenic overlook of the surrounding alluvial plain, but it is quite steep in places as it descends to the bottomland forest and then back up. In several spots, the sequential geologic strata that built the ridge are well displayed—or at least those of the last few hundred thousand years or so. And, there is a final surprise—a complement of trees and plants restricted to this region of Missouri.

Through some curious history and evolution, Crowley's Ridge has acted as an island of refuge for plant communities that were more common in Missouri several thousand years ago, when the climate here was cooler and more moist. Did the alluvial, swampy ground on either side of the ridge inhibit the spread and domination of species from the Ozark hills? Whatever the cause, as at Trail of Tears State Park, the woods of Morris State Park more resemble the forests of the Appalachian Mountains than they do the Ozarks. The entire park is mature sand woodland, a rare natural community in Missouri largely confined to ancient escarpments, ridges, and dissected hills in the Mississippi alluvial plain, such as here at Crowley's Ridge. Most such sites have been extensively logged and converted to crops, pasture, or orchards, but here in Morris, there are still patches of old growth and remnants of the former Malden Prairie.

Oaks, hickories, and cedars are here, to be sure, but tulip poplars, sweetgums, and American beeches also abound. In the understory are red buckeye and Hercules club, natives of the southeastern United States, along with some sedges and grasses not found in any other Missouri state park. The park has more than 325 species of plants, with many at the western or northern extent of their range. But in 2009, a huge ice storm nearly wiped out the park's population of sweetgum trees, and the drought of 2012 killed many of the beeches. Perhaps Mother Nature isn't quite done tinkering with her climate zone and plant range overlaps.

Of course, there is a more recent history to Crowley's Ridge, beginning with extensive use by Native Americans and then its settlement in 1821 by Benjamin Crowley and others who followed, attracted by the deep, well-drained loess soils in an otherwise swampy region. American Indian traces, roads, and railroads followed the higher ground. A military road along the ridge moved troops engaged in the Civil War battles at Chalk Bluff a century and a half ago. In the park is the family cemetery of Jonas Stewart, a Confederate supporter from South Carolina, who was captured at Chalk Bluff and held at a Union encampment near or perhaps in what is now the state park. He became so enamored with the area that he returned with his family after the war to buy a farm and open a grist mill and a cotton gin.

But these are stories for another place and mere blinks of an eye in the geology embraced by Morris State Park, a park that tells the story of a time when this part of Missouri was oceanfront real estate, and where the flora of ten thousand years ago still persists. *

MORRIS STATE PARK • HIGHWAY WW, CAMPBELL

BIG RIVERS

"One who knows the Mississippi will promptly aver—not aloud, but to himself—that ten thousand River Commissions, with the mines of the world at their back, cannot curb it or confine it, cannot say to it, Go here, or Go there, and make it obey; cannot save a shore which it has sentenced; cannot bar its path with an obstruction which it will not tear down, dance over, and laugh at."
—MARK TWAIN, *LIFE ON THE MISSISSIPPI*, 1883

THE LOWER MISSOURI AND MIDDLE MISSISSIPPI Rivers could be Missouri's most consequential landscape features—and they are also among the most altered. Comprising only about 5 percent of the state, the Big Rivers are defined ecologically as the floodplains and terraces of the largest rivers, especially the Mississippi and Missouri but also the lower portions of larger tributaries. These floodplains, with their bottomland forests, wet prairies sloughs, marshes, islands, and sand and mud bars have been severely diminished during the course of the twentieth century by damming, diking, and dredging to deepen, narrow, and stabilize the main channels for commercial barge navigation and flood control, largely under the auspices of the Army Corps of Engineers, advised by the Mississippi River Commission.

Along the Missouri River, for example, scientists have calculated that 50 percent of the original surface area of the river within the boundaries of the state was lost between 1879 and 1972, that the island area was reduced by 90 percent, that some fifty miles of river length were removed by straightening, and that most backwater habitat was eliminated as the margins silted in and accreted, both physically and legally, to the mainland, where they were placed under plow by the owners of adjoining land. Fisheries were devastated, with an 80 percent decline in the commercial harvest between 1947 and 1963 alone, and wildlife has been greatly diminished, with several species such as the least tern and pallid sturgeon virtually eliminated.

Above St. Louis, the Mississippi River has been turned into a series of long pools by the addition of locks and dams, leaving more backwater areas but also creating problems with shifting water levels and deposits of dredge spoil. Below St. Louis, and to some extent above, the Mississippi channel has been greatly constricted by flood walls and agricultural and industrial levees, so that the natural vegetation and the normal cycles of flooding, silting, and drying have been drastically altered, with serious consequences to both natural habitats and man-made structures when levees are breached or overtopped.

As a result, very little natural habitat remains along the big rivers, and what little there is, with several notable exceptions, is underrepresented in the state park system. Until the early 1970s most Missourians had gradually turned their backs on the big rivers, regarding them as barge canals or, worse, as open sewers; the river margins were often invisible behind levees or flood walls or desecrated by urban blight. Even those who realized what had happened, and who cared, regarded the situation as too hopeless for amelioration.

From high in the Missouri State Capitol, the view looks out on the Missouri River flowing downstream toward St. Louis, with Jefferson Landing and the Missouri Pacific Railroad just below, the Governor's Mansion in the middle distance, and the Katy Trail following the river on the opposite shore. *Scott Myers*

During the 1970s, with heightened environmental awareness in the wake of the first Earth Day and with creative and determined leadership by citizen organizations and some agency professionals, public opinion about the big rivers began to turn. The Corps of Engineers also began partnering with other federal and state agencies and conservation organizations to mitigate some of the damage. Since then, the Missouri Departments of Conservation and Natural Resources and various federal agencies have been restoring fish and wildlife habitat and water quality along the rivers, and there is a growing understanding of the need to restore more natural hydrologic function as well. Although more remains to be done, several new parks featuring riparian landscapes and river corridor sites have been acquired along the margins of the big rivers.

Even though the natural features and hydrologic function of the big rivers and their floodplains and terraces have been severely altered and are underrepresented in the park system, the same is not true of the cultural features. In fact, the state has a remarkable string of historically significant parks and sites along the big rivers. Some of them are beyond the bounds of the floodplains but are still close enough to be considered here.

Most social and cultural scholars who have attempted to delineate regions in Missouri have not identified the big rivers as a distinctive area. Yet most everyone recognizes the vital role the rivers played in channeling transportation and settlement in the state, especially during the nineteenth century. Key communities and sites, some of which by natural criteria might be classified as part of the Ozark Border or Glaciated Plains, have been influenced significantly by their proximity to the big rivers. Paradoxically, many of these sites still retain a large measure of their integrity because they were left in the backwater of a century and a half of progress in transportation—by rail, highway, and air—that took the pressure of development away from the cultural borders of the big rivers even as destruction of the natural channels and floodplains was intensifying.

The Big Rivers region logically segments into Mississippi and Missouri River portions, and especially, in terms of physical characteristics and presettlement vegetation, into lower and upper stretches of each river within Missouri. Because most migration and settlement of Missouri in the early nineteenth century came from the upper South and proceeded up the Mississippi and Missouri Rivers, we arrange the Big Rivers essays geographically, proceeding upstream on the Mississippi and then on the Missouri River.

Because several sites on the lower Mississippi have been considered as part of the Mississippi Lowlands, we begin at Trail of Tears State Park in Cape Girardeau County, which commemorates one of the most tragic episodes in Native American relations, the expulsion and forced march of some thirteen thousand Cherokee from Georgia and Tennessee across the Mississippi at Moccasin Springs to Indian Territory in what is today Oklahoma during the devastating winter of 1838 to 1839. Trail of Tears State Park is also a sizable, quite wild representation of the intensely rugged and richly forested river breaks along the Mississippi.

Traveling upstream, we arrive next at the Felix Vallé House State Historic Site. Though located in Ste. Genevieve, which was established about 1750 as the earliest permanent French settlement on the west bank of the Mississippi, the house was built by a Philadelphia merchant in the Federal style and purchased by the Vallé family. It reflects the successful transition of this prominent French family into an American milieu during the nineteenth century. The site also includes several other structures, including the 1792 Bauvais-Amoureux house, built in the traditional French vertical log style and fronting on the culturally significant Big Common Field along the Mississippi.

Farther upstream at Herculaneum, on a high bluff overlooking the Mississippi, is Gov. Daniel Dunklin's grave, a tiny one-acre site that invites consideration not only of the state's fifth governor but also of the fascinating role of these bluffs in the manufacture of lead shot by Moses Austin and other early American entrepreneurs.

In St. Louis, rampant urbanization and, later, massive land clearance for the city's celebratory arch have obliterated most of the early historic structures along the waterfront. But in this great river city with its complex cultural and architectural history, the state has restored the house and inner city neighborhood where the King of Ragtime, Scott Joplin, lived and composed some of his best known works in the earliest years of the twentieth century.

Continuing upstream on the Mississippi, we find an unusual state park and two historic sites in adjacent counties in the northeastern corner of the state. Wakonda, on the floodplain in Lewis County where gravel was mined by the state highway department between 1924 and the early 1980s, was redeveloped as a state park with attractive fishing and swimming lakes for recreation, resulting in an unexpected revival of a scarce natural habitat. In Clark County along an old channel of the Des Moines River near its confluence with the Mississippi is Iliniwek Village State Historic Site, the archaeological site of a large village of Peoria Indians. Here in 1673 Father Jacques Marquette and Louis Jolliet—in this case traveling *down* the Mississippi from the Great Lakes—became the first Europeans to describe setting foot in what is now Missouri while visiting the village. Not much farther up the Des Moines River is the Battle of Athens State Historic Site, focus of the northernmost battle of the Civil War, but significant also for containing the entire street grid and several structures of an antebellum river town.

The Mississippi River portion of the Big Rivers region is represented by rather disparate parks, but the Missouri River has several parks that focus on river ecology and history or, at least, offer visitors a connection with the river, beginning with a landmark site that it shares with the Mississippi. Where the Missouri river converges with the Father of Waters just upstream from St. Louis, the Edward "Ted" and Pat Jones–Confluence Point State Park was dedicated in 2004 on the bicentennial of the Lewis and Clark expedition. In this historically important floodplain park now in process of ecological restoration, visitors can actually venture out along a short point and place a foot in each mighty river.

Along the lower 170 miles of the Missouri River where high quality natural areas are scarce, the Katy Trail provides a marvelous linear connection for a series of significant historic and cultural sites. It also offers a passing glimpse at various features of the natural scene. The trail, formerly a right-of-way for the Missouri-Kansas-Texas Railroad along the north bank of the river, starts at Machens northeast of St. Charles and continues upstream to Boonville before striking off through the countryside to Sedalia and Clinton. Totaling 240 miles, the Katy is the longest rail-to-trail conversion in the nation. And because it follows the lower Missouri for much of its length, it is certainly among the most historic.

State historic sites along the Katy Trail include First Missouri State Capitol, Deutschheim, Clark's Hill, Jefferson Landing, and the Missouri State Museum. Missouri's first state capitol, which occupied the upper floors of a row of commercial buildings along the riverfront in St. Charles for several years in the 1820s, was restored by the state in the 1960s in honor of the state's sesquicentennial and in turn sparked the revitalization of a nine-block historic district near the river. At Deutschheim, the state has restored several buildings to showcase the strong German heritage of settlers in Hermann and surrounding areas beginning about 1838. Then comes Clark's Hill/Norton State Historic Site, a hill near the confluence of the Missouri and Osage Rivers that William Clark described having climbed in June 1804 to reconnoiter the country during his expedition to the Pacific.

At Jefferson City, the state capital since 1826, several restored buildings on the old Jefferson Landing evoke the commercial vitality of the Missouri waterway during the steamboat era in the mid-nineteenth century. Up the hill on the first floor of the state capitol building is the Missouri State Museum, which is operated by Missouri State Parks and serves as a base for guided tours of the state's impressive capitol with its remarkable treasure trove of public art.

About seventy miles farther upstream after the Katy Trail leaves the river at Boonville is another cluster of related sites. Boone's Lick, the salt springs on a tributary stream north of the river where Daniel Boone's sons manufactured salt beginning about 1806, gave its name to the famed Boone's Lick Trail from St. Charles to the interior. Arrow Rock across the river was a thriving mid-nineteenth-century town that was associated for a time with the Santa Fe trade and also a political powerhouse of southern gentry. The state has restored several buildings here, including the Huston Tavern and the home of artist George Caleb Bingham, and also offers access to the river on a trail across a portion of Big Muddy

National Fish and Wildlife Refuge. Sappington Cemetery several miles west is the burial place of Dr. John Sappington of Arrow Rock and his extended family, including three Missouri governors, while nearby Sappington Negro Cemetery is the resting ground of many former slaves and their descendants.

The dividing point between the lower and the upper Missouri River in the state is upstream from Arrow Rock near Glasgow, above which the floodplain is less constricted because of softer, more easily eroded bedrock, and where prairie was more prevalent in the presettlement landscape. This is also the approximate boundary between the northern Ozark Border and the Glaciated Plains to the west and north. The first state park upstream from this juncture is Van Meter, which during the seventeenth and eighteenth centuries was the site of the principal village of the Missouria Indians, from whom the river and the state took their names. Though most of the park is on the uplands, the approach to it is across the broad Missouri floodplain. Remnants of the magnificent hardwood forests testify to the rich loess soils formed from wind picking up silt from the glaciated plains to the west and depositing it in thick mounds here along the river. At the base of these bluffs is a sample of the once expansive wetland marshes of the Missouri floodplain.

Continuing upstream, we arrive at Lexington, the site of a major victory of the Missouri State Guard on behalf of the Confederate cause during the first summer of the Civil War, as Union troops for a time failed to control the vital Missouri River artery. And south of the river a few miles, near Higginsville, is Confederate Memorial State Historic Site, a cemetery and park on the grounds of what was formerly the Confederate Home of Missouri, now a memorial to the fifty thousand Missourians who fought for the Confederacy. Next comes Kansas City, the great metropolis of the nation's breadbasket. Here in a comfortable neighborhood south of the river are the home and studio of the noted regionalist painter Thomas Hart Benton, who died in his studio in 1975 as he was completing his last great mural.

Upriver north of Kansas City, three state parks preserve aspects of the riverine environment. Weston Bend, like Van Meter, offers richly forested Missouri River loess hills, bluff-top trails, original barns where visitors can learn about the region's historic tobacco culture, and access to a small portion of the floodplain. Lewis and Clark State Park, about fifteen miles farther upstream, includes part of the shoreline of an oxbow lake that the famed explorers visited and described on the Fourth of July, 1804, during their epic journey to the headwaters of the Missouri and beyond. Finally, Big Lake State Park, on the shore of the state's largest remaining natural oxbow lake in far northwest Missouri, offers access to the lake and an outstanding remnant marshland rich in bird life.

The state of Missouri developed as the child of these magnificent rivers, which defined her boundaries and channeled her exploration and settlement, even from prehistoric times. Missourians have returned to a stronger awareness of the Big Rivers, and the state parks now better reflect their importance. Don't miss an opportunity to visit these sites and ponder the role of the Big Rivers in the life of the state and the nation. *

The American white pelican is an iconic species along the Mississippi and Missouri Rivers, especially here at the confluence. ***Danny Brown***

Thousands of Cherokee were ferried across the Mississippi River and camped near here during the harsh winter of 1838 to 1839 on the infamous Trail of Tears. *Oliver Schuchard* • Top right: False Solomon's seal, long known for its healing qualities, grows in the rich river breaks in Vancill Hollow Natural Area. *Allison Vaughn*

Trail of Tears State Park

THE VIEW FROM THE OVERLOOK is grand and serene. The Mississippi River stretches lazily north and south. Limestone bluffs three hundred feet high stand guard on the west, and bottomland farms line the eastern side of the valley. You may spot an eagle soaring over the lush green forest that cloaks the rugged hollows that extend through the bluffs to the river.

Regardless of the peaceful vision this sublime view may evoke, it once overlooked one of the sorriest episodes in American history. That infamy gives Trail of Tears State Park its name. Here at Moccasin Springs in the fall and winter of 1838 and 1839, nine contingents of Cherokee were ferried across the icy Mississippi River, a formidable obstacle on the forced march from their Appalachian homeland to a new home in what is today Oklahoma. American Indian tribes subjected to removal crossed the river at a number of different points, including the one here. Many died during that harsh winter, and some are thought to be buried in and around the park.

The park's extensive forests, despite some early logging, resemble the great woods of the Cherokee homeland. Trail of Tears State Park preserves Missouri's best sizable example of what botanists call "western mesophytic" forest. Mesophytic refers to the relative moisture in the soil. Here on the deeper, richer soils protected in the cove ravines along the river, growing conditions mirror those of the Appalachian Mountains to the east.

In comparison to much of the Ozarks, the park features trees of greater size and variety. Oaks abound, but they join many typically Eastern species such as tulip poplar, cucumber magnolia, and American beech. The ground cover is luxuriant with ferns. You may find the rare pennywort, a delicate plant that flowers early in the spring, or see beechdrops, parasitic plants found only near beech trees. The state has set aside a particularly outstanding example of this river-break landscape as Vancill Hollow Natural Area, 300 acres in the middle of the park.

You can find solitude and ample recreation on the nine-mile Peewah Trail in the 1,300-acre Indian Creek Wild Area north of Vancill Hollow and the overlook drive. The steep and rugged hollows of the wild area empty into Indian Creek along the park's northern boundary. The bottomlands of Indian Creek, once cleared for crops, are now jungle-like, featuring patches of giant cane and a profusion of grapevines dangling from large sweetgums and black willows. On the slopes in the labyrinth of hollows are a mature forest of black gum, white oak, bitternut hickory, tulip poplar, sassafras, and deciduous holly. The ridges above the creek, more readily accessible by trail, contain woodlands of post oak, blackjack oak, and shortleaf pine, which park managers have been treating with prescribed fire. The park has been designated an Important Bird Area for its key role in providing habitat for forest birds along the Mississippi flyway.

Perhaps the Cherokee viewed this rugged terrain and dense forest with longing, as it resembled the homeland they were forced to leave. The story of their removal began in 1829 when President Andrew Jackson, responding to pressure from the state of Georgia where gold had just been discovered on Cherokee land, asked Congress for legislation to remove the southern tribes to lands west of the Mississippi. Congress responded a year later with the Indian Removal Act. It is clear that "Old Hickory" strongly believed that American Indians could not be assimilated into the white culture that was bursting the seams of the already settled areas. The irony is that the Cherokee and the other members of the so-called Five Civilized Tribes had already demonstrated a willingness to interact with white culture and to live in peace. Most of the Cherokee leaders could read and write English, and thousands of Cherokee had learned to read and write in their own language since the development of a syllabary a decade earlier by the remarkable Cherokee statesman Sequoyah. The Cherokee lived in houses, had adopted the practice of owning slaves, and farmed. Additionally, acculturation had been furthered by considerable intermarriage of white traders and frontiersmen with native women. Nevertheless, enticed by the potential economic boon of gold mining, Congress dictated that the Cherokee had to go.

Removal did not occur right away, however. Although some Cherokee tribal leaders actually favored relocation and signed Jackson's Treaty of New Echota, Principal Chief John Ross and most of the other chiefs representing over sixteen thousand Cherokee resisted federal and state efforts to remove them. The Cherokee brought legal action and eventually obtained a favorable ruling by the US Supreme Court. However, this only prompted Jackson to move faster. In the spring of 1838, a

Top: A November fog shrouds the Bushyhead Memorial, previously known as the Princess Otahki monument. The local Rotary Club erected it to honor the Cherokee who died at this river crossing. *S. Denise Dowling* • A visitor center exhibit depicts Cherokee women preparing food at a camp. *Missouri State Parks*

THE BUSHYHEAD MEMORIAL

Ice held up a group of Cherokee led by Rev. Jesse Bushyhead, a charismatic Baptist preacher, at the Mississippi River for more than a month. According to legend, his daughter Otahki died, and his wife gave birth to a baby, Eliza Missouri. Otahki was said to have been buried on a knoll above the encampment at Moccasin Springs. Wishing to commemorate the tragedy of the Cherokee, the Cape Girardeau Rotary Club in 1961 erected a monument to "Princess Otahki" and the many others who died at the river crossing.

Later research suggests that there never was an Otahki and that the person buried here is likely Bushyhead's sister, Nancy Bushyhead Walker Hilderbrand, who was listed in an 1835 census of the Cherokee Nation as owner of a farm worth $760 in Candy's Creek, Tennessee. Her first husband was John Walker Jr., a man with mixed heritage, who had met with President Andrew Jackson and was assassinated in 1834 for his role as a treaty advocate; he thought removal was inevitable and wanted the best deal. Nancy's second husband was Lewis Hilderbrand, who was selected to deliver a petition to Washington protesting the removal treaty and signed by nearly sixteen thousand Cherokee. He later led one of the detachments on the Trail of Tears.

Nancy and John had two children before he died, and both reached the new territory without their mother. Years later, one of them told a Cherokee historian that his mother had died on the trail in Missouri. Reverend Bushyhead's infant daughter Eliza Missouri also made it to Indian Territory and became a prominent educator and businesswoman until her death at age eighty-one.

The Princess Otahki monument at the park was renamed the Bushyhead Memorial in 2001.

A natural hill prairie on Sheppard Point overlooks the Mississippi downstream from the Moccasin Springs crossing. *Ron Colatskie* • The rugged river breaks of the 300-acre Vancill Hollow Natural Area feature American beech, tulip poplar, cucumber magnolia, and a luxuriant ground cover. *Tom Nagel*

force of four thousand troops under Gen. Winfield Scott rounded up the remaining Cherokee and placed them in primitive, unsanitary military stockades, awaiting a break in the worst drought ever recorded in the region; more than fifteen hundred died of cholera and measles during confinement. Many others were ill when the forced migration began that fall. Divided into seventeen detachments of about a thousand each, the exodus proceeded across Tennessee, Kentucky, and Illinois.

From the Mississippi, the Cherokee took several routes across Missouri, some of which have been marked as part of the Trail of Tears National Historic Trail, established in 1987. The main route apparently took them through the county seat of Jackson (named for the president who had forced their removal) and then northwest through Farmington, Caledonia, Steelville, and St. James, where the path turned southwest to Waynesville and Springfield and then across the corner of Arkansas to reservations in Oklahoma. One of every four Cherokee died in the stockades or during the forced migration. The remainder arrived a broken and politically divided people. In spite of everything, the Cherokee built a remarkable society in their new homeland and continue to survive as a nation within a nation.

Trail of Tears State Park was a gift to the state by the people of Cape Girardeau County, who authorized a $150,000 bond to purchase more than 3,000 acres in 1956. A handsome visitor center provides exhibits on the natural history of the park and on the Cherokee tragedy. The 3,400-acre park is a superb preserve of an original Mississippi River landscape. It is also a sober reminder of the intolerance of a young country and a memorial to a resilient people who persevered. *

TRAIL OF TEARS STATE PARK • 429 MOCCASIN SPRINGS ROAD, JACKSON

Felix Vallé House State Historic Site

WHEN FATHER ST. PIERRE DULY NOTED in the parish records on February 20, 1793, that he had moved the body of Francois Leclerc from the cemetery in "old" Ste. Genevieve to the cemetery in "new" Ste. Genevieve, he might as well have pronounced the last rites for the old town at the same time. Plans already were being made to transfer the church and the civil administration to the new town, and it is this new town of the 1790s that we cherish today. With wonderful examples of French architecture from both during and after the colonial era scattered among the homes of later American and German settlers, Ste. Genevieve is one of the most attractive and interesting historic towns not only in Missouri but also in North America.

> *"... a eté relevé le corps de François Leclerc du cimeteriere de vielle Sainte Genevieve et transferé dans le cimeteriere de Nouvelle Ste. Genevieve."*—DE SAINT PIERRE, CURÉ

Although receiving scant attention today, just southeast of town lies the big common field and the archaeological remains of the old, original town of Ste. Genevieve, the little French settlement that farmers and traders established around 1750 on the west bank of the Mississippi River. By 1790 it had grown to about nine hundred people, about a third of whom were black or mulatto, living in a three-mile-long settlement strung along the riverbank and exposed to the vagaries of that capricious river. They had been attracted there by *le grand champ*, the rich agricultural land in places nearly a mile wide on the floodplain, which they farmed with slaves and maintained as a common field. The field was divided into long, narrow private lots running from the river to the bluffs but surrounded by a single common fence, which all landholders helped maintain.

After a series of particularly severe floods in the 1780s destroyed many homes, some families began to leave the river bottom and move to higher ground in various places, including what was first known as *Petites Côtes* (Little Hills), a slight rise a few miles northwest of the old town, between the forks of the Gabouri Creek. As more families moved to higher ground, *Petites Côtes* became *Nouvelle Sainte Genevieve*, and after 1793, just Ste. Genevieve. The old village on the bank of the Mississippi had become only a memory—and an archaeological site.

Beginning in the fall of 1796, land-hungry Americans arrived seeking concessions in the hinterland to the west from a suddenly more liberal Spanish officialdom. Spain had secured the west bank of the Mississippi when France lost its empire in North America in the early 1760s, although Spain's imprint on the French colonial society and culture of the area were very light. Then, Spain traded it back to France in 1800, just before Thomas Jefferson's purchase from Napoleon in 1803 of the entire Louisiana Territory, including New Orleans, Ste. Genevieve, St. Louis, and west all the way to the crest of the Rocky Mountains. The purchase unleashed a flood tide of Americans who nearly overwhelmed the French in Ste. Genevieve.

Among the new arrivals, most of whom were from the upper South, was Jacob Philipson of a Philadelphia family, who had migrated to St. Louis to open a mercantile business and then in 1811 moved his business to Ste. Genevieve. Ste. Genevieve was a logical port of trade for

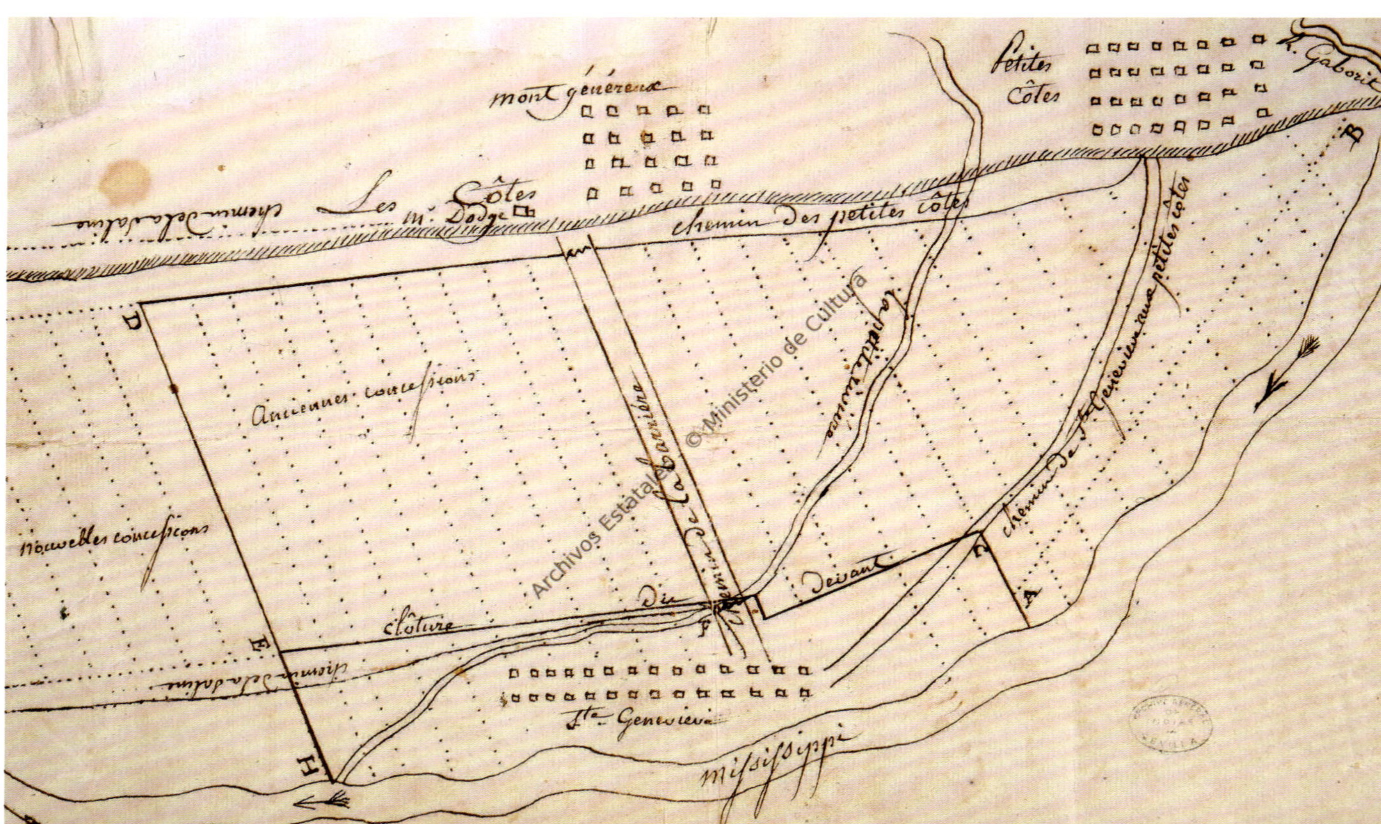

Two front entrances show that Felix and Odile Vallé's home served also as the headquarters for the Menard & Vallé mercantile establishment. *Oliver Schuchard*

This 1793 map attributed to Barthélemy Tardiveau shows old Ste. Genevieve, the Mississippi River, the big common field, and the new town, then known as *Petites Côtes*. North is to the right. *Archivo General de Indias, Seville*

manufactured goods coming west by river from Philadelphia and Pittsburgh and for lead and furs from Missouri's interior going east. In 1818 Philipson built a one-and-a-half-story home and store of local ashlar stone on the southeast corner of Merchant and Second Streets. The Federal-style structure is evidence of the new American influences on the community. The building was divided on the first floor into two distinct areas, one for Philipson's mercantile business and the other for his residence, with two separate front entrances on Merchant Street.

Jean Baptiste Vallé (1760–1849), the last commandant of the post of Ste. Genevieve before the Louisiana Purchase, bought the building from Philipson in 1824. Vallé used it as headquarters for Menard & Vallé, a commercial enterprise involved in much of the fur trade with the Indians of southern Missouri and Arkansas. Head of the leading French family in Ste. Genevieve, Vallé then owned a large portion of the block that included Philipson's stone building. His personal residence on the opposite corner of the block was a typical French colonial vertical log structure built in the 1790s. It still stands, now owned by the National Society of Colonial Dames in Missouri, who have long owned and carefully restored the Bolduc and Bolduc-LeMeilleur houses next door and operate them as the Bolduc House Museum.

Vallé's youngest son, Felix, and his wife, Odile Pratte Vallé, made their home in the stone house for the next fifty years. Felix worked as a clerk for Menard & Vallé in the commercial side of the house and eventually took much of the responsibility for the firm's operation. In the early 1840s when the Menard & Vallé partnership dissolved following the death of Pierre Menard, Felix Vallé founded an enterprise with James

Top: This remarkably accurate diorama built by Lewis Pruneau can be seen in the Bauvais-Amoureux house. It depicts Ste. Genevieve in the 1830s, with Main Street at the right across South Gabouri Creek. You can still see many of these structures. *Susan Flader* • Above: A detail of the diorama shows the Felix Vallé house, its outbuildings, and the Bossier-Shaw house to the right. *Missouri State Parks* • Left: The Felix Vallé house has been restored to how it was when the Menard & Vallé mercantile business occupied part of the building. *Scott Myers*

The person who occupied the Bauvais-Amoureux house for the longest time was Pelagie Amoureux, who had been born a slave in 1805 and freed by the widow of Vital Bauvais in 1832. She lived there from 1852 to 1890. ***Missouri State Parks***

Harrison called the American Iron Mountain Company to mine for iron ore in nearby St. Francois County. Probably not long afterward, Felix and Odile modernized their home, removing the commercial rooms and one of the two front doors and turning it into a center-hall Victorian house.

Across a side street from the Felix Vallé house is a small frame structure known today as the Shaw house, now also part of the state historic site. It was originally built around 1819 by Jean Baptiste Bossier as a commercial structure. Dr. Benjamin Shaw purchased the timber-frame building in 1837 and presumably enlarged it to its present configuration around 1840. Dr. Shaw and his wife, Emile, were contemporaries of the Vallés. Emile, widowed in 1849, continued living in the house for more than fifty years. In this part of town are numerous other historic homes, most privately restored and still lived in, including the home of Dr. Lewis F. Linn, a prominent physician who served as a US Senator from 1833 to 1843. Vallé and Harrison's American Iron Mountain Company thrived, adding a successful rolling mill in St. Louis in partnership with Pierre Chouteau Jr., scion of the founding family of St. Louis. They employed nearly one thousand men in the Iron Mountain vicinity by 1869. Felix Vallé died in 1877, leaving most of his vast estate to his wife. Odile Vallé donated three-fourths of the funds to build the Catholic Church that still stands in the center of town and continued to live in the modest stone house on Merchant Street until her death in 1894.

As early as the 1930s, the federal government recognized the significance of the Felix Vallé house by incorporating architectural drawings of the structure in the Historic American Buildings Survey. In 1970 the family home was donated to the state by descendants of the intermarried Vallé and Rozier families. The Rozier family was descended from Ferdinand Rozier, a Frenchman who had arrived in Ste. Genevieve in 1811 with his business partner, John James Audubon. Audubon dissolved the partnership shortly thereafter to pursue his calling as an artist, but Ferdinand Rozier and his family lived for many years near Felix and Odile Vallé on Merchant Street.

Park officials restored the Felix Vallé house to its original appearance, including reopening the two original front entrances leading to separate sections, and furnished it as it may have been during the 1830s. The house boasts a great expanse of original painted ceiling, protected for more than a century by a plaster ceiling that was placed over it during remodeling around 1850; the newly revealed 1818 paint is covered with thousands of flyspecks, a hint of life before wire screens. Outdoors, the restored sidewalks are gravel—not always popular today but mandated by an early nineteenth century city ordinance as an improvement over the dirt that seemed always to have been either mud or dust.

Two connected outbuildings—a brick one that was likely a wash house and a frame building that was probably a slave cabin—remain in the rear yard, rare survivals of nineteenth-century outbuildings. The wash house has been set up as of circa 1830, while the frame building, currently repurposed, also may some day be restored. An archaeological study of the yard revealed the location of several other significant features, including a building believed to have been the original kitchen and two cisterns.

In 1989 the Shaw house across the street was added to the state historic site for use as an administrative building and a reception and exhibit area for visitors. In the process of converting the building for that purpose, numerous layers of added modern materials were removed from the walls and floors, revealing paint shadows, nail holes, and other

evidence that precisely outlined the previous positions of store counters and shelving—a ghostly vision of the old Bossier store of the early nineteenth century. The site collection even holds Bossier's original business account book. The largely residential property has had a colorful history since the days of Emile Shaw, especially during the Depression years of the 1930s when it was the focal point for a colony of artists attracted to the French heritage and peaceful surroundings of Ste. Genevieve. Because it was altered many times over the years, this house was not set up with period furnishings, but the evidence of its interesting architectural evolution from store to residence was left in view. Few buildings in Ste. Genevieve have been as intimately involved in as many aspects of the community during the last two centuries as the Shaw house, and its use for both administrative and exhibit purposes is pragmatic preservation in action.

There was a certain irony in the fact that a state historic site in the best-preserved French colonial community in the nation consisted of a series of nineteenth-century American-style buildings. This preservation was justified, however, as none of the other museum houses in town were interpreting the interaction of French and Anglo-American culture in the early nineteenth century. And yet, the lack of an eighteenth century French colonial structure—built in the traditional vertical log manner—was a striking gap in park system holdings. These distinctive buildings, with their wall logs set vertically either in a trench or on a sill, with the spaces between the logs filled with small stones and clay or lime (*pierrotage*) or with clay and grass or straw (*bousillage*), are the signature French trait in Ste. Genevieve. State park officials recognized the need for such a building and desired to acquire one for the site.

A farmhouse on a beautiful site fronting on the common field a few miles south of town was among the obvious candidates. The house, near the village of New Bourbon, was discovered in the mid-1980s to have vertical logs beneath its clapboard siding. Tree-ring dating of the logs by a University of Missouri scientist established that they were cut in 1793, and archival research suggested the house may have been built for Pierre Charles Dehault Delassus de Luzières, a high-ranking French nobleman who left France in the aftermath of the French Revolution and arrived in Ste. Genevieve in 1793. He served as commandant of the New Bourbon District, carved out of the Ste. Genevieve District in 1793 for him to administer. Architectural study of the house established that it had the largest floor plan of any house constructed in the French colonial manner in the entire middle Mississippi River valley. The house was owned by descendants of a German family, the Kerns, who had occupied it since the 1850s. They added a second floor in the 1890s. But despite being vacant, it was not for sale.

In early 1993 the Delassus-Kern house was finally offered for sale, and the state agreed to accept it as a gift from an anonymous donor. Before the transaction could be completed, the Mississippi rose out of its banks in one of the greatest floods of modern times, gravely imperiling Ste. Genevieve, St. Louis, and lands along the river. The agricultural levee protecting the common field was one of many to breach that spring, and the Delassus-Kern and many other houses, both historic and modern, on the south side of town stood in floodwater until late September. When the waters finally receded, preservation experts discovered that the old vertical log French houses came through much better than newer frame buildings, and the state park system found itself the recipient of not one but two flood-damaged but largely intact vertical log houses.

In addition to the Delassus-Kern house, the state acquired the Bauvais-Amoureux house, a gift of the French Heritage Relief Committee, formed to raise money for flood-imperiled French heritage sites. Also overlooking the common field, the Bauvais-Amoureux is *poteau en terre*, or "post in ground," a type of construction, once common in the original town along the river, in which the vertical wall logs extend into a trench in the ground to form the foundation. Today, the Beauvais-Amoureux is one of only five such houses known to still exist in North America, three of which are in Ste. Genevieve. Jean Baptiste St. Gemme Bauvais Jr. built it in 1792. It was sold to Benjamin Amoureux and his wife Pelagie in 1852. Pelagie had been born a slave in 1805, owned and perhaps fathered by Bauvais's brother Vital. Vital's widow set Pelagie free in 1832 after Pelagie's common-law marriage to Amoureux; Felix Vallé wit-

Left: The long lots of the big common field are still evident on Google Earth (with north at top), although they are wider today due to land consolidation. ***B.H. Rucker and Tom Vought*** **• Above: Bolduc, Bolduc-LeMeilleur, and Jean Baptiste Vallé houses on Main Street form the most iconic French colonial streetscape in Ste. Genevieve.** ***Bill Naeger*** **• Right: These are some of the thirteen traditional desserts featured at** ***le réveillon,*** **a French Christmas celebration.** ***William Hopkins***

nessed her manumission document. Pelagie, who had six children with Benjamin Amoureux, continued to live in the house until her death in 1890. The house contains no original furnishings, but with its excellently preserved original eighteenth-century features, it illuminates both the technique of vertical log construction and the mixed cultural heritage of its occupants. Additionally, it houses a remarkably accurate diorama constructed by Lewis Pruneau, a nationally known model maker, depicting Ste. Genevieve as it appeared in the 1830s. You will definitely want to see this diorama when you visit Ste. Genevieve.

Meanwhile, the Delassus-Kern house fell victim to historical controversy, which stymied its restoration. A French colonial historian challenged the house's purported connection to Delassus on the grounds that the Delassus house had been both mapped and described at the time as located on a bluff, whereas the extant house was on a terrace at the base of the bluff. In the late 1990s, archaeological excavation around the house in conjunction with a Southeast Missouri State University field school found a gap between Native American artifacts and Euro-American materials from the 1830s, suggesting the house was not on that site until the 1830s. Archaeology on the bluff above found a house foundation, but the dig was too limited to establish its floor plan. The question became: Is it the Delassus house relocated or a house built from salvaged materials of the period? The question remains unresolved, but in either case, it is a significant example of French-style construction, fabricated from logs cut in the 1790s. After decades of inaction, park officials allocated modest funds to stabilize it in 2013.

In 2006, Congress authorized a study of the feasibility of National Park Service involvement in preserving Ste. Genevieve. The NPS considered not only the heart of the historic town, which was one of the first places in the nation to be designated a National Historic Landmark, but also the significance of the common field and the old town archaeological site, a thirty-eight-acre tract, never excavated, that is probably the only remaining portion of the old town not obliterated by channel changes of the Mississippi River. A decision by Congress on NPS recommendations may be years off, but Ste. Genevieve's residents and many friends eagerly await the possibility of enhanced national attention. *

LE RÉVEILLON

The French are noted for fine cuisine and *joie de vivre*, and the staff and volunteers at the Felix Vallé house have a reputation for staging soirées that would rival those Felix and Odile Vallé would have held in the early 1800s. Perhaps the most special is *le réveillon*, a traditional French Christmas celebration that calls for thirteen desserts. After preparing feverishly until the last minute, the hosts don period clothing to welcome visitors to the house, simply decorated with boughs of native shortleaf pine and bathed in candlelight. On the elegant dining table is the *pièce de résistance*: a *bûche de Noël*, a cake shaped as a Yule-log, alongside other sweets from the era: *gâteau de sirop*, a cake made with Louisiana cane syrup; *madeleines*, tiny, shell-shaped cookies; *gâteau St. Honoré*, a cream-puff ring like an ornamented crown, topped with miniature caramelized cream puffs, named for the patron saint of French pastry chefs; *croquembouche* (literally, "melts in the mouth"), a pyramid of the tiny caramelized cream puffs; and on and on to the count of thirteen.

Enjoy a slice of *bûche de Noël* and a chat with other guests, then join in singing French carols—and imagine having spent such a Yuletide evening with Felix and Odile Vallé. Stroll through the village center after the soirée, back to your bed-and-breakfast, and you may discover the intangible sense of Ste. Genevieve's early days lingering in the air.

FELIX VALLÉ HOUSE STATE HISTORIC SITE • 198 MERCHANT STREET, STE. GENEVIEVE

EMILY S.
McILVAINE
DAUGHTER OF
DUNKLIN
FEB. 3, 1820
MAY 16, 1897

Gov. Daniel Dunklin's Grave State Historic Site

ON A HIGH BLUFF overlooking the Mississippi River about a mile north of the town of Herculaneum lies the final resting place of Missouri's fifth governor. Daniel Dunklin (1790–1844) was born in South Carolina, but the pioneer spirit led him to journey west: first to Kentucky, next to Ste. Genevieve, and then to the lead belt in the vicinity of Potosi, where he pursued farming and mining interests. During the War of 1812 he joined the command of Gen. Henry Dodge in Missouri and Illinois territories. In 1815 he married a Kentucky girl named Emily Haley and opened a tavern in Potosi; he also served for four years as the Washington County sheriff. It was at his tavern in 1822 that Dunklin was nominated to the Missouri legislature as a Jacksonian Democrat.

Dunklin was elected governor in 1832 after serving a term as lieutenant governor. A progressive, he championed public education, humane treatment of prisoners, and a state institution for people with hearing and speech disabilities. In 1834 he recommended a state university be founded and supported by the sale of land. Later that year, he submitted to the legislature a report calling for a state system of tax-supported schools, a state board of education, and common schools supported by local taxation on the basis of property ownership. For his success in helping enact the state's first comprehensive public school law in 1835, Dunklin has been called the "father of Missouri public schools." His financing system was adopted in some of the larger cities, and though the sparse populations in small towns and rural areas made such funding difficult, the seed was planted for a later day. While in office, Dunklin also added counties to northwest Missouri through the Platte Purchase.

When President Andrew Jackson offered him the position of US surveyor general for Missouri, Illinois, and Arkansas, Dunklin resigned as governor with three months remaining in his term. Under his federal appointment, he surveyed and named some of the counties south of the Missouri River. His own name was later given to a county in the Bootheel.

Dunklin moved to Jefferson County in 1840 to an estate he called Maje, near the lead-smelter community of Herculaneum. Three years later, Gov. Thomas Reynolds assigned Dunklin the task of establishing the final boundary between Missouri and Arkansas. But before completing the task, Dunklin died of pneumonia on July 25, 1844; he was buried in a small field near Maje.

Some forty years later, his son James L. Dunklin sold the family estate to Charles B. Parsons, superintendent of St. Joseph Lead Company. It was about this time that Dunklin's remains were moved to the present one-acre cemetery on the bluff, which was retained in Dunklin family ownership. There, Governor Dunklin lies between his daughter and son.

The small site, little more than an acre, can be a challenge to reach in the labyrinth of subdivisions south of St. Louis, but in addition to its historical associations, it offers a superb view of the Mississippi, some three hundred feet below. *

MOSES AUSTIN NAMED HERCULANEUM

The town and bluffs of Herculaneum have a long and fascinating history of their own. Moses Austin picked the site where Joachim Creek enters the Mississippi in 1808 as an alternative to French-dominated Ste. Genevieve for use as a depot for shipping lead mined and smelted near Potosi. In 1810 he erected a shot tower on the bluffs north of town, from which molten lead was dropped through a sieve to the water below to form round lead shot. Austin named the new town after the ancient Roman city of Herculaneum, a twin to Pompeii, both of which met a tragic end in the fury of Mount Vesuvius in AD 79. In addition to its claim as the last home and final resting place of Daniel Dunklin, Herculaneum was also the birthplace of Thomas Clement Fletcher (1827-1899), Missouri's first native-born governor, who served during the Reconstruction era immediately following the Civil War.

The small, one-acre family burial plot of Gov. Daniel Dunklin sits high above the Mississippi River at Herculaneum and offers visitors a lovely view for quiet reflection. ***Oliver Schuchard (left) and Missouri State Parks***

GOV. DANIEL DUNKLIN'S GRAVE STATE HISTORIC SITE • DUNKLIN DRIVE, HERCULANEUM

Scott Joplin House State Historic Site

SCOTT JOPLIN WAS THE KING OF RAGTIME, and John S. Stark proclaimed him so. Between them, a composer and his publisher, they had a major hand in the direction and sound of American music in the first decades of the twentieth century.

Scott Joplin was born around 1867 to Jiles and Florence Joplin, a musical family in northeast Texas. He grew up in Texarkana and exhibited musical talent at an early age. He learned to play several musical instruments: the banjo, bugle, cornet, violin, and eventually the piano. As a youngster, Joplin studied with a local Texarkana music teacher, Julius Weiss, who recognized his talent and provided free instruction. Almost no factual information has survived concerning his teen and young adult years. Some musicologists speculate that Joplin took up the life of an itinerant musician, playing piano in bars and honky-tonks in red-light districts in towns along the rail lines, which was an avenue of employment for black musicians in those days. By 1891 he was performing with a Texarkana minstrel group, and in 1893, he toured with the Texas Medley Quartette, a black vocal group.

In 1894 he was living in Sedalia, where he played cornet in the Queen City Cornet Band, led his own six-piece dance band, and still occasionally toured with the Texas Medley vocal group. But he made his mark by playing piano at the 400 Club and Maple Leaf Club, two black social clubs in town where he continued to hone his skills in the free-flowing, improvisational, artistic expression of black musicians from the minstrel tradition. He also attended the George R. Smith College for Negroes, learning the formal structure of classical music and accurate musical notation, so that he could record on paper the African American rhythms he had learned. Joplin eventually became the leader in a new, syncopated musical genre that was becoming a national sensation—ragtime.

Joplin's composition, the "Maple Leaf Rag," became immensely popular and boosted both Joplin and his publisher's prospects. John S. Stark had been an ice cream maker and a piano and organ salesman, and he had taken over a failing music-publishing house in Sedalia. Riding on the success

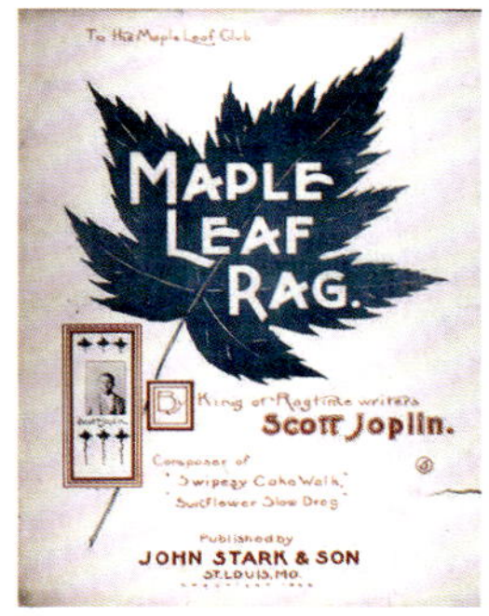

At the turn of the twentieth century, Scott Joplin and his wife moved into the second floor flat of this brick building at 2658 Delmar in St. Louis. ***Peter Ciro Photography*** **• As the last surviving structure known to have been associated with Joplin, it was designated a National Historic Landmark in 1976.** ***Brian Stith*** **Joplin and Stark's fortunes depended upon the sales of sheet music for home performance, not records, tapes, downloads, or any of the technology since. The ones shown here are Joplin's most famous and successful rag compositions along with** ***Treemonisha*****, his most serious operatic work. • The Joplin flat is furnished modestly, as it might have been in 1901, but whether Joplin owned his own piano when he lived here is not known.** ***Missouri Division of Tourism***

of "Maple Leaf," Stark relocated the publishing company to St. Louis and Scott Joplin soon followed.

Musical genius or not, as a black man Joplin had limited options for housing in turn-of-the-century St. Louis. The building he and his new bride, Belle, moved into at 2658A Morgan, now Delmar Boulevard, had in the mid-1800s been part of a prosperous German neighborhood, but by 1900, most German families had moved to neighborhoods farther west. The house had been built as a duplex but later was converted into a four-flat as rental property by enclosing the staircases in each side of the duplex with board partitions so that the second floors could be rented as separate apartments or even single rooms. This area had become the most densely populated part of the city. Older residences had become flats, and new multifamily tenements constructed in the backyards of the older homes now lined the alleys cheek by jowl. Joplin had moved into a busy, bustling neighborhood of the working poor: waiters, janitors, porters, firemen, laborers, and, yes, musicians. A few of the original German families were still there, along with the most recent poor white immigrants to the city, but the district had become increasingly black.

This was the beginning of a productive time for Joplin. He began to perform less and became more of a teacher and composer, although he occasionally performed at Tom Turpin's Rosebud Café. Advertised as the "headquarters for Colored Professionals," the Rosebud was the epicenter of St. Louis ragtime. But more often, he was there to listen to others play and to converse with musician friends, including Louis Chauvin and Tom Turpin. He became a student and friend of Alfred Ernst, director of the St. Louis Choral Symphony Society, with whom he studied classical music. Joplin persevered in his quest to refine and develop syncopated music—ragtime—as serious music, and it was largely his efforts that moved ragtime from the barroom to the white middle-class parlor.

During his time in this second floor flat on Morgan Street, Joplin began work on a major, serious composition, an operatic piece called *A Guest of Honor*. Possibly the historic visit of Booker T. Washington to Theodore Roosevelt's White House inspired it, although Joplin's opera was reputedly set in the beautiful Missouri Governor's Mansion in Jefferson City. Sadly, we may never know for certain, since the original score was lost and only a few short passages have been reconstructed. While living on Morgan Street, he also published some of his most successful rags: "The Entertainer," "Elite Syncopations," "The Strenuous Life," "March Majestic," and "Ragtime Dance." Buoyed by his royalties on these pieces, he left Morgan Street and moved to a larger house on nearby Lucas Avenue in 1903. There, he may have even become the landlord to several other ragtime musicians who listed the same address. Arthur Marshall and Scott Hayden, former students of Joplin's in Sedalia, also had moved to St. Louis and may have lived with the Joplins for a time. Both later coauthored rags with Joplin, and the teacher and his former students became the exemplars of Missouri ragtime.

Joplin was in and out of St. Louis for a few more years, spending time in Sedalia and Chicago, and he enjoyed continued success. New compositions included some of his most popular, among them "The Cascades," a musical tribute to the beautiful waterfalls at the 1904 St. Louis World's

> *"We mean to advertise these as classic rags, and we mean just what we say. They have lifted ragtime from its low estate and lined it up with Beethoven and Bach."* —*John Stark, Publisher*

Fair. He continued his quest to transform classical music to embrace folk and rag themes, and he probably began work on a second opera, *Treemonisha*. In 1907 he moved to New York, where he struggled for years to get his completed second opera performed. He finally produced a trial performance of *Treemonisha* without scenery or orchestra at his own expense. Sadly, it was a disaster and a serious blow to his spirit—he never really recovered. Obsessed with the opera and weakened by disease, he entered

Top: A player piano, also known as a pianola, lets visitors hear Joplin's classic ragtime performance preserved on paper rolls that control the piano. Above: The Joplin flat was lit with gaslights like this one. *Both Brian Stith* • Left: Visitors can try their own ragtime skills in the Joplin house music room, either on a standard piano or by playing a duet via piano rolls on a player piano. Here, ragtime pianists Bryan Wright and John Reed-Torres play at a party at the Joplin house. *Missouri State Parks*

the state hospital, and he died there on April 1, 1917.

The decades after Joplin left were not kind to this area of St. Louis, and the post-World War II era of so-called projects and urban renewal devastated large swaths of the old declining neighborhoods. In the 1950s and 1960s, many of the properties along Delmar Boulevard had fallen into serious disrepair. By 1977 the derelict building at 2658 Delmar was the last remaining structure anywhere known to have been associated with Scott Joplin. The cradle of his most productive and successful period, it was designated a National Historic Landmark. Nonetheless, it had the misfortune to be located in a part of St. Louis that was slated for complete obliteration and transformation for commercial or light industrial uses.

After its landmark designation, Jeff-Vander-Lou, Inc., a not-for-profit neighborhood development corporation, purchased the house and led the charge for preservation. The St. Louis Board of Aldermen eventually appropriated $100,000 for restoration, but the money was tangled in controversy for years. Finally in 1983 after complex negotiations, Jeff-Vander-Lou donated the building to the state for restoration as a historic site.

By the time the transfer was made, time and vandals had nearly destroyed the building while it stood empty. A squatter had built a campfire in the center of the west duplex parlor floor, and the fire burned through two floors and part of the roof. On the east side of the duplex where the Joplin flat was located, the building was in better condition, but a failed roof had caused water damage to paint, plaster, and woodwork. Extensive and expensive restoration over a period of several years gradually returned

Above: The commercial building next door to the Joplin house has been rebuilt as the New Rosebud Café, replicating Tom Turpin's famous club and providing space for performers and ragtime events. ***Brian Stith*** **• Right: In addition to ragtime concerts, lectures, and other performance events, the New Rosebud Café can be engaged for private parties.** ***Missouri State Parks***

the duplex to its former appearance.

A new opening in the brick common wall between the duplex sides allows visitors access to both sides through one entrance. The ground floor of the west unit contains exhibits explaining the history of the house, its restoration, and the neighborhood. On the second floor of this west unit are offices and a small archive room. On the east side, one finds more exhibits about Scott Joplin and his music and a room housing an authentic, operating player piano and a large collection of piano rolls, some actually cut by Joplin. With these rolls, you can listen to Joplin's personal style of playing ragtime. If you're good enough, you can even play a duet on the player piano with Scott Joplin himself—you get to use all the keys he's not using!

Visitors can pass through an opening in the thin boarding that had enclosed the staircase and climb the stairs into a world of turn-of-the-century St. Louis. Lit only with gaslights, the flat where Scott and his new wife, Belle, set up housekeeping is small, with a parlor, a bedroom, and a small kitchen at the back of the house that in grander days had been a maid's bedroom. The flat is provided with period furnishings—used, a little worse for wear, but not junk, befitting Joplin's status as a struggling musician just at the beginning of better times. It seems only right that the flat has a piano, but it isn't known for certain if Joplin was able to afford his own at this time.

As the Joplin house was being restored, the red brick neighborhood surrounding it was rapidly disappearing as the land clearance authority razed building after building. The Joplin house seemed in danger of becoming lost in either an open greensward or a sea of new manufacturing plants, neither of which would convey much sense of the old urban neighborhood that Joplin knew. To protect against a total loss of context, park officials bought the buildings on either side of the Joplin house and several nearby row houses for preservation. Vacant lots in front and behind were purchased to keep new construction for manufacturing firms at a respectable visual distance.

The commercial building on the west side of the Joplin house was rebuilt as the New Rosebud Café, a replica of the bar and gaming club that Scott Joplin frequented. It provides an authentic performance space for ragtime concerts and other special events, and arrangements can be made to rent the New Rosebud Café as a venue for private parties. The sound of syncopated piano frequently reverberates through the building, and there is an occasional cakewalk dance. The site also hosts lectures on African American life in St. Louis in the early 1900s. The building on the east side of the Joplin house is being used as state park offices. Several other period buildings have been stabilized for future use.

Today, the Scott Joplin State Historic Site attracts a variety of visitors, from local school groups learning about life and music in early 1900s St. Louis to out-of-town musical groups to syncopation aficionados, who come from all across America and the world to pay homage to "the king of ragtime." The site is a tribute to the creativity and talent of an enormously gifted musician who called Missouri home, and it celebrates the many rich African American contributions to Missouri's cultural history. *

SCOTT JOPLIN HOUSE STATE HISTORIC SITE • 2658 DELMAR BOULEVARD, ST. LOUIS

Wakonda State Park

WHAT A PARADOX that in the twentieth century, in an industry-fueled search for gravels, Missourians accidentally created an aquatic playground. Through an unlikely series of events beginning with glaciation during the Pleistocene Epoch and involving intensive human manipulation of the landscape, Wakonda State Park has become one of the state's most enticing recreational parks as well as a refuge for one of its most endangered natural communities: the sand prairie.

The landscape near Wakonda in northeast Missouri was shaped by the southward thrust of massive ice sheets and then by their last retreat when the big thaw set in. The retreat of the glaciers and the melt that ensued caused the Mississippi to carve a broad floodplain along which large, concentrated deposits of gravel and sand that had been carried along by the glacier were left behind. These deposits then lay unremarked until Missourians found a widespread need for them.

After World War I, the increasing popularity of the automobile dictated a rapid improvement in Missouri's roads. A new State Highway Commission set a major mission: "To lift Missouri out of the mud!" The obvious and practical method was to gravel the roads. The search was on for

In the Osage and Missouria Indian languages, "Wah'kon-tah" means "something consecrated," as by the Great Spirit.

materials, and soon some alert road builder discovered the extensive and easily mined deposits near LaGrange. They turned out to be the best and largest source of road-surfacing material in the state, with about sixteen million tons of gravel shipped from the site between 1930 and 1965.

As a reminder of the deposits' Pleistocene origins, a mastodon tusk and other fossils of the epoch were excavated in the gravel operations. Another indication of their origins was the Lake Superior agate, which demonstrates how far the glacier carried its collection. This and other stones of various colors gave LaGrange gravel its lithological beauty, a beauty that lives on today. Visitors enjoy searching for interesting geological specimens, but removal of rocks from state parks is prohibited.

Years of dredging scooped out the gravel to deep levels, below the water table in the floodplain, creating lakes. They are clean little lakes because the river water that filled them was filtered through the glacial deposits. The new water bodies soon became popular for fishing and swimming, suggesting to Lewis and Marion county residents a perfect location for a park. The idea grew, and on June 5, 1960, the Highway Commission deeded 257 acres on which it had exhausted the gravel deposits to a receptive State Park Board.

Park officials invited suggestions for a name for the new park. Dr. Carl Chapman, a noted archaeologist at the University of Missouri, suggested Wakonda, derived from an Osage and Missouria word meaning "something consecrated." A river north of the site is named Wyaconda.

Development was slow at first. Not until September 1967 was a contract let for construction of a combination bathhouse and concession. Wakonda boasts the largest natural sand beach of any state park—at least, the sand is natural. It was put there by the glacier and the Mississippi and left behind after decades of gravel excavation. The beach is large enough for swimmers, volleyball, and other activities. As overburden was removed from the gravel beds, it was shoved to the sides of the excavation where it now forms embankments above the open water. Although the landscape is man-made, the well-watered silty soil promotes rapid tree growth, and visitors can enjoy walking and camping in an attractive, largely cottonwood forest that may be younger than themselves.

In 1991 the State Highways and Transportation Commission transferred an additional 740 acres to the state park, including about 220 acres of lakes and ponds created by more recent gravel and sand excavations. The expanse of Wakonda State Park was nearly quadrupled, its lake area enlarged proportionately.

There are now six lakes, and you may rent a johnboat or kayak on several of them. There are also two campgrounds and numerous picnic sites. Since the lakes are inundated during extreme Mississippi River flooding, they contain many different species of fish. Most anglers target largemouth bass, crappie, bluegill, and catfish, but other species may be taken including muskie, spoonbill, walleye, and northern pike. Attracting thousands of waterfowl during spring and fall migrations, Wakonda is also a destination on Missouri's portion of the Great River Birding Trail.

Most intriguing, however, is a 100-acre area of seemingly naturally sculpted sand mounds, which mimic the soil conditions found on now rare natural sand prairies. On these mounds, amazingly, a number of sand-loving prairie and sandbar species have found refuge. Sand grass, sand dropseed, winged pigweed, and an endangered umbrella sedge (*Cypeius schweinitzii*) blanket the undulating sandy mounds, as do the yellow-flowered evening primrose and the prairie sunflower.

Sand prairies were once fairly common on the more stable sandy terraces along the Mississippi, Missouri, and other large rivers. But channelization since the 1920s and conversion of river margins to agricultural land relentlessly eliminated them. By 1949 when Julian Steyermark was making collections for his monumental *Flora of Missouri*, sand prairies and some of their characteristic plants were virtually extinct—except for one small remnant he discovered and described on the lower Des Moines River. Now it turned out that the spoil piles of the LaGrange gravel operations, quite by accident, had created another refuge for some of these species.

How did it happen? Highway department maps carefully marked as to dates of mining reveal that the prairie established itself on spoil piles created very early in the operations—back in the 1920s, when natural sand prairies that could provide a source for windblown seed still existed on

Right: Prairie sunflowers bloom on a once common but now rare sand prairie in Missouri. *Scott Myers* • Left: Kids learn to kayak on Agate Lake during a WOW (Wonders of the Outdoor World) weekend at Wakonda. *Missouri State Parks*

nearby Mississippi River terraces. Just as the last of the natural prairies were destroyed, victims of improvements for barge navigation, the artificial environment in the park was being created. Thus at a most singular moment in time, a window of opportunity opened, and seed from the last of the natural sand prairies took root in a new, artificial environment, one that mimicked precisely the growing conditions necessary for the survival of the sand prairie species. The man-made piles of Wakonda, protected from further disturbance for more than eighty years, became the unheralded savior for a unique, vanishing natural community.

As it turns out, Steyermark's tiny sand prairie on the lower Des Moines River also still exists, having been carefully protected over the years by a family who regarded it as something special. The family agreed to let park naturalists maintain the site and use it as a source of seed for reestablishing yet other species that did not manage to make it on their own to Wakonda. More recently, naturalists discovered some remnants of sand prairie at the newly acquired Iliniwek Village State Historic Site near the junction of the Des Moines and Mississippi Rivers, not far from Steyermark's site, and are working also to restore those.

Mississippi River floods periodically take a toll on the visitor facilities at Wakonda, but the park continues to attract more than 100,000 visitors a year. In addition to swimming, fishing, birding, and boating, the park offers more than seven miles of hiking and biking trails. Several wind along the lakes and through the sand prairies, where those so inclined can marvel at the natural survivors of a most unnatural history. *

WAKONDA STATE PARK • 32836 STATE PARK ROAD, LA GRANGE

Iliniwek Village State Historic Site

IN THE SEVENTEENTH CENTURY when France had an empire in the interior of North America, there was a large region in the center of the continent known to the French as *Le pays des Illinois*, "The Illinois Country." It was a deferential nod to those whose country it was, the dozen or so American Indian tribes of the Illinois Confederation who occupied this vast region that encompassed most of the middle Mississippi valley from Iowa to Arkansas, including eastern Missouri, and up the Ohio River to Indiana.

Of course, "Illinois" is a transcription by early French explorers of a Native American term; today, we know a more nearly correct spelling is "Iliniwek." This Algonquin-related word was used by other Indians to refer to the allied tribes of the Confederation. The meaning of the word "Iliniwek" was that the members of those tribes all spoke a common language that was mutually understood, but the word that the Iliniwek used to refer to themselves was "Inoka," most likely meaning "the people."

Explorers of the interior rarely encountered native peoples who did not already know about Europeans. In addition to trading goods, natives traded information among their tribes, and both goods and information moved westward well ahead of European people. The first European awareness of the Iliniwek began when other American Indians visiting the Jesuit missions on the Great Lakes told the French about the Iliniwek, and then when the Iliniwek themselves made the journey to the missions and even to Quebec. At the Chequamegon mission, a thousand miles from Quebec at the far west end of Lake Superior, Father Jacques Marquette was particularly stirred by the stories he heard from visiting Iliniwek, stories of a great river, "Missisipi" (Marquette's spelling), and of large Iliniwek villages along it, one of which more than three centuries later would become Iliniwek Village State Historic Site in far northeast Missouri. How Father Marquette and his companion Louis Jolliet (also spelled Joliet) came to be visitors in this large Indian village near the mouth of the Des Moines River is one of the great exploration stories of North America.

In Quebec, Gov. Louis de Buade, comte de Frontenac also had an interest in this "great river" because it suggested a possible opportunity. Since finding North America, Europeans had been frustrated in not finding a way around it or through it for a quick route to India and the Far East. It had finally become apparent that there was no passage northwest from Quebec through the ice, but some wondered if the great river flowing south could be a southwest passage to India. Could this river possibly empty into the Gulf of California? There was only one way to find out: the governor selected the young adventurer Louis Jolliet to lead an expedition, in company with Father Marquette and a crew of five voyageurs in two canoes. Marquette and Jolliet made a good pair: it was said that Jolliet "had the courage to dread nothing in a place where everything was to be feared," while Father Marquette had knowledge from the people of the Iliniwek country and could speak their language, despite having never been there.

On the morning of May 17, 1673, Marquette, Jolliet, and their companions left the mission of St. Ignace at the Straits of Mackinac in Michigan and headed southwest, Father Marquette in hope of harvesting Iliniwek souls and Jolliet in search of glory—or at the very least, value for his king and country. They proceeded down Lake Michigan to Green Bay, up the Fox River to a portage, then had to carry their canoes several miles to enter the Wisconsin River. A month later on June 17, they entered into the "Missisipi" near present-day Prairie du Chien with, as Marquette put it, "a joy I cannot express." The Iliniwek visiting his mission had been exactly right about the great river.

On June 25, 1673, while traveling down the Mississippi, they saw a path made by humans along the riverbank near the mouth of a tributary. Leaving their canoes and crew behind, Marquette and Jolliet cautiously followed the path alone on foot. A half-dozen miles inland from the Mississippi along the channel of the Des Moines River, they learned who had made the path—and quite a lot more. Before them lay a village, actually a complex of three villages, with a total of some three hundred dwellings and several thousand Indians. This was an Iliniwek village, more specifically, that of the Peoria, one of the larger tribes in the Iliniwek Confederation. The explorers stood in cautious surprise, watching the village scene until a group of four elderly men walked out to them, bringing the calumet, or peace pipe, in welcome.

After exploring the villages and participating in numerous ceremonies for several days, Marquette and Jolliet took leave of the Peoria, primed with new knowledge of the country and a peace calumet for safe passage, to continue their voyage south where they would eventually learn that the Mississippi River doesn't flow into the Pacific Ocean. When they left the Peoria village, six hundred of the villagers walked with them back down the path to the Mississippi, where their canoes and five voyageurs awaited them. Marquette promised to return the following year and found a mission for the Iliniwek—and he did, at one of their villages on the Illinois River.

For the next three hundred years, no one knew where this Peoria village had been. Then in 1984 a routine archaeological survey for a rural waterline found it, not in Iowa as had been thought, but in Clark County, Missouri. Archaeologists also found a Jesuit ring and Iliniwek artifacts. So among their other accomplishments, Marquette and Jolliet became the first Europeans to tread the ground of what eventually became the state of Missouri. In 1992 the site of the village they visited became a new unit of the Missouri state park system.

Today, the historic site offers tables for picnics, a kiosk featuring attractive graphic panels explaining the Iliniwek, their way of life at the village, and interesting information about the unusual plants and animals that live here, as well as a short trail. Most of the 127-acre site is flat and grass covered—prairie that is being seeded and otherwise managed to encourage the return of the native plant cover. The only concentrated woody vegetation is a strip of trees and brush lining the edge of a slough and oxbow lake, with individual trees scattered sparsely over the landscape, including the ones park managers have left for shade in the picnic area and along the trail. Altogether there is a mile and a half of trail, leading to several areas where archaeological excavations have taken place and to the oxbow lake. The trail has a surface of packed fine gravel as far as the archaeological zone. There, visitors may see the outline on the ground of one of the Iliniwek longhouses. As archaeologists uncovered the traces of the original side posts of the house, new posts were installed into the old postholes, resulting in a physical outline of the house on the ground. On the return loop is a similarly ghosted example of one of the round houses. The oxbow lake and slough, which in 1673 was part of the river, provides views of migratory waterfowl in season and a better sense of this landscape as a prairie component of a riparian corridor.

The valley of the Des Moines River is more modest than that of the Mississippi but is still sizable, about two and a half miles in width at the Iliniwek Village site. The valley floor is nearly flat, with low terraces

Above: Archaeologists determined the locations, and now posts mark the sides and center supports of a longhouse on a sand terrace at Iliniwek Village. The sand prairie is being restored, and here you see sumac, grasses, and other plants. Right: The easy Oxbow Trail at Iliniwek skirts nearly a half mile of an old oxbow of the Des Moines River after passing the longhouse site and before looping back past the site of a round house, also marked with posts. *Both Susan Flader*

intertwined with many still visible extinct river channels, marshy areas, and small oxbow lakes in the process of shrinking into sloughs. This landscape bears unmistakable evidence of the Des Moines having meandered repeatedly back and forth from highland to highland in fairly recent geologic times, filling the valley with sandy soil and gravel, a gift from ancient glaciers.

When Father Marquette said the trail he was following to the village opened into "a pretty prairie," he was quite correct, but he couldn't know how special a prairie it would become, at least in Missouri. It was a sand prairie, distinguished by plants and animals adapted to living in a sandy environment and now a rare type of natural community in Missouri. Today, most of the sand prairie in the state, including on the Des Moines River terraces, has been plowed under and turned to cropland. But here and there on scattered small tracts, some of the sand prairie species

Left: Plains puccoon flourishes on a sand prairie, a rare natural community here in Missouri, at Iliniwek Village State Historic Site. *Bruce Schuette* • Above: The posts mark an Iliniwek round house next to the Oxbow Trail. *Missouri State Parks*

LIFE IN AN ILINIWEK VILLAGE

The Iliniwek people were semi-agriculturalists, concentrating in these large villages in the spring to work the ground and plant their crops, primarily Indian corn or maize, along with beans and squash. These foods were supplemented with gathered natural plant foods and hunted game animals. Once the crops were well established in early summer, most of the villagers departed west on a summer hunt, mainly for bison, and did not return until the crops planted earlier were ready for harvest and storage at the end of summer. Then in late fall, the village broke up into smaller groups that scattered farther afield to enhance their success in hunting small game in the winter landscape. In the spring, they returned to the village to begin the cycle over again, reoccupying the permanent structures. Of these, the most impressive were the longhouses, large enough for several families to occupy, being some sixty feet long and twenty feet wide, built of side posts bent to join overhead in the middle and covered with woven rush matting. A variety of other structures of different shapes and sizes fulfilled other needs of the villagers. The string of dwellings and the several village centers stretched for more than a mile and a half along the Des Moines River.

have survived, and Iliniwek Village State Historic Site is one of those tracts. Within the bounds of the historic site are a number of species of rare sand-adapted plants. The site also hosts several species of native bees whose only known occurrence in the state is here. Thus, the acquisition of this important historic property has also provided the park system with another example of a rare natural community. This combination of natural and cultural resources on the same property requires park system scientists to maintain a careful balance in management techniques so that both archaeological and natural resources are protected, and to ensure that a strategy that enhances one does not harm the other.

When the explorers first arrived at the Peoria village, the "Great Captain" had greeted them in this fashion: "I thank thee, Black Gown [Marquette], and thee, O frenchman [Jolliet] for having taken so much trouble to come to visit us. Never has the earth been so beautiful, or the sun so Bright as today.... Never has our tobacco tasted so good, or our corn appeared so fine, as We now see Them." Perhaps if the chief had been able to see the future, he wouldn't have been so pleased to see his French guests. The future yielded less pleasant dealings with Europeans. In fact, the Iliniwek were here on the west bank of the Mississippi in the first place because European incursion on the East Coast had already forced Native Americans to the west by the 1600s. The Iliniwek were in conflict with these eastern tribes pushing into their territory, while to the west Siouan tribes and the Missouria and the Osage were pushing back in the other direction. The Iliniwek were in a squeeze, and to make matters worse, their friendly relationship with Europeans exposed them to measles and smallpox. The constant warfare with their new neighbors decimated some of the Iliniwek tribes, and whole villages were wiped out by Old World diseases, to which American Indians had no immunity. Scholars estimate there were once more than twelve thousand Iliniwek, but by the early 1800s, they had declined to only a few hundred.

The five major tribes of the Iliniwek Confederation—Peoria, Cahokia, Kaskaskia, Tamaroa, and Michigamea—acted together as a confederation for the last time at the signing of the Treaty of Edwardsville in 1818. By further treaty in 1832, they gave up their claim to all Iliniwek lands in Illinois and Missouri. Today, the Iliniwek Village State Historic Site is a reminder of the vagaries of history and of a time when our part of the world was once part of someone else's world, *Le pays des Illinois.* *

ILINIWEK VILLAGE STATE HISTORIC SITE • ROUTE 26, WAYLAND

Battle of Athens State Historic Site

YOU CAN EASILY IMAGINE THE CANNONBALLS hurtling across the Des Moines River into Iowa, toward the pro-Union home guard, some landing in the river, some in the neighboring state, and one passing right through Joseph Benning's home, earning it the name "cannonball house." In and around the town of Athens in Clark County that August morning in 1861, a battle raged for not quite two hours. When it subsided, northeast Missouri was left in the hands of Union supporters.

One of the early skirmishes of the Civil War—and perhaps the farthest north—the Battle of Athens was a test between two strong-willed and passionate Missourians, David Moore and Martin Green, and their equally passionate partisans. Moore was a veteran of the Mexican-American War and thus had military experience. He had a reputation for fearlessness and profanity with which he bolstered his ardent pro-Union feelings. Immediately after South Carolina batteries fired on Fort Sumter, signaling the start of the Civil War, Moore began recruiting volunteers for a home guard. All over Clark County he posted placards that read:

> *The undersigned is authorized to raise a company of volunteers in this county for Union service. All who are willing to fight for their homes, their country, and the flag of our glorious Union are invited to join him, bringing with them their arms and ammunition. Until the government can aid us, we must take care of ourselves.*
>
> *Secessionists and rebel traitors desiring a fight can be accommodated on demand.*
>
> *D. Moore*

Far right: The restoration of the Thome-Benning house carefully preserved the original hole next to the kitchen door where a cannonball had ripped through the house during the two-hour Battle of Athens in 1861. *Oliver Schuchard* Below: The brick house was built around 1857 by Southern sympathizer William Moreland, who was taken prisoner during the battle. *Jerry Toops* • This battle flag was captured by David Moore and taken to Iowa. It had fifteen stars, but Union troops snipped most off as souvenirs. *State Historical Society of Iowa*

Martin Green, a judge of the Lewis County Court (Lewis is just south of Clark County) and a brother of Missouri's staunchly southern US senator James S. Green, was equally committed—but to the Southern cause. He began recruiting volunteers with even more success than David Moore—even Moore's three sons joined up with Green—because of the very strong pro-Southern views in northeastern Missouri. The areas near the Mississippi and lower Des Moines Rivers that were settled early in effect constituted a northeastern limb of Missouri's "Little Dixie," filled with Kentuckians and Virginians, though as the railroads came closer increasing numbers of families from more northern states migrated to the region. The patriotic zeal and organizing efforts of both men led to an eventual showdown at Athens on August 5, 1861.

Moore had selected Athens, one of the larger towns in Clark County and home to a large contingent of the county's pro-South leaders, as the place to garrison his troops. Not the type to avoid confrontation, he had apparently chosen Athens not only to be close to the railroad north of the river at Croton, Iowa, from which he could be supplied, but also to control his major potential opposition. To garrison up to five hundred soldiers in a town of about five hundred people was no small inconvenience to the locals. Moore solved the problem by confiscating the homes and businesses of Southern sympathizers: George Gray's slaughterhouse, W. H.

Spurgeon's dry-goods store, and the homes of Judge William Baker and the widow Jane Gray among many others.

Green's two thousand volunteers outnumbered Moore's home guard by four to one, but Moore's forces, augmented by some Iowans, were better supplied with muskets and ammunition from federal arsenals. When the smoke cleared, there were a few dozen casualties and the pro-South forces were in retreat. Both Green and Moore went on to other fights: they opposed each other once again at Corinth, Mississippi. They both rose in rank to brigadier general. David Moore lost a leg at Shiloh, while Martin Green lost his life in the defense of Vicksburg.

In northeast Missouri, the big loser was the town of Athens, where bitter feelings remained long after the war. The town lost also, and more decisively, because the Civil War accelerated a change in the transportation focus of the nation from rivers to railroads. Athens never got the railroad bridge it had been banking on; when the railroad finally crossed the Des Moines River in 1887, it was near Revere, seven miles south. Athens went into decline and just about died by the early twentieth century.

One hundred years after the battle, the Athens Park Development Association organized and began purchasing land to commemorate the battle, an idea that had been promoted ever since 1900 when local residents held the first of a nearly annual series of August 5 celebrations. The new association wanted the state to develop the property, but the Park Board's historic sites advisory council demurred on the grounds that the site did not have high priority for preservation. The battle was actually "a relatively unimportant skirmish," the historians said. "The historical personages concerned were not of major importance," and the outcome of the skirmish "did not materially affect the course of the war." Furthermore, the only building that bore any physical evidence of the battle, the Benning (cannonball) house, was "in a serious stage of deterioration."

Here at Athens is nearly the entire town plat of a dynamic mid-nineteenth-century steamboat river port. The town was torn asunder by the Civil War, revived briefly, and then was left behind when railways replaced river traffic.

Undaunted, the association continued to acquire tracts, financed with the proceeds from motorcycle hill climbs it staged annually up a steep embankment along the river. The association's members displayed their local pride as they proclaimed in one of their publications: "Like Martin Green's Rebel Gunners of 1861, this gun crew is out for Big Game. And they rebel against the lassitude and historical short-sightedness that have permitted this priceless heritage of Athens to slip from the community's grasp."

It was not until 1975 that the state accepted the donation of 235 acres, and then as a park rather than a historic site. With a 10-acre lake

Above: The historic site contains most of the town of Athens. The home of Union supporters Calvin and Aliza Stone is at right along Spring Street. The postwar Smith Hotel in the distance faces Virginia Street. *Rachel Hoemann* • Left: The ruins of the Athens Mill along the Des Moines River evoke a time when a grist, saw, or woolen mill was the hub of a community. *Sam Williams*

for swimming, excellent fishing on the river, and a good place for a campground, the property could provide much needed recreation facilities in a corner of the state relatively deficient in public lands. No historic restoration was contemplated, but park officials did encourage the association to substitute battle reenactments for the hill climbs, as events more appropriate to the site and less damaging to the terrain.

In 1981 in the course of an archaeological survey occasioned by the need to run a waterline across the park to the new campground, several discoveries changed the perception of the area. Archaeologists found a number of prehistoric Indian sites and part of a large historic Sauk Indian village that had been occupied as late as the 1830s. They also found evidence of nearly the entire site of Athens as laid out in 1844 by Isaac Gray in nine blocks of eight lots each. By this time, prevailing ideas about what historical phenomena were most significant for preservation and interpretation had evolved from the early 1960s. Drawing largely on studies of communities, what was being called the "new social history" focused on ordinary people and everyday events—history from the ground up—and on processes of change in communities over time. Athens's past fit this bill.

Still standing, in addition to the cannonball house built in 1853 by Arthur Thome and occupied during the war by Joseph Benning, were the Stone house and the Moreland house, the Widow Jane Gray house, and the Smith Hotel. Of the fifty or so businesses in operation by 1860, little remained except for the stone foundation of the Athens grist, saw, and woolen mill down by the river, but the buried remains of other foundations, as well as the street grid, could be explored archaeologically. With this wealth of structural remains and substantial archaeological and archival potential, park officials in 1985 decided to reclassify Battle of Athens as a historic site and began an ambitious research and development plan that has brought the site to more than 400 acres.

Archaeology has now exposed old foundations and roads, which are being stabilized, slightly reconstructed, or outlined with fences and plantings—ghosted, the professionals say—in order to create on the ground a full-size map of the town, one that visitors can walk through guided by street signs at the corners. Park staff have restored or stabilized some of the standing structures—notably the Smith Hotel and the Thome-Benning, Moreland, and Stone houses—and placed signs in the shelter house and elsewhere on the grounds to help orient visitors.

An 1865 tax book for Clark County, discovered by pure chance in the rubble during the 2010 demolition of the old county courthouse in Kahoka, led to better understanding and renaming several buildings. For example, it is now thought that the Smith Hotel, formerly known as the William McKee house and said to have been headquarters for Union forces during the battle, was not built until after the war and that William McKee's house, no longer extant, was close to the cannonball house. There may still be buildings here and there in Clark County that had been moved from Athens after its demise, several of which might eventually be moved back and placed on their original foundations, and park officials plan eventually to develop an interpretive center.

In the meantime, state park naturalists discovered that the forested ravines along the Des Moines River northwest of the town site possess outstanding and unique natural features. These coves shelter a rich flora that includes snow trillium and doll's eyes, relicts of glacial times, and

Top: The dooryard and cellar of an in-law of the prominent Thome family has been preserved. *Missouri State Parks* • Right: The limestone cliff along Stallion Branch is within the Des Moines River Ravines Natural Area. *Jerry Toops* • Above: Snow trillium, a relict of glacial times, shelters here. *Bruce Schuette*

many ferns. The ravines adjoin an upland area of former glacial-loess prairie that is being restored by park managers to reveal an unusually tight transition from open prairie to oak woodland to rich, dense forest to riparian cottonwoods, a combination that must surely have attracted the Sauk and other native peoples as well as white settlers. A forty-acre site is now protected as the Des Moines River Ravines Natural Area, accessible via a two-mile loop trail.

During the sesquicentennial of the Battle of Athens in August 2011, nearly three thousand visitors came to witness a reenactment and to view an original battle flag that had been hand-stitched in 1861 for Martin Green's pro-South regiment by ladies of the LaGrange Garden Club, then captured by David Moore and taken across the river to Iowa. The flag eventually found its way to the Iowa Historical Society in Des Moines, from which it was carefully transported to Athens for the occasion and displayed in the cannonball house.

The Civil War is still vitally important at this site, but instead of celebrating famous historical personages and events of major, decisive significance, we are now invited to explore the war's impact on ordinary people—people like our ancestors—caught in a vortex of change in this seemingly ordinary little river town. *

BATTLE OF ATHENS STATE HISTORIC SITE • ROUTE CC, REVERE

Edward "Ted" and Pat Jones–Confluence Point State Park

IT MAY BE THE MOST WIDELY KNOWN UNKNOWN place in America. Everyone knows about it; several million people live within twenty miles of it. But until Edward "Ted" and Pat Jones–Confluence Point State Park was dedicated in 2004 during the bicentennial of the Lewis and Clark expedition, few people had been there. Every schoolchild in Missouri has learned about the founding of St. Louis at the junction of the two most important rivers in America, yet a visit to the city offered no chance to see this great confluence. Within the city, the rivers join only metaphorically in Carl Milles's famous fountain sculpture, *The Meeting of the Waters*, in front of Union Station. The actual joining of the Missouri and Mississippi occurs in the midst of a marshy plain about twelve miles north of Union Station and the city's great arch.

The French explorer Father Pierre Francois-Xavier de Charlevoix captured the essence of the place in 1721: "I believe this is the finest confluence in the world. The two rivers are much the same breadth, each about half a league: but the Missouri is by far the most rapid, and seems to enter the Mississippi like a conqueror, through which it carries its white waters to the opposite shore without mixing them; afterwards, it gives its color to the Mississippi which it never loses again but carries quite down to the sea." Of course, Father Charlevoix is describing the two rivers themselves, not the surrounding land. The early explorers of this area didn't care much about the land at the confluence, preferring instead to conduct their explorations by canoe on the river highways.

Left: A unique view shows the waters of America's two great rivers as they begin to mingle. The Mississippi is on the right, and the Missouri is on the left. ***Paul Jackson*** **• Above: The point is a rocky spit of land in the midst of what was once a vast marshy plain, now being partially restored.** ***Glenn Curcio***

Perhaps the first person to give serious consideration to the land around the confluence would have been Capt. Don Francesco Rui y Morales. In 1767 after France ceded Louisiana to Spain, Don Antonio de Ulloa, the royal Spanish governor in New Orleans, sent Rui and a crew of soldiers and laborers on a quick, secret mission to the confluence to build two forts, one on each side of the mouth of the Missouri River, to deny the British any opportunity to ascend that stream. In New Orleans this looked good on paper, but when Captain Rui arrived at the confluence, he found that the north bank at the mouth was under nine feet of water.

At Edward "Ted" and Pat Jones–Confluence Point State Park, you can walk out on the narrow rocky spit and plant one foot in the Missouri River and one in the Mississippi River.

What was obvious to the Europeans—and later, Americans—on the scene was that the considerable plain surrounding the confluence in every direction was one large wetland, many square miles of alluvial prairie, with sloughs, ponds, lakes, and marshes, and also with bottomland forest on natural levees along the rivers and on islands, nearly all of which went under water almost every year. Zebulon Pike, boating past the confluence in 1805, described it as "a rich prairie, with small skirts of

Above: This rare *Boltonia* is a type of sunflower adapted to flooding. Found only on prairie wetlands in a restricted area of the middle Mississippi region, it has now become established in the park. *Ken McCarty* • The majestic American white pelican, one of the largest North American birds, may be seen in flotillas on the water or in squadrons in the sky, wheeling above the point. *Lane Richter*

woods." Henri Brackenridge, viewing the tongue of land between the two great rivers in 1811 from atop the rounded loess hills east of St. Charles known as *les Mamelles* (the Breasts), wrote of "the ocean of prairie, with islets at intervals. The whole extent perfectly level, covered with long, waving grass, and at every moment changing color from the shadows cast by the passing clouds.... A hundred thousand acres of the finest land are under the eye at once."

Missouri Department of Natural Resources and park officials long wanted to establish a park at this point, to make available to the public one of Missouri's great geographic and natural wonders and the preeminent river junction in the nation's history. As part of the considerable planning and preparation for the bicentennial of the Lewis and Clark expedition, collaborative funding spurred by an initial donation of $943,000 from the Danforth Foundation and a $1 million grant from the North American Wetlands Conservation Act through the US Department of Interior allowed for acquisition of the first 603 acres in 2001. A lease agreement with Great Rivers Greenway—created in 2000 by the passage of a one-tenth-cent sales tax devoted to the development of an interconnected system of greenways, parks, and trails in St. Louis and St. Charles counties and the city of St. Louis—added an additional 515 acres, and the Greenway also provided a $1.6 million grant for the access road to the park.

The park is named in honor of Edward "Ted" Jones and his wife Pat, who donated funds for this park and the establishment of Katy Trail State Park, which will someday extend to the confluence.

The Jones–Confluence State Park was dedicated on Sunday, May 9, 2004, with a replica pirogue and Lewis and Clark reenactors present for the event. This was most appropriate, as that great Voyage of Discovery began here at the confluence on May 14, 1804. As William Clark wrote, "Set out at 4 oClock P.M. in the presence of many of the Neighbouring inhabitents, and proceeded on under a jentle brease up the Missourie." Although several places had been recommended as suitable for their winter quarters, Clark explained to his brother Jonathan that none was better than the River DuBois camp on the Illinois shore, owing to the abundance of game in the vicinity and its location far enough from the vices and temptations of St. Louis to keep his crew "Clear of the means of Corruption" as they prepared for their epic journey.

Thanks to the voluminous field notes of Missouri's early explorers and land surveyors, we are able to understand what this area was like at the time of European settlement and how it has changed over time. Interestingly, geographers have now reckoned that the location of the Illinois camp from which the expedition set out is now in Missouri, north of today's confluence, and the confluence point itself has moved two miles

downstream from where they entered the Missouri River, as a result of the restless movement of the rivers within their floodplains. Most of what is today parkland was then active river channel with small islands.

While much of today's park was cleared for farming in the 1950s, it remains a unique site with tremendous diversity and recreational opportunities. With Missouri River Recovery Program funding provided by the Army Corps of Engineers, park naturalists have undertaken significant restoration activities since the park's opening in 2004, and the land has begun to more closely resemble descriptions contained in historical accounts. This restoration is designed to work with the existing soils, hydrology, and topography while using native vegetation suited to those conditions. The ultimate goal for the park is the reestablishment of more natural floodplain function including native vegetation and natural wetlands, which will allow visitors to experience something of what early explorers saw when encountering the area more than two centuries ago.

This goal has been complicated by several factors. First, there are multiple oil pipelines traversing the park. Second, the park is surrounded by an agricultural levee that protects lands still being actively farmed;

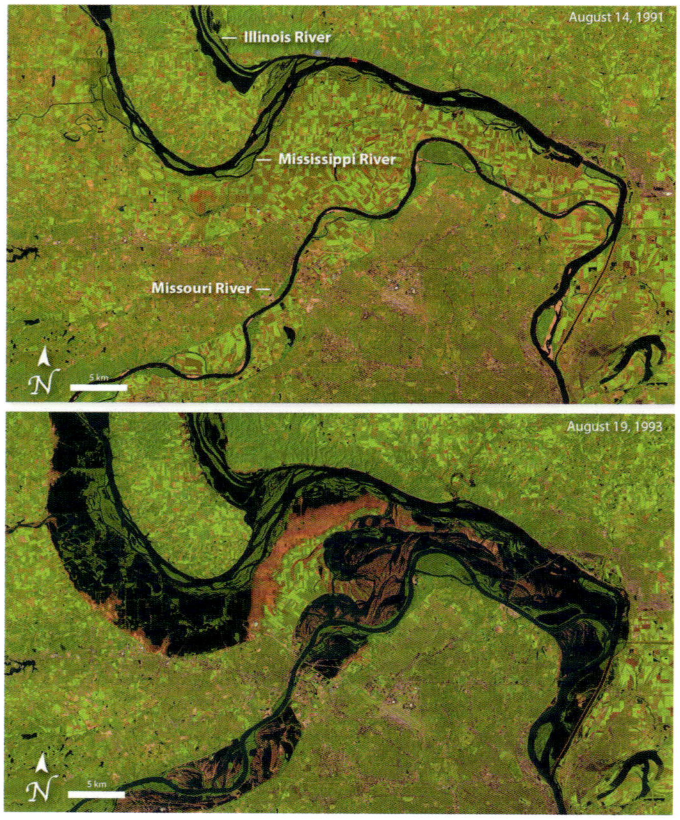

Urban schoolchildren help restore bottomland forests. *Scott McNealy* • The natural riverfront forest is rich and dense with cottonwood, silver maple, willow, and a robust understory, including thickets of giant ragweed. *Ken McCarty* Satellite images show the area in 1991 at normal water levels and in 1993, with the greatest flood recorded on the upper Mississippi already receding. *NASA*

The Edward "Ted" and Pat Jones–Confluence Point State Park is at the tip where the two mighty rivers meet, at the very heart of North America. *Richard Keeling*

the state, when it accepted the property, committed to maintain the levee. To truly restore the natural floodplain would require acquisition of adjacent properties or realignment of the levee so that repairs would not be required on parkland. That would open the possibility that the confluence area over time would revert to what it was like two centuries ago—an active river channel with constantly changing islands—limited only by the Corps of Engineers' mainline levees.

The park has, as was anticipated, experienced frequent flooding; it is so low in elevation that all but the highest areas are likely to flood at some point most years. At least once in every ten years, water can be expected to cover most of the park for at least thirty consecutive days. While minimal infrastructure was developed in the park for this reason, repairs to the paths, the access road, the levee, and the outdoor exhibits have been and will be required on multiple occasions.

With only a dozen feet of vertical relief and roughly ten different soil types, restoration of the park means the re-creation of diverse habitats ranging from sandbars and mudflats to bottomland forest, prairie, marsh, and shrub swamp, all found here before the river was channelized and levees were built. The restoration effort has offered a perfect opportunity to enhance the state park system's urban outreach and environmental education. Much of the restorative tree planting has been done by elementary school classes from north St. Louis and other inner city areas; many of these children experienced state parks and land stewardship for the first time. Confluence Greenway, St. Louis Audubon, and other volunteers have also helped with restoration and monitoring activities.

In addition to the Jones–Confluence State Park, several other sites in the area, most of them recently developed, allow the public to experience the convergence of the nation's two great rivers from different perspectives. Just to the northwest of the park lies the Corps of Engineers 3,700-acre Riverlands Migratory Bird Sanctuary, a popular birding area where the Audubon Center at Riverlands provides visitors with the chance to see and learn about the 325 species of songbirds and waterfowl that live in or migrate through the area.

Across the Mississippi is the National Great Rivers Museum at Melvin Price Locks and Dam, a visitor center operated by the corps, while farther down the Illinois shore across from the confluence are the Lewis and Clark State Historic Site and the Confluence Tower, which offers a panoramic view from 150 feet high.

On the Missouri River just upstream from Confluence Park is the 1,265-acre Cora Island unit of the Big Muddy National Fish and Wildlife Refuge, while directly across the Missouri River from the park is the Missouri Department of Conservation's 4,318-acre Columbia Bottoms Conservation Area, where visitors can experience a more intensively engineered and managed floodplain. Katy Trail State Park currently extends as far east as Machens, about fifteen miles west of the park. The goal is ultimately to link it to the confluence, allowing users one more way to experience this unique area on an interconnected circuit of trails.

But the main attraction in the area by far is the actual rocky point where the two greatest rivers on the continent join together. You can ponder the meeting of these waters and their roles in the exploration and development of the nation. If you are lucky, you may see pelicans wheeling and spiraling above the point, trumpeter swans migrating up or downriver, or a bald eagle standing sentinel in a nearby tree. State parks are often landmarks, and it would be difficult to imagine a single geographic point with more power and meaning than this place. *

EDWARD "TED" AND PAT JONES–CONFLUENCE POINT STATE PARK • 1000 RIVERLANDS WAY, WEST ALTON

Katy Trail State Park

IT'S TWO HUNDRED AND FORTY MILES LONG, but only one hundred feet wide! Now, that's an odd shape for a state park, but that's the Katy Trail. An abandoned railroad converted into a state park, it stretches more than halfway across Missouri, sometimes through woods or open farm fields and in other places squeezed in tight between towering stone bluffs on one side and the Missouri River on the other. For hikers, bicyclists, and on some stretches, equestrians, it is a path through both nature and history as it passes through a tunnel and over more bridges than you can count, leading to villages large and small, historic and picturesque, and even into several larger cities. Of all the units in the Missouri park system, Katy Trail State Park offers the most varied mixture of cultural and natural resources.

Records are made to be broken, so the day will surely come when Missouri's Katy Trail will be surpassed in another part of the country. But as of 1990 when the first resurfaced segments opened for public use and still today, it is the longest rail-to-trail conversion—out of more than 1,600 such conversions throughout the nation—since the movement to preserve old railroad corridors began in the 1960s. It is likely, too, that no other such trail can match the Katy for the historical significance and sheer magnificence of the Missouri River corridor—the pathway for the exploration and settlement of the American West.

The Katy runs through diverse landscapes: dense forests, lush wetlands, deep valleys, steep hills, towering bluffs, remnant prairies, open pasturelands, and gently rolling farm fields.

After the Civil War when the nation's network of railroads was expanding, eastern entrepreneurs organized the Union Pacific Company South Branch to reach and serve the developing agricultural areas of western Missouri, eastern Kansas, and Texas cattle country. In 1870 the South Branch was renamed the Missouri-Kansas-Texas Railway Company. It soon, and ever after, became known as the MKT or, more simply, the Katy.

When competing companies kept the MKT from using the Missouri Pacific line along the south bank of the Missouri River, the company built from Clinton to Moberly, with stops in Sedalia and Boonville for a junction with the North Missouri Railroad (now the Wabash). But that wasn't enough. New management of the Katy after 1888 thought that by building along the north bank of the river from New Franklin, just across the river from Boonville, to Machens east of St. Charles, it could achieve a more direct route to St. Louis. With the same stroke it could open a substantial region of east-central Missouri still dependent on primitive roads, horse-drawn vehicles, and uncertain riverboat service. At Machens, the line would join the Chicago, Burlington, and Quincy for quick entrance to St. Louis and convenient access to Chicago. Construction of the new line began in 1892 and was completed in 1895, just in time for Katy trains to roll into St. Louis's brand new Union Station.

The new rail line transformed the economies of the counties through which it ran. Old towns built on the river boomed; new towns and hamlets quickly sprang up, one about every ten miles or so along the tracks.

Far right: For much of its 240-mile length, the Katy Trail hugs the Missouri River bottoms, often passing at the foot of towering bluffs resplendent with seasonal colors, as here near the mouth of Moniteau Creek at Rocheport. *Frank Oberle*
You might spot the MKT logo on the trail near Rocheport. A marker also calls attention to Native American pictographs on the bluff. *Missouri State Parks*

A few towns such as Mokane and Dutzow that found themselves inconveniently inland picked up and moved to be on the railroad. Holding pens and loading chutes accommodated shippers, and grain elevators appeared beside the tracks at many stations. At Treloar, two of the old elevators still stand, lonely sentinels watching over the trail. In other towns, modern grain bins serviced by trucks have replaced the old elevators. Railroad workers and farmers using the railroad were the lifeblood of these small towns, eating at the restaurants and buying from the general stores.

The railroad industry went into a long decline beginning about 1930 as better roads and ever-bigger trucks began taking away freight business and buses and airlines took away passengers. Railroad companies began consolidating to survive and then abandoning unprofitable lines—often signing the death warrant for smaller towns along the route. In the 1970s and 1980s, passenger trains no longer ran on the Katy line from Sedalia to Machens, and there were fewer and fewer freight trains. In 1986, the MKT Company announced that in August it would file with the Interstate Commerce Commission (ICC)—now known as the Surface Transportation Board—for permission to abandon operations along its Sedalia to Machens route.

Many Missourians knew at once what to do. They had the example of the nature and fitness trail established by the city of Columbia after the MKT abandoned its spur from McBaine to Columbia in 1977. They also had experienced leaders, notably Columbia attorney (and later, mayor) Darwin Hindman, who had marshaled public opinion and persuaded the city to acquire and convert four miles of the abandoned right-of-way from Columbia toward McBaine. The Missouri Parks Association, the Conservation Federation of Missouri, and a dozen or so other conservation and civic groups joined a Katy Trail Coalition.

The state government also reacted quickly and proactively; the park division had tried unsuccessfully for years to secure such an abandonment and did not want to miss this extraordinary opportunity. On September 16,

Hundreds of bicyclists participate in parks-sponsored Katy Trail events. *Missouri State Parks* • Media surround major donor Edward D. "Ted" Jones at a rally for the Katy Trail on the state capitol steps. *Jim Denny*

Gov. John Ashcroft wrote to the director of the Missouri Department of Natural Resources (DNR) endorsing the goal of developing a state-owned biking and hiking trail along the full length of the abandoned line. On the same day—all this had been coordinated, of course—DNR fired off an official request to the ICC, asking the federal agency to bank the 199-mile right-of-way for future railroad use if ever needed and to issue to Missouri a certificate of interim trail use, as the ICC was empowered to do under a 1983 provision of the National Trails System Act of 1968.

Almost as quickly, vociferous opposition boiled up among landowners and in towns along the route. Trail opponents argued that users of the trail would be irresponsible riffraff from the cities, trespassing on neighboring property, stealing, and perhaps committing other crimes. The same arguments had been used against other proposed rail-to-trail conversions—to some extent even along Columbia's MKT nature and fitness trail—and in many instances had forced abandonment of trail plans. Overflow crowds attended legislative hearings in several towns along the route. Both proponents and opponents staged demonstrations on the capitol steps when the legislature debated the issue.

Landowners backed by the Missouri Farm Bureau filed suit in December 1986, contending that under Missouri law, the abandoned land in the right-of-way rightfully must revert to the properties from which it was originally leased or taken by easement. For the state to take the land, their lawyers argued, would be unconstitutional, a "taking without compensation." The Katy Trail Coalition and other organizations intervened with their own attorneys on the side of the state. The case dragged through the judicial process for three years before the US Supreme Court, in a nine-to-nothing decision, affirmed on February 21, 1990, that the National Trails System Act was indeed constitutional, that rail-banking was a legitimate national purpose asserted by the Congress, and that the MKT company had a right to sell the right-of-way to the state for recreational purposes. The supreme jurists also told the landowners, as the lower courts had already told them, that they could take their individual petitions for compensation to the court of claims.

Meanwhile, the Katy right-of-way had become the property of the state after an impatient proponent, Edward D. "Ted" Jones, had given the state $200,000 to buy it, which the state promptly did. A resident of Callaway County midway along the trail, Ted Jones was chairman of a nationwide investment company and a man of genuine vision and commitment. MKT began salvaging the rails and taking up the ties, leaving the ballast of coarse gravel and large rock, upon which a smooth surface could be laid. But while the lawsuit was dragging on, the legislature would appropriate no money for development. DNR posted Keep Out signs. Here and there, landowners erected barriers across the trail to assert their claims of ownership.

DEPOTS OF THE KATY TRAIL

Four railroad stations of notable design remain along the Katy Trail. The largest and most impressive of these is the Sedalia Depot, about all that is left of the once extensive MKT facilities there that included a roundhouse and repair shops, stockyards, and a hospital for company employees. Meanwhile, the depot at Marthasville near the other end of the line is a quaint frame structure with characteristic wide eaves supported by stylized stick bracketing. The only one of its kind left on the abandoned Katy line, it is typical of many that once served small rural towns. The Boonville Depot was built in the Spanish Mission style with stucco walls, a red tile roof, and extended eaves. The St. Charles Depot, slated in 1975 for demolition to build Riverside Drive, was saved, relocated along the Katy in the city's Frontier Park, and restored through the efforts of the South Main Preservation Society and the city. Unfortunately, a fifth depot of historical and architectural interest at North Jefferson, across the river from Jefferson City, was totally destroyed by an arsonist's fire on the night of October 28, 1988. But the other restored depots remain to serve as they always have, as way stations along the route.

Some depots built by the MKT serve today as rest stops for trail travelers. Top: Boonville's depot is Spanish Mission style. ***Ben Nickelson*** **• Above: Sedalia's depot is Romanesque Revival style.** ***Sedalia Heritage Foundation***

Anticipating reluctance by the legislature to appropriate sufficient funds even after the Supreme Court decision and wanting results, Ted Jones pledged $2 million of his own money to restore the bridges and resurface the entire trail with crushed and packed limestone. Jones was present and was honored with a special medallion when Governor Ashcroft on April 28, 1990, ceremoniously opened the first pilot segment of the trail at Rocheport. A monument to Jones was later erected along the trail near Rocheport, but he did not live to see it, having succumbed to cancer. Little more than a year later in December 1991, the Union Pacific Railroad donated to the state 33.6 miles of the old MKT from Sedalia to Clinton, thus extending the trail to more than 230 miles.

Hikers and bicyclists flocked to the completed segments, and parking lots at trailheads were soon overflowing. Businesses sprang up almost overnight in towns along the way to provide food and drink. The people using the trail on any given day are whom you might expect: families walking together, some pushing baby carriages, young couples holding hands, and athletic pedalers zooming along, some alone, some in pairs, some riding tandem on bicycles built for two.

The Katy Trail is also unique among all the state parks in that its corridor traverses three of Missouri's six natural divisions: Big Rivers, Ozark Border, and Osage Plains. Distinctive elements of these landscapes occur in a string of pearls ranging from the 300-foot limestone cliffs near Rhineland to remnant prairies west of Sedalia. Most of the way from Machens and St. Charles to Boonville, the trail hugs the Missouri River bottoms or stretches along the water's edge, and it lies at the foot of steep hills or towering bluffs resplendent with wildflowers, shrubs, and trees. In places, it passes through bottomland forest, and in other places, through croplands reclaimed from the floodplain.

Most of the birds that nest in or migrate through Missouri may be seen along the river corridor, one of the nation's great migratory flyways.

Several major river vantage points provide excellent viewing for great blue herons, bald eagles, egrets, and a host of shorebirds and waterfowl. Bluff-tops and cliff faces are haunts for red-tailed hawks, falcons, turkey vultures, kestrels, and the unique Missouri population of cliff-nesting Canada geese, and indigo buntings flit across the trail at eye level. There are wetlands, U-shaped valleys, and steep canyons carved by tributary streams, which the trail crosses on an array of historic bridges.

On its tangent from Boonville to Sedalia, the trail leaves the river and traverses the Ozark Border through rolling hills, mostly pasture and cropland, but also, especially near the Lamine River, through deep, wooded valleys. On the Osage Plains from Sedalia to Clinton, remnant prairies have been protected for a century by the railroad right-of-way and occasional mowing. More recently, park managers have restored them with the aid of prescribed burns. Some of these prairies are home to the rare, regal fritillary butterfly.

Not only does the trail traverse three different natural divisions, but it is also a pathway through history. From its eastern terminus to Boonville, the trail parallels the river route taken by the Lewis and Clark expedition when it headed west in 1804 to explore uncharted territory. Signs and panels along the way point out their campsites and other noteworthy features, including "uncouth [Indian] paintings of animals" that the explorers recorded having seen on a limestone bluff at the mouth of Moniteau Creek in Rocheport. You can still see faint remnants of some of these pictographs about four miles east of Rocheport today, where a sign alerts trail users to them.

The trail passes through outposts of early settlers such as Louis Blanchette, a French-Canadian fur trader who is said to have built a cabin at St. Charles as early as 1769. Farther upstream is the site of Côte Sans Dessein ("hill without design"), a French village established by Jean Baptiste Roy on a long narrow ridge opposite the mouth of the Osage River. The village was once a prime contender to be the state capital.

Most of the early settlers along the Missouri, though, were Americans from Kentucky, Tennessee, and Virginia who followed the lead of Daniel Boone. The aging Boone, already famous in legend and literature, came from Kentucky in 1799 to take up a land grant offered him by the Spanish government. A monument to the adventurous frontiersman lies near the Katy Trail just east of Marthasville, which is also the site of his original grave. Some of Boone's followers brought with them the culture and traditions of the upper South, including slavery. The Loutre Island Methodist Church in Warren County, constructed in 1841 and 1842 with slave labor, is still in good condition and is a fine example of a southern Protestant church not far from the trail. Many southern homes as well as a few log houses lie in close proximity as well.

Farther upstream, near the western terminus of the Boone's Lick Trail,

Above: A glowering sky threatens an event beside Treloar's historic grain elevator. ***Curt Dennison*** **• Left: Children explore the spring along the trail east of Rocheport. Right: The trail draws bicycles built for two, families with wheelchairs or strollers, runners, and people walking dogs.** ***Both Scott Myers***

the Katy passes the site of Franklin, a starting point of the fabled Santa Fe Trail and the leading city of interior Missouri before the river washed it away in 1827. A number of old historic markers here ended up at the bottom of a gigantic blew hole, a deep hole scoured by the flood of 1993's errant current.

Beginning about 1830, a gradually swelling tide of German immigrants began moving into Missouri, building new communities on both sides of the Missouri River. German culture predominates today in Augusta, Hermann, and some other towns along the lower Missouri, described as Missouri's "Rhineland." Several nineteenth-century homes along the Katy route in St. Charles, Warren, and Montgomery counties reflect German building styles. The trail passes several fine wineries, as well as small town taverns where you can stop for a beer or soda.

Practically every old river town has its historic structures—except places like Providence in Boone County, which was once a thriving community but is now just a few foundation ruins overgrown with brush and trees. Most of Rocheport is a historic district on the National Register of Historic Places. Boonville, where the Katy line turns southwest toward Sedalia, has seven historic districts on the National Register. Some impressive residences built by prosperous farm families in the 1800s are within view of the trail in Cooper County. And Sedalia, once the railhead on the competing Missouri-Pacific line and a destination for cattle drovers out of Texas after the Civil War, has numerous historic buildings.

The art and science of taking railroads over streams reached a zenith in the 1890s, a decade known to civil engineers as the golden age of bridge building. The MKT had to span many creeks and branches, and multiple styles of metal-truss bridges, now floored with planks, remain for trail users to admire and photograph. The trail also goes underground for 243 feet at Rocheport. The tunnel with its picturesque stonemasonry faces was quarried through a hill that left no room between it and the river channel to lay a railroad. It is blessedly cool on a hot summer day, and it's also listed on the National Register of Historic Places.

The Katy was subject to severe flooding in 1993 and again in 1995, with shorter stretches flooded during smaller floods, but state park crews made the repairs required to reopen to the public. Of greater concern is the need to repair or rebuild much of the basic infrastructure of the Katy with its 240 miles of roadbed, 472 bridges, 898 culverts, and 58 structures, many of them more than a century old. Though the nearly $50 million estimated for this work may seem huge, it is dwarfed by the

Above: The trail provides either solitary or social exercise. ***Dennis Coello*** **Left: Almost any outing allows cyclists to cross several of the trail's 472 bridges—count them! Right: The Rocheport tunnel, on the National Register of Historic Places, promises cooling relief on a hot summer day.** ***Both Scott Myers***

remarkable economic impact of the park to the state and especially to many of the small communities and businesses along the route.

A 2012 study of the economic impact of the trail reported that some 400,000 Katy users generate nearly $18.5 million a year through their trail-related spending and support 367 jobs. The Katy Merchants and Communities Association includes more than a hundred businesses that cater to trail users. It is safe to say that many of these businesses and even some of the communities would not exist if it were not for the trail, while others such as Defiance, Hartsburg, and Rocheport have been decidedly revitalized by the trail. A dozen cities have built trail spurs to connect with the Katy. Jefferson City, Hermann, and Washington have or are adding bike lanes on their Missouri River bridges, and Boonville, after many years of struggle and with significant help from Gov. Jay Nixon, in 2013 acquired the historic MKT railroad bridge, an engineering marvel with its 408-foot central lift span still operable, to restore and develop as an attraction in its own right. To protect landscapes along the trail, a Katy Land Trust was established in 2010 to help local landowners protect their farms and forests through conservation easements or other agreements.

Some fifty special events are hosted each year in communities along the trail. The annual Pumpkin Festival organized by Hartsburg, population only about one hundred, draws more than forty thousand people each October, and bicyclists from all over the country and from several nations ride the entire length on the annual week-long Katy Trail Ride sponsored by Missouri State Parks each June. The Katy from St. Charles to Boonville has been designated part of both the longer Lewis and Clark National Historic Trail and the American Discovery Trail, and Missouri's selection in 2013 as the Best Trails State was due in no small part to the Katy Trail. In 2014, the Katy Trail was named by MSN Travel as one of the top ten international cycling destinations.

These accolades can only hint at the wonder of the Katy Trail. The actual experience of it creates an indelible memory, which draws visitors back time and time again. *

KATY TRAIL STATE PARK • TRAILHEADS IN MANY TOWNS

First Missouri State Capitol State Historic Site

THE RESTORATION OF MISSOURI'S FIRST STATE CAPITOL in St. Charles in the 1960s was a catalyst sparking the creation of a fourteen-block historic district surrounding it. This area, known as Historic Main Street, features a variety of shops and restaurants occupying early nineteenth-century buildings along Main Street that were restored with private capital attracted by the newly refurbished historic site. The district, listed on the National Register of Historic Places in 1970, a year after the restored capitol building itself, lies adjacent to the Missouri River just downstream from the I-70 bridge.

A simple Federal-style, two-story brick row housed the capitol complex on South Main Street. The complex is actually two separate but adjoining buildings; arched drives leading through the buildings to the rear yards separate the first floors of each. Originally built in 1819 for commercial and residential purposes, the structures achieved their greatest fame as the seat of Missouri government for five years from 1821 to 1826.

FRONTIER PARK AND THE KATY TRAIL

After passenger trains ceased running on the MKT Railroad through St. Charles in the late 1960s, the company sold part of its land along the river, including the historic depot, to St. Charles for a park—initially called First State Capitol Park but now known as Frontier Park. Then after the MKT in 1986 announced its intent to abandon the line, the Katy Trail State Park was created; the trail and Frontier Park are directly adjacent to First Capitol, separated only by Riverside Drive.

Selection of the new state's temporary capital city was embroiled in the controversy over Missouri's admission to the Union. The serene, park-like setting of the old capitol, as it appears today, belies the stormy nature of the first legislative sessions held there. The legislators—forty-three representatives and fourteen senators—were a mixture of tobacco-chewing frontiersmen and Southern gentry. Before them was no simple task: they had to create a state government out of the Missouri Territory.

The population of the territory had grown rapidly after it was added to the United States with the 1803 Louisiana Purchase, and petitions for statehood appeared as early as 1817. Missouri's admission was part and parcel of the escalating national controversy over slavery and state rights. On March 3, 1820, the US Congress passed legislation that would become known as the Missouri Compromise, whereby Missouri would be admitted as a slave state and Maine would be admitted as a free state. But the debate was far from over.

In the early summer of 1820, delegates from some fifteen counties assembled in St. Louis to draw up a state constitution, and on August 28, the first state election was held. In addition to choosing a governor, a lieutenant governor, and a representative to Congress, voters elected members of the General Assembly. The assembly convened for the first time at the Missouri Hotel in St. Louis on September 19.

The new state constitution provided for a permanent seat of government to be located on the banks of the Missouri River "within forty miles of the mouth of the river Osage." But while Missourians thrust and parried over the location of the permanent capital and while the "City of Jefferson" was being prepared, Missouri's government needed a temporary home. Locating the temporary capital was one of the first tasks of the first legislature.

At least nine towns competed for the honor of being the temporary capital city. Ultimately, St. Charles—a bustling city of about a thousand people and

Left: A drone camera captures the capitol with Frontier Park, the Katy Trail, and the Missouri River just beyond. St. Charles provided access by river and overland to growing parts of the state. ***Paul Jackson*** **• Above: The buildings' second floors housed Missouri's first General Assembly and governor's office.** ***Tom Nagel*** **Right: Students tour the assembly chambers.** ***Jeffrey Bonney***

with excellent access to the most rapidly growing areas of the state both by river and overland via the Boone's Lick Road—was selected for its conspicuous advantages. And its prospects were undoubtedly enhanced when some prominent citizens offered "to furnish free of expenses to the state, rooms suitable for the accommodation of both branches of the General Assembly, and also committee rooms." They had in mind rooms rented by the city and used as a courthouse. On November 25, 1820, Gov. Alexander McNair signed the bill designating St. Charles the temporary capital of Missouri; it served in this capacity until October 1, 1826.

The buildings selected as the capitol were owned by the Peck brothers, Charles and Ruluff—who operated a general store and lived on the first floor of the south building—and by Chauncey Shepard. The senate and the "room" of representatives, as well as Governor McNair's office, were upstairs. Today, all these rooms, including the Peck and Shepard residences and the store, have been restored and furnished to reflect the 1821 to 1826 period.

The legislators first convened in their new capitol on June 4, 1821, in an emergency session. What followed were weeks of debate, probably as rough-hewn as the pine flooring of the Peck brothers' building. The issue of slavery itself was not argued; Missouri would be a slave state. Instead, the debate centered on a controversial clause of the Missouri constitution—article III, section 26—which made it mandatory that the General Assembly pass laws to prevent free African Americans from settling in Missouri.

Congress had made it clear that statehood would be denied unless this clause, which jeopardized the constitutional rights of free black citizens, was deleted. But many of the legislators feared that free black citizens might incite trouble among Missouri's large slave population—nearly one-sixth of the state's sixty-six thousand residents. Finally, the Missouri lawmakers relented to the extent of passing a "Solemn Public Act," which declared that section 26 of the Missouri constitution would never be construed to restrict the constitutional rights of any citizen of any state. On August 10, 1821, President James Monroe proclaimed Missouri the twenty-fourth state.

Four Missouri governors ran the state's affairs from the capitol in St. Charles. McNair was replaced by Frederick Bates, elected in 1824, but Bates died less than a year later. Thereupon, senate president Abraham J. Williams became the temporary governor for a few months until a special election in December 1825 selected John Miller. Miller oversaw the moving of the state government from St. Charles to Jefferson City.

After 1826 the buildings were used for a variety of residential and commercial purposes. By the early part of the twentieth century, the former capitol row—and, indeed, the whole neighborhood—had begun to decay. The site was marked with a plaque by the St. Charles Knights of Columbus in 1921 for the state's centennial celebration. During the next two decades, local Veterans of Foreign Wars and Daughters of the American Revolution groups began efforts to convert the old capitol into a museum, and in 1938 the state planning board prepared a study recommending preservation of the buildings. But nothing happened. Finally in 1961, after much prodding from St. Charles citizens and officials, the state purchased the properties that had housed the old capitol, using money from a special Spanish-American War fund controlled by the governor. The major funds required for restoration—some $600,000—were appropriated by the General Assembly in recognition of the state's upcoming sesquicentennial, after appointment of a high-level First Missouri State Capitol Restoration Commission.

Restoration and furnishing of the structures presented vexing dilemmas to park historians and planners because no records have been found that indicate the uses of particular rooms or describe their appearance or furnishings. State documents relating to the St. Charles sessions of the legislature were apparently destroyed in the spectacular conflagration that leveled Missouri's third state capitol in Jefferson City in 1911. But the process of restoration provided a few clues, such as the size and shape of the original rooms. Nine of the rooms have been restored, and seven are furnished to interpret Missouri's fight for statehood and life in St. Charles in the early 1820s. The restorations have been handled with such care that the buildings seem no older than they were when their halls reverberated with heated debates over state rights and slavery.

In the years following the restoration of First State Capitol, the fourteen-block historic district surrounding it has undergone its own rebirth, building by building, largely with private funds. As St. Charles City and County have grown explosively in recent decades—the county is one of the fastest growing in the nation—the historic district has thrived and attracts nearby residents and visitors from afar on a daily basis.

Today, historic Main Street in front of the capitol and Frontier Park and the Katy Trail behind it play host to an amazing number of festivals and other special events year-round, all of which attract visitors to the historic site, making it one of the most heavily visited sites in Missouri. Just as the first state capitol brought a flurry of activity to the young town on the Missouri River, so too did its restoration spark the continuing economic revival of old St. Charles. *

FIRST MISSOURI STATE CAPITOL STATE HISTORIC SITE • 200 SOUTH MAIN STREET, ST CHARLES

Deutschheim State Historic Site

THE LOWER MISSOURI RIVER VALLEY WAS A BEACON, promoted as a second Germany to thousands of immigrants seeking economic, intellectual, religious, or political freedom. The result was the most intense immigration movement in the history of the state. By 1860, more than half of Missouri's diverse foreign-born residents were German; today, more than a quarter of all Missourians claim some German ancestry, nearly twice as many as the next major ancestry group. Some towns like Hermann, founded in 1838, were conscious efforts to re-create all they held most dear from German towns left far behind. The region from St. Louis to Boonville along the Missouri—and a smaller area along the Mississippi centered around Perry and Ste. Genevieve counties—had become a true *Deutschheim* or German home by the mid-nineteenth century.

Hermann has developed an uncommonly strong sense of pride in its heritage. More than one hundred structures in the small town have been placed on the National Register of Historic Places.

Many of the settlers were attracted to the state by the prose of one of their fellow countrymen. Gottfried Duden had taken up the life of a gentleman farmer in Warren County in the 1820s. His 1829 collection of letters, entitled *Bericht uber eine Reise nach den westlichen Staaten Nordamerikas (Report on a Journey to the Western States of North America)* is broadly—perhaps too broadly—credited with stimulating waves of immigration during the thirty years before the Civil War. A sample of Duden's promotional style explains his appeal:

Carl Procopius Strehly and Eduard Muehl published two German newspapers from Strehly's house in the 1840s and also cultivated grapes in the rear. Strehly built the two-story addition in 1857 for a winery. *Missouri State Parks*

> *I cannot describe the impression that the days of wandering in this river valley have made upon me. One can travel hundreds of miles between gigantic tree trunks without a single ray of sunlight falling upon one's head. The soil is so black here from the plant mold that has been accumulating since primeval days that one seems to be walking on a coal bed.... Settling next to charming hills, near never-failing springs, on banks of small rivers near their junction with large rivers, all depends entirely on the option of the settler without taking the price into consideration.*

Duden warned his fellow countrymen that frontier settlement should not be undertaken lightly, but his romantic descriptions were more compelling than his warnings. After discovering for themselves that opening the frontier was easier to read about than do, some settlers blamed Duden for misleading them, calling his book "Duden's Eden." He revised the book in 1834, using the occasion to lambaste his detractors. Then, disillusioned, he eventually ceased promoting emigration. But the effects of his love for the Missouri valley were lasting; German settlers came and left an indelible mark on Missouri's culture, industry, and politics.

Some of the communities in the Deutschheim region were settled by organized societies of German immigrants, of which seven functioned in Missouri. One such group, the Emigration Society of Giessen, settled near Dutzow. Four years later, upstream and on the opposite side of the river, the *Deutsche Ansiedlungs-Gesellschaft zu Philadelphia* or German Settlement Society of Philadelphia, founded the city of Hermann in Gasconade County. The founding society of Hermann was unique in that it was set up as a joint-stock company advertised throughout the eastern United States and Germany. Members bought shares of stock that entitled them to land in the proposed colony or that could be held in anticipation of profits to be derived from the new "German Athens of the West." The society, organized in 1836, acquired 11,000 acres in Missouri in 1837 and laid out the colony on paper before platting it in 1838. It was to be a culturally integrated, self-supporting economic complex based on farming, industry, and commerce to which Germans could come to preserve their heritage and traditions. About half the members came from the Philadelphia area, but the rest were from twelve other states, Canada, and Germany itself.

Today, Hermann maintains much of the look and charm of a nineteenth-century German river town. Its well-maintained historic district and seasonal events like the Maifest, Oktoberfest, and Kristkindl Markt, along with its wineries, attract many visitors.

Deutschheim State Historic Site began with the Pommer-Gentner house and the Strehly house. Both were donated to the state in 1978 by the Hermann Brush and Palette Club, a local society for historic preservation and the arts. But it is impossible to separate these two houses from their setting—the rest of Hermann. Visitors to Deutschheim can also visit the Historic Hermann Museum at the German School (circa 1871) and the Gasconade County Historical Society Archives and Records Center (1909) or stroll by the White House Hotel (c. 1868), Eitzen House (1850), and the Concert Hall (c. 1878). And tours of Stone Hill Winery and Hermannhof Winery are as colorful as the Rhineland wines they sell. At one time, Stone Hill, founded after 1847, was the third largest winery in the world; the 1856 Hermann production was 100,000 gallons of wine. The industry crashed with Prohibition in 1920, but in recent decades the Missouri wine industry has made an aggressive comeback.

Of the two historic buildings on the tour of the Deutschheim historic

This stately neoclassical home was built in 1840 for the family of Caroline Pommer, widow of one of the organizers of the German Settlement Society of Philadelphia, which platted the colony at Hermann in 1838. *Nick Decker*

site, the Pommer-Gentner house is the earlier, built in 1840 for the family of Caroline Pommer, widow of Charles Pommer, piano maker and one of the organizers of the Philadelphia settlement society, who died prior to the move. It was the first two-story brick house in Hermann, and it is a sterling example of German neoclassicism, featuring Beidermeier furnishings appropriate to what was then the finest house in town. Two of the Pommer sons were trained piano makers. The eldest moved to St. Louis to form a business there, and the other sold furniture from the shop side of the house. Several other sons became carpenters. After a succession of other owners from 1856 to 1882, the house came into the possession of G. Henry Gentner and his wife, who had arrived in Hermann in December 1837, four months before the town was even platted. Arriving as newlyweds with few resources, the Gentners raised their family and prospered on a farm southwest of town in the intervening years.

The Strehly house, on the other hand, is a fine example of German vernacular architecture. It was built over a period of twenty-seven years, beginning about 1842. The core of the modest house—a single story and a half with a deep front porch facing the street in the European tradition—was built by another early stockholder, Andreas Doldt. It was then acquired by Carl Procopius Strehly of Cincinnati in 1843. The house had a stone lower level where Strehly and his brother-in-law and business partner Eduard Muehl operated a full-service printing business; this level opened to the rear on the south-facing hillside where the partners also began cultivating grapes.

They produced two of the earliest German-language newspapers west of the Mississippi: the *Licht-Freund (Friend of Light)* from 1843 to 1847 and the *Wochenblatt (Weekly Paper)* from 1845 to 1855. They also took other printing jobs and produced at least one book by Friedrich Muench, who was a leader of the Giessen Society and frequent contributor to the papers. The *Licht-Freund* was a rationalist and religious biweekly paper edited by Eduard Muehl with readership among German-Americans across the country. It frequently editorialized against Catholics, structured Protestantism, and government regulation; it also promoted the abolition of slavery. Opposition to slavery was widespread in the German communities, and the strong Union sympathies of most German immigrants helped ensure federal control of Missouri during the war. A legacy of the printing business can still be seen when entering the Strehly house: the doorstep is a block of lithographic limestone from the old print shop.

After Muehl died in the cholera epidemic of 1854, Strehly sold the printing business and all their equipment to the Graf family and expanded the wine business. Since 1844, the Hermann town council had encouraged development of the wine industry by making vacant lots available to growers for no money down and with no payments required for five years, later extended to ten years. Carl Strehly and Edward Muehl had taken up several of the wine lots and beginning in 1845 wrote every week in *Wochenblatt* extolling the benefits of investment in grapes.

In 1857, likely with proceeds from the sale of the printing press, Strehly built next to his house a winery complete with a wine production floor, a vaulted brick cellar, and an upper floor for a tavern where his wines could be sold and enjoyed. A wine press and beautiful hand-carved wine cask can still be seen in the winery, and grapevines planted by the Stre-

Right: Period kitchen or vegetable gardens like this *gemüsegarten* in the rear of the Pommer-Gentner house offer a taste of life in a nineteenth-century German community, here with a view of the Missouri River as well. *Cynthia Browne*
Left from top: An arbor behind the Strehly house features Norton grapevines more than one hundred years old planted by the Strehlys and pruned in the nineteenth-century manner. *Missouri State Parks* • The historic site recently acquired a pianoforte built by Charles Pommer in 1838 in Philadelphia just before his death and his family's subsequent move to Missouri. The site has acquired a press similar to what Carl Strehly and Eduard Muehl would have used to publish their newspapers named *Wochenblatt* and *Licht-Freund*. Strehly sold the original equipment after the death of his partner. *Both Cynthia Browne*

hlys in the nineteenth century grace an arbor running downhill the length of the yard. The vines are still pruned according to practices outlined in a book, *The Cultivation of the Native Grape and Manufacture of American Wines*, by nineteenth-century Hermann viticulturist George Husmann.

Strehly joined the house and winery and enclosed the front porch of the house about 1869 to add more rooms. His daughter Rosa, who never married, lived in the house all her life, from 1865 to 1962, first with her parents and later with a nephew; as her income was limited, she made few changes to the structure. When she died, virtually the entire contents of the house went with the building to the Brush and Palette Club, which had in 1952 saved the Pommer-Gentner house from destruction. The club gave both houses to the state in 1978, making possible the establishment of Deutschheim State Historic Site to serve as a museum of Missouri German culture and traditions.

The Strehly house has undergone major conservation and restoration. With its full printing setup, winery, and other furnishings, it provides an extraordinary window into the daily life of a German middle-class family of limited means in the 1860 to 1885 era. The Pommer-Gentner house has been restored to reflect a somewhat wealthier family in the earlier settlement period of the 1830s and 1840s. A half-timbered barn behind the house displays gardening and other tools from the nineteenth century. Period gardens, including a German four-square *gemüsegarten* (kitchen garden) at the rear of the house, offer a lovely place to stroll and to view the Missouri River.

Over the years, the site also acquired several other buildings. The handsome Feldmann-Stark house, built in 1883 by Dr. John Feldmann, a local physician who arrived in Hermann from Vienna in 1852, is used for programming and special events, while the 1902 home of vintner Julius Hundhausen, with its full height window-doors opening onto an iron balcony, is being restored and will serve eventually as a visitor center. The site is supported by a friends group, Deutschheim Verein, which collaborates on special events and programming with other organizations in this history-conscious town, including the Brush and Palette Club, Historic Hermann, the Gasconade County Historical Society, and the German-American Club.

A visit to Deutschheim State Historic Site offers a glimpse into the lives and businesses of several founding families of Hermann, but it also illuminates our deep German heritage throughout Missouri. *

DEUTSCHHEIM STATE HISTORIC SITE • 109 WEST 2ND STREET, HERMANN

Clark's Hill/Norton State Historic Site

CLARK'S HILL IS A TRIPLE-BONUS sort of place, interesting geologically, geographically, and historically. Plus, it provides one of the finest overlook views of the Missouri River valley that can be had. This kind of hill is sometimes called a lost hill, meaning that it stands as an isolated elevation in the midst of level ground, a cut-off remnant of a bluff line that once closely edged the river. As the river meandered over the millennia, it carved its valley ever wider, but here and there, owing to differential softness of the stone or cracks and crevices in it, the water cut through and around the back side of the escarpment, leaving an isolated long, narrow hill parallel to the river. From the top of the hill, another lost hill, the famous Côte Sans Dessein, once promoted as a location for Missouri's capital city, can be seen a few miles downstream.

Clark's Hill joined the Missouri park system in 2002, a thirteen-acre donation in Cole County by William and Carol Norton, who had purchased the property in the mid-1970s. The Nortons had been approached by state park staff about the significance of their property. Stimulated by the national bicentennial commemoration of the 1804 Lewis and Clark Corps of Discovery expedition, history buffs in Missouri scoured the state for extant sites described in the expedition journals, special places that might still evoke the spirit of the famous explorers. There were the obvious ones, of course, places such as St. Louis or St. Charles, but in them the essence of the expedition had been long since overshadowed by subsequent events. Clark's Hill, by contrast, had not changed appreciably in the two centuries since. Well described in the journals as the explorers headed both upriver and back down, it might, for all anyone knew, still be embossed with the boot prints of William Clark. "Others will be able to stand and feel the strength of what's here," Carol Norton said.

When Lewis and Clark approached this place in 1804, they were more concerned with the mouth of the Osage River than the hill. The intersection of the Missouri and the Osage Rivers was a major crossroads in those times, an already well-known landmark. The "limestone rock," as

Clark called it, was more-or-less exactly at the intersection of the rivers, but in front of its sheer stone face, extending for a quarter-mile downstream, was a narrow riverbank, a mere point at its downstream end but about two hundred yards wide at the foot of the hill where it separated the rivers. The expedition camped on this alluvium, later known as the Osage Point, on the nights of June 1 and 2, 1804, and again on their return trip, September 19, 1806. On the morning of June 2, 1804, Clark left the riverbank camp and climbed the hill, which he estimated to have been one hundred feet high. At the top, he enjoyed the view: "a delightful prospect of the Missouri, up and down; also the Osage, up."

Today, the park provides an easy walk to the top of the high riverside bluff via a trail built through the woods by the state park staff. The trail offsets the steepness of the climb by making a few switchbacks, trading length for slope. Once at the top of the hill, visitors follow the trail along the edge of the bluff to the very point of the cliff at the east end, where a viewing platform overlooks the river valley. Along the way, there are wayside markers explaining history and geology, and visitors pass by five Native American burial mounds along the edge of the bluff, three more than the two William Clark reported seeing. This reminds us that Clark climbed the sheer bluff from the river side, not having the more gentle state park path to the top, and so only encountered the two mounds closest to the point overlooking the river junction.

The hill is densely wooded today, just as it was in Clark's time. In order for the captains to make their celestial observations to calculate latitude and longitude at their camp on the Osage Point, they had to cut down four or five trees just to reveal enough open sky. The trail to the top of the hill today begins in a bottomland amidst cottonwoods, willows, and sycamores but passes as it climbs through a more diverse growth of oaks, hickories, and maples, beneath which the typical understory of dogwoods, redbuds, wild plums, and other small brushy species are growing in the dense shade. Eastern red cedars are randomly scattered throughout the woods, both at the bottom and on the hilltop, and in the fall, a surprising number of Osage orange trees proclaim their earlier unassuming presence by the striking appearance of the bright chartreuse "hedge apples" hanging from their limbs. Most of this is second growth, as old maps show a major portion of the hill was once an orchard.

In a few open, sunny clearings, wildflowers such as asters and the rare amethyst shooting star can be seen, and scurrying sounds in the woods along the trail proclaim the presence of the usual birds and small animal wildlife. From the top of the hill, turkey vultures often sail on rising thermal currents, and in winter, eagles sometimes fish the rivers lying just below. Although the valley is always on view, the best look at the rivers themselves is in the wintertime, when the surrounding trees are bare.

Although the site's preoccupation with Lewis and Clark is understandable, there was a second exploring expedition that came across this lost hill: Lieutenant Zebulon Pike led an exploration party sent to the southwestern part of the Louisiana Purchase at nearly the same time as Lewis and Clark were exploring the northwest. In fact, had Pike left St. Louis a month later in 1806 or had Clark climbed the hill a month earlier on his return trip to St. Louis, Clark might have seen the Pike Expedition ascending the Missouri and making the left-hand turn into the mouth of the Osage River, headed west.

When William Clark described the wonderful view of the rivers from the top of the hill, he didn't mention the large island that lay immediately downstream from the point of the hill, in front of the mouth of the Osage River. Often claimed to be the largest island in the Missouri River, in the early nineteenth century it was just called the Big Island, but it later came to be known as Dodd's Island. Most of the time, the Osage

Left: William Clark would have seen a much wider Missouri River than visitors today see, when he climbed the hill on his 1804 expedition. *Missouri State Parks* Right: From Clark's Hill, you can see the Côte Sans Dessein, the hill across the Missouri River that was once promoted as a site for the state's capital city. *Taylor Blair* • A rare species of shooting star adorns the path up the hill. *Allison Vaughn*

River entered the Missouri, turned immediately downstream and flowed along the south side of the island in what was called the Osage chute, while the main flow of the Missouri went around the north side. But depending upon which river was in high water and which was low, the main current of water either flowed in the Missouri channel along the north side of the Big Island or in the Osage chute along the south side. The situation was complicated by a half-dozen smaller islands and sand bars that resulted in the Osage and Missouri combining into a braided stream made up of multiple, shallower water channels separated by strips of land.

A steamboat pilot coming upriver or going down had choices to make, sometimes all of them bad, as he tried to estimate which chute was carrying the most water or had the fewest snags. The Osage chute soon became notorious with riverboat pilots; a steamboat, the *Thomas*

Clark's Hill is above the present confluence of the Osage River on the left and the Missouri River, at the downstream tip of the triangular patch of yellow grain in the distance where the two rivers come closest together. The hill now adjoins a peninsula that is the former Big (or Dodd's) Island. The thin white line is a road on the levee that separates the rivers. Most bottomland along the channelized Missouri River is now in row crops. ***Jim Wark***

Jefferson, chugging up the Missouri in 1820 holed itself on a snag just downstream from Clark's Hill—the very first steamboat ever to sink on the Missouri River. As the years passed, the Osage chute also claimed the *Excel* and the 235-foot-long packet boat *Kate Howard*.

Over the decades, despite the hazard at the Osage River mouth and numerous other dangerous locales along the Missouri's length, more than a thousand different steamboats made at least one ascension of

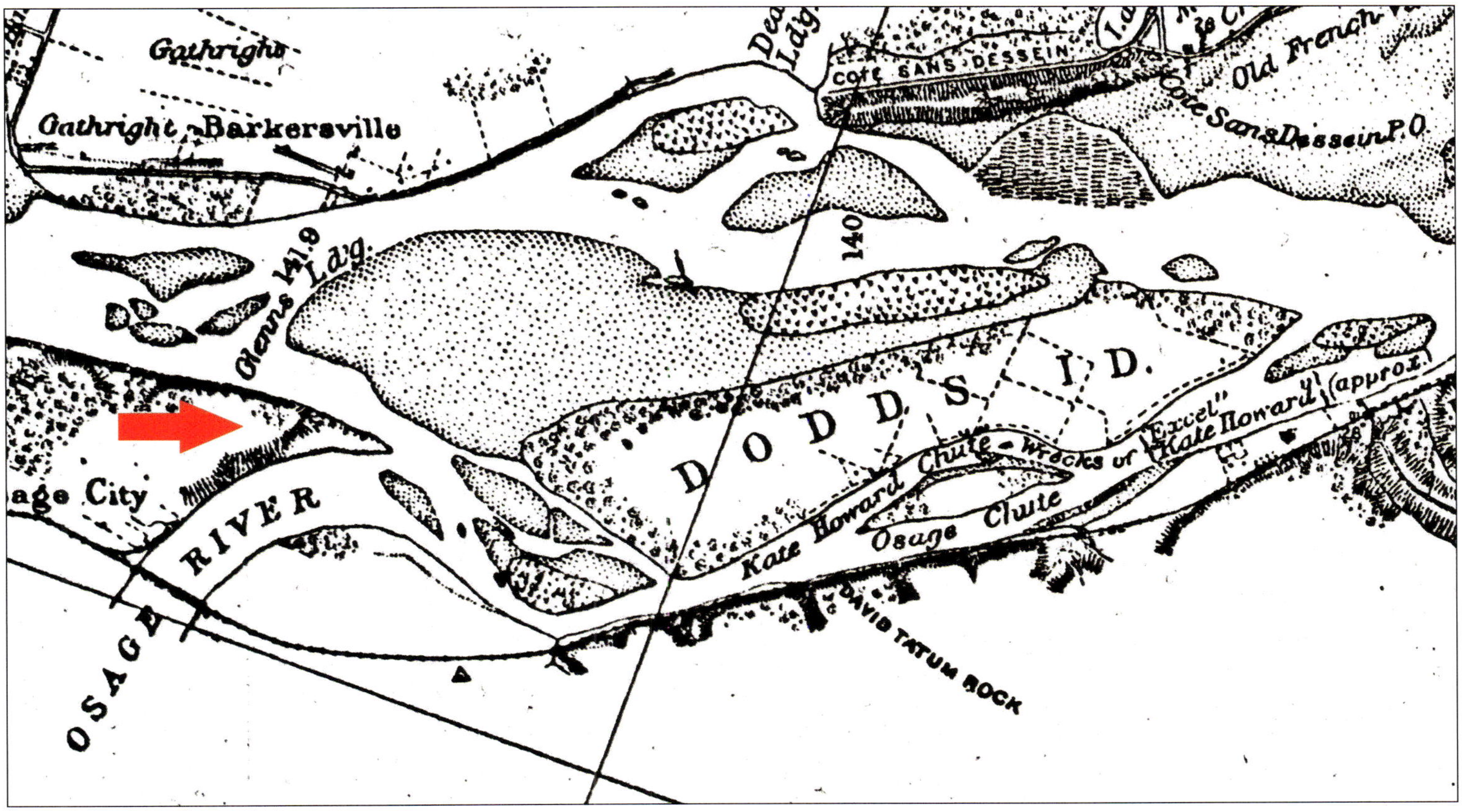

The red arrow marks the top of Clark's Hill; the expedition camp was on the point of bottomland below the bluff. This 1897 drawing shows where the Osage River joined the Missouri River with its many islands and sandbars, before the Corps of Engineers began to channelize the river for barge navigation. *Missouri River Commission* • Taos artist Victor Higgins took some liberties in his 1924 lunette for the Missouri capitol—only Clark climbed the hill—but Higgins depicted the river more as Clark would have seen it than as it appears today. *Lloyd Grotjan*

As the rivers meandered over the millenia, the Missouri River or the Osage River, maybe both, flowed on both sides of Clark's Hill.

the Missouri River. By 1860, the head of navigation extended all the way to Fort Benton in the Montana Territory. Clark's Hill witnessed not only this passing boat traffic on the Missouri but also more than a hundred smaller, rugged steamboats that regularly turned into the Osage River just below the hill, carrying the mail and freight from St. Louis or Jefferson City as far west as Osceola.

The Army Corps of Engineers waged a century-long war with the rivers, improving them for navigation with dikes, revetments, and dredging. William Clark in 1804 estimated the Missouri River, with its multiple channels, was 875 yards wide in front of his hill; today, it has been forced into a single channel less than half that width. Because the flow of the Osage was insufficient at times to scour its chute along the south side of Dodd's Island enough for navigation, the corps tried repeatedly with dikes and revetments to force the Osage to come straight to the Missouri across the upper end of the island, but it was a losing battle. After Bagnell Dam finally ended upstream navigation on the Osage in 1931, the corps allowed the Osage to return to its natural chute. In the 1930s, the corps began to turn Dodd's Island into a peninsula, anchoring it to the base of Clark's Hill, and more than two dozen wing-dikes and a mile of revetment ensured the Missouri channel stayed on its own side.

Clark's Hill is still a wonderful place, awaiting discovery. It provides an invigorating hike up a hill, through the woods, with a nearly perpetual breeze at the top, and a terrific view over the Missouri River valley. It's a great place to think about history and the role of the rivers as Missouri's first highways. While you enjoy the view, think about the eighteenth-century French traders and later settlers who once passed this rocky prominence, and imagine the military expeditions heading up both rivers to explore a newfound frontier. Think about the scores of steamboats that once plied these waters, maybe the *Chippewa* or the *Key West* headed all the way up the Missouri to the Montana territory, or the *Evening Star*, the *Thomas E. Tutt*, or even the *Gee Whiz*, making the hard turn into the Osage and heading west nearly to Kansas. Remember also the three wrecks on the bottom of the river, just below.

The Missouri is more placid now, pinioned between wing dikes and revetments, flowing in its narrow, trough-like channel, well clear of the mouth of the Osage. The peninsula, with a high levee extending down its middle like a spine, guarantees the rivers stay apart until they are finally allowed to mingle, six miles below where they used to meet. Up and down both rivers, the dense bottomland forests are mostly gone now, and a patchwork of crops and plowed fields recedes into the distance. But the hill itself remains the same, as do its five burial mounds, there for a thousand years. *

CLARK'S HILL/NORTON STATE HISTORIC SITE • OSAGE HICKORY STREET, OSAGE CITY

Jefferson Landing State Historic Site

When Capt. Charles B. Maus returned home to Jefferson City in 1865 after Civil War service in the federal army, he decided that the name of the hotel he had built in the 1850s should be changed to more forcefully demonstrate his wartime sentiments. That's how the old Veranda Hotel at the base of Jefferson Street on the Missouri River landing became the Union Hotel, and so also has it come down to us, in part as a testament to the strong pro-Union loyalties of Jefferson City's German population.

The lower end of Jefferson Street had been a lively commercial and transportation hub ever since the state's seat of government moved to Jefferson City in Cole County from St. Charles in 1826. In 1839 James A. Crump built a sturdy three-unit row building of locally quarried stone that served as grocery store, warehouse, tavern, telegraph office, and hotel for the growing state capital traffic.

Missouri was the main conduit of national expansion into the far West, and much of that epic migration went right by the front doors of the hotels at Jefferson Landing—or stopped overnight.

Traffic at that time was more by river than by road, and businesses flourished in the area that became known as "the Landing"—the capital city's primary commercial center and official city wharf. The lower doors of Crump's building were double, providing easy access to freight for the boats that pulled up nearly in front of the building. Built-in hoists above the top-floor doors lifted heavy loads. Crump's Missouri House Hotel, which occupied part of the building, won a reputation as a meeting place for rivermen and legislators.

In 1852, Charles F. Lohman bought a portion of the stone building built by Crump and opened a general store with his brother-in-law, Charles Maus. Three years later, Maus built his own new brick hotel and warehouse building across Jefferson Street from the Crump building. The Missouri House had changed its name to the Pacific Railroad Hotel in 1853, so Maus felt free to name his new establishment the Missouri Hotel, but later changed it to the Veranda Hotel.

In 1856 the Pacific Railroad reached Jefferson City from the east, promising even more prosperity. As a sign of things to come, the construction of the railroad damaged the cobblestone wharf and cut the businesses on the landing off from the river. Indeed, the iron horse would be the end of steamboating on the Missouri River. But for several years thereafter until the railroad pushed on westward, Jefferson City was the rail terminus, and all passengers and freight going upriver transferred to steamboats there. Business boomed along with the state, as Missouri experienced an epic burst of settlement and development, nearly doubling its population from 682,044 to 1,182,012 during the 1850s. During this time, Charles Maus's brother Christopher built a modest brick house a few doors south of his brother's hotel, where Christopher served as a saloonkeeper.

Then came the war. Charles and Christopher Maus enlisted in the Union army, while a third brother is said to have fought for the Confederacy. Lohman stayed behind and bought the rest of the stone building, which has since become known as the Lohman building. He developed one of the city's largest warehouse and mercantile businesses using the building's ground floor. Lohman also built and operated other businesses on the grounds around the large stone structure, among which was an iron foundry that cast plow shares and iron storefronts, including several cast-iron storefronts along High Street.

After the war and then Charles Maus's rechristening of the Union Hotel, Missouri River traffic began a slow but steady decline. Maus and Lohman, no longer tied to the steamboat trade, eventually relocated their commercial activity to Jefferson City's High Street in the mid-1870s. The old hotel, warehouse, and store buildings at the landing served as storage and tenements until the early twentieth century when

Left: The red brick Union Hotel now serves as an Amtrak station with a gallery of Missouri arts and culture on the second floor. The Lohman building is across the street. The two buildings comprise Missouri's oldest intact river landing commercial district. *Missouri State Parks* • Above: This 1861 woodcut shows the notch between the bluffs connecting the city to the river and railroad, with the capitol above and the Lohman building at the center of the wharf. *Harper's Weekly* • Right: The ground floor of the rehabilitated Lohman building displays exhibits illustrating its use as a commercial center. *Missouri State Parks*

they were combined into a large shoe factory. Because of their declining condition, they were almost torn down for the proverbial parking lot in the late 1960s during our national craze for demolishing old buildings.

An alert local citizenry, led by Elizabeth Rozier and with help from the preservation movement all across Missouri, gained a reprieve for this riverfront complex. Four years later, state park officials proposed to restore the buildings to correct period appearance and open them to the public. It was part of an integrated approach to history and culture in the state's capital that would lead eventually to the park system taking over operation of the state museum and conducting public tours of the capitol building. First Lady Carolyn Bond endorsed this plan, and her enthusiastic support led the state bicentennial commission to adopt the Jefferson Landing proposal as the state's official bicentennial project. All three of the remaining historic structures at the landing—the Lohman building, the Union Hotel, and the Christopher Maus home—were restored in time for their dedication on July 4, 1976.

As Missouri's oldest intact river-landing commercial district, Jefferson Landing tells an important story of how Missouri grew during those crucial years of the mid-nineteenth century. Freight shipped to or from Jefferson City or transferred there from rail to steamboat was warehoused in these buildings while awaiting the next leg of a western journey. Maybe things aren't quite as bustling down at the landing these days, but there is a different kind of excitement. While the exteriors of the buildings have been restored to their mid-nineteenth-century appearance, the interiors have been adapted for modern use. A lack of documentary and architectural information made a reconstruction of period interiors impossible. Instead, the focus of Jefferson Landing State Historic Site has been on interpreting some of the original function of the landing as a gathering place and on showcasing Missouri's art, culture, and history.

The ground floor of the Lohman building houses an exhibit area that tells the story of Jefferson City and the landing through immersive exhibits, designed to appear as a mid-nineteenth-century general store and warehouse. Every year, thousands of schoolchildren from all over Missouri tour these exhibits to learn of their capital city's history. The upper floors of the Lohman building hold offices and workshops for the Missouri State Museum and Missouri State Parks. The second floor of the Union Hotel houses a gallery for the exhibition of Missouri arts, culture, and history—appropriately named in honor of the landing's savior, Elizabeth Rozier. The bottom level of the hotel has been restored to something of its old-time commercial bustle through its use as the Amtrak passenger-train station—once again, a gateway to the city.

Just up the hill east of the Christopher Maus home is the Governor's Mansion with its lovely gardens and trees, and to the south are the formal plantings and reflecting pool of the Carnahan Memorial Garden. Across Jefferson Street at the edge of the capitol grounds is the impressive sculptural group representing the Lewis and Clark expedition, added during the bicentennial commemoration of that historical journey, and farther up the hill at the crest is the resplendent Missouri State Capitol.

Originally, all local lines of communication crossed at the landing—steamboat, river ferry, stagecoach, telegraph, and railroad. The hotels, saloons, warehouses, and mercantile establishments provided business activity by day and social activity by night. Today, the site staff is working to reestablish the landing as a gathering place through exhibits and special events both indoors and on the grounds. In this historic setting, Jefferson Landing carries on the age-old tradition of community first fostered by those river workers and statesmen who lived, worked, and spent free time here many years ago. ❋

JEFFERSON LANDING STATE HISTORIC SITE • 100 JEFFERSON STREET, JEFFERSON CITY

DE SOTO

Missouri State Museum

IF YOU ARE VISITING THE STATE CAPITOL for the first time, you may be surprised to discover that your guides wear state park uniforms. In 1976 responsibility for the Missouri State Museum and educational efforts about the capitol and its extraordinary public art were vested in the park division, thanks largely to its successful development of the adjacent Jefferson Landing State Historic Site.

A museum was planned for the capitol from the start. The architects designed a 60-by-112-foot-long museum gallery on each side of the rotunda. On the ground floor, the galleries extend two stories high, with a mezzanine at the second-floor level. Shortly after construction, the Missouri General Assembly defined the themes of the museum galleries. First came the historical museum in the east wing, designated in an act of 1919 as the Missouri Soldiers and Sailors Memorial Hall. Then in 1921 the assembly created the Resources Museum in the west wing to display "the products of the mines, mills, fields, and forests of this state."

The two museums were combined in 1923 and designated collectively as the Missouri State Museum. The museum continued to grow and change over the next five decades, for a time in the 1930s even being called The People's University. Its administration ranged through several state agencies before its 1976 transfer to State Parks. The park division then planned and oversaw a million-dollar renovation of the museum, its first major updating in nearly fifty years, with a special appropriation secured through the efforts of spouses of legislators.

Visitors can learn Missouri's history from both long-term and temporary exhibits. Most of the exhibits, which change regularly to highlight different topics, themes, and eras, include interactive elements as well as artifacts from the museum's vast collections. The museum also presents the state's heritage in educational programming, workshops, and special events of all kinds.

In the Resources Museum, exhibits are arranged according to the six natural divisions of the state, the same ones that are used to organize this book's chapters, with ingenious cutaway dioramas portraying the characteristic landforms and landscapes of each. The Foundations gallery under the governor's stairs in the rotunda focuses on the previous capitols in Jefferson City and on Missouri state government. As in the other galleries, the artifacts rotate over time to bring out different pieces from the museum's collections, such as legislative desks from the capitol destroyed in the 1911 fire, and to feature new donations.

Missouri boasts a truly distinguished state capitol, one that reflects the best of Missouri's people and government. Its setting could hardly be better: in the heartland of the state on a bluff overlooking the broad and fertile valley of the Missouri River, a historic transportation corridor that was a key to the state's development, and backed by a city large enough to provide many urban amenities yet small enough to retain the flavor of rural Missouri.

As Missouri was about to become a state in 1821, a temporary capitol was established at St. Charles, now First Missouri Capitol State Historic Site, until a permanent seat of government could be prepared. The Missouri constitution specified that the new capital city must be located on the Missouri River within forty miles of the mouth of the Osage River. A special commission selected the location in Cole County, and the General Assembly approved the site in 1821 and named it the City of Jefferson in honor of the president who made the Louisiana Purchase.

The first capitol in Jefferson City, which was also where the governor lived, was completed in 1826, an attractive Federal-style structure but only 40-by-60 feet in size. That building, located on the site of the present governor's mansion, burned in 1837 and was replaced in 1840 two blocks away, on the same site as the current capitol, by a much larger Greek Revival structure. This capitol survived the Civil War and was remodeled in the 1880s with a slender wooden dome, but the building was consumed by fire kindled in its dome by lightning on the stormy evening of February 5, 1911. Hundreds of fire-fighting volunteers, prisoners, legislators, and public officials managed to save some state records and artifacts, but the proud old building was ruined.

In retrospect, if a fire had to occur, it could hardly have come at a better time, for Missouri was at the crest of progressive idealism and its governor, Herbert Spencer Hadley, who was the nationally acclaimed prosecutor of the Standard Oil Trust, was determined that Missouri should take its rightful place as a leader among the states.

The old capitol had for years been too small to accommodate the growing functions of state government, but the legislature, tenacious in its heritage of antitax sentiment extending back to the days of Radical reconstruction after the Civil War, had repeatedly declined to expand facilities. Though Governor Hadley, a Republican, had previously been thwarted by conservatives in the Democratic-controlled legislature in his efforts to raise taxes and to create a state park system, he succeeded within two months of the fire in forging a bipartisan legislative coalition to authorize the issuance of $3.5 million in state bonds for a new and much larger capitol. Missouri voters approved the bond issue in August, and Hadley appointed a four-member State Capitol Commission to administer the planning and construction.

The bipartisan citizen commission chaired by Columbia newspaperman E. W. Stephens studied and fought through a series of issues concerning such matters as financing, an architectural competition, and choice of building stone. The commission announced a design competition that drew sixty-eight entrants nationwide and was won by Egerton Swartwout and Evarts Tracy of New York. Their classically symmetrical structure, evocative of the nation's capitol in Washington, DC, is considered a superb example of the Roman Renaissance style of public architecture typical of the early twentieth century. Built of Missouri

A SPECIAL GALLERY FOR VETERANS

The original dedication of the museum to Missouri's soldiers and sailors is reflected in the Missouri Veterans Gallery. Opened in 2007, this gallery honors Missouri's veterans with rotating displays featuring artifacts and stories about their service in wars throughout the state's history. One of the highlights of the museum's holdings is a significant and rare collection of more than six hundred flags. They include some 130 Civil War battle flags, many of which belonged to or were captured by Missouri units on both sides of the war, and nearly a hundred World War I service banners, created for almost every Missouri county. On the World War I banners are the number of men enlisted from the county as well as a gold star for each person who died in service.

A museum of history and resources was planned for the capitol from the start and coordinated with the design and decoration of the building. ***Scott Myers***

Redbud and other native Missouri trees frame the Roman Renaissance-style capitol, built between 1913 and 1917 during a crest of progressive idealism, after a disastrous fire in 1911 destroyed its predecessor. *Oliver Schuchard*

marble from quarries at Carthage and Phenix, it began to rise above the high ground overlooking the river in 1913 and was completed in 1917.

As capitol construction was coming to a close, there came a most pleasant surprise. The special property tax levy that had been earmarked for the capitol bonds was producing more funds than had been expected, while material and labor costs for the well managed project were less than estimated. In response to a request from the commission, the attorney general ruled that these funds could not legally be used for any purposes other than the capitol. Given these circumstances, another commission, the Capitol Decoration Commission chaired by University of Missouri art history Professor John Pickard, was established to use the more than $1 million of surplus funds to decorate the building.

Over the course of eleven years, the Decoration Commission recruited some of the most notable artists of the day from both America and Europe and oversaw the creation of a resplendent collection of murals, stained glass, carvings, castings, and statuary. All of these works relate directly or indirectly to the people and history of Missouri, and the commission took great care to match artists to subjects and to ensure historical accuracy. Frank Brangwyn of London, whom Pickard considered the preeminent mural painter in the world, was commissioned to do the murals in the dome; N. C. Wyeth painted the Civil War battles of Wilson's Creek and Westport; Missourian Frank B. Nuderscher did a lunette of the Eads Bridge in St. Louis, using an optical trick that changes the viewpoint perspective from left to right as one walks past, a favorite of tourists. And a group of artists, the Taos Society, which included Oscar Berninghaus of St. Louis, was commissioned to paint frontier and American Indian scenes, while Henry Reuterdahl's colorful depiction of war at sea, *The Navy Guarded the Road to France*, is a modernist masterpiece.

The decorations of the 1920s were later supplemented by a masterwork of Missouri's Thomas Hart Benton, whom the legislature in 1935 commissioned to paint a mural on the four walls of the house lounge. Benton's *Social History of the State of Missouri* delivers with bold and vivid strokes scenes of everyday life in the state's past, and in so doing, offers a commentary from the perspective of the Great Depression decade on the lofty themes of the rest of the capitol art. Highly controversial at the time, the mural is now Missouri's pride.

The building is literally a museum of public art, remarkable both for its quality and abundance and for faithfully reflecting the state and its people. What is less known, though no less worth pondering, was the constant but successful rearguard action waged by the Pickard commission and others against certain politicians' efforts to divert funds earmarked for the capitol to other needs of a perennially impecunious state.

Tours of the capitol cover all major aspects of the building and its artwork as well as the Missouri State Museum on the first floor. Because the museum was designed for the building, the art was matched to the theme of each gallery. Thus, the art on the ceiling and mezzanines above the Soldiers and Sailors Hall reflects Missouri's military history from the American Revolution through World War I. In each of the arches along the mezzanines, noted Italian artist Carlo Gino Venanzi painted historical characters from eras corresponding to those depicted in nearby lunettes: a Continental soldier, a trapper, a colonial dame, a ranger, a war nurse, a Spanish-American War officer, a World War I soldier, and a naval seaman, each near its corresponding lunette. A timeline of Missouri's history from the first explorations is carved above the alcoves, and engraved above the columns are the names of people important in the state's history: Jefferson, Lewis, Clark, Boone, and others.

The ceiling and mezzanine art in the west wing reflect the themes of the Resources Hall below. The lunettes illustrate the resources and development of the state, with those on the south side portraying eastern Missouri and those on north portraying the western part. Included are lunettes depicting several places that are now state parks, among them Ste. Genevieve, the Confluence, Clark's Hill, Boone's Lick, Ha Ha Tonka, and Osage Village. Medallions show the coats of arms of some of the principal cities of Missouri, while resource types are named in stone above the alcoves: red granite, marble, lead, fruits and cereals, and more. Other engravings highlight the industries that have developed those resources: mining, agriculture, forestry, water power, railroads, manufacturers, dairy, and livestock production.

Much of the excellence of the building is in its exterior design and statuary, including Karl Bitter's bronze relief of the signing of the Louisiana Purchase treaty, which sits on the terrace overlooking the Missouri River, and the Lewis and Clark monument by Columbia sculptor Sabra Tull Meyer, commissioned for the 2003 to 2006 bicentennial of their expedition and located east of the capitol on a hill overlooking Jefferson Landing. The landscaping complements the building, with seasonal floral displays and fine specimens of a large number of native tree species.

While state park staff provide guided tours of all four floors of the capitol and the Missouri State Museum and its artifacts are legally part of the state park system, the building itself and the artwork intrinsic to it are the seat of government and not a state park and thus are cared for by the Missouri Office of Administration and the Missouri State Capitol Commission. It was an irony of history, then, when supporters of the park system in 1990 found themselves calling on other concerned citizens and legislators to prevent an attempted diversion of nearly $1.4 million from the State Park Sales Tax Fund for the purpose of repairing the masonry of the capitol. One could imagine Herbert Hadley, E. W. Stephens, and John Pickard standing alongside them, arguing for the integrity of the dedicated park fund and calling on Missouri officials once again to rise to their responsibility and provide the funds necessary to maintain the capitol and its unparalleled public art.

The Missouri State Museum and the magnificent capitol that houses it represent a triumph of vision and vigilance by Missourians who dared to believe that their state could accomplish something truly great. *

MISSOURI STATE MUSEUM • THE CAPITOL, 201 WEST CAPITOL AVENUE, JEFFERSON CITY

A state park guide introduces school children to Thomas Hart Benton's ***Social History of the State of Missouri*** mural in the house lounge. Children and adults have been fascinated with the cutaway dioramas affording a 3-D view of features of the state's six natural divisions—the same ones used for this book—ever since they were installed in the 1980s, and they still are today. *Both Susan Flader*

Boone's Lick State Historic Site

WHILE LEGENDARY PIONEER DANIEL BOONE spent more time at his home in western St. Charles County in his later years, his sons explored and hunted much of Missouri. In 1805 Nathan and Daniel Morgan Boone began manufacturing salt at a Missouri valley site in what is now southwestern Howard County. Within seven years, the Boone brothers left the salt business, but their enterprise gave these salt springs and this interior region of Missouri a new name. Even today, this part of the state is known as the Boone's Lick Country (often rendered as Boonslick in literature of the period and by some contemporary writers, as well as on the bridge over the Missouri River at Boonville). The trail the Boones blazed from St. Charles to the salt springs, known as the Boone's Lick Trail, was followed by thousands of pioneers who bypassed eastern Missouri to settle the rich farmlands of the Missouri Valley in Howard and neighboring counties.

Salt springs, or salines, were desirable in a frontier society and relatively common in this part of the state, though few were as large or as well-known as Boone's Lick. Lewis and Clark recorded "a large lick and salt spring of great strength" about four miles southeast of "a cliff called the Arrow Rock" on their trip up the Missouri in 1804. The lick the Boones worked was on 400 arpents (340 acres) of a 1798 Spanish land grant to James Mackay, from whom they leased it. When Mackay's grant was challenged in court and voided, the Boones and their partners in the enterprise, James and Jesse Morrison, then purchased several quarter sections of the land.

PRODUCING SALT WAS A LONG PROCESS

Brine, or saline water, from the spring was poured into large kettles that held anywhere from twenty to one hundred gallons each. The brine was then heated over a stone furnace. As it boiled, various bitter compounds would precipitate out at the bottom of the kettles. This "bittern" or "powder scratch" had to be removed periodically with long-handled ladles. As the water continued to evaporate, salt crystallized in the kettle. About two hundred gallons of brine water were required to obtain one bushel of salt. To boil all of this water required hundreds of cords of wood, hauled in from as far as four miles away. The piles of ash scraped out of the furnaces now appear as earthen mounds dotting the site.

In an interview more than four decades later in 1851 with famed frontier historian Lyman Copeland Draper, the aging pioneer Nathan Boone said they initially had six to eight men using forty kettles and one furnace to boil the brine water. They produced twenty-five to thirty bushels of salt a day and boated them to settlements downriver where salt sold readily for two-and-a-half dollars per bushel. As the business grew, Nathan Boone recalled, they added furnaces and kept fifteen to twenty men employed, making 130 bushels a day. They paid each man about fifteen dollars a month.

Daniel Morgan Boone sold out to James Morrison in 1810, and Nathan pulled out two years later when he was appointed captain of the Missouri Rangers in the War of 1812. Forty years later, Nathan would blame their departure from the salt business on insufficient profit and pillaging of "working and beef cattle" by American Indians. After three years of disruption and occasional terror in the settlements, during which the salt operation was damaged and apparently shut down, Nathan Boone was appointed by the territorial government in 1815 to survey the overland route from St. Charles to the interior that he and his brother had earlier blazed, hence the name Boone's Lick Road. A flood tide of settlement surged into the Boone's Lick Country during the next few years.

The Morrisons continued making salt at the lick until 1833. The operation was managed for a time by William Becknell, who also operated a ferry across the Missouri River in the vicinity of Boone's Lick and Arrow Rock beginning in 1818. From the Boone's Lick region in the summer of 1821, Becknell organized an expedition to trap, hunt, and trade in the southern Rocky Mountains. This was the expedition that was met near Raton Pass that November by a detachment of friendly Mexican troops who encouraged them to proceed to Santa Fe. With Mexico newly independent from Spain and hungry for trade goods, it was the storied beginning of the Santa Fe Trail, which brought prosperity and political power to Boone's Lick Country.

After James Morrison advertised Boone's Lick for sale in 1831—apparently with no takers—and an 1833 court reversal of its earlier judgment against the Mackay claim, the record becomes murkier. Despite litigation over a lease to Lindsey P. Marshall and purchase of the site by James and John Marshall at a sheriff's sale in 1850, there is little evidence of commercial activity until after the Civil War when a Marshall relative from Canada, Henry Brown, bought a one-third interest in the property and formed the Boone's Lick Salt Manufacturing Company. After several years of effort, including the drilling of a thousand-foot well, they decided the lick was not salty enough to be profitable. As the nineteenth century drew to a close, W. N. Marshall proposed damming the springs to raise oysters and saltwater fish. The plan failed, supposedly because he could not find adequate fresh water nearby in which the oysters could spawn.

The Daughters of the American Revolution marked the site of Boone's Lick in the early twentieth century, but it remained relatively unknown. Then in 1960, Mr. and Mrs. J. R. Clinkscales of Boonville and Horace Munday donated to the State Park Board two small tracts totaling about seventeen acres that contained what remained of the salt lick. A limited archaeological survey at the time revealed evidence of a rock-lined furnace exposed in cross section by erosion of the banks of Salt Creek, which flows through the site to the Missouri River. There were remains of a box-like structure surrounding the well that had been drilled after the Civil War, remains of another box around the lower salt spring, and various partially buried wooden timbers near the upper spring. The timbers were assumed to be from later activity not related to the early salt industry, on the theory that exposed wood would not have remained intact for 150 years. And that was about it. The site required a visitor to exercise his or her imagination.

Over the following decades, the remains were further eroded until even the rock-lined furnace could no longer be seen. Historical records indicated five springs at the site, but only one still flowed at the surface. Then in 1986 a brief ten-day archaeological investigation led by Robert T. Bray of the University of Missouri at Columbia produced

The trickle of a saline spring and a few remnants of well casings in a valley are the only surface evidence of salt manufacturing by Nathan and Daniel Morgan Boone, sons of the famous explorer and pioneer, and others. ***Oliver Schuchard***

Right: Visitors will spy an old cast-iron salt kettle along the trail to the spring. *Sarah Herrera* • Below: Artist Victor Higgins, from Taos, New Mexico, imagined the scene at Boone's Lick for this lunette entitled *Sons of Daniel Boone Making Salt*, 1807. See it at the State Capitol in Jefferson City. *Missouri State Parks*

Above: A wooden well casing has survived for more than a century, preserved by the saline water. *Missouri State Parks* • Right: Archaeologists remove a hand-hewn octagonal drive shaft for a tread wheel that dipped brine from the spring and lifted it to a wooden flume for transport to the salt furnaces. *Robert T. Bray*

startling results. Bray found not one furnace as in 1961, or two as reported by Nathan Boone, or four as reported by Jesse Morrison, but six. Four years later, another investigation would raise that number to ten. Moreover, the timbers that had been seen at the surface in 1961 turned out to have been from the early activity at the site after all, and the remains of several well casings, two log cabins, and a brine-elevating delivery system were still there underground, perfectly preserved in the waterlogged, briny earth.

Most remarkable of all was a ten-foot-long octagonal shaft superbly hand-hewn from a log, with spindles at the ends and mortises in each face to receive the spokes of a wheel. It was the drive shaft for a tread wheel ingeniously designed to dip brine from the spring and elevate it to a system of wooden flumes that might have extended as far as five hundred feet in order to supply the various furnaces. The 960-pound drive shaft required twelve people to carry it up the hill to be transported to a specially built tank in which it would be conserved, using a then new technique that employed a supersaturated sugar solution. With these and other discoveries made at the site, the secrets of the operations at Boone's Lick are finally beginning to emerge.

The saline water at Boone's Lick not only supported an industry and preserved its remains, but it has also produced a habitat for salt-loving plants and animals. Some of the grasses found around this and other similar licks in Howard and Saline Counties might seem more at home along the seashore. Their names, like salt meadow grass and saltbush, tell the story. In the alkaline waters of Salt Creek just below the lick, the rare plains killifish has found a most suitable home. This is the easternmost population of this two-inch-long topminnow, so named because of its habit of skimming along the water's surface looking for insects. These killifish thrive in water with relatively few other species. The lick is also home to a species of salt-tolerant mosquito that breeds in the briny water.

Archaeological excavations suggest that saline water may have been pumped and distributed by flumes to multiple furnaces, as shown in this diorama in the visitor center at Arrow Rock, across the river from Boone's Lick. ***Michael Dickey***

Boone's Lick State Historic Site now contains about fifty acres set among rolling fields and wooded hills. A kiosk at the parking lot above the springs explains the history of Boone's Lick and the people associated with it. Included are illustrations of how the salt works may have appeared and operated based on the archaeological excavations. A narrow, winding trail leads down into the spring valley. When the weather is right, you can detect the odor of sulfurous vapors rising from the spring from halfway down the hill. One of the original cast-iron salt kettles remains alongside the trail, and signs explain the layout of the significant frontier industry once located here. Remnants of two well casings are still visible on site, and the drive shaft may now be seen in the visitor center museum across the river at Arrow Rock.

Once the scene of a noisy, smoky, bustling frontier industry, Boone's Lick today is off the beaten track and so peaceful that you can easily imagine yourself in another world—the world of the Boones and the Morrisons, scouting out the prospects and laying the foundations for a rich new region of settlement. *

BOONE'S LICK STATE HISTORIC SITE • ROUTE 187, NEAR BOONESBORO

Arrow Rock State Historic Site

AS THE STATE'S FIRST HISTORIC SITE, Arrow Rock holds a place of honor in the state park system. Today, as in the past, it beckons to travelers passing through the Missouri River valley. Visitors enjoy the easygoing, small-town ambience of its current environment with reminders of its nineteenth-century past as a flourishing river port in the heart of the Boone's Lick Country.

The Missouri River was and is the dominant geographic feature of the region, and the river served as a road to empire for France, Spain, and the United States in succession. An important Indian trail known as the Osage Trace crossed the Missouri River here.

The site was noted by Lewis and Clark on their monumental expedition upriver in 1804 and again in 1808 by William Clark, who deemed it "a handsome Spot for a Town" when he camped there on his expedition to construct Fort Osage 130 miles farther upstream. Small enclaves of American settlers became established in the region by 1810. During the War of 1812 when Fort Osage had to be closed for a time, a government fur trading post for the Osage tribe was constructed near Arrow Rock and operated by George Sibley, who had been the agent at Fort Osage.

Arrow Rock appeared as pierre a flèche *or "rock of arrows" on French maps as early as 1732. Arrow Rock takes its name from a flinty landmark bluff along the river that Native Americans used for thousands of years as a place to make flint tools and weapons.*

After the war, settlers flooded into the area "like an avalanche," said Baptist missionary John Mason Peck. A ferry began operating here. One of its earliest owners was David Todd, whose niece would marry Abraham Lincoln, and William Becknell, who managed the Boone's Lick salt works, served for a time as a ferryman. In September 1821, a party led by Becknell crossed on the Arrow Rock ferry and followed the Osage Trace on what became the first successful trading venture to Santa Fe.

Although the bluff above the ferry became a point of departure for wagon trains to Santa Fe led by Becknell and others for a decade after 1821, Arrow Rock was not platted formally as a town until 1829. The plat made by Meredith M. Marmaduke featured a grid pattern of regular blocks with a public square and east-west and north-south streets, beginning at the edge of the bluff with Water Street. The place was confidently named Philadelphia, but that was changed in 1833 by an act of the state legislature to coincide with the more familiar landmark bluff, the arrow rock that gave the place its name.

Among the early residents was Joseph Huston, who had settled in the area in 1819 and went on to serve as both a justice of the peace and a judge for Saline County. In 1834 he built the Federal-style J. Huston Tavern on Main Street that has served for nearly two centuries as a restaurant and gathering place and, at times, as a hotel, dance hall, and mercantile store. George Caleb Bingham, one of America's most well-known artists, moved with his mother to a nearby farm in 1827 and in 1837 built a small brick house at the corner of First and High streets.

Dr. John Sappington, a pioneer in the use of quinine for treating malarial fevers—a scourge in riverine areas—was Saline County's first physician and a rural Arrow Rock resident. His close association with President Andrew Jackson and US Senator Thomas Hart Benton from Missouri, as well as the wealth acquired from his quinine pill business and agricultural pursuits, helped create a family political dynasty that included three Missouri governors—Meredith Miles Marmaduke, Claiborne Fox Jackson, and John Sappington Marmaduke. Probably no other town in the state was more of a powerhouse than Arrow Rock, at the center of the so-called Central Clique or Boone's Lick Democracy that dominated Missouri politics from statehood to the beginning of the Civil War.

In 1843 the Missouri legislature established the Arrow Rock Female Academy, which was replaced by a succession of other schools. A two-story log house believed to have served as a dormitory still survives. Churches of several denominations were organized, and several of their buildings remain throughout the town, as do several lodge halls of fraternal social orders.

Despite all of the surviving architecture of this thriving river port, which boasted a population of more than a thousand by 1860, perhaps nothing better expresses the vitality and vision of this community than the gutters that still grace Main Street today. Quarried limestone blocks were individually shaped and carefully laid in concave troughs by slaves in 1858. The streets were improved with flagstone walks at the intersections and macadam, or crushed rock, surfacing. The business area on the north side of Main Street had a sixteen-foot-wide sidewalk covered with awnings, and many of the commercial buildings rose to two and three stories in height, befitting a town of distinction. There was also an effort to extend Main Street directly to the river by making an enormous cut through the bluff. Known as Godsey's Diggings for the contractor hired to do the job, the project was abandoned as impractical in 1858, leaving only a steep, tree-filled ravine today. Merchants continued to use the earlier road via the Big Spring valley to reach the steamboat landing south of town. But some began laying more ambitious plans for the Louisiana and Missouri River Railroad that was to angle southwest across the state and cross the river, they hoped, at Arrow Rock.

These glowing prospects were dashed by the Civil War, a war in which

Right: Limestone gutters, made of blocks quarried and carved by slaves, line the main street of Arrow Rock near the building known as the Old Courthouse. *Oliver Schuchard* • Left: From an overlook at Arrow Rock, one now sees the bottomland forest of the Big Muddy National Fish and Wildlife Refuge, with the Missouri River confined to a channel on the far side of its floodplain. *Scott McNealy*

J. HUSTON
TAVERN
RESTAURANT
HUSTON MERCANTILE
J. HUSTON
TAVERN
ICE CREAM
SHOP

Left: The Huston Tavern has accommodated western travelers since the 1830s and still serves a hearty fare to its guests. *Mike Kellner* • Above: The Brown Masonic Lodge, restored by Friends of Arrow Rock, now houses a museum that preserves the town's African American history. *Missouri Division of Tourism* Right: Many special events take visitors back to different eras, along a street lined with shops built in the nineteenth century. *Mike Kellner*

many citizens of Arrow Rock took leadership roles, but mostly on the losing side. The town was occupied at various times by soldiers of both sides. Although it escaped major destruction, the town was under martial law and repeatedly harassed by guerrilla raids, disrupting business and making farming in the countryside impossible.

Following the war, railroads rapidly replaced river commerce, but Arrow Rock failed to secure a railroad. The leading families, most now among the vanquished, lost much of the wealth and prestige they had earlier known, and younger sons sought their future elsewhere. A pall settled over the town as the population shrank to six hundred by 1872, the year a series of arson fires wiped out much of the commercial district. Another fire in 1901 again devastated the business district and sealed the fate of the community, which by then had decreased to three hundred people, about half of them black and half white. Arrow Rock was now known as an "ancient town" and many of its structures were threatened with loss to fire, demolition, or neglect.

The seemingly inevitable descent of this once proud town was paralleled in the twentieth century by a gradually rising commitment to preserve some of its storied past. It began with the efforts of the Missouri Society of the Daughters of the American Revolution to mark and commemorate historical trails, principal among them the Boone's Lick and Santa Fe trails, and to identify some of the structures of interest still along their routes. Indeed, in 1912 the DAR, together with the Women's National Old Trails Road Association, furnished a room in Joseph Huston's old hotel as the "Old Tavern Rest Room," with relics useful for "teaching Missouri history to the passerby."

After World War I, the Missouri DAR encouraged the state's political leaders to acquire the Arrow Rock Tavern to ensure its preservation. Their efforts culminated in the purchase of the building and its contents by the state of Missouri in 1923, making the tavern the first building in the state purchased with public funds for historic preservation purposes. The DAR would serve as managers and custodians of the tavern until 1984. In 1926 they conducted a statewide campaign for contributions to match a grant of $6,000 from the General Assembly for restoration of the structure—perhaps the first large-scale citizen campaign for historic preservation in Missouri.

A restoration of the tavern in 1986 took the building as close to its 1840s appearance as possible, with a fish-shaped weather vane still

turning on the roof. Now operated directly by the state park system, the structure still serves as a house museum and full-service restaurant, with the old ballroom upstairs turned into a meeting room.

In 1926 the state acquired about thirty acres south of town around the Big Spring (also known as the Santa Fe Spring), as well as the one-cell vaulted stone jail, and established Arrow Rock State Park. The academy boarding house, a four-room log house constructed in the 1820s and owned by Dr. George Penn during the period of his medical partnership with Dr. John Sappington, was added to state holdings in 1930, and in 1934, the state acquired the George Caleb Bingham house and other significant property fronting on Main Street.

Bingham had served as a trustee of the Arrow Rock town board and, after his Arrow Rock years, as a state representative, state treasurer during the Civil War, and state adjutant general beginning in 1875. He was also the first professor of art at the University of Missouri, a largely honorary position because of his poor health at the time. During his years in and out of public service, he actively painted the portraits, scenes of western life, and realistic canvases depicting frontier politics that made him known nationwide as "The Missouri Artist." Several of Bingham's paintings, engravings, and prints are exhibited at the site's visitor center museum. The Bingham house was renovated in 1936 as a Works Progress Administration (WPA) project. A more authentic restoration based on archaeological research was completed in 1966, and the house was designated a National Historic Landmark in 1968.

WPA workers also built a three-arched stone bridge, picnic facilities, including a shelter house, and a gazebo-like lookout shelter on the bluff

Above: The National Historic Landmark home of Missouri artist George Caleb Bingham is a favorite on tours. Bingham built the home in 1837. *Kathy Borgman* The annual Fourth of July parade and other special events are planned by various Arrow Rock groups. *Scott Granneman* • The large visitor center and museum complex, built in a swale at the edge of town so as not to overshadow historic structures, contains fine exhibits on the Osage and Missouria tribes, the French and Spanish time in the Missouri valley, and the pioneers. *Missouri State Parks*

east of the Bingham home, though you can no longer see the river from there. During the early years of the twentieth century, the river channel shifted to the far side of the flood plain, where it has since been stabilized by the Army Corps of Engineers, so the current no longer runs below the bluff at Arrow Rock but flows a mile from town. Following record floods in 1993, the US Fish and Wildlife Service purchased nearly two thousand acres of bottomland bordering the historic site for the Jameson Island unit of the new Big Muddy National Fish and Wildlife Refuge and has been working with the corps to restore more natural channels and sloughs. The area has reverted to bottomland forest and marshland, more characteristic of the river floodplain when Lewis and Clark passed by in 1804. The walking trails of the refuge and the historic site connect, offering access to the old river landing, the Missouri River, and bird and wildlife viewing opportunities.

In 1959 citizens of Arrow Rock, which had persisted with a population of less than a hundred, joined with others to establish the Friends of Arrow Rock, Inc., a private not-for-profit organization devoted to the preservation and restoration of the town. The first trustees of the friends

Above: The four-room log academy boarding house dating from the 1820s once housed students of the Arrow Rock Female Academy. *Bruce Wicks* • Right: Arrow Rock's quiet, shady streets even today evoke the nineteenth century. The Friends of Arrow Rock now maintain the Masonic and Odd Fellows lodge halls, which face each other across Main Street. *Friends of Arrow Rock* • Left: Local lore holds that the primitive 1873 sandstone city jail, "the old calaboose," was used only once, and then for only a single night. *Jerome Goolsby*

included many notable Missourians, among them Joseph Huston Sr., Gov. John Dalton, and President Harry S Truman. The group's first project was to acquire, restore, and furnish the weather-boarded log building known as the Old Courthouse, which it donated to the state in 1962. Although the evidence does not support the oral tradition that this is the building that served as the Saline County courthouse from 1839 to 1840 or that it inspired George Caleb Bingham's famed painting, *County Election*, the carefully beaded walnut siding suggests that it is one of the older buildings, dating to the early 1830s, and tours of the town take visitors there.

The Friends of Arrow Rock have saved and restored more than a dozen buildings over the years, including the John Sites house and gun shop, a fully functioning nineteenth-century American gun shop. The group leased the Lawless Farm from the state and restored it in 2002, so visitors can compare the lifestyles and technological changes that occurred over time from the Bingham house (1837) to the Sites house (1872) to the Lawless farm (1903). The Friends' efforts have also inspired many private restorations of residences and bed-and-breakfasts in the community and nearby areas. Since 1965 the Friends have conducted tours of the town and its house museums in cooperation with the state historic site. In 1976 the Friends assumed full responsibility for funding tour guides. The group also hosts numerous special events each year, usually in cooperation with park officials, and collaborates closely with the historic site in the development of educational programs for schools, public programs, and special exhibits.

Significantly, the Friends have led efforts to recover the town's black history. Before the Civil War, one-third of Saline County's population was enslaved. The number of "freedmen" moving into postwar Arrow Rock helped to slow the town's otherwise plummeting population. By 1880 black citizens made up more than half of the populace, and they increasingly began establishing their own households, churches, and social institutions. As the black population dwindled in the second half of the twentieth century, the Friends in the 1970s began recording oral histories of black residents and descendants. Ted Fisher and his wife, Virginia, then began to seek out multiple heirs of the unused structures

and purchased several in an effort to save them. When the state proved resistant to his proffered donation of the buildings, the Friends of Arrow Rock stepped up in the 1990s to accept the properties, arrange for archaeological and historical studies in cooperation with former residents and their descendants, and restore the 1869 Brown's Chapel Free Will Baptist Church and the 1881 Brown Lodge (Black Masonic Lodge), the latter now a museum showcasing the culture and contributions of Arrow Rock's black residents. With preservation of these black cultural features, visitors to Arrow Rock gain a more complete understanding of the complex society that once characterized life in this small Missouri town.

The good will and pride among black descendants generated by these efforts led to the state acquiring and adding to the historic site the Sappington Negro Cemetery about five miles west of town. This two-acre cemetery was given in 1856 by Dr. Sappington to Emanuel Banks, and it is the resting place of many of Arrow Rock's black residents from the nineteenth through the mid-twentieth century. The last burial there was in 2006.

The entire town of Arrow Rock, including the state-owned portion, was designated a National Historic Landmark in 1964 in recognition of its distinguished role in American history. In the 1960s, the state purchased and restored the 1847 brick home of Dr. Matthew W. Hall, a member of the state legislature during the crisis of 1861, and in the 1970s, it acquired nearly a hundred additional acres south of town and developed a larger camping area, a small fishing lake, and a walking trail through the wooded bluffs. A long-awaited museum and visitor center was finally constructed in 1991. It presents not only the history of this remarkable place and its inhabitants—American Indian, black, and white—but the larger context of the Boone's Lick Country in state and national history.

In 2006, only months after this national landmark community was named one of a Dozen Distinctive Destinations in the United States by the National Trust for Historic Preservation, the town was threatened by a proposed 4,800-hog concentrated animal feeding operation (CAFO) less than two miles upwind. With a constellation of political forces aligned in support of industrial agriculture and with Department of Natural Resources (DNR) permits already issued for CAFOs within two miles of three state parks—Battle of Athens and Roaring River as well—the only recourse for park supporters was the courts.

Friends of Arrow Rock, the Missouri Parks Association, and other organizations joined in two lawsuits, one federal based on review requirements of the National Historic Preservation Act—the first such proceeding in the nation related to a CAFO—and the other at the state level to establish the duty of the Missouri DNR to protect state parks, even when its permitting obligations conflict. In the state suit, the plaintiffs won summary judgment—a stunning judgment that on appeal was declared moot because the Arrow Rock CAFO construction permit had lapsed after the owner had decided not to proceed. In fact, this made both suits moot. Arrow Rock was saved from the CAFO threat, but Battle of Athens and Roaring River were not. Fortunately, neither the prevailing winds nor the runoff waters from the CAFOs enter those parks.

Arrow Rock was the center of an extraordinary concentration of power and influence in antebellum Missouri and a way station in the development of the American West. Today, with a year-round population of only fifty, it annually attracts well over 100,000 visitors. It maintains its historical ambience through the cooperative efforts of the state, town government, private individuals, and the Friends of Arrow Rock, ensuring that the red brick buildings, white frame homes, and canopied storefronts will continue to fascinate and inspire visitors. *

ARROW ROCK STATE HISTORIC SITE • 39521 VISITOR CENTER DRIVE, ARROW ROCK

Sappington Cemetery State Historic Site

THE HUGE RED CEDARS are visible for a quarter-mile before you arrive at Sappington Cemetery, five miles west of Arrow Rock in Saline County. These magnificent trees were greatly beloved by the pioneers, not only for their associations with scriptural passages, but also as an evergreen reminder of the promise of everlasting life in an otherwise deciduous world. Nearly every pioneer home had one or more in the yard, and every old cemetery in Missouri featured them. They are frequently older than the houses they are standing by, and these at Sappington Cemetery are perhaps older than the first burial. The largest is over two and a half feet in diameter.

Thomas Gray, in his famous "Elegy Written in a Country Churchyard" of 1750, fixed forever in our consciousness the sense of romance and history embodied, literally, in a country burying ground:

The lowing herd wind slowly o'er the lea,
The plowman homeward plods his weary way,
And leaves the world to darkness and to me.

Gray's words perfectly describe a visit to Sappington Cemetery. Even today, when your eye strays away from the limestone-walled enclosure, through the small, wooded grove surrounding it, and onto the high rolling prairie beyond, you see a scene of bucolic peace, the grassland studded with grazing cattle.

This is the heartland of Missouri's Little Dixie, and extending to and beyond the horizon are the sites of the great country estates of the nineteenth century. Their very names—Experiment, Prairie Park, Fox's Castle, Lilac Hill, Val Verde—evoke mental images of an agrarian elite that graced Missouri's antebellum society. The gentry that once lived and laughed and loved and died in those great halls now lie here, beneath our feet.

A first impression of Sappington Cemetery, other than of the neat orderliness of the limestone wall topped by a cast-iron fence, is dominated by the curious elevation of the Sappington vaults and by the size of the huge eastern red cedars that flank them. Dr. John Sappington (1776-1856), after whom the cemetery is named, was a celebrity of his day, not only as Southern gentry but also as a noted physician and a consummate politician. For several decades, he was the power broker of the Boone's Lick Democracy, the so-called Central Clique that controlled Missouri for most of the first half of the nineteenth century. Two of his sons-in-law, who lie nearby, and one grandson became governors of the state.

Sappington made money by promoting quinine as an anti-fever remedy in the treatment of malaria, the most common disease in the Mississippi and Missouri valleys at the time. His unconventional treatment saved thousands of lives and became the standard treatment for nearly a century. He used his money to buy rich Saline County farmland and his enormous prestige to steer the course of events. His daughters married some of the most powerful men in the state—men made more powerful no doubt by their association with John Sappington.

The grave of a Sappington son-in-law and Missouri's eighth governor, Meredith Miles Marmaduke (1791-1864), along with his wife, Lavinia Sappington Marmaduke (1807-1885), are to the left after you enter the cemetery gate. The Marmaduke tombstone consists of twin white columns connected by an arch on which are carved two clasped hands and the single word, "Farewell." Marmaduke was elected lieutenant governor in August 1840, and after Gov. Thomas Reynolds committed suicide on February 9, 1844, Marmaduke served out the remaining nine months in the term. He was a strong Union supporter. His son, John Sappington Marmaduke, however, became a Confederate major general. He also became Missouri's twenty-fifth governor forty years after his father, serving from 1885 to 1887.

Missouri's fifteenth governor, Claiborne Fox Jackson (1806-1862), married not just one but three successive daughters of John Sappington: Jane, Louisa, and Eliza, Jane and Louisa having died young. At the cemetery, he is buried with his third wife, Eliza W. Sappington Jackson (1806-1864). Their graves are marked by two twin pillars inscribed "Gather my Saints together unto me."

Jackson was the doomed protagonist of Missouri's Southern hopes. He began his term as governor on January 3, 1861, during the crisis of secession, and his beliefs compelled him to lead Missouri into alliance with the Confederacy. Federal forces drove the elected state government from Jefferson City in the summer of 1861, and Unionist Hamilton Gamble was appointed provisional governor on July 30. Jackson set up a government-in-exile in Neosho. In October, his government seceded and became the twelfth state in the Confederacy. He died in exile in Little Rock, Arkansas, on December 6, 1862. Some years after the war, his remains were reinterred here.

The land where the two-acre cemetery is located was part of a quarter-section patented by John Sappington in 1837 but deeded to Claiborne Jackson in 1853 when Sappington was distributing most of his property to his children to avoid possible jealousies after his death. The cemetery, which contains 111 headstones, mostly of Sappington kin, was maintained by the family until 1901 and then by the Sappington School Fund, an endowment Sappington established to provide education to indigent or orphan children of Saline County in 1854 before the advent of a local public school system. Offered to the state as early as 1949 for management in conjunction with Arrow Rock, the cemetery finally came into the system in 1970 following the State Park Board's new statutory authority to maintain every grave of a former governor that

Top: Red cedars flank the grave of Boone's Lick power broker Dr. John Sappington. Left: Gov. Claiborne Fox Jackson was Sappington's son-in-law, successively marrying three of his daughters. *Both Oliver Schuchard* Above: The tombstones in the black cemetery are generally more simple, but no less heartfelt. Many graves there are unmarked. *Michael Dickey*

is not within a perpetual care cemetery.

Try to visit the cemetery and the nearby Sappington Negro Cemetery on a late Sunday afternoon in mid-November. You will likely have them entirely to yourself and not hear a sound other than the quiet rustling of the dry but not yet fallen oak leaves and the peculiar swooshing of the breeze passing through the huge red cedars. The low angle of the cool, autumnal sun will heighten the melancholy air of the cemeteries. Here, in these special places, a sense of life in the old Missouri Boone's Lick country is palpable. *

THE SAPPINGTON NEGRO CEMETERY

Across and down the road from Sappington Cemetery is another less imposing burial ground that was also a gift of Dr. John Sappington. In 1856, the last year of his life, he deeded two acres to Emanuel Banks for what became the Sappington Negro Cemetery. There were probably more than twice as many burials there as in the white cemetery, and they continued throughout the twentieth century, though it is not known how many because some grave markers and records have been lost. The markers that still exist are rough limestone or even concrete, not marble, and the fence is just wire to keep out the cows. There are a few cedars, somewhat smaller than those across the road, but still a testament to the love and hope of the survivors. The last officer of the Sappington Negro Cemetery Association donated the cemetery to the state in 2014. It is now a vital part of the record and interpretation of the black heritage of Arrow Rock and helps visitors understand the complexity of society in antebellum Missouri and in the next century.

SAPPINGTON CEMETERY STATE HISTORIC SITE • COUNTY ROAD AA, ARROW ROCK

Van Meter State Park

A FIRST-TIME VISITOR TO VAN METER STATE PARK will likely find the place quiet, maybe even sleepy. Route 122 approaches the park in Saline County across the broad bottomlands of the Missouri River. The park is part of the steep loess hills—known locally as the Pinnacles—that loom up and border that floodplain, overlooking the river and its valley. At the park, you will see a lovely walnut-shaded picnic ground with two Civilian Conservation Corps-era shelters, a small campground, and an eighteen-acre fishing lake—not a very imposing array. But appearances can be deceptive. On a winter afternoon, standing on the hills where the leafless trees allow a view of the mostly bare and hushed Missouri River valley, the sunset across the valley washes the bleak and rugged hills in a persimmon glow. The hills seem to be breathing, and there is almost a yearning in the air.

The first Europeans to touch what is now Missouri are believed to have been Frenchmen—the Jesuit missionary Father Jacques Marquette and the adventurer Louis Jolliet. While exploring the Mississippi River in 1673, they passed the mouth of a great brown behemoth flowing from the west and heard from some friendly Native Americans about a tribe that lived farther up that continent-draining river. Later on, that tribe's name was recorded on their map as *Oumessourit*, a word meaning "people of the big canoes" in one of several rough interpretations. *Oumessourit* evolved thereafter into Missouria or Missouri. Thus was the name for a group of people, a great river, and eventually, a state first recorded in a European language.

About forty years later, another Frenchman, Etienne Véniard sieur de Bourgmond, went to live for a time with these people who had been called the *Oumessourit*. Bourgmond found a proud and vigorous people, who welcomed the Frenchman and helped him establish fur-trading contacts and, eventually, a nearby outpost, Fort Orleans (1723 to 1728), the exact site of which has yet to be found. The Missouria—a Chiwere Siouan people related to the Winnebago, Ioway, and Otoe—had their principal village on the commanding upland at the great bend of the Missouri River in what is today Van Meter State Park. In Bourgmond's time, they numbered at least a thousand families (perhaps up to five thousand people) and exploited all aspects of their environment, both near and far. They hunted bison far out on the prairies, deer in the woodlands, and waterfowl along the river. They fished for sturgeon and gar. They tended corn, beans, and squash on the rich river floodplains. And on the uplands near the village, they gathered walnuts, pecans, pawpaws, plums, and other fruits and nuts from the abundant trees.

In the decades following their initial contact with whites, the Missouria fared poorly. Unlucky alliances in the tangle of competing European powers, ravaging European diseases, especially smallpox, and well-armed rivals like the Sauk and Fox combined to reduce and disperse them. By 1804 when Lewis and Clark passed the Missouria village site during their epic expedition upriver, the site had been long abandoned, the remnant clans having fled to live among their Otoe kindred in what is now Nebraska. In 1910 only thirteen Missouria of full blood survived, and by 1930, no full-bloods remained.

The core of Van Meter State Park was donated to the state in 1932

A Civilian Conservation Corps-era picnic shelter graces a walnut grove on the Van Meter homestead, occupied by the Van Meter family for a century before they gave it to the state in 1932 for a park. *Oliver Schuchard*

Above: Missouri's American Indian Cultural Center at Van Meter contains exhibits developed with descendants of each of the nine tribes that lived in or passed through Missouri. Here, a Kickapoo artist paints a symbol, entitled "Grandfather's Tools," on a buffalo hide on display there. *Missouri State Parks* • Right: Green ash, cottonwood, and whitescale sedge dominate this wet bottomland forest in the Oumessourit Natural Area. *Ken McCarty* • Archaeology students from the University of Missouri excavated a portion of the Missouria village here. The site was designated a National Historic Landmark in 1964. *Robert Bray*

MISSOURI'S AMERICAN INDIAN CULTURAL CENTER

For decades, Van Meter State Park was an out-of-the-way place offering little explanation of its key cultural and natural features. On Earth Day, April 21, 1990, the state dedicated a modest new visitor center that helps travelers understand both the Missouri River valley with its rich loess soil forests and formations and the contributions of visitors such as French explorers, the Van Meter family, and the people called Missouria who provided the state with its beautiful name. Present at the dedication to give a blessing in the Missouria language was ninety-one-year-old Truman Dailey, or Soaring High, from Red Rock, Oklahoma, the last living male of the Otoe-Missouria tribe.

Park officials also secured Lewis and Clark bicentennial funding through the National Park Service to enlarge the visitor center so it could explain the cultural history of each of the nine tribes in Missouri in the early nineteenth century: the Osage, Shawnee, Delaware, Ioway, Ilini-Peoria, Kanza, Kickapoo, Sac, and Fox, with a special focus on the Otoe-Missouria. Now, the center presents cultural exhibits and space for programs by each tribe. In addition, a memorial garden was established near the Van Meter family cemetery for unmarked native burials.

by Annie Van Meter and her brother, Charles Pittman, in memory of her husband, Abel. Abel Van Meter had come to this land in the year of his birth, 1834, with his family and their slaves from Hardy County, Virginia. Abel's father soon became the biggest cattle dealer in west-central Missouri, grazing his livestock on the rich prairie grasses that abounded in the area and driving them to market in St. Louis and other cities. Abel was also a prosperous farmer and livestock dealer who came to own nearly 3,000 acres in the area. Of this, Annie donated 369 acres for the park, and Charles Pittman added another 140 acres.

Ironically, the initial decision to preserve this area as a state park probably had less to do with the Missouria, about whom very little was known at the time, than with a nearby series of ditches, embankments, and mounds known as the Old Fort. The fort had been reported as early as 1878 by G. C. Broadhead, an assistant state geologist, and again in 1910 by Gerard Fowke, representing the Smithsonian Institution. It was thought to be related to the much older Hopewell culture dating to about the time of Christ. In fact, by the 1930s it was considered Missouri's preeminent Hopewell site. Abel and Annie Van Meter were well aware of the site's importance, having hosted Fowke when he worked there in 1906, even though the fort was not on their land.

It is conceivable that Annie was encouraged to donate her land with the thought that leverage could then be placed on the state to acquire the adjoining tract that included the Old Fort—in spite of the fact that the state game and fish commissioner, who was responsible for parks at the time, touted the site solely as a waterfowl-shooting area where a lake

and marsh could be reestablished. At the first meeting of the new Missouri Archaeological Society in 1934, Henry W. Hamilton of Marshall, a passionate amateur archaeologist and astute political lobbyist, was appointed to chair a committee to investigate preservation of the fort, and at every meeting thereafter, the fort was prominently on the agenda. By 1939 the group had negotiated with the landowner, secured an appropriation from the legislature, provided for proper supervision of work on the site, petitioned the governor for approval, and celebrated the Park Board's acquisition of the Old Fort.

Around this time, archaeologists began searching in earnest for the Missouria villages described by Bourgmond and Lewis and Clark. They identified two different sites, both near the park: the village on the Pinnacles, which had earlier been thought to be a considerably older site, and a less prepossessing site known as Gumbo Point on the floodplain a few miles upstream. In the late 1950s, through the efforts of T. M. Hamilton, brother of Henry, portions of the upland village, known as the Utz site after one of the landowners, were added to the park by a donation from Mr. and Mrs. W. P. Lyman and an exchange with another owner. The core of the village site was later transferred to the University of Missouri, which established the Lyman Archaeological Research Center and Hamilton Field School, where studies were made that would dramatically alter prevailing notions about the site. Robert T. Bray was hired jointly by the university and the Park Board to direct the center and to initiate a program of archaeological research there and at other parks and historic sites.

In the course of summer excavations during the 1960s and 1970s that park visitors were welcome to observe, it became apparent that the village site and the Old Fort were closely related. But the fort had not been built two thousand years earlier by Hopewell peoples, nor had the Missouria moved into the area from the Great Lakes region as recently as the seventeenth century, as scholars thought in the early 1960s. Rather, the artifacts suggested that the Missouria Indians had lived in the area since about AD 1400 and that they had built the fort.

Researchers, however, were no longer certain whether the Old Fort was actually a fort or why the Missouria built it. Archaeologists are still not certain exactly when or why the Missouria left their commanding city on the Pinnacles for the seemingly less favorable site on the gumbo. Some think they were using both the uplands and the floodplain seasonally during Bourgmond's time. It is equally unclear why the tribe withered so tragically and faded away. What we do know is that the Missouria were a creative and thriving people during their years on the Pinnacles, and that the site supported them well for some 350 years. The site was designated a National Historic Landmark in 1964.

Why did so many people—the Archaic and Woodland Indians, the Missouria, the French, and the Van Meters—find this locality so attractive? Part of the reason must be the quality of the wind-deposited loess soil that is heaped up into the imposing bluffs that border the river floodplain. Some of the ravines that cut through the loess hills today support rich forests of red oak, basswood, and walnut designated in 1981 as the Van Meter Forest Natural Area. To the west spans the broad valley of the Missouri River, once covered by bountiful wet prairies and marshes interspersed with timber-lined sloughs. This once rich marshland and prairie is now gone, victim of agricultural drainage ditches and levees. But there remains a small remnant of it on the west edge of the park. Once an ancient channel of the Missouri River, this area has been restored with prescribed burns and water-control structures in a levee adjoining the park. An endangered aquatic snail, found nowhere else in the state, lives in this remnant. Giant reed grasses and sedges, knotweeds, bulrushes, and more than a hundred other native plants that once provided substance and sustenance for the Missouria also grow here.

A two-mile loop trail built by the Civilian Conservation Corps in the 1930s winds through the rich woodlands and ravines of the Pinnacles past the Old Fort of the ancestral Missouria and what are thought to be even older Woodland Era burial mounds. The trail was enhanced with updated signs, though the Missouria village (Utz) site was still held by the university and off-limits to the public, the field school having ended in the late 1970s. But when the Utz site was listed as a threatened National Historic Landmark in 2000 because of looting and vandalism in the long-unoccupied facilities, park officials began concerted efforts to secure return of the land to the park so the village site could be protected and shared with the public. The transfer finally occurred in 2006, and with the purchase that same year of several adjoining portions of the Utz site, the park was enlarged to over 1,100 acres.

By this time, the marsh remnant was restored well enough to be combined with the Van Meter Forest, which had been designated earlier, in the new 300-acre Oumessourit Natural Area. Signs line the boardwalk and explain the indigenous wildlife and landscape as the trail traverses the marsh and bottomland woods at the base of the bluff.

There is meaning in the yearning one feels from the hills on a leafless winter afternoon. It may be the yearning of long forgotten people to proclaim themselves, and not to be forgotten. Here in the heart of Missouri is a park that is heavy with the shades of earlier peoples, a place that is, in a real sense, sacred. *

VAN METER STATE PARK • 32146 NORTH HIGHWAY 122, MIAMI

Battle of Lexington State Historic Site

THE CIVIL WAR IN MISSOURI is probably best known for the vicious guerrilla warfare that grew out of the cruel divisions among the state's citizens. Perhaps this degeneration was inevitable given the state's location and the strong and conflicting convictions of the day, but in the early months of the war, there was some hope that it need not be so. The victors write the histories, often leaving the hopes and aspirations of the vanquished little appreciated. Battle of Lexington affords an opportunity to ponder the vision and the virtues of the vanquished, who at Lexington were victors for a time.

An important but often overlooked factor of the Civil War in Missouri was the Missouri State Guard. This organization, which never numbered more than 22,000 men at any one time, was mobilized in defense of the state against what the legislature viewed as an invasion by the hostile armies of the United States. This small force, surrounded on three sides by Northern states and contested within the state by Missouri forces loyal to the Union, defended the Southern cause west of the Mississippi River for the better part of a year. The Missouri State Guard was the only border state army to make so bold a campaign, and it did so with little assistance from the official Confederate States Army.

The leader of the Missouri State Guard was probably the most popular man in Missouri. Sterling Price was a Virginia-born tobacco planter from Chariton County who had served Missouri as legislator and governor and his nation as congressman and brigadier general of Missouri volunteers in the Mexican War. His politics were representative of many—perhaps even most—Missourians: he was a conservative Democrat, opposed to abolition but also passionate about the old Union, as he demonstrated when he presided over the state convention in February 1861, at which Missouri decided there was as yet no cause to secede. But when actual conflict came, Price's Southern loyalty was aroused. He was known for his strong resolve and physical courage, and this was a prime attraction for the men who came to serve in the State Guard.

Reenactors portray the use of William Oliver Anderson's house as a field hospital at the 150th anniversary. ***Scott Myers (left) and Susan Flader (above)***

Price's rough and ready Missourians won for the South two of its most important victories west of the Mississippi. Except for a small but crucial skirmish at Boonville, he and his men were never driven back on a battlefield. After they disbanded in 1862, Missouri State Guard veterans made up the core of some of the most highly regarded and decorated units in the regular Confederate States Army. Yet today, one can search many standard war histories in vain for any reference to this important force.

In many respects, the finest hour of the State Guard was its victory in September 1861 over the federal garrison at Lexington, on the Missouri River. It marked the high tide of hopes for uniting the state behind the pro-South government that Missourians had elected in 1860 and for driving the detested Yankees from the state.

The events leading up to the battle at Lexington had begun in May 1861 when Gov. Claiborne Fox Jackson, with authority from the state legislature, expanded and reorganized the state militia to repel a feared invasion of federal troops following the secession of the deep South states. Union forces, composed mostly of local German volunteers, arrested state troops encamped near the federal arsenal in St. Louis on May 10. An ensuing riot resulted in the deaths of twenty-nine civilians fired on by Union soldiers. After observing that riot firsthand, Sterling Price offered his services to the governor and was appointed major general of the Missouri State Guard. A federal force composed largely of Missourians, including many German volunteers, moved quickly in June to occupy Jefferson City and other major river towns and rail centers.

Price and the growing body of his hastily called green recruits, along with Governor Jackson and other pro-South state officials, were forced to flee to the refuge of far southwest Missouri, where Price drilled the Guard into a rough semblance of an army. Meanwhile, the pro-Union portion of delegates who had been elected in February to decide the issue of secession reconvened in Jefferson City in July, declared state offices vacant, and elected new officials. Missouri now had two governors—Claiborne Jackson and Hamilton Gamble—and two sets of state officials who claimed legitimacy, a situation that would persist throughout the war.

With the reluctant help of Confederate forces stationed in northern Arkansas, Price's State Guard advanced in early August toward Springfield, where it met and defeated a Union army under Gen. Nathaniel Lyon at Wilson's Creek—one of the bloodiest battles of the Civil War. After this victory, the Confederate units returned to Arkansas, leaving Price and the Missouri State Guard to defend their cause against the now thoroughly roused federal government.

In late August, Price led his army north toward the Missouri River. Flush with the success at Wilson's Creek, the Missourians hoped to rally the citizenry in the populous pro-South counties of the Missouri valley. They also hoped to open the Missouri River for the many northern Missourians who would rally to the Southern cause but who were prevented from joining Price by Union control of the river crossings. As Price continued northward, his ranks were swollen with new recruits. His march began to seem a triumphal progress and a portent of a reunified state.

Lexington was, and is, a lovely Missouri River town in Lafayette County. In 1861 it was a prosperous trading center for the tobacco and hemp plantations of the area and one of the largest communities in Missouri. It was also strongly pro-South in sentiment, though with a substantial German population in the rural areas. Recognizing Lexington's importance, federal troops had occupied the town since July, headquartering at the Masonic College campus situated on a ridge that ran toward and overlooked the Missouri River. By early September, the garrison was commanded by a courageous young colonel named James A. Mulligan, an Irishman from Chicago, who strengthened his defenses with an elaborate system of entrenchments and ramparts much too large for his 3,000 troops to defend—an indication perhaps that he anticipated substantial reinforcements.

Not far from these defenses was the stately home of one of Lafayette County's leading families, that of William Oliver Anderson. Anderson owned a factory that processed hemp into rope and bagging, but financial problems led him to serve also as county sheriff. His two-and-a-half-story Greek Revival home had been constructed in 1853 of brick made at the site by slaves. It boasted beautiful millwork, including a handsome stairway of native black walnut, front-porch columns with cast-iron Corinthian capitals, and cast-iron sills and lintels. The property surrounding this fine home with a sweeping view of the river valley included slave quarters, a carriage house, a horse barn, a summer kitchen, a riverside warehouse and wharf, extensive gardens, and an orchard. Married to a cousin of Sterling Price, Anderson refused to take an oath of loyalty to the federal government and was arrested and imprisoned. The house, confiscated by Union troops, was fated to endure bloody turmoil.

Although time has gentled the remains of Union defensive trenches, you can still see their outlines on a hill overlooking the Missouri River. ***B.H. Rucker***

Price arrived within sight of Lexington on September 12. The State Guard had grown by now to 12,000 men and was enlarging daily. Mulligan's federal troops numbered only about 3,500, about half Illinoisans and half Missourians, many of them German or Irish immigrants. After sharp skirmishes on the outskirts of town, Price waited several days for his supply wagons to catch up and then laid siege to the fortified garrison rather than wasting blood and supplies on a frontal assault. "It is unnecessary to kill off the boys here," he supposedly said. "Patience will give us what we want"—a judgment he might have ruefully recalled three years later after his debacle at the battle of Pilot Knob, which today is also a state historic site.

Once the State Guard was in control of the area, recruits flocked in all the faster. With the arrival of Gen. Thomas A. Harris and his 4,000 northeast Missouri men from across the river, each of the Guard's nine divisions was represented at Lexington except the first, which was fighting in southeast Missouri. On September 17, Price moved to surround the federal garrison on College Hill and cut off Mulligan's access both to the river and to drinking water. The siege was on.

With effective blocking of Union lines, the siege warfare took on a casual, almost festive air—at least for those outside the lines. But the bombardment went on night and day, fifty-two hours straight. The reinforcements Mulligan expected never arrived. Most were never sent, but a few were intercepted north of the river by Gen. Mosby Monroe Parsons of Jefferson City and his Sixth Division troops.

The Anderson house, which lay outside the Union entrenchments, was being used by the federals as a hospital. Normally, both sides would have respected the neutrality of such a site. But the Anderson house was in too strategic a location, and it was too far from the regular Union lines to remain unmolested. As a result, it was attacked repeatedly by both sides, as a deep loess gully from the river offered a protected approach almost to the back door. The scars of battle still mark the walls and brickwork of the house, except where a summer kitchen, subsequently removed, absorbed a number of bullets. A bullet may still be found in a piece of door trim, and the path of a cannonball is clearly visible through the attic. Blood still stains the wooden floor of an upstairs bedroom.

At length, the Union troops weakened in the heat and drought of the Missouri September. The story is told that when federal soldiers sent some women for water from a spring east of the Union breastworks, the State Guard men allowed the women to drink all they wanted but would not let them carry any water back to the federal troops. Toward the end, Price's men employed a novel tactic in closing in on the Union entrenchments. They found some large bales of hemp, possibly in Anderson's warehouse, wrestled them into position, soaked them with water to prevent hot shot from setting them ablaze, and rolled them forward as they advanced, shooting safely from behind them. These innovative movable breastworks functioned well enough to earn the siege the nickname Battle of the Hemp Bales. As the bales approached early in the afternoon of September 20, Mulligan was forced to surrender.

The Union troops had fought gallantly from inside their embattled fort, and Price and the State Guard treated them with no less gallantry. In fact, the Battle of Lexington, besides being the high-water mark of the cause of the South in Missouri, was also one of the last Civil War engagements in which the civilities of old-style warfare were so prominently honored. Price took command of a large store of arms, ammunition, and supplies, but federal officers were allowed to keep their swords. Mulligan and his wife were treated as honored guests in Price's entourage. All of the enlisted men were paroled after they had been treated to a speech from Governor Jackson reminding them to go home to Illinois and mind their own business, and to one from General Price commending their bravery.

Hay bales were used during the sesquicentennial reenactment of the Battle of the Hemp Bales, but the museum shows real hemp bales. *Scott Myers*

SEE HEMP BALES AND A SPECIAL SWORD

Today, more than one hundred acres of the original battlefield are preserved in the historic site, including the northern part of the federal entrenchments and the Anderson house. The site offers a self-guided walking tour of noteworthy features and a tour of the house itself, which has been beautifully restored and landscaped to reflect the late 1850s. Visitors are oriented to the site and to the Civil War in Missouri at a visitor center museum and at several kiosks on the grounds. Among featured exhibits in the museum are hemp bales and a special sword. The hemp had to be shipped all the way from China; it was once a leading cash crop in Missouri but currently has stringent licensing requirements. The ornate presentation sword was commissioned by officers under Gen. Thomas A. Harris, who conceived the novel use of hemp bales as movable breastworks. The sword was bought with funds from private donors matched by park funds when it was released from the Augusta Museum of History in Georgia.

Local Union soldiers were released into the community. Commissioned officers were imprisoned at Lexington. The federal entrenchments and State Guard hemp bales kept casualties fairly low, but some sixty-five men in total were killed and nearly two hundred wounded.

In the glow of this victory, the Southern press lionized Price, and the Northern press agonized. Southern sympathizers swelled Price's army to as many as 22,000 Missourians, a good number of whom drifted away when supplies ran out and hard marching resumed. And hard marching did resume before long when in late September Price withdrew to southwest Missouri in the face of federal forces converging from Kansas and St. Louis. These forces ultimately pushed Price out of Missouri entirely in 1862. Claiborne Jackson headed a government-in-exile until his death later that year. Price transferred to regular Confederate service, and eventually some 50,000 Missourians served in Southern armies. Many other Missourians, of course, followed equally strong convictions into the federal army.

After Price's withdrawal, Lexington was retaken by federal troops in October and remained under federal control thereafter except for several short-term occupations by Confederate guerrillas or expeditionary forces. Price himself passed through the area again during his unsuccessful effort to retake the state in 1864.

After the war, the town gradually declined in prominence along with the river trade that had led to its rise, but it retained its Southern charm. The Anderson house was purchased in 1865 by the Tilton Davis family, who lived there for the next fifty years; it is their furniture that may be seen in some of the rooms today.

In the 1920s the Lafayette County Court acquired the Anderson house and a portion of the battlefield, and the Works Progress Administration helped to restore the house during 1933 and 1934 in one of the first government-sponsored efforts at historic restoration in the state. The house was offered to the State Park Board as early as 1939, with the thought that the Daughters of the Confederacy would furnish it and cooperate in attracting visitors. Nonetheless, it remained in county hands until its transfer in 1955 to the Anderson House and Lexington Battlefield Foundation, which in 1958 donated the site to the state. A reenactment of the battle on its centennial in 1961 reportedly attracted 15,000 people.

Lexington is brimming with history and still evokes the atmosphere of the antebellum Missouri river town. Even if you don't have a deep interest in Civil War history but enjoy beautiful Missouri valley scenery, elegant architecture, or an exciting story, you will want to visit Lexington. The contradictions that surround the war in Missouri are many and not easily absorbed, but you will leave with new insights. Maybe too, you will leave with some appreciation for a stalwart body of Missourians who, at the high tide of their soon-to-be-dashed fortunes, proved their capacity to show generosity toward their equally stalwart but vanquished foe. Missouri, and the nation, might not have suffered quite as terribly in the next four years if such antique virtue had continued to prevail. *

LEXINGTON STATE HISTORIC SITE • 1101 DELAWARE STREET, LEXINGTON

Confederate Memorial State Historic Site

IN THE HEART OF MISSOURI'S LITTLE DIXIE, not far from the Missouri River, the Confederate Memorial State Historic Site commemorates more than fifty thousand Missouri soldiers who fought for the Confederate States of America. It is a testimonial also to their wives and daughters, who bore the brunt of the war at home and who a generation or so later took the lead in establishing the home, grounds, and cemetery where so many of the aging Confederate veterans came to live out their last years and be buried. Wandering among the more than eight hundred graves in the cemetery, one may experience a gamut of emotions, strongest among them a deeper understanding of what it meant to be a Missourian and a Southerner in 1861.

It required several decades after the surrender in 1865, while Confederate veterans and their families dealt with the trauma of defeat and began to rebuild their lives, before they were moved to commemorate their lost cause. Then, in an era of annual encampments beginning in the 1880s, veterans who organized as the Ex-Confederate Association of Missouri came together to relive old times and to consider the plight of the less fortunate among them. At their encampment at Higginsville in 1889, they incorporated a Confederate Home Association to select a site and seek funding for a home for their destitute brethren. The following year they purchased a 360-acre farm north of Higginsville, aided by donations from citizens of Lafayette County.

A fascinating chapter of the state's history came to a close on May 9, 1950, when John Graves, the last Missouri Confederate veteran, who had fought with legendary Confederate Gen. Joseph O. Shelby, passed away in the home at the age of 107.

Practically every state that furnished organized troops for the Confederacy established homes for veterans, but Missouri was unique in building and furnishing its home solely through voluntary contributions. This is where the women entered the picture.

Seeking a way to aid the cause of the Confederate Home, Mrs. Abner Cassidy of St. Louis invited nearly one hundred women to the Southern Hotel in that city in January 1891 to organize the Daughters of the Confederacy and to promote a plan for selling tickets at ten cents apiece, each representing "a brick in the Confederate Home." The idea caught on, and soon there were Daughters of the Confederacy chapters in many Missouri communities and then in other states, leading in 1894 to the establishment of a national organization, the United Daughters of the Confederacy. In Missouri, the women held dinners, balls, ice-cream socials, and a strawberry festival, raising money in any way they could to provide cottages and furnishings and then a spacious, colonial-style main building for the Confederate Home. The home was dedicated in 1893 and six months later had 115 residents. The Daughters of the Confederacy subsequently built a hospital, a chapel, and several other buildings, in addition to commissioning a stately granite monument featuring the Lion of Lucerne, erected in the cemetery in 1906.

In 1897, with costs outstripping income, the state of Missouri accepted the home and all the other buildings and farmland into the state hospital system, but a board of trustees made up of Confederate veterans continued to oversee the home and a small endowment fund. In 1925 the board proposed development of a memorial park. About 90 acres of "waste land" at the southern end of the property were landscaped and thousands of trees and shrubs planted, again courtesy of the Daughters of the Confederacy with the help of local schoolchildren. Seven lakes were built and stocked with fish for the veterans. A footbridge, gazebo, and bandstand were constructed, and rocks were hauled in for a rock garden, all at no expense to the state. This Confederate Memorial Park, on state land, was in effect one of Missouri's earliest state parks, though it was not deeded over to the State Park Board until 1949.

Over the years, nearly fifteen hundred residents, including some wives and widows and even a few children of veterans, lived in the home or in the fourteen cottages on the grounds. With gardens behind the cottages, ample cropland, and cattle and other domestic livestock, the place operated fairly self-sufficiently. Many thought the dynamic and impressive institution was the finest such home in the country. Many Missourians remember visiting the home when the last old veterans sat fishing from the lake bank on a warm afternoon, spinning stories of past glory, until the clanging of the commissary bell called them back for supper. But as the old Confederate ranks thinned during the 1930s and 1940s, several attempts were made to close the home or to move in mental patients, children with physical disabilities, or World War II wounded.

In 1951, a year after the last Missouri Confederate veteran at the home had passed away, the Missouri legislature voted to abolish the home, and the few remaining residents, all widows of veterans, were transferred to a nursing facility in Columbia. Most of the old buildings were demolished in 1954 despite local preservation efforts, and the northern part of the grounds, including what was left of the building complex, is now occupied by the Higginsville Habilitation Center administered by the Missouri Department of Mental Health. The United Daughters of the Confederacy gave the cemetery to the State Park Board in 1952, to be managed in conjunction with the memorial park that had been accepted three years earlier. The chapel, threatened with demolition, was saved in 1978 by the Higginsville chapter of the Beta Sigma Phi sorority, who paid to move it back near its original site next to the cemetery on state park land.

In 1993 as the centennial of the soldiers home approached, the Confederate Memorial Friends Association helped to secure legislative approval for transfer to the park of the last remaining building, a two-story brick hospital, and several other structures and additional land. The intent was to restore the building for a visitor center, museum, and offices, but funds have been insufficient to proceed.

As occasionally happens with politically charged Civil War sites, there have been some distractions from the fundamental purpose of this site

Above: The Missouri Daughters of the Confederacy commissioned this monument modeled on the famed Lion of Lucerne in Switzerland, dedicated to Swiss Guards massacred during the French Revolution. Mark Twain described the original as "the most mournful and moving piece of stone in the world." ***Oliver Schuchard*** **• Left: The Confederate Memorial Chapel is one of only two such chapels in the country that still remain to honor the vanquished.** ***David Piet*** **Right: The last veteran at the home was buried with this simple stone.** ***Tom Nagel***

in the form of disagreements over whether or not to grant a request to bury several leg bones of the Confederate guerrilla William Quantrill in the cemetery, despite his lack of connection to either the home or the regular Confederate Army (the bones are there), and when and how to fly or display the Confederate flags (flown on special occasions).

Today, Confederate Memorial Park is administered as a beautiful 135-acre historic site. The simple, one-room frame chapel, one of only two such Confederate memorial chapels still standing (the other is in Richmond, Virginia), has been restored and furnished, with exhibits in the basement about the history of the home and the Confederate cause in Missouri. Some of this has been funded through the Confederate Memorial Park Endowment Fund, a legacy of private fundraising a century ago. The lake area, ever popular for fishing and picnicking, has been restored to look as it did when built by the Daughters of the Confederacy. The fishing is still good, and the grounds are still peaceful.

But most impressive is the carefully manicured cemetery, its more than eight hundred graves of veterans and widows a solemn reminder of loyalty and pride. The simple epitaph on the last old warrior's headstone is itself a lesson in history, and none who see it leave unmindful of the Southern cause in Missouri, or unmoved by the devotion of its followers: "John T. Graves, The Last Of Shelby's Men." *

CONFEDERATE MEMORIAL STATE HISTORIC SITE • 211 WEST FIRST STREET, HIGGINSVILLE

THOMAS HART BENTON HOME & STUDIO
STATE HISTORIC SITE
Missouri Department
of Natural Resources

Thomas Hart Benton Home and Studio State Historic Site

IN THE DEEP WINTER OF 1937, THE COLD WEATHER was heated by a controversy that played loudly across the pages of Missouri's newspapers. The subject of this particular controversy did not concern the ominous situation in Europe or even the national struggle against economic depression. Instead, a war of words was waged over a painting, a mural in the house lounge of the state capitol. This mural, officially titled *A Social History of the State of Missouri*, was a spacious work in a distinguished place by a Missourian of eminent background. It was painted by Thomas Hart Benton, namesake great grandnephew of Missouri's legendary first US senator, "Old Bullion," and son of Maecenas E. Benton, a four-term congressman and Confederate war veteran from the town of Neosho in Southwest Missouri.

The august setting for Benton's mural fueled the passion of those who felt that it did disservice to the state of Missouri:

"Whitewash the murals! They're vulgar! Look at those half-naked dancers!"

"Where are Missouri's favorite sons?"

"Nothing but honky-tonk, hillbillies, and robbers. We're more than a 'coon dog state!"

By the mid-1930s, Tom Benton was no stranger to controversy, and he responded with vigor to his critics. He painted real folks, doing the things that real folks do, along with some of the state's most characteristic folk legends. He captured for all time much of the pungent flavor of the state's history. Today, the Benton mural in the state capitol is one of the most treasured artworks in the state; it inspires thousands of visitors every year. Look upon this broad expanse of vivid color and form, and you will feel its power. After seeing the mural, you will surely want to visit the home and studio of the artist who produced it and who came to be recognized as a preeminent representative of the Regionalist tradition in American art.

Moving to Kansas City was a homecoming for Benton. Born in Neosho in 1889, Benton left home in his teens to pursue an art career; he lived for varying periods in Chicago, Paris, and New York. In the course of his travels, Benton became a recognized painter, though from almost the beginning a combative and controversial one. Benton gradually became disillusioned with much of the artistic establishment and the aura of big city life. When in 1935 the Missouri General Assembly authorized the capitol mural and the Kansas City Art Institute offered him a teaching position, Benton was happy to come home to Missouri with his wife and son and begin the long, colorful, and productive final phase of his career.

If Tom Benton had produced no other work than the capitol mural, he would still deserve a place in Missouri and American art history, but he produced thousands of illustrations, paintings, sketches, and other murals, including one at the Truman Presidential Library in Independence. And shortly after coming home, he published the first edition of his autobiography, *An Artist in America*, which detailed his reactions to the world of art and life and left no question of his love for "the real Missouri." Missourians love Benton best for his true rendering of the common people and the land—especially, perhaps, his native Ozark region.

The home to which Tom and Rita Benton moved in 1939 and where they remained until their deaths in 1975 is located in midtown Kansas City in a fashionable though not exclusive neighborhood in the Westport area. The two-and-a-half-story house is of stone and frame construction. The home is spacious and comfortable and sits amid towering trees and pleasant shrubs and plants.

The rear carriage house served as a garage, and part of it was converted in the 1940s to Benton's art studio. Here in the studio where he spent so many hours, we find today a lingering presence of the artist. He was working in this studio the day he died, January 19, 1975, a heart attack having taken him as he was applying the finishing touches to another of his dynamic murals, *The Sources of Country Music*, for the Country Music Hall of Fame in Nashville.

> *In his capitol mural, Thomas Hart Benton depicted a people and a state that he knew intimately and loved fiercely, but that he was determined not to falsely romanticize or idealize.*

Partly through the care and generosity of Benton's wife, who soon also passed away, and his friends, the artist's studio and home are almost perfectly preserved. They were purchased by the state in 1977 and opened to the public on April 15, 1983, the anniversary of his birth. In the studio, the furniture, paints, sketches, brushes, and even spectacles and a pipe lie about in perfectly natural clutter the way he left them. But if there is a haunting presence here, it is far from morbid. Benton was a vital man of great creativity, and that creative energy is what we feel.

In the home itself, almost all of the Bentons' personal possessions are also left in place. The most common and ordinary of family objects are as casual and visible as if Tom and Rita could walk in and offer us refreshment. In fact, entertaining friends from all over Missouri and well beyond was one of the great joys of household life for the Bentons. They were hosts to a nearly continual stream of guests, and their home had the warm and casual atmosphere that encouraged visitors to return. Thanks to its preservation, it still does. *

Left: Tom and Rita Benton's comfortable home in Kansas City still welcomes guests as it did when it was the family residence. *Ben Nickelson* • Below: This panorama shows Benton's studio in the carriage house behind his home, which looks as casually cluttered as it did the day he died there in 1975. *Jim Steinhart*

THOMAS HART BENTON HOME AND STUDIO STATE HISTORIC SITE • 3616 BELLEVIEW, KANSAS CITY

Weston Bend State Park

FOR SEVERAL YEARS, MISSOURI WAS THE LARGEST state in the Union. While in this enviable position, the state's General Assembly had the temerity in 1831 to petition Congress to expand her boundaries farther.

When the state was first laid out, the northwest boundary was a line straight north from the mouth of the Kansas River to the Iowa territory. The land west of that line to the Missouri River was promised by treaty to Native Americans in perpetuity. The people of this region, the Sac, Fox, Ioway, and others, endured repeated violations of their territory because of the remorseless advance of American pioneers, who settled illegally on the rich Indian lands. In 1837, the local tribes were removed and the land annexed. Out of these lands, known as the Platte Purchase, the counties of Platte, Buchanan, Andrew, Holt, Atchison, and Nodaway were established.

From a particularly pleasant overlook, you can enjoy a sweeping view upriver, downriver, across to the wild bottomland forest of Fort Leavenworth, and six to eight miles westward to distant ridges in Kansas.

Platte was the first of these counties to be organized, and it immediately became a lively scene of settlement and commerce along the Missouri River. The first community to rise was the town of Weston, named for one of its cofounders, Thomas Weston. The town, in turn, provided a name for the great bend of the Missouri River immediately downstream and, much later, for Weston Bend State Park.

In the 1830s and 1840s, Weston grew rapidly. Very quickly the deep loess soils of the surrounding river hills were recognized as ideal for the cultivation of burly tobacco and hemp, the two main plantation crops of the antebellum upper South. Weston thrived on the tobacco and hemp trade and from general river traffic and transportation. The commercial boom raged for several decades, with steamboats calling frequently and enterprising citizens building their fortunes. During this period, two brothers, Benjamin and David Holladay, developed a whiskey distillery just south of town. Then in 1858, the great river that had brought prosperity abruptly changed its course. This left Weston no longer a port, and without rail connections, the town fell into a gradual decline.

Around 1980, when the state was seeking a potential park site on the Missouri River near Kansas City, Platte County officials encouraged them to consider the hills downstream from Weston. The site combined to a rare degree the potential for fulfilling all three goals of the state park system—natural, cultural, and recreational excellence. It includes

From the overlook at Weston Bend, you can see almost the same Missouri River valley scene that would have greeted Lewis and Clark in 1804. ***Ben Nickelson***

Missouri River loess-capped hills and low bluffs. From several points, one can view almost the same Missouri valley scene that greeted Lewis and Clark in 1804, thanks in part to a large expanse of natural bottomland forest preserved on the lands of Fort Leavenworth across the river.

This Platte County hill country also offers excellent outdoor recreation to the greater Kansas City population, with ten miles of trails, including one running alongside a still-used railroad line below the bluffs. Two trail spurs lead to the riverside, and another trail atop the bluffs offers spectacular river views. There is also a paved hiking and biking trail through mature hardwoods on the river hills and a trail that connects the park to historic downtown Weston and the former village of Beverly. An off-leash dog park is the state park system's first; it was a cooperative project between the park and Weston with funding through a grant from the county.

Finally, the cultural heritage of western Platte County will fascinate visitors. The town of Weston might have continued as a boomtown had the river stayed put in 1858, but then it would have been unlikely that so many of her beautiful antebellum buildings would have survived the progress that changed so many towns. The hemp business petered out when slavery was abolished and world competition increased. But the tobacco economy still hangs on. Two large tobacco warehouses are the marketplaces for millions of pounds of the fine-grade white burley that is grown in the region, making Weston the largest tobacco market west of the Mississippi. The telltale elongated drying barns of real tobacco country still dot the ridges of the region. Four of these barns and several old tobacco fields were included in the lands making up the new park.

The park boundary is also directly adjacent to grounds of the McCormick distillery, a direct descendant of the enterprise begun in 1857 by the Holladay brothers. Benjamin (1819–1887) ran a hotel and a store in Weston and became a leading operator in the overland freight and stagecoach business. Like many of their neighbors, the Holladays were former Kentuckians who brought with them knowledge not only of tobacco culture but also of bourbon whiskey. David Holladay is said to have discovered in local springs a source of "sweet" limestone water considered ideal for use in a distillery like those that dotted Kentucky.

The Missouri Department of Natural Resources assembled 1,100-acre Weston Bend State Park through the acquisition of contiguous farms beginning in 1980. In the wake of the 1970s oil crisis, Weston was to have been the system's first demonstration park for energy independence, with cropland for biofuels, an earth-contact staff house, solar panels, and a still to produce alcohol to power park equipment. But the crisis ended, public interest waned, and the effort was dropped.

Even before the park was officially dedicated in the summer of 1990, it attracted 80,000 visitors in 1988 and more than 100,000 in 1989. Visitation now exceeds 150,000 per year. The main entrance road leads past scenic areas, a park office, and a large, well-preserved tobacco-curing barn with outdoor exhibits explaining the history of both tobacco and the Weston area. The park also offers a campground and two picnic shelters. The Bee Creek shelter is a refurbished tobacco barn suitable for large gatherings such as reunions and weddings, while an open shelter accommodates smaller groups.

From an overlook and hiking trails along the park ridges, bluffs, and river, especially early on a quiet morning or near dusk, the visitor is likely to see a profusion of native and migrating birds. The park is the centerpiece of the Iatan-Weston River Corridor Important Bird Area, where more than three hundred species of birds have been recorded; it is a bird-watcher's paradise of bottomland forests, wetlands, upland forests, woodlands, grasslands, and agricultural lands.

Another special feature is a storage cellar and the foundation remains of a trading house likely built in the early 1830s by a notorious French Canadian fur trader named Pensineau directly across the river from Fort Leavenworth. The east bank of the river was still American

Well-ventilated tobacco barns like this one in the park once dotted the hills along the river and dried the fine burley tobacco grown here. ***Missouri State Parks***
Volunteers from Burroughs Audubon in Kansas City teach aspiring young birders at the annual Wings Over Weston festival. ***Christine Kline***

Indian territory at the time, and Pensineau operated a tavern to supply Indians and soldiers with liquor and other necessities, much to the consternation of military authorities. They apparently managed to get a presidential order incorporating this parcel into Fort Leavenworth shortly after the Platte Purchase, thereby putting Pensineau out of business. Hikers may reach the site via North Ridge Trail.

From time to time, freight trains rumble along the Burlington Northern track at the foot of the bluff, and freight barges pass on the river, now narrowed and contained by the Army Corps of Engineers. Although no longer as natural and fractious as when early explorers passed this way or when Weston was a booming river port, the Missouri is still a great river, and awesome to contemplate. ⁎

WESTON BEND STATE PARK • 16600 HIGHWAY 45, WESTON

Lewis and Clark State Park

J*ULY 4TH WEDNESDAY [1804] ussered in the day by a discharge of one shot from our Bow piece, proceeded on, passed the mouth of a Bayeau lading from a large Lake on the S.S. [starboard, or right side] which has the apperance of being once the bed of the river & reaches parrelel for Several Miles.... The before mentioned Lake is clear and Contain great quantities of fish an Gees &. Goslings, The great quantity of those fowl in this Lake induce me to Call it the Gosling Lake.*

—William Clark, in *The Journals of the Lewis & Clark Expedition*

In those youthful days of our national independence, it seemed appropriate to Meriwether Lewis and William Clark and their crew of forty-five patriotic adventurers to begin the day with a salute from the gun mounted on the bow of their keelboat. That same day, they explored the lake, noted the abundance of goslings on the water, and named it Gosling Lake. Although the continual shifting of the river's channel makes identification uncertain, Gosling Lake may well be the oxbow known today as Lewis and Clark Lake in Buchanan County, out on the broad warm floodplain of the Missouri River. The lake and surrounding marsh areas are still attractive to many waterfowl.

> *One of the notable landmarks on the lower Missouri River that Lewis and Clark and their band of explorers encountered on the Fourth of July, 1804, was this beautiful large oxbow lake.*

Among the great treasures of the Corps of Discovery expedition were the detailed accounts of the trip written by the leaders and also by several of the other men. From these journals, we still draw key information about geology, biology, and anthropology. We also can use the journals to locate noteworthy landmarks of the expedition, such as Gosling Lake, and assess how they have fared over time.

In the summer of 1804, the lower Missouri valley was, as it still frequently can be, oppressively hot and uncomfortable. Nevertheless, the journals record a landscape startling to the explorers for its richness and beauty. Enveloping the wide brown river course were rolling hills draped in lush prairies and interspersed with copses of timber. Clark and Lewis comment on the abundant wild game, including deer and turkey, and also on the walnut and "paecaun" (pecan), the wild grapes and raspberries, and the colorful "Parrot queets" (now extinct Carolina parakeets) that wheeled in flocks among the towering riverside trees.

Lewis and Clark State Park, honoring one of the longest expeditions across some of the broadest expanses of the American continent, is one of the smaller state parks in Missouri, less than 200 acres. The lake, at 365 acres, is bigger than the park. Even though it is smaller and probably shallower and less clear than it was in 1804, it still provides good fishing for catfish.

In 1934 a group of Buchanan County sportsmen donated about 50 acres along the southeast shore of what was then known as Sugar Lake to the state for a park. And in 1938, the centennial of William Clark's death, the Park Board renamed this site to honor the leaders of the expedition, both of whom continued to serve the territory that would become the state of Missouri after their return from their epic journey: Meriwether Lewis was appointed governor of the Territory of Louisiana in 1807 and served until his death in 1809, and William Clark served as governor of the Territory of Missouri from 1813 to 1821 and was appointed Superintendent of Indian Affairs by President Monroe in 1822. Upon his death in 1838, Clark was buried in St. Louis's Bellefontaine Cemetery.

As in its sister oxbow lake park, Big Lake in Holt County, the lake has a tendency to fill in with silt during major floods, such as those in 1993 and 2011. As the lake has filled in, it has become more attractive to waterfowl, and one may see numerous ducks, geese, pelicans, and even swans, especially during migration. The great flood of 1993 led to the closing of the Department of Conservation's fish hatchery operation and

Right: Lewis and Clark celebrated the Fourth of July at this oxbow slough they named Gosling Lake on their epic journey up the Missouri River in 1804. ***Oliver Schuchard*** **• Below: A plaza with a compass rosette and stone benches honors the crew of the expedition. Left: A replica of the keelboat the explorers took up the Missouri River can be seen in the park office.** ***Both Ben Nickelson***

the ongoing redesign of park facilities to emphasize the Lewis and Clark expedition, the Missouri River, and the evolution of the local landscape.

The park provides facilities for lakeside picnicking, including a Civilian Conservation Corps–era stone shelter, and a well-appointed campground with friendly little thirteen-lined ground squirrels that scurry around to the delight of campers. A short hiking and biking trail connects the campground with a plaza dedicated in 2004 during the Lewis and Clark bicentennial. The plaza features a walkway suggesting the landscape of the time, complete with meanders, sand bars, and little rolling hills. It overlooks the lake and includes a compass rosette surrounded by stone benches that display the names of members of the Corps of Discovery. A large replica of the keelboat used on the expedition may now be seen in the park office.

Lewis and Clark State Park commemorates an epic exploration, and it offers a pleasant environment in which to enjoy a remnant landscape of that saga of discovery. *

LEWIS AND CLARK STATE PARK • 801 LAKE CREST BOULEVARD, RUSHVILLE

Big Lake State Park

THE BROWN AND BRAWLING MISSOURI RIVER comes down to the state from the Great Plains, burdened with the silt of the high prairies and flowing with energy from the steep eastern slopes of the Rocky Mountains. Formed of meltwater from the great continental ice sheets that covered the country to the north, the river in Missouri has carved a wide valley that has supported an abundance of life ever since the glaciers' retreat. The fertile soils of the Missouri Valley include not only those deposited directly by the flooding river but also loess soils, especially in northwest Missouri. These loess soils were formed from silts picked up by the wind after the glaciers retreated, then deposited in thick mounds along a broad strip bordering the river. These rich but easily erodible soils give the valley its shape and form. They have also shaped and formed its human history.

In its broad floodplain, the Missouri River shifted its course across the yielding alluvium from time to time. After such a shift in course, the old channel often retained water and formed a marsh or an open-water lake. Where such an abandoned channel is the result of the river cutting off a U-shaped bend in its own course, the lake is called an oxbow lake. As recently as a century or two ago, the floodplain of the Missouri River in northwest Missouri was a maze of shallow riverbeds, bottomland forests, wet prairies, marshes, and oxbow lakes teeming with fish, waterfowl, and large game animals. The floodplain was bordered on the east by high-piled mounds of savanna-covered loess. It was a lush and fertile landscape. Since having been channelized and hardened in place by the Army Corps of Engineers, the river no longer creates such a dynamic riparian corridor, but vestiges can still be glimpsed in a few places in the western sections of Atchison, Holt, Andrew, and Buchanan Counties.

Big Lake in Holt County is among the largest remaining natural oxbow lakes along the Missouri River and one of the largest natural lakes of any type in the state.

Big Lake is an oxbow lake with 615 acres of open water and nearby wildlife habitat, and it has been a recreation magnet for many years. Most of northwest Missouri, including the silted-in former river channels, has been devoted to agricultural production, and relatively few areas offer public opportunities for outdoor recreation. Big Lake is such an area, and much of its shoreline is dotted with weekend cabins and fishing camps. In 1932 the state acquired about 100 acres along the eastern shore of the lake for development as one of northern Missouri's first state parks.

The primary attraction at Big Lake was the open water of the lake itself, and all developments have been oriented to viewing, boating, and fishing opportunities in and around this shallow, tree-lined remnant of the Missouri River channel. Facilities included a campground—here in the floodplain, every site is flat—picnic areas, a swimming pool, a boat launch, vacation cabins, a restaurant, and a small motel.

But the Missouri River over the years has had other ideas, occasionally flooding and depositing its silts in and around the new developments, as well as in the lake. A particularly bad flood wreaked havoc in 1952, but the cabins and other facilities were cleaned up and put back to use. Again in the spring of 1984, the river rose out of its army engineer-controlled channel and swept over its floodplain. Temporarily reclaiming ground it had roamed since the Ice Age, the swollen river washed over the park, taking a heavy toll on the facilities—especially the old cabins dating from the earliest days of the park, which were a total loss. Very quickly, new cabins were built in the same lakeshore area, this time on elevated mounds to protect them from future flooding.

The park flooded again during the Great Flood of 1993 and on other occasions, but the most devastating flood events came in 2010 and 2011. As a result of heavy rains upstream, flooding in 2010 caused

significant damage and closure of the park. Although this was a time of greatly reduced staff and financial stringency for both the state and nation, park staff from elsewhere in the system rallied to help in the cleanup in time to reopen by Labor Day. The very next spring, a combination of heavy snowpack in the Rocky Mountains and rains upstream necessitated a major release of water from the Gavins Point Dam in South Dakota, causing the breach of numerous levees downstream.

Hundreds of thousands of migratory waterfowl visit Big Lake every spring and fall. Here is a dramatic concentration of snow geese. ***Tom Uhlenbrock***

Strong currents in the swirling waters did enormous damage to all the facilities. To compound the problem, officials of a nearby railroad had quickly raised the height of the roadbed, but without installing culverts, after the 2010 flood; this, in effect, acted as a dam that

Above: Big Lake, beautiful at sunset, provides one of various popular recreation opportunities for northwest Missourians. ***Stephanie Sidoti*** **• Left: Flooding occurs regularly along the Missouri River, as shown here in 2011 in the vicinity of the park. Indeed, the ecology of the Big Lake oxbow depends on flooding to maintain the largest natural marsh in any state park.** ***Scott Myers*** **• Left below: A great blue heron rises majestically from the marsh.** ***Missouri State Parks***

prevented the water from draining quickly back into the river. Three months of standing floodwaters killed more than fifteen hundred trees in the park and caused further damage to the facilities, necessitating complete closure, this time for several years.

State Parks contracted with a private firm for a redesign of the park, and they proposed a $13 million plan for new facilities, but the state did not have the funds to implement that plan. The park reopened in 2014 with a cleaned-up campground and swimming pool, but a great deal of recovery is still to come. Fortunately, Big Lake State Park has many loyal fans and important natural resources, so there is no doubt that it will survive, but probably never again with so many buildings within reach of an ever-capricious river.

As the Missouri River does what it will, the oxbow lakes, sloughs, and other wetlands continue to attract millions of migratory waterfowl and provide a haven for resident birds and animals. The nearby 6,000-acre Squaw Creek National Wildlife Refuge, established in 1935 on the floodplain and adjacent loess hills east of the park, has long been a major magnet for migratory waterfowl. In 1990, Big Lake State Park secured a significant natural marshland with the addition of a 300-acre wetland portion of the Big Lake oxbow northwest of the existing park. This gave Big Lake the park system's largest natural Missouri River floodplain marsh. It is a refuge for a variety of wetland species, such as the unusual yellow-headed blackbird. Despite additional siltation and the loss of some of the trees on its margins during and after the 2011 flood, the marsh has survived largely intact as a remnant of the extensive pre-agricultural wetlands in this region. Park officials plan eventually to install a boardwalk and bird observation sites in the marsh.

The park visitor will find Big Lake a pleasant, restful place. There always seem to be shorebirds or waterfowl on the lake, and the spring and fall migrations are times of extraordinary excitement in the Missouri valley for both birders and hunters. Squaw Creek has been especially attractive to the beautiful snow geese. These birds make a thunderous display when they come down from the north by the thousands in the fall and again in spring when they gather together and head back north. Other large birds, including bald eagles, come down to the Big Lake vicinity to spend the winter and may frequently be seen soaring over the park. Local authorities pump water from the river to keep the lake deep enough for boating and fishing. The new marsh and a portion of the park known as Scout Island are kept undeveloped, and they are fine places to walk in the mornings and evenings to take in the variety of floodplain plants and birds or to sit on the bank and drop a line for Missouri River catfish.

So, in the midst of heavily farmed northwest Missouri, there is an oasis of recreation, natural landscape, and wildlife. Come in the summer for a lazy camp-out and fishing trip or during spring or fall migration time—or even in winter—to watch the eagles. Missouri would benefit from more and larger parks like Big Lake in the magnificent Missouri valley. *

BIG LAKE STATE PARK • 204 LAKE SHORE DRIVE, CRAIG

OSAGE PLAINS

"On the plains we encountered small troops of five or six deer, prairie hens, woodcocks with long tails.... In the woods huge flocks of parrots flew away as we approached, uttering discordant cries."
—Victor Tixier, *Travels on the Osage Prairies*, 1844

TALLGRASS PRAIRIE, NOW ONE OF THE RAREST ecosystems in Missouri, once covered more than 30 percent of the state and more than 70 percent of the Osage Plains in southwestern Missouri. A prairie region like the Glaciated Plains to the north, the Osage Plains are underlain by shale, sandstone, and limestone of Pennsylvanian age, softer and more easily erodible than the dolomite of the Ozarks. These plains are characterized by deep prairie soils and gently rolling topography with broad, shallow stream valleys and many marshes and sloughs. But unlike the northern plains, the Osage Plains were not covered by the great continental glaciers; hence they are topographically older and biologically more diverse, with a greater proportion of southwestern plants and animals than can be found farther north. (Victor Tixier in the quote above was referring to the upland sandpiper when he mentioned woodcocks, and the parrots were the now extinct Carolina parakeet.) This region grades almost imperceptibly into the adjoining Ozarks, Ozark Border, and Glaciated Plains.

We lead with Prairie State Park in Barton County. At nearly four thousand acres, it's the largest remaining example of native prairie in Missouri and once was home to the powerful Osage people. With over four hundred different species of grasses and wildflowers, the park ecosystem is still being studied and painstakingly restored to reveal the full drama of this stunning and now very rare landscape. Some thirty miles to the northeast is a hilltop site—one of a series of limestone-capped erosional remnants, or monadnocks, common in the region—that was the principal village of the Osage Indians in the seventeenth century when they were first encountered by Europeans, and into the 1700s. Though cropped in places and grazed like the rest of the Osage Plains, the vista is open, and Osage Village State Historic Site is key to understanding the preeminent role of the Osage in the state and region.

Native bison were eliminated from Missouri in the nineteenth century, along with virtually all of the tallgrass prairie that once covered most of the Osage Plains, but they are back in a world of their own at Prairie State Park. ***Scott Myers***

Fifteen miles east of Prairie State Park, in Lamar, is the modest birthplace of Harry S Truman, reminding us that the small towns of Missouri produced more than their share of great leaders. And in Bates County farther north along the Kansas border, on the prairie uplands and in the marshes and sloughs along the Marais des Cygnes River, is the site of a little known but significant Civil War encounter, the Battle of Island Mound. Here, for the first time in that war, African American soldiers, organized as the First Kansas Colored Volunteer Infantry, saw armed action in battle on behalf of the Union.

In Johnson and Pettis counties, where the Osage Plains grade into the Ozarks, are three parks characterized by somewhat rougher land and more woody vegetation. Knob Noster was acquired by the federal government as a Recreation Demonstration Area in the 1930s because of its scarred and impoverished condition after a century of poor agricultural practices and some coal mining; the park illustrates not only the penalties of misuse but also the recuperative potential of the land under careful stewardship, especially in recent years when park system staff have been restoring the long-lost oak woodlands characteristic of this region. Bothwell Lodge, developed by a wealthy Sedalia businessman as a country estate with a castle-like, bluff-top retreat, offers trails with stone steps along wooded slopes for the enjoyment of guests today, in the same way Bothwell's guests enjoyed the place in the past. And extending more than the length of Johnson County westward from its junction with the Katy Trail near Windsor to Pleasant Hill on the outskirts of Kansas City is the still-developing Rock Island Trail State Park. The forty-seven-mile route begins in rough, highly dissected woodlands and moves west through gradually more prairie-like uplands with low, marshy bottoms. It will eventually also extend east from Windsor through the Ozarks to Beaufort west of St. Louis.

The Osage Plains harbor the finest remnants of one of Missouri's most important presettlement landscapes and sites associated with the people who lived there before and after Euro-American settlement. Exploration of this region's parks will expand your vision and also your mind and heart. *

Prairie State Park

FALL MUST BE THE PRETTIEST SEASON on the prairie. Emerald-green grasses turn brilliant orange, red, bronze, and gold. During the summer, they whisper or rustle in the wind. In fall, they rattle and toss to and fro. The land seems restless and alive, its color more intense and consuming than that of forests. Standing in a swale in the midst of this rolling sea of grass, facing the wind and knee-deep in prairie asters, you are just a speck on land that must stretch to somewhere beyond forever. And all around you, engulfed by the open skies, the annual fall pageant of the prairie begins.

First, there are the northern harriers—prairie hawks that the fall prairie attracts like a magnet. Sometimes near, sometimes far, the hawks glide low, slowly skimming over the top of the grass. Or they hover, suspended, barely cresting some windy knoll—listening. Occasionally, one dives into the grass, and a noisy flock of red-winged blackbirds or a covey of quail erupts.

Beneath the prairie hawks, the bison are in a world of their own. In fall, they are in their best condition of the year. It's also breeding season, and the bulls are touchy and cantankerous. Sometimes they fight. The ground shakes and the dust flies when two one-ton animals slam full speed into one another.

Rare and endangered species here are the northern harrier, greater prairie chicken, prairie mole cricket, regal fritillary butterfly, Mead's milkweed, auriculate foxglove, and more.

Deer seem to sprout in the openness. The early morning sun highlights them, ornamenting ridge tops and browsing along the prairie swells and swales. Sometimes you become aware of a collection of eyes, ears, and noses—each looking your way. But since only their heads show, motionless at the surface of that tossing, grassy sea, they look strangely suspended, almost as if the heads are rooted while the land moves around.

Beside them in the distance, a short-eared owl glides home from the hunt, and two coyote heads flash up and are gone with the blink of an eye. They reappear a little farther away, bouncing high for looks above the tall fall grasses. Overhead, shimmering white dots—pelicans—wing their way south.

This is the essence of Prairie State Park, one of the few places left where this tallgrass drama still unfolds so completely. And it happens not just in fall, but daily, with a progression of sights and sounds that become a song of the seasons—living visions of Missouri's natural past preserved in this park for our future.

Even winter is special, with deer everywhere and coyotes howling at night as first one pack and then another sounds off in the distance. The bison in their thick woolly coats have no problem with cold, sleet, or snow, and the tall grasses provide insulation and food for numerous small birds and mammals.

Then, before the last of winter's occasional snow, the early sedges bring a tinge of green among the white spots on the hills. These add an upright dimension to ground cleaned by prairie fires of last year's dead grasses. Soon the green spreads and envelops the land.

Splashes of color appear: scattered bouquets of purple violets, bright sulfur-yellow puccoons, and pale yellow wild indigos. The male prairie chickens begin their booming, inflating their bright orange air sacs with a call that can be heard a half-mile away as they dance and battle for the attention of females. One morning the hillsides are tinted red by Indian paintbrush, and meadowlark and dickcissel songs float on the spring air. Minute grasshopper sparrows busily build nests, and briefly, the buzzing song of the rare prairie mole cricket floats out of the twilight.

By May and June, the grasses begin a growth spurt that easily overtops the low flowers of spring. When knee-deep, they toss and blow in every wind, tirelessly sending waves rippling and racing across the hillsides—then out of sight over the far horizons. Next, a taller series of wildflowers springs through the grass, this time in mass profusion. These easily give late spring the distinction of having the most spectacular flower display of the year. Yellow coreopsis, white beard-tongue, false dragonhead, pale purple coneflower, sensitive brier, prairie phlox, scurfy pea, lead plant, and many more extend in all directions, to every horizon. Bison calves frolic among them in their uncommonly awkward fashion, following their mothers across the park. Northern harriers still dive, but now into blackberry thickets, where their tiny fluff-ball hatchlings are hidden and waiting to be fed.

By midsummer, as these flowers fade, the whole prairie world turns emerald. Now the grasses reign supreme, and the grassy waves still tirelessly race the breeze. When clouds drift, the effect is almost dizzying. In fact, everything seems to move—the hawks, the songbirds, the bison—all building during this time of plenty for the coming winter. As big as the land seems, though, it is sometimes dwarfed by the power and fury of summer thunderstorms. And through it all, the call of the meadowlark becomes the song of the season.

By late August, these millions of grasses send up their seed stalks—four, six, eight, and in wet places, sometimes ten feet. Other late summer blooms, especially sunflowers, reach even higher to display their heads above the grassy sea to the hummingbirds, butterflies, and moths that must pollinate them. By late September, the orange returns, and the fall pageant begins once again.

Prairie State Park is a unique place, dedicated as a living tribute to a nearly extinguished native landscape. Missouri's sweeping prairie panoramas were all but history when this land was acquired in the late 1970s

for a park. With so few fragments left—less than 1 percent of the state's original prairie—it is difficult to imagine that a third of the state's land surface once was prairie. That is, except when standing in one. Then it becomes much easier to appreciate our loss—and to feel the real value of Prairie State Park. For here, on nearly 4,000 native and restored acres, is Missouri's largest remaining prairie and our greatest hope for preserving a sense of the scope of these wild grasslands.

Prairie State Park exists because of a happy conjunction of historical circumstance and people's growing appreciation for the prairie landscape. It is fitting that the park is located in southwestern Missouri's Barton County, for this county had more land in prairie when the white settlers came than any other county in the state—some 86 percent. These western prairies were Osage Indian hunting grounds during the time of their great village on the hill along the Osage River to the north—now Osage Village State Historic Site. The Osage continued to hunt here even after they gave up their lands farther east in the cession of 1808. White settlement began in Barton County as early as the 1820s, but slowly. The lands now in the park were not taken from the public domain until the 1850s, and even then as whole or half-sections under military bounty and swampland acts that tended to encourage speculative purchase by absentee owners. Most of the land in the park was never tilled.

Major development in this area began in 1880 with the coming of the railroad, which provided access to markets for the region's coal and crops. Coal production centered around Mindenmines, only a few miles southwest of the park, but there was only limited disturbance on lands now within the park, most of which has been remediated. More happily, a new industry began to flourish: the cutting and curing of the tall prairie grasses for hay, highly desired as fodder for mules, horses, and cattle. The hay could be shipped by rail to markets near and far. The locals proudly aver that by World War I, when Missouri mules were greatly sought for use in crop production and even by the military overseas, the Schreiner Hay Company of Lamar had grown so successful that it had cornered the market for prairie hay. The company operated out of Prairie

Bison were reintroduced in 1985 and now number about one hundred, providing a rare chance to see them on natural prairie. In fall, the prairie is a riot of earthy colors amid a bronze sea of grasses, here with winged sumac, rough-leaved dogwood, and tall goldenrod. *Both Meagan Duffee*

Elk were reintroduced to the prairie in 1993, and the herd now has about twenty. ***Missouri State Parks*** **• Top right: Blazing stars grace the prairie in summer.** ***Tom Uhlenbrock*** **• Below right: East Drywood Creek is an outstanding prairie headwater stream that flows through the Regal Tallgrass Prairie Natural Area.** ***Ken McCarty*** **• Left: Spring brings the booming of prairie chickens.** ***Jim Rathert***

Center, just southeast of today's park. The need for mules began to decline with the advent of tractors, but a market for the nutritious prairie hay still existed at stables, racetracks, and stockyards.

As recently as the 1960s, more than 30,000 acres of native prairie remained in western Barton County, mostly on land whose owners were proud of their unbroken yet productive hay meadows. But then the chain of benign circumstance began to break. When the price of soybeans soared in the early 1970s, the prairies one by one were put to the plow.

By the late 1970s when state park officials began to seek lands for a prairie park, they feared the best they could do would be an untilled forty-acre tract or two that might in time be restored. But again came a happy conjunction of circumstance. An owner of a key undisturbed tract was suddenly willing to sell, and the Missouri Prairie Foundation and the Nature Conservancy simultaneously became aware of his willingness and the state's interest. A wealthy benefactor from Connecticut, who had fallen in love with the rolling prairie on her visit to Barton County in 1972, offered an interest-free loan to cover the sale price. Within days, a deal was struck for the core 1,520 acres that by 1980 would be dedicated as Prairie State Park. Katharine Ordway, who put up the money, ultimately gave more than $40 million through the Nature Conservancy and other groups to preserve tallgrass prairie throughout the Midwest at a time when it would otherwise have likely faced annihilation. At the park, subsequent donations and acquisitions over the years brought the acreage to nearly 4,000, including several prairie tracts that had never been plowed and others that have been restored.

At Prairie State Park today, careful clearing of brush and controlled burning deliver some of the best wildflower shows in the state, more spectacular even than those that enchanted Katharine Ordway. American bison were reintroduced to the park in 1985, and a small herd of elk was also introduced by 1993. The bison now number up to one hundred, and the elk about twenty. But most important, the park is a place where a prairie landscape can survive—expansive, dynamic, self-renewing, a living tribute to a largely extinct component of our natural past.

Prairie State Park is for people to enjoy. A nature center tells the prairie

To better understand and preserve the prairie, botanists periodically monitor diversity by counting all species within one-tenth-meter quadrants. ***Ron Colatskie*** **• Left: A northern harrier skims low over the grassland.** ***Nopadol Paothong*** **• Indian paintbrush reaches for the big sky.** ***Matt Faupel*** **• The park's 3,646-acre Regal Tallgrass Prairie Natural Area is named after the regal fritillary butterfly, here alighting on a pale purple coneflower.** ***Donna Brunet***

story with displays, a diorama, an aquarium, audiovisual programs, and more. Park staff present programs about the prairie and the American Indians who have lived here, and they answer questions about the prairie or lead walks across it. School groups are common by day, as are visitors on trails or along the roadways in the evening, when bison, deer, and prairie birds are most easily seen. Fifteen miles of foot trails, some short and some long, leave from the visitor center and roadside trailheads. These lace the rolling prairie, from its high, dry ridges to its rich, marshy streams. A picnic ground and a small, reservation-only campground lie along one prairie stream, in a small grove near the visitor center.

A trail from the campground leads to a reservation-only campsite for backpackers out on the prairie. A mile to the east is East Drywood Creek, among the state's most outstanding prairie headwaters streams. The area through which it flows has long been a state natural area. In 2007, following eighteen years of vegetation monitoring that demonstrated the integrity of the park's natural resources, Regal Tallgrass Prairie Natural Area was expanded to include 3,646 acres, almost the entire park, including East Drywood Creek and three other previously designated small natural areas. Prairie State Park is a place where those who wish to immerse themselves in the great North American tallgrass prairie may readily do so. Development has purposefully been kept to a minimum to keep the prairie as natural as possible.

It is a wonder that enough prairie survived to become a state park. But it did, thanks first to the many owners who valued these unbroken grasslands, and then to those who cared enough to preserve a legacy for the future. Park staff over the years have dedicated themselves to restoring and maintaining this extraordinary treasure, carefully pursuing the burning regime so essential for maintaining a prairie. If this legacy is truly to be preserved, however, park scientists realize that this fragmented island ecosystem should be at least doubled in size to provide the habitat needed for species in peril. Also needed is a buffer against changes in land use and other threats from beyond its boundaries. The hope for this park is that it can be large enough, and ecologically viable enough, that the age-old drama of the prairie may forever unfold. ✻

PRAIRIE STATE PARK • 128 NORTHWEST 150TH LANE, MINDENMINES

Osage Village State Historic Site

THE TRIBE MOST FEARED AND RESPECTED by other natives when French-speaking explorers and traders first came to Missouri called themselves the Ni-U-Ko'n-Ska, "Children of the Middle Waters." Among themselves, in humility before their Wah'Kon, or "Mystery Force," they said they were the "Little Ones." The first written record of this tribe derives from the expedition of Louis Jolliet and Father Jacques Marquette down the Mississippi River in 1673. Soon after, the world at large would come to know of this proud and powerful people: the Osage.

Their principal villages were at a junction of waters in western Missouri that they called the Place-of-Many-Swans. This locale is where the streams we know today as the Marmaton, Little Osage, and Marais des Cygnes come together to form the Osage River in Vernon and Bates counties. The Osage were lords of the prairies and woodlands from the Missouri River to the Arkansas River, and from the Mississippi River to the Great Plains. It is startling to consider that this robust, warlike tribe numbering at most ten thousand people so thoroughly dominated such a large region. The land, which they called "The Sacred One," was certainly rich, and the Osage obviously knew how to live on it.

The Osage held sway over a huge territory, including most of what is now Missouri, Arkansas, eastern Kansas, and Oklahoma. On hunting or war expeditions, they wandered even farther.

The Osage may have developed as a tribe in the same territory they occupied when the French encountered them. They spoke a language classed as one of the southern Siouan tongues, related to the Quapaw of northeast Arkansas. As a prairie and woodland people, the Osage used the animals and plants of both the forest and the grasslands. They planted gardens of corn, squash, and beans but also hunted for buffalo, bear, elk, and deer. They gathered walnuts, wild grapes, pawpaws, persimmons, and American lotus or yonquapin, and fished the fertile waters of the rivers and oxbow lakes.

The Osage defended their northern frontier from the Sac and Fox, cooperated with the kindred Missouria and Kansa along the Missouri River, fought more or less continually against the Pawnee on the western plains, and thoroughly intimidated the Caddoan tribes to the south along the Arkansas and Red Rivers.

Osage ceremonies, rituals, and modes of social organization were elaborately tuned to the natural environment. By almost any fair measure, the Osage had "strong medicine." And they apparently looked the part. Almost every chronicler of the early West was impressed by the physical prowess of the Osage. Washington Irving, in his *Tour on the Prairies* (1832), paints a characteristic word portrait:

> *Near by there was a group of Osages: stately fellows; stern and simple in garb and aspect. They wore no ornaments; their dress consisted merely of blankets, leggings, and moccasins. Their heads were bare; their hair was cropped close, excepting a bristling ridge on the top, like the crest of a helmet, with a long scalp lock hanging behind. They had fine Roman countenances, and broad deep chests; and, as they generally wore their blankets wrapped round their loins, so as to leave the bust and arms bare, they looked like so many noble bronze figures. The Osages are the finest looking Indians I have ever seen in the West.*

The arrival of the earliest French traders from the east and of the first stray horses from the southwest probably did not affect the Osage as drastically as the tribes farther west on the plains. Neither the French, the Spanish, nor the British could contest the power of the Osage in their domain. Instead, the Osage were prime trading partners, supplying huge quantities of furs and also captive Indian slaves. Until the nineteenth century, the Osage accounted for over half of the total trade in furs on the Missouri River. The French and Spanish profited from the trade, valued the Osage as buffers between each other and the British, and closed their eyes to the frequent robbing of traders or the killing of weaker Indians and even whites who strayed into confrontations with the "Imperial Osages."

For their part, the Osage tolerated the small infringements of French settlements along their largest rivers, occasionally punished offending settlers or traders, and even adopted a number of stray whites as semi-permanent guests in their villages. They relished the trade that brought them metal tools and weapons, gradually becoming more and more dependent upon them.

When the young United States bought the territory of Louisiana from France in 1803, the old Osage way of life was doomed. American settlers, more aggressive and numerous than French villagers and more persistent and tenacious than French traders or Spanish commandants, pressed hard upon Osage lands. Starting with a treaty in 1808, the Osage began a series of dignified retreats that withdrew them step-by-painful-step from eastern Missouri, then from western Missouri into Kansas in 1823, then into southern Kansas, and finally, after the Civil War, into Oklahoma, where they now live. The Osage domain today is but one oil-rich county in Oklahoma: Osage County.

In the vicinity of the rich prairie, river, marsh, and woodland area known by the Osage as Place-of-Many-Swans in present Vernon and Bates counties, the Osage occupied several village sites over the course of the many years they lived there. During the period from about 1700,

Above: During most of the eighteenth century, Osage Indians had their principal village on a grass-covered hilltop near what they called the Place-of-Many-Swans. ***K.W. Cole*** **• Right: The pits and grooves in this sandstone slab give mute testimony to its use by the Osage for grinding and sharpening.** ***Anne Larsen*** **Left: Mobile exhibits of George Catlin's Osage portraits, painted during his travels in the 1830s, are displayed at special events with Osage connections.** ***Jennifer Sieg***

not long after they first met the French traders, until about 1775, when they moved a few miles away to the south, the lodges of the Little Ones stood on a high, open hilltop that commands a broad, sweeping view of the winding Osage River valley and surrounding hills and groves. This hill is the highest in a chain of isolated, limestone-capped remnant hills that runs roughly northwest to southeast, sitting between two small tributary streams and pointing toward the Osage River to the north. It is this grass-covered hilltop site that is now preserved as Osage Village State Historic Site.

While living in this beautiful setting with their rich lands arrayed before them, the Osage came to know the white traders and their goods very well, trading for several years at Fort Orleans on the Missouri River. They met Etienne de Bourgmond, Claude Charles du Tisné, and Bernard de la Harpe, and they welcomed home the warrior who was taken along with other Native Americans to France to be the object of flattering attention from the Gallic nobility. The Osage sent warriors east in alliance

E. I. Couse, one of the famed Taos Society of Artists, painted several murals for the Missouri Capitol depicting the Osage as a people at peace with the land, reflecting and perhaps aiding the transformation of attitudes about Native Americans in the twentieth century. ***Lloyd Grotjan*** **• In the eighteenth century, the Osage came to depend upon axes, hoes, and other European trade goods such as these excavated from their village site.** ***University of Missouri***

with France to help in the bloody ambush of the English general Edward Braddock, and they came to know, though not very intimately, the Spanish commandants after Charles III took suzerainty over Louisiana. They visited the new village growing up on the Mississippi just below the Missouri that the Spanish called San Luis, but which they always referred to as "Chouteau's town" in deference to their most respected trading partner. During this time, the Little Ones also continued their traditional skirmishes with the tribes that bordered Osage territory, especially the Pawnee on the west. They also carried out their ceremonies of life, hunting in the spring and fall, planting and harvesting their crops, and praying each morning in the predawn darkness as they faced the rising sun.

When the Osage left this home in Missouri, they left no monuments. Soon there was little that might tell the white American settlers of Vernon County that this tall hill had once been the political and cultural center of an empire extending into four states. This was a domain claimed by a people who called themselves the Little Ones but whom others called giants, an empire even respected by the sovereign monarchs of Europe. The Osage themselves retained memories of the Place-of-Many-Swans but did not come back to visit except as occasional individual pilgrims. In time, domestic cattle came to graze the hill. Farm buildings and watering ponds were constructed. The old village site became, for practical purposes, lost to knowledge.

Then in 1941, a young archaeologist from the University of Missouri surveyed the site and confirmed that this hill was indeed a principal village site of the Osage during those historic decades of the eighteenth century. In the archaeological world, the village site took on the name of the Missouri farm family who owned the ground, the Browns. Eventually, further investigations were conducted at the so-called Brown Site—or, even more arcane, at 23VE3, as it was identified in the Archaeological Survey of Missouri. The extent of the site was more precisely defined through excavations over the years, and a wealth of recovered artifacts now documents the village. Here is where the Osage were becoming more and more dependent upon European trade goods, even while maintaining their earlier style of life. Evidence suggests that at its height the village had two to three thousand inhabitants living in about two hundred lodges.

In 1971, the Brown Site was enrolled in the National Register of Historic Places. The Brown family knew its value and safeguarded it from pot hunters. In the late 1970s, the same archaeologist who first confirmed the site, Dr. Carl Chapman, by this time the dean of Missouri archaeologists, alerted the park division and the Archaeological Conservancy, a national preservation organization, that Mrs. Leslie Brown was interested in seeing the site permanently preserved. Mrs. Brown's death brought some urgency to the matter, and the Conservancy, after signing a repurchase agreement with the Missouri Department of Natural Resources in 1981, stepped in and purchased the hundred-acre tract. Then in 1984, thanks again largely to the efforts of Carl Chapman, the state legislature appropriated funds to buy the property.

Above: From their hilltop village in this mostly open landscape, the Osage dominated a wide swath of prairies and woodlands. *Missouri State Parks*
Right: Archaeologist Carl Chapman had a tremendous influence on the site's preservation. Here, he described his archaeological findings to a group gathered to support adding the village site as a state park. *K.W. Cole*

In its lovely setting with its wealth of buried knowledge and because of its pivotal role in so much early Missouri history, Osage Village State Historic Site has a unique part to play in helping Missourians understand their state. Though the site has been left undeveloped in an effort to preserve what remains, the one-mile walking trail with excellent outdoor exhibits helps the visitor not only to visualize the history of the Osage and the relationship of this place to other nearby Osage and early European sites but also to sense something of what life must have been like in this vibrant Native American village .

The site also brings an unusual burden of responsibility. Even beyond the obvious charge of protecting the resource, there is the memory of the Little Ones to be treasured and nourished. The people who once lived on this spot for most of a century shaped our history, but they remain relatively little known. What we know of them from history was written largely by those who coveted their land or feared their strength. The Osage of old Missouri will never have an opportunity to tell their story in their own way, from their own point of view. We must hope that the stories that are told here would find a measure of approval in the hearts of the Little Ones, the Children of the Middle Waters. *

Harry S Truman Birthplace State Historic Site

THE THIRTY-THIRD PRESIDENT of the United States was born May 8, 1884, in a downstairs bedroom of a neat but small frame house in Lamar, the seat of Barton County. The house, purchased for $625, measured only 20-by-28 feet. It had four tiny rooms downstairs and two upstairs, both small and with very low ceilings. It had neither electricity nor indoor plumbing. To call this house modest is to be charitable. Set behind it were a smokehouse, a cistern, and, a little distance away, an outdoor privy, typical of the times in rural areas. The house was at the edge of town, and John Truman also owned the property catty-corner across the street. There, he had a corral and barn and traded horses and mules.

Harry S, whose middle initial was a compromise between the names of his grandfathers, Anderson Shipp Truman and Solomon Young, was the first of three children of John Anderson and Martha Ellen Truman (née Young). Harry himself used the S both with and without a period. The monument at Lamar does not use the period, but the library and museum in Independence do.

> *Truman returned and stood in the town square of Lamar to accept the nomination as candidate for vice president of the United States, as the running mate of Franklin D. Roosevelt. Citizens of the little Osage prairie town, population 3,223, cheered with pride.*

Lamar, first settled and platted in the 1850s, was briefly host to Gov. Claiborne Jackson's rebel force during the Civil War, before the battle of Carthage, then was garrisoned by the Union army, and finally was raided twice by William Quantrill's guerrilla band. Wyatt Earp married a local girl and served as the town's first marshal in 1870, but it was not until 1880 and 1881, when two rail lines reached and intersected at Lamar, that prospects significantly brightened.

Unfortunately, Lamar's bright future didn't include John Truman's business. Evidence shows his ventures did not prosper, and when Harry was only eleven months old, his restless young father pulled up stakes and moved his family south of Kansas City where both he and his wife had grown up, first to Harrisonville, then Belton, and then Grandview. The family moved to Independence, seat of Jackson County, in 1890. There, Harry began his formal schooling and, at age six, first met Elizabeth Virginia (Bess) Wallace, age five. The two were classmates for a long time. Harry fell behind Bess one year when he was ill with diphtheria, but he caught up later by skipping a grade—he was a "bookish" rather than an athletic boy—and both were members of the Independence High School graduating class of 1901.

Attending the 1959 dedication were from left, State Park Director Joe Jaeger, President Harry Truman, and Leland Cox, representing the United Auto Workers, which purchased and donated the site to the state. *Missouri State Parks* • The tiny rooms are furnished appropriately to the period. *Denise H. Vaughn*

College was out of the question. John Truman had switched from livestock trading, which he understood, to the commodities market, which he did not, and lost all his savings including his home in Independence. Harry had to go to work to help keep his brother and sister in school. In 1906 his father and mother returned from a brief farming venture in Henry County to take over management of Grandmother Young's substantial six-hundred-acre farm near Grandview, and they asked Harry to help. For the next eleven years, farming was his work, leavened by a prolonged courtship with Bess Wallace.

Truman's farming career was put on hold with America's entrance into World War I in 1917. In late September, a new field artillery regiment made up of Kansas City and Independence units of the National Guard arrived at Camp Doniphan in Fort Sill, Oklahoma, and was federalized. Harry Truman had been elected first lieutenant. By the next April, they were in France, and Lieutenant Truman, having demonstrated exceptional leadership, was promoted to captain and commander of Battery D. His outfit was in some of the fiercest fighting in the battle of Meuse-Argonne and on the Verdun front, as the Americans helped push the German army back and into collapse. His company, Captain Truman wrote, fired more than ten thousand rounds at "the Hun" and never lost a man. They did lose one gun, but that was because a shell was stuck in it.

Upon Truman's return from overseas in April 1919, he and Bess Wallace lost little time planning their marriage in June, and then Truman and his former canteen sergeant at Camp Doniphan opened a men's clothing store in Kansas City. The business did well at first but failed in 1922 during a period of postwar deflation. Another of Truman's army friends, Lt. James Pendergast, who was a nephew of the Kansas City political boss, Tom Pendergast, helped persuade Harry to run for eastern judge of the Jackson County Court (a position now called commissioner). He won a first term, was defeated for a second, but then was elected for successive terms, eight years in all, as presiding judge of the county. He developed a good record and established a reputation for honesty.

In 1934, with Pendergast backing, Truman won a three-way contest

Harry Truman was born in a downstairs bedroom of this little house in the county seat and up-and-coming railroad town of Lamar in 1884. *Missouri State Parks*

for the Democratic nomination and was elected to the US Senate, demonstrating a surprising appeal in outstate Missouri, thanks no doubt to his small-town and farm roots. Despite his continued loyalty to Pendergast, even after the Boss was indicted for bribe-taking and sent to prison in 1939 for income tax evasion, Truman was reelected to the Senate in 1940, again appealing to rural Missouri and also to labor.

In his second term, he built a national reputation as chairman of the Truman Committee, a special panel set up to monitor World War II contracts and to investigate and expose graft and profiteering. This led President Franklin D. Roosevelt, as he prepared in 1944 to run for a fourth term, to choose the popular and dependable Senator Truman to be his running mate.

Mindful of the support he had received from rural Missouri, Truman came back to Lamar to accept the nomination. By this time, in the midst of World War II, Lamar citizens bragged of several high-ranking native sons and daughters: three rear admirals and the lieutenant commander of the Coast Guard Women's Reserve. Eight months later, Lamar would be able to boast of the president and commander-in-chief.

The man from Missouri became president when Franklin Roosevelt, only eighty-two days into his new term, died of a massive stroke on April 12, 1945. In 1948, Harry Truman was reelected to a full term, upsetting Republican candidate Thomas E. Dewey of New York, whom pollsters had picked as a sure winner.

Events and decisions of national and worldwide significance marked the seven-plus years of the Truman presidency: the dropping of the first atomic bombs to end the war with Japan, the signing of the United Nations charter, the development of the Marshall Plan to rebuild war-ravaged Europe, the formation of the North Atlantic Treaty Organization, the beginning of the so-called police action in Korea, and at home, the evolution of the Fair Deal program of social and economic reform.

Choosing not to run for another term in 1952, Truman returned to live in retirement with Bess in Independence. For many years, he kept up a vigorous life, working daily and writing his memoirs in the Harry S. Truman Library and Museum. He died December 26, 1972, at the age of eighty-eight. Bess outlived him by nearly ten years. Both are buried on the grounds of the Truman Library in Independence.

Throughout his political life, Harry Truman had been a strong supporter of organized labor. In appreciation, the United Auto Workers of America (UAW) bought the birthplace at Lamar in 1957 from descendants of Wyatt Earp, had it restored, and donated it to the state in 1959 for preservation as a historic site. Harry Truman came down from Independence for the dedication on April 19, 1959, along with Gov. James T. Blair, Sen. Stuart Symington, and other dignitaries. "I feel like I've been buried and dug up while I'm still alive," Truman said, "and I'm glad they've done it to me today." He signed the guest book as a "retired farmer."

With no family pieces available from the Trumans' time in Lamar, the house was furnished appropriately for the time of Harry's birth. The period wallpapers, the gingham check cloth on the kitchen table, the rag rugs and the faint odor of the coal oil lamps successfully evoke the era. An Austrian pine planted in the yard by John Truman in honor of Harry's birth thrived for well over a century but then regrettably died. A monument to our thirty-third president, erected by the UAW at the time the house was dedicated, stands nearby.

Over the years, the park division acquired additional nearby lots, including the site of the mule barn owned by Truman's father, with the intention of protecting the immediate area and reconstructing the barn and also an elementary school that was south of the home, if funds were to become available. Local residents became excited by the prospect of a more extensive site that could attract more tourism revenue. But when no funds materialized, they supported a move to have the National Park Service study the birthplace for possible addition to the national system. The 2011 federal study found no justification for adding the birthplace to the complex of Truman sites in Independence and Grandview when state preservation was "more than adequate to the task." The state and the federal government were both strapped for funds.

Meanwhile, the place remains very much as it was when John and Martha Ellen Truman lived there and Harry was born. It just may be that this plain, small house is giving us the best possible understanding of the extraordinary man who thought of himself as "Mr. Citizen." *

HARRY S TRUMAN BIRTHPLACE STATE HISTORIC SITE • 1009 TRUMAN STREET, LAMAR

Battle of Island Mound State Historic Site

OUT AT MISSOURI'S WESTERN EDGE, the hills seem to roll in from Kansas in waves. Although the hills don't amount to much, a small hill commands a big view. In western Bates County, this high, prairie-like landscape is cut by the Marais des Cygnes (Swans) River, offering a considerable contrast, with its low and marshy valley sporting a fair growth of timber.

The boundary between Kansas and Missouri runs through this country, and while only a line on a map, it was an important line, a significant part of the great national debate—a free soil territory on one side, a slave-holding state on the other. The 1820 Missouri Compromise that allowed Missouri to enter the Union as a slave state had forbidden slavery in any of the remaining Louisiana Purchase territory north of the southern boundary of Missouri, but the 1854 Kansas-Nebraska Act had nullified the compromise by allowing Kansans to decide the slavery issue for themselves. Although it delayed a national civil war for a few more years, the act engendered a bloody, vicious conflict along this border as the Kansas decision was contested by Free-Soilers in Kansas and pro-slavery adherents in Missouri, with nothing separating them but a line on the map. By the time Union and Confederate forces fought the Battle of Island Mound in 1862, a local civil war had already raged along the border for nearly a decade.

Eight or nine miles east of this border in Missouri, along the Fort Scott Road, lay the farmstead of Enoch and Christina Toothman. A modest place with a two-room log house and a few outbuildings, it occupied eighty acres of the high prairie land a couple of miles north of the Marais de Cygnes bottom. Enoch Toothman was from Virginia and was known to hold strong pro-Southern views. In fact, the male Toothmans were accused of being at least part-time bushwhackers. Enoch's son John was being held prisoner at Fort Lincoln, just inside Kansas. It was no accident that in the late afternoon of October 27, 1862, a column of blue-clad, Union soldiers—black men, some 240 of them—marched up to the Toothman's dooryard.

Marching his First Kansas Colored Volunteer Infantry troops into Missouri from Fort Lincoln, Capt. Henry Seaman, the officer in command, knew of the Toothmans and knew their farm sat upon the high ground above the Marais des Cygnes, an excellent place to encamp and a base from which to carry out his orders in Missouri. The soldiers commandeered the Toothman house for a headquarters, and the split rail fences from all around were gathered in and restacked as breastworks around the house. The encampment was proudly dubbed Fort Africa.

About two miles south of the Toothman farm, the channels and sloughs of the Marais des Cygnes River meandered through the marshy lowland. In this marsh was Hog Island, a patch of high ground between a channel of the river and one of its wandering sloughs. Hog Island was a favorite safe haven—a place of refuge and rest and for storage of supplies and loot—for the pro-Southern guerrillas that ranged along the border after the Missouri State Guard and the regular Confederate Army evacuated Missouri. In the fall of 1862, the local bands of Turman and Hancock were staying at the island, and they had been joined and presided over by Col. Jeremiah "Vard" Cockrell, back in Missouri recruiting for the Confederate forces in Arkansas. The First Kansas had been sent to Missouri to clear out this so-called nest of guerrillas.

Between the Toothman house and the river bottom were a series of small hillocks, or as they are called locally, mounds, one of which was Island Mound. Hog Island lay on the bottomland just beyond these mounds. The encounter that the historic site commemorates took place on October 29, 1862, on and around the mounds between the Toothman's house on the high ground and the river bottoms below.

After the First Kansas had set up operations at the Toothman homestead, Captain Seaman had satisfied himself, by scouting and interviewing locals, that the Kansans were outnumbered about two-to-one by some four hundred mounted rebel guerrillas. He resolved to sit tight

and wait until cavalry reinforcements came from Fort Scott, a few days' march away, before directly assaulting the rebel camp. Through the day of October 28, some long-distance skirmishing kept both sides at arm's length, but on the afternoon of October 29, the rebels set fire to the tall prairie grass below the Toothman house to obscure their movements.

Captain Seaman sent a small scouting party forward to go around the fire and smoke and from the vantage point of one of the nearby mounds determine what was happening on the mounds and the river bottom below. They were instructed not to take chances and to stay in view of the fort. Ignoring orders, they let their zeal lead them farther afield, out of view and into danger. Hearing increased firing and realizing the scouting party might be in trouble, Seaman sent a larger support group after them. The rescue party found the patrol and joined up with it, but then unwisely moved even farther south, off of the mounds and onto the river bottom, apparently lured by the possibility of some "easy pickings" of isolated rebel pickets.

Several descendants of soldiers who fought in the historic Battle of Island Mound were among other visitors who viewed the Marais des Cygnes bottoms from a neighboring farm after the 2012 dedication of the site. ***Scott Myers***

This small squad of some thirty infantrymen soon found more guerrillas than they had bargained for, when 125 or so rebel horsemen burst from the timber on the bottomland, on a beeline to get between the Union detachment and the fort. The foot soldiers realized they couldn't out-race the cavalry, but went on the double-quick up the hill trying for an embankment or some likely ground upon which to make their stand.

On the flank of Island Mound, still a mile short of Fort Africa and no cover in sight, the beleaguered African American soldiers formed up and

Left: A *Harper's Weekly* illustration in 1863 depicted the First Kansas Colored Volunteer Infantry. Above: At the sesquicentennial of the battle, descendants reflect upon the action here. *Scott Myers* • Above right: These actors appeared in a film produced by Missouri State Parks about the battle. *Missouri State Parks*

got off one volley of musket fire as the rebel cavalry crashed into and over them. With no time to reload, they stood their ground and fought the attacking cavalry hand-to-hand with bayonets and empty muskets, until Captain Seaman was able to bring the balance of his troops forward and drive off the attacking horsemen. After the cavalry withdrew, the black soldiers marched back up the hill in good order to their encampment.

For the first time in the Civil War, former slaves had taken up arms and performed admirably as soldiers on the battlefield. Island Mound wasn't much of a battle by the standards of the Civil War, little more than a skirmish, but an important question of the time was answered: Will they fight? Fight they did.

Of the two-dozen First Kansas soldiers who had withstood the cavalry charge on Island Mound, eight men had been killed and eleven seriously wounded. Sergeant Edward Lowrey, wounded three times by shotgun blasts in the arm and shoulder, managed to kill three of his assailants with the bayonet and butt of his unloaded musket. Fourteen-year-old Manuel Dobson shot one cavalryman, and even though he was shot through both arms, proudly related to his commander: "I brought my gun back." Yes, they would fight. Among other things, it was also the first time an African American officer, Lieutenant Patrick Minor, commanded black troops in action on a battlefield.

The guerrillas took their dead and wounded with them, so their total casualties remain unknown. But one of their captains, Bill Turman, later reported, "Those black devils fought like tigers."

Two days later, the reinforcements arrived, and the First Kansas swept the river bottoms and Hog Island in force, but it was deserted. The guerrillas had moved on to fight another day. The Kansas troops returned to Fort Lincoln, and the affair at Island Mound was left to history, along with the Toothmans and their farm.

Perhaps after the troops left, the Toothman family took apart the defensive works and began the job of rebuilding their rail fences. If so, it would have been for naught. Less than a year later this farm was at the epicenter of a four-county rural area along the Kansas border south of the Missouri River that was completely depopulated pursuant to the infamous General Order No. 11—intended to deprive Confederate guerrillas of support and ruthlessly enforced by Kansas troops creating what became known as the burnt district.

After President Abraham Lincoln's Emancipation Proclamation on

January 1, 1863, the First Kansas Colored Volunteer Infantry was mustered into federal service on January 13 and later designated the 79th Regiment, United States Colored Troops. The regiment had a long and distinguished record throughout the war and mustered out in October 1865, after having participated in a dozen battles or other engagements. Five of its officers and 173 of its enlisted men were killed in combat.

The state bought forty acres of the eighty-acre Toothman farm, the site of Fort Africa, in 2008, in time to prepare it for dedication on the 2012 sesquicentennial of the battle. Park staff have not tried to replicate the site in 1862. There is no contemporary description of the Toothman homeplace, and Fort Africa wasn't much more than the stacked remnants of all the rail fence in the neighborhood. Archaeological investigations have not revealed enough evidence to support reconstruction.

The site today features a short trail—aptly named the Courage Trail—that leads out onto restored prairie where there is a view of the mounds on which the fighting took place on a farm adjacent to the site. Farther beyond, but out of sight behind the hills is the Marais des Cygnes bottomland. Today, the countryside is still very open, but the prairie grasses have been mostly replaced by pastures and fields, and there are more trees on the high ground and fewer on the bottoms. A number of wayside markers with photos and maps explaining the battle are located along the trail. The men of the First Kansas are commemorated in a bronze plaque, and visitors are accommodated with parking, a rest room, and a small pavilion for picnicking. A short stretch of rail fence calls to mind Fort Africa but mainly serves as a reminder that a rail fence was at least half air and didn't provide much protection from bullets.

As far as is known, none of the African American soldiers of the First Kansas ever wrote an account of the battle or published a memoir of their Civil War experiences, so we have no idea of their thoughts as they marched across that bloody border, knowing full well that guerrillas would not take black prisoners. What filled their minds as they marched: trepidation or vindication? We will never know, but we can stand on the ground where they stood and reflect on the landscape where they earned their place in Missouri—and national—history. *

BLACK SOLDIERS AT ISLAND MOUND

Enlisting free black men and ex-slaves as Union soldiers had been debated since the beginning of the Civil War, but it was a step that nearly every leader, for mostly political reasons, had been reluctant to take. Jim Lane, a hot-headed radical Kansas senator and instigator of many ugly border incidents, was determined to make it happen. Acting against President Abraham Lincoln's wishes and Secretary of War Edwin Stanton's orders, Lane assembled two regiments of African Americans in the summer of 1862 as Kansas units. They were the First and Second Kansas Colored Volunteer Infantry. At the Battle of Island Mound, these Kansas state soldiers were not yet part of the federal army.

BATTLE OF ISLAND MOUND STATE HISTORIC SITE • 4837 NORTHWEST COUNTY ROAD, BUTLER

Knob Noster State Park

THERE IS AN OLD, STRIKING PHOTOGRAPH in the park archives in Jefferson City—a scene at Knob Noster sometime during the 1930s. In the warm glow of a campfire, a young woman in a white costume stands ceremonially surrounded by her fellow campers. If you have had the good fortune in your own youth to participate in a similar ceremony—probably the allegorical closing ceremony of a youth camp session—you may be able to call up memories of such an evening. With excitement and anticipation, you would have heard whippoorwills and an occasional barred owl calling from beyond the circle of light, a darkness punctuated by thousands of tiny fireflies and intensified by the magic of the light and warmth, where ceremonies and songs drew you and your friends together. Some of life's most enduring memories can emerge from such circles of summer firelight.

Knob Noster State Park was named for a nearby Johnson County town, which in turn was named in the 1850s for two hillocks, or knobs, near the town, plus some wag's addition of the Latin word for "our," which is "noster," yielding "our knobs."

The group camps of the state parks were conceived during the Great Depression to provide the opportunity for just such experiences for youngsters who might not otherwise be able to enjoy them in a privately run camp. These camps, built mostly by the Civilian Conservation Corps (CCC) and the Works Progress Administration (WPA), are for the most part still functioning today, including two—Camp Shawnee and Camp Bobwhite—at Knob Noster State Park.

From 1936 to 1946, the park was administered by the National Park Service under the name Montserrat as one of its Recreation Demonstration Areas (RDAs), sub-marginal lands restored and developed for recreation near population centers. Montserrat was one of three such RDAs that have become state parks, along with Lake of the Ozarks and Cuivre River. The name Montserrat derived from another adjoining village, smaller than the town of Knob Noster, located north of the park. The park became Knob Noster in 1946 when the National Park Service transferred it to the state.

With labor provided through the work-relief program of the WPA, the federal government between 1938 and 1941 built Shawnee and Bobwhite youth camps, as well as a campground and picnic area, several small lakes, and various bridges and service buildings. Many of these buildings and other structures are still intact today and are listed on the National Register of Historic Places.

Johnson County is mainly an agricultural and ranching county, so how did this tract, 3,300 acres at the time, come to be a candidate for a New Deal program aimed at poor and worn-out lands? While much of the county is indeed rolling prairie now under productive cultivation, a region along the Clearfork Creek tributary of the Blackwater River is fairly rough, centered on a high, limestone-capped erosional remnant known as Bristle Ridge. The sedimentary shale in this area contained coal deposits. Because of overgrazing and poor farming practices on the thin soils of these rolling ridges, coupled with coal mining in places, this vicinity had by the 1930s become scarred and impoverished. With federal acquisition and development, the Montserrat RDA began a useful second life. The effects of erosion were largely reversed, and a somewhat brushy forest reclaimed parts of the area.

But neither the barrenness of the early 1930s nor the more recent brushy aspect accurately represents the original landscape in this area. Knob Noster lies along the eastern fringe of the Osage Plains, and there was originally a broad zone of transition between forest and prairie along such sizable streams as Clearfork Creek in these dissected lands. An eyewitness description of this now vanished savanna and open woodland comes to us in a narrative written by a young Missouri Confederate soldier, Ephraim McDowell Anderson, who marched with his companions through the Knob Noster vicinity in 1861: "The view opens upon boundless and beautiful prairies, dotted with clumps of trees."

By the 1970s, scraggly timber and brush had mostly replaced the open landscape described by Anderson, but park managers have been restoring portions of the earlier landscape. The visitor center contains exhibits that explain the dynamic forces, including fire, that created and are restoring Knob Noster's open woodlands, and signs near some of the burn areas tell the story, too. The park also has a small natural area at Pin Oak Slough, an old oxbow of Clearfork Creek, now home to pin oak,

Camp Fire Girls, an organization founded in 1910, conduct a ceremony at the fire circle at a Knob Noster group camp in the 1930s. *State Park Archives* • The Hawk's Nest Trail passes through an open woodland restored with prescribed fire, which brought out the blue phlox and other wildflowers. *Scott Myers*

Lake Buteo and other small lakes offer fishing, nonmotorized boating, and a good chance to see wildlife. *Scott Myers* • Kansas City children enjoy camp activities. It was the first visit to a state park for some of them. *Shalonn Curls*

swamp white oak, silver maple, and many other species.

This park, now nearly 4,000 acres, attracts over a quarter of a million visitors a year. Most of them come from nearby Whiteman Air Force Base, Warrensburg, Sedalia, and the Kansas City area. Its two group camps have been renovated and can be rented by nonprofit groups. The park offers two fishing lakes and seven trails totaling nearly twenty miles, including longer trails for mountain biking and horses.

Come and set up your camp in the shady public campground. Enjoy some quiet fishing or kayaking in Clearfork or Buteo Lake. Take advantage of a naturalist-led program or guided walk. Bring a mountain bike to ride the Opossum Hollow Trail or your horse to ride the McAdoo Trail. Hike out to a prairie or woodland area, listen to the dickcissels calling in the tall bluestem, and imagine the old Missouri landscape as Ephraim Anderson saw it. In the evening, you can enjoy your own golden campfire. The dark summer night still resounds with whippoorwills and barred owls. The fireflies still flicker like tiny stars, and the glow of a circle of friends or family can still create magical memories. *

KNOB NOSTER STATE PARK • 873 SOUTHEAST 10, KNOB NOSTER

Bothwell Lodge State Historic Site

SEDALIA IS PROBABLY BEST KNOWN to the world at large as the temporary home of ragtime genius Scott Joplin, the place where he wrote the "Maple Leaf Rag," named after a former popular Sedalia nightclub. Missourians probably know Sedalia best as the home of the Missouri State Fair. Thousands of Missouri families over the years have traveled north from Sedalia along Highway 65 after a visit to the fair and have noted the large stone castle standing prominently on a bluff just a few miles north of town. Many have wondered what this building was and who owned it. Any Pettis County local could have told them.

In 1979 the old stone lodge and the surrounding 180 acres—now nearly 250—were dedicated as Bothwell State Park, later changed to Bothwell Lodge State Historic Site. Now the state park system is the caretaker and storyteller for this intriguing old estate. John Homer Bothwell, a Pettis County attorney and businessman, moved to Missouri in 1871. He married the daughter of a prominent Sedalia family, Hattie Ellen Jaynes, in 1884. Hattie died only a few years later after contracting an unknown illness, and he never remarried. Bothwell was active in local politics and served Pettis County in the Missouri General Assembly for four terms, running unsuccessfully for governor in 1904. He also helped to make Sedalia the permanent home of the State Fair.

After purchasing the beautiful bluff-top property in 1896, Bothwell began construction of the home he called Stonyridge Farm. He used native rock from the estate grounds, and the house grew in a rambling fashion. Four independent sections are tied together. In a combination storage area and workroom below the library, a wooden box covers an opening to a shaft that drops directly into a cave below the house. The shaft links the cave to a winding stairwell in the tower, which has doors and windows that can be opened to create a draft that pulls naturally cooled air up into the house.

As a bachelor of means, Bothwell enjoyed both traveling afar and entertaining numerous guests at home. Stonyridge reflected all of this in its informal atmosphere and eclectic furnishings, from Mission style to wicker, with souvenirs from his travels and an occasional stuffed and mounted animal. Bothwell appreciated the natural world, and he grieved that much of the timber atop the ridge had been cut just before he acquired the property. He spent years restoring the native vegetation, and he constructed a half-mile trail along the wooded slope surrounding the lodge. This charming trail was popular with his guests, providing stone steps in steep spots, benches for resting, and a small picnic shelter.

Left: John Homer Bothwell's Stonyridge estate, located north of Sedalia, was added to the state park system in 1974. The structure has been intriguing guests since the turn of the twentieth century. *Oliver Schuchard* • Above: The castle, perched on its high bluff, is surrounded by a short trail that leads guests along the wooded slope. *Kevin Walker* • Top right: The well-appointed library of Bothwell's bachelor aerie still holds many of his books. *Missouri State Parks*

The house is built over two natural caves, with an ingenious shaft into one of them. On hot, humid summer days, a series of small doors and windows were opened, creating a draft that pulled cool cave air up into the house, room by room.

Bothwell prospered into his old age, continuing to provide easygoing hospitality until his death in 1929, and even after. His will provided that the estate should continue to serve as a recreational retreat for his friends and ultimately for the people of Missouri. The state accepted Bothwell Lodge in 1974, and today, it continues to entertain and refresh visitors from far and near.

A trip to this site properly begins with a visit to the lodge, which could be described as an overgrown English cottage. It has three levels and thirty rooms; twenty are visible on tour. If Hattie Bothwell had lived, she might have brought a more delicate touch to the decor, but the furnishings are of good quality and comfortable. A favorite room is the library; when you go inside, it's easy to imagine the widely read and curious Bothwell enjoying the fine woodwork and extensive collection of handsomely housed books, including many first editions from the 1870s and 1880s, as well as the lovely view of the valley below his estate. The cozy fireplace must have made this a favorite retreat in the wintertime, too.

Bothwell's Stonyridge Trail has been refurbished and still offers a pleasant walk. Many of the trees along this forested slope are sugar maples, so fall walks can be especially beautiful among the orange and golden leaves. In 2006, the site opened a longer and more challenging three-mile route, the Radiant Trail, named after a favorite poem of John Bothwell. He believed above all in enjoying nature's radiance and bequeathed his home and grounds to the state so future generations of Missourians could also enjoy them. *

BOTHWELL LODGE STATE HISTORIC SITE • 19349 BOTHWELL STATE PARK ROAD, SEDALIA

Rock Island Trail State Park

THE CHICAGO, ROCK ISLAND, AND PACIFIC RAILROAD was sometimes described as "one railroad too many" in the late nineteenth and early twentieth centuries. It began operations in 1852 as the Chicago and Rock Island Railroad, operating trains between those two cities. It later expanded, with transcontinental aspirations, but Colorado and New Mexico were as close as it ever got to the Pacific. The Rock Island seemed to have left early but arrived late, as its expansions tended to bring it into head-to-head competition with well-established rail lines that had more direct routes, leaving the Rock Island to build over less favorable terrain and more circuitous routes.

In 1902 the Rock Island acquired the St. Louis, Kansas City, and Colorado Railroad to obtain a route from St. Louis to Kansas City competing with the Missouri Pacific and the Missouri-Kansas-Texas railroads. However, the SLKC&C was largely imaginary, existing at the time only from St. Louis to Bland in the eastern Ozarks. Its completion across the upper Ozarks to Kansas City required expensive construction, including an enormous trestle across the Gasconade River valley, scads of other bridges, and no fewer than four tunnels. The line opened for business in 1905, but it was competing with long-established lines that already had more direct routes between Missouri's two largest cities.

This reckless competitiveness all across the Midwest sent the Chicago, Rock Island, and Pacific into receivership three different times, the last being in 1980, when the business was dissolved and its routes sold to other roads in a bankruptcy settlement of mind-boggling complexity. This tangle of railroad business is of interest, of course, because of the 1983 Rails-to-Trails Act, which amended the 1968 National Trails Act to permit the preservation of railroad corridors by long-term, interim use as hiking and biking trails. Missouri's first project was the Katy Trail, after the Interstate Commerce Commission (ICC) granted a certificate of interim trail use from St. Charles to Sedalia in 1987, and later from Sedalia to Clinton across the Osage Plains.

Where the Rock Island roadbed crosses diagonally through the meandering loops of Big Creek east of the former village of Wingate, hikers and cyclists will discover a shady path through bottomland forest. *Google Earth*

State park planners and trail enthusiasts never lost sight of their long-range goal: a hiking and biking trail all the way across Missouri. As it happened, the Southern Pacific Railroad acquired the Rock Island Line in Missouri during the bankruptcy proceedings, then announced its intent to abandon it. In 1993, the Missouri Department of Natural Resources (DNR) filed a formal request with the ICC to secure a 197-mile segment from Owensville in Gasconade County to Kansas City, in large part to make possible a link with the Katy Trail at Windsor, thus allowing for completion of a trail across the state. The Missouri Rail Trail Foundation pledged funds set aside for this acquisition through the foresight of Ted Jones, who had died in 1990. But Union Pacific, which donated the segment of the MKT from Sedalia through Windsor to Clinton that made the link with the Rock Island possible, petitioned the ICC for the twenty-six-mile right-of-way from Kansas City to Pleasant Hill for coal trains, and the ICC approved. Though a local group was still trying to raise funds to restart rail service on the part of the line between Pleasant Hill and Owensville, DNR in 1994 signed a contingent contract with the Southern Pacific for that stretch of line.

When the dust finally settled, Ameren Corporation—an energy company—wound up owning the Rock Island rail line from Pleasant Hill east to Maryland Heights in the St. Louis suburbs, a hedge against possible problems hauling coal from the West for its midwestern power plants. Even though Ameren had no immediate plans to run trains on the western part of the line, it still declined to strike a deal with the state to provide for a link from the Katy Trail at Windsor to Pleasant Hill, from which a series of local trails might extend farther into Kansas City. Then, in the predawn of December 14, 2005, the dam at Ameren's pump storage reservoir on Proffit Mountain in Reynolds County collapsed and the resulting deluge tore the heart out of Johnson's Shut-Ins State Park. The final damage settlement for the disaster included Ameren's somewhat reluctant agreement to license the state to construct a trail from Windsor to Pleasant Hill on its Rock Island right-of-way, but not on the rail bed, along with some $18 million in settlement funds for the purpose, in addition to reconstruction at the Shut-Ins.

In a sort of strange stasis, a disaster in one part of the state park system had created an opportunity in another: finally the vision of a cross-state hiking and biking trail linking St. Louis and Kansas City had come within reach. It wouldn't be simple; Ameren didn't even own much of the land in the right-of-way. The state would have to bargain with dozens of individual landowners and construct new bridges and crossings as well as a safe surface for hikers and bicyclists. Even after Ameren finally agreed in 2011 to abandon the segment under the National Rails to Trails Act so the new trail could be developed on the current rail bed after all, major obstacles remained. Decades of neglect had not been kind to the old Chicago, Rock Island, and Pacific. Sizable trees had grown up between the rails. Bridges had deteriorated, and even the roadbed itself had eroded and washed out in places. But, it is a beautiful forty-seven-mile stretch of Missouri countryside. Even though it wasn't the easiest terrain over which to build a rail line in the first place, as a trail, it will provide a scenic biking and hiking experience of both natural and historical significance.

Names of both current and former towns along the route are intriguing, some obvious, some not so. New Castle? An easy one, surrounded by coal

The nearly mile-long and 100-foot-high Rock Island trestle spans not only the Gasconade River but also its entire valley. *Zachary Gillihan* • An old song about the Rock Island Line has a joke about pigs and pig iron, but here, cows mosey along the bed where locomotives once hauled freight. *Missouri State Parks*

mines. Post Oak? Purely descriptive. Chilhowee? Native American, but how and why? Haddon. Denton. Hadsell. Wingate. Prominent locals? Railroad executives? Trail users will have some history to ponder as they ride.

Some of these small communities will benefit economically from the Rock Island Trail, just as many have from the Katy Trail. Other towns may be too far gone, with not enough of a core left to benefit from the stimulation. The pretty little town of Leeton has a small café, and perhaps a bike repair business might take root there. Chilhowee has three hundred residents, but no café; a dependable stream of trail users could support one, a benefit for locals and travelers alike.

The civil engineers who laid out the Rock Island Line from Windsor to the west were diligent in their profession, keeping the line as level as possible while crossing the fewest number of watercourses. From its intersection with the Katy Trail a short distance northeast of Windsor, the Rock Island curves in a gentle arc northward to Leeton, and from there arcs south again as it proceeds west to Chilhowee, making a twenty-mile-long, shallow S curve. The idea was to follow the high ground, first bending north to avoid the Tebo Creek's upper reaches, which flow south toward the Osage River, and then bowing back south to stay clear of the Blackwater drainage, which flows north toward the Missouri River. The strategy was not without problems. The high ground between the drainages is broken country, and there were many small swales to cross, most containing rivulets or shallow creeks—more than two dozen of them between Windsor and Chilhowee.

The engineering solution to this problem was to raise the rail bed on earthen fills as it crossed the valleys, with culverts below to let the water pass. This allowed the rails to remain relatively level across the low spots, in much the same way as the Romans crossed valleys with their aqueducts. These fills are of varying heights and visual interest and will make for entertaining riding and hiking where they are high and narrow. With careful thinning of brush and smaller trees, users may ride or walk

Hikers and cyclists will enjoy the lofty view from the trestle bridge. *Zachary Gillihan* • Work is underway west of Windsor to convert the former rail line to a trail. *Chris Crocker* • When the Rock Island reached Windsor in 1904, it passed beneath the already existing Katy Railroad. This bridge and underpass is now the junction of the Katy Trail with the Rock Island Trail, as the Katy heads southwest to Clinton and the Rock Island heads west to Kansas City. *Susan Flader* Above right: Missouri already has the longest rail-to-trail conversion in the country with the Katy Trail State Park, but the state will have an almost 400-mile loop when the Rock Island is connected. *Missouri Life*

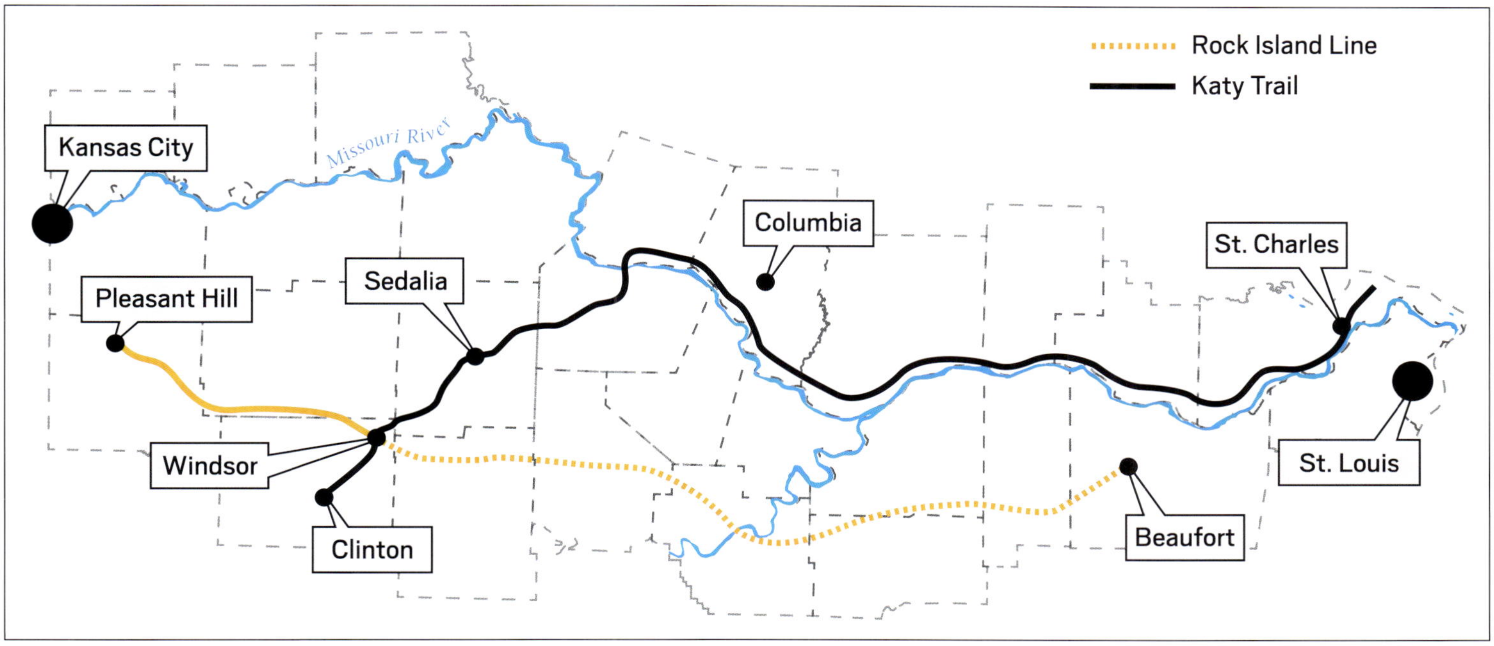

in dappled shade for long stretches, while still having pastoral views of picturesque farmsteads.

Adding historical interest to this portion of the trail are the occasional landscape features that resulted from extensive coal mining in the last century, one of the original justifications for building a railroad through this part of Missouri. Between Leeton and Chilhowee, the abandoned, raised roadbed of the MKT can be seen running parallel and only a few feet away from the Rock Island roadbed, underscoring the Rock Island's problem of coming late to a route where a competing railroad was in place. Near Chilhowee, the character of the countryside changes into a more upland, prairie-like landscape. The horizons open outward, the sky seems larger, and there are fewer swales where the roadbed crosses on fill.

For the next twenty or so miles, the Rock Island bit the bullet. The larger stream crossings that were so carefully skirted from east of Chilhowee became unavoidable farther west, if the line was to reach Kansas City. Beginning just west of the crossroads hamlet of Denton, the route passes through many stretches of low, marshy bottomland. Although much of this bottomland has been drained and is now cultivated, trail users will still have the pleasure of many stretches where the dense forest seems to enclose the right-of-way. Bikers and hikers will pass through a high and dry, leafy tunnel above the swampy ground, while experiencing an entirely different complement of animal and plant life than on the higher ground. In these bottoms are the meander channels of numerous larger creeks with relatively little sign of man-made activity other than the rail bed itself. There is one man-made lake, the Rock Island Lake, over which the dam provides passage for the trail. Veteran trail hands may recognize this as a water supply point for steam locomotives.

In the vicinity of White Oak and Bear Creeks, the route runs for nearly three miles with no road crossings. The county road builders avoided this low, marshy country, though the railroad could not. It was a difficult place to build a railroad. Within a stretch of only seven or eight miles, the Rock Island crossed successively Lost Creek, Hornsby Branch, Crawford Creek, and finally Big Creek—a civil engineer's nightmare of elevated roadbed, mushy ground, driven pilings, and bridges crossing the same meandering streams multiple times. These lush riparian zones make for great cycling and hiking, and with only three road crossings in this whole section of the trail, deep woods solitude is nearly guaranteed.

After the crossing of Big Creek comes the former village of Wingate, and from there the railroad, now the trail, stays in the valley of Big Creek, running parallel to the stream all the way into Pleasant Hill. This section is low and flat, mostly cleared farm ground with a nice stand of timber along the right-of-way. The route makes one last crossing of Big Creek, and it's a dandy, crossing over the creek and under a highway at the same time. From the trailhead at Wingate west into Pleasant Hill, a pilot section of the trail is open for visitor use. Cyclists will find that Pleasant Hill is pleasant indeed—a bicycle-friendly town, with bike lanes, road separations, and special signage. The Rock Island Trail State Park ends here, and from Pleasant Hill on into Kansas City, a new route will be patched together and maintained by a coalition of municipal recreation agencies and organizations.

As plans for the Rock Island route toward Kansas City neared resolution in 2014, Ameren unexpectedly announced its intent to sell its long-held but never used 144-mile stretch of the Rock Island from Windsor east through Eldon and Owensville and on to Beaufort—presumably for the multimillion dollar salvage value of the rails. When communities and organizations along the route, in partnership with the national Rails-to-Trails Conservancy, sought to enter the bidding process in order to establish rail trails, DNR reiterated its interest in the project, sought ever since 1993. Ameren agreed to donate the corridor for a trail, and salvage of the rails is underway. Meanwhile, rail banking was approved in early 2015 for the leg west of Windsor, and work shot ahead. Because the challenge and expense of developing the eastern leg through the Ozarks, which includes three tunnels and a mile-long, 100-foot-high trestle over the Gasconade River, will be enormous, state park officials will likely partner with communities and organizations to foster local initiatives in developing certain stretches.

> *The Rock Island will not only eventually open another scenic trail but also, with the addition of a spur to the Katy Trail from Beaufort via Washington, complete a gigantic continuous loop trail totaling nearly four hundred miles along the river, across the plains, and through the Ozark hills.*

On the Rock Island both west and east of its junction with the Katy Trail at Windsor, there are still engineering problems—bridges and hydrology—and funding and property issues to be resolved. Nonetheless, the time is again coming when, as the old song says: "The Rock Island Line is a mighty good road; The Rock Island Line is the road to ride." *

ROCK ISLAND TRAIL STATE PARK • TRAILHEADS AT WINDSOR AND ELSEWHERE

GLACIATED PLAINS

"This is probably the easiest unsettled country in the world to commence farming in. The emigrant has only to locate himself on the edge of a prairie, and he has the one-half of his farm a heavy forest and the other half a fertile plain or meadow. He has then only to fence in his ground and put in his crop."
—Samuel R. Brown, *Western Gazetteer or Emigrant's Directory*, 1817

THE CONTINENTAL ICE SHEETS covered the northern third of the state reaching about as far south as the Missouri River, which was largely formed by outwash from the melting glaciers. Thus, the land surface of the Glaciated Plains natural division is younger than that of the Osage Plains and other unglaciated portions of the state, with generally deeper soils formed primarily from glacial till and windblown silts or alluvium. Prairie covered about 45 percent of the area, primarily on the more level uplands but with wet prairie along some of the major streams, while savanna, woodland, and forest covered the slopes and many bottomlands. Topography, soils, and vegetation vary considerably within the Glaciated Plains region.

We begin in the east in the Lincoln Hills along the Mississippi River, an area of steep topography with bedrock exposures of Mississippian and Ordovician age. This area of almost Ozark-like ruggedness was a mosaic of oak forest woodland, savanna, and some open prairie in presettlement times. Bluffs, glades, and karst features such as caves and sinkholes have resulted in a biota similar to the Ozarks but with some species more characteristic of areas to the north. The Lincoln Hills are well represented by the substantially restored natural communities of 6,400-acre Cuivre River State Park, with its limestone bluffs, wooded valleys, remnant and restored prairies, and a richly diverse flora and fauna.

Immediately to the west are several parks in more rolling terrain drained by the various branches of the Salt River that flow eastward to the Mississippi. Originally, this was a region of glacial till prairie and savanna, which is now farmland, or in places, mined land. Fitting for an area settled by migrants pushing upstream from the Mississippi, the region is represented by two historic sites and a related park. Far and away the best known denizen of the Salt River hills is Samuel Langhorne Clemens, born in 1835 in Florida, Missouri, in a two-room cabin now enshrined about a quarter-mile away in a modern museum at Mark Twain Birthplace State Historic Site. Mark Twain State Park, which surrounds the birthplace and museum, was assembled in 1924 to preserve his childhood haunts, but in an irony of fate symptomatic of our times, the river valley setting of his youth is now drowned by a huge reservoir named Mark Twain Lake. Fifteen miles west on the Elk Fork of the Salt River is Union Covered Bridge, which preserves a structure from the 1870s.

In the central part of the Glaciated Plains are lands drained by the Chariton and Grand Rivers and their tributaries, which flow south to the Missouri River. This region was originally about half savanna and half woodland and prairie, wooded in the breaks along the stream drainages, but with wet prairies and marshes along the broad floodplains of the major rivers, and dry prairies on the rolling hills. Moving generally westward, we reach Thousand Hills State Park west of Kirksville in a belt of hills that shelters Indian petroglyphs and rare occurrences of the large-toothed aspen, a plant usually found much farther north. Long Branch State Park, on the shores of an Army Corps of Engineers reservoir farther downstream on the Chariton River, presents restored remnants of the savanna and prairie landscape that greeted early settlers, along with reservoir-based recreation.

Rattlesnake master and prairie blazing star festoon Sherwood Prairie in Cuivre River State Park, a small remnant of tallgrass prairie that once was common on the Glaciated Plains. This was the first site in the park system to benefit from prescribed fire beginning in the mid-1970s, but similar vistas can now be seen at other north Missouri parks such as Mark Twain and Long Branch. ***Bruce Schuette***

In the Grand River drainage to the west are several sites associated with military leaders of the World War I era: Gen. John J. Pershing, leader of the American Expeditionary Force in Europe and the highest ranking military officer in US history, and Gen. Enoch Crowder, founder of the Selective Service System.

Three sites associated with General Pershing are in Linn County near Laclede, where he grew up. The Pershing Historic Site in Laclede includes his boyhood home, the one-room Prairie Mound School where he once taught, and several other period buildings. Pershing State Park preserves the childhood landscape in which the general was raised, including superb wet prairie and forested bottomlands along Locust Creek, one of the last sizable stream segments in northern Missouri that has not been channelized. Locust Creek Covered Bridge, which Pershing knew as a boy, sits at the north end of the park, eight hundred feet away from the "improved" channel of Locust Creek, a monument to the wave of stream straightening that afflicted north Missouri from the 1920s to the 1950s.

To the west, Crowder State Park in Grundy County preserves General Crowder's boyhood stomping grounds along the rough, wooded drainages of the Big Thompson River, like Locust Creek a tributary to the Grand. On the border of Caldwell and Clinton Counties, closer to Kansas City, is Wallace State Park near Shoal Creek, which drains to the lower Grand. Wallace, which includes a superb example of old-growth north Missouri upland forest, is a wooded oasis amid fertile farmlands where thousands of Mormons once had settled.

The westernmost portion of the Glaciated Plains is characterized by thick mounds of loess on bluffs along the Missouri River and extending back from it. Because this is some of the richest, though highly erodible, agricultural land in the state, little prairie remains. Watkins Woolen Mill State Historic Site and Park in Clay County near Kansas City provides a fine introduction to the riches of the area. A prosperous agricultural plantation since its settlement by Waltus Watkins in the 1830s, the operation by the 1860s included a major industrial woolen mill with four floors filled with machinery. It is the nation's only nineteenth-century textile factory with its original machinery still intact, and it has been designated a National Historic Landmark.

Much of Missouri's reputation as a leading agricultural state derives from the deep rich soils of north Missouri's Glaciated Plains and the sturdy farmers who settled and developed that land. Park visitors to this region will find expansive vistas of that legacy, still productive and inspiring, but also wooded and watered refuges of earlier landscapes that evoke the fiber of the leaders that this land produced, leaders for Missouri and also for the nation. *

Cuivre River State Park

THE CUIVRE RIVER barely touches the southwestern edge of the state park that bears its name in Lincoln County. But the juxtaposition is dramatic: a high cliff of Mississippian limestone known locally as Frenchman's Bluff drops off sharply to the river. From the vantage point of the park, one can take in a sweeping view of the rich alluvial farmland stretching along the valley.

Such striking topography may, at first, seem out of place north of the Missouri River. The rugged landscape, the rich woodlands, the limestone glades, the upland sinkhole ponds: all seem more representative of the Ozarks region south of the river. But Cuivre (pronounced quiver) River State Park is located at the southern end of a sixty-mile stretch of uplifted bedrock known as the Lincoln Hills. While continental glaciers scoured and buried the land north of the Missouri River with debris, the Lincoln Hills somehow escaped most of this. Glacial erratics are found throughout the hills, yet today, the hills remain a biological island with an assemblage of plants and animals not usually found on the glaciated plains of northern Missouri.

The state park consists of more than 6,400 acres centered on Big Sugar Creek, a tributary of Cuivre River; more than eight miles of Big Sugar within the park have been designated by the Missouri Clean Water Commission as an Outstanding State Resource Water. The creek has carved a lovely valley through limestones formed from warm-sea sediments laid down more than 300 million years ago. That ancient sea was home to multi-armed animals called crinoids or sea lilies. Related to starfish and sea urchins, the crinoids once carpeted the sea bottom, and their fossil remains are plentiful in the Mississippian-age rocks exposed in the park. In fact, the crinoid is now the official state fossil.

Eons after the last crinoid died on the sea floor and turned to stone, and long after the resulting rock formations were uplifted, folded, and eroded, the Cuivre River area was inhabited by humans. American Indians arrived in the area as early as ten thousand years ago, and archaeologists have identified their villages, campsites, burial mounds, and ceremonial areas in and around the park. French explorers and settlers came next, hence the names for the bluff and the river: *cuivre* means copper in French, but some think the river was originally named in honor of Georges Cuvier, a noted French paleontologist and naturalist.

Cuivre River is one of three state parks initially acquired by the National Park Service as Recreation Demonstration Areas (RDAs) through the 1933 National Industrial Recovery Act. RDAs were supposed to provide economic and work relief by developing parks from sub-marginal farmland near cities to give urban residents opportunities for outdoor recreation. Most of the forty-six areas acquired nationwide had been badly abused; the lands at Cuivre had been cutover and eroded, with the valleys planted with crops and the uplands grazed by cattle. Two New Deal agencies, the Civilian Conservation Corps (CCC) and the Works Progress Administration, built many of the park's facilities: the roads, bridges, picnic shelter, and group camps. In 1946 the Cuivre lands, along with RDAs at Lake of the Ozarks and Knob Noster, were transferred to the state.

Group camps—Camp Sherwood Forest, Camp Derricotte, and Camp Cuivre—are a special feature of the park. Generations of eastern Missouri schoolchildren first encountered wild nature through one of the organized school, church, or other group camp sessions at Cuivre River State Park. Most of the campers came straight from the world of asphalt and concrete. The natural world was new to them. Just as the New Deal was attempting to rehabilitate the lands of the park, so too were the group camps

Right: Frenchman's Bluff brings a touch of the Ozarks to the Lincoln Hills of northeast Missouri, and you can reach it by park trails or by road. ***Tom Nagel***
Above: This restored oak-hickory woodland features tickseed sunflowers, elm leaf goldenrod, muhly grass, and wild legumes. ***Bruce Schuette***

ONE OF THE MOST BIOLOGICALLY DIVERSE PARKS

Today, Cuivre River State Park is recognized as one of the most ecologically significant and biologically diverse parks in the Missouri system. More than seven hundred species of native vascular plants occur here, seventy-nine of which rank as "highly conservative" species, meaning they are found only in high quality, undisturbed communities of great conservation value.

The entire park is an Important Bird Area, with 190 species recorded, plus more than eighty kinds of butterflies. The park harbors many species at the edge of their range; such species tend to exhibit greater genetic variability and are critical for maintaining biological diversity.

More than twenty species here have not been found in any other Missouri state park—including eight that have not been found anywhere else in the state—and two species are new to science. In the database of species for the entire Missouri park system, Cuivre River has twice as many animal and plant species entered as any other park.

That's not bad for a park that was acquired as a depleted area, pieced together from more than fifty private holdings in the Great Depression.

Its geologic history and topographic roughness certainly help, as does its proximity to the Mississippi River, which increased the downcutting and weathering of glacial material, exposing preglacial features that created microhabitats attractive to floral and faunal species from both north and south. Its size and relatively long time as a park also help to enhance diversity.

Perhaps the most critical factor has been the decades of active restoration effort here. Several state parks have benefited from long-term stewardship by skilled and dedicated naturalists, but perhaps none more so than Cuivre. Bruce Schuette began here as a summer worker in 1977 and devoted himself to restoring Cuivre until his retirement in 2014. That is rare, and it has made an extraordinary difference here.

The challenge will be to maintain this rigorous attentiveness and care, combined with research and monitoring, in the face of continued threats from invasive species, trampling, and overuse in the most populous area of the state.

Many woodland wildflowers such as wild bergamot (above) and gray-headed coneflower (below) have responded vigorously to controlled burning and dot the savanna-like border of the Lincoln Glade area. *Both Bruce Schuette*

an effort to invigorate the health and imaginations of the young campers.

Camp Sherwood Forest, designed and built in cooperation with the Park and Playground Association of St. Louis, is a perfect example of the traditional New Deal group camp. Fifty-three CCC buildings and other structures still remain, most restored for use. Evoking the Robin Hood theme, the camp consists of four isolated villages—named Ancaster, Locksley Chase, Nottingham, and Fountain Dale—each with five cabins for up to eight campers, two counselors' cabins, and a unit lodge, outdoor kitchen, and shower house, each accessible from the rest of the camp by foot trails through the woods. Central facilities include a dining lodge, recreation hall, infirmary, and administrative buildings, plus an amphitheater and council circle with a flagstone campfire area and split-log seats. Originally operated under the supervision of the Park and Playground Association (forerunner of the Sherwood Forest Camping Association) with assistance from various social agencies and charities, the camp developed a ritualized program intended to instill the spirit of "friendship, cooperation, and learning" and even more, an appreciation of the workings and values of citizenship in children from the inner city. In recent decades, the camps have been available for rental by a wide range of organizations for everything from religious retreats, group gatherings, and family reunions to music or sports camps, and 4-H, scouting, and school activities.

Cuivre River State Park, itself an assemblage of restored and preserved natural communities and cultural resources, is an ideal setting in which to learn the meaning of resource stewardship. One might begin with a trip along the main park roads, where the New Deal relief workers in the 1930s painstakingly constructed masonry check dams, curbing, guttering, and culverts to keep roadside ditches from washing out and to direct the flow from one side of the road to the other. Much of this conscientious engineering is now enrolled, along with Camp Sherwood Forest and other structures, on the National Register of Historic Places.

New Deal workers with the Civilian Conservation Corps or the Works Progress Administration built many structures, now on the National Register of Historic Places. The bridge at the entrance spans Little Sugar Creek. ***Bruce Schuette***

The natural environment has recovered to such a degree that the park now boasts three state natural areas—Big Sugar Creek (56 acres), George A. Hamilton Forest (40 acres), and Lincoln Hills (1,872 acres)—together covering more than 30 percent of the park. There are two state wild areas totaling nearly 3,000 acres, partially overlapping two of the natural areas. Both wild areas straddle Big Sugar Creek—Northwoods is north of Route KK, while Big Sugar Creek is to the south—and both feature a canopy dominated by sturdy white oak.

Big Sugar Creek Natural Area, designated in 1979, extends along and a hundred feet on each side of the northern headwaters of the creek

A misty morning along Big Sugar Creek in the Lincoln Hills Natural Area invites quiet reflection or exploration. *Bruce Schuette* • The hot sun and the cool water beckon swimmers at the Lake Lincoln beach. *Missouri State Parks*

within the Northwoods Wild Area. The creek has a gravel or limestone bottom with a gradient of fourteen feet per mile and is partially spring-fed, like an Ozark stream. However, the springs are intermittent, allowing for warmer water in the pools. The eighteen or more fish species and other aquatic life here show the transition between Ozark and prairie streams. With much of its watershed protected by the park, Big Sugar Creek is one of the least disturbed streams in northeast Missouri. A bottomland forest of sycamore, cottonwood, black walnut, box elder, hackberry, and Ohio buckeye grows along its banks.

Toward the southern end of the park along the main road, the George A. Hamilton Forest Natural Area was designated in 1983 and named after an owner who protected this valley before the park was formed. It features a mature white oak forest, one of the finest mature stands in the Lincoln Hills of north Missouri. Abundant spring wildflowers adorn steep limestone slopes that drain into Big Sugar Creek.

In the large expanse of Big Sugar Creek watershed in the middle of the park, a tiny natural area was designated in 1978 to protect Pickerelweed Pond, a three-quarter-acre upland sinkhole pond. By 1997 the natural area had been expanded to the 1,872-acre Lincoln Hills Natural Area—the park's pride and joy today. Sinkhole ponds are karst topographic features that dot much of the soluble limestone terrain of the Ozarks and this part of Lincoln Hills. Sinkhole ponds have often been misunderstood and abused, whether through drainage, sedimentation, alteration for livestock, or use as convenient dumping grounds. Yet these ponds served—and Pickerelweed Pond still serves—as refuge for some of the park's rarest inhabitants, like the Missouri park system's only known population of the beautiful pickerelweed, a planthopper, and a species of bee that feeds only on the planthopper; the bee cannot be found anywhere else in the state. For some species like the rare ringed salamander, these ponds provide a breeding habitat at the northern extreme of their global range. Pickerelweed Pond was the one sinkhole in north Missouri that retained sufficient integrity to be designated a natural area in 1978. Park staff have since excavated fill from another sinkhole, one that had been filled in the 1940s to create a playing field, thus reestablishing another rare functional sinkhole pond wetland community.

Equally significant, as early as the 1970s, park naturalists began a program of prescribed burning, often accompanied by thinning and removal of invasive species, to restore remnant prairie openings, glades, and woodlands characteristic of the area as described by the earliest travelers and surveyors. The first experimental use of prescribed fire by park naturalists anywhere in the state park system was in 1977 on Sac Prairie just south of the road to Camp Sherwood Forest. The prairie still retained long-dormant seed stock of such species as big bluestem, Indian grass, rattlesnake master, butterfly weed, and prairie blazing star, which responded vigorously after the fire. Even more important, where the fire burned into adjacent woods, woodland wildflowers also responded, leading to the landscape-scale use of fire in woodlands not only at Cuivre but elsewhere in the state park system. The park also contains most of the ecologically significant limestone glades in this quadrant of Missouri, and they also were enhanced by prescribed fire after mechanical clearing of red cedar. Since 1977, some 2,000 acres of prairies, woodlands, and glades have been periodically burned under the supervision of park naturalists. More than 60 percent of total park acreage is in special ecological management areas, tracts designated for various types of stewardship or restoration.

The park offers excellent programs and nature walks headquartered at a visitor center with exhibits on the natural and cultural history of the park and the Lincoln Hills. A dozen different hiking, backpacking, biking, and equestrian trails total some thirty-five miles. The trails take you through the wild areas, the natural areas, to Frenchman's Bluff, and to still other scenic places; you can spend days exploring them. The 50-acre Lake Lincoln is popular for swimming and fishing, and there are numerous campsites and picnic areas.

Even the entrance to Cuivre River State Park is special. Following a narrow corridor of public land north from Route 47, you are gently removed from the asphalt and speed of the workaday world and drawn into the peaceful wooded hills and valleys of Cuivre. When you cross the hand-crafted triple-arched stone bridge over Little Sugar Creek, day-to-day cares seem distant, and you feel somehow reborn. Cuivre River is a park of hope, where nature has regenerated and people may too. *

CUIVRE RIVER STATE PARK • 678 ROUTE 147, TROY

Mark Twain Birthplace State Historic Site

On any list of Missourians who have contributed to our national culture and to world heritage, the name of Samuel Langhorne Clemens, better known as Mark Twain, ranks preeminently. As creator of such masterpieces as *Adventures of Huckleberry Finn, The Adventures of Tom Sawyer,* and *Life on the Mississippi,* he is one of America's foremost storytellers, humorists, and masters of language. While providing the world with enduring wit and wisdom, Mark Twain's imagination remained deeply rooted in his home state. Twain's genius enriches the world, but he remains also the keenest observer and literary interpreter of Missouri.

Huckleberry Finn and Tom Sawyer are not only timeless examples of the quintessential all-American boy, but they are also the best portraits ever penned of nineteenth-century Missouri youth. Jim is not only the symbol for a whole class of long-suffering black Americans, but he is also an exemplar of their human aspirations. Huck and Jim's journey down the river into humanity has become a classic of world literature.

A great artist portrays individual experience so well that universal human experiences are illuminated. No literary artist performed this magic more successfully than Mark Twain. And the specific, individual world of experience that Mark Twain drew upon centered around his boyhood in the Missouri countryside and along the Mississippi River. To a degree, the land and people that shaped his life can still be found in northeast Missouri. And the story of his birth and early childhood are told at one of Missouri's most important shrines: the Mark Twain Birthplace State Historic Site at Florida, Missouri.

In 1835, the Clemens family moved from Tennessee to Monroe County, Missouri, at the suggestion of relatives who had already made the trip. The family settled in the four-year-old village of Florida, between the North and Middle Forks of the Salt River in a region of rolling hills, oak forests, and small prairies. As Twain recalled in his autobiography, the village had "two streets, each a couple of hundred yards long; the rest of the avenues mere lanes, with rail fences and cornfields on either side. Both the streets and the lanes were paved with the same material —tough black mud in wet times, deep dust in dry."

Upon seeing a picture of the simple cabin years later, Mark Twain wrote, "Heretofore, I have always stated that it was a palace, but I shall be more guarded now."

On November 30, 1835, in a rented two-room clapboard cabin, Samuel Langhorne Clemens was born, the sixth child of John and Jane Clemens. That cabin still stands, though its setting has changed dramatically. In 1839 the Clemens family moved to Hannibal on the Mississippi River in Marion County. Even after this move of some thirty miles, young Sam returned to spend summers with his many cousins on his uncle John Quarles's farm, maintained by thirty slaves, just north of Florida. This was the countryside that Sam Clemens roamed, as biographer A. B. Paine recalled, "hunting berries and nuts, drinking sugar-water, tying love knots in love-vine, picking the petals from daisies."

Sam Clemens's world expanded after he left school at the age of twelve, first learning the printing trade in Hannibal, then working as an itinerant printer in several eastern cities, and especially as he earned his living working as a riverboat pilot on the Mississippi River. After the Civil War broke out, in response to the governor's call to activate the state

militia and along with thousands of fellow Missourians, Clemens volunteered to help defend the state against the Yankees. He and some companions formed the short-lived Marion County Rangers. As lieutenant of this company, Clemens spent a few weeks in the summer of 1861 drilling with the Rangers in the hills and draws of Ralls and Monroe Counties, ending up near his birthplace village of Florida. There, they caught word that Col. Ulysses S. Grant and the Twenty-first Illinois Infantry were headed their way with the intent of destroying their militia unit before it could join up with Col. Tom Harris and his Confederate troops.

Clemens quickly abandoned the war and "lit out for the territories." In leaving, he commenced a remarkable set of adventures and launched his career as a writer under the name Mark Twain, a term meaning two fathoms (twelve feet) of river depth, borrowed from his days as a river pilot.

Many who read Mark Twain's works find, in addition to wit, humor, and good-natured insight, an underlying tension of competing values. Some credit part of Mark Twain's creative genius to the artist's conflicting loves for rural simplicity and urban progress, for the Southern flavor of his boyhood and the Yankee respectability he later craved. Could there be a more likely home for such a genius than Missouri?

So, how do we acknowledge the legend? More specifically, how should the state honor this extraordinary son? Not all could agree on an answer. Shortly after Mark Twain died in 1910 at his home in Redding, Connecticut, groups formed to seek appropriate commemoration. The Missouri General Assembly in 1911 authorized a bust and a monument. The bronze bust, created by R. P. Bringhurst, and the monument were erected in 1914 at the corner of Main and Mill streets in Florida. In addition, Merritt Alexander "Dad" Violette, whose mother had known the Clemens family in Florida, bought the seriously deteriorated birthplace cabin in 1915, moved it across the street to property he owned, rehabilitated it, furnished it in a nineteenth-century manner, and opened it to the public. He also ran a girls camp to bring youngsters to Twain's Salt River country. In 1923, at the behest of one of the campers—Ruth Lamson, whose father was a newspaperman in Moberly—a group of northeast Missouri country newspaper editors, backed by Violette, or-

Above: The Mark Twain Shrine with its unusual roof was dedicated in 1960 as the first modern visitor center and museum in the state park system. Far left: Twain was born in this two-room cabin with clapboard siding, now safe from the elements within the shrine. *Both Oliver Schuchard* • Left: Mark Twain reenactor Tom Gilding; Ralph Gregory, age 101, the first site administrator at Mark Twain Birthplace; B.H. Rucker, coauthor of this book; and Henry Sweets of the Mark Twain Museum in Hannibal meet during the centennial of Twain's death and the fiftieth anniversary of the site in 2010. *Susan Flader*

ganized the Mark Twain Memorial Park Association. Within a year, the group raised $15,000 to purchase the core tract for a state park adjacent to Florida, which could memorialize Mark Twain. Violette presented the cabin to the park association in August 1924, and in December, the association transferred both the park and the cabin to the state. This was the first state park north of the Missouri River.

The birthplace cabin itself was moved in 1930 from Florida to the new park, where it was placed on the highest point of Violette's old Hilltop Camp, underneath a primitive frame shelter built to protect it from the weather. In 1960, this inadequate arrangement was abandoned with the dedication of an ultramodern museum building, complete with a hyperbolic paraboloid roof, under which the simple two-room cabin now sits. The contrast between the soaring roof and the little cabin on the red tile floor is striking. One pauses as if in anticipation of a crack of hilarity from the mind that it honors. Perhaps, however, this very contrast helps us to see more starkly the simplicity, almost poverty, into which this exemplary man of letters was born. It also tells us something about how we sometimes choose to honor our legends. Twain's daughter Clara had a hand in selecting the design of the shrine.

An honor of a different sort was the dedication in 1983 of the huge Clarence Cannon Dam and the reservoir that drowns nearly all of the Salt River valley that Sam Clemens came to know as a boy. This 18,600-acre reservoir with the ghosts of forests past still standing in the shallows is Mark Twain Lake, constructed and operated by the Army Corps of Engineers. Maybe this is the ironic and ultimate revenge of the federal army for Sam's initial but short Confederate proclivities.

The museum in the shrine contains a wealth of artifacts and exhibits. An original handwritten manuscript of *The Adventures of Tom Sawyer* and a galley proof with his handwritten notes and corrections are on view. Plus, a public reading room houses an excellent collection of works by and about Mark Twain, as well as foreign-language versions of his works. The Bringhurst bust of Mark Twain originally erected in Florida was moved to the shrine in 1964, and in 1966, the monument was moved from the corner of Main and Mill streets to the spot in Florida where the birthplace cabin originally stood.

Mark Twain Birthplace State Historic Site is a place to ponder the origins of authentic homespun genius. It is also a place to contemplate how we as a society choose to honor our legends and how our choices change over time. *

MARK TWAIN BIRTHPLACE STATE HISTORIC SITE • 37352 SHRINE ROAD, FLORIDA, MISSOURI

Mark Twain State Park

AFTER THE MARK TWAIN MEMORIAL park association formally dedicated its new park in honor of Monroe County's native son in August 1924, it transferred the land to the state. Mark Twain State Park was one of the first parks in the state's new park system and, for years, the only one north of the Missouri River. Some of the hundred-acre park was formerly a girls' camp operated by M. E. "Dad" Violette of Florida, one of the founders of the park association. The park eventually provided a hilltop setting for the relocated birthplace cabin of Mark Twain, which Violette had saved from destruction. Mark Twain was born as Samuel Clemens in 1835 in the tiny settlement of Florida, its remains now surrounded by the park and, since 1983, by the huge Mark Twain Lake.

With the help of the park association and people from the neighborhood, the state improved road access, provided camping and picnic grounds, and constructed a large pen for two bison on loan from the State Fair Board. There was some thought by the late 1930s that the park ought to be enlarged and turned over to the federal government as a national park for north Missouri. From 1938 to 1939, the state acquired more than a thousand acres in eight separate tracts, but the area was destined to remain a state park.

Much of the early development occurred between 1939 and 1942, when Civilian Conservation Corps (CCC) Company 1743, an all-black company that had done superb work at Washington State Park, was transferred here. Some local residents, forgetting the lessons of Huck and Jim, circulated petitions protesting the assignment of blacks to the park, but other citizens, who did remember, circulated counter-petitions and carried the day. The CCC cleared large tracts of land, laid out trails, installed a water system, and developed a beautiful picnic area amid generous shade trees at Buzzard's Roost, a promontory overlooking the Salt River valley, which is today Mark Twain Lake. The picnic ground features a T-shaped, open shelter, built of native limestone, with a large stone fireplace flanked by built-in stone benches with wood seats.

For decades, Mark Twain State Park consisted of rugged, timbered hills surrounding and overlooking the north and middle forks of the scenic Salt River. In these valleys and along these streams, Missourians were invited to play and explore, just as a young Sam Clemens had done. In fact, state park officials built a group camp named Camp Clemens here after World War II, using some of the buildings from Camp Tom Sawyer, the former CCC barracks.

But in 1983, the Army Corps of Engineers completed Clarence Cannon Dam on the Salt River, creating the 18,000-acre Mark Twain Lake and totally changing the character of the park. Enlarged to 2,775 acres by the addition of land leased from the corps, the park is now reservoir-based and provides facilities geared toward water recreation, including boat ramps, a beach, picnic areas, camper cabins, and modern campsites. The most attractive picnicking spot in the park, however, is still the old Buzzard's Roost. Camp Clemens has been closed, and a modern group camp was constructed on land acquired from the corps. The camp is named Camp Colborn, after R. I. "Si" Colborn, the longtime editor of the *Monroe County Appeal* and a State Park Board member

The woody hill fell sharply away ... to a limpid brook which sang along over its gravelly bed and curved and frisked in and out and here and there and yonder in the deep shade of overhanging foliage and vines—a divine place for wading, and it had swimming pools, too, which were forbidden to us and therefore much frequented by us. —AUTOBIOGRAPHY OF MARK TWAIN

Above: Buzzard's Roost once looked across the Salt River valley Sam Clemens loved to roam as a boy. Today, it attracts people to spectacular views of Mark Twain Lake. Left: A winter snow mantles the stone walkway to the Buzzard's Roost overlook, stunning in this season as well. ***Both Missouri State Parks***

The less developed Mark Twain Lake is a beautiful place to view the Milky Way and one of our rarest natural resources—the night sky. The lake provides water fun, including boat ramps, a beach, or simply a peaceful view. *Both Scott Myers*

during the 1950s and 1960s, as well as the leader of the counter-petition effort back in 1939 to bring the black CCC company to the park.

Away from the developments, there is still a large area of fairly wild land. Because of the deep valleys carved by the Salt River and its tributaries, the park has an Ozark-like quality in contrast to most of the rolling glaciated plains of agricultural north Missouri. The extent of the park's woodlands of oak, hickory, and maple, coupled with those owned by the corps around virtually the entire lake, make this area one of the most significant examples of a north-central Missouri forested landscape. The woodlands with their steep hillsides bordering the lake are accessible on five hiking trails totaling more than six miles.

Beyond the reservoir and its wooded fringe, the lovely rolling fields and farms and the friendly people of Monroe County are still there, and the country still offers the perfect setting for a lazy summer of fishing, swimming, and dreaming. *

MARK TWAIN STATE PARK • 37352 SHRINE ROAD, FLORIDA, MISSOURI

Union Covered Bridge State Historic Site

FOR ALL THE ROMANTIC IMAGES they continue to inspire, covered bridges were, in fact, utilitarian. Their roofs provided shelter against the weather, not so much for the convenience of travelers but to protect the wooden structure of the bridge. These bridges proved structurally sound for years, but without the covers, moisture would quickly have rotted the joints where the large timbers intersect. Union Covered Bridge, one of the four remaining covered bridges in Missouri, clearly shows the care and planning that went into its construction.

On September 17, 1871, officials of the Monroe County Court opened the Union Covered Bridge to traffic. The new bridge replaced a dilapidated, uncovered structure spanning the Elk Fork of the Salt River near Union Church, where the Paris-Fayette road crossed the stream. The bridge continued to carry vehicles for almost a hundred years.

Joseph C. Elliott from Payson, Illinois, won the county contract for construction of the bridge in 1870; records at the courthouse show $5,000 allocated for two bridges. Elliott eventually built five covered bridges in Monroe County, crossing the North, Middle, South, and Elk Forks of the Salt River. Of these, only Union remains.

All five had been constructed using a support system called the Burr arch truss. Patented by Theodore Burr of Torringford, Connecticut, the Burr arch truss produced bridges of great structural integrity. In addition to the usual truss made of vertical and diagonal members, Burr's design added wooden arches to each side of the trusses. This combination of truss and arch created a bridge as strong as it was handsome, since either the arches or the trusses alone were capable of supporting the entire bridge, almost like wearing both a belt and suspenders. But Elliott went even further: his bridges also featured double arches on each side.

Although the trusses carrying the floor of the bridge rested on top of the stone abutments at each end of the bridge, the arches on each side passed through the floor and were braced against the sides of the stone piers farther below; each system of support was independent of the other. To form the arches, Elliott fitted multiple timbers, cut from local oak, together with bolts. Then the timbers were sawed on two sides and shaped to the necessary curve with an adze. The careful observer can still see the blade marks left by the builders. Where the large wooden members of the truss connected with each other, the joints were fastened together with wooden pins called treenails or trunnels. Many covered bridges were covered with board-and-batten siding, but the Union bridge sports a slightly dressier siding of clapboards, topped by a wood-shingled roof.

Amazingly, two of Elliott's bridges—Union and Mexico—were still carrying traffic in the 1960s, almost a century later. The active era came to a close for the Union covered bridge when a dump truck with a load of gravel from the nearby quarry partially broke through the bridge floor but, luckily, did not completely destroy the bridge in the process.

The Mexico bridge's end was more catastrophic. On July 9, 1967, a raging flash flood destroyed it. Ironically, the state legislature had just that year authorized the Missouri State Park Board to take ownership and preserve the state's remaining covered bridges, and the Mexico bridge, along with the Union bridge, had been slated for transfer to the park system on July 12. Some of the Mexico bridge timbers were salvaged, however, and used on Union bridge a year later when it was partially restored by state park authorities.

Since acquiring the four remaining bridges in 1967, the state park system restored them all initially, repaired them after repeated flood events, and defended them against vandalism and arson. For nearly half a century, these once utilitarian structures have added beauty and grace to Missouri's state parks. Perhaps they always will, "The good Lord willin' an' the crick don't rise." *

THE KISSING BRIDGE

I like a bridge that sports a roof
Well thatched with cedar shingle:
They're just as good for married folks
And better for the single.
For where may country lad and lass,
Their work-day world forgetting,
Have better chance for holding hands
And altruistic petting.

Thus did the poet Daniel L. Cady explain one reason for the popularity of covered bridges in nineteenth-century America. Such "kissing bridges" provided a refuge for lovers, but they also sheltered weary travelers seeking some shade as well as highwaymen ready to relieve the unsuspecting of their valuables. Still today, birds and other animals make their home within the clapboards. And every covered bridge has been the source of local superstitions, a residence of ghosts, goblins, and trolls.

The bridge is the only one of Missouri's four remaining covered bridges to feature the Burr double-arch truss. *Oliver Schuchard (left) and Missouri State Parks*

UNION COVERED BRIDGE STATE HISTORIC SITE • 20700 MONROE COUNTY ROAD 962, PARIS

Thousand Hills State Park

IN THE YEARS FOLLOWING WORLD WAR II, the northeast Missouri community of Kirksville faced a number of challenges. Two seemed to be related: how to provide fresh clean water for a population that had more than doubled since 1900, and how to provide outdoor recreation opportunities for that same population, which included the growing ranks of students at Northeast Missouri State Teachers College (now Truman State University). The town leaders knew they had some advantages. There was Big Creek, a large stream west of town that flowed through wooded, hilly land. There was lively interest in the region in bringing some of the benefits of public recreation land to this portion of the state. And there was the legacy of Dr. George Mark Laughlin.

George Laughlin had been born in nearby Ralls County in 1872. He moved to Kirksville in Adair County as a young man to study osteopathic medicine with the founder of this new branch of medicine, Dr. A. T. Still. Laughlin flourished in his endeavors, married Still's daughter, and built a remarkable career as an administrator of hospitals, medical schools, and clinics. In addition to medicine, Laughlin had an interest in land, and he eventually developed a large farm west of town that he called Thousand Hills Farm.

The land west of Kirksville includes a rugged belt of hills that runs north and south between rolling expanses of Missouri prairie lands. This belt is located west of the Grand Divide between the Salt River drainage east to the Mississippi and the Chariton drainage south to the Missouri, and it has always been a refuge for wildlife, plants, and humans. The hills surrounding Big Creek valley supported a natural vegetation of mixed oak and hickory woodland, savanna, and tallgrass prairie.

AMERICAN INDIAN PETROGLYPHS

The American Indians who used this area left behind highly realistic rock carvings of deer, opossums, snakes, lizards, at least four different birds, arrows, and other figures on a prominent sandstone outcrop overlooking the valley. You can see the petroglyphs in the shelter above. Because these carvings lack the stylization and the symbols of status and power that distinguish Mississippian petroglyphs, like those at Washington State Park, archaeologists believe people of the earlier Late Woodland period, around AD 400 to 900, may have made them. *George Denniston*

Most of the ambitious early American settlers tended to bypass this land at first in favor of less rugged terrain, but some folks did call the hills home. Later, they also exploited the valley for its clay deposits and coal reserves. The little town of Novinger, just northwest of the hills, still bears the stamp of its heritage in late-nineteenth-century mail-order miners' cabins. About the same time, Laughlin's Thousand Hills Farm brought quality livestock, including Aberdeen Angus cattle and Berkshire hogs, to the area.

Laughlin died in 1948, and the following year Kirksville leaders conceived a solution to their problems of water supply and recreation—a large freshwater lake on Big Creek in the rugged Thousand Hills country. The groundwater from the Pennsylvanian bedrock of northern Missouri is unfit for most municipal and agricultural uses, and the water in the glacial drift is often too saline as well, so that most water must come from surface sources—hence the need for impoundments, especially near urban areas. The Laughlin heirs concurred with the plan and donated 1,000 acres of the old farm. The city raised funds to purchase another 1,500 acres. By 1952, a 600-acre reservoir named Forest Lake was completed, using an abandoned coal mine and rock quarry. Then the whole tract was turned over to the state, and in 1953 Thousand Hills State Park in Adair County was dedicated. The city retained ownership of the lake proper to ensure that its function as a water-supply reservoir would continue.

Most of the original facilities at the park were built between 1955 and 1964, and they generally reflect the park style of that era. During the same period, the park also gradually grew to more than 3,200 acres. Among the 1970s additions to the park was a dining lodge on a lovely spot overlooking

Above: Wiry spike rush and other marsh plants line the shore of 600-acre Forest Lake in Thousand Hills State Park. The lake has a marina where you can rent boats and buy supplies, and you can enjoy fishing, swimming, hiking, and bird-watching along the seventeen miles of shoreline. *Oliver Schuchard* • Left: Forest Trail is among fourteen miles of trails that provide access to the wooded uplands encircling Forest Lake as well as to other park features. *Scott Myers*

Forest Lake. Over the years, this lodge has developed into one of the finest restaurants in northeast Missouri, with a reputation for excellent food, reasonable cost, and a beautiful setting.

The park is, naturally, centered around Forest Lake with its seventeen miles of shoreline, and many of the activities here are on or in the water. A marina provides boat rentals and supplies. Fishing and swimming are good, and so is bird-watching along the shore. Fully furnished cabins are available, if you are not in the mood to camp.

You will also want to visit the petroglyphs and walk the trails. The petroglyphs are enclosed in a shelter for protection against vandalism and the elements, but windows along an outside ramp allow you to view them even when the building is not open. If you are adventurous, take the rugged, ten-mile Thousand Hills Trail, which nearly encircles the lake and wanders through hundreds of acres of oak woodland and savanna. Northern Missouri was once more than half savanna and prairie. Few remnants remain, so park naturalists have been restoring and managing these at Thousand Hills with prescribed fire. The trail also takes you into an isolated little valley where a rare tree grows. The large-toothed aspen is a northern species, and most of its range is far to the north. But a small colony of this beautiful and delicate visitor grows in protected seclusion here at Thousand Hills. Wildlife abounds in the park. Deer, turkey, red fox, coyotes, barred and great-horned owls, and various ducks are fairly easy to see if you know when to expect them, and other rarer species like bald eagles and ospreys occasionally appear. Speak to the park naturalist to help make your visit really special.

Thousand Hills is a unique state park with its mission shared between Kirksville and the state. The arrangement works to benefit both the city and the people of Missouri. So plan a visit, and spend a day exploring the park's cultural and natural treasures. *

THOUSAND HILLS STATE PARK • 20431 ROUTE 157, KIRKSVILLE

Long Branch State Park

IN THE EARLY 1800s, pioneers from the Appalachian hills and valleys of North Carolina and Kentucky followed Daniel Boone into Missouri, and some of them continued on into the area north of the Missouri River. Traveling westward along the Salt River, a Mississippi River tributary, or northward from the Missouri River via the Chariton River, they converged on an ancient American Indian trade route that followed high ground marking the geographical divide between the Mississippi and Missouri drainages, known as the Grand Divide. Thus, they found the land that is now Randolph, Macon, and Adair counties, and it reminded them of home. Skilled woodsmen and farmers settled first in the timbered valleys of the rivers and creeks, felling logs to build houses and barns and clearing the bottomlands for crops.

In 1965, Congress authorized a dam, a multipurpose project for flood control, water supply, and recreation for the area. The Army Corps of Engineers actually constructed the dam on the East Fork Little Chariton, a few miles south of the point where the waters of Long Branch joined its flow, but in the annals of federal public works it was Long Branch Dam. The 2,450-acre reservoir it formed is Long Branch Lake, and the park in Macon County is Long Branch State Park, which surrounds the lower reaches of the reservoir.

After the dam was completed in 1980, the corps leased 550 acres of the shoreline area to Missouri for a state park. The federal agency also signed an agreement with the Missouri Department of Natural Resources to share equally the cost of developing and operating recreational facilities. Among the facilities are picnic areas, campgrounds, a swimming beach, several boat ramps, and a marina.

In 1987 the state park grew to more than 1,800 acres by lease of additional corps land. The new acreage includes the southern part of the historic Bee Trace area between the two arms of the reservoir and additional lands on the eastern side, the so-called Macon area. The dam and park lie just north of Highway 36, scarcely west of Macon.

Some 640 acres of the Bee Trace area, where settlers harvested honey, lie within the park. The area is mostly open woodland interspersed with native prairie, a once common savanna landscape now rare in northern Missouri. Here, great old white oaks that were saplings when the first settlers came in search of honey loom over an open understory of prairie grasses, sedges, and wildflowers. Core drillings have revealed one tree that has stood for more than 250 years, and several range up to nearly two centuries in age. It was the white and bur oaks—given their tendency to have hollow trunks and limbs—that provided homes for the wild honeybee.

Paradoxically, the construction of the dam came none too soon to save remnants of northern Missouri's once vast tallgrass prairie and oak savanna. Now that the Bee Trace area is within a state park, prescribed fires and removal of scrub brush from old farm pastures and woodlots have restored its health and species diversity, making it northeastern Missouri's most important prairie and savanna landscape. Some 385 acres in the Bee Trace area and an additional 44 acres of prairie on the southwest side of the park have been designated as the Chariton River Hills Natural Area, with more than 250 native plant species and an abundance of birds. The 7.5-mile Bee Trace Trail and the 1.5-mile Little Chariton Prairie Trail provide access to the natural area.

Long Branch State Park also reveals considerable evidence of occupation by American Indians. The drainages are so narrow and steep-sided that there are sites on almost every hill. Just as the environment of northern Missouri was highly structured with narrow fingers of wood-

THE BEE TRACE TRAIL

Between the East Fork Little Chariton River and its sizable tributary, Long Branch, settlers discovered open woodlands well populated with hollow trees that provided nesting places—natural hives—for the American honeybee, first introduced by Europeans but naturalized here. A road through the woods became known as the Bee Trace, the original meaning of "trace" being a beaten path or trail. Settlers came here in the autumn to fell the bee trees and chop them open to harvest the honey. Before the culture and processing of sorghum cane became common, the delectable product of the bee was the sweetening agent most accessible to pioneers. Of course, if they chopped the tree to get the honey, they destroyed the tree and, often, its colony of bees.

Bee trees are scarce now, but portions of the Bee Trace area are still preserved in Long Branch State Park.

Rattlesnake master blooms among 200-year-old white oaks on this remnant of north Missouri savanna in the Bee Trace area. Honeybees and bats favored hollow trees in these open woodlands and native prairies. ***Ken McCarty***

The West Chariton Prairie unit of the Chariton River Hills Natural Area at Long Branch offers a glimpse of the prairie landscape of native grasses and wildflowers that once covered much of northern and western Missouri. *Scott Myers*

Families enjoy the natural sand beach at Long Branch. *Ben Nickelson*

land extending along the streams, with the broad sweep of prairie beyond, so too were the locations of American Indian sites. From the Early Archaic period through the Middle Woodland, about nine thousand to fifteen hundred years ago, most sites were occupied seasonally in late summer and fall for large-scale processing of nuts, as indicated by the unusually high concentrations of nutting stones in proportion to projectile points. During the Late Woodland period, the Indians congregated in larger communities along the Missouri River in the summer and fall, and they used the Long Branch area in the winter when they broke into smaller groups. Then during the Mississippian cultural tradition of larger, more permanent towns around Cahokia, Illinois, about AD 900 to 1400, Long Branch seems to have been used only for small hunting and fishing camps. On the Chariton River not far from the park, archaeologists have investigated a stone dam and weir that served as a fish trap, possibly built by Missouria or Osage Indians.

Pioneer families hunted the abundant native game and exploited the rivers for fish and fur. For a century or more, the waters were productive, but after World War II, the streams of northern Missouri degraded for subsistence or recreation. Channelization and intensive farming turned them into heavily silted waterways, and drainage from coal mines soured their waters.

The Army Corps of Engineers project was welcomed by locals. Macon needed water, and Long Branch Lake with its sparkling blue water satisfied an ancestral hunger for a good fishing hole. It has become famous for lunker black bass, walleye, and catfish. It is popular also for boating, water-skiing, and swimming. A visit to Long Branch can help you appreciate the environment that is and was north Missouri. *

LONG BRANCH STATE PARK • 28615 VISITOR CENTER ROAD, MACON

Gen. John J. Pershing Boyhood Home State Historic Site

IT REQUIRES A REAL EFFORT of our modern-day imaginations to appreciate the thunderous impact of the arrival of US military forces in Europe in June 1917. Isolationist America had at last decided to enter the Great War against the Kaiser and his allies. President Woodrow Wilson knew that his choice of leader for the American Expeditionary Forces was crucial: he appointed Gen. John J. "Black Jack" Pershing from Missouri.

General Pershing was a soldier's soldier and not given to fanfare, but he understood the importance of symbolism—and his arrival in Europe was a triumph in international diplomacy. The single most powerful moment took place at a small ceremony in a Parisian cemetery. After accepting an official welcome to Paris, the American general and his first small contingent of combat troops marched to the resting place of the French officer who had fought with the American colonies during their revolution against Britain. On America's Independence Day, July Fourth, descendants of the Marquis de Lafayette met the general and his party at the Picpus Cemetery and led them to the gravesite. There, in a simple gesture, the leader of the American army that had come across the ocean to help France in her hour of need placed a wreath of roses upon the tomb of the gallant French soldier, with the words: "Lafayette, we are here." All of France erupted in an outpouring of emotion for America and her general. The striking utterance was widely attributed to Pershing, though he himself credited a colonel on his staff.

> *"The place seems like home to me and it always will. I've been away a long time and there have been many changes, but this is home."*
> —GENERAL PERSHING, UPON VISITING LACLEDE LATE IN HIS LIFE

General Pershing was astute not only in public ceremony but in conducting warfare. Most historians credit Pershing with masterful handling of the American army in France, which tilted the tide of war against the Germans. He was lionized at the time, even touted for president, and upon completion of his European assignment, the US Congress conferred upon him the rank and title of General of the Armies of the United States, a rank higher than that of any other American general. In 1976, during the American Revolution Bicentennial, George Washington was accorded the rank and title posthumously.

The nation's highest-ranking military officer was a fighting soldier. Graduating from West Point in 1886, he built a career that stretched from the wars with American Indians in his youth to his death in 1948 at the dawn of the nuclear age. He began his career leading cavalry against the Apache chief Geronimo, and he mentored many of the officers who would become the nation's leading generals in World War II, including Gen. Dwight D. Eisenhower. During that remarkable span of service, Pershing led the African American soldiers of the Tenth Cavalry—the source of his nickname Black Jack—against American Indians and bandits in Montana. During the Spanish and Philippine wars with the United States, he fought against Spaniards at San Juan Hill and against revolutionary Emilio Aguinaldo in the Philippines and later served as a military observer with the Japanese during the Russo-Japanese War. In 1906 he was promoted by President Theodore Roosevelt directly from captain to brigadier general over 862 more senior officers. After serving in other assignments in France and again in the Philippines, he commanded the Mexican border operations against Pancho Villa. Pershing then led American troops in World War I, after which he served as army chief of staff until his retirement in 1924.

In retirement he served in many capacities, including as chairman of the American Battlefield Monument Commission from 1924 until his death, and in 1932 he won the Pulitzer Prize for his memoirs. He was an outspoken advocate for aid to the United Kingdom both before and after American entry into World War II.

He also married and had four children, three of whom died with their mother in a tragic fire at the Presidio in San Francisco in 1915 on the eve of his greatest achievements. Through all his remarkable exploits, John Pershing always remembered the north Missouri countryside from which he came, and he returned to his hometown of Laclede whenever he could.

John Joseph Pershing was the firstborn son of a northern father, John Fletcher Pershing of Pennsylvania, and a southern mother, Ann Elizabeth Thompson of Tennessee. Born in 1860 near Laclede in Linn County, young John Pershing's earliest memory was of the cruel violence of the Civil War that divided the people of Linn County. There was a Confederate raid on Laclede when he was five years old. Pershing's father was a strong Union man. His mother's brother was a Confederate soldier.

After the war, the growing Pershing family continued operating a general store and farming but moved into town to live. The comfortable frame house at the corner of State (now Pershing Drive) and Warlow

The heroic-scale bronze sculpture by Carl Mose is flanked by a wall and granite tablets honoring the service of all veterans, but especially those who served under General Pershing in World War I. *Stephanie Sidoti*

For his service as leader of the American forces in World War I, John J. Pershing earned the rank and title of General of the Armies, becoming the highest-ranking military officer in American history. He insisted that American troops fight under American command. Pershing spent his youth during the 1860s and 1870s in this home in the small north Missouri town of Laclede. ***Oliver Schuchard***

Streets was home during Pershing's boyhood, and he called it his "real home" for the rest of his life. Johnny Pershing grew into Jack Pershing and was a great favorite among the boys of the vicinity for his high spirits and friendly ways, but he also won over adults because he was hard-working and trustworthy.

While still in his teens, Jack Pershing took on the responsibility of teaching at the Prairie Mound School nine miles south of town. He also attended the Kirksville Normal School and might have become a Missouri lawyer if he had not in 1881 noticed an opportunity to take an examination for entrance into the US Military Academy at West Point. After entering the army, Pershing's duties across the continent and the world would make him only an occasional visitor to his hometown. His career became the heritage of the whole nation, and when he died in 1948, he was buried in Arlington National Cemetery just as his World War I comrades were, with a plain, government-issued headstone.

Back in Laclede, the Pershing family eventually moved out of its old home on State Street in 1885. Other families lived in the house, and it had fallen into a state of disrepair by 1952, when it was purchased by the state through the good offices of the Pershing Memorial Park Association as a shrine to the memory of General Pershing and the American soldiers of World War I. The house, which is described as carpenter Gothic, was restored under the direction of John Albury Bryan, an architect and longtime guru of historic preservation in Missouri. It was dedicated on September 13, 1960, the one-hundredth anniversary of Pershing's birth, with the US Army Band "Pershing's Own," which he founded, and numerous dignitaries in attendance. In 1977, the Pershing home was designated a National Historic Landmark.

It went through additional restoration in 2000 and has been furnished to recapture the era of Pershing's youth in the 1870s. Around the house, original features of the grounds have been restored, including the smokehouse, root cellar, well, and privy. To preserve the character of the neighborhood, the state has acquired adjoining property and expanded the scope of the site. Near the home is a bronze statue of Pershing by sculptor Carl Mose. Originally created for the state capitol grounds, it was legislatively transferred and moved to the Pershing home in 1968. The statue is flanked by a Wall of Honor and granite tablets honoring the military service of veterans, with special designation for those who served under Pershing's command in World War I. Among the names is Frank Buckles—affectionately known as Pershing's Last Patriot—who was born in Bethany forty miles from Laclede and was the last surviving American Doughboy when he visited the Pershing site on Memorial Day 2008, three years before his death at the age of 110.

The old Prairie Mound School where young Pershing had taught, which had faced demolition in its original location south of town, was relocated to the site and restored to hold exhibits about Pershing's life. The Pershing Park Memorial Association still exists and continues to support the site with fundraising campaigns and special events.

In 2010, a special dedication took place on the anniversary of the general's 150th birthday, with military and political dignitaries from six nations in attendance. During the ceremony, Laclede was joined with the city of Souilly, France, in the international Sister City program. Souilly was the site of Pershing's headquarters during the Meuse-Argonne campaign, the largest commitment of US troops in the Great War.

Laclede has struggled to survive as a town in the years since Pershing's father served as postmaster and community leader. Like many small farm belt and railroad communities, it has been a victim of the changing technologies and economics of agriculture and transportation. But the little village, population 415 in 2010, is determined not to perish. With the completion of the four-lane US Highway 36 as part of the Chicago-Kansas City Expressway, the town gained a new lease on life. The residents love their community, and they honor the memory of their most famous son. All those who recall or imagine small-town life with fondness and those who are curious about the place where a great American soldier got his start will enjoy a trip to the Pershing home in Laclede. *

GEN. JOHN J. PERSHING BOYHOOD HOME STATE HISTORIC SITE • 1100 PERSHING DRIVE, LACLEDE

Pershing State Park

A CHILDHOOD FRIEND OF GEN. JOHN J. PERSHING remembered years later that "he knew the best places to shoot squirrels or quail, knew where to find the hazel or hickory nuts. He knew where the coolest and deepest swimming pools in the Locust, Muddy, or Turkey Creeks were." Thus, when the patriotic members of the Gen. John J. Pershing State and National Park Association pondered in 1930 how to commemorate the World War I hero from Missouri, who was still living, they quickly resolved that the most suitable memorial would be a park amidst the wilds that young Jack Pershing had loved to roam.

For the young people of Laclede in the 1870s, there was no better place for outdoor adventure than the old Canfield property just west and south of town. This sprawling Linn County ranch bordered the winding Locust Creek with its mill and its swimming and fishing holes, and it included the low ridges, tall forests, and open prairies typical of north Missouri in the 1870s. In 1930 this "Jack Pershing Country" still boasted its free-flowing stream and bottomland forest. The old Canfield tract was the obvious choice for the core of the proposed memorial park.

A MONUMENT TO MOTHERS

The park opened in 1940—a year after a second great twentieth-century conflict had erupted and a year before American youth would again be drawn into the maelstrom. That same year, the American War Mothers of Missouri dedicated a monument in the center of the park to American mothers, who like Pershing's, gave sons to the war. Sculpted of white marble by John Slitz, a federal prisoner at Fort Leavenworth in Kansas, the War Angel carries a torch of liberty, wears a laurel wreath, and has an American flag draped about her shoulders.

The association originally had hoped to establish a national military park at the site, but this was not to be—in part because National Park Service policy prevented commemoration of living people. The focus thus shifted to the state. Members of the association envisioned a recreation ground for legionnaires as well as the general public, a place with a good-size lake, a golf course, a landing strip, a large auditorium, and other facilities suitable for encampments of veterans. Enthusiastic support for the park idea spread across Missouri, and in 1937 the state General Assembly approved funds for purchase of the initial 1,800 acres, though without the funds or intention to develop the site to the extent envisioned by the promoters.

The Civilian Conservation Corps helped Missouri develop this park, and it opened in the summer of 1940. It is difficult to imagine a more fitting memorial to the spirit of Gen. John J. Pershing than to preserve a portion of the environment that shaped him in his youth. The march of agricultural progress across northern Missouri has now rendered this remnant of north Missouri prairie and forest a rare jewel, surrounded by

miles and miles of row crops and clipped pastures.

Locust Creek runs through the heart of the park. The creek is actually a small river that originates in Iowa and flows southward through north-central Missouri until it joins the Grand River, a tributary to the Missouri. Along most of its length today, Locust Creek, like most north Missouri streams, has been channelized and straightened, deprived of its wildlife habitat and natural beauty. But here in Pershing State Park, the winding stream still flows lazily across its broad and level floodplain. Across the centuries, the meandering creek has formed and reformed oxbow lakes, sloughs, and small ponds. Along its shores, one of the last old-growth forests in north Missouri towers over the creek and adjacent low ridges. Early promotional literature for the memorial park boasted of a gigantic national champion cottonwood tree. That stately tree died

years ago, but the even more significant bottomland forest of which it was a part still stands. Two years after establishment of the interagency Missouri Natural Areas Committee in 1977, two natural areas won designation along the creek in the park: the 80-acre Cordgrass Bottoms Natural Area, featuring cordgrass prairie and marsh surrounded by wet bottomland forest, and the 330-acre Locust Creek Natural Area, the most ecologically rich and complete floodplain system remaining in north Missouri, with a full complex of bottomland forest, shrub swamp, slough, marsh, and oxbow lakes.

Away from the forest corridor along Locust Creek, an even rarer scene awaits explorers of Pershing Park. Out on the wide floodplain of Locust Creek are hundreds of acres of remnant lowlands covered not in forest but in wetland prairie and marsh. Wet bottomland prairies were once abundant along the broad river valleys of north Missouri. Because their soggy soils and tendency to flood discouraged farming, large expanses of such prairies persisted even after most of the upland prairies had been plowed under. In this realm of slough grass, southern blue flag, and yellow giant hyssop, a whole community of life flourished under the Missouri sun. Marsh wrens, American bitterns, and red-winged blackbirds nested in the tall grasses and reeds. Ducks, geese, and shorebirds by the thousands congregated around the ponds and sloughs. Deer—and in an earlier age, bison and elk—wandered through grasses shoulder high

False asters bloom amid a profusion of tickseed sunflowers on the broad wetland prairie at Pershing State Park. Bottomland wet prairie, once prevalent in north Missouri, has disappeared nearly everywhere except here. ***Ken McCarty***

A boardwalk in Pershing State Park leads through the marsh and bottomland forest to the prairie beyond. *Scott Myers* • Wild sweet William carpets the ground in the loess and glacial till soil of this north Missouri woodland at the park. Park naturalists burn the area about every two years. *Ken McCarty*

or taller. Close to the ground, fox snakes and massasauga rattlesnakes hunted for mice. And every year, the rains would bring the streams up and out to replenish the moisture in the soils.

Eventually, north Missouri farmers mastered the arts of ditching, draining, and plowing these wet prairies, and a whole world passed away. Pershing State Park features one of the largest wet prairies left in northern Missouri, and the only one along an unaltered section of meandering stream. Some park advocates in the 1930s proposed draining the creek or damming it for a lake, but park officials in the late 1930s sensed the special value of the natural stream and the virgin prairie. By the 1950s, however, pressure mounted from local farmers to plow part of the Locust Creek bottoms for soybeans, and park officials, in a moment of weakness, relented. Fortunately, the farming episode was short-lived because of the gumbo soil, and many prairie plants reestablished themselves naturally. But the wet prairie and bottomland forest at Pershing, today more rare and precious than ever, are still threatened, and their annual renewal by floodwaters is impeded by agricultural levees, drainage ditches, and heavy erosion and siltation from beyond the park borders.

There was always seasonal flooding along Locust Creek—it's in the nature of streams on north Missouri's glaciated plains. But in 1995, another heavy flood after the great, prolonged floods of 1993 deposited the first of what would become a seemingly endless series of massive logjams in the park; these would eventually spur concerted action to deal with problems in the entire watershed of Locust Creek. Earlier logjams had concentrated at a railroad trestle over the creek just north of Highway 36, where railroad crews broke them up. But when the railroad ceased operations and crews removed the trestle, the logs began to jam up in the park during large floods, where it became the responsibility of park managers to remove them.

Then an even more ominous problem came to light through engineering studies that explored stream hydrology and options. Sedimentation over the decades, ever since the channelization of Locust Creek in the 1920s, had built up the floodplain in the park so that it was some twelve feet higher in elevation than a drainage ditch—Higgins Ditch—west of the park, also begun in the 1920s by a farmer with his mules. Furthermore, the ditch was cutting its way upslope toward Locust Creek north of Highway 36. In the drought year of 2007, the "headcut" (an abrupt vertical drop that continues eroding and migrating upstream) reached Locust Creek and captured almost all its low-water flow, creating a major crisis—and local public consternation—that would lead to emergency funds for acquisition of additional lands surrounding the park, the installation of temporary structures in the ditch to control the headcutting, and a large Environmental Protection Agency grant for design and construction of more comprehensive solutions.

Not only did the park add nearly 1,700 acres of long-sought additional tracts to the north, west, and east, but the problems became the catalyst for the development and funding of major programs to work with landowners, agencies, and organizations in the entire 1.5 million-acre watershed. The Lower Grand River watershed, of which Locust Creek accounts for about 80 percent, was selected as a priority project of the Mississippi River Basin Healthy Watersheds Initiative administered by the Natural Resources Conservation Service (NRCS), with an initial grant of more than $5 million for incentives to encourage conservation practices on private lands. The Lower Grand was also selected as a pilot watershed for a new Department of Natural Resources (DNR) program of stakeholder-driven planning and funding known as Our Missouri Waters. DNR and state park officials are also partnering with other nearby public landholdings, including the US Fish and Wildlife Service's Swan Lake National Wildlife Refuge and the Missouri Department of Conservation's Fountain Grove Conservation Area, to restore more natural hydrologic function.

Within Pershing State Park, embracing some 5,250 acres by 2012, NRCS provided about $1 million to restore newly acquired farmland to mimic former oxbows, sloughs, terraces, and other wetland topography. AmeriCorps crews worked with park staff to harvest and sow seeds of prairie and marsh species and transplant cordgrass plugs. Within a year, several sandpiper species plus yellowlegs, bitterns, golden plovers, fish crows, and thousands of ducks were already using the newly reclaimed areas. The restoration process will continue, as it has for decades, on the original wet prairie and marshland areas of the park. Although the Cordgrass Bottoms Natural Area had to be delisted in 2014 because it was covered with six feet of sediment, obliterating the cordgrass and other components of its community, park naturalists were proposing expansion of the Locust Creek Natural Area to include more than one thousand acres of wet prairie and bottomland forest.

Blue-winged teal and snow geese circle the prairie in spring and fall, and snow-white flocks of pelicans rest on hidden ponds. More than two hundred species of birds have been recorded at Pershing Park. In September, thousands of orange monarch butterflies migrate languidly across the sunny prairie, drifting and dallying above nodding ranks of sawtooth and tickseed sunflowers. One of the great sensations of this prairie is space, broad and flat across the waving grasses. An old wood-decked iron bridge leads park visitors across Locust Creek and then through the bottomland forest—either six miles along the creek to the adjoining Fountain Grove Conservation Area, or on a boardwalk to a prairie overlook. This is the best place to touch the long-lost world of northern Missouri wilderness.

Today, Pershing State Park offers plentiful picnic sites on the breezy uplands above the creek as well as a shady campground. The well-manicured recreation area with the War Angel statue hosts a superb display of pink redbud in the spring, and there are several small fishing ponds. From the campground, a short trail leads down to the remains of the old gristmill where a dam across Locust Creek once provided the power to turn the buhrstones. The pool above the dam was a favorite swimming hole, a place for youngsters, most likely including Jack Pershing himself, to cool off and pass time. The mill and the dam are long gone, but the creek is still there, as are the forest and the prairie.

Pershing the general was one of a kind, and so, too, is the park that commemorates him. *

PERSHING STATE PARK • 29277 HIGHWAY 130, LACLEDE

Locust Creek Covered Bridge State Historic Site

BEREFT OF NOT ONLY A ROAD BUT ALSO A RIVER, the longest remaining covered bridge in the state sits a few miles west of Gen. John J. Pershing's hometown of Laclede, a reminder of how times have changed in north Missouri. By the 1970s, what were once rising approaches to either end of the bridge in Linn County could no longer be discerned, nor could the stone abutments that excavations would later prove were there. The road leading to the bridge and what was once the channel of Locust Creek were barely visible as faint traces. All had been buried in silt from eroded fields swept down the waterway through the artificially straightened channel all the way from southern Iowa and Missouri counties to the north.

The bridge is remarkably well preserved, considering it was built in 1868, although much restoration was necessary. This is the longest of the four covered bridges surviving in Missouri (all now state historic sites), 151 feet from end to end, 16 feet wide, and 20 feet to the gable. It was built of white pine using the Howe truss method, as were most of the once numerous covered bridges in the state. According to Linn County records, the construction cost was "not to exceed $5,000."

Running parallel to the Hannibal and St. Joseph Railroad, completed before the Civil War, the bridge was situated on what would become the main east-west road across northern Missouri. Built in the days of horses and buggies, the roadway in 1897 accommodated the Buffalo Soldiers Bicycle Corps of the Twenty-fifth Infantry, crossing on their trek from Fort Missoula, Montana, to St. Louis to prove the effectiveness of the bicycle in moving infantry more rapidly than marching. At about the same time, Pershing acquired his lifelong nickname, Black Jack, for his role leading the Tenth Cavalry Regiment of Buffalo Soldiers in Montana and in the Battle of San Juan Hill in Cuba during the Spanish-American War.

Near the turn of the century, with the advent of the automobile, many booster organizations were formed to promote improved roads in their locales. Gradually, some local groups coalesced into larger organizations promoting not only local highway development but also transcontinental corridors for travel and tourism. Among the most vigorous groups were the Lincoln Highway Association, the National Old Trails Road Association, and the Pikes Peak Ocean to Ocean Highway Association. Each proposed their favored and competing routes across America, vying for the dollars and prestige that transcontinental travel would bring. The Pikes Peak Ocean to Ocean Highway included the old Hannibal to St. Joseph road across Missouri, which crossed Locust Creek Covered Bridge.

> *A large red and white sign with the bold black letters PP-OO was likely once nailed to the bridge, as the Pikes Peak Ocean to Ocean Highway crossed the creek here.*

The PP-OO Association promoted its route as "The Appian Way of America, the military-commercial main-line across the United States," comparing it with ancient Rome's most famous road. In a February 1919 meeting of the association, which had recently relocated its headquarters from Colorado to St. Joseph, the Missouri delegates wanted to rename the Missouri portion of the route, by then designated as Route 8, to "The Pikes Peak Ocean-to-Ocean Highway—The Pershing Transportation Route." General Pershing cabled his approval from somewhere in France, on behalf of the troops. In a burst of patriotic fervor, the association voted to rename the entire route from New York to Los Angeles with the Pershing sobriquet. But it would not make much difference for long.

Model Ts, then Model As, rattled across the plank floor in the late 1910s and 1920s, soon outnumbering the horse-drawn wagons and buggies. Federal funding had begun to vastly extend the network of good roads, and in 1926, by common agreement of the states and the federal government, a consistent numbering system for federal highways was adopted. Most of the transcontinental routes that had been stitched together from various old pioneer traces were broken up with different segments receiving different number designations. The trail names and their supporting groups faded, and in 1930, the Pikes Peak Ocean to Ocean Highway was replaced across Missouri by Highway 36, built one mile to the south. The venerable covered span was about to become a relic.

A Model A Ford like those that traveled over the bridge in its heyday appeared at the celebration of the bridge's restoration in 2003. *Wayne Murrell*

More engineering enterprises contributed to the bridge's present strange setting. From the 1920s into the 1950s, stream-straightening fever afflicted north Missouri, including Locust Creek. Through most of its northern reaches, the creek was stripped of its meanders and converted into a long drainage ditch. The straightened channel was located a quarter mile to the east of the covered bridge, leaving the bridge to span a dry bed or, in wet times, a temporary slough. Channelization extended as far as the railroad a half-mile south then skipped the creek course through Pershing State Park south of Highway 36.

The silt-laden floodwaters, rushing down the "improved" Locust Creek chute, piled up north of the tracks, spread over the floodplain, submerged the old road, crept up the side of the old bridge, and dropped the topsoil carried from eroded farmlands up north. The silt buildup was so dramatic that one could scarcely imagine the earthen ramps that were once necessary to provide access to the bridge, or that once a dozen or more feet separated the bottom of the bridge from the surface of the stream below.

The Linn County government stopped maintaining the road to the bridge in 1960. Trees now growing on the old right-of-way and in the former creek channel are fifty or more years old. The bridge was deeded

Pershing State Park now surrounds the high and dry historic site, home of the longest covered bridge remaining in the state. ***Kyle Spradley***

to the state for preservation as a historic site in 1968, one hundred years after its completion. After an initial stabilization and partial restoration, it was added to the National Register of Historic Places in 1970.

A new approach route from the west was completed and dedicated in 1989. It includes a sturdy footbridge across Higgins Ditch—another engineered intervention—several hundred yards to the west. A kiosk with informative panels was also installed. Then in 1991, the park division raised the structure three feet, rebuilt the abutments, and constructed new approaches, so that the bridge would again look more like a bridge and also to lift the bottom of the bridge chords off the ground, where they would be less exposed to flooding and soil moisture.

In 2002, after years of planning and with funds from the federal Intermodal Surface Transportation Act, the bridge went through a complete restoration, including raising it another six feet to keep it above frequent floods in the Locust Creek basin. A new study found that the original piers of the bridge were fifteen feet below the newly constructed piers. During restoration, the bridge was suspended from a steel I-beam structure while the floor supports were replaced. For a few months, it was the world's only suspended covered bridge. The old timbers were so huge that replacement timbers had to be brought in from Canada, as trees of that size were no longer cut by commercial operators in the United States.

In recent years, the once sleepy roadway crossing northern Missouri has been replaced with a four-lane highway, part of the Chicago-Kansas City Expressway. Today, some eight to ten thousand visitors per year pull off the highway and walk the quarter mile from the parking lot to see the bridge.

At one time, there was talk of moving the abandoned and isolated bridge to Pershing State Park several miles to the south. But here is where memories were made at square dances, at weddings held in it, and at picnics enjoyed nearby, and here, small boys, including Jack Pershing and his brothers, played and swam and fished in Locust Creek. Here was the hoped-for transcontinental highway. Here the bridge remains, with more than fifteen feet of accumulated silt obliterating the creek bed, as a dramatic testimony to past misuse of the land and to our frequent folly in trying to improve on nature's drainage patterns.

Ultimately, it was Pershing State Park that moved to the old bridge, having been expanded to surround the bridge site as part of an effort to deal more wisely with Locust Creek and to restore the health of its watershed *

LOCUST CREEK COVERED BRIDGE • 16957 DART ROAD, LACLEDE

Crowder State Park

GEN. ENOCH CROWDER, a native north Missourian, was born just before the Civil War near the small town of Edinburg in Grundy County. He developed into a highly intelligent though severe military man and is remembered primarily as the "father of the Selective Service." As judge advocate general, Crowder drafted the Selective Service Act of 1917, and as provost marshal general, he directed its implementation.

A Military Man Who Understood the Civic Spirit of a Free People— EPITAPH FOR GEN. ENOCH HERBERT CROWDER

General Crowder's other exploits included his participation in the efforts to corral Geronimo's Apaches in the 1880s; his indirect role in the arrest and subsequent death of Sitting Bull in 1890; his service as head of the military government of the Philippines, where he drafted new laws to help create a fair and impartial legal system; and his vigorous involvement in the affairs of our country's Latin neighbors, especially Cuba, where he helped create a provisional government after the island became a republic. General Crowder was held in extremely high regard for his legal erudition, his devotion to duty, and his principled dedication to fairness as he saw it.

There is general consensus that the Selective Service System was a key factor in the United States' victorious role in World War I. The law that established the draft, an extension of the idea of the citizen soldier, inspired one waggish county clerk to versify about the local sheriff named Burke and himself, when he was "drafted" into helping to implement it: "Who was it built up this army, that set the whole world free? / Who inducted them into service? It was Crowder, and Burke, and me."

The leader of American forces in World War I and a fellow north Missourian, Gen. John J. Pershing, who was born one year later in a neighboring county, commented following Crowder's death in 1932: "Professionally his exceptional record speaks for itself.... I had a high regard for him, both as a man and an officer." He is buried in Arlington Cemetery.

So, besides Crowder State Park in Grundy County near Edinburg, there is also the army's Camp Crowder near Neosho—now Crowder College—and the University of Missouri's Crowder Hall on its Columbia campus; after graduating from West Point, Crowder taught military tactics in Columbia while attending law school.

The original 640-acre memorial park honoring Enoch Crowder was purchased with a $10,000 legislative appropriation in 1938, just a few years after the general's death. It includes a wonderfully representative tract of northern Missouri hills formed through dissection of glacial till plains. Located just a few miles from the old Crowder homestead, the park adjoins the Big Thompson, a major tributary of the Grand River, and it is generally forested due to the fairly rugged drainages near the river.

Most of the surrounding region is rich farmland, but within the refuge of the park are impressive stands of hardwoods, including sugar maple, walnut, and stately white and red oaks. There is also a small area of restored upland prairie. Like most streams in north Missouri, the river was channelized in the 1920s. But it has begun to reassert its natural right to meander, and the stretch of it in the park once again sports twists and bends with sandbars and gnarled driftwood snags. All along its banks, a rich bottomland forest of silver maple, cottonwood, river birch, and green ash shades a valley floor where the rare ostrich fern spreads its delicate lime-green foliage. Leatherwood, a deciduous shrub species of the deep Ozarks, also grows here. Orchids and ferns may be seen on shaded sandstone ledges carved by the Big Thompson River. The park has several mounds built by prehistoric native peoples, and it was still occupied by the Sac and Fox tribes when the first American settlers showed up.

The Crowders, who arrived from Ohio by way of Iowa just before Enoch Crowder's birth in 1859, were not the first migrants to the area. The first settler of Grundy County, Dr. William Preston Thompson, gave the Big Thompson River its name. In 1991, an extension to Crowder Park of more than 1,200 acres was acquired to preserve a meandering stretch of the Big Thompson with its high quality bottomland forest, and the ruins of Dr. Thompson's old brick home still stood in this tract. Thompson was a Virginia-born physician who was a brigadier general during the War of 1812 and a member of the Virginia legislature and the US Congress before coming in 1821 to Ray County, where he continued to play a prominent role in public affairs. He moved to this northern hinterland in 1833, and his house was built soon thereafter by slaves from clay dug on the site and molded into bricks, then set in a Flemish bond pattern. In building this house, Thompson extended southern culture to a frontier region well removed from the prevalent centers of Missouri's southern settlement. However, one of his sons died fighting for the Union in the Civil War, as did Enoch Crowder's namesake uncle.

The house was in poor condition when the land was acquired, with the roof partially collapsed into the house, parts of the brick walls badly deteriorated, the woodwork and plaster mostly gone, and the floors unstable with parts missing. Some fragments of woodwork could still be seen, including a few remnant hand-carved walnut sunburst corner blocks for door and window frames that offered mute testimony that this was once a showplace of the region.

Above: The classic park landscape here is a fitting memorial to the north Missouri farm boy who implemented the Selective Service System in 1917. *Oliver Schuchard* • Far left: Bordering a portion of the park, the Big Thompson River is beginning once again to meander across the glacial till plain. *Don Schultehenrich* Left: Winter snow mantles a Civilian Conservation Corps bridge. *Anna Persell*

After a period of study and planning, park officials decided not to attempt a restoration of the house, particularly in such a remote location and with constrained finances, but to stabilize the ruins, somewhat in the manner of the castle at Ha Ha Tonka. Officials opted to erect a security fence and provide informative panels for hikers and equestrians visiting the house and the nearby family cemetery by trail. Members of the Grundy County Historical Society and a newer group, Friends of the Thompson House, were not satisfied with this decision, however, as they envisioned a full-blown reconstruction. After another period of discussion and negotiation, park officials agreed to a land swap by which they transferred the house and five acres to the Friends of the Thompson House, which has been raising funds locally for work on the house. The house and cemetery may still be viewed from the Thompson River Trail.

The recreational facilities at Crowder, begun by the Civilian Conservation Corps and continued after the war by contract labor, are centered upon a 20-acre man-made lake that offers fishing, boating, and a lovely setting for picnics. A campground sits on the hill above the lake, and one of the park system's fine group camps, Camp Grand River, sits upon a broad ridge above the Big Thompson tributary of the Grand. The 1,900-acre park has more than seventeen miles of interconnected hiking, biking, and equestrian trails and receives well over 100,000 visitors a year.

Commemorative parks such as Crowder preserve a collective memory of our shared ideals from the past and of the leaders who embodied them. It is good for us to know whom we have honored in earlier times, and why. We would do well to accurately interpret the character and deeds of those we have commemorated and seek to understand the role they played in their time and place. ✻

CROWDER STATE PARK • 76 NORTHWEST ROUTE 128, TRENTON

Wallace State Park

IF YOU TRAVEL IN NORTHWEST MISSOURI, you will no doubt be impressed by the fertile farmlands there. Scattered throughout the region, however, are also areas of rough, hilly land, especially near some of the streams. One of the most lovely of these forested oases of natural land is preserved in Wallace State Park near the town of Cameron in Clinton County, not far northeast of Kansas City.

Wallace was one of the second-generation parks, and only the second to be acquired north of the Missouri River, after Mark Twain State Park. Land was considerably more expensive in north Missouri than in the Ozarks. Its initial 120 acres were purchased in 1932 for a state recreation area from William J. Wallace and other family members and neighbors. Now about 500 acres, the park includes beautiful forested hills and more than a mile of the valley of Deer Creek.

William Wallace's father, James, a native of Tennessee, had fought as a young man in the Black Hawk War of 1832 and subsequently migrated to Missouri, settling in what is now far western Caldwell County. The legislature carved Caldwell County out of the sparsely settled northern reaches of Ray County in December 1836, specifically as a haven for the Mormons, who had already been driven out of Independence into Clay County, where non-Mormon settlers were now agitating for them to leave and where the Mormons were equally determined to remain. Mormons flooded by the thousands into Caldwell County, especially after their faith's founder Joseph Smith arrived in March 1838 and proclaimed their principal settlement, Far West, the new gathering place of the Latter-Day Saints, as the Mormons are also known. Far West, about five miles east of the Wallace farm, quickly became second in population only to Liberty among western Missouri cities. By this time, some Mormons were intimidating original settlers and spilling beyond the bounds of Caldwell County. Violence erupted from both sides. Then during the fall of 1838, Missourians united in a sorry episode of vigilante and militia action to drive the Mormons from the state. The Mormons fled to Nauvoo, Illinois, and then in 1846 began their trek to the Great Salt Lake.

Wallace family tradition holds that James Wallace arrived in the area before the dramatic migration of the Mormons and took part in anti-Mormon activity, though no evidence has been found to substantiate this. Records at Far West were destroyed during the Mormon War, and those in the new courthouse at Kingston were lost to fire in 1860. We do know that his family was established in Caldwell County by the census of 1850, and that he, his brother David, and his four sons eventually acquired some 600 acres on both sides of the Caldwell-Clinton county line, a portion of which became this state park in Clinton County.

The early facilities in Wallace State Park—roads, trails, picnic area, landscaping, and the like—were developed with the assistance of the Works Progress Administration and the National Youth Administration. Later, a small lake was constructed along a tributary of Deer Creek. This attractive lake, nestling in its little valley, is known as Lake Allaman after a former Park Board member. It has been a favorite of visitors and offers swimming, boating (electric motors only), and fishing. But it is also subject to heavy siltation, a common malady because of the erodible soils on the glaciated plains of north Missouri, and it requires periodic renovation.

Several interconnected hiking trails totaling six miles can help you explore the lake, the gentle hills, and the Deer Creek valley. You may be lucky enough some summer morning to find a mother whitetail and her fawn drinking from the waters of Deer Creek. If you camp overnight, you may hear the call of the barred owl along the creek or the howl of coyotes in the distance. The park provides visitors with numerous picnic sites, several playgrounds, and two shelter houses popular with families for reunions, birthdays, and weddings. In addition to the forested campground, youth groups may choose from one of three special-use areas for a primitive camping experience. On weekends, there are park programs at the campground amphitheater.

This was Mormon country in the 1830s, before they were forced to leave. Some historians believe one of the Mormon trails crossed the creek on the limestone shelves at Rocky Ford in the park.

About twenty miles southwest of Wallace State Park, a 60-acre tract of land, also administered by the park, exhibits an outstanding example of north Missouri's original oak woodlands that were once scattered throughout the northern prairies. Known as Trice-Dedman Memorial Woods in honor of its previous owners, it was preserved through the research efforts of the University of Missouri and the care of the owners; it is now owned by The Nature Conservancy of Missouri, which has leased it to the park division since 1981.

The tract features mature woodland dominated by old-growth white oaks—some of them perhaps the original trees of the open white oak woods early naturalists described. Shagbark hickory and northern red oak may also be found on the uplands, with hackberry, box elder, and Ohio buckeye in lower areas. In the spring, you may find an abundance of Jacob's ladder, Dutchman's breeches, and other wildflowers. In many places, the low, green umbrella leaves of the Mayapple carpet the soft ground. This is a place for nature education, for research on means to secure oak reproduction, and for a rare look at an old-growth tract. Like the rest of Wallace State Park, it is also a place for healthy recreation and simple contemplation of nature in a peaceful setting. *

The park is a lovely wooded oasis in north Missouri's rolling farmland. ***Oliver Schuchard*** **• Lake Allaman offers good swimming, fishing, and boating with electric motors. Six miles of trails can help you explore the park.** ***Lana Woody***

WALLACE STATE PARK • 10621 NORTHEAST HIGHWAY 121, CAMERON

Watkins Woolen Mill State Historic Site and Park

"GOING . . . GOING . . . GONE! Sold to the man for six hundred dollars." When the auctioneer's hammer fell on that warm, late spring afternoon in May 1958, it was both an end and a new beginning for the Watkins farm and its famous woolen mill. This auction was the sale of the last intact piece of one of Missouri's best-known antebellum land holdings. It also began a new era for the property, once known as Bethany Plantation, soon to become an outstanding state historic site and park—and a National Historic Landmark.

The story began in 1830, when a young Waltus Watkins immigrated to Liberty from Kentucky and built a small cotton-spinning mill. In his youth, he'd been an apprentice in the mechanical trades, and now he planned to operate a mill of his own, along with small plants for milling grain and sawing lumber. These enterprising plans went awry, as cotton cannot be grown successfully in northern Missouri's climate and the expense of shipping in baled cotton was too great. The mill was converted to wool carding and spinning and operated for a number of years until halted by a fire.

In 1839, Watkins moved his growing family from Liberty to the country, settling in northeast Clay County. Today, the state historic site encompasses some 1,500 acres of Watkins's land and preserves a large portion of it as a historic farmstead, appearing about as it did in the 1870s. The landscape is high and rolling—hilly, but gently so. The hilltops and ridges today are largely pasture, still open land, although no longer covered with native grasses. The slopes, deeper ravines, and lower elevations still hold dense stands of timber, now second-growth, without the occasional giant oaks, huge walnuts, and native elms that once towered above the general forest canopy. This mosaic of prairie braided with forest drew settlers like a lodestone. It was just as attractive as the Kentucky bluegrass, and by comparison, it was practically free.

Today, a visitor arriving at Watkins Woolen Mill sees first the impressive visitor center, built in the early 1990s. It not only provides an introduction to the site through exhibits, artifacts, and audiovisual programs but also houses offices and museum-quality storage for a valuable collection of original Watkins family manuscripts and artifacts.

The exhibits feature photographs, models, and artifacts, such as original yarns spun at the mill along with fabrics and blankets made from them. Inside a glass room, several textile machines turn slowly, on idler pulleys powered by belts from a revolving line shaft overhead. This exhibit will be the first clue for visitors that the mill is not the quaint, moss-covered water mill they might have imagined. Watkins Mill is the industrial revolution exemplified—all steam power, speed, and cast iron. Oddly, it is a factory on a farm.

Watkins Woolen Mill, constructed in 1860 on the eve of the Civil War, is the best preserved nineteenth-century textile factory in the country. It has four floors of original machinery and is now a National Historic Landmark. ***Ben Nickelson***

The visitor center features antique textile and farm machines, working models, museum exhibits, and a collection of original yarn, cloth, and blankets made in the mill. ***John Browning*** **• The four-mile paved path around Williams Creek Lake is the single most popular feature of the recreation area.** ***Tom Nagel***

After exiting the visitor center, you find yourself in a narrow country lane, lined with split-rail fences and bleating sheep. This place is the bucolic world Waltus Watkins moved his family to in 1839. By 1846, his 80 acres had grown to 640, of which 450 acres were under cultivation. By his death in 1884, this home farm had grown to about 1,200 acres, and it was the centerpiece of a holding that totaled over 3,600 acres in several counties. Watkins called this place Bethany, and for a while, he held a federal appointment as postmaster for it.

Fully 95 percent of everything here is original. The park division has reconstructed only minor features—a few outbuildings, sheds, fences, all determined by archaeological research—so that a more understandable context is created for the original structures remaining. A flock of lazy sheep and some busy chickens enable us to better visualize this world.

It isn't clear whether Waltus was thinking of Bethany as the sort of plantation he had known in Kentucky or whether his post office reveals plans to found a town. He once referred to "my plantation" in an advertisement, but the place is best described as having been a very large, diversified farm. In its heyday, the farm had a high degree of self-sufficiency, raising nearly everything needed for subsistence but also producing a plantation-like excess for sale: honey by the hundred-weight, fruit by the ton, and in some years, as much as 400 acres of hemp. Watkins owned several slaves, mostly employed in domestic tasks or chores such as milking. They may also have assisted with farming, but so far as is known, none worked in the mill, which was run by thirty to forty skilled workers and their families, some of whom were provided housing in a row of small houses near the mill known as Smokey Row and elsewhere on the farm.

Down the lane is the house that Watkins began in 1850 to replace

his earlier log home. Even from a distance, the house is inviting—handmade red brick, green shutters, white trim, and a wood shingle roof. A whitewashed fence encloses long, straight rows of hard maples and red cedars running from the house down to the lane. This house was not so much a mansion as a large, comfortable country home.

The house has an understated simplicity, trimmed plainly in walnut or cherry wood, with few moldings and little ornamentation, the stark white plaster everywhere contrasting with the beauty of this warm, mellow woodwork. Family letters tell that the windows and possibly other millwork for the house were contracted for by a brother-in-law in Kentucky and shipped to Clay County by steamboat. The house is furnished almost entirely with original family pieces spanning the full period of their occupancy.

In a day of large families—Waltus had eleven children, two of whom died in infancy—and long visits by relatives and friends, houses had to accommodate a variety of living arrangements. On the ground floor of the home are large double parlors flanking the circular stair, a large dining room, an indoor kitchen, and a small bedroom. Sleeping rooms are on the second and third floors. To a modern visitor, it may seem unhandy that the second floor of the house is divided in half and that the two big bedrooms in the front of the house, at the top of the circular stairway, have no corridor or doors that connect to the three smaller bedrooms in the rear. To go from a front bedroom to a back one, a trip down the circular stair and back up a different one is required. Of the three small rear bedrooms, two are en suite, with their own staircase. The third rear bedroom, above the kitchen, is accessed from the dining room via its own steep, narrow set of steps. Past this small bedroom, this same narrow stairway turns at a landing and leads to the third floor, where the many boys of the family—and perhaps some hired hands—slept in a large dormitory room. These arrangements, which seem so inconvenient, were a nineteenth-century concession to modesty and privacy, whereby family and guests, and boys and girls, were easily segregated.

From the balcony over the front porch, you can look out over a view that Waltus Watkins himself probably savored. Just below at the bottom of the hill is the woolen mill, the centerpiece of the state historic site, with its bright red metal roof, pinkish brick walls, and white woodwork belying its 150-plus years. Hiding behind the trees a half-mile to the east are the Franklin School and the Mount Vernon Church, built in 1856 and 1871 respectively. Waltus provided the land, served as building commissioner for the construction of both, and funded a major portion of their cost. These two buildings have been fully restored. Today, students on school field trips visit the old academy and sometimes relive a school day from the 1870s. Likewise, modern couples occasionally come to say their vows in the church, just as in days past.

From top: The Franklin School was built in 1856 in an unusual octagonal style. *Missouri State Parks* • The produce from many acres of peach, pear, and apple orchards was dried for preservation in trays in the fruit drying house. In the large brick smokehouse, pork was cured. The Watkinses would have butchered as many as one hundred hogs every year. The carcasses were scalded and lard rendered in these cast-iron kettles. *Both Denise Tschida* • Top right: The Watkins family would have had big gardens. Today, historic site staff raise heirloom varieties of plants and trade seeds with other historic sites in an effort to keep vintage vegetables from becoming extinct. *John Browning*

The Watkins home was begun in 1850 and finished four years later, when the staircase was completed. The bricks were made on site, and walnut cut on the farm provided most woodwork. *Denise Tschida* • The sweeping circular staircase at the entry, constructed with oak treads and walnut trim, is the most striking feature of the house, which has little other ornamentation. *Cindy Browne*

Farther south and west of the church and school lies the recreation zone of the historic site, some 800 acres devoted to camping, picnicking, and other outdoor activities. The wooded campground has one hundred units nicely spaced among the trees. Here in the midst of rapidly urbanizing Clay County, the variety of plant and animal life is quite a surprise. Birders have reported species here, such as the painted bunting, Connecticut warbler, and the rare black scoter, which had not been seen for years in other areas of northwestern Missouri. White-tailed deer are sure to be seen, and raccoons, opossums, and even beavers are possible delights for the careful observer.

This area is the most rugged part of the original Watkins property, and a small valley lent itself to the creation of a lake. Williams Creek Lake, now universally enjoyed, was once the subject of controversy among Watkins Mill supporters. The Williams Creek ravine, because of its steepness, had seemingly never been farmed or logged during its long ownership by the Watkins family. As a result, it stood full of huge and ancient oaks, some more than three feet wide, with sycamores and cottonwoods twice that diameter interspersed. The Watkins Mill Association had used a "save the oaks" theme as one element in its campaign for the bond issue that had purchased and donated the acreage to the state. But the 1960s was an era of lake building in state parks, and officials favored a lake. The ravine seemed an obvious place. A Conservation Department forester called in for advice pronounced the oaks "over mature" and down they

This view of Watkins Mill shows the skilled workers' houses on Smokey Row in the background and the wool shed in front of the mill. Watkins purchased as much as 25,000 pounds of wool annually and stored it here until it was needed in the mill. *Historical Atlas of Clay County Missouri 1877*

came, aided by a $100,000 grant from the Soil Conservation Service. Swimmers today play in the water and sun on the sand beach, unaware of the old argument. But in such argument, the differences in philosophy between and within agencies and over time may be revealed.

The combination of history and recreation works well together at Watkins Mill. The park provides a place for a picnic or a shady bit of relaxation following a tour of the historic site, or in reverse, those camping for the weekend find a trip through the mill an interesting diversion. Camping is a part of the history of the Watkins farm; more than a century ago, the farm hosted the Missouri Valley Foxhunters Association. A tent city was erected, complete with barbershop and movie theater, and several thousand people camped for two weeks, listening to the baying of hounds and telling tall tales.

A tour of the mill begins at the front door, and upon stepping in from the bright sunshine, you get an immediate impression of great age; in the dim light, the softened edges of old brick flooring and wooden doorjambs worn smooth with time meet the eye. The slightly acrid odor of damp brick and old wood mingles with the oily scent of lanolin from sheep's wool, soaked deeply into the wooden floors and machinery. Near the front door is the mill office. There, you enter a mercantile world, complete with the store counter and walnut yardstick used for measuring yard goods, deep bins to hold bolts of finished cloth, and a hanging shelf above for displaying other sundries. Overhead, items of original store stock hang on nails. A letterpress and a tall bookkeeper's desk proclaim this was indeed the "office and sales room at the mill" that some advertisements proclaimed.

Upstairs, the second floor is mainly about weaving. Whitewashed walls, which enhanced visibility by reflecting light, surround lines of looms: from narrow simple looms of 1860 vintage that produced yard goods to wide looms for weaving blankets. Then come the most modern machines in the mill—fancy looms of the 1880s, set to weave patterned cloth, the pattern controlled by a chain-and-cam version of early automation. In the corner of this room sit two unimposing machines with tongue-twister names: ring-frame ply twisters. These particular examples are thought to be the only ones left in the world of their once common type.

The third floor is devoted to carding and spinning. A long row of carding machines—with rotating cylinders covered with sharp wire teeth—brushed and straightened fleece before its transformation into yarn and then cloth. Across the room, two rows of spinning machines mark a midpoint in industrial evolution. Known as spinning jacks, each spins 216 threads at a time, a leap forward from Richard Arkwright's famous spinning jenny, which prepared 16 threads simultaneously.

Back on the first floor are all of the wet-finishing machines needed to convert the raw cloth into the fine, salable product we see in stores. Here is a zone of mainly wooden machines for fulling, washing, dyeing, pressing, and napping. These machines have a homemade, antique look but were state of the art for their time. The fourth floor attic with its low ceiling is not open to visitors, but long racks studded with tenter hooks are still there, awaiting cloth to stretch and dry.

Waltus Watkins was never one to waste things, and thus the window sills of the mill are made from the packing crates in which the looms were shipped. The boards that form the wooden enclosure surrounding the main power sheave clearly show the stenciled legend "Not Contraband," displaying their origin as crating lumber that once enclosed mill machinery being shipped into an embargoed Missouri in the 1860s.

Behind this board enclosure can be seen the huge ten-foot-diameter main power sheave for the entire factory. This cast-iron wheel drove a belt of twenty-inch-wide leather that was connected to a power-distribution center on the second floor, from which in turn every machine

HOW WATKINS MILL WAS SAVED

Potential buyers and curious spectators crowded the entry room of the old mill in 1958, awaiting an auction that would ultimately lead to the creation of this state historic site. The Watkins farm had been promoted as a state park as early as 1938, after the death of the last of Waltus Watkins's sons, but in 1945, the heirs sold the entire farm to ranching interests from Texas. Now, thirteen years later, the property was for sale again. At this auction, the home estate was likely to be sold in parcels, breaking up the large farm that Watkins began acquiring in 1839.

Three curious employees of Allis-Chalmers Gleaner Combine Works in Independence were among those planning to attend. At the last minute, George Reuland had to cancel, but Lee Oberholtz and Forest Ingram went on, carrying with them Reuland's casual request to "buy a souvenir for me." When the afternoon ended, the request was more than satisfied—in a burst of enthusiasm and for a little more than $600, they had bought the entire contents of the mill, four floors loaded with rare, century-old textile equipment and machinery.

The next day, the three formed the nonprofit Watkins Mill Association to deal with the enormous task of removing all contents of the mill within thirty days, the land with the mill on it having been sold to a different bidder. But the winning bidder's check bounced, and the second-place bidder, George Stilley, agreed to sell the mill and the Watkins home to the association, while he retained the farm ground. By this bit of luck, the old machines were not only saved but also saved intact in their historic environment.

With the leadership of the Watkins Mill Association and the help of hundreds of volunteers, a several year effort culminated in the successful Clay County bond issue that allowed the Watkins Mill and most of the original farm to become part of the state park system on January 1, 1964. Today, the association remains an active partner, supporting the state in making Watkins Mill available to the public.

Top: Fancy looms convert yarns into cloth in a pattern controlled by an automated program, and each loom is powered by a belt from an overhead line shaft. Above: Converting fleece to cloth requires carding, where it is loosely combed into long soft ropes called rovings, ready to be spun into yarn. Above right: The carriage of the spinning jack travels forward, stretching and twisting 216 rovings, turning each into six feet of yarn, then repeats the process over and over. ***All Ron Ginther***

in the building was driven by line shafts and belts. The sheave is mounted on an iron axle that passes through the brick wall into the engine room immediately outside.

The tour of the mill concludes in the engine room at the rear of the building. From here, a steam engine, powered by a thirty-foot iron boiler salvaged from a sunken steamboat, provided the power to run all three floors of machinery. The shaft piercing the wall into the mill is surmounted by a sixteen-foot-diameter flywheel weighing four tons. The many scars in the brick wall are a lasting remembrance of those who had to turn it by hand with pry bars when the engine would occasionally stop on dead center. It could not be restarted with steam power until rotated off-center by manpower.

Nowadays, when early retirement often begins at fifty-five, it is not easy to understand the determination of a man who began the largest undertaking of his life at that age—risking everything he owned, at a time when cash was hard, credit practically nonexistent, and the outbreak of civil war at any moment a virtual certainty. This amazing survival of nineteenth-century industrial America is a fitting memorial to the determination and strength of the man who willed it into existence. *

WATKINS WOOLEN MILL STATE HISTORIC SITE AND PARK • 26600 PARK ROAD NORTH, LAWSON

Bibliography Information

MATERIAL FOR THE ESSAYS IN THIS BOOK has been drawn from a wide array of sources both documentary and secondary, as well as from personal observations and interviews. Authors have visited each park once or several times in the course of preparing these essays, and talked with park staff and other knowledgeable persons. This essay includes types of sources available for research as well as suggestions for further reading on a variety of topics addressed in this book and on many of the parks and historic sites.

Archival Resources. Park officials made available archival and current files on the individual parks, including correspondence, reports, plans, clippings, and for some parks and historic sites, archival materials from previous owners of the property. This material has been supplemented by ancillary research for a history of the system as a whole, using annual agency reports, minutes, correspondence, land acquisition records, and other data. For the earlier years of the system, when park archives are thin, the papers of several Missouri governors and other materials in the Western Historical Manuscript Collection (now the State Historical Society of Missouri Research Center at Columbia) and the Missouri State Archives at Jefferson City are quite rich. These have been supplemented with newspapers available at the State Historical Society and, for the period after 1945, with clippings from the files at the Missouri State Library, as well as with census records, county histories, and other items. To list all these resources individually is beyond the scope of this essay.

The Movement for Public Parks. Perhaps the most suggestive work on the intellectual context of the movement for public parks is Norman T. Newton, *Design on the Land: The Development of Landscape Architecture* (Cambridge: Harvard University Press, 1971), while architect Albert Good chaired a committee to select examples from parks nationwide for what would become the classic guide to CCC-era "parkitecture": Albert Good, *Park and Recreation Structures, Parts I-III* (National Park Service, 1938). The most insightful history of the national park system, on which many state systems including Missouri's are modeled, is Richard West Sellars, *Preserving Nature in the National Parks: A History* (New Haven CT: Yale University Press, 1997; 2009). For historic sites, a classic work is Charles B. Hosmer Jr., *Presence of the Past: A History of the Preservation Movement in the United States before Williamsburg* (New York: Putnam, 1965) and *Preservation Comes of Age: From Williamsburg to the National Trust, 1926—1949*, 2 vols. (Charlot-

The Missouri River is known for its memorable sunsets, seen here from the Bonne Femme Bridge on the Katy Trail. ***Randal Clark***

tesville: University Press of Virginia, 1981). The best approach to urban parks in Missouri is through Caroline Loughlin and Catherine Anderson, *Forest Park* (Columbia: Junior League of St. Louis and University of Missouri Press, 1986); William H. Wilson, *The City Beautiful Movement in Kansas City* (Columbia: University of Missouri Press, 1964); and Edward C. Rafferty, "Orderly City, Orderly Lives: The City Beautiful Movement in St. Louis," *Gateway Heritage* 11:4 (Spring 1991): 40-65.

The National Conference on State Parks published several comprehensive reports on state park systems: Raymond H. Torrey, *State Parks and Recreational Uses of State Forests in the United States* (Washington, DC, 1926); and Beatrice Ward Nelson, *State Recreation: Parks, Forests and Game Preserves* (Washington, DC, 1928). For an overview of postwar recreation issues see the reports of two major national commissions: Outdoor Recreation Resources Review Commission, *Outdoor Recreation for America* (Washington, DC: USGPO, 1962), and President's Commission on Americans Outdoors, *Americans Outdoors: The Legacy, the Challenge* (Washington, DC: Island Press, 1987). Freeman Tilden offers a classic personal interpretation with essays on selected parks nationwide in *The State Parks: Their Meaning in American Life* (New York: Alfred A. Knopf, 1962). For a study of contemporary state park issues as of 1989, see Phyllis Myers, *State Parks in a New Era*, 3 vols. (Washington, DC: The Conservation Foundation, 1989), and for an excellent, more recent history and critique of the movement for state parks see Ney C. Landrum, T*he State Park Movement in America: A Critical Review* (Columbia: University of Missouri Press, 2004, 2013).

Missouri State Park System History, Inventories, and Plans. Numerous articles published in magazines and newspapers have discussed individual Missouri parks, but few have dealt with the system as a whole. Periodicals that have carried articles about parks and related themes over the years include *Bulletin of the Missouri Historical Society, Gateway Heritage, Grassroots, Missouri Archaeological Society Quarterly, Missouri Archaeologist, Missouri Game and Fish News, Missouri Conservationist, Missouri Historical Review, Missouri Life, Missouri Magazine* (1928-1938), *Missouri Preservation News*, and *Ozarks Watch. Missouri Resource Review*, published since 1982 by the Missouri Department of Natural Resources (DNR), features a park or park theme in each issue, while *Heritage*, the newsletter of the Missouri Parks Association (1983 to date), is the best source for news about the park system and park issues in recent decades (see parks.missouri.org).

Carl Chapman traced the history of archaeological research in Missouri, much of which was at sites now in the park system, in "Digging Up Missouri's Past," *Missouri Historical Review* 61:3 (April 1967): 348-63, while Michael O'Brien revisited the subject in his book-length *Paradigms of the Past: the Story of Missouri Archaeology* (Columbia: University of Missouri Press, 1996). Ronald W. Johnson discussed the park division's early involvement in preservation of historic sites in two articles, "Historic Preservation in Missouri: Origins and Development through the Second World War," *Bulletin of the Missouri Historical Society* 32:4 (July 1976): 222-46, and "Historic Preservation in Missouri: A Recent View," *Midwest Quarterly* 18:1 (October 1976): 64-77. Greg Iffrig and Paul Nelson discussed a new approach at that time to resource management in "Savannah Stewardship in Missouri State Parks," *Missouri Prairie Journal* 5:1-2 (October 1983): 3-12. Park philosophy and issues are explored in *First Missouri Conference on State Parks, June 15-17, 1984: Proceedings*, edited by Susan Flader (Missouri Parks Association, 1984).

Paul W. Nelson prepared a "Natural Heritage Inventory of Missouri State Parks" (DNR, 1980), which categorized and listed sites for natural areas, rare and endangered species, and special ecological management areas. Richard H. Thom and Greg Iffrig followed in 1985 with *Directory of Missouri Natural Areas* (many of which are in state parks), issued by the Missouri Natural Areas Committee, revised in 1996, and now available on-line: http://mdc.mo.gov/discover-nature/places-go/natural-areas. See also Michael Leahy, *Discover Missouri Natural Areas: A Guide to 50 Great Places* (Missouri Department of Conservation, 2011). These works were in turn based on natural area inventories initiated by Dr. William Elder of the University of Missouri-Columbia in the 1970s, extended to the entire state by the L-A-D Foundation under the general direction of R. Roger Pryor, and further refined through an ongoing computerized methodology developed by the Nature Conservancy under sponsorship first by the Department of Natural Resources and then by the Department of Conservation. For the world underground see James and Treva Gardner, "An Inventory and Evaluation of Missouri State Park Cave Resources" (report, DNR, 1982). And for a conceptual framework see Paul W. Nelson's "Natural History Themes for the Missouri State Park System" (DNR, 1985).

A major survey of CCC and WPA architecture in the parks resulted in the nomination of nearly 350 structures to the National Register of Historic Places: James M. Denny and Bonita Marie Wright, "Emergency Conservation Work (E.C.W.) Architecture in Missouri State Parks, 1933-1942, Thematic Resources" (1984). A sobering park-by-park assessment of internal and external threats was issued as *Challenge of the '90s: Our Threatened State Parks*, 2 vols, (1991). The DNR in 1991 also issued a draft "Missouri State Park and Historic Site System Expansion Plan," containing an analysis of the system and suggested criteria for expansion.

The central office maintains planning documents for all parks and historic sites, including general management plans, conceptual development plans, natural and cultural resource management and interpretation plans, and nominations or plans for special features, such as natural areas, wild areas, special ecological stewardship areas, the National Register of Historic Places, and National Natural and Historic Landmarks. Missouri State Parks also has or is developing computerized inventories of floral and faunal species, archaeological sites and artifacts, historic sites and artifacts, and lands and buildings. Following a recent inventory of more than 230 trails, the park division published T*rails of Missouri State Parks* (2012), complete with maps.

Missouri Landforms and Natural Resources. Characteristic landforms of Missouri are discussed in several classic works: Carl O. Sauer, *The Geography of the Ozark Highland of Missouri*, (The Geographic Society of Chicago, Bulletin No. 7, 1920; reprint New York: Greenwood Press, 1968); J. Harlen Bretz, *Caves of Missouri* (Rolla: Division of Geological Survey and Water Resources, 1956, 2012); H. Dwight Weaver and Paul A. Johnson, *Missouri: The Cave State* (Jefferson City: Discovery Enterprises, 1980); Jerry D. Vineyard and Gerald L. Feder, *Springs of Missouri* (Rolla: Missouri Division of Geological Survey and Water Resources, 1974); Walter A. Schroeder, *Missouri Water Atlas* (Jefferson City: Missouri Department of Natural Resources, 1982); Thomas R. Beveridge, *Geologic Wonders and Curiosities of Missouri*, Educational Series No. 4, revised by Jerry D. Vineyard (Rolla: Missouri Division of Geology and Land Survey, 1990); Jon L. Hawker, *Missouri Landscapes: A Tour Through Time*, Educational Series No. 7 (Rolla: Missouri Department of Natural Resources, Division of Geology and Land Survey, 1992); A. G. Unklesbay and Jerry D. Vineyard, *Missouri Geology: Three Billion Years of Volcanoes, Seas, Sediments, and Erosion* (Columbia: University of Missouri Press, 1992); H. Dwight Weaver, James N. Huckins, and Rickard L. Walk, *The Wilderness Underground: Caves of* *the Ozark Plateau* (Columbia: University of Missouri Press, 1992); and Charles G. Spencer, *Roadside Geology of Missouri* (Mountain Press Publishing Company, 2011).

The dean of botanical studies in Missouri was Julian Steyermark, whose key works are *Studies of the Vegetation of Missouri: I. Natural Plant Association and Succession in the Ozarks of Missouri*, Field Museum of Natural History, Botanical Series 9:5, Publication 485 (Chicago, 1940); *Vegetational History of the Ozark Forest*, University of Missouri Studies, 31 (Columbia, 1959); and *Flora of Missouri* (1963), now revised and published in three volumes by George Yatskievych as *Steyermark's Flora of Missouri* (St. Louis: Missouri Botanical Garden Press, 1999–2013). The occurrence of prairie in the state has been expertly mapped and analyzed by Walter A. Schroeder in *Presettlement Prairie of Missouri*, Natural History Series No. 2 (Jefferson City: Missouri Department of Conservation, 1982). For glades see Paul W. Nelson and Jane A. Fitzgerald, *Glade Conservation Assessment for the Interior Highlands and Interior Low Plateaus of the Central Hardwoods Region* (Central Hardwoods Joint Venture, 2013), available on-line. Several handy guides to trees, wildflowers, ferns, orchids, aquatic plants, and other flora have been published by the Missouri Department of Conservation.

Regarding the role of fire in Missouri ecosystems, see A. P. Beilmann and L. G. Brenner, "The Recent Intrusion of Forests in the Ozarks," *Annals of the Missouri Botanical Garden* 38 (1951): 261–82; and Douglas Ladd, "Re-examination of the Role of Fire in Missouri Oak Woodlands," in *Proceedings of the Oak Woods Management Workshop* (Charleston: Eastern Illinois University, 1991), 67–80. For a discussion of the use of prescribed burns in restoring and maintaining Missouri natural communities, especially as applied in state parks, see Ken McCarty, "Ecological Management," in Paul W. Nelson, T*he Terrestrial Natural Communities of Missouri* (Missouri Natural Areas Committee, 2010), 38–61.

The best guide to Missouri mammals is by Charles W. Schwartz and Elizabeth R. Schwartz, *The Wild Mammals of Missouri* (Columbia: University of Missouri Press, 1959; Revised editions 1981, 2002). For birds see Brad Jacobs, *Birds in Missouri* (Jefferson City: Missouri Department of Conservation, 2001). See also Conservation Department guides to fishes, naiads, reptiles and amphibians, butterflies, and other fauna.

For a report on the biodiversity of the state, see Timothy Nigh et al., T*he Biodiversity of Missouri* (Jefferson City: Missouri Department of Conservation, 1992). For species of conservation concern see Francis T. Holt et al., *Rare and Endangered Species of Missouri*, rev. ed. (Jefferson City: Missouri Department of Conservation, 1984) and checklists of "Missouri Species and Communities of Conservation Concern," now issued annually by MDC (2014).

Missouri History and Cultural Resources. For Missouri archaeology see Carl H. Chapman, *The Archaeology of Missouri* (Columbia: University of Missouri Press, Vol. 1, 1975; Vol. 2, 1980); Michael J. O'Brien and W. Raymond Wood, *The Prehistory of Missouri* (Columbia: University of Missouri Press, 1998); and Carol Diaz-Granados and James R. Duncan, *The Petroglyphs and Pictographs of Missouri* (University of Alabama Press, 2000). More accessible for the general reader is Carl H. Chapman and Eleanor F. Chapman, *Indians and Archaeology of Missouri* (Columbia: University of Missouri Press, 1964; Revised Edition 1983).

Among the numerous surveys of Missouri history, the most consistently helpful is David D. March, *The History of Missouri*, 4 vols. (New York: Lewis Historical Publishing Company, 1967). David Thelen's *Paths of Resistance: Tradition and Dignity in Industrializing Missouri* (New York: Oxford University Press, 1986; reprint Columbia: University of Missouri Press, 1991) offers insight on the political culture of the state. The several volumes of the University of Missouri Press series *A History of Missouri*, by William E. Foley, Perry McCandless, William E. Parrish, Lawrence O. Christensen, Gary R. Kremer, Richard S. Kirkendall, and Lawrence H. Larsen are also useful, as are one-volume surveys by Duane G. Meyer, Paul C. Nagel, and William E. Parrish et al. For those interested in parks and historic sites, the outstanding WPA guide, *Missouri: A Guide to the "ShowMe" State* (1941), supervised by Charles van Ravenswaay, is still indispensable; it was reissued in 1986 by the University Press of Kansas as *WPA Guide to 1930s Missouri*. See also Lawrence O. Christensen et al., *Dictionary of Missouri Biography* (Columbia: University of Missouri Press, 1999).

Missouri's pivotal role in the central conflict of American history continues to engage the national imagination. The literature regarding Civil War Missouri is vast and ever-growing, stimulated in recent years by 150th anniversary observances. Besides interpretations of the guerrilla conflict and new studies of various battles and campaigns and biographies of notable generals, there are also now new investigations about African American soldiers, life on the home front, and women's experiences. Many of these studies can be related directly or indirectly to Missouri historic sites. Much of this new scholarship is motivated by a worldview quite far removed from that of earlier investigations.

Official records and other contemporaneous material about the five battles commemorated in the park system—Carthage, Athens, Lexington, Island Mound, and Pilot Knob—may be found in US War Department, *The War of the Rebellion: A Compilation of the Official Records of the Union and Confederate Armies* (128 volumes, 1880–1901) and Frank Moore, ed., *The Rebellion Record: A Diary of American Events, with Documents, Narratives, Illustrative Incidents, Poetry, etc.* (12 volumes, 1861–1868), both available online. For a Missouri overview, see Louis Gerteis, *The Civil War in Missouri: A Military History* (Columbia: University of Missouri Press, 2012)

The history of Missourians' relationship to their natural resources can be approached through Charles Callison, *Man and Wildlife in Missouri: The History of One State's Treatment of Its Natural Resources* (Harrisburg, Pa.: Stackpole, 1953; reprint Jefferson City: Missouri Department of Conservation, 1981); James F. Keefe, *The First 50 Years* (Jefferson City: Missouri Department of Conservation, 1987); and Susan L. Flader, ed., *Toward Sustainability for Missouri Forests* (St. Paul MN: USDA Forest Service North Central Research Station, 2004).

Natural Division Frameworks. The regionalization scheme of natural divisions that provides the organizational framework for this book was developed by the Missouri Natural Areas Committee; see Richard H. Thom and James H. Wilson, "The Natural Divisions of Missouri," *Transactions, Missouri Academy of Science* 14 (1980): 9–23. This regionalization was in turn based on schemes developed in Sauer, *Geography of the Ozark Highland of Missouri* (1920), Arthur B. Cozzens, "Analyzing and Mapping Natural Landscape Factors of the Ozarks Province," *Academy of Science of St. Louis Transactions* 30:2 (1939): 37–63; James E. Collier, "Geographic Regions of Missouri," *Annals of the Association of American Geographers* 45 (December 1955): 368–92; and other regional studies in the fields of geology, soils, vegetation, zoogeography, and so forth.

More recently, a cooperative effort of state and federal agencies and organizations in Missouri has been developing a spatially nested ecological classification system that integrates patterns in landforms, geology, soils, and vegetation from broad continental ecoregions through landscapes to local levels; see Timothy A. Nigh and Walter A. Schroeder, *Atlas of Missouri Ecoregions* (Jefferson City: Missouri Department of Conservation, 2002). Parallel with these classification efforts has been the development of an increasingly sophisticated natural community classification system for Missouri led by Paul Nelson, formerly of the natural history program in the state park system; see Paul W. Nelson's *The Terrestrial Natural Communities of Missouri* (Jefferson City: Missouri Natural Areas Committee, 1985; revised editions 1987, 2005, 2010), which characterizes eighty-nine distinct communities and includes numerous examples from state parks.

Although there is no comparable widely accepted division of the state based on history and culture, Walter A. Schroeder developed a map of cultural regions of Missouri for the reissue of the *WPA Guide to 1930s Missouri* (University of Kansas Press, 1986), which overlaps in significant respects with the natural divisions used in this book.

The natural divisions, the Missouri ecoregions, and the natural communities classifications developed by Nelson and others have served since the 1980s as the basis for the state park natural history program, including natural history aspects of state historic sites.

Ozarks. The best place to start reading about the Ozarks and the Ozark Border is with the trenchant observations of the early nineteenth-century traveler Henry Rowe Schoolcraft, published in several volumes: *A View of the Lead Mines of Missouri* (New York: Charles Wiley & Company, 1819); and *Journal of a Tour into the Interior of Missouri and Arkansas* (1821), reissued as *Schoolcraft in the Ozarks*, ed. Hugh Park (Van Buren, Ark.: Press-Argus Printers, 1955). Other key works offering insight on the Ozarks include Sauer's *Geography of the Ozark Highland;* Vance Randolph, *The Ozarks: An American Survival of Primitive Society* (New York: Vanguard Society, 1931); Otto Ernst Rayburn, *Ozark Country* (New York: Duell, Sloan and Pearce, 1941); Russel L. Gerlach, *Immigrants in the Ozarks: A Study in Ethnic Geography* (Columbia: University of Missouri Press, 1976); and Milton D. Rafferty, *The Ozarks: Land and Life* (1980; 2nd edition, 2001).

For more information on the geology and the diverse flora of the parks at the core of the Ozarks in the St. Francois Mountains—Elephant Rocks, Taum Sauk, Johnson's Shut-ins, and Sam Baker—see Cheryl M. Seeger, "St. Francois Mountains Geologic History" (unpublished, Missouri Division of Geology, c. 2011), the St. Francois Mountains Natural Area Nomination (1996), Paul W. Nelson, "Flora of Johnson's Shut-Ins State Park, Reynolds County, Missouri" (M.S. thesis, Southern Illinois University, Carbondale, 1977), and draft natural resource management plans for Elephant Rocks (c2005) and Johnson's Shut-ins (c2000). Theodore Pease Russell wrote regular columns of historical vignettes and personal observations on this part of the Ozarks in the nineteenth century; these have been edited and annotated by James F. Keefe and Lynn Morrow as *A Connecticut Yankee in the Frontier Ozarks: The Writings of Theodore Pease Russell* (Columbia: University of Missouri Press, 1988).

Studies of the Battle of Pilot Knob include Cyrus A. Peterson, *Pilot Knob: The Thermopylae of the West* (1964, 2nd edition, 2000), and Walter E. Busch, *Fort Davidson and the Battle of Pilot Knob: Missouri's Alamo* (Charleston: The History Press, 2010). See also the Fort Davidson interpretive plan (2002). Among the biographies of Sterling Price is Robert E. Shalhope, *Sterling Price: Portrait of a Southerner* (Columbia: University of Missouri Press, 1971).

For the Meramec River, along which there are five state parks (Onondaga, Meramec, Robertsville, Route 66 and Castlewood), see James P. Jackson, *Passages of a Stream: A Chronicle of the Meramec* (Columbia: University of Missouri Press, 1984), and "Meramec State Park Natural Resource Management Plan" (c 2008). George C. Suggs, Jr., offers brief essays on Dillard and Bollinger mills in *Water Mills of the Missouri Ozarks* (Norman: University of Oklahoma Press, 1990), and Priscilla Evans puts the mills in historical context in "Merchant Gristmills and Communities, 1820-1880: An Economic Relationship," *Missouri Historical Review* 68 (April 1974): 317-26. See also Bonnie Stepenoff, "National Register of Historic Places Nomination for Dillard Mill Historic District" (2014).

Carol A. Fuller, Barbara Farnsworth, Gordon Todd Maupin, Theresa L. Hilton, and Kathleen Lee Hornberger have written master's theses at Southwest Missouri State University on aspects of the vegetation of several state parks, respectively Ha Ha Tonka (1986, 1998), Montauk (1975), and Roaring River (1979, 1980). See also natural resource management plans for Ha Ha Tonka (c2003) and Bennett Spring (2009). Ralph McCanse has written a beautifully evocative narrative poem, *Waters over Linn Creek Town* (New York: Bookman Associates, 1951), on the country that is now inundated by Lake of the Ozarks, and H. Dwight Weaver has seven books of history and vintage images of the Lake of the Ozarks region, including *A Pictorial Guide to Ha Ha Tonka State Park* (Osage River Trails, 2011), *Lake of the Ozarks: The Early Years* (Arcadia Publishing, 2000), *History and Geography of Lake of the Ozarks* (Vols. I & II, Osage River Trails, 2005, 2008), and *Osage Beach* (Arcadia Publishing, 2012), all of which discuss the early history of sites in state parks.

The Current River country, which includes Montauk and Current River state parks, is depicted in Leonard Hall's classic *Stars Upstream: Life along an Ozark River* (1958; rev. ed., University of Missouri Press, 1969), and in *Two Ozark Rivers: The Current and the Jacks Fork*, with photographs by Oliver Schuchard and text by Steve Kohler (Columbia: University of Missouri Press, 1984). See also natural and cultural resource management plans for Current River State Park and the National Register nomination for the Alton Club (2005). For background on the Pioneer Backcountry, see Jim Guldin, Greg Iffrig, and Susan Flader, eds., *Pioneer Forest—50 Years of Sustainable Uneven-Aged Forest Management in the Missouri Ozarks* (Asheville NC: USDA Forest Service Southern Research Station, 2007).

For the early history of the Wappapello region, see James and Cynthia Price, "Greenville on the St. Francis" (Center for Archaeological Research, Southwest Missouri State University, 1979). The best approach to Grand Gulf is through Luella Agnes Owen, *Cave Regions of the Ozarks and Black Hills* (1898; reprinted with an introduction by Jerry Vineyard, New York: Johnson Reprint Corp., 1970), which also discusses caves in the vicinity of Table Rock Lake. "Tourism in the White River Valley," where Table Rock and Roaring River state parks are located, was the subject of a special issue of *OzarksWatch* 3:4 (Spring 1990) and Lynn Morrow and Linda Myers-Phinney, *Shepherd of the Hills Country: Tourism Transforms the Ozarks, 1880s-1930s* (Fayetteville: University of Arkansas Press, 1999). See also the Roaring River Hills Wild Area management plan (2003) and, for Big Sugar Creek in the Elk River Hills, the natural and cultural resource management plans (2008, 2009).

For Nathan Boone, see Carole Bills, ed., *Nathan Boone: The Neglected Hero* (Republic, Mo.: Western Printing Co., 1984) and R. Douglas Hurt, *Nathan Boone and the American Frontier* (Columbia: University of Missouri Press, 2000). Olive Boone is portrayed in Margot Ford McMillen and Heather Roberson, *Called to Courage: Four Women in Missouri History* (Columbia: University of Missouri Press, 2002). See also the natural resource management plan for the site (c2009). The Civil War in the Ozarks, including the Battles of Carthage and Pilot Knob, is the subject of a special double issue of *OzarksWatch*, 4:4 and 5:1 (Spring-Summer 1991).

The prehistory of the Springfield Plateau area represented by Stockton, Pomme de Terre, and Harry S Truman parks was the subject of an intensive interdisciplinary study reported in *Prehistoric Man and His Environments: A Case Study in the Ozark Highland*, ed. W. Raymond Wood and R. Bruce McMillan (New York: Academic Press, 1977). See also a two-volume draft cultural resource report by Curtis H. Synhorst prepared for this study (1977). For controversies over hydroelectric dams in the region, see Leland and Crystal Payton, *Damming the Osage: The Conflicted Story of Lake of the Ozarks and Truman Reservoir* (Lens & Pen Press, 2012).

Ozark Border. For an indication of some of the special features of Hawn and St. Francois parks in the Ozark Border, see John A. Karel and William H. Elder, "A Natural Area Survey of the Southeast Missouri Regional Planning District" (University of Missouri Cooperative Wildlife Research Unit, Columbia, 1976); and Mary Kay Solecki, "The Vegetation and Floristics of Hawn State Park, Ste. Genevieve County, Missouri" (MS thesis, Southern Illinois University, Carbondale, 1981). See also the natural resource management plans for Hawn (c2000), St. Francois (c2001) and St. Joe (2012) state parks.

Early excavations at Mastodon State Historic Site are discussed in M. G. Mehl, *Missouri's Ice Age Animals,* Education Series No. 1 (Rolla: Missouri Division of Geological Survey and Water Resources, 1962), and subsequent excavations in Russell W. Graham, "Final Report on Paleontological and Archaeological Excavations and Surface Surveys at Mastodon State Park" (Illinois State Museum, Springfield, 1981). For the petroglyphs at Washington State Park see Ronald J. Wyatt, "A Study of Three Petroglyph Sites along Big River in the Eastern Ozark Highland of Missouri" (paper, Harvard University, 1959).

Missouri's mining history, represented at Missouri Mines, St. Joe, and Finger Lakes, is summarized by Jo Burford in "Underground Treasures: The Story of Mining in Missouri," *Official Manual, State of Missouri, 1977-1978*, 1-33. See also Henry C. Thompson, *Our Lead Belt Heritage* (Flat River, Mo.: News-Sun, 1955) and Robert E. Faust, "Lead Belt Progressives: The Struggle for Social and Environmental Reform in Missouri Mining Communities" (PhD dissertation, University of Missouri-Columbia, 2003).

For the parks along the lower Meramec River—Castlewood, Route 66, Don Robinson, and Robertsville—see the "Meramec River Greenway Concept Plan" (unpub., St. Louis Co. Department of Planning, Sept. 2003). Castlewood, St. Joe, and Finger Lakes—all in the Ozark Border—were among the featured case studies in a Heritage Conservation and Recreation Service handbook on *Land Conservation and Preservation Techniques* by Timothy Fox (USDI, 1979). For Castlewood, see also a website on the Kiefer Creek Restoration Project: http://kiefercreek.weebly.com/about-the-watershed.html. The Times Beach disaster at what is now Route 66 State Park has been well covered nationwide and may readily be searched on the Internet; see, for example, "Times Beach, Missouri Votes Itself out of Existence," *The New York Times*, April 3, 1985," and William Powell, "Remember Times Beach: The Dioxin Disaster, 30 Years Later," *St. Louis Magazine*, December 3, 2012. See also Great River Associates, Inc., *Meramec River US 66 Bridge J-0421 Historic Structure Report* (2011); Quinta Scott and Susan Kelly, *Route 66: A Highway and its People* (Norman: University of Oklahoma Press, 1988); and Michael Cassity, *Route 66 Corridor National Historic Context Study* (2004). For Don Robinson State Park, see the natural resource management plan (2013) and the *LaBarque Creek Watershed Conservation Plan* (Friends of LaBarque Creek Watershed, 2009).

For Babler, see the National Register nomination for "E.C.W. Architecture in Missouri State Parks" (1985) and the natural resource and ecological stewardship management plans (2011 and 2013). Excavations at Graham Cave are reported in Wilfred D. Logan, *Graham Cave: An Archaic Site,* Missouri Archaeological Society Memoir No. 2 (1952) and Walter E. Klippel, *Graham Cave Revisited: A Reevaluation of Its Cultural Position during the Archaic Period*, Missouri Archaeological Society Memoir No. 9 (1971).

For a history of the mills at Rock Bridge, see Amahia Mallea, "Rock Bridge Mills in the Nineteenth Century" (2002), and for an account of the origins of the park, see Gene Baumann, "In Memory of Carol," *The Optimist Magazine* (February 1967). See also the park's natural resource management plan (2005) and the *Bonne Femme Watershed Plan* (Bonne Femme Stakeholder Committee, 2007), summarized by Robert Lerch, Roxie Campbell, and Terry Frueh, "Successful Stakeholder-led Watershed Planning," *NSS News*, (April 2008). For Finger Lakes, see the park's conceptual development plan (2005).

Mississippi Lowlands. A good overview of the history of the Mississippi Lowlands is Leon Parker Ogilvie, "The Development of the Southeast Missouri Lowlands" (PhD dissertation, University of Missouri-Columbia, 1967). For a classic if iconoclastic interpretation see Thad Snow, *From Missouri: An American Farmer Looks Back*, ed. Bonnie Stepenoff (Columbia: University of Missouri Press 2012; originally published in 1954). Paul A. Korte and Leigh H. Fredrickson have traced the "Loss of Missouri's Lowland Hardwood Ecosystem" in *Transactions of the 42nd North American Wildlife and Natural Resources Conference* (March 1977): 31-41.

For the champion trees at Big Oak Tree, see James P. Jackson, "A Park of Champions," *American Forests*, 69:5 (May 1963): 9, 62-63; and for an analysis of the vegetation see Wanda S. Oskins Doolen, "The Vascular Flora of Big Oak Tree State Park, Mississippi County, Missouri" (MS thesis, Central Missouri State University, 1984). See also the park's natural resource management plan (2006) and Craig L. Shafer, "Values and Shortcomings of Small Reserves," *Bioscience,* 45:2 (Feb. 1995), 80-88, for which Big Oak was featured on the cover.

Indian use of the lowland environment is considered in R. Barry Lewis, *Mississippian Exploitative Strategies: A Southeast Missouri Example* (Columbia: Missouri Archaeological Society Research Series No. 11, 1974), while excavations at Towosahgy are reported in James E. Price et al., "Archaeological Investigations in Three Areas of the Towosahgy State Historic Site, 23MI2, Mississippi County, Missouri, 1989" (University of Missouri, American Archaeology Division, June 1990). Robert A. Shaddy studied "The Hunter-Dawson Families in Southeast Missouri" in a University of Missouri-Columbia paper in 1987. For Morris State Park, see the cultural and draft natural resource management plans (2008, c2011).

Big Rivers. The best starting points for the Big Rivers are undoubtedly Mark Twain's *Life on the Mississippi* (1883) and *The Journals of the Lewis and Clark Expedition* (1803-1806). The definitive thirteen-volume edition of the journals is edited by Gary E. Moulton and published by the University of Nebraska Press; for the Missouri portion, see Vol. 1: *Atlas of the Lewis and Clark Expedition* (1983) and Vol. 2: *August 30, 1803-August 24, 1804* (1986). For a path-breaking computer-assisted re-creation of the natural landscape and settlement patterns of the time in maps and text based on original sources see James D. Harlan and James M. Denny, *Atlas of Lewis and Clark in Missouri* (Columbia: University of Missouri Press, 2003). The Mississippi River as far north as St. Louis and parts of the Missouri are also admirably described in A*n Account of Upper Louisiana*, written by Nicholas de Finiels in 1803 and edited by Carl J. Ekberg and William E. Foley (Columbia: University of Missouri Press, 1989).

Quinta Scott, *The Mississippi: A Visual Biography* (Columbia: University of Missouri Press, 2009), offers a superb history and photographic interpretation of changes along the entire course of the Mississippi River with a special focus on numerous efforts at restoration of habitat and hydrologic function in recent decades. For the Missouri River, see Don Pierce, *Exploring Missouri River Country* (Jefferson City: Missouri Department of Natural Resources, ca. 1982); and John L. Funk and John W. Robinson, *Changes in the Channel of the Lower Missouri River and Effects on Fish and Wildlife,* Aquatic Series No. 11 (Jefferson City: Missouri Department of Conservation, 1974).

For an account of the tragedy commemorated at Trail of Tears State Park, see Theda Perdue and Michael Green, *The Cherokee Nation and the Trail of Tears* (Penguin Library, 2008), and Joan Gilbert, *The Trail of Tears Across Missouri* (Columbia: University of Missouri Press, 1996). See also Tiffany Patterson, "Cherokee Trail of Tears in Missouri, 1837-1839" (National Register Nomination, 2013), and Trail of Tears draft natural resources management plan (2011).

For Ste. Genevieve and its hinterlands see Walter Schroeder, *Opening the Ozarks: A Historical Geography of Missouri's Ste. Genevieve District,*

1760-1830 (Columbia: University of Missouri Press, 2002); Carl J. Ekberg, *Colonial Ste. Genevieve* (Gerald MO: Patrice Press, 1985), *French Roots in the Illinois Country* (Urbana: University of Illinois Press, 1998), and *A French Aristocrat in the American West: The Shattered Dreams of De Lassus de Luzieres* (Columbia: University of Missouri Press, 2010); James Baker, "Menard & Valle and Ste. Genevieve's Early 19th Century Merchants," paper delivered at Fur Trade Symposium, 1989; Bonnie Stepenoff and Debbie Bibb, *The Delassus-Kern House* (Jefferson City: MDNR Division of State Parks, 2003); Bonnie Stepenoff, *From French Community to Missouri Town: Ste. Genevieve in the Nineteenth Century* (Columbia: University of Missouri Press, 2006); Mary Susan Green, "The Material Culture of a Pre-Enclosure Village in Upper Louisiana: Open Fields, Houses, and Cabinetry in Colonial Ste. Genevieve, 1750-1804" (MA thesis, University of Missouri-Columbia, 1983); and Susan C. Boyle, "Did She Generally Decide? Women in Ste. Genevieve, 1750-1805," *William and Mary Quarterly*, 3d series, 44 (October 1987): 775-89. See also the historic site's cultural and natural resource management plans (2008, 2007).

Scott Joplin and his musical tradition are discussed in Susan Curtis, *Dancing to a Black Man's Tune: A Life of Scott Joplin* (Columbia: University of Missouri Press, 1994, 2004) and Edward A. Berlin, *King of Ragtime: Scott Joplin and His Era* (New York: Oxford University Press, 1996).

For Iliniwek, the place to start is Fr. Marquette's journals and map in Reuben Gold Thwaites, ed., *The Jesuit Relations and Allied Documents*, Vol. LIX (Cleveland: Burrows Bros. Co., 1899); see also Raphael N. Hamilton, SJ, *Marquette's Explorations: The Narratives Reexamined* (Madison: University of Wisconsin Press, 1970). Archaeological excavations are reported in Larry D. Grantham, "The Illini Village of the Marquette and Jolliet Voyage of 1673," *The Missouri Archaeologist*, Vol. 54:1-20, and Kathleen L. Ehrhardt, "Linking History and Prehistory in the Midcontinent: Archaeological Investigations at Marquette and Jolliet's 'Peourea,'" *Papers in Honor of Dr. Howard D. Winters*, ed. by Anne-Marie Cantwell and Lawrence Conrad (Springfield IL: Illinois State Museum and Center for American Archaeology, 2004). See also the site's general management plan and draft natural resource management plan (1997, 2008). For Battle of Athens see Leslie Anders, *The Twenty-First Missouri: From Home Ground to Union Regiment* (Westport, Conn.: Greenwood Press, 1975), and Ben F. Dixon, *The Battle of Athens*, a 1991 reprint by the *Hometown Journal* of Kahoka, Missouri, of a local historian's articles about the battle. See also the site's draft natural resource management plan (2013).

The history of the Confluence area may be traced in numerous early historical accounts and subsequent studies, including those previously cited. See also Ken McCarty et al., "Revegetation and Restoration Plan" (MDNR 2004). *The Katy Railroad and the Last Frontier* by V. V. Masterson (1952; Columbia: University of Missouri Press, 1988) offers an account of the railroad that once ran along the Missouri River on what is now the Katy Trail, while James M. Denny et al. prepared an extensive report on cultural resources along the route from Sedalia to Machens, Missouri (DNR, 1986), and Brett Dufur frequently revises his *Complete Katy Trail Guidebook* (10th edition, 2013). For an account of the successive structures that have served as Missouri's capitol, including First State Capitol in St. Charles, see Marian Ohman, *The History of Missouri Capitols* (Columbia: University of Missouri Extension Division, 1982).

The German culture celebrated at Deutschheim is best approached through Charles van Ravenswaay's monumental *Arts and Architecture of German Settlements in Missouri: A Survey of a Vanishing Culture* (Columbia: University of Missouri Press, 1977, reprinted with an introduction by Adolf Schroeder, 2006). Original sources from the period include Gottfried Duden, *Report on a Journey to the Western States of North America*, ed. James W. Goodrich et al. (Columbia: State Historical Society of Missouri and University of Missouri Press, 1980), and *Hold Dear, As Always: Jette, A German Immigrant Life in Letters*, ed. Adolf E. Schroeder and Carla Schulz-Geisberg (Columbia: University of Missouri Press, 1988). For a history and portrait of Hermann, see Anna Kemper Hesse, ed., *Little Germany on the Missouri: The Photographs of Edward J. Kemper, 1895-1920* (Columbia: University of Missouri Press, 1998).

Clark's Hill may be approached through the Lewis and Clark journals; Elliott Coues, *The Expeditions of Zebulon Montgomery Pike: To Headwaters of the Mississippi River, Through Louisiana Territory, and in New Spain, During the Years 1805-6-7* (New York, Francis P. Harper, 1895); and annual reports of the Missouri River Commission, especially 1897. For Jefferson Landing, see Eldon Hattervig, "Jefferson Landing: A Commercial Center of the Steamboat Era," *Missouri Historical Review* 74:3 (April 1980): 277-99. The magnificent public art that is part of the original design of the Missouri State Museum, as well as other art in Missouri's current state capitol is treated in John Pickard, *Report of the Capitol Decoration Commission, 1917-1928* (Jefferson City, 1928) and beautifully depicted and discussed in Bob Priddy and Jeffrey Ball, *The Art of the Missouri Capitol: History in Canvas, Bronze, and Stone* (Columbia: University of Missouri Press and Missouri State Capitol Commission, 2011). See also Nancy Edelman, *The Thomas Hart Benton Murals in the Missouri State Capitol* (Jefferson City: Missouri State Council on the Arts, 1975).

The history and archaeology of the "Boone's Lick Salt Works, 1805-33," were reviewed by Robert T. Bray in *Missouri Archaeologist* 48 (December 1987): 1-65. For a superb historical study, see Lynn Morrow, "Boone's Lick in Western Expansion: James Mackay, the Boones, and the Morrisons," *Boone's Lick Heritage Quarterly*, 13:3:3-4 (Fall-Winter 2014), 4-32. For Arrow Rock see Charles van Ravenswaay, "Arrow Rock, Missouri," *Bulletin of the Missouri Historical Society* 15:3 (April 1959): 203-23; Dorothy J. Caldwell, *Missouri's National Historic Landmarks: Village of Arrow Rock and George Caleb Bingham Home* (Arrow Rock: Friends of Arrow Rock, Inc., 1968); and Michael Dickey, *Arrow Rock: Crossroads of the Missouri Frontier* (Arrow Rock: Friends of Arrow Rock, Inc., 2004). Studies of leading residents of the area include E. Maurice Bloch, *The Paintings of George Caleb Bingham: A Catalogue Raisonné* (Columbia: University of Missouri Press, 1986), and Nancy Rash, *The Painting and Politics of George Caleb Bingham* (New Haven: Yale University Press, 1991); Thomas B. Hall, Jr. and Thomas B. Hall III, *Dr. Sappington of Saline County, Missouri, 1776-1856*, (Arrow Rock: Friends of Arrow Rock, 1975, 1986); Lynn Morrow, "John Sappington: Southern Patriarch in the New West" (paper, University of Missouri-Columbia, 1985); and William H. Lyon, "Claiborne Fox Jackson and the Secession Crisis in Missouri," *Missouri Historical Review* 58 (July 1964): 422-41. See also the site's cultural resource and interpretation plans (2005). For African American history and archaeology see Timothy E. Baumann, " 'Because that's Where my Roots Are': Searching for Patterns of African American Ethnicity in Arrow Rock, Missouri" (PhD dissertation, University of Tennessee-Knoxville, 2001), and Baumann's "A Historical Perspective of Civic Engagement and Interpreting Cultural Diversity in Arrow Rock, Missouri," *Historical Archaeology* 45:1 (2011), 114-34. See also Friends of Arrow Rock, Inc., "Sappington Negro Cemetery" (unpublished, 2001).

For Van Meter State Historic Site see Jean Tyree Hamilton, "Abel J. Vanmeter, His Park and His Diary," *Bulletin of the Missouri Historical Society* 28:1 (October 1971): 3-37; Robert T. Bray, "The Missouri Indian Tribe in Archaeology and History," *Missouri Historical Review* 55:3 (1961): 213-25; Dale R. Henning, "Development and Interrelationships of Oneota Culture in the Lower Missouri River Valley," *Missouri Archaeologist* 32

(1970): iii-180; and Michael Dickey, *The People of the River's Mouth: In Search of the Missouria Indians* (Columbia: University of Missouri Press, 2011). See also the National Register nomination for the Utz Site (c1980).

One way to approach the Battle of Lexington is through the eyes of a participant, Ephraim McDowell Anderson, *Memoirs: Historical and Personal; Including the Campaigns of the First Missouri Confederate Brigade* (1868; reissued with annotations by Morningside Press, 1972). See also Neil Haddock, "Embattled Mansion," *Missouri Life* 5:1 (1977): 19-23; Larry Wood, *The Siege of Lexington, Missouri: The Battle of the Hemp Bales* (The History Press, 2014); and Lexington Historical Society, *The Battle of Lexington: Fought in and around the City of Lexington, Missouri* (2012). Regarding Confederate Memorial see Elizabeth Ustick McKinney, "The Confederate Home: Its Origin and Objects," in *The Confederate Mail Carrier* by James Bradley (Mexico, Mo., 1894), 231-61, and three volumes by Wade F. Ankesheiln: *The Heart is the Heritage: The Story of the Founding of the Confederate Home of Missouri* (Llumina Press, 2007), and *800 Voices: Each with a Story to Tell,* Vols. I and II (Two Trails Publishing, 2009).

The best place to start among the numerous biographies and studies of Thomas Hart Benton is certainly with his own autobiography, *An Artist in America* (1937; 4th edition, University of Missouri Press, 1983). For a haunting account of his life and work, see Karen Ann Marling, *Tom Benton and His Drawings: A Biographical Essay and a Collection of His Sketches, Studies, and Mural Cartoons* (Columbia: University of Missouri Press, 1985). See also R. Douglas Hurt and Mary K. Dains, eds., *Thomas Hart Benton: Artist, Writer, Intellectual* (Columbia: State Historical Society of Missouri, 1989).

For an in-house illustrated historical timeline of the Army Corps of Engineers Kansas City District, which had a significant impact on Weston Bend, Lewis and Clark, and Big Lake state parks, see *Heartland Engineers: A Century of Superior Service 1907-2007* (USACE 2009).

Osage Plains. The prairie plains of western and northern Missouri have been relatively little celebrated, but see Walter Schroeder's superb *Presettlement Prairie of Missouri* for maps of early prairies and a discussion of early travelers who described the prairie landscape. Denyse K. Sturges, "Prairie State Park: A Public Land History" (paper, University of Missouri-Columbia, 1985), traces the beginnings of the lands that became the park, while James H. Shortridge provides insights into the business that kept the lands in prairie in "Prairie Hay in Woodson County, Kansas: A Crop Anomaly," *Geographic Review* 63:4 (October 1973): 533-52.

Probably the finest account of the natives who roamed the western prairies is *The Osage: Children of the Middle Waters* by John Joseph Mathews (Norman: University of Oklahoma Press, 1961). See also Washington Irving's description of his encounters in *A Tour of the Prairies* (1835), ed. John Francis McDermott (Norman: University of Oklahoma Press, 1956); Carl H. Chapman, "The Origin of the Osage Indian Tribe: An Ethnographic, Historical and Archaeological Study" (Ph.D. dissertation, University of Michigan, 1959); and Willard H. Rollings, *The Osage: An Ethnohistorical Study of Hegemony on the Prairie-Plains* (Columbia: University of Missouri Press, 1995).

Though there is little known about the Truman Birthplace, a good place to start with the man is *The Autobiography of Harry S. Truman*, ed. Robert H. Ferrell (Boulder: Colorado Associated University Press, 1980). See also Ferrell's edition of Truman's letters to his wife, *Dear Bess: The Letters from Harry to Bess Truman, 1910—1959* (New York: Norton, 1983), and biographies by Margaret Truman, *Harry S. Truman* (New York: William Morrow, 1973) and David McCullough, *Truman* (Simon and Schuster, 1992).

For a historical introduction to the contested border along which the Battle of Island Mound was fought, see Jeremy Neely, *The Border Between Them: Violence and Reconciliation on the Kansas-Missouri Line* (Columbia: University of Missouri Press, 2007). Accounts of the battle itself may be found in the *Official Records* and in Moore's *Rebellion Records* (previously cited). For the history of the Rock Island, see Bill Marvel, *The Rock Island Line* (Bloomington: Indiana University Press, 2013).

Glaciated Plains. Bonnie Stepenoff has written about youth camps, a key aspect of Cuivre River State Park, as well as Lake of the Ozarks and Knob Noster, in "The New Deal's Camp Sherwood Forest: An Incubator of Democracy," *Gateway Heritage* 11:3 (Winter 1990-1991): 52-59. See also the Cuivre River natural resource management plan (2004) and the Lincoln Hills Natural Area nomination (1997). The most obvious place to start on Mark Twain is with *The Adventures of Tom Sawyer* (1876) and *Adventures of Huckleberry Finn* (1885), but don't neglect *The Gilded Age: A Tale of To-Day* (1873-1874), written with Charles Dudley Warner and set in part in Sam Clemens's Salt River country. See also his posthumously published *Mark Twain: Autobiography,* 2 vols. (New York: Harper and Brothers, 1924). Albert Bigelow Paine reported on his effort to find the birthplace cabin in Florida in *Mark Twain: A Biography*, 3 vols. (New York: Harper & Brothers, 1912). Concerning the saga of the cabin and the park, see Ralph Gregory, *M. A. "Dad" Violette: A Life Sketch*, a pamphlet printed in Perry, Missouri, in 1969. The Salt River country has been the subject of a major multidisciplinary study sponsored by the Army Corps of Engineers, summarized in Michael J. O'Brien, ed., *Grassland, Forest, and Historical Settlement: An Analysis of Dynamics in Northeast Missouri* (Lincoln: University of Nebraska Press, 1984). For the history of the dam see Michael D. Shulse, "The History and Development of the Clarence Cannon Dam and Reservoir, 1957-1968" (M.A. thesis, Northeast Missouri State University, 1975), and for the efforts of local folks to come to terms with the Mark Twain legend see Ron Powers, *White Town Drowsing* (Boston: Atlantic Monthly Press, 1986).

The military men honored by north Missouri parks are the subjects of a number of biographies, including Everett T. Tomlinson, *The Story of General Pershing* (New York: D. Appleton and Company, 1920); Donald Smythe, *Pershing: General of the Armies* (Bloomington: Indiana University Press, 1986); and David A. Lockmiller, *Enoch H. Crowder: Soldier, Lawyer and Statesman,* University of Missouri Studies 27 (Columbia, 1955). Pershing's autobiography, *My Experience in the World War,* 2 vols. (New York: Frederick A. Stokes Co., 1931), won the Pulitzer Prize. For an assessment of flooding and sedimentation along Locust Creek, which passes through both Locust Creek Covered Bridge and Pershing State Park, see HDR Engineering, Inc., *North Central Missouri: Locust Creek Watershed Study Final Report* (Prepared for the Army Corps of Engineers and Missouri Department of Natural Resources, November 2013). See also the park's draft management plan (c 2001).

The trauma of the Mormons in the vicinity of Wallace State Park is recounted in Stephen C. LeSueur, *The 1838 Mormon War in Missouri* (Columbia: University of Missouri Press, 1987). Dorothy Caldwell has written about Watkins Mill in "Missouri National Historical Landmarks, Part III: Watkins Mill," *Missouri Historical Review* 63:3 (April 1969): 364-77, as has B. H. Rucker in "Watkins Mill," *The Harbinger* 3:5 (December-January, 1970-1971): 15-19, but see especially Ann M. Sligar, *Waltus Watkins and His Mill* (Lawson MO: Watkins Mill Association, 2002) and Louis W. Potts and Ann M. Sligar, *Watkins Mill: Factory on the Farm* (Kirksville: Truman State University Press, 2004).

Visitor Facilities. Current brochures on various types of visitor facilities at parks statewide may be secured at the parks or by writing to Missouri State Parks, P.O. Box 176, Jefferson City, MO 65102, but the most complete and up-to-date source is the Missouri State Parks website: http://mostateparks.com/. Almost all state parks and historic sites have a robust website, which may be most readily found by searching on the name of the park or site. *

Index

Abbreviations used in this index:
Co. County
SHS State Historic Site
SP State Park

FROM LEFT: SUSAN FLADER, JOHN KAREL, OLIVER SCHUCHARD, B. H. RUCKER

About the Authors

SUSAN FLADER is professor emerita of American western and environmental history at the University of Missouri-Columbia. She has written or edited ten books and numerous articles, including works on Aldo Leopold and on Missouri parks and forests. She has been active in the Missouri Parks Association since its founding, serving three times as president and many years as editor. She has also lectured throughout the United States and abroad, chaired the Aldo Leopold Foundation, and served as president of the American Society for Environmental History and with numerous other national and state conservation and professional organizations.

JOHN A. KAREL is president of the L-A-D Foundation, of which he has been a director since 1982. A visionary resource steward with degrees in history and resource management, he served from 1976 as a DNR park planner, from 1979-1985 as state park director, and then from 1987 to 2014 as director of Tower Grove Park in St. Louis. Founder and leader of the Missouri Wilderness Coalition since 1978, he has served also as an officer of other environmental, historic preservation, and park organizations, including the National Association for Olmsted Parks, the Foundation for Restoration of Ste. Genevieve, and the Missouri Parks Association.

B. H. RUCKER, a native Ozarkian with deep roots in the state, devoted his entire working life to Missouri State Parks. He began his career conducting archaeological research at Watkins Mill and stayed on to direct the development of the historic site. He was long-time chief of historic preservation and cultural resources for Missouri State Parks and served a stint as interim state park director. While much of his superb writing went uncredited, his breadth of knowledge, steel-trap memory, and flair for storytelling have made him indispensable to state parks, the Missouri Parks Association, and both editions of this book.

R. ROGER PRYOR (1945-1999) was a leading voice for conservation and the environment in St. Louis, the state, and beyond. He was executive director and policy director of the Missouri Coalition for the Environment for decades and was an early leader of the St. Louis Open Space Council and the Sierra Club, for which he served as Midwest regional vice president. A celebrated raconteur and musician with degrees in geology and biology, he conducted extensive natural area surveys of Missouri in the 1970s, and wrote more than two hundred articles on environmental issues for newspapers and magazines.

CHARLES CALLISON (1913-1993) had a distinguished career as a conservation leader, serving as chief of information for the Missouri Department of Conservation in the 1930s, executive secretary of the Conservation Federation of Missouri in the 1940s, then conservation director of the National Wildlife Federation, executive vice-president of the National Audubon Society, and president of the Public Lands Institute. He wrote hundreds of articles, including editorials for *The New York Times*, and several books, including *Man and Wildlife in Missouri*, and was a founder of the Missouri Parks Association and its editor until his death.

OLIVER SCHUCHARD is professor emeritus of art at the University of Missouri at Columbia and a noted landscape photographer. Deeply influenced by his studies with Ansel Adams, he has worked with the large-format camera in both black and white and color and in both minute detail and panorama to render images of the landscape. His photographs have appeared in numerous books, magazines, and exhibitions, and he has produced several book-length interpretations of his native state and beyond, including *Missouri*, *Two Ozark Rivers*, and *The Landscape in Black and White: Oliver Schuchard Photographs, 1967-2005*.